*f*P

ALSO BY NORMAN PODHORETZ

Doings and Undoings

Making It

Breaking Ranks

The Present Danger

Why We Were in Vietnam

The Bloody Crossroads

Ex-Friends

My Love Affair with America

The Prophets

The Commentary Reader (editor)

The
Norman Podhoretz
Reader

A Selection of His Writings from
the 1950s through the 1990s

Edited by Thomas L. Jeffers

With an Introduction by Paul Johnson

FREE PRESS
New York London Toronto Sydney

FREE PRESS
A Division of Simon & Schuster, Inc.
1230 Avenue of the Americas
New York, NY 10020

FREE PRESS and colophon are trademarks of Simon & Schuster, Inc.

For information about special discounts for bulk purchases,
please contact Simon & Schuster Special Sales:
1-800-456-6798 or business@simonandschuster.com

Book design by Ellen R. Sasahara

Manufactured in the United States of America

1   3   5   7   9   10   8   6   4   2

Library of Congress Cataloging-in-Publication Data

Podhoretz, Norman.
[Selections. 2004]
The Norman Podhoretz reader: a selection of his writings from the 1950s through the 1990s/
edited by Thomas L. Jeffers; with an introduction by Paul Johnson
p.   cm.
Includes bibliographical references and index.
I. Podhoretz, Norman. II. Jeffers, Thomas L., 1946–.
PS29.P63 A25 2004
818'.5403—dc22   2003049332
ISBN 0-7432-3661-0

"Simone de Beauvoir as Novelist" was originally published as "Experience of Our Time" in *The New Yorker,* September 15, 1956.

"Huck Finn's Literary Journey" was originally published as "The Literary Adventures of Huck Finn" in *The New York Times Book Review* (December 6, 1959). Copyright © 1959 by The New York Times Co. Reprinted by permission.

"In Defense of Editing" was originally published in *Harper's,* October 1965.

The following articles originally appeared in *Commentary* magazine and are reprinted by permission: "J'Accuse" (September 1982), "Israel—with Grandchildren" (December 1995), "Neoconservatism: A Eulogy" (March 1996), *Lolita,* My Mother-in-Law, the Marquis de Sade, and Larry Flynt" (April 1997), "Philip Roth, Then and Now" as "The Adventures of Philip Roth" (October 1998), "A Dissent on Isaiah Berlin" (February 1999), "What Happened to Ralph Ellison" (July–August 1999).

"A Foul-Weather Friend to Norman Mailer" is reprinted with the permission of Free Press, a Division of Simon & Schuster Adult Publishing Division, from *Ex-Friends: Falling Out with Allen Ginsberg, Lionel and Diana Trilling, Lillian Hellman, Hannah Arendt, and Norman Mailer* (pp. 178–220). Copyright © 1999 by Norman Podhoretz. All rights reserved.

"My New York" originally appeared in *National Review,* June 14, 1999, pp. 35–41, and is reprinted by permission.

"Was Bach Jewish?" originally appeared in the December 1999 issue of *Prospect.*

"God and the Scientists" was originally published as "Science Hasn't Killed God" in *The Wall Street Journal,* December 1999.

TO NEAL KOZODOY

Contents

The
Norman Podhoretz
Reader

Introduction

Paul Johnson

A BOOK that needs to be written is *The Rise and Fall of the New York Intellectuals*. It is an important phenomenon in American history. Its story is virtually confined to the twentieth century. Before 1900 the New York intellectual elite virtually did not exist, or at any rate had no coherence or special identity. It was a product of the muckraking epoch and still more of the First World War and the triumphant ideologies which emerged from it—Communism in Russia, fascism in Italy, Nazism in Germany—and of the peculiar American version of democratic ideology, the New Deal. The heyday of the New York intellectuals lasted from the 1930s to the 1970s, at the end of which decade the emergence of Reaganism and Thatcherism introduced a new game of intellectual cards. The consequent collapse of the Soviet Union and international Communism at the end of the 1980s left the New York intellectual without a global battlefield on which to fight. The explosion of international terrorism as the new threat to democracy and civilization at the beginning of the twenty-first century cleared the intellectual stage of all its traditional characters and left it bare for a new drama and cast.

Among the outstanding exponents of New York intellectual life during its golden age was Norman Podhoretz. I say "was" not because he is played out—far from it. Rather it is the drama in which he first starred that has come to a natural end, as all historical epochs must. He and his skills and energy—and his appetite for intellectual battle—survive to participate in the new encounters which are taking shape.

Moreover, Podhoretz is a rather special member of the group. I am inclined to call him the archetype of the New York intellectual. He was born in Brooklyn and educated in the city, and has in his bones and genes its granitic concentration on the self and the idea. Among the intellectuals, he is a polymath rather than a specialist. He is not primarily a literary critic, as were Edmund Wilson and Lionel Trilling. He is not a novelist, like Mary McCarthy and Norman Mailer. Nor is he a historian, like Arthur Schlesinger Jr. and Jacques Barzun, or a politician like Daniel P. Moynihan. He is, rather, protean. An inspiring editor of the intellectual monthly *Commentary* for thirty-five years (from 1960 to 1995), he has always been— unlike, say, Robert Silvers of the *New York Review of Books*—a great deal more than an editor. He is a thinker and writer and polemicist, a geopolitician and student of religious ideas, an autobiographer of genius, a man who reacts sharply to the news as it pours from the press and the airwaves, who thinks deeply, angrily, and sincerely about it, and commits his thoughts into vivid and penetrative argument.

Podhoretz has two virtues that make him especially valuable. First, he is honest, to himself and to his readers. It is a shocking honesty, of the kind George Orwell always displayed and relished. In 1967, at the height of the mad-bad sixties, Podhoretz published *Making It,* the blow-by-blow account of how he got to the top of the New York intellectual tree and acquired power over its lower branches. New York intellectuals are notoriously ambitious and pushy but they maintain the convention that they are merely a group of disinterested idealists. Podhoretz's book asserted that the intellectual ladder was climbed in much the same way as the corporate one. So it was seen as a disgraceful betrayal of his caste, and everyone read it either in anger or in joy.

Making It was followed in 1979, just before the Reagan era opened and after a decade of precipitous decline in American power and self-confidence, with *Breaking Ranks.* Here was another intimate and unsparing account of how Podhoretz tore himself away from his left-wing roots and severed his connection with the predominant body of the New York intelligentsia. This, too, caused a sensation and constituted treason to the Left, worse compounded by the almost exultant tone of his discovery that he was a free man again. Both books were all the more effective for having been written in blood and toil and sweat, and in agony of spirit. They took not just honesty but moral courage, qualities in short supply among intellectuals.

PODHORETZ'S second salient virtue is independence of mind. He always thinks for himself. Conformity is the professional deformation of intellectuals, just as selfishness is of royalty, snobbery of aristocracy, complacency of the bourgeoisie, and thoughtlessness of the workers. And this sheeplike conformity to the current received ideas of the intellectual trendsetters is all the more debilitating in that it is carefully masked and vehemently denied. Podhoretz thinks for himself because, like Luther, he "can do no other." His thoughts are deep, sinewy, often very direct and even strident, but equally often surprising and unexpected, never predictable. When you come to the end of a Podhoretz article and argument you feel you have got the real man, every time. There is no cant, nothing phony, no hidden agenda, nothing withheld, no tactical dodges, just the awkward or angular or disconcerting or simple truth, as he sees it. Here again, the comparison with Orwell springs to mind.

THERE IS A third point which needs to be made about Podhoretz. In New York, as in Paris and other writers' capitals on the European continent, intellectuals play for keeps. Breaking ranks is a fateful step, not just politically and ideologically but socially and culturally. It means severing friendships, even changing neighborhoods and acquiring a new range of acquaintances—as well as a new set of enemies. I was in Paris when Sartre and Camus broke up, and great was the fallout thereof and woeful the personal cost, especially for poor Camus. I recall, too, that when Jacques Soustelle took exception to de Gaulle's policy on Algeria and told him "All my friends think my way," the General, one of the few intellectuals to make an outstanding head of state, firmly replied: "Well then, Soustelle, get yourself new friends!"

Now we do things differently in England. We try not to let ideological disagreements disturb our social life or the ecumenical serenity of our clubs. Politics, let alone ideas, are not that important. When I left the Labor Party, rather noisily, in the mid-1970s, I did not sever a single old friendship. Americans and continentals are sometimes astonished to encounter politicians and thinkers of all persuasions at my wife's parties. We think people should come before ideas: it is our strength, as well (some would say) as our weakness.

Podhoretz had to adapt to the New York adversarial system, of course, to some extent at least. It was painful, because he rightly sets a high value on friendships. Indeed, he and his gifted and accomplished wife, Midge Decter, his faithful companion in all his battles, are famous for their "troops of friends." Hence, although Podhoretz did eventually see most of his old attachments weaken or dissolve, he found the strength of the ties sufficiently tenacious to write a remarkable book about them. *Ex-Friends* describes, with his characteristic honesty, and in places tenderness, his falling-out with Lillian Hellman, Lionel and Diana Trilling, Norman Mailer, Hannah Arendt, and Allen Ginsberg. It is a penetrating reflection on what happens when private and public passions conflict.

I THINK I have written enough to show that, as a New York intellectual, Podhoretz is both the archetype and sui generis. He is not a man you can put into a category or include in a definition or make the basis for a worthwhile generalization. He is formidable but friendly; honest, frank, and unrelenting, but warm and kindly in his personal relationships; loyal to all who deserve loyalty but in the last resort only to truth. To use my old army definition, he is a good man to share a slit-trench with.

He has recently been studying the old Hebrew prophets to some purpose, and has published a powerful book about them, not lacking in contemporary wisdom, as you may well suppose. He is a bit of a prophet himself, gritty and angular, nonconformist and egregious, a purveyor of harsh and often unwelcome truth. When I read him, I always see his earnest, worried, anxious, and desperately sincere prophet's face behind his words, begging me to hear him before it is too late. I ask readers of this collection to approach it in the same spirit, with the man before their eyes.

A Bibliographical Note

THE following pieces by Norman Podhoretz, whether discrete essays or chapters from books, represent only a small portion of what he produced between the early 1950s and the end of the twentieth century. Nonetheless, I believe that readers already familiar with his work will find this one-volume retrospective freshly illuminating. And I also believe it will stand as a tempting invitation to readers who have yet to make his acquaintance.

Everything is presented in toto, mainly because each selection is so tightly written that cutting without doing serious damage to the whole was—as I discovered in undertaking the effort—impossible. And except for a very few, very minor cosmetic changes, everything appears here as originally published, with the pieces arranged decade by decade, rather than by genre or by topic. As a result, they reflect not only the march of history through the second half of the twentieth century—a history primarily American and primarily literary, cultural, and political—but also the unfolding of his own sensibility and the evolution of his ideas and attitudes. Within each decade, however, the ordering isn't always chronological; rather, pieces have been grouped in accordance with the logic of thesis or subject.

Here, in any event, is the bibliographical information readers should have, in order of appearance in this volume. (In the case of pieces that were subsequently collected in *Doings and Undoings* or *The Bloody Crossroads*, I have not cited the magazines in which they were first published.)

"The Adventures of Saul Bellow," 1953–59. In *Doings and Undoings: The Fifties and After in American Writing,* 205–27. Farrar, Straus & Giroux, 1964.

"Simone de Beauvoir as Novelist" (originally titled "Experience of Our Time"), *The New Yorker,* 15 September 1956, 156–62.

"The Know-Nothing Bohemians," 1958. In *Doings and Undoings,* 143–58.

"Huck Finn's Literary Journey" (originally titled "The Literary Adventures of Huck Finn"), *New York Times Book Review,* 6 December 1959.

"My Negro Problem—and Ours," 1963. In *Doings and Undoings,* 354–71.

"Hannah Arendt on Eichmann," 1963. In *Doings and Undoings,* 335–53.

"In Defense of Editing," *Harper's,* October 1965, 143–47.

"The Brutal Bargain," from *Making It,* 3–27. Random House, 1967.

"After Modernism, What?" (originally titled "The Literary Light as Eternal Flame"), *Saturday Review,* 24 August 1974, 90–98.

"Prologue: A Letter to My Son" and "Postscript," from *Breaking Ranks,* 3–17, 361–65. Harper & Row, 1979.

"J'Accuse," *Commentary,* September 1982, 21–31.

"Whose Immorality?" from *Why We Were in Vietnam,* 174–210. Simon & Schuster, 1982.

"Kissinger Reconsidered," 1982. In *The Bloody Crossroads,* 139–66. Simon & Schuster, 1986.

"If Orwell Were Alive Today," 1983. In *The Bloody Crossroads,* 50–68.

"An Open Letter to Milan Kundera," 1984. In *The Bloody Crossroads,* 167–83.

"The Terrible Question of Aleksandr Solzhenitsyn," 1985. In *The Bloody Crossroads,* 184–208.

"Israel—with Grandchildren," *Commentary,* December 1995, 38–47.

"Neoconservatism: A Eulogy," *Commentary,* March 1996, 19–27.

"*Lolita,* My Mother-in-Law, the Marquis de Sade, and Larry Flynt," *Commentary,* April 1997, 23–35.

"Philip Roth, Then and Now" (originally titled "The Adventures of Philip Roth"), *Commentary,* October 1998, 25–36.

"What Happened to Ralph Ellison," *Commentary,* July–August 1999, 46–58.

"A Foul-Weather Friend to Norman Mailer," from *Ex-Friends,* 178–220. Free Press, 1999.

"A Dissent on Isaiah Berlin," *Commentary,* February 1999, 25–37

"My New York," *National Review,* 14 June 1999, 35–41.

"Was Bach Jewish?" *Prospect,* December 1999, 21–24.

"God and the Scientists" (originally titled "Science Hasn't Killed God"), *Wall Street Journal,* 30 December 1999.

I WISH to express appreciation for abundant assistance from Jessica Demovsky, my capable research assistant, who did a lot of draft-reading and précis-writing for me, and from Milton Bates, my friend and colleague, who made many useful suggestions for the editor's notes.

—TLJ

The 1950s

Editor's Note

"I AM an American, Chicago born—Chicago, that somber city." Those, of course, are the affirmative first words of Saul Bellow's novel, *The Adventures of Augie March* (1953), and in the 1950s they stood, for many readers, Jewish and otherwise, whose parents might have been born in Kraków or Naples, as a declaration of citizenship. Certainly that is how Norman Podhoretz read them. Brooklyn born in 1930, of parents who had come to America from Galicia (then part of Poland, now of Ukraine), he grew up in Brownsville, a neighborhood populated not only by other Jewish immigrants from Eastern Europe but by blacks recently arrived from the South and by Italians not long off the boat from Sicily. Many Jewish families Americanized their names when they settled in—Podhoretzes becoming Podhursts, for example—but not this Podhoretz family, difficult to pronounce though most people found the name. (The right way is Pod-hór-etz, aspirating the "h.") Julius Podhoretz was a milkman, his wife Helen a homemaker busy raising Norman and his sister Mildred (1924–2002). Yiddish was spoken at home more often than English, which is why, having as a kindergartener told a teacher that he was "goink op de stez," (going up the stairs), he was put in a remedial English class. There, happily, he was taught to speak standard English, with the Yiddish accent removed. Whatever traces of a Brooklyn accent may have remained began in turn to fade under the instruction of gifted teachers, and the general milieu, in high school, Columbia College, and (concurrently) the College of Jewish Studies at the Jewish Theological Seminary. Three fellowship years followed at Cambridge in England, where the young man from Brooklyn was, by his tongue, regarded simply as a well-educated American.

It wasn't a question of Henry Higgins giving Eliza Doolittle a dialect makeover. It was, for Podhoretz, a question of being offered a chance to hear, speak, and above all read and think about the literature that had been written in English. If Hebrew was God's first language, he has neatly said, then English was His second. That mystic sense of the power of a literary tradition did him no harm at Columbia, where in the late 1940s he was Lionel Trilling's favorite student, or at Cambridge, where in the early 1950s it was, if anything, intensified under F. R. Leavis, who offered this rare young American his austere tutelage. An incomparable pair of mentors. Not forgetting their inspiration during his couple of years in the army, Podhoretz soon went to work "writing for a living" for such serious magazines as *Partisan Review,* the *New Yorker,* the *New Republic,* and above all *Commentary,* which, the day after he was discharged from the army, in the closing weeks of 1955, made him an assistant editor. In 1960, shortly after the death of Elliot E. Cohen, who had created the magazine in 1945, Podhoretz became editor. He was thirty years old.

The pieces collected here to represent his writing during the 1950s, like those in the other sections of this *Reader,* can only begin to indicate Podhoretz's range and depth. But it's safe to say that in the beginning he promised fair to become exactly what, under Trilling and Leavis, he had set out to be—a literary critic. Not in the academic sense: unlike most of the legendary figures of that New Critical era—Cleanth Brooks, R. P. Blackmur, Allen Tate—he didn't become a professor. He followed the model of H. L. Mencken or Edmund Wilson, a model that a Trilling or a Leavis (in whose *Scrutiny* Podhoretz, then all of twenty-one, had made his debut as a professional, appropriately enough with an essay about Trilling entitled "The Arnoldian Function in American Criticism") could also practice, of writing for general-audience publications in a manner that specialists could appreciate and the laity understand. He was naturally helped by his editorial job at *Commentary,* but he must have burned midnight oil by the barrel reading books well enough to review them with an intelligence as stunningly precocious, I think, as Mencken's or Wilson's had been two or three generations earlier. In 1956 he wrote seven substantial pieces, in 1957 he wrote thirteen, in 1958 nine—which averages a piece every forty days or so, most of them on contemporary American fiction, the rest on European fiction, Jewish culture, and even television drama.

A few words about the four pieces here. "The Adventures of Saul Bellow" adds to and ties together his earlier reviews of Bellow's novels, including the controversial analysis of *Augie March* he did in 1953 for *Commentary*—an analysis which, while hardly as negative as most interested parties remember it as being, did not find that National Book Award winner to be all that everyone, including Podhoretz himself, had hoped it would be.

It was one thing, per that opening declaration I've quoted, to want to affirm the hero's (and the author's) sense of belonging to America, celebrating America itself as (in Podhoretz's words) "the only protection against the infinitely greater menace of Soviet totalitarianism," and, for all its philistinism, as a country whose "virtues" made for a civilization *worth* celebrating. But it was another thing to bring that affirmation off, consistently, page by page. In this passage or that, Podhoretz argues, Bellow displays a great mastery of ideas, while stylistically he's "perhaps the greatest virtuoso of language the novel has seen since Joyce." Too often, however, the beyond-alienation claims sound like windy-city bluster, manifest tellingly in "the forced spontaneity of the prose." The larky, willed optimism of the book is revealed, too, by the action: the hero "goes through everything and undergoes nothing."

Bellow's best, it then seemed to the young Podhoretz, was *Seize the Day* (1956). This short novel, he contends, falls short of greatness only because Bellow doesn't give full rein to his bitterly tragic response to life. It is a response that in *Augie* is comically directed at the utopians who, the protagonist reflects, "simply cannot understand how little help there is for being human." What we get in *Seize the Day*, by contrast, is merely the hero weeping in his longing for love; what we should have got, Podhoretz asserts, is a fit of "murder."

Which is provocative but hardly, I believe, the judgment that the mature Podhoretz would render. Nor does it seem consistent even with the author of "The Know-Nothing Bohemians." Here Podhoretz evokes the Bohemians of the 1920s and 1930s—Ernest Hemingway, F. Scott Fitzgerald, Sinclair Lewis, et al.—who fled the Midwest to New York or Paris or London in quest of a civilization marked by "intelligence, cultivation, spiritual refinement," and splendidly contrasts them with the Bohemians of the 1950s—Allen Ginsberg and especially, in this essay, Jack Kerouac—whose preferences were for "primitivism, instinct, energy, 'blood.'" This was also what Norman Mailer was then portentously touting as a "revolution backward toward being." It was a philosophy that misunderstood—or, rather, distorted—D. H. Lawrence; an aesthetic that mangled Walt Whitman: "It isn't the *right* words [Kerouac] wants (even if he knows what they might be), but the first words, or at any rate the words that most obviously announce themselves as deriving from emotion rather than cerebration."

The upshot is vagueness punctuated by bop ejaculations such as "wild" or "crazy," now and then intensified by "really." Sounding like Leavis "placing" the effusions of Shelley, Podhoretz snaps the hipsters to attention:

> [W]riting that springs easily and "spontaneously" out of strong feeling is *never* vague; it always has a quality of sharpness and precision because it is in the nature of strong feelings to be aroused by specific objects. The notion that a diffuse, generalized, and unrelenting enthusiasm is the mark of great sensitivity and responsiveness is utterly fantastic, an idea that comes from taking drunkenness or drug addiction as the state of perfect emotional vigor.

What the Beats wanted to be spontaneous about, aside from verbal expression, were sex and violence—the first in anxious attempts to "perform" so as to bring about "'good [simultaneous] orgasms,' which are the first duty of man and the only duty of woman"; the second, evident more in Ginsberg than in Kerouac, in thrashings out against "repressive" laws protecting property or banning hallucinogens and sex with minors.

This is an exceptionally prescient essay, as one looks toward the countercultural revolutions of the 1960s. And taking a long view of the prior decades, Podhoretz rightly notes "that there is a close connection between ideologies of primitivistic vitalism and a willingness to look upon cruelty and bloodletting with complacency, if not downright enthusiasm."

The short, hitherto uncollected pieces on Simone de Beauvoir's *The Mandarins* and Mark Twain's *The Adventures of Huckleberry Finn* are remarkable examples of, first, how to review a novel by setting it in a larger cultural and political frame and, second, how to revisit a classic in a fashion that makes its timeless theme timely. Reading Podhoretz on de Beauvoir reminds us why many French intellectuals after World War II became pro-Soviet, and what was tragically wrong with that. It also shows us that the young critic, however willing to shake a stick at capitalist complacencies and aesthetic backwardness, was never a candidate for what sentimentalists would later call "the romance of American Communism."

Indeed, even when, toward the end of this decade, he would begin moving leftward from the "revisionist" or "cold-war" liberalism he had espoused since coming under Trilling's influence at Columbia, his anti-Communist passions would remain intact, rooted as they were in an anti-Jacobin preference for hard facts, starting with the human costs and benefits tallied by the Communists. (His commitment to capitalism as a form of freedom in itself, and as more beneficial economically to more people than socialism in any of its varieties, would only develop much later.)

But already in the 1950s, among the hard facts of life Podhoretz grasped, as one may learn from his short statement on *Huck Finn,* is that concepts of good and evil aren't merely social conventions. They derive, transhistorically, from the "state of nature," which Twain limns, contra Thomas Hobbes, in the life of responsibility, love, loyalty, and generosity Huck and Jim share on the raft, away from the slave-owning, murderously feuding "civilization" on shore. That Podhoretz could read *Huck Finn* in such transcendental terms is worth remembering when, in coming decades, he calls for racial equality less out of political convenience than out of a conviction that it's an eternal good, or when, in only an apparent paradox, he defends Western, and specifically American, civilization precisely because it is, this side of any state of nature, the best defender of Twain's natural law.

—TLJ

THE ADVENTURES OF SAUL BELLOW

MOST SERIOUS CRITICS TODAY
—at least those who have concerned themselves at all with current writing—would probably single out Saul Bellow as the leading American novelist of the postwar period. There are many reasons for this. First of all, Bellow is an intellectual, by which I do not only mean that he is intelligent, but also that his work exhibits a closer involvement with ideas than the work of most other writers in this period. Alfred Kazin, one of his warmest admirers, for example, calls attention to the fact that Bellow's characters "are all burdened by a speculative quest, a need to understand their particular destiny within the general problem of human destiny," and he compares Bellow to "'metaphysical' American novelists like Melville, for he identifies man's quest with the range of the mind itself." Nor is it simply that Bellow is concerned with ideas; the concern itself operates on a high level of sophistication and complexity—higher, even, than Norman Mailer's, if not more audacious. He is an educated, exquisitely self-conscious writer, at the opposite pole from someone like James Jones, and yet not in the least academic or Alexandrian. His books, whatever else we may say of them, *mean* something: they are charged with the urgency and the passion of a man to whom the issues he writes about are matters of life and death. And finally, Bellow is a stylist of the first order, perhaps the greatest virtuoso of language the novel has seen since Joyce.

But these qualities alone do not account for the special, almost personal, interest that serious critics have always taken in Bellow. For an adequate explanation, we also have to look, I believe, at the changing historical context out of which his novels have come and in terms of which their impact has been registered. Bellow began writing fiction at a time when the literary avant-garde in this country had reached a point of sheer exhaustion, and when the moral and social attitudes associated with it no longer seemed relevant either to life or to literature—and he was the first gifted American novelist to search for another mode of operation and a more viable orientation to the world of the postwar period. Since a large and influential body of intellectuals was engaged on a similar quest, Bellow naturally assumed a position as spokesman and leader. There is, indeed, a sense in which it may even be said that the validity of a whole new phase of American culture has been felt to hang on whether or not Saul Bellow would turn out to be a great novelist.

The direction in which Bellow would find himself going in search of this new orientation was evident as far back as his first novel, *Dangling Man,* a short bitter book about a Chicago intellectual who is told to hold himself in readiness for the army and then waits around in lonely idleness for nearly a year before the draft board finally acts. If we think of *Dangling Man* as a war novel, we can see how far Bellow's starting point was from Mailer's, to whom the experience of war offered an opportunity for establishing continuity with the past—with, that is, the conventions of naturalism and the progressive ideas that were its traditional ally. The war for Bellow did not mean an exposure to the great realities of hardship, violence, and death; nor did it mean a confrontation between the virtuous individual and the vicious instrument of a vicious society. On the contrary: it meant the disruption of continuity with the past, the explosion of a neat system of attitudes that had for a time made life relatively easy to manage. These attitudes can be summed up in the word "alienation," provided we understand that the term refers not merely to the doctrines of a small group of radicals bred on Marx, but to the hostile posture toward middle-class society adopted by nearly all the important writers of the modern period, whatever their particular political persuasion. T. S. Eliot and Ezra Pound on the Right, or the largely nonpolitical Hemingway, Fitzgerald, and Faulkner, were no less "alienated" from the America of the 1920s and 1930s than John Dos Passos and James T. Farrell on the Left. What distinguished the 1930s in this regard is simply that a temporary alliance was struck between the avant-garde in literature and radicalism in politics, so that a phenomenon like *Partisan Review* could develop, and a critic like Edmund Wilson could conclude his book on symbolism with the assertion that Marxism had provided a "practical" answer to the questions posed by the modernist movement. Those writers and intellectuals who decided around the time of the Moscow trials that Stalin had betrayed the revolution might altogether have lost their faith in the possibility of a practical solution to the spiritual problems of the age if not for the fact that a third alternative presented itself in the form of a new proletarian revolution led by Trotsky. With America's entry into the war, however, the few shreds of revolutionary hope that had managed to survive the end of the decade disintegrated completely. Yet the collapse of revolutionary hopes only killed the belief in a *practical* or political solution to the spiritual problems of the age; it did not kill the problems themselves, nor did it destroy the sharpness with which writers and intellectuals experienced those problems. (That was left to the 1950s to accomplish.)

From this perspective, we can see why *Dangling Man* ought to be called a prescient book. Published in 1944, it was one of the first expressions of the dislocation that set into American intellectual life during the 1940s, when a great many gifted and sensitive people were quite literally dangling, like the Joseph of Bellow's novel, between two worlds of assumption and were forced back upon themselves to struggle with all the basic questions that had for so long been comfortably settled. At twenty-seven Joseph has not only repudiated the radicalism of his immediate past, but has come to believe that there can be no political answers to problems of the spirit. There is, he admits, something about modern society that creates special and unprecedented difficulties for the individual who aspires to the best that mankind has been able to accomplish—to wholeness of being, grace of style, and poise of spirit. But he also feels that we abuse the present too much: surely it must still be possible to do again what so many others have done before. Though he continues to "suffer from a feeling of strangeness, of not quite belonging to the world," he refuses to accept alienation as a strategy for getting by. Alienation, he says, "is a fool's plea. . . . You can't banish the world by decree if it's in you. . . . What if you declare you are alienated, you say you reject the Hollywood dream, the soap opera, the cheap thriller? The very denial implicates you," and if you decide that you want to forget these things, "The world comes after you. . . . Whatever you do, you cannot dismiss it." It may even be that it is a "weakness of imagination" that prevents people from seeing "where those capacities have gone to which we once owed our greatness." Nevertheless, a man must protect himself from the world, and if he has no recourse either to alienation as a style of life or to political activism, how is he to live? Perhaps, Joseph thinks, "by a plan, a program . . . an ideal construction, an obsessive device." But it would be better to get along without such an "exclusive focus, passionate and engulfing," partly because there is always "a gap between the ideal construction and the real world, the truth," and partly because "the obsession exhausts the man," often becoming his enemy.

What Bellow is attempting to do here, then, is challenge the standard idea of the heroic that dominates twentieth-century literature in general and the fiction of the 1930s in particular: the idea that under modern conditions rebellion is the only possible form of heroism. He is saying, in effect, that all the traditional modes of rebellion (including—and perhaps especially—the simple act of conscious dissociation from society) have been robbed of their relevance by the movement of history. Heroism as Bellow envisages it in *Dangling Man* would consist in accepting the full burden of time and place, refusing to hold oneself aloof, and yet managing not to be overwhelmed or annihilated. The image he has in mind, in other words, is neither Prometheus nor Ahab, but Beethoven, Shakespeare, Spinoza—men who have achieved (to use the phrase that was soon to become so fashionable) the tragic sense of life. It goes without saying that Joseph is very far from this goal; but he has the ambition, and the main thing that happens to him in the course of the novel is that he is pushed by suffering into recognizing that the sober, balanced, Olympian attitudes of his earlier self were an evasion rather than a stage in his progress. In a word, he discovers evil—the reality that must be contended with before the tragic sense of life can develop. He also discovers how far he still has to go and how pitifully ill-equipped he is for making the journey—which means that he has experienced a necessary humiliation. At the end, he hurls himself with a kind of joyous bitterness into the army and the war, hoping to learn through "regimentation of spirit" what he had been unable to learn as an isolated "free" man.

Yet it is hard to believe that Joseph will do very much better in the army than he managed to do in his lonely room. He is too self-consciously eager for further humiliation, too ready to extract the wisdom from suffering before it even comes to a boil, too little endowed with the robust toughness that would be needed to make him a plausible candidate for the destiny to which he aspires. Thus, what Bellow has actually succeeded in creating in Joseph is not a character whose job it will be to find a way of realizing the highest human possibilities under modern conditions, but an extraordinarily intelligent portrait of a type that was to come into great prominence in the years following World War II. Joseph is still the alienated modern man who has been a leading figure in the literature and social thought of the twentieth century, but he differs from his immediate ancestors in lacking a plan or program or obsessive device to justify, support, and enrich his estranged condition. Like Mailer's Lovett in *Barbary Shore,* he is doomed to alternate bursts of aimless hysteria and pathological apathy; and again like Lovett, he is forced to drag himself through the world without the help of the past and without a sense of wide future possibilities. ("I, in this room, separate, alienated, distrustful, find in my purpose not an open world, but a closed, hopeless jail. My perspectives end in the walls. Nothing of the future comes to me.") As he himself observes, "the greatest cruelty is to curtail expectations without taking away life completely," and it is to this cruelty that he is exposed, the more so because he can find nothing in the life he leads to "hold and draw and stir" him. Whereas the answer to this predicament was once art (but he is not an artist) or revolution (but revolution is impossible), Joseph's answer is to accept the society of which he is inescapably a part and to work toward transcending it. The fact that this answer exists within the novel only as an abstractly stated proposition rather than a concrete presence, is, of course, a major failing, just as it is the main reason for the book's imaginative thinness. Written in the form of a journal, *Dangling Man* hardly ventures beyond the consciousness of the central character and is so highly self-involved that even when Bellow does move outside Joseph's mind and into the world around him, the novel remains cheerless and claustral, giving the impression of a universe barren of people and things, a kind of desert beaten by the wind and sleet of a foul Chicago winter.

Cheerlessness also characterizes the world of Bellow's second novel, *The Victim* (1947). Here the Chicago winter gives way to a New York summer, and instead of emptiness we get a sense of crowds milling, seething, and sweating. "On some nights New York is as hot as Bangkok" is the opening sentence, and this association of the city with an exotic primitive place is unobtrusively reinforced throughout the narrative, until we begin to understand that what we have in *The Victim* is a vision of the city as a tiny village surrounded on all sides by a jungle that threatens at any moment to spill over and engulf the precarious little human oasis at its center. This is New York seen through the eyes of a writer overwhelmed by the sheer animality of the human species, and nagged by the suspicion that "civilization" may be a gigantic and desperate illusion—and an illusion that is becoming more and more difficult to sustain.

Discussing the conviction he once had of the mildness of his own character and trying to rationalize his horror of violence, Joseph tells us in *Dangling Man* that the famous passage from Hobbes which describes life in the State of Nature as "nasty, brutish, and short" was always present to his mind, and one imagines that the same passage was always present to Bellow's mind as he was writing *The Victim*. The central figure, Leventhal, is a man of even greater spiritual timidity than Joseph, though not being an intellectual, he has no theories to bolster his timidity. He goes through life with the feeling of having "got away" with something, by which he means that he might very easily have fallen among "that part of humanity of which he was frequently mindful—the lost, the outcast, the overcome, the effaced, the ruined." But it gradually becomes clear in the course of the novel that what Leventhal really fears is crossing over a certain boundary of the spirit, beyond which lies not merely failure, but violence and the darker passions: he is afraid of being "drowned at too great a depth of life." In order to keep from drifting out of the shallow water, he has always resorted to various psychological tricks ("principally indifference and neglect"), and *The Victim* is about a crisis that crashes through his wall of defenses and jolts him into reconsidering his life and his character. The crisis takes the form of his pursuit by the down-and-out anti-Semite of patrician origin, Kirby Allbee, who accuses Leventhal of having maliciously caused his ruin, and (less importantly) Leventhal's simultaneous involvement in the illness and death of his brother's child. With great subtlety and brilliance Bellow traces the process by which Leventhal is drawn into acknowledging responsibility for Allbee, not because Allbee's accusations against him are justified (they are not), but because he learns to recognize a kinship with Allbee himself, who embodies everything he most fears in the world and in his own soul.

From a purely literary point of view, *The Victim* represents a great step forward for Bellow. Whereas in *Dangling Man* we get the feeling that the few dramatic incidents included are brought in only to create the spurious impression that Joseph's theoretical speculations are anchored in the events of his life, in *The Victim* the abstract metaphysical questions that are so important to Bellow arise naturally and spontaneously (and ingeniously) out of the story. The book, moreover, is beautifully constructed and paced, so that Leventhal's growing sympathy for the repulsive Allbee sneaks up on the reader as insidiously and surprisingly as it sneaks up on him. The subplot is managed with less dexterity; there is something perfunctory and perhaps a little schematic about it, as though Bellow thought it necessary to provide Leventhal with an experience of death in case his crisis should seem lacking in dimension and profundity.

From the point of view of Bellow's quest for a new orientation to the world around him, however, *The Victim* is not so much an advance over *Dangling Man* as a companion piece to it. If *Dangling Man* challenges the strategy of alienation under the altered conditions of the postwar period, *The Victim* launches an assault on the prudence, caution, and spiritual timidity that Bellow believes to lie behind alienation in a postradical world. "You people take care of yourselves before everything," Allbee says to Leventhal. "You keep your spirit under lock and key. . . . You make it your business assistant, and it's safe and tame and never leads you toward anything risky. Nothing dangerous and nothing glorious. Nothing ever tempts you to dissolve yourself." There is, of course, a certain justice in the charge, as Leventhal goes on to discover, but there is also something to be said in his favor. He lives by a sensible idea of responsibility as against Allbee's insistence that no one can be held responsible for the terrible things that happen to him, and he knows far better than Allbee that a price has to be paid for avoiding the awful dangers of "cannibalism." At the same time, however, Leventhal has been denying the darker sides of his nature, and it is these that he learns to respect and acknowledge in the course of his relations with Allbee. He comes to see that if Allbee is an animal and a monster, so too is he an animal and a monster, capable of savagery and malice and gratuitous cruelty, and he also comes to recognize that his timidity has robbed him of warmth and sympathy and the capacity to reach into the being of another.

Yet it is important to notice that these profound lessons carry no startling practical consequences. In an epilogue to the novel, we come upon Leventhal some years later, and the only change that has taken place is that "Something recalcitrant seemed to have left him; he was not exactly affable, but his obstinately unrevealing expression had softened. . . . And, as time went on, he lost the feeling that he had, as he used to say, 'got away with it.'" In other words, he is now more at peace with himself than before. He has not ventured into the "depths" that he once feared would drown him; he has merely (like a successfully analyzed patient) learned something about himself that has helped him come to terms with the world and make a settlement. During his difficulties with Allbee, he had reflected that "Everybody wanted to be what he was to the limit. . . . Therefore hideous things were done, cannibalistic things. Good things as well, of course. But even there, nothing really good was safe. . . . There was something in people against sleep and dullness, together with the caution that led to sleep and dullness." *The Victim* is concerned with criticizing "the caution that led to sleep and dullness," but Bellow wishes to do so in a complicated way, never blinking at the "cannibalistic things" that can erupt once this caution is overthrown. In the end, he does not advocate that it be overthrown; all he does is recommend that the anticautious impulses be acknowledged and accepted, and it is perhaps his feeling that nothing more ambitious can be offered that accounts for the oppressively pessimistic tone of the novel. I call it oppressive because it is a pessimism over the human condition even darker than Freud's in *Civilization and Its Discontents.* In *The Victim,* the making of a settlement (that is, the stifling of the instincts) is seen as bringing no positive rewards or compensations of any significance—no increase of energy through sublimation, no powerful Faustian drive; it merely has the negative virtue of preventing the outbreak of "cannibalism." Nor is Bellow's pessimism here of a piece with the grim view of life that led Hobbes to insist on the necessity of a strong social authority. Bellow wants no strong authority to enforce repression, and he knows that such authorities as do exist are—deservedly—in a seriously weakened condition. *The Victim* is thus highly characteristic of the postwar ethos, restricting itself to a consciousness of how difficult and complicated things are and seeing little hope of remedial action of any kind whatever. Taking itself as a tragic view of life, this attitude is in reality a form of the very cautiousness and constricted sense of possibility that Bellow attacks both in *Dangling Man* and *The Victim.*

BY THE EARLY 1950S, however, while Bellow was working on *The Adventures of Augie March,* the ethos of which his first two novels had been among the early premonitions was also in process of consolidating itself, and as its outlines grew clearer, it gained steadily in confidence and militancy. The first stage (reflected, it may be, in the pessimism of *The Victim*) was an almost reluctant admission that America had become the only protection against the infinitely greater menace of Soviet totalitarianism. But what began as a grim reconciliation to the lesser of two evils soon turned into something rather more positive, ranging from the jingoism of a few ex-radicals who traveled as far to the Right as they could go, to the upsurge of an exhilarating new impulse to celebrate the virtues of the American system and of American life in general. So powerful was this new impulse that it even found its way into the pages of *Partisan Review,* which had always been the very symbol of the attitudes now under attack.

The spiritual atmosphere of this phase of American cultural history was fully captured and expressed for the first time in a novel by *The Adventures of Augie March,* which perhaps explains why the book was greeted with such universal enthusiasm and delight when it appeared in 1953. The attitudes of what its enemies called "the age of conformity" and its friends "the age of intellectual revisionism" were all there; the prevailing tone of the age was there; and a new Bellow, reborn into exuberance and affirmation, was there too. "I am an American, Chicago born," ran the opening words of the novel, and anyone who knew Bellow's earlier work immediately understood him to be asserting that he had managed to cut through all the insoluble problems over the proper relation of the self to society with which he had been wrestling for ten years—cut through them to this wonderfully simple declaration of his identity. The man who had been dangling had finally come to rest in a new maturity of style and vision; the victim of a cruel universe offering only the consolations of an uneasy settlement was now rushing headlong into a world of possibility: he was discovering the richness and glory of the life around him, and everywhere he looked there were treasures to reap. Instead of being deposited into a bleak Chicago or a threatening New York, we are swept in *Augie* through whole continents, each more vividly colored than the other. Instead of being greeted by puny characters forever taking their own pulses and dragging themselves onerously from one day to the next, we are introduced in *Augie* to huge figures like the crippled Einhorn whom Bellow belligerently compares to Caesar, Machiavelli, Ulysses, and Croesus ("I'm not kidding when I enter Einhorn in this eminent list"); like Grandma Lausch, who is portrayed as a giant among formidable old women; and like Thea Fenchel, who is reviving the art of falconry and captures poisonous snakes with her bare hands. Most important of all, perhaps, we get a new prose style, the first attempt in many years to experiment with the language in fiction. In contrast to earlier experiments, however, this one expresses not an attempt to wall off the philistines, but precisely a sense of joyous connection with the common grain of American life. And finally, there was the form of the novel itself. Bellow had done his duty by the well-made novel, writing in the shadow of the accredited greats who were sanctioned both by the academy and the literary quarterlies—Flaubert, Kafka, Gide, Henry James—and again he anticipated a widespread feeling in his implicit declaration that this tradition had become a burden rather than a help. For *Augie* he looked back to another tradition—the picaresque, with its looseness of structure, its saltiness of language, its thickness of incident, its robust extroversion. And the fact that one of the greatest of all American novels (whose title is echoed by his own) itself derived from the tradition made it all the more obvious that he had hit upon the right mode for a novel that was setting out to discover America and the American dream anew.

In certain respects, Augie March is a familiar figure, an image of modern man living in a hopelessly fluid society, forced to choose an identity because he has inherited none, unable to find a place for himself. He is rootless, cut off, even (if you like) alienated. But far from responding to this situation with the usual anxiety, he is "larky and boisterous," and his rootless condition makes life endlessly adventurous and endlessly surprising. His uncertainty about his own identity, moreover, is represented as a positive advantage, leading not to the narcissistic self-involvement of a Joseph or a Leventhal, but rather to a readiness to explore the world, a generous openness to experience. Nor is his optimism superficial or blind. He understands that there are powerful arguments against his position, and he knows that optimism is a faith which, like any other, must be maintained in the teeth of the opposing evidence. "What I guess about you," one of his friends tells him, "is that you have a nobility syndrome. You can't adjust to the reality situation. . . . You want to accept. But how do you know what you're accepting? You have to be nuts to take it come one come all. . . . You should accept the data of experience." Augie's reply is significant: "It can never be right to offer to die, and if that's what the data of experience tell you, then you must get along without them."

Here, then, was the hero Bellow had been looking for since the start of his literary career; here, it seemed, was a way out of the impasse at which the mode of alienation had arrived—a way that offered the possibility of participating fully in the life of the time without loss of individuality, a way that pointed toward a fusion of mind and experience, sophistication and vitality, intelligence and power. Since this was also the way that so many of Bellow's contemporaries had marked out for themselves, it is not surprising that they should have approached *The Adventures of Augie March* with a ready disposition to take the novel's pretensions wholly at face value. Yet the truth is that like the ethos of which it was the most remarkable reflection, *Augie* was largely the product not of a state of being already achieved, but rather of an effort on Bellow's part to act as though he had already achieved it. As a test case of the buoyant attitudes of the period, in other words, *Augie* fails—and it fails mainly because its buoyancy is embodied in a character who is curiously untouched by his experience, who never changes or develops, who goes through everything yet undergoes nothing.

The strain it cost Bellow to maintain this willed buoyancy becomes most strikingly evident in the prose style he invented for *Augie*. It is a free-flowing style that makes use of three apparently incongruous rhetorical elements—cultivated, colloquial, and American-Jewish—each deriving from a different side of Augie's character and announcing, in the very fact of their having been brought together, the new wholeness of being to which Bellow had always aspired. When it works, as it does at many isolated moments in the novel, this style is capable of extraordinary effects:

[Mama] occupied a place, I suppose, among women conquered by a superior force of love, like those women whom Zeus got the better of in animal form and who next had to take cover from his furious wife. Not that I can see my big, gentle, dilapidated, scrubbing, and lugging mother as a fugitive of immense beauty from such classy wrath . . .

But the rightness, the poise, and the easy mastery of this passage are not typical of *Augie* as a whole. More often Bellow seems to be twisting and torturing the language in an almost hysterical effort to get all the juices out of it:

The rest of us had to go to the dispensary—which was like the dream of a multitude of dentists' chairs, hundreds of them in a space as enormous as an armory, and green bowls with designs of glass grapes, drills lifted zigzag as insects' legs, and gas flames on the porcelain swivel trays—a thundery gloom in Harrison Street of limestone county buildings and cumbersome red streetcars with metal grillwork on their windows and monarchical iron whiskers of cowcatchers front and rear. They lumbered and clanged and their brake tanks panted in the slushy brown of a winter afternoon or the bare stone brown of a summer's, salted with ash, smoke, and prairie dust, with long stops at the clinics to let off clumpers, cripples, hunchbacks, brace-legs, crutch-wielders, tooth and eye sufferers, and all the rest.

The frantic and feverish pitch betrays the basic uncertainty that I have been pointing to in the Bellow of *Augie March:* it tells us that there was simply not enough real conviction behind the attitudes out of which the novel was written. And it tells us to expect the radical shift of mood that did indeed come over Bellow in his next book, *Seize the Day.*

PROBABLY IT WOULD be foolish to relate this change too closely to the parallel shift in mood that occurred among American intellectuals in general during the same period. Nevertheless, the parallel is worth noticing, for it suggests that the optimism of the intellectuals about America was as strained and willed as the prose of *Augie March* itself. The irrepressible doubts that lurked on the underside of the new optimism were bound to emerge once more as the dreary Eisenhower years wore on, but when they did emerge, it was in a form very different from the ones they had taken in the decades before World War II. To be sure, the old idea that the modern world was suffering from a "loss of values" came back again, but even that idea soon began to seem inadequate to account for the dimensions of the spiritual vacuum that many intellectuals saw lying beneath the surface prosperity and apparent confidence of the Eisenhower Age. The more and more frequent outbreaks of juvenile violence; the sharp rise in the consumption of narcotics (including legal drugs like tranquillizers and sleeping pills); the fantastic divorce rate; the suicides; the breakdowns—all this showed how great a gap had developed between the realities of experience in America and the moral vocabulary of the age.

It is against this background, I think, that the upsurge during the late 1950s of various forms of antirationalism must be understood. The sudden popularity of Zen, Reichianism, and existentialism reflected the growth of a conviction that the source of our trouble lay deep in the foundations of Western civilization—deeper than politics could reach, deeper than a mere opposition to capitalist society or middle-class values could cure. We were a people so far removed from nature, so lost in abstraction, so cut off from the instinctual that only—as Norman Mailer put it—a "revolution backward toward being" could save us. Bellow, of course, has never gone as far in this direction as Mailer—he has too skeptical a mind to go far in any theoretical direction—but his last two novels, *Seize the Day* and *Henderson the Rain King,* seem to indicate an equally strong awareness on his part of the depth to which the contemporary crisis has cut. The world of *Seize the Day,* indeed, might fairly be compared with the world of Mailer's *The Deer Park,* for each in its own way is an image of a society at the end of its historical term, a civilization whose particular compromise with nature has all but broken down.

Like *The Victim, Seize the Day* is set in New York, but if Bellow once saw the city as a tiny village holding out desperately against the surrounding jungle, here he sees it as "the end of the world, with its complexity and machinery, bricks and tubes, wires and stones, holes and heights." So far has the divorce of man from nature proceeded that "the fathers are no fathers, and the sons no sons," and money—that most refined of all abstractions—rules in place of the natural affections. Communication is no longer possible under these circumstances ("Every other man spoke a language entirely his own, which he had figured out by private thinking"), and there is no telling "the crazy from the sane, the wise from the fools, the young from the old or the sick from the well." Love has disappeared along with communication, and what remains is a world full of lonely men, "a kind of hell [or] at least a kind of purgatory. You walk on the bodies. They are all around. I can hear them cry *de profundis* and wring their hands . . . poor human beasts."

This, then, is a civilization on the edge of collapse:

> Seven percent of this country is committing suicide by alcohol. Another three, maybe, narcotics. Another sixty just fading away into dust by boredom. Twenty more who have sold their souls to the Devil. Then there's the small percentage of those who want to live. That's the only significant thing in the whole world today. Those are the only two classes of people there are. Some want to live, but the great majority don't. . . . They don't, or else why these wars? I'll tell you more. . . . The love of the dying amounts to one thing; they want you to die with them.

The central figure of the story, Tommy Wilhelm, is one of those who want to live, though it is part of Bellow's complex purpose to reveal this fact only gradually both to the reader and to Wilhelm. He is presented at first as a weak, blundering, self-destructive man riddled with self-pity and totally lacking in the resources of character that would enable him to redeem the mess he has made of his life. Only when we reach the closing scene do we realize that his desperate appeals to his father for help and his wild gamble on the commodities exchange were unconsciously motivated (like all the crucial decisions he has ever made) by a saving impulse to liberate himself from the false values that have always dominated his soul. These values are money and success, the pursuit of which has perverted a whole civilization, turning millions of people into slaves of the social system, enemies of themselves, monsters with murder in their hearts who go resentfully and hideously to their graves never knowing why life has been so bitter. Indeed, there is probably no more frightening picture of old age in literature than the one Bellow draws in *Seize the Day*—the men like Wilhelm's father meanly and coldly and selfishly clutching at his withered life, or like the retired chicken farmer Rappaport ("I'm older even than Churchill"), who sits day after day at the commodities exchange greedily waiting for a rise in rye or barley or lard. This is what the pursuit of success and money finally amounts to in the world of *Seize the Day*, and it is what Wilhelm—as he dimly comes to recognize in the closing pages—has always resisted by blundering over and over again into failure.

Because of its masterful concentration, its vividness of detail, its brilliance of characterization, and its grandeur of theme, *Seize the Day* probably deserves its reputation as the best thing Bellow has so far done. It is so good, in fact, that one wonders what prevents it from being great. My guess would be that Bellow was putting the brakes on himself in writing the story, that he allowed a certain timidity in the face of his own most powerful response to life—and I mean to life, not to the historical circumstances of the moment—to soften the impact of his material. This response, to judge by all those things in his work that carry the most conviction, is one of angry resentment and bitterness—precisely the kind of bitterness that is expressed in the terrible words in *King Lear:* "As flies to wanton boys are we to the gods./They kill us for their sport." Even the comic side of his talent participates in this bitterness, for comedy in Bellow's fiction is almost always directed against the utopian theorizers (like Robey, Thea Fenchel, and Bateshaw in *Augie March*), who simply cannot understand how little help there is for being human. For some reason, however, Bellow has never been willing to give his bitterness free rein; he is always trying to stifle it or qualify it, and it is this refusal of anger, I believe, that robs *Seize the Day* of the great power it might have had.

The answer to Wilhelm's predicament, we are given to understand, is love, and we gather from the description of a momentary revelation he had once experienced that by love Bellow means something like the Christian agape. And with a good many Christian writers, he seems to believe that a man's capacity to "seize the day"—that is, to live fully in the present—depends on his capacity to know himself as kin to all other men. The nature to which Bellow wishes to return in *Seize the Day* is not the instinctual nature that Norman Mailer talks about, but nature as the theologians have conceived of it: a harmonious universe ruled over by God, a universe in which man has reassumed his proper place in the cosmic hierarchy. "We are bleeding at the roots, because we are cut off from the earth and sun and stars, and love is a grinning mockery, because, poor blossom, we plucked it from its stem on the tree of Life, and expected it to keep on blooming in our civilized vase on the table." This is not, of course, Bellow; it is D. H. Lawrence. Yet the passage fairly characterizes the doctrinal core of *Seize the Day,* and another remark of Lawrence's points toward the "positive" values implied in the novel: "Augustine said that God created the universe new every day; and to the living, emotional soul this is true. Every day dawns upon an entirely new universe, every Easter lights up an entirely new glory of a new opening in utterly new flower. And the soul of man and the soul of woman is new in the same way, with the infinite delight of life and the ever-newness of life."

But this is a theory, and Bellow, we know, is skeptical of theories, which is perhaps one reason why he puts these sentiments, cruelly vulgarized, into the mouth of Dr. Tamkin, a charlatan, a fake, and a liar. Making Tamkin the spokesman of his own views, however, is perhaps also his way of saying that today even those who know the truth are caught up in the false values of our civilization—the churches, as it were, are corrupt, the prophets are fools and probably a little crazy. Nevertheless, the fact that he is skeptical of the theory does not prevent Bellow from allowing it to inhibit the response which his story, in its primary emotional impact, demands. "You see," Tamkin tells Wilhelm, "I understand what it is when the lonely person begins to feel like an animal. When the night comes and he feels like howling from his window like a wolf." And Wilhelm agrees. "One hundred falsehoods," he says to himself of Tamkin's remarks, "but at last one truth. Howling like a wolf from the city window. No one can bear it any more. Everyone is so full of it that at last everyone must proclaim it. It! It!" What the reader waits for in *Seize the Day* is exactly this howl, some expression of wrath, some violent uproar which would release the "great knot" in Wilhelm's chest that has been strangling him by inches, and which would express the full extent of Bellow's outrage at life. It never comes. All Bellow gives us at the end is a fit of weeping that, he says, carries Wilhelm "toward the consummation of his heart's ultimate need." We have already been told what this need is—it is love. If, however, Bellow had been ruthless in following out the emotional logic of *Seize the Day*, it would almost certainly have been murder—and *Seize the Day* would almost certainly have become a great book.

IN *Henderson the Rain King*, Bellow's latest novel, the ideology of love does not so much inhibit him as obscure his central intention. Returning to the loose picaresque mode of *Augie March*, Bellow tells the story of a middle-aged millionaire, the ne'er-do-well scion of an old patrician family, who runs off to Africa in a state of crisis and is transformed by a series of fantastic adventures he encounters there. The Africa of the novel bears very little relation to the real Africa; it is an imaginary place, and Bellow might have avoided a certain amount of misunderstanding if he had given it an imaginary name. Similarly, if he had presented Henderson in frankly allegorical terms instead of confusing the issue by making him a Hudson Valley aristocrat, he would not have left himself open to the charge of having failed to create a believable hero, or of having failed at the end to put Henderson's regeneration to the test back in the "real" world. In my opinion, while

Henderson is obviously not believable as a Hudson Valley aristocrat, he is completely convincing as an allegorical personification of the vague malaise, the sense of aimless drift and unused energy, that seems to afflict a prosperous and spiritually stagnant society like our own. And while Henderson's regeneration cannot be accepted as a total transformation of character, it seems to me wholly credible as an *experience,* the kind of experience that religious converts speak of when they say they have been reborn.

The important question is: to what, precisely, is Henderson reborn? Here and there, and especially in the concluding pages, Bellow makes several pious gestures in the direction of Love, but this only confuses the issue even further, for if anything Henderson is saved by being reborn into more rather than less self-involvement. The transforming revelation he experiences with the help of King Dahfu is that the world from which he has fled is not to be confused with reality: reality is in the self and not in the circumstances or conditions that surround the self. "The world of facts is real, all right, and not to be altered. The physical is all there, and it belongs to science. But then there is the noumenal department, and there we create and create and create." A voice inside him had been crying *"I want! I want! I want!"* He had never known what it wanted, but now he knows:

> It wanted reality. How much unreality could it stand? . . . We're supposed to think that nobility is unreal. But that's just it. The illusion is on the other foot. They make us think we crave more and more illusions. Why, I don't crave illusions at all. They say, Think Big. Well, that's baloney of course, another business slogan. But greatness! That's another thing altogether. . . . I don't mean pride, or throwing your weight around. But the universe itself being put into us, it calls out for scope. The eternal is bonded onto us. It calls out for its share. This is why guys can't bear to be so cheap.

WITH *Henderson,* then, Bellow seems to have come very close to surrendering the idea that the world of postwar America is a rich and inviting world and that the strategy of alienation is—as he called it in *Dangling Man*—a fool's plea. He is still resolutely nonpolitical, for when he talks in *Henderson* about the "world of facts" that cannot be altered, he makes no effort to exempt the world of social facts from the category of the unalterable. So, too, he is still fixed on the notion that it is only spiritual timidity or—to take another phrase from *Dangling Man*—"a weakness of imagination" that robs us of the capacity to achieve true wholeness of being, true grace of style, true poise of spirit. For all that, however, *Henderson,* properly understood, represents a further stage in Bellow's development away from the forced affirmations of *Augie March*—here, at least, as in *Seize the Day,* he writes with a sharp awareness of the extent to which the problems of contemporary life are more than merely a matter of individual pathology. What one awaits is a novel by Bellow that would unambiguously locate the source of the malaise that afflicts Joseph, Leventhal, Wilhelm, and Henderson in the institutions under which they are forced to live—in that particular "world of facts" which belongs not to science but to politics, not to nature but to history, not to the realm of the physical but to "the noumenal department" where we "create and create and create." Bellow could find no better target than this for the rage that is contained within him and that has perhaps always been stifled only for lack of its proper object.

SIMONE DE BEAUVOIR AS NOVELIST

*T*HE MANDARINS, SIMONE DE Beauvoir's massive new novel about a number of people who bear a close resemblance to Sartre, Camus, and their followers, may very well be the most relentlessly thoroughgoing roman à clef since the eighteenth century. Indeed, virtually nothing in the book but the names of the characters appears to derive from her imagination. We can find several reasons to explain this compulsive reliance on real people and events. One of them, in my opinion, is Mlle. de Beauvoir's deficiency as a novelist; her real talent is for the manipulation of abstract ideas, not the exploration of human relationships and the nuances of feeling. Her grasp of the concrete and the sensuous is so weak, her conception of character so abstract, her sense of drama so static that she seems able to simulate reality only by straying as little as possible from what she has seen and heard. (I would be willing to bet that a fair portion of the dialogue in *The Mandarins* is transcribed from memory.) When she strikes out on her own, attempting to render the quality of an experience, the invariable result is a lapse into banality. In a writer of Mlle. de Beauvoir's sophistication and literacy, this cannot be attributed to mere clumsiness of style or simple lack of taste. There is a total collapse of critical self-awareness in much of the writing that is all the more embarrassing because it goes hand in hand with an almost religious determination to be honest. But Mlle. de Beauvoir's air of being the voice of an age and her certainty that the spiritual, intellectual, political, and even sexual adventures of the group with which she has been associated represent the Experience of Our Time are too powerful to permit the detachment that might have made honesty possible.

With typical French tidiness, Mlle. de Beauvoir divides the Experience of Our Time into two categories, the public and the private. She employs the device of changing the narrative point of view in alternate chapters from the third person to the first, presumably to let us see the public dimension of her characters impersonally and then to expose their private lives through the direct observation of the heroine, who is, to boot, a practicing psychoanalyst. Everyone, then, is examined in turn as a figure in the drama of history and as a creature who eats, drinks, and falls in and out of love.

The third-person plot focuses on Henri Perron, a distinguished writer, a hero of the Resistance, and the editor of an influential newspaper, who is drawn reluctantly into the political upheavals of the postwar world by Robert Dubreuilh, one of the two "greatest minds" of this century. Dubreuilh has a taste for power and a deep conviction that the intellectual can influence the course of events. Consequently, he organizes the S.R.L., a pro-Soviet, anti-American political movement that remains independent of the Communist party in order to assert its disapproval of minor aspects of the Soviet system. Perron agrees with Dubreuilh that justice, equality, and the future of civilization are the exclusive property of the Left, while reaction, privilege, indifference to human suffering, and hostility to culture are a monopoly of the Right, which is led, of course, by America. Both men, that is, are dogmatic Marxists who see the class struggle as the fundamental fact of history and to whom the proletarian revolution is therefore an absolute. But they are also fierce intellectuals, committed just as deeply to another absolute—Culture. For Dubreuilh, the two absolutes are perfectly compatible, but they never manage to get along so well in Perron's mind. Partly because he has no stomach for politics, partly because he is disturbed by Communist tactics, but mainly because politics interferes with his writing (he longs to work on a "light novel" and an "insignificant book"), Perron resists Dubreuilh's efforts to get his full support for the S.R.L., and he finally wrecks the movement by admitting in his newspaper that the Soviet Union maintains slave-labor camps. Dubreuilh takes this as a betrayal of the higher truth embodied in the Revolution and publicly denounces Perron for having sold out to the Right. The breakup of the S.R.L. is a severe blow to Dubreuilh, leading him to the conclusion that Culture has become temporarily irrelevant in the modern world, that the leftist intellectual can do nothing to further the revolutionary cause, and that he had better give up writing, for the Revolution has made Literature obsolete. This position is rather like the one Perron puzzles out for himself while undergoing a few crises of his own. In the end, the two friends are reconciled and, despite their feeling of impotence, plunge into political journalism all over again, in the belief that the intellectual must try to serve both Literature and the Revolution as best he can, even though he knows that the two ideals do not always serve each other.

This part of the novel is done with far more authority than the first-person chapters. It consists mostly of discussions and debates, the only form of discourse with which Mlle. de Beauvoir really feels at home. Yet her attempts to convey Perron's and Dubreuilh's moral crisis suffer from her eagerness to generalize it, without further ado, into a symbol of the modern predicament:

> But now, he had to admit to himself that he was a mature man: young people treated him as an elder, adults as one of them, and some even treated him with respect. Mature, bounded, finite, himself and no one else, nothing but himself. But who was he? In a way, his books would ultimately decide; but on the other hand, he had to know the truth about himself in order to write them. At first sight, the meaning of those months he had just lived through was quite clear, but if you looked more closely everything became hazy. Helping people to think straight, to live better lives—was his heart really set on it, or was it only a humanitarian daydream? Was he really interested in what happened to others, or only in soothing his own conscience?

This abstract bloodlessness is typical of *The Mandarins*. It is what makes the love stories that comprise the private world of the novel seem wholly false, and what turns Dubreuilh, Perron, and their hangers-on into disembodied minds who daily confront the absolutes to prepare themselves for an imminent apocalypse. They are all pure spirits living on intimate terms with the Right, the Left, the Bourgeoisie, the Proletariat—words that represent not human beings but categories of thought, elements of a philosophical problem on which a stand must be taken.

The assumption of an attitude in the face of irreconcilable contradictions—this is all Mlle. de Beauvoir cares about in politics, and it is all that matters to her in love, which in *The Mandarins* constitutes the whole range of private life. The first-person chapters concentrate on three women—the narrator, Anne Dubreuilh (Robert's wife); her eighteen-year-old daughter, Nadine; and Perron's mistress of ten years' standing, Paula. During a visit to America, Anne falls in love with a novelist named Lewis Brogan, but she is unwilling to leave her husband, and her attempt to lead two lives simultaneously results in her losing Brogan. She returns to Paris in despair, and is on the point of committing suicide when she manages to strike an Existentialist attitude toward her situation ("It's strange. I would die alone; yet it's the others who would live my death"), and—true to the philosophical bias of the novel—this enables her to go on living. Nadine, too, is saved from an impulse to destroy herself, by choosing to become a mother, though she has no real desire for domesticity and children.

Paula, on the other hand, lacks the intelligence to recognize the true nature of her predicament, and moves from self-deception to madness and finally into a kind of living death. But Paula has a deeper meaning than Mlle. de Beauvoir may have intended. Paula is the woman entirely absorbed in love and cut off from any attachment to the world of history and culture; she has given up her career as a singer and made her passion for a man into the whole of reality. She represents absolute immersion in private life, in immediate personal concerns, and this Mlle. de Beauvoir regards as a form of madness. The antithesis to Paula is Dubreuilh, who has no private life at all. He hasn't slept with his wife for ten years, and his benevolent indifference to her is exceeded only by his refusal to worry about his daughter. So unencumbered is he by necessities of the flesh that during the war he was able to work efficiently in an unheated room, since he could generate his own heat from within. His complete absorption in public life makes him the most disembodied of all the Mandarins—and this, in Mlle. de Beauvoir's eyes, is greatness.

But the private world to which she is so hostile is the sphere of the concrete, the domain of simple fact, and a novelist turns his back on the concrete at the risk of sterility and lifelessness. Yet the concrete is not only the novelist's proper preserve; it is also the sphere of politics, that pursuit which lives or dies by its sense of fact. So Mlle. de Beauvoir's inability to respond to the concrete (an inability that all the amassing of documentary details cannot conceal) does more than explain the failure of *The Mandarins* as a work of art; it goes far toward accounting for the special political temper of which the book is an expression. The political writings of Sartre and his followers since the war have been marked by a persistent refusal to allow fact to influence abstract ideology in judging either the Soviet Union or the United States. Ironically, one of the main attractions of Marxism for many French intellectuals had been its "realism," its apparent orientation toward the hard facts of material life. After the war, the French intellectual, who, like Perron, in 1935 had considered himself the center of the universe, found that he had become "an insignificant citizen of a fifth-rate power," and this loss of status bred the sense of impotence that lurks in Mlle. de Beauvoir's Existentialism (the universe "is nothing but a huge place of exile"), not to mention Sartre's. It also gave rise to the guilt that overcame the intellectual at the discovery that the things he cherished were irrelevant to the great majority of mankind, who were too busy trying to feed themselves to develop an interest in Culture. To identify himself with the cause of the downtrodden, and to sacrifice his love of ideas and beauty to a concern with the "price of sardines," was his way of making amends for the "selfishness and thoughtlessness" of his prewar life.

How this admirable resolve could have been translated politically into an enthusiasm for the Soviet Union is a question *The Mandarins* inadvertently answers. The same contempt for fact, the same bondage to abstraction, the same atrophy of respect for the concrete that define *The Mandarins* both in its character as a work of art and in its vision of reality permitted Sartre's group to believe—in the teeth of the most obvious evidence—that support of the Communists meant support of the downtrodden. The French intellectual has stared long and hard at the Soviet Union without ever detecting the lineaments of the totalitarian power; all he can see is an incarnation of the "Left"—an abstraction that bears as much relation to the facts of Soviet life and policy as an image of the "counterrevolutionary Right" does to American realities. (Learning that the Soviet Union uses slave labor hardly affects Perron's and Dubreuilh's belief that the Communist state is devoted to justice, equality, and civilization; their quarrel is over the wisdom of telling the truth, not over the true nature of Stalin's regime.) In *The Mandarins,* one might say, Mlle. de Beauvoir reveals herself and her friends as direct descendants of the Jacobins, to whose pathological passion for the abstract Edmund Burke ascribed their tolerance of a tyranny no less cruel than the one they had set out to destroy. And in this sense, as a document of contemporary Jacobinism, *The Mandarins* truly represents an Experience of Our Time.

THE KNOW-NOTHING BOHEMIANS

ALLEN GINSBERG'S LITTLE VOLUME of poems, *Howl,* which got the San Francisco renaissance off to a screaming start, was dedicated to Jack Kerouac ("new Buddha of American prose, who spit forth intelligence into eleven books written in half the number of years . . . creating a spontaneous bop prosody and original classic literature"), William Seward Burroughs ("author of *Naked Lunch,* an endless novel which will drive everybody mad"), and Neal Cassady ("author of *The First Third,* an autobiography . . . which enlightened Buddha"). So far, everybody's sanity has been spared by the inability of *Naked Lunch* to find a publisher,* and we may never get the chance to discover what Buddha learned from Neal Cassady's autobiography, but thanks to the Viking and Grove Presses, two of Kerouac's original classics, *On the Road* and *The Subterraneans,* have now been revealed to the world. When *On the Road* appeared last year, Gilbert Millstein commemorated the event in the *New York Times* by declaring it to be "a historic occasion" comparable to the publication of *The Sun Also Rises* in the 1920s. But even before the novel was actually published, the word got around that Kerouac was the spokesman of a new group of rebels and Bohemians who called themselves the Beat Generation, and soon his photogenic countenance (unshaven, of course, and topped by an unruly crop of rich black hair falling over his forehead) was showing up in various mass-circulation magazines, he was being interviewed earnestly on television, and he was being featured in a Greenwich Village nightclub where, in San Francisco fashion, he read specimens of his spontaneous bop prosody against a background of jazz music.

Though the nightclub act reportedly flopped, *On the Road* sold well enough to hit the best-seller lists for several weeks, and it isn't hard to understand why. Americans love nothing so much as representative documents, and what could be more interesting in this Age of Sociology than a

---

*It did, of course, find one a few years after this piece was written.

novel that speaks for the "young generation"? (The fact that Kerouac is thirty-five or thereabouts was generously not held against him.) Beyond that, however, I think that the unveiling of the Beat Generation was greeted with a certain relief by many people who had been disturbed by the notorious respectability and "maturity" of postwar writing. This was more like it—restless, rebellious, confused youth living it up, instead of thin, balding, buttoned-down instructors of English composing ironic verses with one hand while changing the baby's diapers with the other. Bohemianism is not particularly fashionable nowadays, but the image of Bohemia still exerts a powerful fascination—nowhere more so than in the suburbs, which are filled to overflowing with men and women who uneasily think of themselves as conformists and of Bohemianism as the heroic road. The whole point of Herman Wouk's *Marjorie Morningstar* was to assure the young marrieds of Mamaroneck that they were better off than the apparently glamorous luftmenschen of Greenwich Village, and the fact that Wouk had to work so hard at making this idea seem convincing is a good indication of the strength of prevailing doubt on the matter.

On the surface, at least, the Bohemianism of *On the Road* is very attractive. Here is a group of high-spirited young men running back and forth across the country (mostly hitchhiking, sometimes in their own second-hand cars), going to "wild" parties in New York and Denver and San Francisco, living on a shoestring (GI educational benefits, an occasional fifty bucks from a kindly aunt, an odd job as a typist, a fruitpicker, a parking-lot attendant), talking intensely about love and God and salvation, getting high on marijuana (but never heroin or cocaine), listening feverishly to jazz in crowded little joints, and sleeping freely with beautiful girls. Now and again there is a reference to gloom and melancholy, but the characteristic note struck by Kerouac is exuberance:

> We stopped along the road for a bite to eat. The cowboy went off to have a spare tire patched, and Eddie and I sat down in a kind of homemade diner. I heard a great laugh, the greatest laugh in the world, and here came this rawhide oldtimes Nebraska farmer with a bunch of other boys into the diner; you could hear his raspy cries clear across the plains, across the whole gray world of them that day. Everybody else laughed with him. He didn't have a care in the world and had the hugest regard for everybody. I said to myself, Wham, listen to that man laugh. That's the West, here I am in the West. He came booming into the diner, calling Maw's name, and she made the

sweetest cherry pie in Nebraska, and I had some with a mountainous scoop of ice cream on top. "Maw, rustle me up some grub afore I have to start eatin myself or some damn silly idee like that." And he threw himself on a stool and went hyaw hyaw hyaw hyaw. "And throw some beans in it." It was the spirit of the West sitting right next to me. I wished I knew his whole raw life and what the hell he'd been doing all these years beside laughing and yelling like that. Whooee, I told my soul, and the cowboy came back and off we went to Grand Island.

Kerouac's enthusiasm for the Nebraska farmer is part of his general readiness to find the source of all vitality and virtue in simple rural types and in the dispossessed urban groups (Negroes, bums, whores). His idea of life in New York is "millions and millions hustling forever for a buck among themselves . . . grabbing, taking, giving, sighing, dying, just so they could be buried in those awful cemetery cities beyond Long Island City," whereas the rest of America is populated almost exclusively by the true of heart. There are intimations here of a kind of know-nothing populist sentiment, but in other ways this attitude resembles Nelson Algren's belief that bums and whores and junkies are more interesting than white-collar workers or civil servants. The difference is that Algren hates middle-class respectability for moral and political reasons—the middle class exploits and persecutes—while Kerouac, who is thoroughly unpolitical, seems to feel that respectability is a sign not of moral corruption but of spiritual death. "The only people for me," says Sal Paradise, the narrator of *On the Road,* "are the mad ones, the ones who are mad to live, mad to talk, mad to be saved, desirous of everything at the same time, the ones who never yawn or say a commonplace thing, but burn, burn, burn like fabulous yellow roman candles exploding like spiders across the stars. . . ." This tremendous emphasis on emotional intensity, this notion that to be hopped-up is the most desirable of all human conditions, lies at the heart of the Beat Generation ethos and distinguishes it radically from the Bohemianism of the past.

The Bohemianism of the 1920s represented a repudiation of the provinciality, philistinism, and moral hypocrisy of American life—a life, incidentally, which was still essentially small town and rural in tone. Bohemia, in other words, was a movement created in the name of civilization: its ideals were intelligence, cultivation, spiritual refinement. The typical literary figure of the 1920s was a Midwesterner (Hemingway, Fitzgerald, Sinclair Lewis, Eliot, Pound) who had fled from his hometown to New York or Paris in search of a freer, more expansive, more enlightened way of life than was possible in Ohio or Minnesota or Michigan. The political radicalism that supplied the characteristic coloring of Bohemianism in the 1930s did nothing to alter the urban, cosmopolitan bias of the 1920s. At its best, the radicalism of the 1930s was marked by deep intellectual seriousness and aimed at a state of society in which the fruits of civilization would be more widely available—and ultimately available to all.

The Bohemianism of the 1950s is another kettle of fish altogether. It is hostile to civilization; it worships primitivism, instinct, energy, "blood." To the extent that it has intellectual interests at all, they run to mystical doctrines, irrationalist philosophies, and left-wing Reichianism. The only art the new Bohemians have any use for is jazz, mainly of the cool variety. Their predilection for bop language is a way of demonstrating solidarity with the primitive vitality and spontaneity they find in jazz and of expressing contempt for coherent, rational discourse which, being a product of the mind, is in their view a form of death. To be articulate is to admit that you have no feelings (for how can real feelings be expressed in syntactical language?), that you can't respond to anything (Kerouac responds to everything by saying "Wow!"), and that you are probably impotent.

At the one end of the spectrum, this ethos shades off into violence and criminality, main-line drug addiction and madness. Allen Ginsberg's poetry, with its lurid apocalyptic celebration of "angel-headed hipsters," speaks for the darker side of the new Bohemianism. Kerouac is milder. He shows little taste for violence, and the criminality he admires is the harmless kind. The hero of *On the Road,* Dean Moriarty, has a record: "From the age of eleven to seventeen he was usually in reform school. His specialty was stealing cars, gunning for girls coming out of high school in the afternoon, driving them out to the mountains, making them, and coming back to sleep in any available hotel bathtub in town." But Dean's criminality, we are told, "was not something that sulked and sneered; it was a wild yea-saying overburst of American joy; it was Western, the west wind, an ode from the Plains, something new, long prophesied, long a-coming (he only stole cars for joy rides)." And, in fact, the species of Bohemian that Kerouac writes about is on the whole rather law-abiding. In *The Subterraneans,* a bunch of drunken boys steal a pushcart in the middle of the night, and when they leave it in front of a friend's apartment building, he denounces them angrily for "screwing up the security of my pad." When Sal Paradise (in *On the Road*) steals some groceries from the canteen of an itinerant workers' camp in which he has taken a temporary job as a barracks guard, he comments, "I suddenly began to realize that everybody in America is a natural-born thief"—which, of course, is a way of turning his own stealing into a bit of boyish prankishness. Nevertheless, Kerouac is attracted to criminality, and that in itself is more significant than the fact that he personally feels constrained to put the brakes on his own destructive impulses.

Sex has always played a very important role in Bohemianism: sleeping around was the Bohemian's most dramatic demonstration of his freedom from conventional moral standards, and a defiant denial of the idea that sex was permissible only in marriage and then only for the sake of a family. At the same time, to be promiscuous was to assert the validity of sexual experience in and for itself. The meaning of Bohemian sex, then, was at once social and personal, a crucial element in the Bohemian's ideal of civilization. Here again the contrast with Beat Generation Bohemianism is sharp. On the one hand, there is a fair amount of sexual activity in *On the Road* and *The Subterraneans*. Dean Moriarty is a "new kind of American saint" at least partly because of his amazing sexual powers: he can keep three women satisfied simultaneously and he can make love any time, anywhere (once he mounts a girl in the back seat of a car while poor Sal Paradise is trying to sleep in front). Sal, too, is always on the make, and though he isn't as successful as the great Dean, he does pretty well: offhand I can remember a girl in Denver, one on a bus, and another in New York, but a little research would certainly unearth a few more. The heroine of *The Subterraneans*, a Negro girl named Mardou Fox, seems to have switched from one to another member of the same gang and back again ("This has been an incestuous group in its time"), and we are given to understand that there is nothing unusual about such an arrangement. But the point of all this hustle and bustle is not freedom from ordinary social restrictions or defiance of convention (except in relation to homosexuality, which is Ginsberg's preserve: among "the best minds" of Ginsberg's generation who were destroyed by America are those "who let themselves be fucked in the ass by saintly motorcyclists, and screamed with joy,/who blew and were blown by those human seraphim, the sailors, caresses of Atlantic and Caribbean love"). The sex in Kerouac's books goes hand in hand with a great deal of talk about forming permanent relationships ("although I have a hot feeling sexually and all that for her," says the poet Adam Moorad in *The Subterraneans*, "I really don't want to get any further into her not only for these reasons but finally, the big one, if I'm going to get involved with a girl now I want to be permanent like permanent and serious and long termed and I can't do that with her"), and a habit of getting married and then duly divorced and remarried when another girl comes along. In fact, there are as many marriages and divorces in *On the Road* as in the Hollywood movie colony (must be that California climate): "All those years I was looking for the woman I wanted to marry," Sal Paradise tells us. "I couldn't meet a girl without saying to myself, What kind of wife would she make?" Even more revealing is Kerouac's refusal to admit that any of his characters ever makes love wantonly or lecherously—no matter how casual the encounter it must always entail sweet feelings toward the girl. Sal, for example, is fixed up with Rita Bettencourt in Denver, whom he has never met before. "I got her in my bedroom after a long talk in the dark of the front room. She was a nice little girl, simple and true [naturally], and tremendously frightened of sex. I told her it was beautiful. I wanted to prove this to her. She let me prove it, but I was too impatient and proved nothing. She sighed in the dark. 'What do you want out of life?' I asked, and I used to ask that all the time of girls." This is rather touching, but only because the narrator is really just as frightened of sex as that nice little girl was. He is frightened of failure and he worries about his performance. For *performance* is the point—performance and "good orgasms," which are the first duty of man and the only duty of woman. What seems to be involved here, in short, is sexual anxiety of enormous proportions—an anxiety that comes out very clearly in *The Subterraneans,* which is about a love affair between the young writer, Leo Percepied, and the Negro girl, Mardou Fox. Despite its protestations, the book is one long agony of fear and trembling over sex:

> I spend long nights and many hours making her, finally I have her, I pray for it to come, I can hear her breathing harder, I hope against hope it's time, a noise in the hall (or whoop of drunkards next door) takes her mind off and she can't make it and laughs—but when she does make it I hear her crying, whimpering, the shuddering electrical female orgasm makes her sound like a little girl crying, moaning in the night, it lasts a good twenty seconds and when it's over she moans, "O why can't it last longer," and "O when will I when you do?"—"Soon now I bet," I say, "you're getting closer and closer"—

Very primitive, very spontaneous, very elemental, very beat.

For the new Bohemians interracial friendships and love affairs apparently play the same role of social defiance that sex used to play in older Bohemian circles. Negroes and whites associate freely on a basis of complete equality and without a trace of racial hostility. But putting it that way understates the case, for not only is there no racial hostility, there is positive adulation for the "happy, true-hearted, ecstatic Negroes of America."

> At lilac evening I walked with every muscle aching among the lights of 27th and Welton in the Denver colored section, wishing I were a Negro, feeling that the best the white world had offered was not enough ecstasy for me, not enough life, joy, kicks, darkness, music, not enough night. . . . I wished I were a Denver Mexican, or even a poor overworked Jap, anything but what I was so drearily, a "white man" disillusioned. All my life I'd had white ambitions. . . . I passed the dark porches of Mexican and Negro homes; soft voices were there, occasionally the dusky knee of some mysterious sensuous gal; and dark faces of the men behind rose arbors. Little children sat like sages in ancient rocking chairs.

It will be news to the Negroes to learn that they are so happy and ecstatic; I doubt if a more idyllic picture of Negro life has been painted since certain Southern ideologues tried to convince the world that things were just as fine as fine could be for the slaves on the old plantation. Be that as it may, Kerouac's love for Negroes and other dark-skinned groups is tied up with his worship of primitivism, not with any radical social attitudes. Ironically enough, in fact, to see the Negro as more elemental than the white man, as Ned Polsky has acutely remarked, is "an inverted form of keeping the nigger in his place." But even if it were true that American Negroes, by virtue of their position in our culture, have been able to retain a degree of primitive spontaneity, the last place you would expect to find evidence of this is among Bohemian Negroes. Bohemianism, after all, is for the Negro a means of entry into the world of the whites, and no Negro Bohemian is going to cooperate in the attempt to identify him with Harlem or Dixieland. The only major Negro character in either of Kerouac's two novels is Mardou Fox, and she is about as primitive as Wilhelm Reich himself.

The plain truth is that the primitivism of the Beat Generation serves first of all as a cover for an anti-intellectualism so bitter that it makes the ordinary American's hatred of eggheads seem positively benign. Kerouac and his friends like to think of themselves as intellectuals ("they are intellectual as hell and know all about Pound without being pretentious or talking too much about it"), but this is only a form of newspeak. Here is an example of what Kerouac considers intelligent discourse—"formal and shining and complete, without the tedious intellectualness":

We passed a little kid who was throwing stones at the cars in the road. "Think of it," said Dean. "One day he'll put a stone through a man's windshield and the man will crash and die—all on account of that little kid. You see what I mean? God exists without qualms. As we roll along this way I am positive beyond doubt that everything will be taken care of for us—that even you, as you drive, fearful of the wheel . . . the thing will go along of itself and you won't go off the road and I can sleep. Furthermore we know America, we're at home; I can go anywhere in America and get what I want because it's the same in every corner, I know the people, I know what they do. We give and take and go in the incredibly complicated sweetness zigzagging every side."

You see what he means? Formal and shining and complete. No tedious intellectualness. Completely unpretentious. "There was nothing clear about the things he said but what he meant to say was somehow made pure and clear." *Somehow.* Of course. If what he wanted to say had been carefully thought out and precisely articulated, that would have been tedious and pretentious and, no doubt, *somehow* unclear and clearly impure. But so long as he utters these banalities with his tongue tied and with no comprehension of their meaning, so long as he makes noises that come out of his soul (since they couldn't possibly have come out of his mind), he passes the test of true intellectuality.

Which brings us to Kerouac's spontaneous bop prosody. This "prosody" is not to be confused with bop language itself, which has such a limited vocabulary (Basic English is a verbal treasure-house by comparison) that you couldn't write a note to the milkman in it, much less a novel. Kerouac, however, manages to remain true to the spirit of hipster slang while making forays into enemy territory (i.e., the English language) by his simple inability to express anything in words. The only method he has of describing an object is to summon up the same half-dozen adjectives over and over again: "greatest," "tremendous," "crazy," "mad," "wild," and perhaps one or two others. When it's more than just mad or crazy or wild, it becomes "really mad" or "really crazy" or "really wild." (All quantities in excess of three, incidentally, are subsumed under the rubric "innumerable," a word used innumerable times in *On the Road* but not so innumerably in *The Subterraneans.*) The same poverty of resources is apparent in those passages where Kerouac tries to handle a situation involving even slightly complicated feelings. His usual tactic is to run for cover behind cliché and vague signals to the reader. For instance: "I looked at him; my eyes were watering with embarrassment and tears. Still he stared at me. Now his eyes were blank and looking through me. . . . Something clicked in both of us. In me it was suddenly concern for a man who was years younger than I, five years, and whose fate was wound with mine across the passage of recent years; in him it was a matter that I can ascertain only from what he did afterward." If you can ascertain what this is all about, either beforehand, during, or afterward, you are surely no square.

In keeping with its populistic bias, the style of *On the Road* is folksy and lyrical. The prose of *The Subterraneans,* on the other hand, sounds like an inept parody of Faulkner at his worst, the main difference being that Faulkner usually produces bad writing out of an impulse to inflate the commonplace while Kerouac gets into trouble by pursuing "spontaneity." Strictly speaking, spontaneity is a quality of feeling, not of writing: when we call a piece of writing spontaneous, we are registering our impression that the author hit upon the right words without sweating, that no "art" and no calculation entered into the picture, that his feelings seem to have spoken themselves, seem to have sprouted a tongue at the moment of composition. Kerouac apparently thinks that spontaneity is a matter of saying whatever comes into your head, in any order you happen to feel like saying it. It isn't the *right* words he wants (even if he knows what they might be), but the first words, or at any rate the words that most obviously announce themselves as deriving from emotion rather than cerebration, as coming from "life" rather than "literature," from the guts rather than the brain. (The brain, remember, is the angel of death.) But writing that springs easily and "spontaneously" out of strong feelings is *never* vague; it always has a quality of sharpness and precision because it is in the nature of strong feelings to be aroused by specific objects. The notion that a diffuse, generalized, and unrelenting enthusiasm is the mark of great sensitivity and responsiveness is utterly fantastic, an idea that comes from taking drunkenness or drug addiction as the state of perfect emotional vigor. The effect of such enthusiasm is actually to wipe out the world altogether, for if a filling station will serve as well as the Rocky Mountains to arouse a sense of awe and wonder, then both the filling station and the mountains are robbed of their reality. Kerouac's conception of feeling is one that only a solipsist could believe in—and a solipsist, be it noted, is a man who does not relate easily to anything outside himself.

Solipsism is precisely what characterizes Kerouac's fiction. *On the Road* and *The Subterraneans* are so patently autobiographical in content that they become almost impossible to discuss as novels; if spontaneity were indeed a matter of destroying the distinction between life and literature, these books would unquestionably be It. "As we were going out to the car Babe slipped and fell flat on her face. Poor girl was overwrought. Her brother Tim and I helped her up. We got in the car; Major and Betty joined us. The sad ride back to Denver began." Babe is a girl who is mentioned a few times in the course of *On the Road;* we don't know why she is overwrought on this occasion, and even if we did it wouldn't matter, since there is no reason for her presence in the book at all. But Kerouac tells us that she fell flat on her face while walking toward a car. It is impossible to believe that Kerouac made this detail up, that his imagination was creating a world real enough to include wholly gratuitous elements; if that were the case, Babe would have come alive as a human being. But she is only a name; Kerouac never even describes her. She is in the book because the sister of one of Kerouac's friends was there when he took a trip to Central City, Colorado, and she slips in *On the Road* because she slipped that day on the way to the car. What is true of Babe who fell flat on her face is true of virtually every incident in *On the Road* and *The Subterraneans.* Nothing that happens has any dramatic reason for happening. Sal Paradise meets such-and-such people on the road whom he likes or (rarely) dislikes; they exchange a few words, they have a few beers together, they part. It is all very unremarkable and commonplace, but for Kerouac it is always the greatest, the wildest, the most. What you get in these two books is a man proclaiming that he is *alive* and offering every trivial experience he has ever had in evidence. Once I did this, once I did that (he is saying) and by God, it *meant* something! Because I *responded!* But if it meant something, and you responded so powerfully, why can't you explain what it meant, and why do you have to insist so?

I think it is legitimate to say, then, that the Beat Generation's worship of primitivism and spontaneity is more than a cover for hostility to intelligence; it arises from a pathetic poverty of feeling as well. The hipsters and hipster lovers of the Beat Generation are rebels, all right, but not against anything so sociological and historical as the middle class or capitalism or even respectability. This is the revolt of the spiritually underprivileged and the crippled of soul—young men who can't think straight and so hate anyone who can; young men who can't get outside the morass of self and so construct definitions of feeling that exclude all human beings who manage to live, even miserably, in a world of objects; young men who are burdened unto death with the specially poignant sexual anxiety that America—in its eternal promise of erotic glory and its spiteful withholding of actual erotic possibility—seems bent on breeding, and who therefore dream of the unattainable perfect orgasm, which excuses all sexual failures in the real world. Not long ago, Norman Mailer suggested that the rise of the hipster may represent "the first wind of a second revolution in this century, moving not forward toward action and more rational equitable distribution, but backward toward being and the secrets of human energy." To tell the truth, whenever I hear anyone talking about instinct and being and the secrets of human energy, I get nervous; next thing you know he'll be saying that violence is just fine, and then I begin wondering whether he really thinks that kicking someone in the teeth or sticking a knife between his ribs are deeds to be admired. History, after all—and especially the history of modern times—teaches that there is a close connection between ideologies of primitivistic vitalism and a willingness to look upon cruelty and bloodletting with complacency, if not downright enthusiasm. The reason I bring this up is that the spirit of hipsterism and the Beat Generation strikes me as the same spirit which animates the young savages in leather jackets who have been running amok in the last few years with their switchblades and zip guns. What does Mailer think of those wretched kids, I wonder? What does he think of the gang that stoned a nine-year-old boy to death in Central Park in broad daylight a few months ago, or the one that set fire to an old man drowsing on a bench near the Brooklyn waterfront one summer's day, or the one that pounced on a crippled child and orgiastically stabbed him over and over and over again even after he was good and dead? Is that what he means by the liberation of instinct and the mysteries of being? Maybe so. At least he says somewhere in his article that two eighteen-year-old hoodlums who bash in the brains of a candy-store keeper are murdering an institution, committing an act that "violates private property"—which is one of the most morally gruesome ideas I have ever come across, and which indicates where the ideology of hipsterism can lead. I happen to believe that there is a direct connection between the flabbiness of American middle-class life and the spread of juvenile crime in the 1950s, but I also believe that juvenile crime can be explained partly in terms of the same resentment against normal feeling and the attempt to cope with the world through intelligence that lies behind Kerouac and Ginsberg. Even the relatively mild ethos of Kerouac's books can spill over easily into brutality, for there is a suppressed cry in those books: kill the intellectuals who can talk coherently, kill the people who can sit still for five minutes at a time, kill those incomprehensible characters who are capable of getting seriously involved with a woman, a job, a cause. How can anyone in his right mind pretend that this has anything to do with private property or the middle class? No. Being against what the Beat Generation stands for has to do with denying that incoherence is superior to precision; that ignorance is superior to knowledge; that the exercise of mind and discrimination is a form of death. It has to do with fighting the notion that sordid acts of violence are justifiable so long as they are committed in the name of "instinct." It even has to do with fighting the poisonous glorification of the adolescent in American popular culture. It has to do, in other words, with one's attitude toward intelligence itself.

HUCK FINN'S LITERARY JOURNEY

"Persons attempting to find a motive in this narrative will be prosecuted," wrote Mark Twain in a notice at the head of *The Adventures of Huckleberry Finn;* "persons attempting to find a moral in it will be banished; persons attempting to find a plot in it will be shot." This month marks the seventy-fifth anniversary of the publication of *Huckleberry Finn,* and by now the number of candidates for prosecution, banishment, and shooting must be very large indeed—far larger than Mark Twain could ever have anticipated. No other American novel (with the possible exception of *Moby-Dick*) has been so thoroughly ransacked for motives and morals, so lovingly examined, so jealously claimed as an ally in so many different polemical campaigns.

In the early years of the century, Van Wyck Brooks (who had not yet become the leading patriot of American culture) cited it in support of his contention that the crudity of life in the West had combined with the emasculating gentility of the East to cripple the genius of Mark Twain and prevent his proper development as an artist. Some time later, Bernard de Voto, rushing to the defense of the West, pointed to *Huckleberry Finn* itself to refute Brooks, and far from indicting American life for the destruction of Mark Twain, gave it full credit for having produced and nourished him.

More recently, the issue has shifted to deeper ground, and *Huckleberry Finn* is now read as a key to the very essence of the American imagination, a central document of our most primitive impulses. A few years ago, Leslie Fiedler gained a greater degree of notoriety than it is usually given to literary critics to achieve by suggesting that the relation between Huck and Jim expresses the homosexual attraction toward Negroes which Mr. Fiedler discovered hidden in the furthest recesses of the American unconscious. (It is amusing to speculate on the punishment Mark Twain might have thought up for *this* kind of motive hunting had he been prescient enough to know that it would some day come into fashion.)

Other contemporary critics, more restrained than Mr. Fiedler though

hardly less exuberant, have spoken of Huck as an archetype or a mythic figure who embodies the nostalgia for innocence and the fantasy of flight
from maturity that are said to be so characteristic of the American soul.

Sooner or later, it seems, all discussions of *Huckleberry Finn* turn into
discussions of America—and with good reason. Mark Twain was the quintessential American writer, quintessential because he was more or less untutored—"a natural," as Wright Morris puts it, "who learned to write the way
a river pilot learns the feel of a channel." And Richard Chase, in his
remarkable book on the American novel, observes that *Huckleberry Finn* is
constantly engaged in an "exorcism of false forms" through parody and
burlesque, and that the chief exorcism performed by the novel is done
upon "European culture itself."

Why did Mark Twain find it necessary to exorcise European culture?
Partly, of course, in order to liberate himself from the grip of an approved literary style that bore no relation to living American speech, but also, in my
opinion, because what he had to say about life could not have been said by a
writer whose attitudes had been molded by the European sense of things.

Someone once quipped that the whole of philosophy is a footnote to
Plato, and it might be remarked with equal justice that the whole of European literature is a commentary on the first sentence of Aristotle's *Politics*.
Man, says European literature in a thousand different ways and in tones
ranging from dismay to jubilation—man is by *nature* a social animal. To
conceive of the individual as existing apart from society is an illusion or at
best a convenient fiction; there is no State of Nature and there never was
one. It was this idea more than anything else, I believe, that Mark Twain
was trying to exorcise in *Huckleberry Finn*. He was asserting through the
image of life on the raft that the State of Nature is a reality, and he was
asserting through the character of Huck that the distinction between the
individual and society is a true distinction and a necessary one.

Lionel Trilling, in his brilliant introduction to *Huckleberry Finn*, takes
rather a different view of the matter. Mr. Trilling, of course, recognizes that
the novel is built on an opposition between nature and society, but he cautions us against thinking of that opposition as absolute. Huck, he tells us,
"is involved in civilization up to his ears," and his flight from society "is but
his way of reaching what society ideally dreams of for itself." This interpretation, I should say, is itself in need of exorcism, for it is an attempt to
assimilate *Huckleberry Finn* into what I have characterized as the European
sense of things.

Surely the fact that Huck "has not run away from Miss Watson and the Widow Douglas and his brutal father to a completely individualistic liberty" only proves that Mark Twain's idea of the State of Nature is not Freud's or Hobbes's. And surely the fact that "responsibility is the very essence of Huck's character" only proves that Mark Twain differs from Mr. Trilling in his view of what belongs to nature and what to civilization. The truth is that all the virtues civilization claims for itself (and which Mr. Trilling claims for it)—responsibility, love, loyalty, generosity, and so on— are seen in *Huckleberry Finn* as properties of the State of Nature. Civilization, to be sure, has usurped credit for them, but what else does this novel demonstrate over and over again if not that civilization is really their mortal enemy?

No more devastating comment has ever been made on the fraudulent pretensions of civilization than the great scene in which Huck struggles with himself over the question of whether to turn Jim back to Miss Watson. Huck, of course, is not consciously a rebel against the values of his society, and he never doubts that he has done wrong in helping a runaway slave to escape. After he discovers that the Duke and the King have sold Jim back into captivity, he decides that the hand of Providence has slapped him in the face, "letting me know my wickedness was being watched all the time from up there in heaven, whilst I was stealing a poor old woman's nigger that hadn't ever done me no harm." He tries to console himself with the reflection that "I was brung up wicked, and so I warn't so much to blame," but he is too honest to accept this as an adequate excuse, and finally he scrawls a note to Miss Watson telling her where she can find Jim.

The passage that follows the note is one of the supreme moments in all of literature:

> I felt good and all washed clean of sin for the first time I had ever felt so in my life, and I knowed I could pray now. But I didn't do it straight off, but laid the paper down and set there thinking—thinking how good it was all this happened so, and how near I come to being lost and going to hell. And went on thinking. And got to thinking over our trip down the river; and I see Jim before me all the time: in the day and in the night-time, sometimes moonlight, sometimes storms, and we a-floating along, talking and singing and laughing. But somehow I couldn't seem to strike no places to harden me against him, but only the other kind.

And he goes on remembering details of their voyage down the river together, until his glance falls on the note he has just written to Miss Watson. "It was a close place. I took it up, held it in my hand. I was a-trembling, because I'd got to decide, forever, betwixt two things, and I knowed it. I studied a minute, sort of holding my breath, and then says to myself: 'All right, then, I'll *go* to hell'—and tore it up. It was awful thoughts and awful words, but they was said. And I let them stay said; and never thought no more about reforming."

We must not be misled by the humor of the concluding lines into supposing that Huck's belief in his own damnation is perfunctory or insincere. Mark Twain is using the device of comic exaggeration—reaching all the way down into hell—in order to make the contrast between the "civilized" values and Huck's natural feelings as stark as he possibly can.

The contempt for civilization that breathes through every page of *Huckleberry Finn*—both the particular civilization Mark Twain was writing about and civilization in general—is only matched in intensity by the reverence for nature embodied in the character of Huck and in the image of the river. The Mississippi, as Mr. Trilling rightly observes, is a god in this novel, and those who attune themselves to its ways are able to share in its power, its vitality, and its beauty. There is also danger in the river and destruction and loneliness, for the god has his sullen moods and refuses to be placated. But though the river can maim and kill, it cannot do what society invariably does: it cannot warp a man's feelings into ugly and unnatural shapes, and it cannot distort the clarity of his vision of the truth.

Now that I have succeeded in adding myself to the violators of Mark Twain's ordinance against finding motives in *Huckleberry Finn*, I might as well follow Huck's example and go the whole hog in wickedness by looking for a moral, too. The moral, I think, will be obvious to anyone who feels the sharpness of the opposition Mark Twain sets up between nature and society. *Huckleberry Finn* is a celebration of the instinctive promptings of the individual against the conditioned self, and a refutation of the heretical idea that reality can be equated with any given set of historical circumstances. This heresy has become even more powerful today than it was seventy-five years ago, and there can be no better protection against the morality of "adjustment" than Mark Twain's uncompromising, hardheaded insistence on the distinction between nature and society.

For that matter, it might be a good idea to pass a law requiring social workers, guidance counselors, and all the members of certain schools of psychoanalysis to read *Huckleberry Finn* at least once a year. There is no telling what might happen if the proponents of adjustment were forced into periodic contemplation of a character who is more civilized than his mentors and more mature than his elders precisely by virtue of his refusal to submit to their notion of what is necessary, "natural," and real.

The 1960s

FROM the start, Podhoretz has consistently defended a belief in the primacy of natural law. In the early 1950s, and again from the 1970s onward, that belief demanded of him a passionate defense of American civilization. But in the late 1950s, as is evident from the essays on Bellow and Twain, his emphasis on the virtues of American civilization began giving way to a new stress on its failings and deficiencies.

This shift, along with a parallel but more narrowly political change in his thinking, led by the early 1960s to Podhoretz's emergence as one of the intellectual leaders in the quest for a new radicalism—new in that it would be untainted by the Communist sympathies that had perverted the radicalism of the 1930s, and radical in that it would be aimed at "perfecting" American society. Accordingly, in *Commentary* he began promoting, and in some cases rescuing from obscurity, a number of writers who would soon become pipers of the young—among them Paul Goodman, James Baldwin, and Norman O. Brown. Later he would express serious public doubts about most of these writers, but for now he did much as an editor to establish and spread their influence.

He would in time also have grave second thoughts about some of the ideas in his own writings of this period, and in general about the utopian perspective that informed them. And yet, in spite of this temporary infatuation with utopianism, his approach to the problems of the day remained refreshingly free of cant. No doubt the reason was that, while more capable than most writers of cerebrating upon abstract principles, he always weighed them on the scales of his immediate experience—the pleasures and pains felt during the decades that had taken him from Brownsville to the Columbia campus, or from his rooms at Cambridge to the editor's chair at *Commentary.*

Those decades are the subject of *Making It,* whose first chapter, included here, begins with a sentence that would become famous: "One of the longest journeys in the world is the journey from Brooklyn to Manhattan." In describing that journey, *Making It* unforgettably exemplifies Podhoretz's saving trust in his own experience not only over abstraction but also over the conflicting ideas of others. As such, the book represents a further development of the form Podhoretz first used in "My Negro Problem—and Ours." It is a form he has sometimes called (rather inelegantly, as he himself acknowledges) "auto-case history" in that, unlike straightforward autobiography, it strictly limits itself to as much of his personal experience as can shed light on the theme or the problem being explored.

As its provocative title defiantly proclaims, the problem being explored in *Making It* is ambition, or the hunger for success. In arguing that it's a hunger no less fierce among writers and intellectuals than among other Americans, Podhoretz recognizes, as he says in the preface, that he's betraying a "dirty little secret" (a then little-known phrase he borrowed from D. H. Lawrence—writing about sex—and that would now enter into general circulation). He also recognizes that by drawing on his own career to examine the pursuit, and the achievement, of success in America, he is opening himself up to accusations "of self-inflation and therefore of tastelessness." Actually, as "The Brutal Bargain" poignantly demonstrates in its account of the subtle "treason" to family and childhood friends that the "journey from Brooklyn to Manhattan" entails, Podhoretz is fully alive to the costs of success, even as he refuses to surrender to the "dirty little secret" by piously and hypocritically denigrating its benefits.

This complicating aspect of the book was for all intents and purposes entirely disregarded in the many attacks on it, including the one by Podhoretz's then close friend Norman Mailer (see page 399). Nor is this the only reason that the attacks, taken together, seem acts of bad faith. Twentieth-century Anglo-American writers may discountenance success, the hoped-for extrinsic outcome of ambition, in favor of intrinsic values—things supposedly good in themselves, regardless of whether other people are willing to admire or even buy them. But virtually all of Western literature, from the Greeks until the Romantics (and much since), is plainly of the opinion that "wealth, power, and especially fame," in Podhoretz's list of the various forms success can take, "are immensely desirable things to have." Obviously these winnings can be badly invested, and evil things can flow from them. But just as obviously, they can be well invested, and from them good things can flow. Naturally, then, Podhoretz wanted to be successful—to achieve not money or power, but fame. Fame in service of personal gratification, certainly, but in my judgment, in service of something greater.

That service was, first of all, as an editor. In his essay, "In Defense of Editing," Podhoretz declares, rightly I believe, that at *Commentary* he has been defending nothing less than the English language. Because the specialized journals had become unreadable (and if that was true in the 1960s, a perusal—one cannot say a "reading"—of *Social Text* or *Critical Inquiry* will confirm that it's even truer today), it was now the general-audience magazine editor's responsibility "to reconstruct [the] shattered common language" and keep it alive.

The immediate background to Podhoretz's understanding of his task was surely the then-dubbed "two cultures" debate between physicist turned novelist C. P. Snow and F. R. Leavis. Snow bemoaned the widening divide between science and the humanities—their mutual unintelligibility, but especially the failure of humanists to make the effort to grasp the work of scientists—and Leavis acidulously replied that there is only one culture, and that it isn't called science.

But the deeper background, I suspect, would be Podhoretz's sympathy with the position forwarded in George Orwell's "Politics and the English Language" (1946), that justly eminent appeal for concreteness, directness, and candor in expression. Totalitarianism and other forms of tyranny flourish on euphemism—calling mass killings or deportations "ethnic cleansing," for instance; therefore, seeing and naming the object as it really is can be a weapon for political liberty. Similarly, the endeavor "to reconstruct [the] shattered common language" that physicists and historians, mathematicians and classicists once spoke around the not-altogether-mythic High Table affirms a world of shared information and ideas, which, too, is political liberty's ally.

The rejection of euphemism meant that Podhoretz's "My Negro Problem—and Ours" at first seemed to contain something to offend everyone: liberal integrationists, black nationalists, and Jews. Later it would seem to contain something to please, if not everyone, then those who thought whites were incurably racist. Not that Podhoretz had said *that:* he had said that whites were sick and twisted in their feelings about blacks. But this was taken as "the functional equivalent" of white racism (I'm quoting a 1993 "Postscript" not included here) and was thought to justify black apathy: since they could do nothing to change white racism, there was in effect nothing that blacks could do for themselves.

This, however, is to fall back upon generalizations. The genius of the

1963 essay, the first one Podhoretz felt he was writing entirely in his own voice and in his own "auto-case history" form, resides in its street-level particulars—the etiology of "my" problem with Negroes, as African Americans were then called by themselves as well as by others, going back to his encounters with them as a boy in Brownsville. What as an adult he read in the liberal, integrationist press didn't jibe with what he could remember from the 1930s and 1940s: the Jews he knew weren't rich, they were poor; and the blacks, while hardly rich (who in Brownsville was?), weren't persecuted, they were persecutors. Baited, bullied, and beaten by blacks, the child Podhoretz naturally feared and hated them, just as, noting their physical grace in sports or dance, or their ability to thumb the nose at authorities, he envied them. Podhoretz may have flirted on the streets with a rather mild form of delinquency, but at home and at school he was a "good boy," a striver who frequently wished he might say "to hell with it" as most of the blacks did. For they were "*really* bad, bad in a way that beckoned to one, and made one feel inadequate."

And if whites looked upon blacks in this faceless way, blacks returned the favor: to them, James Baldwin had said, all whites were "jailers" to be hated, and their self-repressive discipline something to be shunned as Uncle Tom-ish. To study in school was to act white, just as to go (in a term not yet invented) "wilding" in the park was to act black. Reciprocal fear, hatred, and envy were in any event no basis for living together, which is why Podhoretz believed that both the integrationist program and Baldwin's pleas for love were doomed. Ergo Podhoretz's very American, and very desperate, assimilationist proposal: let the races blend together through mixed marriages. Had the maintenance over the centuries of a separate Jewish identity been worth the cost of the persecutions it entailed, culminating in the murder of six million by the Nazis? And if the answer might possibly be No, why should black people, whose history as a distinct race seemed to Podhoretz less rich than that of the Jews, wish to remain separate?

Two rejoinders from Ralph Ellison stopped this interracialist proposal in its tracks: first, white-black marriages would lead not to the disappearance of racial difference but to the production of more babies who would simply be looked on as black; second, black culture in America had produced music, literature, religion, folklore, etc., in which great pride could and should be taken. (See p. 362 below.) Rather than cast their culture off as—in Podhoretz's word—a "stigma," blacks ought to continue building upon it. Podhoretz took both points. Where he went next in thinking about race and ethnicity we will see in later sections of this *Reader.*

The other front in the ethnic wars that concerned Podhoretz in the 1960s, as it had before and would after, is where Jews must defend themselves against non-Jews or, as in "Hannah Arendt on Eichmann," against other Jews. His subtitle, "A Study in the Perversity of Brilliance," contrasts Arendt's cleverness and moral ambiguity with Baldwin's eloquence and moral melodrama. Moral ambiguity is what modernist literature had taught intellectuals to appreciate: Baldwin's story of good egalitarian vs. evil racist was by that standard uninteresting because simplistically "sentimental." How brilliant, yet also how perverse, was Arendt's story of the evil but banal Nazi, not the Jew as virtuous martyr but the Jew as executioner's accomplice.

By perverse, Podhoretz means false. The Final Solution, he insists, was not a utilitarian means to a rational end, say of winning the war. On the contrary: as he reminds Arendt, the Nazis fanatically ignored the greater utility of sending more soldiers to the front in 1944–45, and instead diverted trains to transport Jews to the death camps. The Final Solution, then, was a monomaniacal means to an irrational end, namely the wholesale slaughter of European Jewry. Arendt blames Jewish leaders for collaborating with their persecutors when, she avers, determined opposition would have saved countless lives.

Podhoretz demonstrates that Jewish cooperation doesn't begin to account for six million dead, and that such cooperation as took place merely replicated the attempts by the appeasers in England and France during the 1930s to deal with Hitler as a "statesman." They all assumed "that the Nazis were rational beings and that their aims must therefore be limited and subject to negotiation." This is a theme Podhoretz will return to again and again: when opposed by a party whose aims are limitless—the Soviets who wanted to dominate the West, the Arabs who want to drive Israel into the sea—one cannot negotiate without falling into a trap. Negotiation entails compromises and trade-offs, the stuff of rational problem solving. Nazi, Soviet, or Palestinian eliminationism is interested not in compromise but in total victory.

The immediate point, however, was in reaction to Arendt's relentless brief against the Jews, who, whether going to their death, running a country, or prosecuting a trial, could do nothing right. Enough apology and recrimination, Podhoretz insisted: the Jewish leaders did what they did, and were what they were. "None of it mattered in the slightest to the final result. Murderers with the power to murder descended upon a defenseless people and murdered a large part of it. What else is there to say?"

One more thing, actually, and Podhoretz himself says it. It is that the time has come to reexamine Arendt's theory of totalitarianism. In later years (see the section of this *Reader* covering the 1980s), he will reexamine his own reexamination of how the theory of totalitarianism applies to Communism in general and the Soviet Union in particular. But there will be no second thoughts about the element of the theory that reduces individuals to machines ("banal" functionaries), and induces us to forget what, as Podhoretz puts it, we know about "the Nature of Man." Which is that people make and are responsible for moral choices: "uninteresting though it may be to say so, no person could have joined the Nazi party, let alone the S.S., who was not at the very least a *vicious* anti-Semite; to believe otherwise is to learn nothing about the nature of anti-Semitism"—or anti-any-bodyism, whether the anybody is a race, a class, an ethnic group, or a religious community. Such hatreds are "evil"—the once-foundational moral concept is one Podhoretz has repeatedly tried to revivify, as he has the concept of "good"—and that is why, to recur to the end of "My Negro Problem," he asserts that, should his daughters have proposed to marry black husbands, he would have suppressed his *own* "sick feelings" and supported what *appeared* to be the last best hope, miscegenation.

As for the Jews, they are people who, like all other mortal beings, are capable of moral evil and moral good. They should therefore let up on themselves and cease feeling that they have to be morally superior in order to justify their very existence. Nevertheless, Podhoretz will subsequently go on to contend that in defending themselves against aggression, the Jews of Israel have behaved rather better than most. But that's an issue that will come to the fore in due course.

—TLJ

MY NEGRO PROBLEM—AND OURS

If we—and . . . I mean the relatively conscious whites and the relatively conscious blacks, who must, like lovers, insist on, or create, the consciousness of the others—do not falter in our duty now, we may be able, handful that we are, to end the racial nightmare, and achieve our country, and change the history of the world.

—JAMES BALDWIN

TWO IDEAS PUZZLED ME DEEPLY as a child growing up in Brooklyn during the 1930s in what today would be called an integrated neighborhood. One of them was that all Jews were rich; the other was that all Negroes were persecuted. These ideas had appeared in print; therefore they must be true. My own experience and the evidence of my senses told me they were not true, but that only confirmed what a daydreaming boy in the provinces—for the lower-class neighborhoods of New York belong as surely to the provinces as any rural town in North Dakota—discovers very early: *his* experience is unreal and the evidence of his senses is not to be trusted. Yet even a boy with a head full of fantasies incongruously synthesized out of Hollywood movies and English novels cannot altogether deny the reality of his own experience—especially when there is so much deprivation in that experience. Nor can he altogether gainsay the evidence of his own senses—especially such evidence of the senses as comes from being repeatedly beaten up, robbed, and in general hated, terrorized, and humiliated.

And so for a long time I was puzzled to think that Jews were supposed to be rich when the only Jews I knew were poor, and that Negroes were supposed to be persecuted when it was the Negroes who were doing the only persecuting I knew about—and doing it, moreover, to *me*. During the early years of the war, when my older sister joined a left-wing youth organization, I remember my astonishment at hearing her passionately denounce my father for thinking that Jews were worse off than Negroes. To me, at the age of twelve, it seemed very clear that Negroes were better off than Jews—

indeed, than *all* whites. A city boy's world is contained within three or four square blocks, and in my world it was the whites, the Italians and Jews, who feared the Negroes, not the other way around. The Negroes were tougher than we were, more ruthless, and on the whole they were better athletes. What could it mean, then, to say that they were badly off and that we were more fortunate? Yet my sister's opinions, like print, were sacred, and when she told me about exploitation and economic forces I believed her. I believed her, but I was still afraid of Negroes. And I still hated them with all my heart.

It had not always been so—that much I can recall from early childhood. When did it start, this fear and this hatred? There was a kindergarten in the local public school, and given the character of the neighborhood, at least half of the children in my class must have been Negroes. Yet I have no memory of being aware of color differences at that age, and I know from observing my own children that they attribute no significance to such differences even when they begin noticing them. I think there was a day—first grade? second grade?—when my best friend Carl hit me on the way home from school and announced that he wouldn't play with me anymore because I had killed Jesus. When I ran home to my mother crying for an explanation, she told me not to pay any attention to such foolishness, and then in Yiddish she cursed the *goyim* and the *schwartzes,* the *schwartzes* and the *goyim.* Carl, it turned out, was a *schwartze,* and so was added a third to the categories into which people were mysteriously divided.

Sometimes I wonder whether this is a true memory at all. It is blazingly vivid, but perhaps it never happened: can anyone really remember back to the age of six? There is no uncertainty in my mind, however, about the years that followed. Carl and I hardly ever spoke, though we met in school every day up through the eighth or ninth grade. There would be embarrassed moments of catching his eye or of his catching mine—for whatever it was that had attracted us to one another as very small children remained alive in spite of the fantastic barrier of hostility that had grown up between us, suddenly and out of nowhere. Nevertheless, friendship would have been impossible, and even if it had been possible, it would have been unthinkable. About that, there was nothing anyone could do by the time we were eight years old.

ITEM: The orphanage across the street is torn down, a city housing project begins to rise in its place, and on the marvelous vacant lot next to the old orphanage they are building a playground. Much excitement and anticipation as Opening Day draws near. Mayor La Guardia himself comes to dedicate this great gesture of public benevolence. He speaks of neighborliness and borrowing cups of sugar, and of the playground he says that children of all races, colors, and creeds will learn to live together in harmony. A week later, some of us are swatting flies on the playground's inadequate little ball field. A gang of Negro kids, pretty much our own age, enter from the other side and order us out of the park. We refuse, proudly and indignantly, with superb masculine fervor. There is a fight, they win, and we retreat, half whimpering, half with bravado. My first nauseating experience of cowardice. And my first appalled realization that there are people in the world who do not seem to be afraid of anything, who act as though they have nothing to lose. Thereafter the playground becomes a battleground, sometimes quiet, sometimes the scene of athletic competition between Them and Us. But rocks are thrown as often as baseballs. Gradually we abandon the place and use the streets instead. The streets are safer, though we do not admit this to ourselves. We are not, after all, sissies—that most dreaded epithet of an American boyhood.

ITEM: I am standing alone in front of the building in which I live. It is late afternoon and getting dark. That day in school the teacher had asked a surly Negro boy named Quentin a question he was unable to answer. As usual I had waved my arm eagerly ("Be a good boy, get good marks, be smart, go to college, become a doctor") and, the right answer bursting from my lips, I was held up lovingly by the teacher as an example to the class. I had seen Quentin's face—a very dark, very cruel, very Oriental-looking face—harden, and there had been enough threat in his eyes to make me run all the way home for fear that he might catch me outside. Now, standing idly in front of my own house, I see him approaching from the project accompanied by his little brother who is carrying a baseball bat and wearing a grin of malicious anticipation. As in a nightmare, I am trapped. The surroundings are secure and familiar, but terror is suddenly present and there is no one around to help. I am locked to the spot. I will not cry out or run away like a sissy, and I stand there, my heart wild, my throat clogged. He walks up, hurls the familiar epithet ("Hey, mo'fucker"), and to my surprise only pushes me. It is a violent push, but not a punch. Maybe I can still back out without entirely losing my dignity. Maybe I can still say, "Hey, c'mon Quentin, whaddya wanna do *that* for? I dint do nothin' to *you*," and walk away, not too rapidly. Instead, before I can stop myself, I push him back—a token gesture—and I say, "Cut that out, I don't wanna fight, I ain't got nothin' to fight about." As I turn to walk back into the building, the corner of my eye catches the motion of the bat his little brother has handed him. I try to duck, but the bat crashes colored lights into my head.

The next thing I know, my mother and sister are standing over me, both of them hysterical. My sister—she who was later to join the "progressive" youth organization—is shouting for the police and screaming imprecations at those dirty little black bastards. They take me upstairs, the doctor comes, the police come. I tell them that the boy who did it was a stranger, that he had been trying to get money from me. They do not believe me, but I am too scared to give them Quentin's name. When I return to school a few days later, Quentin avoids my eyes. He knows that I have not squealed, and he is ashamed. I try to feel proud, but in my heart I know that it was fear of what his friends might do to me that had kept me silent, and not the code of the street.

ITEM: There is an athletic meet in which the whole of our junior high school is participating. I am in one of the seventh-grade-rapid-advance classes, and "segregation" has now set in with a vengeance. In the last three or four years of the elementary school from which we have just graduated, each grade had been divided into three classes, according to "intelligence." (In the earlier grades the divisions had either been arbitrary or else unrecognized by us as having anything to do with brains.) These divisions by IQ, or however it was arranged, had resulted in a preponderance of Jews in the "1" classes and a corresponding preponderance of Negroes in the "3's," with the Italians split unevenly along the spectrum. At least a few Negroes had always made the "1's," just as there had always been a few Jewish kids among the "3's" and more among the "2's" (where Italians dominated). But the junior high's rapid-advance class of which I am now a member is overwhelmingly Jewish and entirely white—except for a shy lonely Negro girl with light skin and reddish hair.

The athletic meet takes place in a city-owned stadium far from the school. It is an important event to which a whole day is given over. The winners are to get those precious little medallions stamped with the New York City emblem that can be screwed into a belt and that prove the wearer to be a distinguished personage. I am a fast runner, and so I am assigned the position of anchorman on my class's team in the relay race. There are three other seventh-grade teams in the race, two of them all-Negro, as ours is all-white. One of the all-Negro teams is very tall—their anchorman waiting silently next to me on the line looks years older than I am, and I do not recognize him. He is the first to get the baton and crosses the finishing line in a walk. Our team comes in second, but a few minutes later we are declared the winners, for it has been discovered that the anchorman on the first-place team is not a member of the class. We are awarded the medallions, and the following day our homeroom teacher makes a speech about how proud she is of us for being superior athletes as well as superior students. We want to believe that we deserve the praise, but we know that we could not have won even if the other class had not cheated.

That afternoon, walking home, I am waylaid and surrounded by five Negroes, among whom is the anchorman of the disqualified team. "Gimme my medal, mo'fucker," he grunts. I do not have it with me and I tell him so. "Anyway, it ain't yours," I say foolishly. He calls me a liar on both counts and pushes me up against the wall on which we sometimes play handball. "Gimme my mo'fuckin' medal," he says again. I repeat that I have left it home. "Le's seach the li'l mo'fucker," one of them suggests, "he prolly got it *hid* in his mo'fuckin' *pants.*" My panic is now unmanageable. (How many times had I been surrounded like this and asked in soft tones, "Len' me a nickel, boy"? How many times had I been called a liar for pleading poverty and pushed around, or searched, or beaten up, unless there happened to be someone in the marauding gang like Carl who liked me across that enormous divide of hatred and who would therefore say, "Aaah, c'mon, le's git someone else, *this* boy ain't got no money on 'im"?) I scream at them through tears of rage and self-contempt, "Keep your fuckin' filthy lousy black hands offa me! I swear I'll get the cops." This is all they need to hear, and the five of them set upon me. They bang me around, mostly in the stomach and on the arms and shoulders, and when several adults loitering near the candy store down the block notice what is going on and begin to shout, they run off and away.

I do not tell my parents about the incident. My teammates, who have also been waylaid, each by a gang led by his opposite number from the disqualified team, have had their medallions taken from them, and they never squeal either. For days, I walk home in terror, expecting to be caught again, but nothing happens. The medallion is put away into a drawer, never to be worn by anyone.

OBVIOUSLY experiences like these have always been a common feature of childhood life in working-class and immigrant neighborhoods, and Negroes do not necessarily figure in them. Wherever, and in whatever combination, they have lived together in the cities, kids of different groups have been at war, beating up and being beaten up: micks against kikes against wops against spicks against Polacks. And even relatively homogeneous areas have not been spared the warring of the young: one block against another, one gang (called in my day, in a pathetic effort at gentility, an "S.A.C.," or social-athletic club) against another. But the Negro-white conflict had—and no doubt still has—a special intensity and was conducted with a ferocity unmatched by intramural white battling.

In my own neighborhood, a good deal of animosity existed between the Italian kids (most of whose parents were immigrants from Sicily) and the Jewish kids (who came largely from East European immigrant families). Yet everyone had friends, sometimes close friends, in the other "camp," and we often visited one another's strange-smelling houses, if not for meals, then for glasses of milk, and occasionally for some special event like a wedding or a wake. If it happened that we divided into warring factions and did battle, it would invariably be halfhearted and soon patched up. Our parents, to be sure, had nothing to do with one another and were mutually suspicious and hostile. But we, the kids, who all spoke Yiddish or Italian at home, were Americans, or New Yorkers, or Brooklyn boys: we shared a culture, the culture of the street, and at least for a while this culture proved to be more powerful than the opposing cultures of the home.

Why, *why* should it have been so different as between the Negroes and us? How was it borne in upon us so early, white and black alike, that we were enemies beyond any possibility of reconciliation? Why did we hate one another so?

I suppose if I tried, I could answer those questions more or less adequately from the perspective of what I have since learned. I could draw upon James Baldwin—what better witness is there?—to describe the sense of entrapment that poisons the soul of the Negro with hatred for the white man whom he knows to be his jailer. On the other side, if I wanted to understand how the white man comes to hate the Negro, I could call upon the psychologists who have spoken of the guilt that white Americans feel toward Negroes and that turns into hatred for lack of acknowledging itself as guilt. These are plausible answers and certainly there is truth in them. Yet when I think back upon my own experience of the Negro and his of me, I find myself troubled and puzzled, much as I was as a child when I heard that all Jews were rich and all Negroes persecuted. How could the Negroes in my neighborhood have regarded the whites across the street and around the corner as jailers? On the whole, the whites were not so poor as the

Negroes, but they were quite poor enough, and the years were years of Depression. As for white hatred of the Negro, how could guilt have had anything to do with it? What share had these Italian and Jewish immigrants in the enslavement of the Negro? What share had they—downtrodden people themselves breaking their own necks to eke out a living—in the exploitation of the Negro?

No, I cannot believe that we hated each other back there in Brooklyn because they thought of us as jailers and we felt guilty toward them. But does it matter, given the fact that we all went through an unrepresentative confrontation? I think it matters profoundly, for if we managed the job of hating each other so well without benefit of the aids to hatred that are supposedly at the root of this madness everywhere else, it must mean that the madness is not yet properly understood. I am far from pretending that I understand it, but I would insist that no view of the problem will begin to approach the truth unless it can account for a case like the one I have been trying to describe. Are the elements of any such view available to us?

At least two, I would say, are. One of them is a point we frequently come upon in the work of James Baldwin, and the other is a related point always stressed by psychologists who have studied the mechanisms of prejudice. Baldwin tells us that one of the reasons Negroes hate the white man is that the white man refuses to *look* at him: the Negro knows that in white eyes all Negroes are alike; they are faceless and therefore not altogether human. The psychologists, in their turn, tell us that the white man hates the Negro because he tends to project those wild impulses that he fears in himself onto an alien group which he then punishes with his contempt. What Baldwin does not tell us, however, is that the principle of facelessness is a two-way street and can operate in both directions with no difficulty at all. Thus, in my neighborhood in Brooklyn, I was as faceless to the Negroes as they were to me, and if they hated me because I never looked at them, I must also have hated them for never looking at me. To the Negroes, my white skin was enough to define me as the enemy, and in a war it is only the uniform that counts and not the person.

So with the mechanism of projection that the psychologists talk about: it too works in both directions at once. There is no question that the psychologists are right about what the Negro represents symbolically to the white man. For me as a child the life lived on the other side of the playground and down the block on Ralph Avenue seemed the very embodiment of the values of the street—free, independent, reckless, brave, masculine, erotic. I put the word "erotic" last, though it is usually stressed above all others, because in fact it came last, in consciousness as in importance. What mainly counted for me about Negro kids of my own age was that they were "bad boys." There were plenty of bad boys among the whites—this was, after all, a neighborhood with a long tradition of crime as a career open to aspiring talents—but the Negroes were *really* bad, bad in a way that beckoned to one, and made one feel inadequate. *We* all went home every day for a lunch of spinach and potatoes; *they* roamed around during lunch hour, munching on candy bars. In winter *we* had to wear itchy woolen hats and mittens and cumbersome galoshes; *they* were bareheaded and loose as they pleased. *We* rarely played hooky, or got into serious trouble in school, for all our street-corner bravado; *they* were defiant, forever staying out (to do what delicious things?), forever making disturbances in class and in the halls, forever being sent to the principal and returning uncowed. But most important of all, they were *tough;* beautifully, enviably tough, not giving a damn for anyone or anything. To hell with the teacher, the truant officer, the cop; to hell with the whole of the adult world that held *us* in its grip and that we never had the courage to rebel against except sporadically and in petty ways.

This is what I saw and envied and feared in the Negro: this is what finally made him faceless to me, though some of it, of course, was actually there. (The psychologists also tell us that the alien group which becomes the object of a projection will tend to respond by trying to live up to what is expected of it.) But what, on his side, did the Negro see in me that made me faceless to *him?* Did he envy me my lunches of spinach and potatoes and my itchy woolen caps and my prudent behavior in the face of authority, as I envied him his noontime candy bars and his bare head in winter and his magnificent rebelliousness? Did those lunches and caps spell for him the prospect of power and riches in the future? Did they mean that there were possibilities open to me that were denied to him? Very likely they did. But if so, one also supposes that he feared the impulses within himself toward submission to authority no less powerfully than I feared the impulses in myself toward defiance. If I represented the jailer to him, it was not because I was oppressing him or keeping him down: it was because I symbolized for him the dangerous and probably pointless temptation toward greater repression, just as he symbolized for me the equally perilous tug toward greater freedom. I personally was to be rewarded for this repression with a new and better life in the future, but how many of my friends paid an even higher price and were given only gall in return.

We have it on the authority of James Baldwin that all Negroes hate whites. I am trying to suggest that on their side all whites—all American whites, that is—are sick in their feelings about Negroes. There are Negroes, no doubt, who would say that Baldwin is wrong, but I suspect them of being less honest than he is, just as I suspect whites of self-deception who tell me they have no special feeling toward Negroes. Special feelings about color are a contagion to which white Americans seem susceptible even when there is nothing in their background to account for the susceptibility. Thus, everywhere we look today in the North we find the curious phenomenon of white middle-class liberals with no previous personal experience of Negroes—people to whom Negroes have always been faceless in virtue rather than faceless in vice—discovering that their abstract commitment to the cause of Negro rights will not stand the test of a direct confrontation. We find such people fleeing in droves to the suburbs as the Negro population in the inner city grows; and when they stay in the city we find them sending their children to private school rather than to the "integrated" public school in the neighborhood. We find them resisting the demand that gerrymandered school districts be rezoned for the purpose of overcoming de facto segregation; we find them judiciously considering whether the Negroes (for their own good, of course) are not perhaps pushing too hard; we find them clucking their tongues over Negro militancy; we find them speculating on the question of whether there may not, after all, be something in the theory that the races are biologically different; we find them saying that it will take a very long time for Negroes to achieve full equality, no matter what anyone does; we find them deploring the rise of black nationalism and expressing the solemn hope that the leaders of the Negro community will discover ways of containing the impatience and incipient violence within the Negro ghettos.

BUT THAT IS by no means the whole story; there is also the phenomenon of what Kenneth Rexroth once called "crow-jimism." There are the broken-down white boys like Vivaldo Moore in Baldwin's *Another Country* who go to Harlem in search of sex or simply to brush up against something that looks like primitive vitality, and who are so often punished by the Negroes they meet for crimes that they would have been the last ever to commit and of which they themselves have been as sorry victims as any of the Negroes who take it out on them. There are the writers and intellectuals and artists who romanticize Negroes and pander to them, assuming a guilt that is not properly theirs. And there are all the white liberals who permit Negroes to blackmail them into adopting a double standard of moral judgment, and who lend themselves—again assuming the responsibility for crimes they never committed—to cunning and contemptuous exploitation by Negroes they employ or try to befriend.

And what about me? What kind of feelings do I have about Negroes today? What happened to me, from Brooklyn, who grew up fearing and envying and hating Negroes? Now that Brooklyn is behind me, do I fear them and envy them and hate them still? The answer is yes, but not in the same proportions and certainly not in the same way. I now live on the Upper West Side of Manhattan, where there are many Negroes and many Puerto Ricans, and there are nights when I experience the old apprehensiveness again, and there are streets that I avoid when I am walking in the dark, as there were streets that I avoided when I was a child. I find that I am not afraid of Puerto Ricans, but I cannot restrain my nervousness whenever I pass a group of Negroes standing in front of a bar or sauntering down the street. I know now, as I did not know when I was a child, that power is on my side, that the police are working for me and not for them. And knowing this I feel ashamed and guilty, like the good liberal I have grown up to be. Yet the twinges of fear and the resentment they bring and the self-contempt they arouse are not to be gainsaid.

But envy? Why envy? And hatred? Why hatred? Here again the intensities have lessened and everything has been complicated and qualified by the guilts and the resulting overcompensations that are the heritage of the enlightened middle-class world of which I am now a member. Yet just as in childhood I envied Negroes for what seemed to me their superior masculinity, so I envy them today for what seems to me their superior physical grace and beauty. I have come to value physical grace very highly, and I am now capable of aching with all my being when I watch a Negro couple on the dance floor, or a Negro playing baseball or basketball. They are on the kind of terms with their own bodies that I should like to be on with mine, and for that precious quality they seem blessed to me.

The hatred I still feel for Negroes is the hardest of all the old feelings to face or admit, and it is the most hidden and the most overlarded by the conscious attitudes into which I have succeeded in willing myself. It no longer has, as for me it once did, any cause or justification (except, perhaps, that I am constantly being denied my right to an honest expression of the things I earned the right as a child to feel). How, then, do I know that this hatred has never entirely disappeared? I know it from the insane rage that can stir in me at the thought of Negro anti-Semitism; I know it from the disgusting prurience that can stir in me at the sight of a mixed couple; and

I know it from the violence that can stir in me whenever I encounter that special brand of paranoid touchiness to which many Negroes are prone.

THIS, THEN, is where I am; it is not exactly where I think all other white liberals are, but it cannot be so very far away either. And it is because I am convinced that we white Americans are—for whatever reason, it no longer matters—so twisted and sick in our feelings about Negroes that I despair of the present push toward integration. If the pace of progress were not a factor here, there would perhaps be no cause for despair: time and the law and even the international political situation are on the side of the Negroes, and ultimately, therefore, victory—of a sort, anyway—must come. But from everything we have learned from observers who ought to know, pace has become as important to the Negroes as substance. They want equality and they want it *now,* and the white world is yielding to their demand only as much and as fast as it is absolutely being compelled to do. The Negroes know this in the most concrete terms imaginable, and it is thus becoming increasingly difficult to buy them off with rhetoric and promises and pious assurances of support. And so within the Negro community we find more and more people declaring that they want *out:* people who say that integration will never come, or that it will take a hundred or a thousand years to come, or that it will come at too high a price in suffering and struggle for the pallid and sodden life of the American middle class that at the very best it may bring.

The most numerous, influential, and dangerous movement that has grown out of Negro despair with the goal of integration is, of course, the Black Muslims. This movement, whatever else we may say about it, must be credited with one enduring achievement: it inspired James Baldwin to write an essay which deserves to be placed among the classics of our language. Everything Baldwin has ever been trying to tell us is distilled in *The Fire Next Time* into a statement of overwhelming persuasiveness and prophetic magnificence. Baldwin's message is and always has been simple. It is this: "Color is not a human or personal reality; it is a political reality." And Baldwin's demand is correspondingly simple: color must be forgotten, lest we all be smited with a vengeance "that does not really depend on, and cannot really be executed by, any person or organization, and that cannot be prevented by any police force or army: historical vengeance, a cosmic vengeance based on the law that we recognize when we say, 'Whatever goes up must come down.'" The Black Muslims Baldwin portrays as a sign and a warning to the intransigent white world. They come to proclaim how deep is the Negro's disaffection with the white world and all its works, and Baldwin implies that no American Negro can fail to respond somewhere in his being to their message: that the white man is the devil, that Allah has doomed him to destruction, and that the black man is about to inherit the earth. Baldwin of course knows that this nightmare inversion of the racism from which the black man has suffered can neither win nor even point to the neighborhood in which victory might be located. For in his view the neighborhood of victory lies in exactly the opposite direction: the transcendence of color through love.

Yet the tragic fact is that love is not the answer to hate—not in the world of politics, at any rate. Color is indeed a political rather than a human or a personal reality and if politics (which is to say power) has made it into a human and personal reality, then only politics (which is to say power) can unmake it once again. But the way of politics is slow and bitter, and as impatience on the one side is matched by a setting of the jaw on the other, we move closer and closer to an explosion, and blood may yet run in the streets.

Will this madness in which we are all caught never find a resting place? Is there never to be an end to it? In thinking about the Jews I have often wondered whether their survival as a distinct group was worth one hair on the head of a single infant. Did the Jews have to survive so that six million innocent people should one day be burned in the ovens of Auschwitz? It is a terrible question and no one, not God himself, could ever answer it to my satisfaction. And when I think about the Negroes in America and about the image of integration as a state in which the Negroes would take their rightful place as another of the protected minorities in a pluralistic society, I wonder whether they really believe in their hearts that such a state can actually be attained, and if so *why* they should wish to survive as a distinct group. I think I know why the Jews once wished to survive (though I am less certain as to why we still do): they not only believed that God had given them no choice, but they were tied to a memory of past glory and a dream of imminent redemption. What does the American Negro have that might correspond to this? His past is a stigma, his color is a stigma, and his vision of the future is the hope of erasing the stigma by making color irrelevant, by making it disappear as a fact of consciousness.

I share this hope, but I cannot see how it will ever be realized unless color does *in fact* disappear: and that means not integration, it means assimilation, it means—let the brutal word come out—miscegenation. The Black Muslims, like their racist counterparts in the white world, accuse the "so-called Negro leaders" of secretly pursuing miscegenation as a goal. The racists are wrong, but I wish they were right, for I believe that the wholesale merger of the two races is the most desirable alternative for everyone concerned. I am not claiming that this alternative can be pursued programmatically or that it is immediately feasible as a solution; obviously there are even greater barriers to its achievement than to the achievement of integration. What I am saying, however, is that in my opinion the Negro problem can be solved in this country in no other way.

I HAVE TOLD the story of my own twisted feelings about Negroes here, and of how they conflict with the moral convictions I have since developed, in order to assert that such feelings must be acknowledged as honestly as possible so that they can be controlled and ultimately disregarded in favor of the convictions. It is *wrong* for a man to suffer because of the color of his skin. Beside that clichéd proposition of liberal thought, what argument can stand and be respected? If the arguments are the arguments of feeling, they must be made to yield; and one's own soul is not the worst place to begin working a huge social transformation. Not so long ago, it used to be asked of white liberals, "Would you like your sister to marry one?" When I was a boy and my sister was still unmarried I would certainly have said no to that question. But now I am a man, my sister is already married, and I have daughters. If I were to be asked today whether I would like a daughter of mine "to marry one," I would have to answer: "No, I wouldn't *like* it at all. I would rail and rave and rant and tear my hair. And then I hope I would have the courage to curse myself for raving and ranting, and to give her my blessing. How dare I withhold it at the behest of the child I once was and against the man I now have a duty to be?"

HANNAH ARENDT ON EICHMANN
A Study in the Perversity of Brilliance

O NE OF THE MANY IRONIES
surrounding Hannah Arendt's book, *Eichmann in Jerusalem: A Report on
the Banality of Evil*, is involved in the fact that it should have been serialized
in the *New Yorker* so short a time after the appearance in the same magazine
of James Baldwin's essay on the Black Muslims. A Negro on the Negroes, a
Jew on the Jews, each telling a tale of the horrors that have been visited
upon his people and of how these horrors were borne; and each exhorting
the prosperous, the secure, the ignorant to understand that these horrors
are relevant to them. The two stories have much in common and they are
both, in their essentials, as old as humankind itself—so old and so familiar
that it takes a teller of extraordinary eloquence, or else of extraordinary
cleverness, to make them come alive again. Baldwin is all eloquence; there
is nothing clever in the way he tells the story of the Negro in America. On
the one side are the powerless victims, on the other the powerful oppressors; the only sin of the victims is their powerlessness, the only guilt is the
guilt of the oppressors. Now, this black-and-white account, with the traditional symbolisms reversed, is not the kind of picture that seems persuasive
to the sophisticated modern sensibility—the sensibility that has been
trained by Dostoevsky and Freud, by Nietzsche and Kierkegaard, by Eliot
and Yeats, to see moral ambiguity everywhere, to be bored by melodrama,
to distrust the idea of innocence, to be skeptical of rhetorical appeals to Justice. And indeed, not even Baldwin's eloquence, which forced many of his
readers to *listen* for once, could overcome the dissatisfaction many others
felt at the moral simplicity of the story as he told it. For as he told it, the
story did not answer to their sense of reality; it was an uninteresting story
and a sentimental one.

Precisely the reverse is true of Hannah Arendt's telling of the story of
how six million Jews were murdered by the Nazis. If Baldwin is all eloquence and no cleverness, Miss Arendt is all cleverness and no eloquence;

and if Baldwin brings his story unexpectedly to life through the bold tactic of heightening and playing exquisitely on every bit of melodrama it contains, Miss Arendt with an equally surprising boldness rids her story of melodrama altogether and heavily underlines every trace of moral ambiguity she can wring out of it. What she has done, in other words, is translate this story for the first time into the kind of terms that can appeal to the sophisticated modern sensibility. Thus, in place of the monstrous Nazi, she gives us the "banal" Nazi; in place of the Jew as virtuous martyr, she gives us the Jew as accomplice in evil; and in place of the confrontation between guilt and innocence, she gives us the "collaboration" of criminal and victim. The story as she tells it is complex, unsentimental, riddled with paradox and ambiguity. It has all the appearance of "ruthless honesty," and all the marks of profundity—have we not been instructed that complexity, paradox, and ambiguity are the sign manifest of profundity?—and, in addition, it carries with it all the authority of Miss Arendt's classic work on *The Origins of Totalitarianism.* Anyone schooled in the modern in literature and philosophy would be bound to consider it a much better story than the usual melodramatic version which, as it happens, was more or less the one relied upon by the prosecution at the Eichmann trial, and which Miss Arendt uses to great effect in highlighting the superior interest of her own version. But if this version of hers can from one point of view be considered more interesting, can it by the same token be considered truer, or more illuminating, or more revealing of the general situation of man in the twentieth century? Is the gain she achieves in literary interest a matter of titillation, or is it a gain to the understanding?

Let us be clear about these questions: they cannot be answered by scholarship. To the extent that *Eichmann in Jerusalem* parades as history, its factual accuracy is of course open to critical examination. But it would be unwise to take the scholarly pretensions of the book at face value. This is in no sense a work of objective historical research aimed at determining "the way things really were." Except in her critique of the trial itself, which she attended, Miss Arendt's sources are for the most part secondary ones (she relies especially on Raul Hilberg's *The Destruction of the European Jews*), and her manipulation of evidence is at all times visibly tendentious. Nevertheless, a distorted or exaggerated picture drawn in the service of a suggestive thesis can occasionally bring us closer to the essential truth than a carefully qualified and meticulously documented study—provided that the thesis accords reasonably well with the evidence. The point to begin with, then, is Miss Arendt's thesis, and the problem to settle is whether it justifies the distortions of perspective it creates and the cavalier treatment of evidence it impels.

According to Miss Arendt, the Nazis, in order to carry out their genocidal plan against the Jews, needed Jewish cooperation and in fact received it "to a truly extraordinary degree." This cooperation took the form of "administrative and police work," and it was extended by "the highly assimilated Jewish communities of Central and Western Europe" no less abundantly than by "the Yiddish-speaking masses of the East." In Amsterdam as in Warsaw, in Berlin as in Budapest, Miss Arendt writes,

> Jewish officials could be trusted to compile the lists of persons and of their property, to secure money from the deportees to defray the expenses of their deportation and extermination, to keep track of vacated apartments, to supply police forces to help seize Jews and get them on trains, until, as a last gesture, they handed over the assets of the Jewish community in good order for final confiscation.

All this has long been known. What is new is Miss Arendt's assertion that if the Jews (or rather, their leaders) had not cooperated in this fashion, "there would have been chaos and plenty of misery but the total number of victims would hardly have been between four and a half and six million people."

So much for the Jews. As for the Nazis, carrying out the policy of genocide required neither that they be monsters nor pathological Jew haters. On the contrary: since the murder of Jews was dictated by the law of the state, and since selfless loyalty to the law was regarded by the Germans under Hitler as the highest of virtues, it even called for a certain idealism to do what Eichmann and his cohorts did. Miss Arendt in this connection quotes the famous remark attributed to Himmler: "To have stuck it out and, apart from exceptions caused by human weakness, to have remained decent, that is what has made us hard." Eichmann, then, was telling the truth when he denied having been an anti-Semite: he did his duty to the best of his ability, and he would have performed with equal zeal even if he had loved the Jews. Thus also, the Israeli prosecutor Gideon Hausner was absurdly off the point in portraying Eichmann as a brute and a sadist and a fiend: Eichmann was in actual fact a banal personality, a nonentity whose evil deeds flowed not from anything in his own character, but rather from his position in the Nazi system.

This system is, of course, known as totalitarianism, and it is totalitarianism that brings the two halves of Miss Arendt's thesis together. Long ago, David Rousset, Bruno Bettelheim, and Miss Arendt herself taught us that securing the complicity of the victim is one of the distinguishing ambitions of totalitarian states, and her tale of Jewish complicity here is offered (at least on the surface) as yet another illustration of this point. Long ago, too, she and her colleagues taught us that totalitarian states aim at the destruction of common-sense reality and the creation of a new reality molded to the lineaments of the official ideology, and her conception of Eichmann as an ordinary man whose conscience was made to function "the other way round" is similarly set forth in illustration of the more general point. Obviously, though, this ordinary man could not have been turned into so great and devoted a perpetrator of evil if the system had not been so tightly closed—if, that is to say, there had been voices to protest or gestures of resistance. Such voices as existed, however, were in Miss Arendt's judgment pathetically small and thin, and such gestures of resistance as were displayed she finds relatively insignificant. Not only did "good society everywhere" accept the Final Solution, with "zeal and eagerness," but the Jews themselves acquiesced and even cooperated—as we have seen—"to a truly extraordinary degree." Here, then, is the finishing touch to Miss Arendt's reading of the Final Solution, and the explanation she gives for dwelling on Jewish complicity: this chapter of the story, she says, "offers the most striking insight into the totality of the moral collapse the Nazis caused in respectable European society—not only in Germany but in almost all countries, not only among the persecutors but also among the victims."

An interesting version of the story, no doubt about that. But let us look at it a little more closely. Assuming for the moment that Jewish leadership did in fact cooperate with the Nazis "to a truly extraordinary degree" (the degree is the point under contention), why did the Nazis *want* their cooperation? A reader of *The Origins of Totalitarianism* might have expected Miss Arendt to reply that they wanted it for its own sake. And indeed, she does quote David Rousset to this effect in dealing with the "cruel and silly question," as she calls it, that Hausner kept putting to his witnesses at the trial ("Fifteen thousand people were standing there and hundreds of guards facing you—why didn't you revolt and charge and attack?"). The passage from Rousset is crucial and worth quoting again:

> The triumph of the S.S. demands that the tortured victim allow himself to be led to the noose without protesting, that he renounce and abandon himself to the point of ceasing to affirm his identity. And it

is not for nothing. It is not gratuitously, out of sheer sadism, that the S.S. men desire his defeat. They know that the system which succeeds in destroying its victim before he mounts the scaffold . . . is incomparably the best for keeping a whole people in slavery. In submission. Nothing is more terrible than these processions of human beings going like dummies to their deaths.

Yet when Miss Arendt arrives a hundred pages later at the matter of "Jewish help in administrative and police work," considerations of a strictly mundane and thoroughly utilitarian nature suddenly enter as the decisive ones. The Nazis wanted Jewish help, for without it, "there would have been either complete chaos or an impossibly severe drain on German manpower."

Coming from Miss Arendt, this is surprising—"to a truly extraordinary degree," we might say. It is surprising because one of the major points she makes in *The Origins of Totalitarianism* is that the Nazi will to murder every Jew in Europe was so powerful that resources badly needed at the front in 1944 and early 1945 were tied up so that the ovens of Auschwitz could be kept working at full capacity. Certainly it was more *convenient* for Eichmann that the Jews took some of the burdens upon themselves that would otherwise have fallen to him. But to contend that such burdens would have put enough strain on German resources to force the Nazis to ease off on the Jews is ridiculous by Miss Arendt's own account.

For by her own account, the Nazis were determined at almost any cost to "cleanse" Europe of the Jews; nothing in their program had higher priority. But was there no possibility of stopping them? Miss Arendt now argues that there was. Whenever they encountered determined opposition, she says, they backed down, and she cites France, Italy, Belgium, Bulgaria, and (most glorious of them all) Denmark, where the Nazis succeeded in deporting only a comparatively small proportion of the resident Jews. In Holland, Romania, Hungary, Poland, and the Ukraine, on the other hand, the slaughter was near complete. Looking at all these countries, one can readily agree that the determining factor in the number of Jews murdered was the amount of resistance (either active or passive) offered to the Final Solution. The important question to be decided, however, is: resistance by *whom?* Miss Arendt knows, of course, that it was the attitude of the local populace that made the main difference—where they were willing to cooperate in the rounding up and deportation of Jews, most Jews were deported, and where they were unwilling to cooperate, fewer Jews were deported. But since Miss Arendt wishes us to believe that the Nazis could never have killed as many as six million Jews without Jewish help, she tries very hard to convey the impression that what the Jews themselves did in any given country mattered significantly, too. And it is here that she becomes most visibly tendentious in her manipulation of the facts. In explaining, for example, why not a single Belgian Jew was ever deported (though thousands of stateless Jews living in Belgium were), she tells us how the Belgian police and the railwaymen quietly sabotaged deportation operations, and then adds: "Moreover, among those who had fled were all the more important Jewish leaders . . . so that there was no Jewish Council to register the Jews—one of the vital prerequisites for their seizure." But there *was* a Jewish Council in Belgium. There was also one in France, and Miss Arendt simply neglects to mention it. Quite right, too, for the U.G.I.F. made no more difference to the situation in France than the Association des Juifs en Belgique made to the situation in Belgium, or than any other *Judenrat* made to the situation in any other country.

So far as the *Judenräte* were concerned, the chief difference between Western countries like Belgium and France on the one hand, and the Eastern territories on the other, was that the Germans did not set up ghettos in the West. The reason is suggested in Léon Poliakov's account of the role of the French *Judenrat*: "In France you never had a situation where Jews were systematically presiding over the deportation of other Jews. [For] *the attitude of the French population, which strenuously opposed the policy of segregation and isolation of the Jews, made such degradation impossible*" [my italics]. In any case, the Nazis may indeed have backed down somewhat when they encountered opposition from the Danish king or the Italian army or the Bulgarian people, but even there only somewhat. (Hilberg: "The increasing recalcitrance of the French administration . . . finally resulted in a German decision to employ all the available forces of the Security Police for an all-out drive against the remaining Jews.") As for Jewish opposition, all *it* ever did was bring out more German troops. Certainly the Nazis showed little concern over the drain on their manpower when the Warsaw Ghetto revolted.

But not only is Miss Arendt wholly unwarranted in emphasizing Jewish cooperation as a significant factor in the number of victims claimed by the Final Solution; the irony is that her insistence on doing so also involves her in making the same assumption about the Nazis that lay behind Jewish cooperation itself. This assumption was that the Nazis were rational beings and that their aims must therefore be limited and subject to negotiation.

When one of the most notorious of the Jewish leaders—Jacob Gens of Vilna—declared that "with a hundred victims I save a thousand people, with a thousand ten thousand," he was saying precisely what the heads of all the major European governments had said about Hitler. "Herr Hitler," as the *London Times* always referred to him in the 1930s, was after all a statesman; he had grievances, some of them legitimate; if a few of these grievances were satisfied, his anger would be "appeased," and war could be averted. As many historians have pointed out, the policy of appeasement was not in itself foolish or evil; it was a perfectly traditional diplomatic tactic, and its foolishness in this case lay in the fact that it was being applied to an aggressor who was not politically prudential and whose aims were not of the traditionally limited kind. The mistake of the appeasers, in other words, stemmed from their failure to recognize the unprecedented and revolutionary character of the Nazi regime. Almost every Jewish leader in Europe made the same mistake regarding the intentions of the Nazis toward them and their people—a mistake that the Nazis incidentally did everything they could to encourage.

If, then, we ask why Jewish leadership cooperated with the Nazis, the answer would seem to be that they were following a policy of appeasement, and that there was nothing in the least "extraordinary" about this. That, however, is not the answer we get from Miss Arendt; her answer is more interesting and complicated and paradoxical. A distinction must be made, she argues, between the Jewish masses and the Jewish leaders. It was "cruel and silly" of Hausner to ask why the masses went passively to their deaths, "for no non-Jewish group or people had behaved differently." But it is apparently compassionate and intelligent to ask much the same question of the Jewish leaders, even though no non-Jewish leaders had behaved differently. In any event, having raised the issue, Miss Arendt finds herself afflicted for the only time in the book with an attack of speculative diffidence and tells us nothing—literally nothing—about why so many Jewish leaders should have cooperated in the destruction of their own people and (since hardly any of them managed to survive) in their own ruin as well. "Wherever Jews lived, there were recognized Jewish leaders, and this leadership, almost without exception, cooperated in one way or another, for one reason or another, with the Nazis." *In one way or another, for one reason or another.* Period. "[We] can still sense how they enjoyed their new power. . . . We know how the Jewish officials felt when they became instruments of murder. . . . We know the physiognomies of the Jewish leaders during the Nazi period very well." Do we, now? Then pray, Miss Arendt, what did they look like? Give her exactly thirteen lines—four and a bit each for the incredible Chaim Rumkowski of Lodz, the many-sided Leo Baeck of Berlin, and the tortured Adam Czerniakow of Warsaw—and her picture is complete. And why not? The Jews in Miss Arendt's interesting and complicated and paradoxical and ruthlessly honest version of the story are a people curiously without psychology (except of the darker sort, leading to self-destruction), and a people curiously without a history (except of the disabling sort, leading to hopeless inadequacy). When they act—whether it be going to their death, or running a country, or prosecuting a trial—a mere glance at them is enough to produce a confident judgment. And again, why not, when the judgment will almost invariably be adverse?

For what is Miss Arendt really saying when she tells us that "if the Jewish people had . . . been unorganized and leaderless, there would have been chaos and plenty of misery but the total number of victims would hardly have been between four and a half and six million people"? Why, she is saying that if the Jews had not been Jews, the Nazis would not have been able to kill so many of them—which is a difficult proposition to dispute. I do not think I am being unfair to Miss Arendt here. Consider: the Jews of Europe, even where they were "highly assimilated," were an organized people, and in most cases a centrally organized people. This was a fact of their condition no less surely than sovereign nationhood was a fact of the French condition. Yet I doubt that Miss Arendt would ever take it into her head to declare that if the French people had not been organized into a nation-state, they could never have been sold out to the Nazis by Pétain and Laval. Throughout this book, Miss Arendt is very nasty about Zionists and Zionism, but the only sense one can glean from her argument is a grain of retroactive Zionist sense. The Jews, she is implying, should have known that anti-Semitism rendered their position in the Diaspora untenable, and they should therefore either have set up a state of their own or renounced their communal existence altogether. She does not explain how such renunciation could have saved them from the Nuremberg Laws. Nor does she tell us why the slaughter of Jews in occupied Russia should have been so complete even though there was no central Jewish leadership or communal organization in the Soviet Union.

But it is unnecessary to pursue the absurdities of Miss Arendt's argument on this issue, just as it is unnecessary to enter once again into the endless moral debate over the behavior of the Jewish leaders—the endless round of apology and recrimination. They did what they did, they were what they were, and each was a different man. None of it mattered in the slightest to the final result. Murderers with the power to murder descended upon a defenseless people and murdered a large part of it. What else is there to say?

IN STARK CONTRAST to the Jews, whose behavior in Miss Arendt's version of the story self-evidently explains and condemns itself, the Nazis—or anyway Adolf Eichmann—need the most careful and the most imaginative attention before they can be intelligently judged. The irony here is of course obvious, and even the Eichmann trial to some extent fell victim to it. As Harold Rosenberg once put it:

> Why should this self-styled nobody who had hurled into silence so many of the subtlest and most humane intellects of Europe have been permitted to elaborate on each trait of his character, his opinions on all sorts of matters, including Kant's categorical imperative, and his conception of himself as Pontius Pilate and as a "romantic," his reaction to his wife's reading the Bible, his drinking of mare's milk and *schnapps?* One question would have sufficed to complete the formulation of his culpability: "Weren't you the head of Sec. IV B4 of RSHA charged with the extermination of the Jews of Europe, and did you not carry out the function assigned to you to the best of your ability?"

This, in Rosenberg's view, was the main defect of the trial, and it flowed from Gideon Hausner's persistent efforts to prove that Eichmann was subjectively vicious, as well as a perpetrator of objectively criminal deeds. Miss Arendt also disapproves of these efforts by Hausner, but her complaint is against Hausner's particular conception of Eichmann's character and not against the opportunity he gave him to speak. Far from being offended at the idea that *this self-styled nobody who had hurled into silence so many of the subtlest and most humane intellects of Europe* should have been permitted to discourse himself at such great length, Miss Arendt helps the discourse along, develops it, refines it, and in the end virtually justifies it. By this I do not mean that she defends Eichmann, as some of her critics have stupidly charged: she does nothing of the kind anywhere in her book, and she says plainly in the closing chapter that he was guilty of participation in mass murder and deserved to hang. What she does do, however, is accept Eichmann's account of himself and of his role in the Final Solution as largely true. In some sense, he *was* an "idealist"; in some sense, he was *not* an anti-

Semite; and the degree of his responsibility for the murder of the six million, while sufficient to hang him, *was* relatively insignificant, and certainly nowhere near what the prosecution claimed. By building Eichmann up into a fiendish Jew-hater and a major Nazi figure, Miss Arendt believes, the prosecution missed the whole point of his crimes, of the system which made them possible, and of the lessons to be drawn for the future.

Taking Eichmann pretty much at his own word, then (except when his own word conflicts with her reading of his character), Miss Arendt treats us to a genuinely brilliant portrait of the mind of a middle-echelon Nazi and, by extension, of the world that produced him and gave him the power to do the things he did. And around this theme of Eichmann's "banality" other themes gather: the almost universal complicity of Christian Europe, and especially of the German people, in Nazism (for in diminishing Eichmann's personal responsibility for the Final Solution, she enlarges the area of European responsibility in general); and the almost total consequent unwillingness of the Federal Republic to prosecute and mete out adequate punishment to Nazi war criminals still at large and in many cases flourishing (Miss Arendt, it should be noted, presents perhaps the most severe indictment of Adenauer's Germany that has yet been seen this side of the Iron Curtain, and whatever comfort the book may bring to the Germans in some respects, it is bound in the main to infuriate them).

The brilliance of Miss Arendt's treatment of Eichmann could hardly be disputed by any disinterested reader. But at the same time, there could hardly be a more telling example than this section of her book of the intellectual perversity that can result from the pursuit of brilliance by a mind infatuated with its own agility and bent on generating dazzle. The man around the corner who makes ugly cracks about the Jews is an anti-Semite, but not Adolf Eichmann who sent several million Jews to their death: *that* would be uninteresting and would tell us nothing about the Nature of Totalitarianism. Similarly, the behavior of the Jewish leaders under the Nazis was "extraordinary," but Adolf Eichmann was ordinary, even unto banality; otherwise, he tells us nothing about the Nature of Totalitarianism. Did he have no conscience? Of course he had a conscience, the conscience of an inverted Kantian idealist; otherwise he tells us nothing about the Nature of Totalitarianism. But what about his famous statement that he would die happy because he had sent five million "enemies of the Reich" to their graves? "Sheer rodomontade," sheer braggery—to believe it is to learn nothing about the Nature of Totalitarianism. And his decision to carry on with the deportations from Hungary in direct defiance of Himmler's order that they be stopped? A perfect example of the very idealism that teaches us so much about the Nature of Totalitarianism.

No. It finally refuses to wash; it finally violates everything we know about the Nature of Man, and therefore the Nature of Totalitarianism must go hang. For uninteresting though it may be to say so, no person could have joined the Nazi party, let alone the S.S., who was not at the very least a *vicious* anti-Semite; to believe otherwise is to learn nothing about the nature of anti-Semitism. Uninteresting though it may be to say so, no person of conscience could have participated knowingly in mass murder; to believe otherwise is to learn nothing about the nature of conscience. And uninteresting though it may be to say so, no banality of a man could have done so hugely evil a job so well; to believe otherwise is to learn nothing about the nature of evil. Was Hausner right, then, in repeatedly calling Eichmann a liar? Yes, he was right, however successfully Eichmann may have deceived himself by then, and however "sincere" he may have thought his testimony was.

And the Nature of Totalitarianism? What Miss Arendt's book on the Eichmann trial teaches us about the Nature of Totalitarianism is that the time has come to reexamine the whole concept. Apart from the many other weaknesses it has revealed since the days when it was first developed to distinguish between the "simple" dictatorships of the premodern era and the ideologically inspired revolutionary regimes of Stalin and Hitler, the theory of totalitarianism has always been limited in its usefulness by the quasi-metaphysical and rather Germanic terms in which it was originally conceived. For what the theory aimed at describing was a fixed essence, not a phenomenon in flux, and the only changes it saw as possible within the totalitarian structure were those leading toward a more perfect realization of the totalitarian idea itself. (One consequence of this—and it speaks worlds about the limitations of the theory in general—was that many students of Soviet society refused for a long time to credit the significance of the liberalizing tendencies that were so obviously becoming manifest under Khrushchev: once a totalitarian state always a totalitarian state, unless, of course, it could be overthrown by force.)

But since the perfect totalitarian state did not yet exist, how did the theorists of totalitarianism know what it would look like in a fully realized condition? The answer is that they knew from the Nazi concentration camps, which, as they rightly understood, had in part been set up to serve as models and as "laboratories" for experimenting with techniques of absolute domination. Here was where totalitarianism stood nakedly revealed; here was its essential meaning; here was what the system was really all about.

So far, so good. The trouble began with a tendency to speak of Nazi Germany and Soviet Russia as though they had already attained to the perfection of vast concentration camps, and as though the Nazis in their style and the Communists in theirs had already been transformed into the new men of the transvalued totalitarian future. Yet on the basis of a somewhat more optimistic view of human nature than is implicit in the theory of totalitarianism (which substitutes for the naive liberal idea of the infinite perfectibility of man the equally naive idea of the infinite malleability of man), one may be permitted to doubt that the whole world could under any circumstances ever be made over into a concentration camp. As it is, Soviet Russia seems to be moving in the other direction. And so far as the Third Reich is concerned, it lasted for less than thirteen years and conquered only a small section of the globe, with the result that: (1) Nazi Germany never had a chance to seal itself off completely from outside influences; and (2) the people who participated actively in Nazism *knew* they were being criminal by the standards under which they themselves had been raised and that also still reigned supreme in the "decadent" culture of the West.

This is why it is finally impossible to accept Miss Arendt's conception of Eichmann's role and character. Eichmann was not living in the ideal Nazi future, but in the imperfect Nazi present, and while we can agree with Miss Arendt that, as a mere lieutenant colonel, he probably did not enjoy the importance that the Israeli indictment attributed to him, neither can he have been quite so banal as she makes him out to be. After all, there *was* enough opposition to the Final Solution to have persuaded him that not everyone looked upon the murdering of Jews as a fine and noble occupation, and after all, he *was* a first-generation Nazi and an important enough one to have been trusted with a large measure of administrative responsibility for a top-priority item in the Nazi program. Now, if we are not to lose our own minds in the act of trying to penetrate into the psychology of the Nazi mind, we must be very careful to keep it clear that this item of the Nazi program—the "cleansing" of Europe, and ultimately the whole world, of Jews—was literally insane. It is one thing to hate Jews, but it is quite another to contemplate the wholesale slaughter of Jews; it is one thing to believe that no nation-state can be healthy when it contains "alien" elements, but it is quite another to decide upon the murder of eleven million people (the estimated target of the Final Solution) as a means of achieving ethnic homogeneity. Ponder the difference between the Germans and the Romanians in this connection. The Romanians were the worst anti-Semites in Europe and were delighted to join in the butchering of Jews, until they discovered that there was money to be made from the saving of Jews, whereupon they began saving Jews: this is pathological anti-Semitism bounded by rational limits. The Germans, on the other hand, regarded the Jews, whom they had rendered utterly helpless with a stroke of the pen, as dangerous enemies, and they were so convinced of the necessity to do away with these enemies that they were willing to let the war effort suffer rather than let up: this is pathological anti-Semitism bounded by no rational limits. Insanity, in short.

It is in this insanity, I believe, and not in the pedestrian character of Adolf Eichmann, that whatever banality attaches to the evil of the Final Solution must be sought. And because Hitler and his cohorts were madmen on the Jewish question, there is probably little of general relevance we can learn from the Final Solution beyond what the Nuremberg trials established concerning the individual's criminal accountability when acting upon superior orders, even within a system guided by insane aims. There is, however, much to be learned from the Final Solution about other matters, and principally about anti-Semitism. When Miss Arendt speaks of the amazing extent of the moral collapse that the Nazis caused "everywhere," she must be referring specifically to the Jewish question. The will to fight the German armies did not collapse everywhere, and the will to defend democracy against the Nazi onslaught stood up well enough to triumph in the end; the only collapse that took place "everywhere" was a collapse of the will to prevent the Nazis from wiping the Jews off the face of the earth. Here again, Miss Arendt can be refuted out of her own mouth, for acquiescence in the Final Solution (as she demonstrates) was far from universal in Europe (though it may well have been nearly universal in Germany). The fact remains, however, that there was acquiescence enough to allow this insane Nazi ambition to come very close to succeeding. Nobody cared about the Gypsies because nobody ever thinks about the Gypsies—except the police. But how did it happen that nobody cared about the Jews when everyone seems always to be thinking about the Jews? The question surely answers itself, and the answer incidentally provides the justification for Ben-Gurion's statement that one of the purposes of the Eichmann trial was to make the nations of the world ashamed.

Miss Arendt dislikes that statement, but no more than she dislikes every other statement Ben-Gurion made about the trial. She is also unhappy with the trial itself—the fact that Eichmann was tried before an Israeli court instead of an international tribunal, the substance of the indictment, the way Hausner handled the prosecution, the way Servatius conducted the defense. The only aspect of the trial that pleases her is that the judges behaved with scrupulous regard for the interests of Justice: she is as unstinting in her praise of them as she is relentless in her contempt for Hausner and Ben-Gurion ("the invisible stage manager of the proceedings"). A few of Miss Arendt's criticisms of the trial seem reasonable, but given the animus she exhibits from the very first sentence of the book, it becomes extremely difficult to look upon these criticisms as anything other than further instances of the inordinate demands she is always making on the Jews to be better than other people, to be braver, wiser, nobler, more dignified— or be damned.

This habit of judging the Jews by one standard and everyone else by another is a habit Miss Arendt shares with many of her fellow Jews, emphatically including those who think that the main defect of her version of the story is her failure to dwell on all the heroism and all the virtue that the six million displayed among them. But the truth is—*must* be—that the Jews under Hitler acted as men will act when they are set upon by murderers, no better and no worse: the Final Solution reveals nothing about the victims except that they were mortal beings and hopelessly vulnerable in their powerlessness. And as with the victims, so with those who were lucky enough to survive the Holocaust. There is no special virtue in sheer survival, whatever Bruno Bettelheim may say, and there is no martyrdom in sheer victimization, whatever certain sentimentalists among us may think.

The Nazis destroyed a third of the Jewish people. In the name of all that is humane, will the remnant never let up on itself?

IN DEFENSE OF EDITING

I̲t seems to have become the fashion lately for writers who have had difficulties with one magazine or another to complain in public about the terrible treatment they have received at the hands of insensitive editors. B. H. Haggin not long ago voiced such a complaint in *Partisan Review* against Robert Hatch of the *Nation;* more recently in the *Hudson Review,* Hans J. Morgenthau had a go at me. As it happens, both Haggin and Morgenthau were speaking out of what might easily be regarded as personal pique, but the question they raised—Are editors necessary?—is nevertheless an interesting one, touching as it does on the general state of discourse in America and the whole issue of the maintenance of standards. To take up that question, one has to discuss aspects of the editorial process that were perhaps better kept private, but now that they are being made public from the point of view of the aggrieved author, they might just as well be talked about from the point of view of the working editor as well. And the only way for a working editor to begin talking honestly about them is to attempt an answer to the question as it was put in more positive form by John Fischer in the June *Harper's:* What do editors do?

Most people, I imagine, if they think about it at all, think that the job of an editor is to pick and choose among finished pieces of work which have been submitted to him and deliver them to the printer; that is to say, he acts as a middleman between individual authors and an expectant public. In the six years that I have been editing *Commentary,* there have indeed been occasions when my job corresponded roughly to that conception of it. But the editorial process is usually far more complicated. Typically, between the receipt of a manuscript at the offices of almost any magazine and the dispatch of a publishable article to the printer fall the shadows—of *doubt,* of *deliberation,* of *labor,* of *negotiation.*

Doubt: Every magazine that deserves the name has a character, a style, a point of view, a circumscribed area of concern, a conception of how discourse ought to be conducted; if it lacks these things, it is not a magazine but a periodical anthology of random writings. Obviously the editor's personality, his cast of mind, his biases, his interests are crucial to the formation of this character. Yet once it has been formed—if it has been truly formed—it takes on an independent existence of its own, resisting even the editor's efforts to change or qualify it. It is enormously important for him to fight his own magazine, to keep it from becoming hardened and predictable, to keep it open and mobile. Yet if he whores too avidly after strange gods, desiring this man's art and that man's scope, the magazine will avenge itself by refusing to assimilate the foreign substance. Instead of achieving surprise, he will achieve a tasteless incongruity, like a woman with the wrong hairdo; instead of looking more flexible and lively, his magazine will take on an uncertain and affected air. This is why phrases like "Not for us" or "Unsuitable" so often accompany rejected manuscripts. They are used partly to soothe the wounded feelings of authors, but there is a truth in them by which magazines live or die.

To understand that magazines have their own insistent characters is to understand why the vast majority of the articles they publish are likely to be commissioned. (The strictly literary magazines are an exception, for the obvious reason that poems and stories, unlike articles, are not as a rule written to order. But even a literary magazine can only become a real magazine—that is, acquire a character—by going after particular writers whom the editor values more highly than others; that, too, may perhaps be regarded as a form of commissioning.)

If an established writer or a regular contributor comes to a magazine with a proposal that the editor likes, he will naturally be told to go ahead. But before he is told to go ahead, the editor will indicate to him how he thinks the subject ought properly to be handled: "properly," of course, meaning the editor's conception of how the intrinsic demands of the subject can best be reconciled with the demands of the magazine's character.

The other, more common, form of commissioning follows not upon the writer's initiative but upon the editor's. The editor—or, mysteriously, the magazine itself—decides that an article is needed on a given subject and he looks for someone who can do it as far as possible in the "right" way. This search for the right writer sets what is one of the editor's most interesting problems, but it can be exhausting; often the writer he wants is a busy man who must be cajoled, flattered, harassed, nagged. And even with cajolery, flattery, harassment, and nagging, the search ends half the time in failure, either because no one can be found, or because the person who eventually is found never delivers, or worse, turns out to be the wrong writer. With enough experience, however, an editor will know where to go, and with enough luck he will snare his man. Still, he has to be very lucky indeed or very inspired in his choice of the writer to get the piece *he* is dreaming of (and almost miraculously lucky to get it on the promised date). It happens once in a great while. But the typical conclusion to this phase of the editorial process is the delivery of a manuscript which only faintly approximates the editor's ideal conception, or else differs radically from it. Thus *Doubt,* and then . . .

Deliberation: Is it right for *us?* Can it be made right for us? How? Will the author be willing to revise it? Can he revise it on time? Will he let us revise it? Are we willing to risk offending a valuable contributor by pushing very hard? Are we being unfair or too rigid? Should we perhaps publish the piece more or less as it is? Are we perhaps a little crazy? Such are the questions that are struggled with at editorial conferences or via interoffice memos. Finally, when the manuscript may have gone the rounds of the editorial staff a second time (the conference having left everyone thoroughly uncertain), a decision, enthusiastic or grudging, is reached. A letter is written or a telephone conversation held or a lunch date arranged. "This is what we think still needs to be done. Will you do it?" If yes, the whole process is repeated when the revised version comes in. Or, if no: "Will you let us do it, then? Naturally you'll have an opportunity to check the edited version." If yes to that, the phase of deliberation gives way to . . .

Labor: One edits a manuscript by trying to correct the flaws that inevitably appear when it is subjected to the minutest scrutiny of which the editor is capable. In America (and indications are that this is beginning to happen in England, too), the overwhelming majority of the flaws to be corrected are either technical or minimally aesthetic: flaws of grammar, flaws of syntax, flaws of structure, flaws of rhetoric, flaws of taste.

But the deficiencies that tend to show up on a ruthlessly close study of a manuscript may be substantive, too. Under the editorial microscope things that were not visible to the naked eye—neither the editor's nor the author's—suddenly make an unexpected appearance. One sentence does not logically follow from the next; the paragraph on page 8 only makes sense if it is transposed to page 6 and stitched in with a clever transition to cover the seam; a point which seemed persuasive on a first reading turns out to need bolstering with more documentation (or the irrelevancies surrounding it have to be peeled away); an argument which looked reasonable before is now revealed as contradicting another argument elsewhere in the piece, or to have ignored or distorted the evidence on the other side of the case.

Some of these deficiencies—the logical and structural ones—can be remedied by the editor himself if he has acquired a truly inward grasp of what the author is trying to say and show and evoke. But it must be left to the author to fill in gaps, to add further information, to take up new questions that have arisen, to shore up weaknesses that have become evident. Accordingly the edited version of his article will be sent to him with a letter explaining what has been done to the manuscript and why, asking him to make sure that no inaccuracies have crept in through the editing, and requesting that he deal with the substantive problems which have emerged upon careful scrutiny. The phase of *Labor* has come to a close, and what remains is . . .

Negotiation: Seeing the edited manuscript, the author, as likely as not, is more than a little outraged. This is, after all, *his* article; he takes responsibility for it; it is to appear under his name. By what right does anyone presume to tamper with it? (On the other hand, some authors, curiously enough including many who write very well, are often grateful for editing.) When the outrage subsides, however, he will begin to wonder whether there might not perhaps be a certain justice in the criticisms reflected in the editing; not all, of course, but some. Adjustments will naturally have to be made here and there, but on the whole the edited version will do.

Just as the editor may have been worrying about the possibility of losing both article and author by pressing too hard on the manuscript, so on his side the author may be worried lest he lose his chance of publishing the piece and disaffect the editor. There is a clash of interests and vanities here which does not differ greatly in principle from the clash of opposing groups in politics, and it is ordinarily settled in much the same way as political struggles are—by negotiation. The author accepts most of the editing but insists on certain points (the restoration of a passage that has been cut or of a formulation that has been changed), the editor agrees, and the piece is at long last sent to the printer.

Thus is the editorial process completed—so far as this one article is concerned. There may be as many as fifteen or twenty other pieces in the same issue. Not all of them will have involved so much effort. Two or three will have required only a little touching up or none at all; several others will have needed considerable editing but not in every sentence; still others will have needed more editing than the editor—knowing the author would object, and on balance wanting the piece even in an imperfect state—dared to do. (Reading such pieces in proof, or even in print, the editor can hardly control his pencil.)

It takes, then, a great deal of work, an enervating concentration on detail, and a fanatical concern with the bone and sinew of the English language to edit a manuscript—to improve an essentially well-written piece or to turn a clumsily written one into, at the very least, a readable and literate article, and, at the very most, a beautifully shaped and effectively expressed essay which remains true to the author's intention, which realizes that intention more fully than he himself was able to do. In addition to work, manuscript editing takes time—and time is critical to an enterprise that lives under the pressure of deadlines. And in addition to time, it takes a combination of sympathy—getting inside someone else's mind—and rigor—resistance to being swallowed up by that other mind, once inside— that is extremely difficult to maintain.

Is it all worth it? Over and over again one asks oneself that question, tempted as one is to hoard some of the energy that goes into editing for thinking one's own thoughts or doing one's own writing. One asks oneself whether anyone would know the difference if one simply sent all those pieces to the printer after a perfunctory reading. And one asks oneself whether anyone really cares about writing of this kind as writing. For all editors have had the experience of publishing inadequately edited pieces that were praised beyond their deserts, and articles they knew to be classics of their type that were scarcely noticed and certainly not valued at their proper worth. If such articles (which are not edited—one has no impulse to tamper with perfection) are not appreciated, what hope is there that lesser (edited) pieces will be?

In the end an editor is thrown back, as any man doing any job faithfully must be, on the fact that *he* cares and that he can therefore do no other. He cares about the English language; he cares about clarity of thought and grace of expression; he cares about the traditions of discourse and of argument. It hardly needs to be said that even good editors will sometimes bungle a job and that bad editors invariably will, but it nevertheless remains true that the editorial process is a necessity if standards are to be preserved and if the intellectual life in America is not to become wholly compartmentalized and ultimately sterile in spirit.

Apocalyptic as this may sound, I believe it to be an accurate statement of the case. It is no secret that the number of people in this country who can write an acceptable piece of exposition in literate English is astoundingly low. But if one goes beyond that minimal requirement and asks for a piece of exposition whose virtues include clarity, economy, coherence, and grace, one is hard put to find it even among professional journalists or professors of English, let alone professors of economics or sociology. (One is, however, rather more likely to find it among the professors of history who as a class are for some reason the best writers in the academy today.) Whatever the causes of this sorry condition may be, the fact is that it exists, and until it is remedied the only alternative to (competent) editing must be a further debasement of our language and a further loosening of our already tenuous hold on the traditions of civilized public discourse.

In our culture—I exaggerate only slightly—those who know cannot write, and those who can write do not know. An editor who wants an article on a given subject which seems important to him at a given time has very little trouble locating people with impeccable credentials and unquestionable authority. Since such people are rarely good writers, however, he has three choices as an editor: he can decide not to get a piece on the subject at all; he can resign himself to publishing one that is gratuitously unreadable and guilty of grave offenses against the art of exposition; or he can edit. To opt for the first choice is to lose opportunities; to opt for the second is to behave irresponsibly both toward the readers of his magazine and toward the standards of his profession; to opt for the third is to risk error and arrogance for the sake of creating the monthly illusion that we live in a world where a certain mode of serious discussion can still take place. What is today an illusion was once a reality; but without the illusion—that is, the sense of what is possible—before our eyes, how will we ever make it a reality again?

Apart from standards, there is also the matter of American intellectual life itself. Once upon a time—or so it now seems—all educated men spoke the same language and therefore were able to communicate with one another. They strolled together in marketplaces or ate together at High Table conversing all the while, wittily, on all manner of things. These educated men were all equally philosophers, equally theologians, equally scientists. But then one day, in the very midst of a conversation, they suddenly discovered that something strange had happened: they could no longer understand one another. They all wondered why they had been punished in this mysterious way by the multiplication of tongues (which soon came to be known as "disciplines"). Some blamed it on the growth of an idolatrous cult of Science among their fellows; others blamed it on the laziness and complacency of the littérateurs. The argument still rages today, but the "disciplines" are if anything farther apart than they were in that far-off time when the common language was first shattered into a hundred isolated fragments.

In my view, the primary responsibility of the magazine editor is to participate in the struggle to reconstruct that shattered common language. There *must* be a language in which all but the most highly technical matters can be discussed without distortion or falsification or watering down; there *must* be a language impartially free of all the various jargons through which the "disciplines" maintain their proud and debilitating isolation; there *must* be a language in which the kinship of these disciplines is expressed and revealed and reaffirmed.

A man who does not believe in the possibility of such a language cannot edit a magazine (though he may be able to edit a specialized journal of one kind or another). For from the belief in the possibility of such a language everything else that makes an editor follows: the conception of a culture as organic—as one and not many—and therefore accessible in all its modalities to the general intelligence; the correlative conviction that by the exercise of his general intelligence a man can determine what the important issues are even in areas in which he has no special training; the arrogance to assert that *this* is the relevant point rather than *that;* the nerve to tell others how to discuss things which they know more about than he does.

And so we come back to where we began: to manuscript editing. John Fischer is right in stressing qualities like intuition, curiosity, and enthusiasm when he talks about the process by which an editor decides on subjects to be covered, problems to be investigated, issues to be raised. But it is manuscript editing and manuscript editing alone that makes it possible for these subjects to be covered properly, these problems to be investigated adequately, these issues to be raised incisively.

(I should add that the article you have just read was commissioned and deliberated upon, but not edited. Perhaps—I hope not—it should have been.)

FROM *MAKING IT:*
THE BRUTAL BARGAIN

ONE OF THE LONGEST JOURNEYS in the world is the journey from Brooklyn to Manhattan—or at least from certain neighborhoods in Brooklyn to certain parts of Manhattan. I have made that journey, but it is not from the experience of having made it that I know how very great the distance is, for I started on the road many years before I realized what I was doing, and by the time I did realize it I was for all practical purposes already there. At so imperceptible a pace did I travel, and with so little awareness, that I never felt footsore or out of breath or weary at the thought of how far I still had to go. Yet whenever anyone who has remained back there where I started—remained not physically but socially and culturally, for the neighborhood is now a Negro ghetto and the Jews who have "remained" in it mostly reside in the less affluent areas of Long Island—whenever anyone like that happens into the world in which I now live with such perfect ease, I can see that in his eyes I have become a fully acculturated citizen of a country as foreign to him as China and infinitely more frightening.

That country is sometimes called the upper middle class; and indeed I am a member of that class, less by virtue of my income than by virtue of the way my speech is accented, the way I dress, the way I furnish my home, the way I entertain and am entertained, the way I educate my children—the way, quite simply, I look and I live. It appalls me to think what an immense transformation I had to work on myself in order to become what I have become: if I had known what I was doing I would surely not have been able to do it, I would surely not have wanted to. No wonder the choice had to be blind; there was a kind of treason in it: treason toward my family, treason toward my friends. In choosing the road I chose, I was pronouncing a judgment upon them, and the fact that they themselves concurred in the judgment makes the whole thing sadder but no less cruel.

When I say that the choice was blind, I mean that I was never aware—

obviously not as a small child, certainly not as an adolescent, and not even as a young man already writing for publication and working on the staff of an important intellectual magazine in New York—how inextricably my "noblest" ambitions were tied to the vulgar desire to rise above the class into which I was born; nor did I understand to what an astonishing extent these ambitions were shaped and defined by the standards and values and tastes of the class into which I did not know I wanted to move. It is not that I was or am a social climber as that term is commonly used. High society interests me, if at all, only as a curiosity; I do not wish to be a member of it; and in any case, it is not, as I have learned from a small experience of contact with the very rich and fashionable, my "scene." Yet precisely because social climbing is not one of my vices (unless what might be called celebrity climbing, which very definitely is one of my vices, can be considered the contemporary variant of social climbing), I think there may be more than a merely personal significance in the fact that class has played so large a part both in my life and in my career.

But whether or not the significance is there, I feel certain that my long-time blindness to the part class was playing in my life was not altogether idiosyncratic. "Privilege," Robert L. Heilbroner has shrewdly observed in *The Limits of American Capitalism*, "is not an attribute we are accustomed to stress when we consider the construction of our social order." For a variety of reasons, says Heilbroner, "privilege under capitalism is much less 'visible,' especially to the favored groups, than privilege under other systems" like feudalism. This "invisibility" extends in America to class as well.

No one, of course, is so naive as to believe that America is a classless society or that the force of egalitarianism, powerful as it has been in some respects, has ever been powerful enough to wipe out class distinctions altogether. There was a moment during the 1950s, to be sure, when social thought hovered on the brink of saying that the country had to all intents and purposes become a wholly middle-class society. But the emergence of the civil-rights movement in the 1960s and the concomitant discovery of the poor—to whom, in helping to discover them, Michael Harrington interestingly enough applied, in *The Other America,* the very word ("invisible") that Heilbroner later used with reference to the rich—has put at least a temporary end to that kind of talk. And yet if class has become visible again, it is only in its grossest outlines—mainly, that is, in terms of income levels—and to the degree that manners and style of life are perceived as relevant at all, it is generally in the crudest of terms. There is something in us, it would seem, which resists the idea of class. Even our novelists, working in a genre for which class has traditionally been a supreme reality, are largely indifferent to it—which is to say, blind to its importance as a factor in the life of the individual.

In my own case, the blindness to class always expressed itself in an outright and very often belligerent refusal to believe that it had anything to do with me at all. I no longer remember when or in what form I first discovered that there was such a thing as class, but whenever it was and whatever form the discovery took, it could only have coincided with the recognition that criteria existed by which I and everyone I knew were stamped as inferior: we were in the *lower* class. This was not a proposition I was willing to accept, and my way of not accepting it was to dismiss the whole idea of class as a prissy triviality.

Given the fact that I had literary ambitions even as a small boy, it was inevitable that the issue of class would sooner or later arise for me with a sharpness it would never acquire for most of my friends. But given the fact also that I was on the whole very happy to be growing up where I was, that I was fiercely patriotic about Brownsville (the spawning ground of so many famous athletes and gangsters), and that I felt genuinely patronizing toward other neighborhoods, especially the "better" ones like Crown Heights and East Flatbush which seemed by comparison colorless and unexciting—given the fact, in other words, that I was not, for all that I wrote poetry and read books, an "alienated" boy dreaming of escape—my confrontation with the issue of class would probably have come later rather than sooner if not for an English teacher in high school who decided that I was a gem in the rough and who took it upon herself to polish me to as high a sheen as she could manage and I would permit.

I resisted—far less effectively, I can see now, than I then thought, though even then I knew that she was wearing me down far more than I would ever give her the satisfaction of admitting. Famous throughout the school for her altogether outspoken snobbery, which stopped short by only a hair, and sometimes did not stop short at all, of an old-fashioned kind of patrician anti-Semitism, Mrs. K. was also famous for being an extremely good teacher; indeed, I am sure that she saw no distinction between the hopeless task of teaching the proper use of English to the young Jewish barbarians whom fate had so unkindly deposited into her charge and the equally hopeless task of teaching them the proper "manners." (There were as many young Negro barbarians in her charge as Jewish ones, but I doubt that she could ever bring herself to pay very much attention to them. As she never hesitated to make clear, it was punishment enough for a woman of her background—her family was old Brooklyn and, she would have us understand, extremely distinguished—to have fallen among the sons of East European immigrant Jews.)

For three years, from the age of thirteen to the age of sixteen, I was her special pet, though that word is scarcely adequate to suggest the intensity of the relationship which developed between us. It was a relationship right out of *The Corn Is Green,* which may, for all I know, have served as her model; at any rate, her objective was much the same as the Welsh teacher's in that play: she was determined that I should win a scholarship to Harvard. But whereas (an irony much to the point here) the problem the teacher had in *The Corn Is Green* with her coal-miner pupil in the traditional class society of Edwardian England was strictly academic, Mrs. K.'s problem with me in the putatively egalitarian society of New Deal America was strictly social. My grades were very high and would obviously remain so, but what would they avail me if I continued to go about looking and sounding like a "filthy little slum child" (the epithet she would invariably hurl at me whenever we had an argument about "manners")?

Childless herself, she worked on me like a dementedly ambitious mother with a somewhat recalcitrant son; married to a solemn and elderly man (she was then in her early forties or thereabouts), she treated me like a callous, ungrateful adolescent lover on whom she had humiliatingly bestowed her favors. She flirted with me and flattered me, she scolded me and insulted me. Slum child, filthy little slum child, so beautiful a mind and so vulgar a personality, so exquisite in sensibility and so coarse in manner. What would she do with me, what would become of me if I persisted out of stubbornness and perversity in the disgusting ways they had taught me at home and on the streets?

To her the most offensive of these ways was the style in which I dressed: a T-shirt, tightly pegged pants, and a red satin jacket with the legend "Cherokees, S.A.C." (social-athletic club) stitched in large white letters across the back. This was bad enough, but when on certain days I would appear in school wearing, as a particular ceremonial occasion required, a suit and tie, the sight of those immense padded shoulders and my white-on-white shirt would drive her to even greater heights of contempt and even lower depths of loving despair than usual. *Slum child, filthy little slum child.* I was beyond saving; I deserved no better than to wind up with all the other horrible little Jewboys in the gutter (by which she meant Brooklyn College). If only I would listen to her, the whole world could be mine: I could win a scholarship to Harvard, I could get to know the best people,

I could grow up into a life of elegance and refinement and taste. Why was I so stupid as not to understand?

In those days it was very unusual, and possibly even against the rules, for teachers in public high schools to associate with their students after hours. Nevertheless, Mrs. K. sometimes invited me to her home, a beautiful old brownstone located in what was perhaps the only section in the whole of Brooklyn fashionable enough to be intimidating. I would read her my poems and she would tell me about her family, about the schools she had gone to, about Vassar, about writers she had met, while her husband, of whom I was frightened to death and who to my utter astonishment turned out to be Jewish (but not, as Mrs. K. quite unnecessarily hastened to inform me, my kind of Jewish), sat stiffly and silently in an armchair across the room, squinting at his newspaper through the first pince-nez I had ever seen outside the movies. He spoke to me but once, and that was after I had read Mrs. K. my tearful editorial for the school newspaper on the death of Roosevelt—an effusion which provoked him into a full five-minute harangue whose blasphemous contents would certainly have shocked me into insensibility if I had not been even more shocked to discover that he actually had a voice.

But Mrs. K. not only had me to her house; she also—what was even more unusual—took me out a few times, to the Frick Gallery and the Metropolitan Museum, and once to the theater, where we saw a dramatization of *The Late George Apley,* a play I imagine she deliberately chose with the not wholly mistaken idea that it would impress upon me the glories of aristocratic Boston.

One of our excursions into Manhattan I remember with particular vividness because she used it to bring the struggle between us to rather a dramatic head. The familiar argument began this time on the subway. Why, knowing that we would be spending the afternoon together "in public," had I come to school that morning improperly dressed? (I was, as usual, wearing my red satin club jacket over a white T-shirt.) She realized, of course, that I owned only one suit (this said not in compassion but in derision) and that my poor parents had, God only knew where, picked up the idea that it was too precious to be worn except at one of those bar mitzvahs I was always going to. Though why, if my parents were so worried about clothes, they had permitted me to buy a suit which made me look like a young hoodlum she found it very difficult to imagine. Still, much as she would have been embarrassed to be seen in public with a boy whose parents allowed him to wear a zoot suit, she would have been somewhat less embarrassed than she was now by the ridiculous costume I had on. Had I no consideration for her? Had I no consideration for myself? Did I want everyone who laid eyes on me to think that I was nothing but an ill-bred little slum child?

My standard ploy in these arguments was to take the position that such things were of no concern to me: I was a poet and I had more important matters to think about than clothes. Besides, I would feel silly coming to school on an ordinary day dressed in a suit. Did Mrs. K. want me to look like one of those "creeps" from Crown Heights who were all going to become doctors? This was usually an effective counter, since Mrs. K. despised her middle-class Jewish students even more than she did the "slum children," but probably because she was growing desperate at the thought of how I would strike a Harvard interviewer (it was my senior year), she did not respond according to form on that particular occasion. "At least," she snapped, "they reflect well on their parents."

I was accustomed to her bantering gibes at my parents, and sensing, probably, that they arose out of jealousy, I was rarely troubled by them. But this one bothered me; it went beyond banter and I did not know how to deal with it. I remember flushing, but I cannot remember what if anything I said in protest. It was the beginning of a very bad afternoon for both of us.

We had been heading for the Museum of Modern Art, but as we got off the subway, Mrs. K. announced that she had changed her mind about the museum. She was going to show me something else instead, just down the street on Fifth Avenue. This mysterious "something else" to which we proceeded in silence turned out to be the college department of an expensive clothing store, de Pinna. I do not exaggerate when I say that an actual physical dread seized me as I followed her into the store. I had never been inside such a store; it was not a store, it was enemy territory, every inch of it mined with humiliations. "I am," Mrs. K. declared in the coldest human voice I hope I shall ever hear, "going to buy you a suit that you will be able to wear at your Harvard interview." I had guessed, of course, that this was what she had in mind, and even at fifteen I understood what a fantastic act of aggression she was planning to commit against my parents and asking me to participate in. Oh no, I said in a panic (suddenly realizing that I *wanted* her to buy me that suit), I can't, my mother wouldn't like it. "You can tell her it's a birthday present. Or else I will tell her. If I tell her, I'm sure she won't object." The idea of Mrs. K. meeting my mother was more than I could bear: my mother, who spoke with a Yiddish accent and of whom, until that sickening moment, I had never known I was ashamed and so ready to betray.

To my immense relief and my equally immense disappointment, we left the store, finally, without buying a suit, but it was not to be the end of clothing or "manners" for me that day—not yet. There was still the ordeal of a restaurant to go through. Where I came from, people rarely ate in restaurants, not so much because most of them were too poor to afford such a luxury—although most of them certainly were—as because eating in restaurants was not regarded as a luxury at all; it was, rather, a necessity to which bachelors were pitiably condemned. A home-cooked meal was assumed to be better than anything one could possibly get in a restaurant, and considering the class of restaurants in question (they were really diners or luncheonettes), the assumption was probably correct. In the case of my own family, myself included until my late teens, the business of going to restaurants was complicated by the fact that we observed the Jewish dietary laws, and except in certain neighborhoods, few places could be found which served kosher food; in midtown Manhattan in the 1940s, I believe there were only two and both were relatively expensive. All this is by way of explaining why I had had so little experience of restaurants up to the age of fifteen and why I grew apprehensive once more when Mrs. K. decided after we left de Pinna that we should have something to eat.

The restaurant she chose was not at all an elegant one—I have, like a criminal, revisited it since—but it seemed very elegant indeed to me: enemy territory again, and this time a mine exploded in my face the minute I set foot through the door. The hostess was very sorry, but she could not seat the young gentleman without a coat and tie. If the lady wished, however, something could be arranged. The lady (visibly pleased by this unexpected—or was it expected?—object lesson) did wish, and the so recently defiant but by now utterly docile young gentleman was forth-with divested of his so recently beloved but by now thoroughly loathsome red satin jacket and provided with a much oversize white waiter's coat and a tie—which, there being no collar to a T-shirt, had to be worn around his bare neck. Thus attired, and with his face supplying the touch of red which had moments earlier been supplied by his jacket, he was led into the dining room, there to be taught the importance of proper table manners through the same pedagogic instrumentality that had worked so well in impressing him with the importance of proper dress.

Like any other pedagogic technique, however, humiliation has its limits, and Mrs. K. was to make no further progress with it that day. For I had had enough, and I was not about to risk stepping on another mine. Knowing she would subject me to still more ridicule if I made a point of my revulsion at the prospect of eating nonkosher food, I resolved to let her order for me and then to feign lack of appetite or possibly even illness when the meal was served. She did order—duck for both of us, undoubtedly because it would be a hard dish for me to manage without using my fingers.

The two portions came in deep oval-shaped dishes, swimming in a brown sauce and each with a sprig of parsley sitting on top. I had not the faintest idea of what to do—should the food be eaten directly from the oval dish or not?—nor which of the many implements on the table to do it with. But remembering that Mrs. K. herself had once advised me to watch my hostess in such a situation and then to do exactly as she did, I sat perfectly still and waited for her to make the first move. Unfortunately, Mrs. K. also remembered having taught me that trick, and determined as she was that I should be given a lesson that would force me to mend my ways, she waited too. And so we both waited, chatting amiably, pretending not to notice the food while it sat there getting colder and colder by the minute. Thanks partly to the fact that I would probably have gagged on the duck if I had tried to eat it—dietary taboos are very powerful if one has been conditioned to them—I was prepared to wait forever. And in fact it was Mrs. K. who broke first.

"Why aren't you eating?" she suddenly said after something like fifteen minutes had passed. "Aren't you hungry?" "Not very," I answered. "Well," she said, "I think we'd better eat. The food is getting cold." Whereupon, as I watched with great fascination, she deftly captured the sprig of parsley between the prongs of her serving fork, set it aside, took up her serving spoon and delicately used those two esoteric implements to transfer a piece of duck from the oval dish to her plate. I imitated the whole operation as best I could, but not well enough to avoid splattering some partly congealed sauce onto my borrowed coat in the process. Still, things could have been worse, and having more or less successfully negotiated my way around that particular mine, I now had to cope with the problem of how to get out of eating the duck. But I need not have worried. Mrs. K. took one bite, pronounced it inedible (it must have been frozen by then), and called in quiet fury for the check.

Several months later, wearing an altered but respectably conservative suit which had been handed down to me in good condition by a bachelor uncle, I presented myself on two different occasions before interviewers from Harvard and from the Pulitzer Scholarship Committee. Some months after that, Mrs. K. had her triumph: I won the Harvard scholarship on which her heart had been so passionately set. It was not, however, large enough to cover all expenses, and since my parents could not afford to make up the difference, I was unable to accept it. My parents felt wretched but not, I think, quite as wretched as Mrs. K. For a while it looked as though I would wind up in the "gutter" of Brooklyn College after all, but then the news arrived that I had also won a Pulitzer Scholarship which paid full tuition if used at Columbia and a small stipend besides. Everyone was consoled, even Mrs. K.: Columbia was at least in the Ivy League.

The last time I saw her was shortly before my graduation from Columbia and just after a story had appeared in the *New York Times* announcing that I had been awarded a fellowship which was to send me to Cambridge University. Mrs. K. had passionately wanted to see me in Cambridge, Massachusetts, but Cambridge, England, was even better. We met somewhere near Columbia for a drink, and her happiness over my fellowship, it seemed to me, was if anything exceeded by her delight at discovering that I now knew enough to know that the right thing to order in a cocktail lounge was a very dry martini with lemon peel, please.

II

LOOKING BACK NOW at the story of my relationship with Mrs. K. strictly in the context of the issue of class, what strikes me most sharply is the astonishing rudeness of this woman to whom "manners" were of such overriding concern. (This, as I have since had some occasion to notice, is a fairly common characteristic among members of the class to which she belonged.) Though she would not have admitted it, good manners to Mrs. K. meant only one thing: conformity to a highly stylized set of surface habits and fashions which she took, quite as a matter of course, to be superior to all other styles of social behavior. But in what did their superiority consist? Were her "good" manners derived from or conducive to a greater moral sensitivity than the "bad" manners I had learned at home and on the streets of Brownsville? I rather doubt it. The "crude" behavior of my own parents, for example, was then and is still marked by a tactfulness and a delicacy that Mrs. K. simply could not have approached. It is not that she was incapable of tact and delicacy; in certain moods she was; and manners apart, she was an extraordinarily loving and generous woman. But such qualities were neither built into nor expressed by the system of manners under which she lived. She was fond of quoting Cardinal Newman's definition of a gentleman as a person who could be at ease in any company, yet if anything was clear about the manners she was trying to teach me, it was that they operated not inadvertently but by deliberate design to set one at ease *only* with others similarly trained and to cut one off altogether from those who were not.

While I would have been unable to formulate it in those terms at the time, I think I must have understood perfectly well what Mrs. K. was attempting to communicate with all her talk about manners; if I had not understood it so well, I would not have resisted so fiercely. She was saying that because I was a talented boy, a better class of people stood ready to admit me into their ranks. But only on one condition: I had to signify by my general deportment that I acknowledged them as *superior* to the class of people among whom I happened to have been born. That was the bargain—take it or leave it. In resisting Mrs. K. where "manners" were concerned, just as I was later to resist many others, I was expressing my refusal to have any part of so brutal a bargain. But the joke was on me, for what I did not understand, not in the least then and not for a long time afterward, was that in matters having to do with "art" and "culture" (the "life of the mind," as I learned to call it at Columbia), I was being offered the very same brutal bargain and accepting it with the wildest enthusiasm.

I have said that I did not, for all my bookishness, feel alienated as a boy, and this is certainly true. Far from dreaming of escape from Brownsville, I dreaded the thought of living anywhere else, and whenever my older sister, who hated the neighborhood, began begging my parents to move, it was invariably my howls of protest that kept them from giving in. For by the age of thirteen I had made it into the neighborhood big time, otherwise known as the Cherokees, S.A.C. It had by no means been easy for me, as a mediocre athlete and a notoriously good student, to win acceptance from a gang which prided itself mainly on its masculinity and its contempt for authority, but once this had been accomplished, down the drain went any reason I might earlier have had for thinking that life could be better in any other place. Not for nothing, then, did I wear that red satin jacket to school every day. It was my proudest possession, a badge of manly status, proving that I was not to be classified with the Crown Heights "creeps," even though my grades, like theirs, were high.

And yet, despite the Cherokees, it cannot be that I felt quite so securely at home in Brownsville as I remember thinking. The reason is that something extremely significant in this connection had happened to me by the time I first met Mrs. K.: without any conscious effort on my part, my speech had largely lost the characteristic neighborhood accent and was well on its way to becoming as neutrally American as I gather it now is.

Now whatever else may be involved in a nondeliberate change of accent, one thing is clear: it bespeaks a very high degree of detachment from the ethos of one's immediate surroundings. It is not a good ear alone, and perhaps not even a good ear at all, which enables a child to hear the difference between the way he and everyone else around him sound when they talk, and the way teachers and radio announcers—as it must have been in my case—sound. Most people, and especially most children, are entirely insensitive to such differences, which is why anyone who pays attention to these matters can, on the basis of a man's accent alone, often draw a reasonably accurate picture of his regional, social, and ethnic background. People who feel that they belong in their familiar surroundings—whether it be a place, a class, or a group—will invariably speak in the accent of those surroundings; in all likelihood, indeed, they will never have imagined any other possibility for themselves. Conversely, it is safe to assume that a person whose accent has undergone a radical change from childhood is a person who once had fantasies of escaping to some other world, whether or not they were ever realized.

But accent in America has more than a psychological or spiritual significance. "Her kerbstone English," said Henry Higgins of Eliza Doolittle, "will keep her in the gutter to the end of her days." Most Americans probably respond with a sense of amused democratic superiority to the idea of a society in which so trivial a thing as accent can keep a man down, and it is a good measure of our blindness to the pervasive operations of class that there has been so little consciousness of the fact that America itself is such a society.* While the broadly regional accents—

---

*On the other hand, the *New York Times* reported on May 8, 1966, that "A real-life Professor Higgins" had "descended upon Harlem in search of Eliza Doolittles." The *Times* went on: "Every Saturday afternoon the portly 45-year-old professor of comparative education at Teachers College of Columbia University, Dr. George Z. F. Bereday, directs 10 Negro girl seniors from Benjamin Franklin High School on the upper East Side in a series of classes in grooming, dress, make-up, speech, poise, rhythmics, and general deportment and culture." Explained Dr. Bereday: "The theory is that there are factors other than skin color in racial discrimination. These factors are class differences and they are more immediately manageable. They oil their hair and chew gum. Maybe a girl can get a good job as a secretary, but if her hair smells like coconut oil. . . ." (Dr. Bereday himself speaks with a thick Polish accent, which makes him acceptably foreign rather than unacceptably lower class.)

New England, Midwestern, Southern—enjoy more or less equal status and will not affect the economic or social chances of those who speak in them, the opposite is still surely true of any accent identifiably influenced by Yiddish, Italian, Polish, Spanish—that is, the languages of the major post–Civil War immigrant groups, among which may be included American Irish. A man with such an accent will no longer be confined, as once he would almost automatically have been, to the working class, but unless his life, both occupational and social, is lived strictly within the milieu in whose tone of voice he speaks, his accent will at the least operate as an obstacle to be overcome (if, for example, he is a schoolteacher aspiring to be a principal), and at the most as an effective barrier to advancement (if, say, he is an engineer), let alone to entry into the governing elite of the country. For better or worse, incidentally, these accents are not a temporary phenomenon destined to disappear with the passage of the generations, no more than ethnic consciousness itself is. I have heard third-generation American Jews of East European immigrant stock speaking with thicker ethnic coloring even than their parents.

Clearly, then, while fancying myself altogether at home in the world into which I was born, I was not only more detached from it than I realized; I was also taking action, and of a very fundamental kind, which would eventually make it possible for me to move into some other world. Yet I still did not recognize what I was doing—not in any such terms. My ambition was to be a great and famous poet, not to live in a different community, a different class, a different "world." If I had a concrete image of what greatness would mean socially, it was probably based on the famous professional boxer from our block who had moved to a more prosperous neighborhood but still spent his leisure time hanging around the corner candy store and the local pool room with his old friends (among whom he could, of course, experience his fame far more sharply than he could have done among his newly acquired peers).

But to each career its own sociology. Boxers, unlike poets, do not undergo a cultural change in the process of becoming boxers, and if I was not brave enough or clever enough as a boy to see the distinction, others who knew me then were. "Ten years from now, you won't even want to talk to me, you won't even recognize me if you pass me on the street," was the kind of comment I frequently heard in my teens from women in the neighborhood, friends of my mother who were fond of me and nearly as proud as she was of the high grades I was getting in school and the prizes I was always winning. "That's crazy, you must be kidding," I would answer. They were not crazy and they were not kidding. They were simply better sociologists than I.

As, indeed, my mother herself was, for often in later years—after I had become a writer and an editor and was living only a subway ride away but in a style that was foreign to her and among people by whom she was intimidated—she would gaze wistfully at this strange creature, her son, and murmur, "I should have made him for a dentist," registering thereby her perception that whereas Jewish sons who grow up to be successes in certain occupations usually remain fixed in an accessible cultural ethos, sons who grow up into literary success are transformed almost beyond recognition and distanced almost beyond a mother's reach. My mother wanted nothing so much as for me to be a success, to be respected and admired. But she did not imagine, I think, that she would only purchase the realization of her ambition at the price of my progressive estrangement from her and her ways. Perhaps it was my guilt at the first glimmerings of this knowledge which accounted for my repression of it and for the obstinacy of the struggle I waged over "manners" with Mrs. K.

For what seemed most of all to puzzle Mrs. K., who saw no distinction between taste in poetry and taste in clothes, was that I could see no connection between the two. Mrs. K. knew that a boy from Brownsville with a taste for Keats was not long for Brownsville, and moreover would in all probability end up in the social class to which she herself belonged. How could I have explained to her that I would only be able to leave Brownsville if I could maintain the illusion that my destination was a place in some mystical country of the spirit and not a place in the upper reaches of the American class structure?

Saint Paul, who was a Jew, conceived of salvation as a world in which there would be neither Jew nor Greek, and though he may well have been the first, he was very far from the last Jew to dream such a dream of transcendence—transcendence of the actual alternative categories with which reality so stingily presents us. Not to be Jewish, but not to be Christian either; not to be a worker, but not to be a boss either; not—if I may be forgiven for injecting this banality out of my own soul into so formidable a series of fantasies—to be a slum child but not to be a snob either. How could I have explained to Mrs. K. that wearing a suit from de Pinna would for me have been something like the social equivalent of a conversion to Christianity? And how could she have explained to me that there was no socially neutral ground to be found in the United States of America, and that a distaste for the surroundings in which I was bred, and ultimately (God forgive me) even for many of the people I loved, and so a new taste for other kinds of people—how could she have explained that all this was inexorably entailed in the logic of a taste for the poetry of Keats and the painting of Cézanne and the music of Mozart?

The 1970s

Editor's Note

THE 1970s began for Podhoretz in the same way that the 1960s had ended: writing for *Commentary*—for three years short monthly pieces under a heading called "Issues," and later much longer articles. He also frequently appeared in the *New York Times* either as an essayist or as an Op-Ed columnist. Much of his late 1970s work on American foreign policy culminated in *The Present Danger* (1980). But the major book, a turning point in the intellectual history of the period, was *Breaking Ranks: A Political Memoir* (1979). Here Podhoretz, seamlessly weaving together personal experience and public issues, provided a provocative account of how and why, on a series of political and cultural questions, he had parted company with the radical movement of the 1960s that he himself helped to launch and spread, and parted, too, with many of his close friends who remained attached to the ideas and attitudes on which that movement had been built.

One of the factors leading to this break was fatherhood. In 1956 he had married Midge Decter, also a writer and editor, going on to raise her two small daughters, Rachel and Naomi, from her first marriage, along with another daughter, Ruth, and a son, John, who soon came along. With four children to worry about, he found himself forced to look at the radical movement (and especially its cultural side) in terms of its effects on them, and indeed on children, adolescents, and young adults generally. Ultimately, he also found himself forced to explain to them, and to himself, both his original commitment to the movement and his subsequent disillusion and dissent from it. Hence *Breaking Ranks,* whose "Prologue" and "Postscript"—half history lesson, half exhortation—addressed directly to his son John, by then a teenager, and by extension to anyone born after 1945, are included here.

First, though, comes the hitherto uncollected "After Modernism, What?" While Podhoretz appeared to have given up literary criticism—from 1965 to 1985 he would scarcely write a word about a novelist qua novelist—he hadn't ceased to care about the state of contemporary literature. And not least because of his intense need, which Matthew Arnold thought inseparable from human nature, for stories beautifully told.

What disturbed Podhoretz about the early 1970s climate was its hyping of the bohemian know-nothingism he had written about in the 1950s. It was a climate congenial to Norman O. Brown's repudiation of books (because they allegedly forced us to see the world through the eyes of the dead instead of freshly through our own), and also to the claim that "good writing" was itself reactionary or "counterrevolutionary" (the idea being that the beauties of art undermine outrage at social evils). After noting that the good writing of Dickens, say, had if anything aroused readers' outrage, or that good books have more often than not enabled readers to behold the world afresh, Podhoretz admits that, like any great art, literature "is most often antipolitical in its influence, a dampener of activist ardors, a chastener of utopian greed," insofar as it insists on our grasping the world as it really is.

At this point Podhoretz cites a distinction of T. S. Eliot that goes, surely, to the heart of his own sensibility, political as well as literary: "In criticism you are responsible only for what you want, [but] in creation you are responsible for what you can do with material which you must simply accept." The material is precisely "life as the artist knows it in his own time and place," and the given emotions and feelings of the artist himself. He doesn't see them as virtues to be enlarged or vices to be diminished (that's the stuff of utopians or fantasists); he "simply" takes them as his subject. "No wonder then," Podhoretz says, "that radicals who seek as earnestly to transform themselves as to transform society have generally been hostile to literature."

The closing paragraphs of "After Modernism, What?" inquire into the forms literature had assumed in a period of (a) highbrow boredom with the achievements of modernism, which had come to seem commonplace and academically reproducible; and (b) what one might call bourgeois feelings of antibourgeois alienation, the popularization of the modernist brief against middle-class life, otherwise known as (sub)urban self-hatred. The turgidities and the tarting up of the obvious that marked the sociologists' writing, the ill-disguised agitprop of the serious magazines, and the ego displays of the New Journalism: none of these once-promising modes of discourse had filled the void left by the high modernist writers, and no resurgent Trollopian realism had appeared, either. Podhoretz ends with something like a sober Micawber statement of faith in the market: there is a distinct consumer need for realistic stories well told, and writers who can satisfy that need are bound to turn up.

Realism is the theme of *Breaking Ranks,* and the "Prologue" is, again, a primer for boomers. They conceivably know something about the evils of right-wing totalitarianism, since they after all grew up watching movies about World War II, but their ignorance of left-wing totalitarianism seems boundless. Therefore Podhoretz retells the tale of how many liberals in the mid-1930s joined the Communists (who then represented themselves not as fiery revolutionaries but as harmless "liberals in a hurry") in various "popular-front" organizations, which crashed in 1939 when Stalin allied himself with Hitler; or how many of the same liberals in the 1940s discovered that Stalin's "proletarian internationalism" not only subordinated each country's Communist party to the Moscow death star but also annexed, through a combination of coups and invasion threats, an entire bloc of countries in Eastern Europe. In addition, most (if by no means all) artists and scientists had by then figured out that Communism meant less, not more, freedom for the likes of them.

During World War II and afterward, accordingly, one saw formerly Communist or fellow-traveling intellectuals becoming broadly patriotic. If, as the young Mary McCarthy surprised herself by grasping, it *mattered* that the Allies, led by America, win the war against the Axis Powers, then, as we saw with Saul Bellow in the 1950s, it mattered that America and the other Western democracies win the Cold War—Podhoretz after September 11, 2001, would take to calling it World War III—against the Communist powers. Being for America was no less necessary if one wanted to defeat left-wing totalitarianism than it had been in the struggle to eliminate the right-wing variety.

This is something Podhoretz understood as early as the late 1940s, when he was just coming of age. The burden of *Breaking Ranks* is to explain what he had learned being "for America" entailed, and this *Reader* tries to cover those lessons in later decades. By including the "Postscript" to *Breaking Ranks,* it can amplify the running theme of Podhoretz's realism—that is, as against left- or right-wing radicalism's hatred of the world and of human nature as they actually are, an acceptance. If you are white and male and middle-class, well, there you are: embrace those facts and build your life on them. Or to put it negatively, don't reject yourself: don't try to pass yourself off as black, brown, or yellow; female or bisexual; super rich or super poor. If, furthermore, you are an intellectual, then do your intellectual work—thinking, reading, writing—and if you can, produce "literary master-pieces." You needn't "change the world": indeed, the better you think, read, and write, the more you'll understand that on the whole the world can't be changed for the better through political revolution, or overnight. You'll also understand that it's more often than not a dangerous thing to try to out-Shelley Shelley—the Romantic who had called poets "the unacknowledged legislators of the world"—by insisting (in Podhoretz's play on Shelley's for-mulation) that "they had to be acknowledged, [that] they had to exercise actual political power." As William F. Buckley Jr. famously quipped, better to be governed by the first two thousand names in the Boston phone book than by the combined faculties of Harvard and MIT—or any other group of poet-intellectuals bent on dismantling the world as it is and building an "ideal" one.

The "spiritually literate" idea (as Podhoretz calls it) that there exists an unchanging nature of things to which we are best off submitting is anath-ema to many, who equate it with a primitive species of religious funda-mentalism, or worse. But this is to dispute without understanding Podhoretz's perspective, a philosophy rooted in the creation, cultivation, and enjoyment of life—against death. Though those words unfortunately echo the title of one of Norman O. Brown's books, this philosophy is, I think, another indication of an enduring insight Podhoretz got from study-ing with Leavis and reading Lawrence. But it probably derives above all from a key verse in Deuteronomy—"I have set before you life and death, . . . therefore choose life"—that he will repeatedly cite nearly a quar-ter of a century later in his book, *The Prophets: Who They Were, What They Are* (2002).

The "politics of interest" that Podhoretz recommends at the close of *Breaking Ranks* follows from his own fundamental Deuteronomic choice. If you choose life, you accept, and in only a few instances elect, who you are: of this race, that sex; of this ethnic group, that religion; of this voca-tion, that nation. And by marrying and raising children, you strengthen the interests of the wider group you are part of. "That this is all the tran-scendence of self that mortal beings can hope to achieve through action in the public realm, I now believe with all my heart," Podhoretz writes. "But is it, for all that, a politics of selfishness?" The answer is no, and in the spirit of James Madison it comes down to this: no one individual or group can pursue happiness—compete for the world's goods, temporal and spiritual—unless all individuals and groups are free to do the same. "I" and "mine" matter immensely, but the larger "we" of American democracy, which guarantees the right to pursue those freedoms, matters still more.

—TLJ

AFTER MODERNISM, WHAT?

THE FIRST QUESTION TO CONSIDER in thinking about the future of literature is whether literature has any future at all. Fifty years ago T. S. Eliot said that the novel was dead, but he did not say that literature was dead; he said that a particular form of narrative art which had developed in response to the needs and purposes of a particular age would "no longer serve" and that another form would therefore inevitably be taking its place. Similarly, when in the 1930s Edmund Wilson declared that verse was a "dying technique," he did not mean that poetry was disappearing; indeed, he explicitly argued that poetry would go on being written, but in modalities other than verse. Today, however, we hear it said on all sides that literature itself—not a particular form or genre but the entire "medium" of structured verbal discourse—is finished, obsolete, through. Print, we are told, will be unable to survive the competition of television and of the technological marvels already being prepared for the "delivery" of entertainment and information. Some day soon we will all be equipped with machines which at the flick of a switch can serve up any film, lecture, or encyclopedia entry we may choose. In this technological context, books will become as obsolete as hand-lettered parchment scrolls, and print will be confined to a bare minimum of strictly utilitarian functions.

The eyes of those who accept this vision of the future perceive its outlines already taking shape not merely on the drawing boards of the engineers but in the minds and hearts of the young. This new generation, though the best educated of all generations the world has ever seen (or so those who have reared and educated it modestly persist in claiming), cares less about books than about films, less about reason than about feeling, less about words than about images, less about high culture than about low. In this, it is alleged, they are already "tuned in" to a future in which literature will simply cease to exist.

What are we to make of these prophecies? Are they true? The possibility cannot be dismissed out of hand. Certainly the technology on which they depend is there, or is on the point of being developed—though doubts can still be entertained as to whether it will ever be economically feasible to wire every household into the central systems of distribution.

In the meantime, while print is supposed to be growing obsolete, more books than ever before are being published and sold and (presumably) read. Far from declining, the publishing business is booming, with paperbacks especially now rolling off the presses in unprecedented numbers and being distributed through every conceivable outlet. Not so many years ago, books were hard to find in the United States; today they are hard to escape. There is no town so small nor hamlet so remote that it does not offer an astonishing number and variety of books for sale at relatively reasonable prices. In what sense such a situation can be interpreted as a portent of the obsolescence of print baffles the mind.

But what of the youth? Certainly books are the last thing one associates with those hordes of young people who flooded the landscape of the 1960s and dominated its consciousness. One heard that they did occasionally read: Hesse and Vonnegut, Brown and Marcuse, the *I Ching* and the *Kama Sutra*. But one also gathered that these favored exceptions were valued precisely to the degree that they were literary assaults on literature, subverters as it were from within, celebrators in discourse of the nondiscursive, apostles of the nonverbal spreading their gospel in words. In any case, it was agreed by all who spoke for the young, who relentlessly told us what "they were trying to tell us," that books were not their "thing."

One wonders, however, how representative these highly publicized young people who either belonged to or fellow-traveled along with the counterculture were of their own generation, let alone of the generations to come. The media said they were *the* young, and everyone believed the media, and yet in 1972 Richard Nixon—Richard Nixon!—carried 50 percent of the youth vote against George McGovern, who had been expected by all the spokesmen to carry the whole generation. Evidently at least half of that generation did not identify itself in any way with the Woodstock Nation or the counterculture. And if they did not stand for their own generation, neither did the young of the counterculture represent the wave of the future. We are less than halfway through the 1970s, and already the counterculture has faded from the scene. It has left its mark and its legacies, most vividly in the area of sexual mores, but almost everything about it now seems as dated as yesterday's slang—than which nothing ever dates so sadly. More and more the counterculture looks like the product of a unique moment in history which is unlikely to recur rather than the beginning of a new era in the development of the human species. The "mutants" of the sixties have been succeeded in the colleges not by more extreme versions of themselves but by yet another new generation which is once again "hitting the books" that should by now have been moldering beneath another inch or two of dust.

The idea that literature has no future, then, need not be taken very seriously. What does need to be taken seriously, however, is the fact that this idea has achieved so widespread an acceptance. For those who predict the death of literature are not announcing a development over which they have no control; they are hoping to bring about what they pretend merely to foresee. Some of these "prophets" would wish to see literature die because books are in their view a major instrument of human enslavement. Thus Norman O. Brown: "We are in bondage to authority outside ourselves: most obviously . . . in bondage to the authority of books. . . . This bondage to books compels us not to see with our own eyes; compels us to see with the eyes of the dead, with dead eyes. . . . There is a hex on us, the specters in books, the authority of the past; and to exorcise those ghosts is the great work of magical self-liberation." But not only do books serve to perpetuate our enslavement to the authority of the past, they also reinforce our subjugation to the tyranny of mind, of reason, of logic, and all this too must be exorcised if the spirit is ever to be free. All the books, says Brown (meaning it, I suspect, more than metaphorically), must be burned: "In the fire of the holy madness even books lose their gravity, and let themselves go up into the flame."

Norman O. Brown sees books as an obstacle to revolution of the most far-reaching kind—a revolution against the human condition itself—but others would like to see literature die on more narrowly political grounds. "Good writing is counter-revolutionary," said a radical feminist toward the end of the 1960s, and her sentiments were echoed by a professor of literature who denounced the subject he teaches for blunting our outrage at the status quo and for encouraging us to make our peace with things as they are. Of course great works of literature—the novels of Dickens, for example—have often had the opposite effect; they have provoked the outrage of their readers and stimulated a demand for social or political reform (just as, despite Norman O. Brown, books have often *helped* people to see with their own eyes). Nevertheless there is no denying that literature—and in fact art in general and especially the greatest art—is most often antipolitical in its influence, a dampener of activist ardors, a chastener of utopian greeds.

T. S. Eliot once put the matter with his characteristic sharpness: "In criticism you are responsible only for what you want, [but] in creation you are responsible for what you can do with material which you must simply accept." This "material" which the artist "must simply accept," and which he teaches us to accept—to accept and not to struggle against—is life as the artist knows it in his own time and place. (No wonder, then, that Lenin, who loved music, also kept himself on a meager diet of it.) But the material in question, says Eliot, includes "the emotions and feelings of the writer himself," which are also "simply material which he must accept—not virtues to be enlarged or vices to be diminished." (No wonder, then, that radicals who seek as earnestly to transform themselves as to transform society have generally been hostile to literature.)

It is, in short, because we have been living in an age of radical activism that predictions of the death of literature have been so widely propagated and so readily accepted; and so far as the future is concerned, we can be sure that whenever the activist temper flares up again, literature will be held in suspicion and disesteem. But for many people the idea that literature is finished has also seemed plausible for reasons having more to do with the history of culture than with the history of politics. To put the point as plainly as possible, such people find themselves bored by almost everything that passes for literature today. Of course some people have always been bored by literature, and boredom in any event usually says more about the person bored than about the thing he is bored by. But it is another matter when *literary* people find themselves bored by literature, when people who have devoted their lives to studying and teaching and even writing literature, people for whom literature had always been a passion and even a lust, can hardly bring themselves to read a new novel, let alone a new volume of verse. The poets read, or at least review, each other, but does anyone else read new poetry anymore? As for fiction, which has been the dominant literary mode in our culture for about a century now, it still has a relatively large audience, but it too has begun to bore many who were once in love with it. Nearly twenty years ago, Leslie Fiedler, a famous and brilliant critic, opened an article in a leading literary magazine with the admission that the sight of a group of new novels aroused in him "a desperate desire to sneak out to a movie. How respectable the form has become, how predictable!" In its day this was a shocking statement, an offense against the regnant pieties of the literary world, but by now such sentiments have themselves become respectable and predictable. Susan Sontag, another famous critic, also admitted to being bored by the new novels she was reading, but, unwilling out of some atavistic loyalty to pronounce literature dead on that account, she developed an ingenious theory according to which boredom became a new form of interested response. And then there was Richard Poirier, a teacher of literature, an editor, and a much-published critic, who could say of a recent modernist novel which he himself had praised as a work of genius that "if I hadn't promised to review it I might not have finished it at all."

What precisely was it that had gone wrong? What had become boring about literature? For Poirier, who bravely admitted to boredom with many established classics of the past, nothing essential had changed, but in the case of critics like Fiedler and Sontag, whose main interest has been the modernist movement, with its emphasis on formal experimentation, the problem was that "the tradition of the new," as Harold Rosenberg called it, had worn itself out—becoming, so to speak, more traditional than new. And indeed nothing seems more quaintly old-fashioned today, more rearguard, than the self-styled avant-garde. When Pound and Eliot and Joyce and the other founding fathers of literary modernism undertook to "make it new," the point of their formal experiments was to break through literary conventions grown stale into a new apprehension of reality and to find a new way of bringing order to the special chaos of modern life. But for a long time now, the literary conventions standing in the way of a fresh and newly ordered perception of the world have been those of the modernist movement itself, which have become as stylized and academic—and boring—as the conventions against which it once declared a war of independence.

Modernism meant formal experimentation, but it also meant a certain attitude toward the modern world. Whether (like Pound and Eliot) their politics were of the Right, or whether (like Aragon and the early Dos Passos) their politics were of the Left, all the writers of the modernist movement were united in their hostility toward "bourgeois society" and what we call today its "middle-class values." They were, in a word, "alienated," and out of the torments of this sense of estrangement—for most of them a new and unsettling experience—they were often able to wrest a detached perspective on a world from which they felt, and very often actually were, excluded. As the decades went on, however, the antibourgeois attitudes associated with modernism increasingly became the commonplace pieties of the literary world (and by the mid-sixties, of the educated middle class as a whole), growing in the process as respectable and predictable as the literary conventions through which they were endlessly and tiresomely repeated. There were moments when it seemed impossible to find a new novel which did not celebrate the superiority of its author to the world from which he had miraculously sprung, and whose only point in describing that world was to expose it as even shallower and less interesting than he could confidently expect his audience already to think. This may have been good for radical politics, but it was bad for modernist writing.

Nor has the exhaustion of modernism been accompanied in literature by a revitalization of realism. Around the same time that Leslie Fiedler was complaining about the decline of the avant-garde in fiction, Lionel Trilling was registering another kind of complaint having to do, not with matters of form, but with questions of substance. Literature, said Trilling, had "voluntarily surrendered" what had previously been one of its "most characteristic functions, the investigation and criticism of morals and manners." I myself subsequently lamented the degree to which the novel had given up its old effort to bring us "news" of worlds with which we were unfamiliar; and more recently Tom Wolfe offered a similar but even more aggressive indictment: "By the sixties, about the time I came to New York, the . . . novelists had abandoned the richest terrain of the novel: namely, society, the social tableau, manners and morals, the whole business of 'the way we live now,' in Trollope's phrase."

What all of us were lamenting was the demise of the realistic novel, and each of us had a candidate to propose as its successor in the enterprise of investigating and criticizing manners and morals and bringing news of the way we live now. Trilling, much impressed with David Riesman's *The Lonely Crowd,* nominated sociology. I myself, pointing to the essays of James Baldwin and others, thought that magazine articles and reportage, "of all things," were taking over what the novel had "voluntarily surrendered." And Wolfe, thinking of himself and writers like Gay Talese and George Plimpton, put the New Journalism forward as the legitimate heir of the great traditions of realistic fiction.

All of us, I now think, were right in our complaint about fiction and wrong in our choice of alternatives. Trilling was wrong about sociology: instead of telling us more and more about the way we live now, the sociologists have been telling us less and less, and much of what they have been telling us we already know. I was wrong about magazine articles: instead of developing in the direction of a deeper and more extensive investigation of the manners and morals of our time, magazines have increasingly engaged in political agitation and moralistic exhortation, with articles degenerating into veiled sermons and editorials. And Wolfe was wrong about journalism: instead of serving in the spirit of Balzac as "secretaries" of American society, the New Journalists (ironically, but perhaps not so surprisingly, following the example of the novelists before them) have become increasingly narcissistic, with every subject or assignment presenting another occasion for the display of their personalities and for the assertion of their superiority to the rest of the world.

The past fifty years, then, have seen the displacement of realism by modernism, the exhaustion in its own turn of the modernist impulse, and a somewhat desperate search for a new form in which the old ambition of literature to record "the way we live now," to set it all down in rich and precise detail, to see the world as in itself it really is, can be renewed and reinvigorated.

In the light of this experience, what can we expect the next fifty years to bring? There is obviously no way of knowing for sure, but my own guess is that imaginative literature will once again offer itself as the means by which the perennially insistent hunger for showing us how we live and what we are like can best be satisfied. I think this will happen because the logic of literary history points toward it. There is no other way for literature to go, except perhaps to the grave, and I do not believe that literature will go to its grave, not only because the case for believing that literature has no future is so weak, but also—and mainly—because it is impossible to imagine a world in which words will cease to delight and stories will cease to be told.

FROM *BREAKING RANKS:*
PROLOGUE

A LETTER TO MY SON

Dear John:

The other day, reminded by some passing remark that I used to be a radical—indeed that I visibly and enthusiastically participated in the swing to radicalism in the early 1960s—you asked me with astonishment in your voice whether I had ever really believed "all that stuff." The thought of your father in connection with "all that stuff" evidently strikes you as a contradiction in terms. No wonder. All your conscious life you've known me as an opponent of the New Left and the counterculture and their various descendants in the liberal culture. For all your precocity you could never fully understand why I always seemed to be against everything everyone else in the world—your teachers, your classmates, your friends—seemed to be for. I would try to explain whenever you asked me, but it was all so complicated and you were just too young to take it in. You're a little less young now, however, and maybe the time has come for a fully detailed account.

I'll begin by answering your question of the other day. Yes, once upon a time I really did believe in all that stuff. In fact, I played a not inconsiderable part in spreading it around, beginning with a number of articles I wrote in the late 1950s and then, much more importantly, through *Commentary* after I became its editor in 1960. But the minute I say even that much, one of those complications arises that you were until recently too young to understand. Because all that stuff was both the same as it is today and entirely different. That is, the ideas were more or less the same, but the context, the circumstances, the background were all different, and this had the effect of giving a different feel to those ideas than they have today.

For one thing, they were new when I first encountered them. They were also daring and a little dangerous: they could get you into trouble. Not so much, I hasten to add, with the FBI or the House Un-American Activities Committee as with one's fellow intellectuals.

You see, in the late fifties the important forces in the intellectual world—magazines like *Partisan Review, Commentary,* and *Encounter,* and writers like Lionel Trilling, Hannah Arendt, Reinhold Niebuhr, Arthur Koestler, Sidney Hook, Leslie Fiedler, Saul Bellow, etc., etc., etc.—were against radicalism. That doesn't mean (as again you've been led to imagine) that they were on the Right or that they were conservative in the sense, say, that William F. Buckley Jr. and *National Review* were. On the contrary, they were all liberals. This was even true of *Encounter,* which turned out to have been subsidized secretly by the CIA up until the late 1960s. But (still another complication) the CIA was itself a liberal organization. Yes, yes, I know, it did illiberal things. Nevertheless the people who ran it were liberals. For example, the officer who headed the division that was responsible for *Encounter* had come to the CIA from a high position in the United World Federalists, than which nothing could have been more liberal. In any case, whatever its connection with *Encounter* may have been, the CIA had no connection whatsoever with *Partisan Review* or *Commentary,* even though both of them had a point of view similar to *Encounter*'s. I've already said that it was a liberal point of view, and it was; but if you really want to understand it, you have to think of it more in terms of what it was against than of what it was for. And what it was against was Communism.

The reason the anti-Communism of those liberals has to be stressed is that—to complicate matters still further—there were also liberals in America who were *not* anti-Communist—who were, to tell the truth, favorably disposed toward the Communists. They weren't Communists themselves, but they were generally sympathetic to the Communists. These liberals—fellow travelers, they were called—thought the Communists were on the same side as they were, only more zealous and more impatient (faults for which they could easily be forgiven, and even admired and envied).

The Communists, for their part, had no such illusions. To them liberalism was nothing more than the political ideology of the bourgeoisie and therefore marked for destruction in the revolution ahead. But around 1935, when Stalin began to get worried about the growing military power of Nazi Germany, he decided that he had better move toward an alliance with the "bourgeois" democracies—specifically the United States, Britain, and France—in case of war with Hitler. At that point the Communist parties in those three countries, all of which took their orders from Moscow, changed their line. In America (and there were similar developments in Britain and France) they dropped all talk of revolution, they represented themselves as patriots (the slogan of the American Communist party was

"Communism Is Twentieth-Century Americanism"), and they began
encouraging the idea that they were nothing more than "liberals in a
hurry." As for the Soviet Union, it was portrayed as a democratic country
and Stalin as a benevolent figure leading his people out of the backwardness of czarist times toward a richer, fuller, and happier life.

Nobody knows how many American liberals were fooled by propaganda
like this. But enough of them were, certainly, to make a difference. For
example, the two leading liberal weeklies in America, the *Nation* and the
New Republic, became loyal apologists for Stalin, constantly printing pieces
that praised his many accomplishments and denouncing as reactionaries
and fascists anyone who called those accomplishments into question or
tried to expose the bloodiness and repression behind the smiling façade.
No one today denies that Stalin murdered millions of peasants who resisted
his plan to expropriate their land and organize them into collective farms
where they would all become employees of the state. But the fellow-traveling liberals (not to mention the "liberals in a hurry") of the 1930s denied it
and vilified as liars and worse those who tried to tell the world what was
happening. Nor does anyone today deny that the Soviet Union under
Stalin was a police state in which all political opponents were either murdered or imprisoned in the Gulag Archipelago, a vast network of concentration camps that, according to Solzhenitsyn's estimate (he, as you know,
spent eleven years in the Gulag himself), eventually offered gruesome hos-
pitality to an estimated sixty million people. Yet the fellow travelers of the
1930s denied this, too, and denounced reports of it as fascist propaganda.

Who were these "fascists" and "reactionaries"? You might think they
were rich businessmen or sinister capitalists like the character played by
Edward Arnold in *Mr. Smith Goes to Washington,* that old Frank Capra
movie you're seen so many times on television. But you would be wrong.
Mostly they were intellectuals, and a lot of them had once themselves been
Communists who had joined the party in the belief that it stood for social
justice and democracy and who had then eventually come to know better.
Many others had never been Communists but were members of rival
socialist parties who also opposed Communism (or Stalinism) as a betrayal
of the ideals in which they all as followers of Marx claimed to believe.

As time went on, a few of these anti-Communists of the Left moved all
the way over to the Right and became what it is fair to call conservatives.
One such, an ex-Communist, was Whittaker Chambers, who became
famous when he accused Alger Hiss of having been a Communist spy while
occupying an important position in the State Department. Another was

James Burnham, who had been a follower of Leon Trotsky, Stalin's defeated rival, and then wound up as an editor of *National Review* and a defender of Joe McCarthy. A third was Will Herberg, who had belonged to a tiny sub-division of the Communist movement, the Lovestoneites, and eventually became an influential Jewish theologian as well as an important political conservative. And there were others of whom you've probably heard, among them the novelist John Dos Passos, who was a radical when he wrote *U.S.A.* and then became a conservative in later years, and the critic Max Eastman, who began by translating the works of Trotsky from Russian into English and ended by writing articles for the very conservative *Reader's Digest.*

But if some anti-Communists of the Left became conservatives, most of them did not. Some became, or remained, socialists; others became liberals. For example, Jay Lovestone, the leader of the little group to which Will Herberg had once belonged, wound up working for the liberal trade-union movement. Sidney Hook, the author of one of the first important books on Marx written by an American and one of the fiercest and most consistent critics of Communism, continued through thick and thin to regard himself as a socialist. And so did Philip Rahv and William Phillips, the two chief editors of *Partisan Review* who (like the magazine itself) remained sympathetic to radicalism in one form or another after their break with the Communist party in the early thirties.

All these people had one thing in common. Whether they became conservatives, socialists, or liberals, their ruling passion tended to be a hatred of Communism and a suspicion of Communists. Having been Communists themselves, or having seen and dealt with Communists at close range, they had all come away from the experience with the conviction that Communism was a great evil—as great an evil as Nazism and possibly even greater.

There were those who came to feel this way as early as the 1920s when reports of repression and brutality first began circulating in the West—many of them brought out by refugees who had themselves participated in the making of the Russian Revolution in the fond hope that it would bring socialism and democracy to their country. For others the turning point was the Moscow Trials, when Stalin purged and murdered many of his associates on false charges of treason; and for still others the break came when in 1939 Stalin signed a pact with Hitler. Can you imagine the shock that was caused by this incredible event? How could Stalin have done such a thing? Explanations and rationalizations were of course offered and a surprisingly large number of people accepted them. But for many others, this was the end of the line. Not even Hitler's invasion of the Soviet Union two years later, and the fact that Stalin was now allied with the democratic world in the fight against fascism, could repair the moral damage that signing a pact with Hitler had done to Stalin's reputation and to the reputation of the Communists in America and elsewhere who had justified the pact as a necessary maneuver.

What the anti-Communist intellectuals were saying, in short, was that Communism in the Soviet Union had led not to justice, equality, and freedom but to a system of dictatorial control as thoroughgoing as any the world had ever seen. In fact, except for Nazism the world had never seen anything quite like the Communist system. Older-style dictatorships were mainly interested in concentrating all political power in their hands, but they were generally willing to permit a certain amount or even a great deal of freedom in other areas of life—religion, for example, or the arts. But in these new systems—to which the word totalitarianism was beginning to be applied—everything was controlled and no freedom was allowed in any area of life. A single political party ruled the state and the state ruled all of life.

From the point of view of the anti-Communist intellectuals, one of the worst things about this system was the ruthlessness with which it suppressed freedom of thought and freedom of speech. These were, after all, the freedoms that concerned them most closely as intellectuals; and in fact one of the main reasons why so many intellectuals were attracted to Communism in the first place was their belief that in a Communist society people like them—educated people, cultivated people—would be better off than they felt themselves to be under capitalism. In America, for instance, everything was, or seemed to be, run by businessmen. Intellectuals had no status, no power, no money. At worst they were ridiculed and sometimes harassed; at best they were tolerated and ignored. But in a "socialist" society where private property was abolished and the pursuit of profits put to an end, people who cultivated the nonmaterial values would become more and more important, and art and thought would flourish as they never had before. Marx himself had even said that under Communism factory workers would spend their leisure time reading and writing poetry.

This was the theory, but the Soviet reality was something else again. For a few brief years after the Russian Revolution, there was a cultural flowering, but soon the totalitarian darkness descended. Experimentation in the arts was suppressed in the Soviet Union no less thoroughly than in Nazi Germany. The best writers were silenced; some, like Isaac Babel and Osip

Mandelstam, were murdered, and others were forced either to be still or to write according to the dictates of the party bureaucrats. Painting, too, was made to conform to the canons of "socialist realism"—a style that was neither socialist nor realistic, but rather an idealized and sentimental representation of approved scenes and subjects (portraits of Lenin and Stalin, workers building socialism, and so on). Great composers like Shostakovich and Prokofiev were humiliated and forced to apologize and revise their work when they violated the equivalent of these aesthetic rules in music.

Nor was it only the arts that were subjected to this kind of control. Philosophers, historians, sociologists, psychologists—all had to toe the "party line," all had to say what they were in effect told to say and to keep silent about everything else. Not even scientists were safe. A charlatan named Lysenko, for instance, was given the highest honors for "proving" that genetic changes could be induced by changes in the environment—an idea that conformed to the party line but contradicted all the scientific evidence accepted by geneticists everywhere else in the world.

Up until the end of the Second World War, what mainly concerned the anti-Communist intellectuals was the internal character of the Soviet regime. But right after the war, a new anxiety arose over what looked very much like the beginning of a campaign by the Communists to extend their control far beyond the borders of the Soviet Union itself. The victorious Russian armies, moving toward Berlin, had already occupied all the countries of Eastern Europe and, in violation of wartime pledges, had set up governments run by local Communist leaders who took their orders from Moscow and were kept in power by Soviet troops. Then, in Czechoslovakia, the only democratic country in Eastern Europe, the Communists staged a coup and all of Western Europe began to feel threatened.

To make matters even more ominous, the "popular-front" line, stressing the loyalty of the various national Communist parties to their countries of origin and their commitment to peaceful democratic change, was now dropped. "Proletarian internationalism"—that is, the principle that all Communist parties owed their primary allegiance to the Soviet Union— was back, and the fear of Czech-style coups on the one hand and outright Soviet invasion on the other became very great throughout the whole of Western Europe.

It was to prevent any such thing from happening that the United States undertook two major initiatives. It created a military alliance called NATO to defend Western Europe against the threat of a Soviet invasion. And it set up a huge system of economic aid called the Marshall Plan, which, by speeding the reconstruction of the war-torn European democracies and turning them into prosperous modern societies, would (or so it was hoped) deprive the Communists in those countries of opportunities for political subversion.

Here, then, an effort was mounted by the United States and its allies to hold the line against any further advances by the Soviet Union, whether operating on its own through military invasion or indirectly through the agency of local Communist parties. This policy was known as "containment," and the struggle to which it addressed itself also had a name: the Cold War.

It will not surprise you to hear that the anti-Communist intellectuals enlisted in that war on the side of the United States. But it did surprise some of them. What surprised them was not, of course, that they were against the Communists: they had been against the Communists all along, or at least for some years past. But being *for* the United States was a new experience to many of these people. All their lives they had thought of themselves as virtual foreigners in this country, as aliens—hence the term "alienated" was so often applied to intellectuals in America. As it happens, the community of anti-Communist intellectuals in America included a large number of Jews (and so, on the other side, did the community of fellow travelers), and no doubt this had something to do with their feelings of alienation. In those days there was still a great deal of open hostility to Jews in America and Jews were still excluded from many positions of power and influence. Even as late as the 1950s colleges and professional schools had unacknowledged but strictly enforced quotas limiting the number of Jews who could be admitted (I myself entered Columbia in 1946 under a 17 percent quota). Many firms would not hire Jews; many social clubs barred Jews from membership; Jews were unable to get rooms in many hotels or rent apartments in many buildings or buy houses in many neighborhoods. Even in the world of culture restrictions were still in force. At Columbia, for example, Lionel Trilling was the first Jew ever to be appointed to a professorship in the English department; and despite the fact that he had already done very distinguished work in the field, his appointment was resisted on the theory that as a Jew he lacked the background to understand English literature as fully as a "rooted" person of Anglo-Saxon ancestry quite naturally would. (This, I remind you, happened not in the Middle Ages but in my own lifetime and to a man you yourself actually knew.)

But it would be wrong to ascribe the alienation of the intellectuals in America entirely or even largely to Jewishness. For one thing, not all the intellectuals were Jewish; in fact many, and perhaps most, were WASPs from old American families whose position at the head of American society had been challenged by the rise of a new breed of Americans in the years after the Civil War. These old WASP families felt that the country was being stolen away and changed into a place that had no room for the likes of them. Edmund Wilson, who was probably the most important literary intellectual of his time, came out of just such a background, and in one of his essays he describes the difficulties his father and his uncles, educated at schools like Exeter and Andover and such colleges as Princeton and Yale and trained "for what had once been called the learned professions," experienced in trying "to deal with a world in which this kind of education and the kind of ideals it served no longer really counted for much."

Like the Jews down at the bottom of the social ladder, then, the old WASP families at the top had reasons of their own to feel alienated at a certain period in the history of this country. But whether they were Jews or WASPs, intellectuals had cause enough as intellectuals to feel like foreigners in America during that same period—the period running roughly from the end of the Civil War up through the end of the Second World War. It was during those years that America moved into the forefront of the modern world. This was the time when the West was opened up and settled, when the great railroads were built, when all the great industries were established—and many of the great fortunes. It was a time when, as Calvin Coolidge notoriously said during his term as president in the late 1920s, the business of America was business. So it was, and that meant that nothing else was valued very highly—certainly not intellectual and cultural pursuits or the "oddballs" who pursued them. Intellectuals were ridiculed and despised. They were impractical. They were effeminate. They had—in a famous American phrase—"never met a payroll."

If I've given you the impression that the intellectuals were merely passive, pathetic victims and martyrs who took all this lying down, let me immediately set things straight. They didn't take it lying down; they responded by developing a critique of America as a country in the grip of false and corrupting values. "The exclusive worship of the bitch-goddess SUCCESS," said the great philosopher William James, "is our national disease." By the worship of success, James meant the worship of money, and this diagnosis of the American condition was confirmed by practically every important American writer of the period. Not only that, but it was extended into a merciless assault on practically every aspect of the national life. There was nothing good to be said about America, except perhaps that it had a certain raw energy and vitality. For the rest, in addition to being moneygrubbing and materialistic, it lacked any of the civilized graces. It was a "bourgeois" country, a narrow-minded country, a puritanical country, a philistine country. What else could one expect when it was dominated by businessmen and run entirely for their benefit? In such a country it was a badge of honor to be estranged or alienated; it signified a stubborn devotion to the higher things in life.

So powerful were these feelings of estrangement that they persisted right into the Second World War, when some intellectuals (including a few Jews!) saw no reason to "support" America even in a fight against so obviously greater an evil as Nazi Germany. But as the war went on, things began to change. Mary McCarthy once described the happiness she experienced when, as a young writer associated with *Partisan Review* and sharing the stock attitudes of contempt for and estrangement from "bourgeois society," she suddenly realized one day that she cared about the outcome of the war, that she wanted the United States to win.

A few years later, in 1952, *Partisan Review* ran a symposium with the title "Our Country and Our Culture," and the fact that a magazine which had always stood as the very symbol of the alienated intellectual could speak of America as *our* country in itself said more about the changing attitudes of the intellectuals than anything the contributors to the symposium had to say. Not that what they had to say contradicted the spirit of the new sense of personal identification with America expressed in the title. On the contrary. Though very few went quite so far as Mary McCarthy had recently done in an essay for *Commentary* called "America the Beautiful" (with only a protective touch of irony), many of them found virtues in the country and even in its culture to which they had previously been blind.

So democratic America was "our country" now, a bulwark of freedom against both Nazi and Communist totalitarianism. Amazing as this discovery about America was, what amazed the anti-Communist intellectuals even more was how well "our country" worked. During the Great Depression of the thirties, almost everyone thought that the American economic system—capitalism, in a word—had reached a point of collapse, just as its critics, especially the Marxist ones, had always predicted it would. According to these critics, only the war had saved it by absorbing into the armed forces millions who would otherwise have been unemployed and by stimulating production through the temporary need for guns, tanks, and planes. Since these were only temporary expedients, however, the economy was bound to sink back into a depression again once the war was over. But not only did this confident prophecy fail to come true; the very opposite occurred. There was no depression after the war. Instead there was prosperity—more of it than anyone had ever seen before either in America or anywhere else; and more people were getting a share of this prosperity than anyone had ever thought possible under either capitalism or any other economic system. Henry Wallace had been considered a visionary when he said (as vice president under Roosevelt) that there would be sixty million jobs in America after the war; but during the fifties that goal was reached, and the number was growing all the time.

Included among these—and this probably came as the greatest surprise of all—were jobs even for intellectuals. It had always been difficult in the past for intellectuals to earn their living as intellectuals. Of those who lacked inherited wealth, a small number had been able to support themselves by teaching or by contributing to the handful of magazines which provided a market for serious writing. Everyone else either gave up or was forced to do intellectual work in the hours left over from an unrelated job (one of the great American poets of our time, Wallace Stevens, was a lawyer for an insurance company; another, William Carlos Williams, practiced medicine) or had to manage (like several of our best novelists, including William Faulkner and F. Scott Fitzgerald) by doing hack work for the movies and the popular magazines. This situation also began to improve in the years after the Second World War. As prosperity increased, more and more young Americans were being sent to college, which meant that more and more people had to be hired to teach them, and this in turn meant the opening up of a large new source of jobs for intellectuals.

But the expansion of higher education did more than provide teaching jobs for the intellectuals. It also helped to create a much larger public for serious writing (and for the arts in general) than had ever existed before. "Quality paperbacks"—that is, inexpensive reprints of literary classics, many of which had scarcely been available before even in expensive editions—now began to flood the bookstores. Difficult contemporary works (by authors like James Joyce, T. S. Eliot, and William Faulkner), which had previously been of interest to only a minuscule number of readers, also began attracting a relatively large audience, while several younger writers like Saul Bellow and Mary McCarthy, whose work had previously been confined to the "little" magazines, were now suddenly appearing on the best-seller lists and being courted by magazines catering to very large audiences.

Thus, America was becoming "our country" to the anti-Communist intellectuals not just in the sense that they now had a stake in its political system and because they also for the first time had a stake in its economic system; there was the equally astonishing fact that America now had a reciprocal stake in them. The old contempt for intellectuals so characteristic of an earlier day was gradually giving way to a new regard for "brains" and education and the people who had them. Whatever the reasons for this development may have been, intellectuals were more and more looked up to instead of down upon, and were more and more being sought out for advice and guidance by the government, by foundations, and even by corporations. In short, from having been virtual outcasts and pariahs, the intellectuals were becoming a respected group in American society.

To all this the anti-Communist intellectuals responded by moving—to borrow the title of a book later written about American fiction in the postwar period—"beyond alienation" and toward a new sense of identification with and sympathy for the country of which they were now an increasingly important part. If in the past they had been anti-Communist (or anti-Soviet—it came to the same thing at a time when all Communists everywhere were controlled by the Soviet Union) and uncertain about America, they were now anti-Communists and committed to America. They continued, most of them, to think of themselves as men of the Left or as liberals, but liberals who differed from the fellow-traveling species in their ideas about the Soviet Union.

Even the poet and literary critic Delmore Schwartz, who as late as the *Partisan Review* symposium of 1952 had insisted on the continuing relevance of the idea of alienation, and on the need to maintain the "critical nonconformism" which had traditionally characterized the intellectual's attitude toward American society, began experiencing a change of mind. Here is how he put the case in a lecture on "The Present State of Modern Poetry" delivered in 1958:

> Since the Second World War and the beginning of the atomic age, the consciousness of the creative writer, however detached, has been confronted with the specter of the totalitarian state, the growing poverty and helplessness of Western Europe, and the threat of an inconceivably destructive war which may annihilate civilization and mankind itself. Clearly when the future of civilization is no longer assured, a criticism of American life in terms of a contrast between avowed ideals and present actuality cannot be a primary preoccupation and source of inspiration. For America, not Europe, is now the

sanctuary of culture; civilization's very existence depends upon America, upon the actuality of American life, and not the ideals of the American Dream. To criticize the actuality upon which all hope depends thus becomes a criticism of hope itself.

Now if you want to understand my own political development, the first thing you have to bear in mind is that it was on these attitudes toward Communism on the one side and America on the other that I cut my teeth as a young intellectual. It was from here that my odyssey to radicalism began, and it was back to a remarkably similar set of attitudes that my gradual revulsion from radicalism eventually took me.

To be sure, where I stand today is not precisely where I stood twenty-five years ago. How could it be when so much has happened both to the world and to me in the course of those extraordinarily unsettling years? But there is no way I can truly explain the differences both gross and subtle, both large and small, without telling the whole story of how and why I went from being a liberal to being a radical and then finally to being an enemy of radicalism in all its forms and varieties.

That I define my present position in such negative terms does not mean that it is a wholly negative position; not at all. But I do so because I still have trouble finding a positive political label for myself. The label I usually use when I am forced to use one at all is "centrist" or "centrist liberal"; the label almost everyone else uses in describing me or the general point of view I hold is "neoconservative." But whatever its most appropriate name, my present position is very hard to describe in terms of abstract propositions or doctrines. There, too, the whole story has to be told.

It is that story I want to tell in this book. Obviously I want to tell it because I would like you to understand who and what I am. But I also believe that in the story of my own radicalization and deradicalization, and of what I saw going on around me in the process, there is a larger story about the political culture of this country that needs to be faced and absorbed if we are ever to recover our health as a nation after the fevers and plagues of the two decades just past. I have a rather different conception of the nature of those fevers and plagues—and therefore of the possible cures—than is generally accepted by the conventional wisdom of the moment. But once again, I can only explain by telling the whole story.

FROM *BREAKING RANKS:*
POSTSCRIPT

<hr />

T HERE YOU HAVE IT, JOHN, THE
story of how I came to believe "all that stuff," how I came to hate and fear
it, and how it both acquired and lost an amazing amount of power within
the space of twenty years. Not that its power is entirely gone; far from it.
But I don't have to tell you that. From listening to your teachers and your
friends and their parents, you know better than I how many of the things I
used to believe when I was part of a tiny group of radicals in the early sixties have become the conventional wisdom of the seventies. You know from
your own experience that if the Movement is dead, which in a formal sense
it certainly is, it died as much because it won as because it lost. Its ideas and
attitudes are now everywhere.

But when I say that radicalism is still alive, I have in mind something
deeper and more general than the particular doctrines of the New Left and
the counterculture and the habits and the mores and the tastes and the
fashions to which they gave rise. To the extent that these doctrines have
become an orthodoxy in so many American circles, they have inevitably
lost their radical bite; and to the extent that the American way of life has
undergone a marked change under their influence, the "counter" culture
no longer has anything to be counter to.

Where then does radicalism now live? Exactly where it has always lived:
not primarily in doctrines and not in the outward signs of manner and
dress, but in self-hatred and self-contempt. It was out of an infection of
self-hatred and self-contempt—disguised, to be sure, by the various gospels
of expanding human possibility preached by early prophets like Norman
O. Brown, Norman Mailer, and Paul Goodman—that the radicalism of
the sixties was born; and as it grew and spread, the infection grew and
spread until it reached the proportions of an epidemic. The young were
especially vulnerable. They had been inoculated against almost every one of
the physical diseases which in times past had literally made it impossible for

so many to reach adulthood. But against a spiritual plague like this one they were entirely helpless. Indeed, so spiritually illiterate had the culture become that parents were unable even to recognize the disease when it struck their own children, and so confused were they that they went on insisting, even when the evidence of sickness and incapacity stared them full in the face, that the children were models of superior health.

In the case of the white young, the contemptuous repudiation of everything American and middle class was mistaken for a form of idealism when it really represented a refusal to be who they were and to assume responsibility for themselves by taking their place in a world of adults. The case of the black young was more complicated because unlike their white counterparts they had real external oppressions to contend with. But this only made it easier to mistake the plague for health when it struck them in the form of a refusal to accept any responsibility whatever for their own condition—to trace its ills entirely to the actions of whites and to look entirely to external forces for the cure. In the case, finally, of the intellectuals, the third major group that proved especially vulnerable, self-hatred took the form of a repudiation not so much of who as of what they were. To be an intellectual—a scholar, a thinker, an artist, a writer—was not good enough. Not even "the production of literary masterpieces" was good enough: one had to change the world. Nor was it even good enough to be, as Shelley had said the poets were, the unacknowledged legislators of the world: they had to be acknowledged, they had to exercise actual political power.

After sweeping so many away, the plague seems to have run its course among the young, among the blacks, and among the intellectuals. People of your own generation seem to be growing up reasonably well and seem eager rather than bitterly unwilling to take their places in the world; in the black community, leaders like Jesse Jackson have begun to preach an ethic of self-help and individual responsibility; and in the universities there is a new emphasis on intellectual activity as its own justification and its own reward.

But if the plague seems for the moment to have run its course among these groups, it rages as fiercely as ever among others: among the kind of women who do not wish to be women and among those men who do not wish to be men. The same spiritual illiteracy that made it so easy for so many to mistake the self-hatred into which their own children or they themselves had fallen in the sixties for political idealism now makes it easy to misread the female self-hatred so evident in elements of the women's movement, or the male self-hatred pervading the gay rights campaign, as self-acceptance expressing itself politically in the demand for acceptance by others. Yet there can be no more radical refusal of self-acceptance than the repudiation of one's own biological nature; and there can be no abdication of responsibility more fundamental than the refusal of a man to become, and to be, a father, or the refusal of a woman to become, and be, a mother.

In an individual the ultimate expression of self-hatred is suicide—the murder by its own hand of the hated self. Thus it was that the sixties saw a huge rise in the number of suicides among the young, both white and black, and an untold increase in the number of unrecorded suicides through drugs and other "accidents"—all taking place in the context of a culture in which suicide was virtually encouraged by being romanticized (in, for example, the cult of Sylvia Plath) as an expression of superior sensitivity and therefore as an affirmation of life. "Whom the gods wish to destroy," wrote Euripides, "they first make mad"—mad enough, in this application of the rule, to mistake death for life and life for death.

But if the plague, unchecked, causes death by suicide in individuals, it can also attack the vital organs of the entire species, preventing men from fathering children and women from mothering them. Here the disease, unchecked, leads not to the destruction of the individual's will to live (though it may) but to the destruction of the individual's will to propagate and reproduce. Thus it was that when the plague invaded women as women and men as men, the birth rate began to fall precipitously and the number of abortions soon exceeded the number of births. There was a message in the fact that in an age when contraception had become so easily available and so effective, abortion should have remained so prevalent a form of birth control: it was almost as though the species were trying to force itself to recognize the symptoms of the plague behind the cunning deceptions by which it had been tempted into the service of sterility. And just as the rise in the number of individual suicides before had been accompanied and further encouraged by the rise of a veritable cult of suicide, so now sterility was promoted in ways both direct and devious: through warnings about overpopulation; through a harping on the difficulties and miseries of raising a family as compared with the pleasures and excitements of the unencumbered life; through the rise of new therapies like est and "self-help" books which elevated selfishness into the single most important of all moral imperatives. This identification of sterility with vitality is what links the new narcissism of the Me Decade to Women's Lib and the gay-rights movement, and it is what links all of them to the radicalism of the sixties.

By the same token, it is what distinguishes them from the politics of interest that I have come to see as the only antidote to the plague and the only effective protection against ever catching it again. The politics of interest promises neither salvation nor the experience of spiritual transcendence that radicalism pretends to offer. It promises only the satisfactions that come from acting out of respect for oneself and out of responsibility toward those extensions of oneself—one's family and the groups and communities to which one belongs, whether by birth or by voluntary choice—that an openness to life inevitably creates. That this is all the transcendence of self that mortal beings can hope to achieve through action in the public realm, I now believe with all my heart. But is it, for all that, a politics of selfishness? Not if it is pursued in the context of a pluralistic society like our own. In this society the assumption is that the politics of interest not only serves the purpose of civil peace by providing the best way to resolve conflicting claims; it also works to preserve and protect political liberty itself. For as James Madison explained in the best statement of the case for the American Constitution ever made, it is only where liberty exists that the politics of interest can flourish and only where the politics of interest flourishes that liberty can exist.

What I am trying to say is that if the politics of interest goes beyond individual selfishness in embracing the claims of family, community, and group, it also embodies and simultaneously broadens into an instrument of political liberty. At least it does in the American constitutional system, and for those of us who are determined to keep faith with the men who ordained that system "in order to form a more perfect Union, establish Justice, insure domestic Tranquility, provide for the common defense, promote the general Welfare, and secure the Blessings of Liberty to ourselves and our Posterity."

Ourselves—the summons is to me. *Posterity*—the summons is to you.

The 1980s

Editor's Note

THE war in Vietnam: from the mid-1960s, several years after American troops intervened, to 1975, when the United States withdrew, it often seemed that no one could talk about anything else. One reason Podhoretz wrote *Why We Were in Vietnam* (1982), the final chapter of which, "Whose Immorality?," is included here, is that after the North's victory, everyone seemed to want to talk about anything but. Understandably, since the war should have embarrassed even those critics who applauded the American defeat. For they had throughout their protests engaged in double-think: violence committed by American troops and their allies, like their alleged violations of international law, was always evil, while violence committed by Communist forces, like their real violations of international law, was always good. It's a very human reaction, as old as war itself: if "our guys" do it, whoever our guys happen to be, then they are justified, while if "their guys" do it, they aren't. Podhoretz—who had been a very early member of the antiwar movement and had then come to reexamine his position as that movement grew increasingly infected with anti-Americanism—reopens the question of which guys ought really to be ours. We were in Vietnam, he now argues, not to rape and pillage, nor to assert and extend the white man's hegemony over Southeast Asia. We were there at the behest of the idealistic Wilsonian side of the American character, to protect the authoritarian South against the totalitarian regime of the North and its Vietcong allies. The government of the South was no democratic paradise, but the potential for greater economic and political freedoms was present and worth cultivating.

Unfortunately, our idealistic purposes were never vigorously formulated. President Lyndon Johnson, in particular, concentrated on a "realistic," power-politics *raison de guerre*—we were holding the line in Vietnam in order to contain China, etc.—perhaps because he and his advisers thought the moral case was so obvious. To them, remembering the murderous brutalities of Stalin's purges or Mao's Great Leap Forward, it may have been obvious; but not to the young protesters on the campuses or to their older professors and the growing flock of Senate doves, who either cynically "forgot" about those murderous Communist brutalities or had naively never noticed. In any event, the moral argument was imprudently ceded to the doves, whose denunciations of our methods of killing the enemy and, collaterally, the civilians it hid among, were so unrelenting as to make America seem, to their unhistorical imaginations, a new Nazi Germany, and the Marine Corps kin to the Waffen S.S.

Podhoretz brings the discussion back to facts, comparing the number of civilian casualties in Vietnam to those in World War II and the Korean War, and confronting the accusation of "war crimes" allegedly committed by our troops in Vietnam with what happened in those earlier and bloodier conflicts. He also shows that some critics, blindly enthralled by the dream of a perfect world through socialism, actually wanted America to lose, while others, convinced that anti-Communism was not a cause worth killing and dying for, wanted America at any rate not to win, but swiftly to withdraw.

Podhoretz believes that anti-Communism, or (to put it positively) the political and economic freedom afforded by democracy, *is* worth killing and dying for. His main insistence, then, is that America's being "in" Vietnam was not immoral. On the contrary, it was, as President Ronald Reagan frankly said, "noble." The immorality lay in the heart of the antiwar movement, and in Congress, which ignobly abandoned our peace-treaty commitments to what remained of the government in the South.

Reagan and the "neoconservatives," whose ranks Podhoretz had eventually joined after breaking with the Left, emerged from the turmoil over Vietnam understanding (1) that we ought never to have gone "in" unless we meant to prevail—staying nervelessly "out" altogether would have been better than suffering the humiliation of a self-inflicted defeat—and (2) that, nevertheless, the United States remained the defender of democratic freedoms in the world. We had in the middle of the century vanquished the totalitarianism coming from the Right; the job of finishing the totalitarianism coming from the Left remained.

Just *how* to proceed with that job—indeed *whether* it was our moral obligation to proceed—is the question tying together the essays on Henry Kissinger, George Orwell, Milan Kundera, and Aleksandr Solzhenitsyn.

Originally published between 1982 and 1985, all were then collected in *The Bloody Crossroads: Where Literature and Politics Meet* (1986), title and subtitle deriving from one of Trilling's phrases. It's a useful metaphor for the *engagé* critic's task, which is, on the one hand, to discriminate between "literature" and other kinds of writing, and between good literature and great; and on the other, to consider the social realities within which a literary work has been created, and which it partly reflects.

Accordingly, before arguing with Kissinger's policies, Podhoretz takes pains to affirm that the former secretary of state's memoirs are not merely among the highest examples of political autobiography, where the competition includes Winston Churchill and Charles de Gaulle; they are "among the great works of our time," period. This, literarily, because Kissinger offers

> writing that is equally at ease in portraiture and abstract analysis; that can shape a narrative as skillfully as it can paint a scene; that can achieve marvels of compression while moving at an expansive and leisurely pace. It is writing that can shift without strain or falsity of tone from the gravitas befitting a book about great historical events to the humor and irony dictated by an unfailing sense of human proportion.

Would that we could consistently say the same of the writing of our leading novelists, or of Russia's. Podhoretz differentiates the achievements of Solzhenitsyn the novelist, who in *The Red Wheel* cycle is hoping to give us an epic about the Russian Revolution analogous to Tolstoy's on the Napoleonic invasion, from his achievements as a historian and autobiographer. The characters and situations in the novels, *One Day in the Life of Ivan Denisovich* partially excepted, are dead on the page, while those in the nonfictional works *The Gulag Archipelago* and *The Oak and the Calf* are, like the narrator's voice, so vivid as to be there off the page as well as on.

Podhoretz does not refer to Ezra Pound, but in trying to understand his perspective on these matters, we could do worse than tweak one of Pound's dicta: politics is part of every day's "news"; but the only politics that becomes literature is "news that *stays* news." The perdurable political news of Kissinger's memoirs is at one level the story of his (and Nixon's) conception of détente. As American power declined relative to that of the Soviets, we would check them obliquely with our new friendship with China, while directly we would bribe them with economic benefits—rewards for "moderate" behavior. Diplomacy and money would do what our conventional weapons might not be able to do, and what our nuclear weapons morally should not do.

At a deeper level, in Podhoretz's view (though not in Kissinger's), the perdurable news of these memoirs is not only that détente failed, but that, given the nature of our adversary, it was bound to fail. Like the European statesmen before Munich or the Jewish leaders after, trying to "deal with" Hitler as a reasonable man in charge of a normal government (see "Hannah Arendt on Eichmann"), Kissinger and Nixon tried to deal with the Soviet dictators. Yet totalitarians on the Left are no more amenable to negotiation than those on the Right: they are driven by ideology, they want "total" victory, they are not finally interested in compromise. All negotiations end up benefiting the totalitarians, not because they are shrewder or because they cheat, but "because in any negotiation between a party with limited aims and a party with unlimited aims, the party with limited aims is bound to lose in the very nature of things." Therefore, the democratic power must either defeat the totalitarian (or, Podhoretz would now surely add, terrorist) powers, or throw in the sponge. Jaw-jawing toward treaties, or having weapons inspections, can postpone but cannot cancel that inevitable choice.

Which is why in these several essays Podhoretz endeavors to concentrate his reader's mind on the necessity of war, hot or cold, with the totalitarianism of the Left. If the president and his advisers explain why we are fighting, the large majority of the rest of us will follow, just as we did in, say, the morally motivated Civil War and World War II. Podhoretz the literary critic may have been a realist, but when the subject becomes international relations, he is very much a Wilsonian idealist. Thus, he hopes for a change of regime in the Soviet Union that will give its people their inalienable right as human beings to quest for happiness in their own free way. Why, the moral question is, should we in the West have this precious opportunity and others not?

The brilliance of "If Orwell Were Alive Today" rests in Podhoretz's ability to sort through the inconsistencies among the positions that, between 1930 and 1950, the great English essayist took on particular political problems. Of course Orwell declared himself a socialist, but early on he grew suspicious of the vegetarian-variety English socialist's disdain for ordinary people, who evidently needed socialism imposed on them for their own good. Similarly, in the late 1930s and then through the 1940s, he noted that the pacifists always came from the Left—making them "objectively pro-Fascist" vis-à-vis Hitler or pro-Communist vis-à-vis Stalin, and, like the later critics of the American presence in Vietnam, guilty of doublethink about violence. The Soviets' armies were all right because they were defending Communism; the West's armies were wicked because they were defending capitalism.

But what consistently marks Orwell's writings, most famously in his novels *Animal Farm* and *Nineteen Eighty-Four,* is his uncompromising opposition to totalitarianism, his love of liberty and equality of opportunity, and therefore—absent an illusory "third force"—his siding with America. Neutrality between the superpowers was in any event a practical impossibility. As he urged in 1947, wishing like everyone else that atomic war would not break out: look at the map and remember "what happened to the neutrals in the last war." He was good at facing unpleasant facts. That's why it wasn't harebrained in the mid-1980s for Podhoretz to claim that Orwell, had he lived long enough to observe the socialist failure to provide either bread, freedom, or equality, and the capitalist success in providing all three, would have moved from Left to Right.

This is what Podhoretz urges Kundera expressly to do, noting that such a move is implicit in the Czech writer's novels. Not only has Kundera, contrary to the left-leaning scribblers of Orwell's day or ours, identified himself with ordinary people and their workaday lives: like Flaubert, he has set out to discover "the *terra* previously *incognita* of the everyday." He has also understood that the disease of Czech Communism, like the Russian strain, grew less from "hunger and oppression" than from "the utopian fantasy of a return to Paradise." Leftist Western intellectuals have defanged Kundera's critique of Communism by turning it on their own capitalist culture, as if the two systems were morally equivalent. The purpose of Podhoretz's open letter is to persuade the novelist to disavow any such equation.

The essay on Solzhenitsyn, besides locating the greatness of the writer in his nonfiction books, describes the thought of an anti-Communist who is even more passionate than Orwell or Kundera, but who is problematically quirky in his own way. For his prophetic denunciations of Communism in Russia are balanced by equally acerbic denunciations of the West. The trouble, in Solzhenitsyn's view, is not so much that we are materialistically self-indulgent, though he says we are in spades. It's that we have shunned our responsibility to do what is necessary to defeat Communism, and so to save the world from the enslaving tyranny that produced the Gulag. His "terrible question" is whether we will have the sort of courage he had when he survived the Gulag in order to memorialize its countless victims. That conservative American politicians like Reagan did have the courage, during the 1980s, to reject détente and successfully push for victory in the Cold War is our great good luck. But I would add that since then a fanatic Islamic fundamentalism has reminded us that cancerous ideas can still go far toward destroying any and all of the civilizations currently clashing, and Solzhenitsyn's question about our courage remains terrible.

Finally, a word about the previously uncollected "J'Accuse" (whose title is of course borrowed from Émile Zola's protest against the persecution of Alfred Dreyfus). This essay, which has been called "one of the great polemics of our time," is about the reaction to the Israeli incursion into Lebanon in 1982; as such, it stands apart in subject matter from the other writings of the eighties included here. Yet "J'Accuse" is still organically related to those pieces. There is the same assault on doublethink (or the double standard, as Podhoretz calls it here); the same insistence on bringing the discussion back to the facts of the case; the same argument against appeasement; the same emphasis on the correlative courage needed to confront totalitarianism (and terrorism); and the same reversal of conventional liberal opinion as to which party in this particular war deserves to be praised as moral and which should be stigmatized as immoral. And it's a measure both of the validity and the prescience of Podhoretz's analysis of when and how anti-Zionism crosses over into anti-Semitism that it could be applied almost word for word to the things that would be said twenty years later about Israel's efforts to defend itself against terrorist attack.

—TLJ

J'ACCUSE

THE INCURSION BY ISRAEL INTO
Lebanon in June 1982 triggered an explosion of invective against the Jewish state that in its fury and its reach was unprecedented in the public discourse of this country. In the past, unambiguously venomous attacks on Israel had been confined to marginal sectors of American political culture like the *Village Voice* and the *Nation* on the far Left and their counterparts in such publications of the far Right as the Liberty Lobby's *Spotlight*. Even when, as began happening with greater and greater frequency after the Six-Day War of 1967, Israel was attacked in more respectable quarters, care was often taken to mute the language or modulate the tone. Usually the attack would be delivered more in sorrow than in anger, and it would be accompanied by sweet protestations of sympathy. The writer would claim to be telling the Israelis harsh truths for their own good as a real friend should, on the evident assumption that he had a better idea than they did of how to insure their security, and even survival. In perhaps the most notable such piece, George W. Ball (of whom more later) explained to the readers of *Foreign Affairs* "How to Save Israel in Spite of Herself." No matter that Ball warned the Israelis that unless they adopted policies they themselves considered too dangerous, he for one would recommend the adoption of other policies by the United States that would leave them naked unto their enemies; no matter that he thereby gave the Israelis a choice, as they saw it, between committing suicide and being murdered: he still represented himself as their loyal friend.

And so it was with a host of other commentators, including prominent columnists like Anthony Lewis of the *New York Times,* academic pundits like Stanley Hoffmann of Harvard, and former diplomatic functionaries like Harold Saunders. To others it might seem that their persistent hectoring of Israel was making a considerable contribution to the undermining of Israel's case for American support and thereby endangering Israel's very existence. Nevertheless they would have all the world know that they yielded to no one in their commitment to the survival of Israel. Indeed, it was they, and not Israel's "uncritical" supporters, who were Israel's best friends in this country. As a matter of fact, they were even better friends to Israel than most Israelis themselves who, alas, were their "own worst enemies" (an idea which recently prompted Conor Cruise O'Brien, the former editor of the *Observer* of London, to remark: "Well, I suppose Israelis may be their own worst enemies, but if they are, they have had to overcome some pretty stiff competition for that coveted title").

This kind of thing by no means disappeared from the public prints with the Israeli move into Lebanon. In the thick file of clippings I have before me there are many expressions of "anguish" and "sadness" over the damage Israel was doing to its "image" and to its "good name." In a fairly typical effusion, Alfred Friendly wrote in the *Washington Post* (of which he was formerly the managing editor):

> Perhaps it was expecting more than was possible—that Israel should remain the country with a conscience, a home for honor, a treasury for the values of mind and soul. At any rate, it is so no longer but merely a nation like any other, its unique splendor lost . . . its slaughters are on a par with . . . Trujillo's Dominican Republic or Papa Doc's Haiti. Still absent are the jackboots, the shoulder boards, and the bemedalled chests, but one can see them, figuratively, on the minister of defense [Ariel Sharon]. No doubt Israel is still an interesting country. But not for the reasons, the happy reasons, that made it such for me.

In addition to lamenting Israel's loss of moral stature as a result of Lebanon, these great friends of Israel condemned the resort to "unselective and disproportionate violence" (Anthony Lewis) on the ground that it "cannot serve the spirit of Israel, or its true security."

But the sympathetic protestations of this particular species of friend—including even Lewis, perhaps the most unctuous of them all—became more perfunctory and more mechanical in the weeks after the war began. One got the feeling that they were offered mainly for the record or to fend off criticism. And in any case, the preponderant emphasis was no longer on the putative damage Israel was doing to itself by its wicked or stupid policies. The focus was now unmistakably on the evils Israel was committing against others, as in this passage from a column by Richard Cohen in the *Washington Post:*

Maybe the ultimate tragedy of the seemingly nonstop war in the Middle East is that Israel has adopted the morality of its hostile neighbors. Now it bombs cities, killing combatants and noncombatants alike—men as well as women, women as well as children, Palestinians as well as Lebanese.

Israel's "true friends," then, were liberated by Lebanon to say much more straightforwardly and in more intemperate terms than before what they had all along felt: that Israeli intransigence and/or aggressiveness and/or expansionism are the main (and for some, the only) source of the Arab-Israeli conflict and therefore the main (or only) obstacle to a peaceful resolution of that conflict.

Even if this were all, it would have increased the volume and intensity of the attacks on Israel to an unprecedented level. But what made matters much worse was the proportionate escalation and increasing respectability of the attacks from quarters that had never pretended to a friendly concern with Israel.

To be sure, apologists for the PLO who had always been ugly about Israel—Edward Said, Alexander Cockburn, and Nicholas von Hoffman, to mention three prominent names—had been getting a more and more deferential hearing in recent years. Books by Said like *The Question of Palestine* had been widely and sympathetically reviewed in the very media he indiscriminately denounces for being anti-Arab; Cockburn, whose weekly pieces in the *Village Voice* have set a new standard of gutter journalism in this country (and not merely in dealing with Israel), has been rewarded with regular columns in *Harper's* and the *Wall Street Journal* (where in exchange for access to a respectable middle-class audience he watches his literary manners); and von Hoffman, who is only slightly less scurrilous than Cockburn, has also found a hospitable welcome in *Harper's* and a host of other mainstream periodicals both here and abroad (not to mention the television networks). Writing to a British audience in the *Spectator* of London (for which he does a regular column), von Hoffman exulted openly in this change:

> Where before it was difficult to print or say something that was critical of Israeli policies and practices, the barriers are now coming down. Some writers used to believe—rightly or wrongly—that to expound a Palestinian point of view was to risk blacklisting. Now many have become emboldened. . . .

But if they were becoming "emboldened" before Lebanon, their tongues now lost all restraint. Von Hoffman himself is a case in point, having been emboldened in another piece in the *Spectator* to compare Lebanon to Lidice and the Israelis to the Nazis: "Incident by incident, atrocity by atrocity, Americans are coming to see the Israel government as pounding the Star of David into a swastika."

Whether von Hoffman published these words in the United States, I do not know, but by his own account he could easily have found an outlet. "Where once, among the daily press, only the *Boston Globe* could be counted on to print other points of view as a matter of consistent policy . . . now other voices are becoming somewhat more audible."

Somewhat? According to one estimate, of the first nineteen pieces on the war in Lebanon to appear on the *New York Times* Op-Ed page, seventeen were hostile to Israel and only two (one of them by me) were sympathetic. I have not made a statistical survey of the *Washington Post* Op-Ed page, but my impression is that the balance there was roughly the same. In short, not only did the kind of virulent pieces formerly confined to the *Village Voice* and other yellow journals of the Left and Right increase in number and intensity; such pieces now also began appearing regularly in reputable papers and magazines.

Thus, no sooner had the Israelis set foot in Lebanon than Edward Said was to be found on the Op-Ed page of the *New York Times* declaring that Sidon and Tyre had been "laid waste, their civilian inhabitants killed or made destitute by Israeli carpet bombing," and accusing Israel of pursuing "an apocalyptic logic of exterminism." The comparison of Israel with the Nazis here was less brazen than in von Hoffman's piece, but William Pfaff more than made up for it in the *International Herald Tribune*: "Hitler's work goes on," he began, and concluded with the prediction that Hitler might soon "find rest in Hell" through "the knowledge that the Jews themselves, in Israel, have finally . . . accepted his own way of looking at things." The famous spy novelist John Le Carré was imported from England by the *Boston Globe* to deliver himself of similar sentiments:

> Too many Israelis, in their claustrophobia, have persuaded themselves that every Palestinian man and woman and child is by definition a military target, and that Israel will not be safe until the pack of them are swept away. It is the most savage irony that [Prime Minister Menachem] Begin and his generals cannot see how close they are to

inflicting upon another people the disgraceful criteria once inflicted upon themselves.

Finally, the syndicated cartoonist Oliphant, like Cockburn in the *Wall Street Journal*, portrayed besieged west Beirut as another Warsaw ghetto, with the PLO in the role of the Jews and the Israelis in the role of the Nazis.

Many other writers were also "emboldened" by Lebanon, but not quite enough to compare the Israelis with the Nazis. Alfred Friendly, in the passage quoted above, only compared them to Trujillo and Duvalier. Hodding Carter, in the *Wall Street Journal*, invoked Sparta (though his use of language like "Several Lebanese towns have been pulverized by the tactics of total war [and] tens of thousands of Lebanese have been killed or injured since the blitzkrieg was launched" suggested that Sparta was not really the state he had in mind). And Joseph C. Harsch, in the *Christian Science Monitor*, brought up Communist Vietnam: "Vietnam is imperial. It dominate[s] its neighbors Laos and Cambodia. In that same sense Israel is now the dominant power in its own area." Extending this ingenious comparison, Harsch wrote:

> Israel's major weapons come from the U.S. Israel's economy is sustained by subsidies from the U.S. . . . It depends on Washington, just as Vietnam depends for major arms and for economic survival on Moscow. Neither Israel nor Vietnam could dominate their neighborhoods if the support of their major patrons were withdrawn.

But the prize for the most startling comparison of all goes to Mary McGrory of the *Washington Post*, who was reminded of the dropping of atomic bombs on Hiroshima and Nagasaki. More startling still, Miss McGrory said that in her opinion what the Israelis were doing in Lebanon was worse. Addressing Begin directly she wrote:

> You were trying to save your own troops. We understand that. We are, after all, the country that dropped atomic bombs on Hiroshima and Nagasaki. . . . But grant us that we were up against a mighty, if weakened, war machine and a totally mobilized nation. You were punishing a wretched country that reluctantly shelters factions, which, while hostile to you, could not wipe you off the face of the earth, however much they might want to.

What are we to make of words and images like these? How are we to explain them? How are we to understand what they portend?

There are well-wishers of Israel, among them a number of Jews, who recoil in horror from the idea that the Israelis are no better than Nazis, but who believe that Israel under Menachem Begin and Ariel Sharon has brought all this violent abuse on itself. Even though the degree of condemnation is excessive, say these anxious well-wishers, the Israelis have only themselves to blame for besmirching their "good name." Yet I would suggest that the beginning of wisdom in thinking about this issue is to recognize that the vilification of Israel is the phenomenon to be addressed, and not the Israeli behavior that supposedly provoked it. I say supposedly because when a reaction is as wildly disproportionate to an event as this one was, it is clearly being fed by sources other than the event itself.

But what am I or anyone else to say to those for whom there is nothing obvious about the assertion that in this particular case the reaction was disproportionate? From such people one is tempted to turn away in disgust. Yet difficult as it may be to entertain, even for as long as it takes to refute it, the loathsome idea that Israel is to the Palestinians as the Nazis were to the Jews, the world evidently still needs to be reminded of the differences.

To begin with, then, the Nazis set out to murder every Jew on the face of the earth, and wherever they had power to do so, they systematically pursued this objective. Is this what the Israelis have tried to do to the Palestinians? If so, they have gone about it in a most peculiar way.

In Germany under the Nazis, the Jews were first stripped of their civil and political rights and then sent to concentration camps where virtually all of them were put to death. For more than thirty-five years, by contrast, Palestinian Arabs living in the state of Israel have enjoyed Israeli citizenship and along with it a degree of civil and political liberty, not to mention prosperity, unknown to Arabs living in any country under Arab sovereignty.

For fifteen years, moreover, about a million Palestinians on the West Bank and Gaza have been in the power of Israel under military occupation. Have squads of gunmen been dispatched to shoot them down in the fashion of the *Einsatzgruppen* who murdered an approximately equal number of Jews in those parts of the Soviet Union occupied by the Nazis? Have the West Bank Palestinians been rounded up and deported to concentration camps in preparation for being gassed, as happened to some three million Jews living in other countries occupied by Nazi Germany? The Nazis in less than six years managed to kill more than five million Jews in occupied territory. How many Palestinian Arabs have been killed by the Israelis in fifteen years? A hundred? And if even that many, has a single civilian been killed as a matter of policy? Again, the fact is that the Palestinians living even under Israeli military occupation, and even since the recent political offensive against PLO influence on the West Bank, have enjoyed a greater degree of civil and political liberty than any of their brother Arabs living anywhere else *except* in Israel as Israeli citizens.

It is or ought to be obvious, then, that any comparison between the way Israel has treated the Palestinians and the way the Nazis dealt with the Jews is from a rational perspective, let alone morally, disproportionate to a monstrous degree. Anyone who makes such a comparison cannot possibly be responding to the facts of the case and must be driven by some other impulse.

But what about the comparisons of Israel with Sparta, or Haiti, or Communist Vietnam? Are they any the less disproportionate? If so, it is only because nothing could match the intellectual and moral excess of equating Jews with Nazis. Still these comparisons are sufficiently outlandish in their own right.

Sparta, to start with the least repellent of them, was a police state so dedicated to war and so single-mindedly devoted to the martial values that any male child deemed unfit to become a soldier was taken to the mountains and abandoned to his death. Israel is a democracy with an army made up largely of civilian reservists to whom nothing is more distasteful than going to war and to whom peace is the highest value. As for Haiti or the Dominican Republic under Trujillo, they have so little in common with Israel in any respect that bringing their names into the discussion can only be seen as an effort to sneak by with the absurd charge that Israel is no longer a democratic country.

Apparently, though, not even this charge was too absurd to surface openly in the public prints. Thus, Douglas S. Crow, professor of religion, no less, at Columbia University, wrote in a letter to the *New York Times* of Israel's "posturing as a bastion of democracy." But if Israel, where all citizens, including Arabs, have the right to vote and where all individuals and parties, including the Communists, enjoy a full range of liberties—speech, press, assembly, and so on—is not a bastion of democracy, where shall such a bastion be found?

THE SAME POINT can be made of the analogy with Communist Vietnam, where there is even greater repression than in Trujillo's Dominican Republic and perhaps even greater economic misery than in Haiti. To compare Israel—which can indeed be described as a bastion of democracy—with what is by all accounts one of the most Stalinist regimes in the entire Communist world, is a sufficiently gross travesty. But is the comparison Joseph C. Harsch makes between the behavior of the two states toward their respective neighbors any more justifiable?

Both, says Mr. Harsch, are "imperial" states using military forces to dominate the countries of the region. That this is an apt characterization of Communist Vietnam very few will nowadays contest. Two years after signing a peace treaty with South Vietnam, the Communist regime of the North invaded and conquered the South. Not content with that, Vietnam proceeded to invade Cambodia where it installed another puppet regime, while keeping some forty thousand troops in Laos to insure its domination over the Communist regime there. Nor could Vietnam claim to be acting defensively: neither South Vietnam nor Cambodia nor Laos posed any threat to Hanoi.

If we now ask what this set of relationships has in common with the relations between Israel and its neighbors, the answer can only be: nothing whatever. One grows weary of reciting the facts of the Arab-Israeli conflict over and over again. But the controversy generated by Lebanon demonstrates that, far from being tiresomely familiar, they are still unknown by some and forgotten or deliberately ignored by others for whom they are politically inconvenient.

In 1947, then, the United Nations adopted a partition plan for Palestine, dividing it into a Jewish state and a Palestinian one. The Jews accepted the plan; the Arabs rejected it. The form this rejection took was a war against the new Jewish state of Israel launched by the armies of five neighboring Arab states, with the aid and encouragement of all the others. Israel successfully fended off this assault and begged its neighbors to make peace with it. But they all refused, rededicating themselves instead to the elimination of any trace of a sovereign Jewish state from the region.

Living in consequence under siege, with a coalition of nineteen nations pledged to its destruction, Israel maneuvered as best it could. In 1956, it joined forces with the British and the French in an attack on Egypt which left the Israelis in control of a stretch of the Sinai desert. But in response to American pressure, all three parties soon withdrew, and Israel in particular returned the Sinai to Egypt (without any quid pro quo). So much for the first instance of Israeli "expansionism" or "imperialism" and the only one to which these epithets have even a remotely plausible claim.

The next episode occurred in 1967, when Egypt took a series of actions clearly spelling an intention to resort once again to military force whose explicit objective was—as its then leader, Nasser, put it—"the destruction of Israel." After waiting for about two weeks while the United States and others worked unsuccessfully to avert a war in which they might be "wiped off the map" (Nasser's language again) if the Arabs struck the first blow, the Israelis launched a preemptive attack. Six days later, thanks to a brilliant campaign, they found themselves in possession of territory formerly belonging to or occupied by Egypt (the Sinai), Syria (the Golan Heights), and Jordan (the West Bank).

To the Arabs and their apologists, this was another instance of expansionism and imperialism. But since virtually no one doubts that Nasser provoked the 1967 war or believes that there would have been a war at all if not for his closing of the Straits of Tiran (among other actions he took), how can it be regarded as an imperialistic operation by Israel? In any case, Israel begged King Hussein of Jordan to stay out of the war once it started, and if he had agreed, the Israelis would not have been obliged to respond to his attack and they would not have ended the war in control of the West Bank.

Even so, Israel once again, as it had been doing since the day of its birth, asked only for recognition and face-to-face negotiations with its Arab neighbors. Such negotiations would have resulted in the return of occupied territories with whatever minor boundary adjustments security might dictate. Yet once again, as they had from the beginning, the Arab states refused, responding this time with the famous three No's of Khartoum: No recognition, No negotiation, No peace.

Finally, seven years later and after yet another war—this one unambiguously started by Egypt in a surprise attack—Anwar Sadat (Nasser's successor) called what had been universally regarded in the Arab world as Israel's "bluff" by offering recognition and face-to-face negotiations. Almost overnight, Israel responded by agreeing to return every inch of Egyptian territory and then honored the agreement. So much for imperialism.

NOW comes Lebanon. To show that Israel is behaving toward Lebanon as Vietnam has behaved toward Cambodia, Joseph C. Harsch writes:

> Israel has now decreed that there must be no more "foreign" military forces in Lebanon. That means that Israel wants all Palestinian and Syrian armed units out of Lebanon, leaving Lebanon in the hands of elements which would be sympathetic to Israel and to its interests.

There are so many astonishing features in these two sentences that one hardly knows where to begin. In the first place, why the quotation marks around the word foreign? Is Harsch trying to suggest that the "Palestinian and Syrian armed units" are indigenous or native to Lebanon? In the second place, what is illegitimate about Israel's desire to leave Lebanon "in the hands of elements which would be sympathetic to Israel and to its interests"? In view of the fact that those "elements" would be the Lebanese people themselves, there can be nothing wrong in leaving Lebanon in their hands; and in view of the fact that before Lebanon was taken over by the PLO and the Syrians it was sufficiently "sympathetic to Israel and its interests" to live peacefully alongside Israel, a more accurate way of putting the case would be to say that Israel hopes to free Lebanon from the domination of foreign forces who have turned an unwilling Lebanon into a battlefield of their war against Israel.

But of course putting it that way would defeat the purpose of portraying Israel as an imperialistic power imposing its will upon a helpless neighbor. And it would also show the falsity of describing the war as an invasion of Lebanon. Yes, the Israelis did invade Lebanon in the sense of sending military forces across the Lebanese border. But if we are looking for analogies, a better one than any fished up in recent weeks would be the invasion of France by Allied troops in World War II. The purpose was not to conquer France but to liberate it from its German conquerors, just as the purpose of the Israelis in 1982 was to liberate Lebanon from the PLO.

Harsch and many of his colleagues may not know this, but the Lebanese people do. In spite of the sufferings inflicted upon them by the war, and in spite of the fact that they have no love for Israel, they have greeted the Israelis as liberators. Representative Charles Wilson, a Texas Democrat who is so far from being reflexively pro-Israel that he voted for the AWACS sale to Saudi Arabia and intends to vote for the Jordanian arms sale, testified after a visit to Lebanon in July to

> the universal enthusiasm with which the Lebanese welcomed the Israeli army. . . . I mean it's almost like a liberating army. . . . It was astonishing. I expected this, somewhat, from the Christian population. But I didn't expect it from the Muslim population. . . . And in talking to a group of people, some of whom had lost their homes, some of whom had lost relatives, they said it was awful. But they said that all in all, to be free of the PLO it was worth it.

One can see why. According to a news story by David K. Shipler in the *New York Times,* the PLO, whose "major tool of persuasion was the gun," ruled over a large part of Lebanon, terrifying and terrorizing the local populace, Christian and Muslim alike. It took over land and houses, it confiscated automobiles, it stole at will from the shops, and anyone who complained was likely to be shot. Operating as a state within a state, the PLO humiliated local Lebanese officials and displaced them with its own police and "people's committees."

On top of all this, writes Shipler, the PLO "brought mercenaries in from Bangladesh, Sri Lanka, Pakistan, and North African countries. By all accounts the outsiders were crude, undisciplined thugs." And then there were the killings. "Before the PLO," one Lebanese woman told Shipler, "we used to be pro-Palestinian. . . . [But] when we saw the Palestinians were killing us and threatening us and having barricades and shooting innocent people, then came the hatred."

Rowland Evans and Robert Novak, whose column has always been notorious for its pro-Arab bias, arrived at the same assessment: "Once incorruptible, its extraordinary success in accumulating arms and money . . . had made the PLO itself an occupying power . . . permeated by thugs and adventurers."

IF THIS DISPOSES OF the idea that a Vietnam-like Israel was imposing its imperial will upon Lebanon, it does not dispose of the charge that the war in Lebanon was imperialistic in a different sense—that Israel's purpose, as Anthony Lewis (among many others) charges, was "to exterminate Palestinian nationalism" in preparation for annexing the West Bank.

Here again, before taking up the substance, one is forced to begin by pointing to the form in which the charge is expressed. By using the word "exterminate"—a word which is inescapably associated with what the Nazis did to the Jews—Lewis contrives to evoke the comparison while covering himself by designating "Palestinian nationalism" rather than the Palestinian people as the victim. But even in this form the charge is an outlandish misrepresentation. For the *maximum* objective of the Begin government is to establish Israeli sovereignty in the West Bank while allowing to the Palestinians living there a degree of control over their own civil and political affairs far greater—once more the point must be stressed—than they have ever enjoyed in the past, or than Arabs enjoy in any country under Arab sovereignty. This is "to exterminate Palestinian nationalism"?

And even this—to repeat, Begin's *maximum* objective—is subject by Begin's own commitment to negotiation. That is, in signing the Camp David agreement of 1978, Begin has obligated the state of Israel to settle the question of sovereignty after five years of negotiations among all the interested parties, including the West Bank Palestinians. This means that whether Begin and Sharon like it or not, they or their successors might well find themselves turning over the West Bank to Jordan or to a new Palestinian leadership willing, unlike the PLO, to live in peace both with Israel and Jordan.

It is precisely the hope of encouraging such a leadership to emerge that lies behind the two-sided strategy of destroying the PLO as a military force in Lebanon and as a political force on the West Bank. I urge anyone who doubts this to read "How to Make Peace with the Palestinians" by Menahem Milson.* In that article Milson said that Israeli policy on the West Bank had in the past inadvertently led to the strengthening of the PLO's influence there. He therefore advocated a new policy aimed at weakening the PLO so that the "silenced majority"—which in his judgment wished to live in peace with Israel—could make itself heard. The end result was to be a demand by the Palestinians on the West Bank that King Hussein repudiate the PLO as "the sole representative of the Palestinian people" and resume his old role as their spokesman.

After reading that article, Begin and Sharon appointed Milson (then a professor of Arabic literature at the Hebrew University) to the post of civil administrator of the West Bank, from which position he has been putting the policy outlined in the article into practice. The PLO and its apologists have naturally done everything in their power to sabotage and discredit Milson. But the political war against the PLO was proceeding on the West Bank as the military campaign against the PLO in Lebanon was being launched.

No one can say what the eventual disposition of the West Bank will be. What one can say with complete assurance, however, is that so long as the only alternative to Israeli occupation is a Palestinian state ruled over by radical forces pledged to the destruction of Israel, then no Israeli government—no matter who might be its prime minister—will be permitted by Israeli public opinion to withdraw. But one can also say, though with less assurance, that if an alternative should present itself, then no Israeli government, including one headed by Ariel Sharon, would be permitted by Israeli public opinion to absorb the West Bank.

Commentary, May 1981.

Israelis have different reasons for wanting to rid themselves of the West Bank. Some fear the effects of continued occupation on the character of Israel as a democratic society; others fear the effects on the character of Israel as a Jewish state of adding so many Arabs to its demographic mix; still others are convinced that continued occupation is a formula for continued war.

But whatever their motives, many or (as I read Israeli public opinion) most Israelis would favor withdrawal from the West Bank provided they were reasonably confident that the successor regime would be willing to live in peace with a neighboring Jewish state (and provided also, probably, that Jews who wished to go on living in Judea and Samaria would have the same right to do so as Arabs have in Israel). Elimination of the radical rejectionist Palestinians—whether or not they call themselves the PLO—is a precondition for any such resolution of the Palestinian problem. Consequently if Begin and Sharon succeed in their objective of destroying the PLO, they may well make it impossibly difficult for Israel to annex or absorb the West Bank—not because of pressures coming from Washington but because of pressures coming from within Israel itself.

ALL THIS, HOWEVER, is for the future. Returning to the present and to the war in Lebanon, we still have to face the charge that Israel was waging a wanton and indiscriminate campaign against defenseless civilians.

In the early days of the war, words like "holocaust" and even "genocide" freely circulated in the media, along with horrendous estimates of the number of civilians killed or rendered homeless by Israeli arms. At first it was said that 10,000 people had been "slaughtered" in southern Lebanon and 600,000 turned into refugees. But no sooner had these figures been imprinted on the public mind than it was revealed that the local Lebanese authorities themselves put the *total* population of the area in question at 510,000—almost 100,000 fewer than were supposedly driven out of their homes. Israel claimed that there were 20,000 refugees and perhaps 2,000 casualties, of whom more than half were only wounded. Correspondents and other visitors to Lebanon soon confirmed that the original figures were "extreme exaggerations" (Shipler), while casting evenhanded doubt on the much lower Israeli figures. Even though "discussions with local officials and residents of the cities tend to reinforce the Israeli estimates of casualties there," wrote Shipler, "the Israeli figures exclude a lot."

Thus arose what came to be called "the numbers game." But the damage to Israel had already been done. In any case, what did it matter, asked Mary

McGrory, what the exact figures were? Whatever the precise numbers, "it is already too many." In her open letter to Begin, she asked:

> Does Israel's security have to be purchased by the slaughter of innocents? . . . We have been seeing every night pictures of wounded babies and old men. We read about people standing outside devastated apartment buildings, wearing masks against the stench of corpses, waiting to go in to claim their dead. They were a threat to you? Yes, we know, your planes dropped leaflets before they dropped the bombs. But why did you have to bomb their cities at all? People in apartment buildings may be PLO sympathizers or even devoted adherents of Yasir Arafat. But they were unarmed civilians.

Indeed they were, but Miss McGrory's letter might better have been directed to Arafat than to Begin. For (in Shipler's words):

> The huge sums of money the PLO received from Saudi Arabia and other Arab countries seem to have been spent primarily on weapons and ammunition, which were placed strategically in densely populated civilian areas in the hope that this would either deter Israeli attacks or exact a price from Israel in world opinion for killing civilians. Towns and camps were turned into vast armories as crates of ammunition were stacked in underground shelters and antiaircraft guns were emplaced in schoolyards, among apartment houses, next to churches and hospitals. The remains could be seen soon after the fighting, and Palestinians and Lebanese can still point out the sites.

This strategy of hiding behind civilians was entirely natural for the terrorist organization whose greatest exploits in the past invariably involved hijackings and the killing of innocent bystanders. Having held airplanes and buildings hostage, the PLO—as the American Lebanese League declared in a newspaper advertisement—was now holding much of Lebanon itself hostage, and especially west Beirut. Who, the League asked, gave "the PLO authority to insist that Lebanese civilians die with them?" Certainly not the Lebanese civilians themselves.

It is also important to note that under international law (specifically Article 28 of the Geneva Convention of 1948), "the presence of a protected person may not be used to render certain points or areas immune from military operations," and the responsibility for civilian casualties or damage rests on the party, in this case the PLO, who thus uses protected persons or areas. What the other side, in this instance Israel, is required to do is exactly the kind of thing Miss McGrory derides in her reference to the dropping of leaflets: that is, warn the civilians so that they have a chance to leave the area or otherwise protect themselves.

While scrupulously observing this requirement, the Israelis also took other steps to minimize civilian casualties, some of which led to an increase in their own casualties. This is why Miss McGrory's citation of the bombing of Hiroshima and Nagasaki is so bizarre. As it happens, I myself agree with her in thinking that the United States was justified in that action (because the result was to shorten the war and to save many more lives than were lost in the two raids). But the whole point of the bombing of Hiroshima and Nagasaki was to wreak indiscriminate damage which would terrorize the Japanese into surrendering. The Israelis were doing almost exactly the opposite in Lebanon. Their strikes were so careful and discriminating that whole areas of southern Lebanon were left untouched. If they really had been carpet bombing, both the levels of destruction and the number of casualties would have been greater.

That a left-wing liberal like Mary McGrory should be driven into comparing Israel's military tactics in Lebanon with the dropping of the atom bomb on Hiroshima and Nagasaki is demented enough. But that she should go on to defend the use of the atom bomb by the United States (which in any other context she would surely condemn) in order to score an invidious point against Israel is a measure of how far her animus extends. It literally knows no bounds.

OBVIOUSLY A REACTION like this can no more have been provoked by the facts of Israel's behavior than the comparisons of Israel with Nazi Germany. Nor can the relatively milder denunciations of Israel as comparable to Sparta or Haiti or Vietnam be taken as a rational response to what Israel has done. What then can explain them?

In thinking about this question while reading through dozens of vitriolic attacks on Israel, I have resisted the answer that nevertheless leaps irresistibly into the mind. This answer, of course, is that we are dealing here with an eruption of anti-Semitism. I have resisted because I believe that loose or promiscuous use of the term anti-Semitism can only rob it of force and meaning (which is what has happened to the term racism). In my judgment, therefore, it should be invoked only when the case for doing so is clear and precise. When that condition is met, however, I also believe that one has a duty to call the offending idea by its proper name.

Not everyone agrees, not even Meg Greenfield, who in *Newsweek* happily endorses "plain talk about Israel" and who as editor of the *Washington Post* editorial page has certainly done a lot of plain talking herself. Miss Greenfield sees it as a "good thing" that the "resentful, frustrated, expedient silences" Americans have maintained over Israel have now been "interrupted by outraged, emotional condemnations of what Israel is doing." Some of this, she acknowledges, is excessive: "This comparison [of the Israeli invasion] to Nazi policy, for instance, has been as disproportionate in its way as the military violence it complains of." But the rest is understandable, and is anyway not to be confused with being anti-Israel or anti-Semitic. Indeed these very accusations have intensified the pent-up resentments which are now exploding into what Miss Greenfield calls "no-holds-barred attacks on the Israeli action."

In other words, though we are to have "plain talk about Israel," and though such talk is healthy when directed against Israel, we are not to have equally plain talk about the attacks on Israel. To say that such "no-holds-barred attacks" on Israel are anti-Israel is unhealthy, and to say that they are anti-Semitic is even worse.

George W. Ball also rules out any use of the term anti-Semitism:

> I long ago made it a practice not to answer any letter questioning my position on Middle East problems that contains the assertion or implication that I have said or written anything anti-Semitic. That accusation, in my view, is a denial—I might even say an evasion—of rational argument.

Yet when he goes on to explain why it is absurd to accuse him of anti-Semitism, he brings forth so shallow a conception of what the term means that it can only be described as historically illiterate. Anti-Semitism, according to Ball, is the dislike of Jews; it is therefore a sufficient refutation to point out that some of his best friends are Jewish, and that all his life he has admired the Jews for their contribution to the arts, to intellectual life, and to liberal political causes.

That a man of George Ball's experience and education should regard this as an adequate account of anti-Semitism reveals an astonishing blind spot. But this blindness is an advantage, enabling Ball to accuse American Jews of dual loyalty—a classic anti-Semitic canard that also surfaced in the debate over the AWACS—and then indignantly and self-righteously to deny that this makes him an anti-Semite.

Unlike Ball, Conor Cruise O'Brien, who has a habit of speaking plainly on all subjects, does believe that some critics of Israel are "motivated by some kind of anti-Semitic feeling, possibly unconscious." In some instances, he concedes, it may be that what is at work is "genuine compassion for suffering Arabs, expressing itself in terms of a generous hyperbole." But in most others "there are indications to the contrary." These indications include the absence of any concern for the civilian casualties in the war between Iraq and Iran, and the silence that greeted the killing of an estimated twenty thousand Sunni Muslims recently by President Assad of Syria in the city of Hama. (To O'Brien's examples may be added the indifference to the one hundred thousand people killed in the internecine strife in Lebanon since 1975 on the part of virtually all of those who have wept over the civilian casualties in Lebanon since the Israelis went in.) O'Brien suggests, however, that a term other than anti-Semitic is needed because "the people in question are . . . extravagantly *philo*-Semitic these days, in their feelings for the Arab-speaking branch of the Semitic linguistic family." He proposes "anti-Jewism," and he offers a test by which it can be detected in the discussion of Israel: "If your interlocutor can't keep Hitler out of the conversation, . . . feverishly turning Jews into Nazis and Arabs into Jews—why then, I think, you may well be talking to an anti-Jewist."

The trouble is that the term "anti-Jewist" cannot be applied to those like George Ball who are loud in their protestations of friendship for the Jewish people, and who might even agree that comparing the Israelis with the Nazis deserves to be called anti-Semitic.

LET ME THEREFORE propose that we retain the historically sanctioned term anti-Semitism and let me outline a more general criterion for identifying it than the one O'Brien suggests. Historically anti-Semitism has taken the form of labeling certain vices and failings as specifically Jewish when they are in fact common to all humanity: Jews are greedy, Jews are tricky, Jews are ambitious, Jews are clannish—as though Jews were uniquely or disproportionately guilty of all those sins. Correlatively, Jews are condemned when they claim or exercise the right to do things that all other people are accorded an unchallengeable right to do.

As applied to the Jewish state, this tradition has been transmuted into the double standard by which Israel is invariably judged. The most egregious illustration is the UN resolution condemning Zionism as a form of racism. According to the thinking of this resolution, all other people are entitled to national self-determination, but when the Jews exercise this right, they are committing the crimes of racism and imperialism. Similarly, all other nations have a right to insure the security of their borders; when Israel exercises this right, it is committing the crime of aggression. So, too, only Israel of all the states in the world is required to prove that its very existence—not merely its interests or the security of its borders, but its very existence—is in immediate peril before it can justify the resort to force. For example, whereas the possibility of a future threat to its borders was (rightly in my opinion) deemed a sufficient justification by the United States under John F. Kennedy to go to the brink of nuclear war in the Cuban missile crisis of 1962, the immense caches of arms discovered in PLO dumps in southern Lebanon have not persuaded many of the very people who participated in or applauded Kennedy's decision that the Israelis were at least equally justified in taking action against the PLO in Lebanon.

Criticisms of Israel based on a double standard deserve to be called anti-Semitic. Conversely, criticisms of Israel based on universally applied principles and tempered by a sense of balance in the distribution of blame cannot and should not be stigmatized as anti-Semitic, however mistaken or dangerous to Israel one might consider them to be. A good example can be found in the editorials published in the *New York Times* on Lebanon. Unlike the consistently superb editorials on Lebanon in the *Wall Street Journal,* the ones in the *Times* have been harsh on Israel, they have often been unfair, and they have pointed toward policies that would jeopardize Israel's security. But they have not been guided by the usual double standard, and therefore cannot and should not be stigmatized as anti-Semitic.

Criticisms of Israel that *are* informed by a double standard, on the other hand, deserve to be called anti-Semitic even when they are mouthed by Jews or, for that matter, Israelis. That being Jewish or possessing Israeli citizenship guarantees immunity from anti-Semitic ideas may seem a plausible proposition, but it is not, alas, borne out by experience. Like all other human beings, Jews are influenced by the currents of thought around them; and like all other minority groups, they often come to see themselves through the eyes of an unsympathetic or hostile majority. Jews are of course the majority in Israel, but the state itself is isolated among the nations, and subjected to a constant barrage of moral abuse aimed at its delegitimation. This seems finally to be taking the inevitable psychological toll in the appearance among Israelis of the term fascist in talking about their own society, when by any universal standard it is among the two or three countries in the world least deserving of this epithet.

To be sure, very few Israelis have reached the point of blaming the Arab-Israeli conflict largely on Israel or Menachem Begin or Ariel Sharon. But a number of American Jews have been adding their own special note to the whining chorus of anti-Israel columnists, State Department Arabists, and corporate sycophants of Saudi Arabia which has grown more raucous over Lebanon than ever before. The misleading impression has been created that these "dissenters" reveal a serious split within the American Jewish community over Israel. In fact, however, with a few notable exceptions they represent the same minority of roughly 10 or 15 percent which has all along either opposed Israel (because as socialists they considered Zionism a form of reactionary bourgeois nationalism or because as Reform Jews they disliked nationalism for other reasons), or else came to support Israel grudgingly and only on condition that it comport itself in accordance with their political ideas. It is these people who have latterly been congratulating themselves on their courage in "speaking out" against Israel. A few of them—those who live and work within the Jewish community—are actually dissenting. But most of the rest live in milieux like the university or work in professions like journalism in which defending Israel takes far more courage than attacking it.

Not only do these people invoke a double standard in judging Israel: they proudly proclaim that they do. "Yes, there is a double standard. From its birth Israel asked to be judged as a light among the nations." These words come from one of the endless series of columns Anthony Lewis has written on the war in Lebanon. Lewis is Jewish, and even though he makes no public point of it, I single him out here because his thinking is typical of the way Jewish "dissenters" who have been signing ads and giving interviews see not only the war in Lebanon but the Arab-Israeli conflict as a whole.

Thus, while he usually pays his rhetorical respects to the Arab refusal to recognize Israel, Lewis's emphasis is always on the sins of Israel, whether real or imaginary. And while piously proclaiming his great friendship for Israel, he harasses it relentlessly and obsessively, justifying himself in this by hiding behind the political opposition in Israel or behind Zionist heroes of the past like Justice Brandeis. (Others use the Bible for these purposes, humbly comparing themselves to the prophets of old: "[The] biblical tradition of criticism and dissent should now guide public practice," two young Jewish academics declared on the Op-Ed page of the

Times. "Jeremiah's polemics indicate that a government's foreign and security policies, as well as societal inequity and immorality, are grounds for legitimate dissent.")

But is it true that "From its birth Israel asked to be judged as a light among the nations," or even as the socialist paradise dreamed of by so many of Israel's Jewish "friends" on the Left? No doubt there have been Zionist enthusiasts who indulged in such rhetoric, but it is a historical travesty to claim that this was the animating idea behind the Jewish state. If perfection had been the requirement, it would have been tantamount to saying that an imperfect Israel had no right to exist; and since imperfection in human beings is unavoidable, Israel would have been sentencing itself to an early death from the day of its birth.

In any event, the opposite is more nearly true: that the purpose of Israel was to *normalize* the Jewish people, not to perfect them. The Jewish state was to create not a utopia but a refuge from persecution and a haven of security in which Jews who chose or were forced to settle there could live a peaceful and normal life. Thanks to the refusal of the Arab world to agree to this, the Jews of Israel have instead had to live in a constant state of siege. It would have been fully understandable if under those conditions Israel had become a garrison state or military dictatorship. Yet no such development occurred. Founded as a democracy, it has remained a democracy, a particularly vital variant of the species—the only one in the Middle East and one of the few on the face of the earth.

In reminding ourselves of that enormous and wondrous fact, we come to the greatest irony of this entire debate. Although Israel is no more required than any other state to justify its existence through what Anthony Lewis or anyone else, myself included, considers good behavior; and although elementary fairness dictates that Israel not be condemned for doing things that all other nations are permitted to do as a matter of course; even so, even judged by the higher standard that Lewis and his ilk demand, the truth is that Israel *has* become a light unto the nations.

THUS, IN REMAINING a free democratic society while surrounded by enemies and forced to devote an enormous share of its resources to defense, Israel has demonstrated that external threats do not necessarily justify the repression of internal liberties. For casting this light, in whose glare the majority of the nations of the world stand exposed, Israel not surprisingly wins no friends at the UN.

If its persistence in democratic ways under the most unpromising cir-

cumstances has helped win Israel the enmity of the Third World, the fierce-
ness of its will to live is what has made it a scandal and a reproach to its fellow democracies in the Western world. For in the glare of *that* light, the
current political complexion of the Western democracies takes on a sickly,
sallow, even decadent look. We in the West confront in the Soviet Union a
deadly enemy sworn to our destruction, just as Israel does in the Arab
world. But whereas the Israelis have faced the reality of their peril and have
willingly borne the sacrifices essential to coping with it, we in the West
have increasingly fallen into the habit of denial, and we have shown ourselves reluctant to do what the survival of our civilization requires. We tell
ourselves that the danger comes from our own misunderstanding and mis-
perception; we castigate ourselves for being the main cause of the conflict;
we urge unilateral actions upon ourselves in the hope of appeasing the
enemy.

It is a rough rule of thumb that the more deeply this complex of attitudes is rooted in an individual or a group or a nation, the more hostility
it will feel toward Israel. I readily admit that other factors also come into
play. Anxiety over oil or business connections in the Arab world often
turn people against Israel who might otherwise admire it precisely for setting the kind of examples of realism and courage they would wish the
West to follow. Secretary of Defense Caspar Weinberger is perhaps one
such case and there are others scattered through the Defense Department,
the State Department, and the White House. There are also so-called
hardliners where the Soviet Union is concerned (Evans and Novak come
to mind) who have always believed that a tilt away from Israel and a more
"evenhanded" policy in the Middle East is necessary if we are to contain
the spread of Soviet power and influence in that region. This idea dies so
hard that it may even survive the tremendous blow it has suffered in
Lebanon.

On the other side, one can find many American Jews and liberal politicians concerned about Jewish support who back Israel even though in most
other situations they tend to sympathize with forces comparable to the
PLO (such as the guerrillas in El Salvador) and even though they are great
believers in the idea that all disputes can and should be settled through
negotiation.

Even allowing for these complications, however, one can still say that
the more committed to appeasement of the Soviet Union a given party is,
and the more it opposes "military solutions to political problems," the
more hostile it will be to Israel. Thus the West European governments—

the very governments which are so eager to prop up the Soviet economy, to ignore Afghanistan and Poland, and to ratify Soviet military superiority in Europe through arms-control negotiations—are far less friendly to Israel than is the American government. And within the United States itself, the people who are most sympathetic to the European point of view on the issue of the Soviet threat are among those least friendly to Israel.

These are the same Americans who also tend to pride themselves on having learned "the lessons of Vietnam"—lessons which, as Terry Krieger points out in a brilliant piece in the *Washington Times,* Israel has now dramatically refuted. For Israel has shown that military force is sometimes necessary; that the use of military force may also be beneficial; and that a Soviet client, "whether it be a guerrilla force or a terrorist organization," can be defeated by an American ally. This, Krieger thinks, is why such people have turned on Israel with vitriolic fury: "Those Americans who have denounced Israel's invasion of Lebanon eventually may forgive Israel for defending itself, but they may never forgive Israel for illuminating our own confusion and cowardice."

Again Anthony Lewis offers himself as a good illustration. Indeed, the terms in which he has denounced Israel's invasion of Lebanon are strongly reminiscent of the hysterical abuse he used to heap on the United States in Vietnam. This being so, it is worth remembering that Lewis called the Christmas 1972 bombing of Hanoi—in which by the estimate of the North Vietnamese themselves no more than sixteen hundred were killed—"The most terrible destruction in the history of man" and a "crime against humanity." It is worth recalling, too, that only days before the Khmer Rouge Communists would stake a claim to precisely that description by turning their own country into the Auschwitz of Asia, Lewis greeted their imminent seizure of power with the question: "What future possibility could be more terrible than the reality of what is happening to Cambodia now?" Yet with that record of political sagacity and moral sensitivity behind him, Lewis has the effrontery to instruct Israel on how to insure its security, and he has the shamelessness to pronounce moral judgment upon the things Israel does to protect itself from the kind of fate at the hands of the Arabs that has been visited by the Communists upon South Vietnam and Cambodia.

THE BIBLE TELLS US that God commanded the ancient Israelites to "choose life," and it also suggests to us that for a nation, the choice of life often involves choosing the sacrifices and horrors of war. The people of contemporary Israel are still guided by that commandment and its accompanying demands. This is why Israel is a light unto other peoples who have come to believe that nothing is worth fighting or dying for.

But there is more. In the past, anti-Semitism has been a barometer of the health of democratic societies, rising in times of social or national despair, falling in periods of self-confidence. It is the same today with attitudes toward Israel. Hostility toward Israel is a sure sign of failing faith in and support for the virtues and values of Western civilization in general and of America in particular. How else are we to interpret a political position that, in a conflict between a democracy and its anti-democratic enemies, is so dead set against the democratic side?

Even on the narrower issue of American interests, George Ball, Anthony Lewis, and those who share their perspective are so driven by their animus against Israel as to think that (in Lewis's astonishing words) "Looking at the wreckage in Lebanon, the only people who can smile are the radicals and the Russians." Yet consider: Israel, an American ally, and armed with American weapons, has defeated the Syrians and the PLO, both of them tied to and armed by America's enemy, the Soviet Union. Are the Russians insane that this should cause them to smile? The military power of the PLO, representing the forces of radicalism and anti-Americanism in the Middle East, has been crushed; and (unless Ball and the others, who are so desperate to save it, should work their will) its power to terrorize and intimidate may also be destroyed, leaving the way open for such forces of moderation as may exist in the Arab world to come forward. How should this make the radicals smile and the United States weep? Egypt, America's best friend in the Arab world, has been strengthened and the policy of accommodation it has pursued toward Israel has been vindicated in comparison with the rejectionist policies of Syria and the PLO. Can this be good for the Russians and damaging to American interests?

George Ball says that it can be and it is. But this is so palpably absurd that it cannot be taken as the considered judgment of an informed and objective mind. Therefore if it is proper to indict anyone in this debate for bias and insufficient concern for American interests, it is Ball who should be put in the dock and not the Jewish defenders of Israel against whom he himself has been pleased to file this very indictment.

In the broadside from which I have borrowed the title of this essay, Émile Zola charged that the persecutors of Dreyfus were using anti-Semitism as a screen for their reactionary political designs. I charge here that the anti-Semitic attacks on Israel which have erupted in recent weeks are also a cover. They are a cover for a loss of American nerve. They are a cover for the acquiescence in terrorism. They are a cover for the appeasement of totalitarianism. And I accuse all those who have joined in these attacks not merely of anti-Semitism but of the broader sin of faithlessness to the interests of the United States and indeed to the values of Western civilization as a whole.

FROM *WHY WE WERE IN VIETNAM:*
WHOSE IMMORALITY?

LOOKING BACK ON THE ENTIRE story of the Vietnam War, one can, if one wishes, make the consoling point that everyone on all sides of the argument turned out to be wrong about its political character and its implications.

Those supporters of American intervention who thought the problem was to contain Chinese expansionism were wrong: shortly after the Americans left, Communist Vietnam was at war with Communist China, thereby vindicating those opponents of American intervention who had always stressed the ancient enmity between the two countries.

But this was only a partial vindication. Those who said that Hanoi was not a Chinese proxy also tended to think that the Vietcong was not a North Vietnamese proxy, and about this *they* were wrong. To be sure, the National Liberation Front (NLF), true to its character as a front, included elements that were not Communist, as well as Communists and sympathizers who thought they were fighting "for democracy, freedom, and peace" and who believed that the fall of Saigon would lead to "a domestic policy of national reconciliation, without risk of reprisal, and a foreign policy of nonalignment." But Doan Van Toai—whose words I have just quoted, who was arrested and jailed many times for leading student demonstrations against the Thieu regime and against American involvement, and who never joined the Vietcong only because the NLF felt he could be more useful as an intelligence agent—was deceived about this, as were what he calls "the most prestigious intellectuals in the West." Shortly after the North Vietnamese army conquered the South, the Provisional Revolutionary Government (PRG, into which the NLF had been transmuted) was disbanded; and far from being appointed to positions of power in the new Vietnam, many of its members were arrested. "Today," wrote Doan Van Toai in 1981, "among 17 members of the Politburo and 134 members of the Vietnamese Communist party, not a single one is from the

NLF" (though there were a few "who had been North Vietnam Communist party representatives with the NLF").[1]* Although not all members of the NLF knew it then, they had indeed been acting as proxies for Hanoi, and those who persisted in thinking otherwise were eliminated in the end as unreliable. In the view of General Fred C. Weyand, this might even have been one of the purposes of the Tet offensive of 1968: "Applying the test of *cui bono* (for whose benefit) it can be seen that the real losers of Tet-68 were the South Vietnamese Communists (the Vietcong or PRG) who surfaced, led the attacks, and were destroyed in the process. . . . Just as the Russians eliminated their Polish competitors [with] the Warsaw uprising, the North Vietnamese eliminated their Southern competitors with Tet-68. They thereby insured that the eventual outcome of the war would be a South Vietnam dominated and controlled, not by *South* Vietnamese Communists, but by the *North* Vietnamese."[2] Be that speculation as it may, the fact remains that the war in Vietnam was a case of external aggression, and those who said that it was merely a civil war were wrong.

On the issue of the Soviet role in Vietnam, everyone was wrong as well. In its earliest stages, the insurgency in South Vietnam was seen as a "war of national liberation" of the kind Nikita Khrushchev explicitly predicted would lead to the triumph of Communism in the Third World (then known as the undeveloped world). As such, it represented to supporters of American intervention a case of attempted Soviet expansionism at a third remove (that is, through Beijing to Hanoi and through Hanoi to the Vietcong). But the Sino-Soviet split made nonsense of the idea that the Russians could be using the Chinese to further their own imperialistic aims. One of the greatest of all the ironies of the Vietnam War, however, is that it ended by vindicating the original idea that a Communist victory would be tantamount to an expansion of Soviet power. Having won the war with the help of Soviet arms, and then having conquered Laos and Cambodia, Hanoi went on to ally itself with the Soviet Union against "the Chinese menace," at which point (in the words of a high official of the Singapore government, S. Rajaratnam) the Vietnamese found themselves "fighting for a Soviet Indochina."[3] Yet by the time the people who had predicted some such result of an American defeat in Vietnam were thus vindicated, all but a very few had long since changed their minds and gone over to the other side.

But what of the notorious domino theory? Here, too, everyone was

---

*Numbered notes can be found on pp. 191–94.

wrong. Those who said that the fall of Vietnam to Communism would be followed by the fall of Laos and Cambodia were right, but they were wrong in thinking that the dominoes would topple all throughout Southeast Asia "at least down to Singapore but almost as certainly to Djakarta," in Lyndon Johnson's words.[4] This does not, however, mean that the domino theory has been "discredited," as is so often glibly claimed. For believers in the domino theory turned out to be right in thinking that an American defeat in Vietnam would give encouragement to other Communist insurrections or "wars of national liberation" backed by the Soviet Union. Thus, no sooner had Vietnam fallen than Soviet proxies in the form of Cuban troops appeared in Angola to help the Communist faction there overwhelm its pro-Western rivals in a civil war. With local variations, the same pattern was repeated over the next few years in Ethiopia, Mozambique, South Yemen, and Afghanistan, all of which were taken over by Communist parties subservient to or allied with the Soviet Union with the help of Soviet proxies or massive infusions of Soviet arms. Still, if the domino theory was in one sense vindicated by Vietnam, it was not in the sense most of its proponents foresaw.

From a strictly political point of view, then, no one (to borrow a phrase from George McGovern's campaign for the presidency in 1972) was "right from the start." The fall of Vietnam to Communism led to some of the consequences that had been predicted, but not to others.

Nor was anyone "right from the start" about the consequences for the United States of a defeat in Vietnam. On the one hand, those who predicted the upsurge of a new isolationism were right. The new isolationism became powerful enough to capture the Democratic party—the party that had given the nation the Truman Doctrine, the Korean War, and the Vietnam War—and thus managed to establish itself in the very center of American political life for the first time since 1941.

Admittedly, when George McGovern, as the Democratic candidate for the presidency in 1972, campaigned under the all but explicitly isolationist slogan "Come Home, America," he was defeated by Nixon in one of the great landslides in American electoral history. Nevertheless, the new isolationism remained strong enough to produce results in the form of a weakening of "the imperial Presidency"—that is, the main institutional capability the United States possesses for conducting an overt policy of intervention to contain the spread of Communism—and then of the CIA, the main institutional capability the nation possesses for conducting a covert policy of containment. It is true that these assaults on the powers of the presidency and the CIA were triggered by the abuses exposed in connection with the Watergate scandal. But it would be naive to suppose that they did not reflect a new impulse within the political culture of the United States to pull back from the responsibilities of containment by making any future act of anti-Communist interventionism much more difficult (if not indeed impossible) to undertake.

That this was the animating purpose behind the twin assaults on "the imperial Presidency" and the CIA came out very clearly when in 1975 Congress cut off a nascent effort by President Gerald Ford and his secretary of state, Henry Kissinger, to help the pro-Western guerrillas in Angola in their struggle against the Soviet-backed faction there (which finally triumphed after Cuban troops, acting as Soviet proxies, intervened in force). With the election of Jimmy Carter in 1976, the retreat from containment was given full presidential sanction. In his first major foreign-policy address, Carter—not content with even the severe reduction in the scope of containment already accomplished by the Nixon Doctrine—congratulated the nation on having overcome its "inordinate fear of Communism" and went on to assert that "historical trends have weakened the foundation" of the two principles that had guided American foreign policy in the past: "a belief that Soviet expansion was almost inevitable and that it must be contained."[5]

On this issue, then, Lyndon Johnson and some of his chief advisers like Dean Rusk and Walt Rostow, who worried about a resurgence of isolationism, were right.

On the other hand, Johnson was wrong in predicting that this resurgence would be accompanied by "a divisive debate about 'who lost Vietnam'"[6] and a concomitant resurgence of McCarthyism. This fear that American intervention in Vietnam would give rise to a new McCarthyism was expressed as early as 1962 by Hans J. Morgenthau and as late as the closing stages of the war by Henry Kissinger. Yet nothing of the sort ever developed—at least not on the Right. After the war was over, military men like General William Westmoreland defended themselves by saying that they had lost because the politicians had denied them the means by which to win, but hardly anyone seemed to listen. In the army itself no "stab-in-the-back" syndrome ever developed after Vietnam;[7] instead there was a great deal of soul-searching, self-criticism, and strategic analysis. Nor did a stab-in-the-back theory take hold in the country at large: one need only compare the obscurity and even disgrace into which Westmoreland fell to the adulation that greeted General Douglas MacArthur when he made similar complaints about the limitations imposed on him in Korea by the politicians.

As to insinuations of disloyalty and even treason, if they were promiscuously thrown around in the wake of Korea, the situation after Vietnam was in this respect characterized by extreme prudishness. Not only were critics of the war spared accusations of disloyalty; they were celebrated as prophets to whom the country should have listened and heroes who had shown the courage to "tell the truth to power."

Even opponents of the war who had openly sided with the Vietcong and Hanoi—who had marched with Vietcong flags, who had parroted the propaganda of the Communists in speeches and articles and books, who had visited Hanoi and had come back with reports of how well American prisoners of war were being treated, and who had denounced their own country as an aggressor and a perpetrator of crimes against humanity— were spared the wrath of public opinion, not to mention prosecution, for acts that at any other time and in any other country would certainly have been regarded as treason. More than spared: Tom Hayden, who had done most of these things, was received at the White House by President Jimmy Carter; Ramsey Clark, who had done most of these things, was sent on a diplomatic mission by the same President Carter; Jane Fonda, who had done most of these things, was rewarded with greater and greater popularity, higher and higher fees, and more and better prizes.

Indeed, in another of the reversals of role to which the war kept giving rise, the only substantial signs of McCarthyism in the Vietnam era appeared on the Left. Thus the investigations of the CIA by several congressional committees in the 1970s were a mirror image of the congressional investigations of Communists in the 1950s. Like the committees of the McCarthy period, those investigating the CIA featured daily leaks of sensational revelations to a cooperative press, which then helped spread the idea that the Communist once supposedly under every American bed had been replaced by a CIA agent.

Thus, too, attributions of guilt by association—another feature of McCarthyism—became as standard in the writings of the Left as they had been in such right-wing publications of the 1950s as *Red Channels*. For example, when Jeane Kirkpatrick was appointed ambassador to the United Nations by Ronald Reagan in 1981, an article in the *Nation*[8] (subsequently quoted in many other magazines of the Left) connected her with the CIA through her husband, Evron Kirkpatrick, whose brother had allegedly been a high official of the agency. But the official in question (Lyman Kirkpatrick) was not Evron Kirkpatrick's brother or any relation at all. Here, then, was a classic McCarthyite smear: the assumption of guilt by association with even the evidence of association turning out to be false.

If, moreover, McCarthyism means character assassination based on accusations for which there is no solid foundation, the charges of war crimes against both the military and the civilian leadership of the country can also be seen as a symptom of its resurgence on the Left. According to Nixon, Ronald Reagan told him at the time that "CBS under World War II circumstances would have been perhaps charged with treason" for the way it was handling the Christmas bombing of Hanoi in 1972,[9] but Reagan never said any such thing in public, and if he had, he would have been ignored or shouted down. So much for McCarthyism of the Right. On the Left, however, accusations of the most serious kind were freely made and widely circulated with impunity, often by means of self-appointed kangaroo courts whose deliberations were respectfully treated by people who had in the past professed outrage at the violation of due process by congressional investigators. Indeed, what Guenter Lewy calls "a veritable industry publicizing alleged war crimes"[10] emerged both in the United States and abroad (in the form of the International War Crimes Tribunal organized by Bertrand Russell).

This activity was by no means confined to fringe groups on the Left. In 1970, ten congressmen sponsored a conference in Washington on "War and National Responsibility" in which other congressmen and senators participated along with such nonradical luminaries as Hannah Arendt, Benjamin V. Cohen, Hans J. Morgenthau, Louis Pollak, and Telford Taylor. Though some of the forty participants did not agree that the United States was committing war crimes in Vietnam, few disagreed strongly, and all were only too willing to lend their presence to a conference in which the dominant view was that of Richard A. Falk (professor of international law at Princeton): "The evidence is so abundant and so unambiguous that war crimes *are* being committed in Vietnam by the United States Government that there is no longer any excuse for silence or acquiescence on the part of American citizens."[11] Said the editors of the volume that emerged from the conference (whose title, *War Crimes and the American Conscience,* dispensed with the cautious euphemism of the conference's title): "It would have been inconceivable only a few years ago that a serious and searching discussion of war crimes—including American war crimes—could be conducted under congressional auspices at the Capitol of the United States."[12] Again, so much for McCarthyism of the Right.

To say that a book like *War Crimes and the American Conscience* was a species of McCarthyism is to say that the charges it made were irresponsible and that the way it made those charges showed contempt for the rules of evidence and for the procedures by which accusations can fairly be judged. Of course such conferences and tribunals were not courts of law and were bound by no rules other than those they themselves decided upon; in that sense they had a "right" to do what they did. Nevertheless, in exercising that right, they freely defamed and slandered individuals and groups on the basis of false or faulty or tainted evidence, and witnesses of dubious credibility, in proceedings presided over by biased judges.

The Russell tribunal, for example, was convened, as Russell himself put it, "in order to expose . . . barbarous crimes . . . reported daily from Vietnam."[13] This assumption of guilt before trial was further strengthened by the membership of the tribunal, which was made up entirely of such outspoken supporters of North Vietnam as Jean-Paul Sartre, Stokely Carmichael, Dave Dellinger, and Isaac Deutscher. Not surprisingly, the proceedings largely "relied on evidence supplied by VC/NVA sources or collected in North Vietnam by persons closely aligned politically with the Communist camp."[14] So biased was the entire enterprise that even a radical antiwar activist like Staughton Lynd declined to participate, and even to Richard Falk it seemed "a juridical farce" (which did not prevent him from saying shortly thereafter that it had done a good job of turning up evidence of American war crimes and had "developed persuasively some of the legal implications it seems reasonable to draw from that war").[15]

In the United States itself, similar enterprises were launched. One such was the Vietnam Veterans Against the War (VVAW), whose activities included holding hearings all over the country. At one of these hearings, in Detroit in 1971, more than a hundred veterans were reported to have testified to "war crimes which they either committed or witnessed." Senator Mark Hatfield inserted the transcript of the proceedings into the Congressional Record and demanded an investigation of the charges by the Naval Investigative Service (since mostly marines had been involved). This investigation yielded the following: a refusal by many of the witnesses to be interviewed (despite assurances that they would not be questioned about atrocities they themselves might have committed); inability on the part of one witness to provide details of the atrocities he had described at the Detroit hearings; and "sworn statements of several veterans, corroborated by witnesses,"[16] that they had not even attended the hearings at which they allegedly had testified.

But if from a procedural point of view, these (and many others that could be cited) are examples of left-wing McCarthyism, the substantive allegations of criminality "established" by such procedures go beyond McCarthyism in the strict sense. For what the war-crimes industry did was to charge people who had committed certain acts with violating laws that these acts did not in fact violate. (It would be as though a member of the Communist party had been accused of committing a crime in joining the party even though membership in the Communist party was never against the law in the United States.)

For example, one of the crimes with which the United States was most frequently charged was connected with the practice of clearing areas of civilians and then declaring them "free-fire zones" (or "specified strike zones")—that is, areas that could be bombarded by planes and artillery at will. The refugees thus "generated" were placed in camps, and anyone who remained behind was considered Vietcong. Once the area was cleared, evacuees were free to return to their homes, and efforts were made by the authorities to help them do so.

According to an interreligious committee of American theologians (including among others a black Protestant, Martin Luther King Jr.; a white Protestant, Harvey Cox; a Roman Catholic, Robert F. Drinan; and a Jew, Abraham Joshua Heschel), this practice was a crime—a "violation of Article 49 of the Civilians Convention of 1949, an article framed to avert repetition of the forcible relocations that took place in World War II."[17] Yet as was so often the case with such confidently asserted accusations by public figures with no special knowledge either of military matters or of international law, this indictment was based on a faulty or ignorant interpretation of the law.

For one thing, the article of the Geneva Convention invoked here applies only to armed international conflict; yet these theologians and those who agreed with them regarded Vietnam as a civil war and therefore had no intellectual right to subject it to laws applicable only to wars between different nations. But assuming that the Vietnam War was an international conflict—as both the United States and South Vietnam claimed it was—and applying Article 49 of the Geneva Convention Relative to the Protection of Civilian Persons in Time of War, we find that this article unambiguously permits the evacuation of civilians from a combat zone and can even be read to *require* "total or partial evacuation of a given area if the security of the population or imperative military reasons so demand."[18]

Other international codes subsequently added their weight to this requirement, as when in 1956 the International Committee of the Red Cross proposed that belligerents "protect the civilian population subject to their authority from the dangers to which they would be exposed in an attack—in particular by removing them from the vicinity of military objectives and from the threatened areas."[19] So, too, the secretary general of the United Nations in 1970 (while the war was still going on) proposed that the General Assembly "call on all authorities involved in armed conflicts of all types to do their utmost to insure that civilians are removed from, or kept out of, areas where conditions would be likely to place them in jeopardy or expose them to the hazards of warfare."[20]

The lavish use of firepower by the United States in Vietnam undoubtedly caused destruction of property and civilian casualties. But did it constitute a war crime? Professor Falk had no doubt that it did. The American way of fighting the war, he charged, involved "the massive use of cruel tactics directed indiscriminately against the civilian population in flagrant violation of the minimum rules of war."[21] The same group of theologians who were so certain that the United States was guilty of violating Article 49 of the Geneva Convention were equally certain that American actions in Vietnam also violated "the minimal standards of constraint established by the Hague Convention of 1907 and the Geneva Conventions of 1929 and 1949." In short, "our nation must be judged guilty of having broken almost every established agreement for standards of human decency in time of war."[22]

The tactics condemned here were developed in order to fight an enemy, the Vietcong, whose own tactics involved "clutching the people to their breast" by converting rural hamlets into fortified strongholds that were camouflaged to look like peaceful villages; by disguising themselves as civilians; and by using villagers of all ages and both sexes—little children, women, old men—to plant mines and booby traps and engage in other military activities. As it happens, all *these* practices are clearly forbidden by the laws of war, which seek to ensure that innocent civilians are not taken for combatants. Consequently, resistance fighters are required to carry arms openly and have "a fixed distinctive sign recognizable at a distance," and "the presence of a protected person may not be used to render certain points or areas immune from military operations."[23] Professor Falk, so tender of international law when American actions were under consideration, argued that the Vietcong was justified in disregarding these rules on the ground that adherence to the Geneva Convention would have made it impossible for the guerrillas to fight effectively. They had "no alternative other than terror," and they could not wear uniforms or take the care required by international law of wounded or captured enemies. On the other hand, "the cumulative effect of counterguerrilla warfare is necessarily barbaric and inhumane to such an extent as to taint the entire effort with a genocidal quality."[24] Or, in the succinct formulation of Gabriel Kolko, a leading revisionist historian of the Cold War: "The war crime in Vietnam is the war itself."[25]

Again, this idea was not confined to the radical fringe of the antiwar movement. One of the leading "moderate" critics of the war, Hans J. Morgenthau, made much the same point about the nature of the American military effort: "We are not fighting an army. We are not even fighting a group of partisans in the woods, as the Germans did in Yugoslavia. We are fighting an entire people. And since everyone in the countryside of Vietnam is to a lesser or greater degree our potential enemy, it is perfectly logical to kill everyone in sight."[26]

By these criteria, there was no point in arguing over whether this or that American battlefield tactic violated this or that provision of the laws of war: the very act of fighting against the Vietcong was intrinsically or by definition criminal and therefore gave rise by a "perfectly logical" progression to subsidiary criminal acts. What difference could it then make to Falk or Morgenthau that the laws of war *permit* attacks upon a village or town that is occupied by a military force or has been fortified, or upon civilian homes used to store war materials, or even hospitals if (in the language of the Geneva Convention) "they are used to commit, outside their humanitarian duties, acts harmful to the enemy"[27] and due warning has been given to cease such use? Could it make any difference that the American commander who destroyed an entire village in response to a single sniper's bullet was within his legal rights so long as he was honestly exercising his best judgment as to the size of the enemy force, even though (as the Nuremberg tribunal declared) "the conclusion reached may have been faulty"?[28]

None of this would make any difference to Falk, or to Kolko, or to Morgenthau, or to another "moderate" member of the antiwar movement, Jonathan Schell, whose reports in the *New Yorker* were so influential in establishing the impression of indiscriminate use of American firepower against civilians in South Vietnam (they even influenced Robert McNamara when he was still secretary of defense).[29] At the conference on war crimes convened by the ten congressmen, Schell said there were only two alternatives for the United States: "The first is simply to leave and to permit the Vietcong or the North Vietnamese or some combination of them to take over at their leisure." This he found "regrettable," but the second alternative was much worse: it was "to continue what we are now doing—to commit more massacres and to destroy other provinces as we have destroyed Quang Ngai. This course of action—that is to say, our present course of action—leads to the total destruction of the society in South Vietnam."[30]

In other words, whether or not the American effort to save South Vietnam from Communism was intrinsically criminal, it could not be pursued without leading to genocide. Just as we were being forced to destroy the country physically in order to save it, so we were wiping out its entire population for the same purpose.

Of all the crimes with which the United States was charged, genocide was the most serious. Genocide means murdering, or trying to murder, an entire people, and it was in order to reinforce the charge that the United States was doing precisely this in Vietnam that the statistics of bombs dropped and ordnance used were so regularly compared to the tonnages used in World War II (as though such statistics had anything to do with the genocidal program the Germans carried out against the Jews by means of gas chambers); and this is also why the talk of indiscriminate attacks on civilians was so steady and so loud.

Yet at the very time charges of genocide were being made, it was known that the population of South Vietnam was *increasing*. Indeed, no less fervent an antiwar activist than Daniel Ellsberg, speaking in 1970, cautioned against use of the term "genocide" by the movement "even if it is strictly warranted," because "the population of South Vietnam has almost surely increased each year in the last five."[31] So had the population of North Vietnam, despite charges that American bombing was taking a heavy toll of civilian casualties. According to the *United Nations Demographic Yearbook 1974,* the population of South Vietnam went from 16.12 million in 1965 to 19.95 million in 1973, and that of North Vietnam from 18.71 million in 1965 to 22.70 million in 1973; the annual rates of growth were roughly double that of the United States. "This fact," comments Lewy, "makes the charge of genocide a bit grotesque."[32]

But what about indiscriminate and excessive firepower resulting in an unusually high number of civilian casualties? Here, too, the charge can be characterized as "a bit grotesque." According to Lewy's calculations— which are generous in their definition of civilian and extremely cautious in their reliance on official "body counts"—"the Vietnam War during the years of active American involvement was no more destructive of civilian life, both North and South, than other armed conflicts of this century and a good bit less so than some, such as the Korean War."[33] Whereas as many as 70 percent of those killed in Korea were civilians, in Vietnam the proportion was at most 45 percent, which was approximately the level of civilian casualties in World War II. And of course a substantial percentage of these civilians were killed not by the Americans or the South Vietnamese but by the Vietcong and the North Vietnamese, especially after 1969, when there was a steady decline in American bombing and shelling and combat increasingly occurred farther away from areas in which the rural population lived.[34]

The fact that American battlefield tactics were not in themselves criminal does not mean that the laws of war were never violated in Vietnam. The most notorious such violation was the massacre of anywhere from two hundred to four hundred inhabitants—most of them old men, women, and children—of the hamlet of My Lai in the village of Son My in March 1968. These executions were justified by no military necessity and were carried out against nonresisting and unarmed persons, and they therefore constituted acts of murder not only under international law but under the specific directives of the American command in Vietnam. Moreover, they were committed in the wake of other violations of these directives, including the failure to issue a warning prior to an attack on a village or hamlet and the concomitant failure to make "maximum effort . . . to minimize noncombatant casualties during tactical operations."[35] For over a year this atrocity was concealed; then an American soldier, who was not connected with the division of which the offending company was a part and who had heard about the massacre, brought it to the attention of the authorities.

Was the My Lai massacre characteristic of the way all "search-and-destroy" missions were carried out? Some said that it was. For example, the psychiatrist Robert Jay Lifton, a well-known antiwar activist, declared: "My Lai epitomizes the Vietnam War . . . because every returning soldier can tell of similar incidents, if on a somewhat smaller scale. . . ."[36] Three other psychiatrists agreed: *"The most important fact about the My Lai massacre is that it was only a minor step beyond the standard, official, routine U.S. policy in Vietnam."*[37] And Hans J. Morgenthau was "firmly convinced that what happened in My Lai and elsewhere were not accidents, or deviations . . . , but the inevitable outgrowth of the kind of war we are waging."[38]

Yet no evidence existed at the time—and none has materialized since—to substantiate the charge that My Lai was typical. Nor is it likely, given the number of antiwar journalists reporting on Vietnam, that if other such atrocities had occurred, they could have been kept secret. Telford Taylor, who had been a prosecutor at Nuremberg and was now a strong opponent of the war, disputed the judgment of Lifton and others on this point: "It has been said that 'the massacre at Son My was not unique,' but I am unaware of any evidence of other incidents of comparable magnitude, and the reported reaction of some of the soldiers at Son My strongly indicates that they regarded it as out of the ordinary."[39]

So, too, Daniel Ellsberg, who believed the war was criminal and even saw himself (having been a government official) as a potential defendant in a war-crimes trial: "My Lai was beyond the bounds of permissible behavior, and that is recognizable by virtually every soldier in Vietnam. They know it was wrong: No shots had been fired at the soldiers, no enemy troops were in the village, nobody was armed. The men who were at My Lai knew there were aspects out of the ordinary. That is why they tried to hide the event, talked about it to no one, discussed it very little even among themselves."[40]

The other question raised by My Lai was the question of responsibility. The officer in charge, Lieutenant William Calley, who was tried and convicted and punished for the crime, not surprisingly found defenders in political circles that considered such actions justified by the circumstances in which they had been committed. But in what may seem paradoxical at first sight, perhaps his most fervent defenders came out of the ranks of the antiwar movement because they feared that by assigning guilt to Calley or other individuals, the truly guilty parties would be absolved. Said the team of three psychiatrists led by Edward M. Opton Jr.: *"The major responsibility and guilt for the massacre lie with the elected officials who make U.S. policy in Vietnam and with the high military officials who have misled both elected officials and the general public as to what they have been doing under the name of those policy directives."* In addition to elected officials and high military officials, *"America's citizens share in the responsibility for My Lai. . . . We as a people do bear much of the responsibility for My Lai. The guilt is in large part collective."*[41] Lifton, too, believed that the guilt was collective, that the American people shared in a "moral or criminal culpability . . . in relationship to the Vietnam War . . . since all of us are part of America and we, one way or another, live in the American realm and contribute to national and military efforts. . . ."[42]

This revival of the doctrine of collective guilt by a movement generally called "liberal" was one of the more bizarre cultural phenomena of the Vietnam period. For nothing could be more repugnant to the moral and legal tradition of liberalism than the idea that an individual can be held responsible for an act he himself did not commit. But the underlying reasoning—that "My Lai epitomizes the Vietnam War" because "the war crime in Vietnam is the war itself"—is a reminder that the discussion of My Lai and other atrocities was disingenuous. The point was not to expose instances of wrongdoing, or to institute training and command procedures that would more effectively deter violations of the law and punish them more severely when they occurred; the point was to discredit the entire American effort to save South Vietnam from Communism.

This is why convincing refutations of the charge that the United States was committing war crimes could be so easily shrugged off by many who had either voiced the charges themselves or nodded in agreement when they were voiced by others. For example, when Lewy's *America in Vietnam* came out in 1978, the response from those former members of the antiwar movement who even bothered to notice was to dismiss his meticulous examination of the issue of war crimes as "legalistic," and then to shift the ground immediately to the question of morality. Leaving it "for the lawyers to decide" how well Lewy had made his case "that American military operations were conducted in substantial conformity with the laws of war," Terry Nardin and Jerome Slater, two academic reviewers with a clear antiwar point of view, went on to assert that "no legal expertise is needed, however, to see the fallacy of Lewy's further conclusion that because the American way of war was not illegal, it was not immoral. It is simply a *non sequitur* that whatever is not prohibited by the laws of war is therefore morally acceptable."[43]

The political theorist Michael Walzer concurred: "In fact, Lewy argues only the legal case, as if morality were a realm to which scholarly qualification doesn't extend. . . . The task Lewy sets for himself turns out to be surprisingly simple, for the laws of war are so vaguely stated and so radically incomplete that a brief for the defense is readily put together. Lewy's brief is 'legalistic' in the common sense of that word, but I would hesitate to say it is wrong. . . . The result, however, is likely to leave the reader more uncomfortable with the law than easy with the war."[44] Finally, Theodore Draper: "It is a continuing shame . . . that the shamefulness of this war should be incidentally mentioned in a book designed to cover up the shame by taking refuge in narrow and dubious legalisms."[45]

Having conceded in the face of Lewy's analysis that "the charge made by some radicals at home that we were fighting a genocidal war in Vietnam was both ignorant and silly," these critics can then blithely assert that

"though he scores easy victories against what we might call the gesticula-
tions of the Left—the rhetorical exaggerations and the anti-American or
self-hating extravagances of the peace movement—he leaves its core position untouched."[46] Namely, that the war was "a study in military immorality" (Walzer), that "the manner in which it was fought constituted a
dramatic collapse of both reason and morality" (Nardin and Slater), that it
was marked by "immoral conduct" (Draper).

What Draper and the others then do is fall back on a rehearsal of the
familiar catalogue of horrors to which the war in Vietnam gave rise. Quoting from Lewy himself—not that they needed him for this purpose—they
describe once again how the designation of a given area as a "free-fire zone"
led to the "generating" of refugees, the vast majority of whom were old
people, women, and children; how numbers of these were killed because
they insisted on returning to their homes after being sent to squalid refugee
camps. They speak of how "the fatuous policy of 'body counts' encouraged
the indiscriminate lumping of combatants and noncombatants," of how
"American military doctrine called for methods that were insensitive to
political and human costs"; they emphasize—again taking terms and
examples out of Lewy's own book—American "atrocities" and "massacres"
and the lenience with which the perpetrators of these crimes were treated
by the military courts. They cite the astronomical statistics of bomb tonnages dropped both on South and on North Vietnam, and they speak of
how South Vietnam was turned by these bombs and by napalm and defo-
liants and herbicides into "a barren wasteland."[47]

In dwelling on the horrors of the war in Vietnam, these critics provide
ample confirmation of Lewy's argument "that the suffering inflicted upon
large segments of South Vietnam's rural population during long years of a
high technology warfare . . . undermined the efforts of the Saigon regime
to win the allegiance of the people . . . and contributed to the spread of a
feeling of resignation, war-weariness, and an unwillingness to go on fighting against the resolute opponent from the North."[48]

What then accounted for the use of such "counterproductive" tactics?
Reading the critics, one gets the impression that it was all a matter either of
the innate immorality of the military or—what often comes to the same
thing in their analyses—the product of the workings of an inflexible
bureaucracy. Yet there was a reason that so much firepower was employed
in Vietnam. "The American way of war," as it came to be called in the
polemics of the period, was based on the motto "Expend Shells Not
Men."[49] Was it immoral of American commanders to follow this rule? The

antiwar movement thought so, and Lewy's critics still do. "The American way of war was largely responsible for the very high civilian death toll," says Walzer.[50] To rely, as the Americans did, "on massive firepower is not merely a disproportionate response to enemy fire; it is a response that shifts the burden of war from the soldier, who would otherwise have to assume the risks of entering the village to root out enemy soldiers, to the civilian population," write Nardin and Slater (who cite Walzer's book, *Just and Unjust Wars,* as their moral authority).[51] The implication is that it was immoral for American commanders to be more concerned with the lives of their own men than with the lives of Vietnamese who might have been part of the elusive enemy force.

Leaving aside the fact that the civilian death toll in Vietnam was *not* "very high" as compared with Korea and World War II (to repeat: the proportion of civilian deaths was much lower in Vietnam than in Korea and roughly the same as it was in World War II), there is something bizarre in charging an American officer with immorality for adopting methods whose purpose was to minimize American casualties. By normal standards, the men in the field surely had a better case when they made the opposite complaint about the rules of engagement (ROE) which restricted their use of firepower in order to minimize civilian casualties. According to Roger Hilsman, "The military fretted under the limitations, citing incidents in which they took casualties that might have been avoided with more thorough preparatory bombing."[52] These limitations included cumbersome clearance procedures for calling in artillery fire or air strikes—procedures which, in the judgment of Senator Barry Goldwater (who thought they and not the air strikes were shameful) "had as much to do with our casualties as the enemy themselves."[53] No wonder, then, that the rules of engagement were often violated in practice by commanders in the field who—in a tradition that was in the past held to be a special moral glory of the American military—were determined to do everything in their power to protect the men for whose lives they were responsible.

Because of this, stupid though the American way of war no doubt was in the political context of Vietnam—where it served to arouse the hostility of the very people whose "hearts and minds" were being courted and whose support was a necessary ingredient of victory—it could not reasonably be considered immoral. Nor could it even be considered extraordinarily brutal. Writing in 1970, not, obviously, to defend the United States, but out of the expectation that things might yet get worse both in Vietnam and elsewhere, Daniel Ellsberg warned his fellow activists in the antiwar movement that "an escalation of rhetoric can blind us to the fact that Vietnam is . . . no more brutal than other wars in the past—and it is absurdly unhistorical to insist that it is. . . ."[54]

Even granting to writers like the sociologist Peter L. Berger that "the war was marked by a distinctive brutality . . . flowing in large measure from its character as a war of counterinsurgency,"[55] Ellsberg's point was so obviously true that it poses a difficult intellectual problem. One can easily enough understand how the young of the 1960s—who were in general notoriously deficient in historical knowledge or understanding, and who therefore tended to look upon all the ills around them, including relatively minor ones, as unique in their evil dimension—would genuinely imagine that never in all of human experience had there been anything to compare in cruelty and carnage with the war in Vietnam. But how did it happen that so many of their elders and teachers, who did have historical perspective and had even lived through two earlier and bloodier wars, should have taken so "absurdly unhistorical" a view of Vietnam? The answer is, quite simply, that they opposed—or had turned against—the American effort to save South Vietnam from Communism. Being against the end, they could not tolerate the very means whose earlier employment in Korea and in World War II they had not only accepted but applauded.

In World War II, as Lewy says, "despite the fact that the Allies . . . engaged in terror-bombing of the enemy's civilian population and generally paid only minimal attention to the prevention of civilian casualties— even during the liberation of Italy and France—hardly anyone on the Allied side objected to these tactics." The reason was that "the war against Nazism and fascism was regarded as a moral crusade in which the Allies could do no wrong. . . ."[56]

So, too, with the Korean War, in which practically all the major population centers were leveled, dams and irrigation systems were bombed, napalm was used, and enormous numbers of civilians were killed. Yet there was no morbidly fascinated dwelling on those horrors in the press, and very little moral outrage expressed. For the Korean War was seen as an extension of World War II not merely in the strategic sense of representing a new phase in the resistance to aggression through the principle of collective security, but also in being part of a moral crusade against Communism. As such it was a continuation of the struggle against totalitarianism, whose first battles had been fought and won in the Second World War.

The fact that this aspect of the Korean War was rarely emphasized in the official pronouncements, which tended to dwell upon the strategic element, does not mean that it was considered less important. It means rather that it was taken so entirely for granted as to need little if any explicit stress. The consensus of the period was that Communism represented an evil comparable to and as great as Nazism. This was the feeling in the country at large, and it was even the prevalent view within the intellectual community where Communism was regarded—not least by many who had earlier embraced it—as the other great embodiment of totalitarianism, the twentieth century's distinctive improvement upon the despotisms and tyrannies of the past. In one of the most influential books of the Korean War period, *The Origins of Totalitarianism,* Hannah Arendt brought Nazism and Communism together under the same rubric as systems of total control (in contrast to the traditional despotisms which exercised lesser degrees of domination over the individuals living under them). Indeed, Arendt went even further, arguing that Hitler, for all his anti-Communist passion, had looked admiringly to Lenin and Stalin for lessons in the practical implementation of his own brand of totalitarianism.

To go to war in order to contain the spread of Communism was therefore on the same moral plane as going to war against Nazism had been, "and those who fought such a war could do no wrong" either. "There was hideous bloodletting in Korea," wrote Richard H. Rovere in 1967, "and few liberals protested it";[57] he himself had celebrated the Korean War as "a turning point in the world struggle against Communism."[58] Having then believed that "we had an obligation" to go to the aid of the government in South Vietnam when it was threatened by a combination of internal and external Communist aggression, by 1967 he had come to feel that the American role was indefensible. "People who used to say there are things worse than war now say there are things worse than Communism and that the war in Vietnam is one of them."[59] Rovere himself was clearly one of those people, and their number was now legion. It was because they no longer thought that Communism was so great an evil that they saw the American war against it as a greater evil than it truly was, either by comparison with other wars, or more emphatically, in relation to the political system whose extension to South Vietnam the war was being fought to prevent.

2.

HERE THEN we arrive at the center of the moral issue posed by the American intervention into Vietnam.

The United States sent half a million men to fight in Vietnam. More than fifty thousand of them lost their lives, and many thousands more were wounded. Billions of dollars were poured into the effort, damaging the once unparalleled American economy to such an extent that the country's competitive position was grievously impaired. The domestic disruptions to which the war gave rise did perhaps even greater damage to a society previously so self-confident that it was often accused of entertaining illusions of its own omnipotence. Millions of young people growing to maturity during the war developed attitudes of such hostility toward their own country and the civilization embodied by its institutions that their willingness to defend it against external enemies in the future was left hanging in doubt.

Why did the United States undertake these burdens and make these sacrifices in blood and treasure and domestic tranquillity? What was in it for the United States? It was a question that plagued the antiwar movement from beginning to end because the answer was so hard to find. If the United States was simply acting the part of an imperialist aggressor in Vietnam, as many in the antiwar movement professed to believe, it was imperialism of a most peculiar kind. There were no raw materials to exploit in Vietnam, and there was no overriding strategic interest involved. To Franklin Roosevelt in 1941 Indochina had been important because it was close to the source of rubber and tin, but this was no longer an important consideration. Toward the end of the war, it was discovered that there was oil off the coast of Vietnam and antiwar radicals happily seized on this news as at last providing an explanation for the American presence there. But neither Kennedy nor Johnson knew about the oil, and even if they had, they would hardly have gone to war for its sake in those pre-OPEC days when oil from the Persian Gulf could be had at two dollars a barrel.

In the absence of an economic interpretation, a psychological version of the theory of imperialism was developed to answer the maddening question: *Why are we in Vietnam?* This theory held that the United States was in Vietnam because it had an urge to dominate—"to impose its national obsessions on the rest of the world," in the words of a piece in the *New York Review of Books,*[60] one of the leading centers of antiwar agitation within the intellectual community. But if so, the psychic profits were as illusory as the economic ones, for the war was doing even deeper damage to the national self-confidence than to the national economy.

Yet another variant of the psychological interpretation, proposed by the economist Robert L. Heilbroner, was that "the fear of losing our place in the sun, of finding ourselves at bay, . . . motivates a great deal of the anti-Communism on which so much of American foreign policy seems to be founded." This was especially so in such underdeveloped countries as Vietnam, where "the rise of Communism would signal the end of capitalism as the dominant world order, and would force the acknowledgment that America no longer constituted the model on which the future of world civilization would be mainly based."[61]

All these theories were developed out of a desperate need to find or invent selfish or self-interested motives for the American presence in Vietnam, the better to discredit it morally. In a different context, proponents of one or another of these theories—Senator William Fulbright, for example—were not above trying to discredit the American presence politically by insisting that *no* national interest was being served by the war. This latter contention at least had the virtue of being closer to the truth than the former. For the truth was that the United States went into Vietnam for the sake not of its own direct interests in the ordinary sense but for the sake of an ideal. The intervention was a product of the Wilsonian side of the American character—the side that went to war in 1917 to "make the world safe for democracy" and that found its contemporary incarnations in the liberal internationalism of the 1940s and the liberal anti-Communism of the 1950s. One can characterize this impulse as naive; one can describe it, as Heilbroner does (and as can be done with any virtuous act), in terms that give it a subtly self-interested flavor. But there is no rationally defensible way in which it can be called immoral.

Why, then, were we in Vietnam? To say it once again: because we were trying to save the southern half of that country from the evils of Communism. But was the war we fought to accomplish this purpose morally worse than Communism itself? Peter L. Berger, who at the time was involved with Clergy and Laymen Concerned About Vietnam (CALCAV), wrote in 1967: "All sorts of dire results might well follow a reduction or a withdrawal of the American engagement in Vietnam. Morally speaking, however, it is safe to assume that none of these could be worse than what is taking place right now." Unlike most of his fellow members of CALCAV, Berger would later repent of this statement. Writing in 1980, he would say of it: "Well, it was *not* safe to assume. . . . I was wrong and so were all those who thought as I did." For "contrary to what most members (including myself) of the antiwar movement expected, the peoples of Indochina have, since 1975, been subjected to suffering far worse than anything that was inflicted upon them by the United States and its allies."[62]

To be sure, the "bloodbath" that had been feared by supporters of the war did not occur—not in the precise form that had been anticipated. In contrast to what they did upon taking power in Hanoi in 1954 (when they murdered some fifty thousand landlords), or what they did during their brief occupation of Hué during the Tet offensive of 1968 (when they massacred three thousand civilians), the Communists did not stage mass executions in the newly conquered South. According to Nguyen Cong Hoan, who had been an NLF agent and then became a member of the National Assembly of the newly united Communist Vietnam before disillusionment drove him to escape in March 1977, there were more executions in the provinces than in the cities and the total number might well have reached into the tens of thousands. But as another fervent opponent of the war, the *New York Times* columnist Tom Wicker, was forced to acknowledge, "what Vietnam has given us instead of a bloodbath [is] a vast tide of human misery in Southeast Asia—hundreds of thousands of homeless persons in United Nations camps, perhaps as many more dead in flight, tens of thousands of the most pitiable forcibly repatriated to Cambodia, no one knows how many adrift on the high seas or wandering the roads."[63]

Among the refugees Wicker was talking about here were those who came to be known as "the boat people" because they "literally threw themselves upon the South China Sea in small coastal craft. . . ."[64] Many thousands of these people were ethnic Chinese who were being driven out and forced to pay everything they had for leaky boats; tens of thousands more were Vietnamese fleeing voluntarily from what Nguyen Cong Hoan describes as "the most inhuman and oppressive regime they have ever known."[65] The same judgment is made by Truong Nhu Tang, the former minister of justice in the PRG who fled in November 1979 in a boat loaded with forty refugees: "Never has any previous regime brought such masses of people to such desperation. Not the military dictators, not the colonialists, not even the ancient Chinese overlords."[66]

So desperate were they to leave that they were willing to take the poor chance of survival in flight rather than remain. Says Nguyen Cong Hoan: " . . . Our people have a traditional attachment to their country. No Vietnamese would willingly leave home, homeland, and ancestors' graves. During the most oppressive French colonial rule and Japanese domination, no one escaped by boat at great risk to their lives. Yet you see that my countrymen by the thousands and from all walks of life, including a number of disillusioned Vietcongs [*sic*], continue to escape from Vietnam; six out of ten never make it, and for those who are fortunate to make it, they are not allowed to land."[67] Adds one of the disillusioned who did make it, Doan Van Toai: "Among the boat people who survived, including those who were raped by pirates and those who suffered in the refugee camps, nobody regrets his escape from the present regime."[68]

Though they invented a new form of the Communist bloodbath, the North Vietnamese (for, to repeat, before long there were no southerners in authority in the south, not even former members of the NLF and the PRG) were less creative in dealing with political opposition, whether real or imagined. The "re-education camps" they had always used for this purpose in the north were now extended to the south, but the result was not so much an indigenous system of Vietnamese concentration camps as an imitation of the Soviet Gulag. (*The Vietnamese Gulag,* indeed, was the name Doan Van Toai gave to the book he published about the camps in 1979.) The French journalist Jean Lacouture, who had supported the Communists during the war to the point (as he now admitted) of turning himself into a "vehicle and intermediary for a lying and criminal propaganda, [an] ingenuous spokesman for tyranny in the name of liberty,"[69] now tried to salvage his integrity by telling the truth about a re-education camp he was permitted to visit by a regime that had good reason to think him friendly. "It was," he wrote, "a prefabricated hell."[70]

Doan Van Toai, who had been in the jails over which so much moral outrage had been expended in the days of Thieu, describes the conditions he himself encountered when he was arrested by the Communists: "I was thrown into a three-foot-by-six-foot cell with my left hand chained to my right foot and my right hand chained to my left foot. My food was rice mixed with sand. . . . After two months in solitary confinement, I was transferred to a collective cell, a room 15 feet wide and 25 feet long, where at different times anywhere from 40 to 100 prisoners were crushed together. Here we had to take turns lying down to sleep, and most of the younger, stronger prisoners slept sitting up. In the sweltering heat, we also took turns snatching a few breaths of fresh air in front of the narrow opening that was the cell's only window. Every day I watched my friends die at my feet."[71]

He adds: "One South Vietnamese Communist, Nguyen Van Tang, who was detained 15 years by the French, eight years by Diem, six years by Thieu, and who is still in jail today, this time in a Communist prison, told me: . . . 'My dream now is not to be released; it is not to see my family. My dream is that I could be back in a French prison 30 years ago.'"[72]

No one knows how many people were sent to the Vietnamese Gulag. Five years after the fall of Saigon, estimates ranged from 150,000 to a million. Prime Minister Pham Van Dong, who so impressed Mary McCarthy with his nobility in 1968, told a French magazine ten years later that he had "*released* more than one million prisoners from the camps,"[73] although according to the figures of his own government he had arrested only 50,000 in the first place.

These prisoners naturally included officials of the former government of South Vietnam, but many opponents of the Thieu regime could also be found among them, some of whom were by 1981 known to have died in the camps. One such was Thic Thien Minh, "the strategist of all the Buddhist peace movements in Saigon, . . . who was sentenced to 10 years in jail by the Thieu regime, then released after an outpouring of protest from Vietnamese and antiwar protesters around the world," and who died after six months of detention by the Communists in 1979. Another was Tran Van Tuyen, a leader of the opposition to Thieu in the Saigon Assembly. A third was the philosopher Ho Huu Tuong, "perhaps the leading intellectual in South Vietnam," who died in a Communist prison in 1980. All these—along with other opponents of Thieu possibly still alive, like Bui Tuong Huan, former president of Hué University; Father Tran Huu Thanh, a dissident Catholic priest; and Tran Ngoc Chau, whose own brother had been a North Vietnamese agent—were arrested (and of course held without trial) "in order," says Doan Van Toai, "to preempt any possible opposition to the Communists."[74]

Before the Communist takeover, there had been a considerable degree of political freedom in South Vietnam which manifested itself in the existence of many different parties. After the North Vietnamese conquest, all these parties were dissolved; as for the NLF, "they buried it," in the bitter words of Truong Nhu Tang, "without even a ceremony," and "at the simple farewell dinner we held to formally disband the NLF in late 1976 neither the party nor the government sent a representative." The people of Vietnam, who "want only the freedom to go where they wish, educate their children in the schools they choose and have a voice in their government," are instead "treated like ants in a colony. There is only the opportunity to follow orders strictly, never the opportunity to express disagreement. Even within the [Communist] party, the principle of democracy has been destroyed in favor of the most rigid hierarchy. Stalinism, discredited throughout most of the Communist world, flourishes under the aged and fanatic Vietnamese leadership."[75]

Reading these words, one recalls Susan Sontag, Mary McCarthy, and Frances FitzGerald expending their intellectual energies on the promulgation of theories of Vietnamese culture calculated to deny that the people of

Vietnam cared about freedom in the simple concrete terms set forth by Truong Nhu Tang. One recalls Sontag saying that "incorporation" into a society like that of North Vietnam would "greatly improve the lives of most people in the world." One also recalls that both Sontag and McCarthy were troubled by the portraits of Stalin they saw all over the North; they were there, Sontag thought, because the Vietnamese could not bear to waste anything. Perhaps that is also how she would explain why portraits of Soviet leaders began appearing in public buildings, schools, and administrative offices throughout South Vietnam after 1975, and why the following poem by To Huu, president of the Communist Party Committee of Culture and a possible successor to Pham Van Dong,[76] was given a prominent place in an anthology of contemporary Vietnamese poetry published in Hanoi in the 1970s:

> *Oh, Stalin! Oh, Stalin!*
> *The love I bear my father, my mother, my wife, myself*
> *It's nothing beside the love I bear you.*
> *Oh, Stalin! Oh, Stalin!*
> *What remains of the earth and of the sky!*
> *Now that you are dead.*[77]

Written on the occasion of Stalin's death, this poem no doubt earned its place in an anthology twenty years later by virtue of its relevance to the spirit of the new Communist Vietnam. For if the Vietnamese Communist party is Stalinist, so is the society over which it rules. "Immediately after the fall of Saigon, the Government closed all bookshops and theaters. All books published under the former regimes were confiscated or burned. Cultural literature was not exempt, including translations of Jean-Paul Sartre, Albert Camus and Dale Carnegie[!]. . . . The new regime replaced such books with literature designed to indoctrinate children and adults with the idea that the 'Soviet Union is a paradise of the socialist world.'"[78]

As with books, so with newspapers. Under the old regime, under constant attack throughout the world for its repressiveness, there had been *twenty-seven* daily newspapers, three television stations, and more than twenty radio stations. "When the Communists took over," writes the political analyst Carl Gershman, "these were all closed down, and replaced by two official dailies, one television channel, and two radio stations—all disseminating the same government propaganda."[79]

All the other freedoms that existed, either in full or large measure, under the Thieu regime were also eliminated by the Communists. Freedom of movement began to be regulated by a system of internal passports, and freedom of association was abolished to the point where even a large family gathering, such as a wedding or a funeral, required a government permit and was attended by a security officer.

Freedom of religion, too, was sharply curtailed. The Buddhists, who were so effective an element in the opposition to Diem, soon learned that there were worse regimes than his. A Human Rights Appeal drafted by the Unified Buddhist Church and smuggled out by the Venerable Thich Manh Giac when he escaped by boat, charged that the government, "pursuing the policy of shattering the religious communities in our country, . . . has arrested hundreds of monks, confiscated hundreds of pagodas and converted them to government administration buildings, removed and smashed Buddha and Bodhisattva statues, prohibited celebration of the Buddha's birthday as a national holiday, . . . and forbidden monks to travel and preach by ordering restrictions in the name of 'national security.'"[80]

Unlike demonstrations by Buddhists in 1963, this appeal fell on deaf ears; whereas a raid on a Buddhist temple led directly to the overthrow of Diem, a similar raid by the Communist police in April 1977 went unnoticed; and whereas the self-immolation of a single Buddhist monk in 1963 attracted the horrified attention of the whole world, the self-immolation of twelve Buddhist nuns and priests on November 2, 1975, in protest against Communist repression, received scarcely any notice either in the United States or anywhere else.

When all this is combined with the terrible economic hardships that descended upon Vietnam after 1975—hardships that were simultaneously caused by the new regime and used by it to justify resettling millions of people in the so-called New Economic Zones, remote jungle areas where they worked "in collective gangs at such tasks as clearing land and digging canals,"[81] under primitive living conditions with little food and rampant disease—it is easy to see why a sense of despair soon settled over the country. Truong Nhu Tang: "The fact is that today Communism has been rejected by the people and that even many party members are questioning their faith. Members of the former resistance, their sympathizers and those who supported the Vietcong are disgusted and filled with bitterness. These innocent people swear openly that had they another chance their choice would be very different. The common [*sic*] heard expression is: 'I would give them not even a grain of rice, I pull them out of their hiding holes and denounce them to the authorities.'"[82]

The Buddhist human-rights appeal conveyed much the same impression: "Since the liberation thousands have committed suicide out of despair. Thousands have fled the country in small boats. Hospitals are reserved for cadres; civilians hardly have a chance to be hospitalized in case of sickness, while more than two hundred doctors remain in detention. Schoolchildren under fourteen have been assigned to collect pieces of scrap material in big garbage heaps and other places during the summer vacation. . . . A country that used to export rice has no rice to eat, even though the number of 'laborers' has now increased about ten times." The government, the appeal went on to say, prohibits "creative thinking and participation of independent groups. Totalitarianism destroys all possibility of genuine national reconciliation and concord."[83]

Some years after these words were written, a great and angry dispute broke out in the United States over the question of whether there was any practical validity or moral point in the distinction between authoritarianism and totalitarianism. Not surprisingly, those who dismissed the distinction as academic were in general veterans of the antiwar movement, who still refused to see that (as Gershman said in 1978) "for the Vietnamese, the distinction between a society that is authoritarian . . . and one that is totalitarian" turned out to be anything but academic.[84]

Peter L. Berger, one of the few former members of the antiwar movement who recognizes that "the transformation of Saigon into Ho Chi Minh City now offers a crystal-clear illustration of the difference between authoritarianism and totalitarianism, both in terms of political science and political morality," expresses amazement at "the persistent incapacity of even American professors to grasp a difference understood by every taxi driver in Prague." He believes that this incapacity derives in large part from a strong ideological interest in hiding "the fact that totalitarianism today is limited to socialist societies"—a fact that "flies in the face of the socialist dream that haunts the intellectual imagination of the West. . . ."[85]

I have no doubt that Berger is right about this. But where Vietnam in particular is concerned, there is a strong interest not only in protecting the socialist dream in general but, more specifically, in holding on to the sense of having been on the morally superior side in opposing the American struggle to prevent the replacement of an authoritarian regime in the south with a totalitarian system. The truth is that the antiwar movement bears a certain measure of responsibility for the horrors that have overtaken the people of Vietnam; and so long as those who participated in that movement are unwilling to acknowledge this, they will go on trying to discredit the idea that there is a distinction between authoritarianism and totalitarianism. For to recognize the distinction is to recognize that in making a contribution to the conquest of South Vietnam by the Communists of the north, they were siding with an evil system against something much better from every political and moral point of view.

Some veterans of the antiwar movement have protected themselves from any such acknowledgment of guilt by the simple expedient of denying that there is any truth in the reports by refugees like Doan Van Toai, Nguyen Cong Hoan, and Truong Nhu Tang or journalists like Lacouture. Noam Chomsky, for example, speaks of "the extreme unreliability" of these reports,[86] and he is echoed by William Kunstler, Dave Dellinger, and other inveterate apologists for the Vietnamese Communists. Peter Berger compares such people to "individuals who deny the facts of the Holocaust" and rightly considers them "outside the boundaries of rational discourse."[87]

There are, however, others—like the editors of the socialist magazine *Dissent,* Irving Howe and Michael Walzer—who are fully aware of the horrors that have followed the American withdrawal and the Communist conquest, and who are at least willing to ask, "Were We Wrong About Vietnam?" But of course their answer to this question is No. They were right because they were against both Saigon *and* Hanoi; they were right "in refusing to support the imperial backers of both." What then did they support? "Some of us . . . hoped for the emergence of a Vietnamese 'third force' capable of rallying the people in a progressive direction by enacting land reforms and defending civil liberties." But since, as they admit, there was very little chance of any such alternative, to have thrown their energies into opposing the American effort was tantamount to working for the Communist victory they say they did not want. Nevertheless, they still congratulate themselves on being against the evils on both sides of the war: "Those of us who opposed American intervention yet did not want a Communist victory were in the difficult position of having no happy ending to offer—for the sad reason that no happy ending was possible any longer, if ever it had been. And we were in the difficult position of urging a relatively complex argument at a moment when most Americans, pro- and antiwar, wanted blinding simplicities."[88] This is not moral choice; this is moral evasion—irresponsible utopianism disguised as moral realism. Given the actual alternatives that existed, what did the urging of "a relatively complex argument" avail for any purpose other than to make those who urged it feel pleased with themselves? If it served any purpose at all for the people of South Vietnam, it was to help deliver them over to the "blinding simplicities" of the totalitarianism Howe and Walzer so piously deplore and whose hideous workings they are now happy to denounce and protest against, even though there is no one in Ho Chi Minh City or Hanoi to listen or to hear.

Another veteran of the antiwar movement, Professor Stanley Hoffmann of Harvard, who also sees "no reason not to protest the massacres, arbitrary arrests, and persecutions perpetrated by the regimes that have taken over after our exit," nevertheless urges "those who condemned the war . . . to resist all attempts to make them feel guilty for the stand they took against the war." It was not, says Hoffmann, the antiwar movement that contributed to these horrors, but rather the people (led by Nixon and Kissinger) who were supposedly fighting to prevent them. True as this was of Vietnam—where "a monstrously disproportionate and self-destructive campaign" only added "to the crimes and degradation of eventual Communist victory"—it was even truer of Cambodia. "All those who, somehow, believe that the sufferings inflicted on the Cambodian people, first by the Pol Pot regime, and now by the Vietnamese, retrospectively justify America's attempt to save Phnom Penh from the Reds" were instructed by Hoffmann in 1979 to read a new book "showing that the monsters who decimated the Cambodian people were brought to power by Washington's policies."[89]

The book Hoffmann was referring to, *Sideshow: Kissinger, Nixon and the Destruction of Cambodia,* by the English journalist William Shawcross, sought to demonstrate that those Americans who fought to stop the Communists from coming to power in Cambodia were responsible for the crimes the Communists committed when the fight against them was lost. They can be held responsible, not as one might imagine because they did not fight as hard as they should have, or because in the end they deserted the field, but on the contrary because they entered the field in the first place. By attacking—first by bombing, then by invading—the North Vietnamese sanctuaries in Cambodia, the Americans (that is, Nixon and Kissinger) not only drove the Communists deeper into Cambodia, thereby bringing the war to areas that had previously been at peace. They also intensified the rage and bitterness of the Khmer Rouge (as the Cambodian Communists under Pol Pot were called), thereby turning them into perhaps the most murderous rulers ever seen on the face of the earth.

Sideshow is a brilliantly written and argued book. Indeed, not since Hannah Arendt's *Eichmann in Jerusalem*—which shifts a large measure of responsibility for the murder of six million Jews from the Nazis who committed the murders to the Jewish leaders who were trying to save as many of their people as they could—has there been so striking an illustration of the perverse moral and intellectual uses to which brilliance can be put.

There are, for example, the clever distortions and omissions that enable Shawcross to charge the Nixon administration with having destabilized the neutral government of Prince Norodom Sihanouk by bombing the sanctuaries (when in fact Sihanouk welcomed these attacks on the Communist military bases within his own country which he himself was not powerful enough to banish) and with causing large numbers of civilian casualties by the indiscriminate pattern of the bombing raids (when in fact care was taken to minimize civilian casualties). But what is fully on a par of perversity with Hannah Arendt's interpretation of the Jewish role in the genocidal program of the Nazis against them is the idea that Pol Pot and his followers needed the experience of American bombing and the "punishment" they subsequently suffered in the war against the anti-Communist forces of Cambodia to turn them into genocidal monsters.

This idea about the Khmer Rouge can easily enough be refuted by the simple facts of the case. Thus, according to Kenneth Quinn, who conducted hundreds of interviews with refugees from Cambodia, the Khmer Rouge began instituting the totalitarian practices of their revolutionary program in areas they controlled as early as 1971.[90] So, too, Father François Ponchaud, who was in Phnom Penh when the Communists arrived and whose book *Cambodia: Year Zero* Shawcross himself calls "the best account of Khmer Rouge rule":[91] "The evacuation of Phnom Penh follows traditional Khmer revolutionary practice: ever since 1972 the guerrilla fighters had been sending all the inhabitants of the villages and towns they occupied into the forests to live, often burning their homes so they would have nothing to come back for."[92]

Indeed, as Shawcross himself points out, this revolutionary program was outlined in uncannily clear detail in the thesis written at the University of Paris in 1959 by Khieu Samphan, who would later become the Khmer Rouge commander in chief during the war and the head of state afterward. But Shawcross, in line with his own thesis that it was the war that made "the Khmer Rouge . . . more and more vicious,"[93] stresses that "the methods this twenty-eight-year-old Marxist prescribed in 1959 for the transformation of his country were essentially moderate."[94] In support of the same thesis, he quotes Quinn to the effect that "the first steps to change radically the nature of Khmer society" that the Khmer Rouge took in 1971 were "limited."[95]

What Shawcross fails or refuses to see is what Ponchaud understands about such moderate methods and limited steps—namely, that they remained moderate and limited only so long as the Khmer Rouge lacked the power to put them into practice. "Accusing foreigners cannot acquit the present leaders of Kampuchea," Ponchaud wrote (before the Vietnamese invaded Cambodia and replaced the Khmer Rouge Communists with a puppet Communist regime of their own); "their inflexible ideology has led them to invent a radically new kind of man in a radically new society." Or again: "On April 17, 1975, a society collapsed; another is now being born from the fierce drive of a revolution which is incontestably the most radical ever to take place in so short a time. It is a perfect example of the application of an ideology pushed to the furthest limits of its internal logic."[96]

The blindness to the power of ideas that prevents Shawcross from recognizing ideology as the source of the crimes committed against their own people by the Khmer Rouge is his greatest intellectual sin. It is a species of philistinism to which many contemporary intellectuals (who, as intellectuals, might be expected to attribute a disproportionate importance to the role of ideas) are paradoxically prone, and it takes the form of looking for material factors to account for historical developments even when, as in this case, the main causal element is clearly located in the realm of ideas.

But this sin is exceeded in seriousness by the moral implications of Shawcross's book. As Peter W. Rodman (who has been an aide to Henry Kissinger both in and out of government) says in concluding a devastating critique of Shawcross's scholarship: "By no stretch of moral logic can the crimes of mass murderers be ascribed to those who struggled to prevent their coming into power. One hopes that no craven sophistry will ever induce free peoples to accept the doctrine that Shawcross embodies: that resistance to totalitarianism is immoral."[97]

Yet it is just this "craven sophistry" that Stanley Hoffmann reaffirms in the very face of the horrors that have befallen the peoples of Indochina under Communist rule: "As Frances FitzGerald put it," he writes, "our mistake was in creating and building up 'the wrong side,' and we were led by that mistake to a course of devastation *and* defeat."[98] One can almost forgive Anthony Lewis for asking "What future possibility could be more terrible than the reality of what is happening to Cambodia now?"[99] since he asked this question before the Khmer Rouge took over. One can almost forgive the *New York Times* for the headline "Indochina Without Americans: For Most, A Better Life" on a piece from Phnom Penh by Sydney H. Schanberg[100] since it was written before the Khmer Rouge had begun evacuating the city and instituting a regime that led to the death of nearly half the population of the country. Such writers should have known enough about the history of Communism to know better, and they should now be ashamed of their naiveté and of the contribution they made to the victory of forces they had a moral duty to oppose. Nevertheless, they were not yet aware of what Hoffmann already knew when he *still* described the Communists as the right side in Indochina and still denounced those who resisted them as immoral and even criminal. This is almost impossible to forgive.

In May 1977, two full years after the Communist takeover, President Jimmy Carter—a repentant hawk, like many members of his cabinet, including his secretary of state and his secretary of defense—spoke of "the intellectual and moral poverty" of the policy that had led us into Vietnam and had kept us there for so long. When Ronald Reagan, an unrepentant hawk, called the war "a noble cause" in the course of his ultimately successful campaign to replace Carter in the White House, he was accused of having made a "gaffe." Fully, painfully aware as I am that the American effort to save Vietnam from Communism was indeed beyond our intellectual and moral capabilities, I believe the story shows that Reagan's "gaffe" was closer to the truth of why we were in Vietnam and what we did there, at least until the very end, than Carter's denigration of an act of imprudent idealism whose moral soundness has been so overwhelmingly vindicated by the hideous consequences of our defeat.

NOTES

1. Doan Van Toai, "A Lament for Vietnam," *New York Times Magazine,* 29 March 1981.
2. General Fred C. Weyand, quoted in Harry G. Summers Jr., *On Strategy* (Carlisle Barracks, Pa: U.S. Army War College, Strategic Studies Institute, 1981), p. 61.
3. S. Rajaratnam, *Wall Street Journal,* 1 June 1981.
4. Lyndon Baines Johnson, *The Vantage Point* (New York: Holt, Rinehart & Winston, 1971), p. 151.
5. Jimmy Carter, speech at Notre Dame, May 1977.
6. Johnson, *The Vantage Point,* p. 152.
7. Summers, *On Strategy,* p. 7.
8. Alan Wolfe, "Jeane's Designs," *Nation,* 7 February 1981.
9. Richard Nixon, *RN: The Memoirs of Richard Nixon* (New York: Grosset & Dunlap, 1978), p. 740.
10. Guenter Lewy, *America in Vietnam* (New York: Oxford University Press, 1978), p. 224.
11. Richard A. Falk, in Erwin Knoll and Judith Nies McFadden, eds., *War Crimes and the American Conscience* (New York: Holt, Rinehart & Winston, 1970), p. 6.
12. Knoll and McFadden, *War Crimes and the American Conscience,* p. vii.
13. Bertrand Russell, quoted in Lewy, *America in Vietnam,* p. 312.
14. Lewy, *America in Vietnam,* p. 224.

15. Richard A. Falk, quoted in Lewy, *America in Vietnam*, p. 312.
16. Lewy, *America in Vietnam*, p. 317.
17. Quoted in Lewy, *America in Vietnam*, p. 227.
18. Geneva Convention Relative to the Protection of Civilian Persons in Time of War, 12 August 1949, in "Treaties Governing Land Warfare," Air Force pamphlet, 21 July 1958, p. 150, quoted in Lewy, *America in Vietnam*, p. 227.
19. International Committee of the Red Cross, *Draft Rules for the Limitation of Dangers Incurred by the Civilian Population in Time of War* (Geneva: 1956), article II, quoted in Lewy, *America in Vietnam*, p. 229.
20. Quoted in Lewy, *America in Vietnam*, p. 229.
21. Richard A. Falk, quoted in Lewy, *America in Vietnam*, p. 230.
22. Clergy and Laymen Concerned About Vietnam, quoted in Lewy, *America in Vietnam*, p. 230.
23. Geneva Convention, 12 August 1949, article 28, p. 145, quoted in Lewy, *America in Vietnam*, pp. 230–31.
24. Richard A. Falk, ed., *The Vietnam War and International Law* (Princeton: Princeton University Press, 1969), vol. II, p. 240, quoted in Lewy, *America in Vietnam*, pp. 271–72.
25. Gabriel Kolko, in Knoll and McFadden, *War Crimes and the American Conscience*, p. 99.
26. Hans J. Morgenthau, in Knoll and McFadden, *War Crimes and the American Conscience*, p. 15.
27. Geneva Convention, 12 August 1949, article 19, p. 141, quoted in Lewy, *America in Vietnam*, p. 231.
28. Quoted in Lewy, *America in Vietnam*, p. 232.
29. Paul H. Nitze, in W. Scott Thompson and Donaldson D. Frizzell, eds., *The Lessons of Vietnam* (New York: Crane, Russak & Co., 1977), p. 199.
30. Jonathan Schell, in Knoll and McFadden, *War Crimes and the American Conscience*, p. 68.
31. Daniel Ellsberg, in Knoll and McFadden, *War Crimes and the American Conscience*, p. 83.
32. Lewy, *America in Vietnam*, p. 301.
33. Ibid., p. 304.
34. Ibid., p. 448.
35. Ibid., p. 326.
36. Robert Jay Lifton, in Knoll and McFadden, *War Crimes and the American Conscience*, p. 104.
37. Edward M. Opton Jr., Nevitt Sanford, and Robert Duckles, in Knoll and McFadden, *War Crimes and the American Conscience*, pp. 113–14. [Italics in original]
38. Hans J. Morgenthau, in Knoll and McFadden, *War Crimes and the American Conscience*, p. 110.
39. Telford Taylor, *Nuremberg and Vietnam* (New York: Bantam Books, 1971), p. 139.
40. Daniel Ellsberg, in Knoll and McFadden, *War Crimes and the American Conscience*, p. 130.
41. Edward M. Opton Jr., Nevitt Sanford, and Robert Duckles, in Knoll and McFadden, *War Crimes and the American Conscience*, pp. 117–18. [Italics in original]
42. Robert Jay Lifton, in "Questions of Guilt," *Partisan Review,* Fall 1972.
43. Terry Nardin and Jerome Slater, "Vietnam Revisited?" *World Politics,* April 1981.
44. Michael Walzer, review of *America in Vietnam*, by Guenter Lewy, *New Republic,* 11 November 1978.
45. Theodore Draper, "Ghosts of Vietnam," *Dissent,* Winter 1979.
46. Walzer, review of *America in Vietnam*.
47. Draper "Ghosts of Vietnam" Walzer, review of *America in Vietnam*.
48. Quoted in Walzer, review of *America in Vietnam*.

49. Lewy, *America in Vietnam,* p. 269.
50. Walzer, review of *America in Vietnam.*
51. Nardin and Slater, "Vietnam Revisited," *World Politics,* April 1981.
52. Roger Hilsman, *To Move a Nation* (New York: Doubleday & Co., 1967), p. 444, quoted in Lewy, *America in Vietnam,* p. 303.
53. Barry Goldwater, quoted in Lewy, *America in Vietnam,* p. 303.
54. Daniel Ellsberg, in Knoll and McFadden, *War Crimes and the American Conscience,* p. 82.
55. Peter L. Berger, "Indochina and the American Conscience," *Commentary,* February 1980.
56. Lewy, *America in Vietnam,* p. 223.
57. Richard H. Rovere, in "Liberal Anti-Communism Revisited," *Commentary,* September 1967.
58. Richard H. Rovere, quoted in William Manchester, *American Caesar* (New York: Dell Publishing Co., 1979), p. 808.
59. Richard H. Rovere, in "Liberal Anti-Communism Revisited."
60. Jason Epstein, "The CIA and the Intellectuals," *New York Review of Books,* 20 April 1967.
61. Robert L. Heilbroner, "Counterrevolutionary America," *Commentary,* April 1967.
62. Berger, "Indochina and the American Conscience."
63. Tom Wicker, *New York Times,* 8 July 1979, quoted in Charles Horner, "America Five Years After Defeat," *Commentary,* April 1980.
64. Carl Gershman, "After the Dominoes Fell," *Commentary,* May 1978.
65. Nguyen Cong Hoan, Hearings before the Subcommittee on International Organizations of the House Committee on International Relations, 26 July 1977, pp. 145–67.
66. Truong Nhu Tang, "Vietnam, the Myth of a Liberation," unpublished ms., 1981.
67. Nguyen Cong Hoan, Hearings before the Subcommittee on International Organizations.
68. Doan Van Toai, "A Lament for Vietnam."
69. Jean Lacouture, interview with François Fejto, in *Il Giornale Nuovo* (Milan), quoted in Michael Ledeen, "Europe—The Good News and the Bad," *Commentary,* April 1979.
70. Jean Lacouture, quoted in Gershman, "After the Dominoes Fell."
71. Doan Van Toai, "A Lament for Vietnam."
72. Ibid.
73. Quoted in Doan Van Toai, "A Lament for Vietnam."
74. Doan Van Toai, "A Lament for Vietnam" Gershman, "After the Dominoes Fell."
75. Truong Nhu Tang, "Vietnam, the Myth of a Liberation."
76. *Foreign Report,* 16 July 1981.
77. To Huu, quoted in Doan Van Toai, "A Lament for Vietnam."
78. Doan Van Toai, "A Lament for Vietnam."
79. Gershman, "After the Dominoes Fell."
80. Quoted in Gershman, "After the Dominoes Fell."
81. Gershman, "After the Dominoes Fell."
82. Truong Nhu Tang, "Vietnam, the Myth of a Liberation."
83. Quoted in Gershman, "After the Dominoes Fell."
84. Gershman, "After the Dominoes Fell."
85. Berger, "Indochina and the American Conscience."
86. Quoted in Gershman, "After the Dominoes Fell."
87. Berger, "Indochina and the American Conscience."
88. Irving Howe and Michael Walzer, "Were We Wrong About Vietnam?" *New Republic,* 18 August 1979.
89. Stanley Hoffmann, "The Crime of Cambodia," *New York Review of Books,* 28 June 1979.

90. Peter W. Rodman, "Sideswipe," *American Spectator,* March 1981.
91. William Shawcross, "Shawcross Swipes Again," *American Spectator,* July 1981.
92. François Ponchaud, *Cambodia: Year Zero* (New York: Holt, Rinehart & Winston, 1978), p. 21, quoted in Rodman, "Sideswipe."
93. Shawcross, "Shawcross Swipes Again."
94. William Shawcross, *Sideshow* (New York: Pocket Books, 1979), p. 243.
95. Kenneth Quinn, quoted in Shawcross, "Shawcross Swipes Again."
96. Ponchaud, *Cambodia: Year Zero,* pp. xvi, 192, quoted in Rodman, "Sideswipe."
97. Rodman, "Sideswipe."
98. Hoffmann, "The Crime of Cambodia," *New York Review of Books,* 28 June 1979.
99. Anthony Lewis, *New York Times,* 17 March 1975, quoted in Rodman, "Sideswipe."
100. *New York Times,* 13 April 1975, quoted in Rodman, "Sideswipe."

KISSINGER RECONSIDERED

READING *YEARS OF UPHEAVAL,* the second volume of Henry Kissinger's memoirs, was for me a less overwhelming experience than reading its immediate predecessor, *White House Years.* But that was only because my astonishment at what Kissinger was capable of as a writer had already worn off by the time I had finished *White House Years* itself.

Kissinger in his disarming fashion likes to quote the reviewer of one of his early scholarly works who (allegedly) said: "I don't know if Dr. Kissinger is a great writer, but anyone who gets through this book is certainly a great reader." If the remark was ever in fact made, it was an exaggeration. Kissinger as a professor wrote in a serviceable academic style, which was no worse than the prose of most of his colleagues in the fields of political science and international affairs. On the other hand, he was certainly not as lively or as lucid a stylist as certain of his academic colleagues. Be that as it may, if memory serves, there was little if anything of a literary nature in his earlier work to prepare us for *White House Years.* We did, however, have *White House Years* to prepare us for *Years of Upheaval* which, although self-contained in the sense of being entirely intelligible on its own, is really a continuation (though not yet the completion) of the same book. When in due course the third and final volume comes out, we will have a single unit running to some four thousand densely printed pages. And it will be—it already is—one of the great works of our time.

I use the word "great" both reluctantly and advisedly: reluctantly, because I do not wish to contribute to the inflationary tendencies which have debauched the language of literary criticism as surely as they have the currency of monetary exchange; but advisedly, because in this case the epithet for once designates the true value being claimed.

There is also another reason to insist on the word "great" here, and that is the failure of so many who have written about these memoirs to give them their proper due. It is one thing to quarrel with Kissinger about his ideas and his policies; I will be doing just that myself. But it is quite another matter when no awareness is shown of the high intellectual distinction with which those ideas are explicated and the policies defended. And it is altogether scandalous when people who presumably care about books as much as they do about politics are unable to recognize or unwilling to acclaim a masterwork when they see one because they are blinded or moved by political bias. Yet with an occasional, and surprising, exception like Christopher Lehmann-Haupt and Stanley Hoffmann, the reviewers, first of *White House Years* and now of *Years of Upheaval,* have either been unremittingly hostile or grudging in their acknowledgment of what Kissinger has done here.

Admittedly the length of these volumes is a problem, if only because they demand more time than most of us nowadays are willing to give to a book. Yet as an editor who has been known to cut a manuscript now and again and to judge the briefer version an improvement, I would have found it very difficult to shorten either *White House Years* or *Years of Upheaval* without sacrificing something good. It is true that in order to make *Years of Upheaval* self-contained, Kissinger goes over a certain amount of territory already traversed in *White House Years.* But aside from such patches of repetition, these volumes are astonishingly free of either padding or gratuitous detail. One might well say of them what Dr. Johnson said of *Paradise Lost,* that "none ever wished it longer than it is," while at the same time recognizing that they are not too long for what they deliver.

This does not mean that every page is equally interesting. So much ground is covered, so many subjects are explored in such rich and sometimes technical detail, that inevitably every reader will come upon sections that seem arid or dull. But even those sections (for example, discussions of the debate over SALT, or some of the minute-by-minute accounts of Kissinger's negotiations with foreign governments) are necessary to the historical record. Moreover, they always reward careful attention and often turn out to be as fascinating as they appear forbidding. Indeed, not the least stunning of Kissinger's talents as a writer is his ability to do justice to the technical complexities of a subject like arms control while making those complexities clear to any lay reader who is willing to slow down a bit and invest a little extra intellectual effort.

The paradox is that Kissinger unwittingly discourages the reader from exerting himself on such occasions by making it so easy for him the rest of the time. Hard as it is to pick these volumes up (in addition to being so long and looking so forbidding, they weigh about five pounds each), it is harder still to put them down. A reader who approaches them as a duty will invariably be rewarded with a pleasure: a wonderful story told wonderfully well.

It is not, however, as might have been expected, the story of Kissinger's spectacular career. There is almost nothing of a personal nature here. From time to time he refers to his origins as a Jewish refugee from Germany, or his years as a Harvard professor and as an adviser to Nelson Rockefeller. He tells us, too, how he happened to be hired by Richard Nixon in 1968 as national security adviser, and he explains why Nixon later decided to appoint him secretary of state. But whereas Kissinger provides dozens of character sketches throughout these two volumes, the best of them breathtaking in their evocative power, and the least of them shrewd in their psychological insight, he shows no such gift for self-portraiture and no inclination toward the introspective. On the evidence of these memoirs, one would have to conclude that this man—who has become legendary for his arrogance and egomania—is, if anything, abnormally deficient in curiosity about himself. His interest in everyone and everything else in the world, by contrast, seems inexhaustible.

To convey some idea of how this combination of qualities works to control and color Kissinger's narrative style, let me take as a random example the account in *Years of Upheaval* of his first visit to Saudi Arabia in 1973, only two weeks after the oil embargo had been declared.

He begins here, as always, by setting the political context—in this instance Nixon's desperate desire to get the embargo lifted, not only for its own sake, but in order to demonstrate his mastery of foreign policy and hence buttress "his claim to continue in office" just at the point when "Watergate was winding its inexorable way through congressional and judicial procedures." Having spelled out the domestic political forces that influenced the workings of the episode, Kissinger then goes on to place it in its local setting by means of an analysis of Saudi Arabia in which history, geography, religion, and national psychology are interwoven and interrelated in a tour de force of compression and lucidity. Then comes a typical humorous description of his reception, accompanied by a disquisition on the cultural implications of the physical and architectural surroundings which are themselves presented with a vividness beyond the literary powers of a good many contemporary novelists:

> Faisal's palace was on a monumental scale. Preceded by two sword carriers, I was taken to a tremendous hall that seemed as large as a football field. Dozens of the distinguished men of the Kingdom

(women, of course, being strictly segregated) in identical black robes and white headdresses were seated along the walls, immobile and silent. There was incense in the air, circulated by the air conditioning. What seemed like a hundred yards away on a slightly raised pedestal sat King Faisal ibn Abd al-Aziz Al Sa'ud, aquiline of feature, regal of bearing. He rose as I entered, forcing all the princes and sheiks to follow suit in a flowing balletlike movement of black and white. He took one step toward me: I had to traverse the rest of the way. I learned later that his taking a step forward was a sign of great courtesy. At the time, I was above all conscious of the seeming eternity it took to reach the pedestal.

In one respect, this passage is untypical, since it leads straight into a rare reference to Kissinger's personal background ("His Majesty and I sat side by side for a few minutes overlooking the splendid assemblage while I reflected in some wonder what strange twists of fate had caused a refugee from Nazi persecution to wind up in Arabia as the representative of American democracy"). But we soon discover, what we might already have suspected, that the reference is not a gratuitous touch. It is there because it is essential to a full appreciation of the outlandish aspect of Kissinger's encounter with Faisal, who proceeds to tell him that

> Jews and Communists were working now in parallel, now together, to undermine the civilized world as we knew it. Oblivious to my ancestry—or delicately putting me into a special category—Faisal insisted that an end had to be put once and for all to the dual conspiracy of Jews and Communists. The Middle East outpost of that plot was the State of Israel, put there by Bolshevism for the principal purpose of dividing America from the Arabs.

Kissinger's comment on this outburst—the smile playing over the prose, the wit, the wry self-deprecation both concealing and revealing enormous self-confidence—is characteristic of the way he talks about himself throughout these memoirs:

> It was hard to know where to begin in answering such a line of reasoning. When Faisal went on to argue that the Jewish-Communist conspiracy was now trying to take over the American government, I decided the time had come to change the subject. I did so by asking

His Majesty about a picture on the far wall, which I took to be a decorative work of art. It was a holy oasis, I was informed—representational art being forbidden in Islam. This faux pas threw Faisal into some minutes of deep melancholy, causing conversation around the table to stop altogether. In the unearthly silence my colleagues must have wondered what I had done so quickly to impair the West's oil supplies. I did not help matters by referring to Sadat as the leader of the Arabs. His Majesty's morose reaction showed that there was a limit beyond which claims to Arab solidarity could not be pushed.

After a few more amusing details about the way this weird conversation was conducted, Kissinger, modulating smoothly into a serious key, composes a little essay on the mind and character of King Faisal so thoroughly informed by sympathetic imagination that it even manages to make a kind of sense out of the speech on Communism and Zionism:

> However bizarre it sounded to Western visitors, [Faisal's speech] was clearly deeply felt. At the same time it reflected precisely the tactical necessities of the Kingdom. The strident anti-Communism helped reassure America and established a claim on protection against outside threats. . . . The virulent opposition to Zionism reassured radicals and the PLO and thus reduced their incentive to follow any temptation to undermine the monarchy domestically. And its thrust was vague enough to imply no precise consequences: it dictated few policy options save a general anti-Communism.

The section on this visit to Riyadh then moves toward its conclusion with a meticulous account of the negotiating sessions between Faisal and Kissinger, which, like the dozens of other such accounts scattered throughout these memoirs, gives a superlative picture of how diplomacy is actually conducted.

What we have here is writing of the very highest order. It is writing that is equally at ease in portraiture and abstract analysis; that can shape a narrative as skillfully as it can paint a scene; that can achieve marvels of compression while moving at an expansive and leisurely pace. It is writing that can shift without strain or falsity of tone from the gravitas befitting a book about great historical events to the humor and irony dictated by an unfailing sense of human proportion.

KISSINGER THE WRITER, then, has established a secure claim to greatness. But that is not the claim he is staking in these memoirs. What he wants, above all, is to explain and defend his achievements as a diplomat or (to use the word he himself generally prefers) a statesman. On this point, too, his memoirs are a surprise. For what they reveal is that if Kissinger did achieve greatness in this area, it was as a practitioner of the art of diplomacy and not as the "conceptualizer" he was always praised for being.

The reason this is surprising, of course, is that he was, after all, an intellectual rather than a professional diplomat. He had studied and taught and written about international affairs, but when he became Nixon's chief adviser on foreign policy in 1968 he had had very little practical experience in diplomacy or the conduct of high-level negotiations. During the Kennedy and Johnson administrations he had done a certain amount of consulting and he had participated on a relatively low level in one or two diplomatic missions. But that, so far as we can tell from the memoirs, was all.

Of McGeorge Bundy, who blazed the trail Kissinger was to follow from Harvard to the post of national security adviser, Arthur Schlesinger Jr., could say with typical Cambridge smugness: "I had seen him learn how to dominate the faculty of Harvard University, a throng of intelligent and temperamental men; after that training, one could hardly doubt his capacity to deal with Washington bureaucrats." But unlike Bundy, who had been a dean, Kissinger had only been a professor. Hence he had not even had a chance to learn the game of power in the interdepartmental conflicts of the academic jungle before graduating into the real jungles of international conflict where the stakes are so much higher and the talents required to play are of an entirely different order.

Because Kissinger is so incurious—or perhaps only reticent—about himself, we learn nothing from these memoirs that would help us understand how this intellectual, this professor, with no practical diplomatic experience to speak of, could with perfect assurance and a poise that would normally require many years of training to develop, leap overnight and in one bound into the topmost reaches of international statesmanship. There is nothing here to explain how this naturalized American, still speaking with a heavy German accent and (presumably) still carrying the burdens of uncertainty and inner doubt that afflict all refugees and to which even native-born American Jews of Kissinger's generation have so often been prey, could, again overnight, begin dealing on equal terms with all the major figures of the age.

As in the passage quoted above about his first meeting with King Faisal of Saudi Arabia, Kissinger is fond of poking gentle fun at himself for the gaucheries and faux pas he always seems to be committing on his breathless and bewildering diplomatic rounds from one country to another, each with its own manners and mores and hence with its own innumerable opportunities for getting things wrong. In one place he talks out of turn; in another he fails to follow the right procedure in reviewing the troops who have come to honor him; in a third he elicits a pained response for his American obtuseness in missing a subtle signal during the course of a negotiation. But it goes without saying that this easy willingness to tell funny stories at his own expense is the surest mark of a supreme self-confidence.

And indeed, far from being thrown by the requirements of his job as the official envoy of the United States of America and the main shaper of its relations with the rest of the world, he demonstrates a mastery that is all but incredible. In the same month, or the same week, or even on the same day, he will turn his attention to the technicalities of the SALT negotiations, the intricacies of the Arab-Israeli conflict, the problems of the Atlantic Alliance, and the niceties of the developing relationship with China. When he is traveling, especially during the "shuttle diplomacy" that he conducted in 1973 after the Yom Kippur war between Israel and Egypt, and then Israel and Syria, he maintains an alert sense of the issues and the personalities he is dealing with, while simultaneously supervising all the other business of his office.

Sleepless, racked by jet lag, assailed by a multitude of crises, he never seems to tire to the point of losing his edge or growing impatient with the nuances that are—so he repeatedly tells us—the lifeblood of diplomacy. He always seems to know where he is, he always seems to keep a fascinated and wary eye on his interlocutor, he is rarely at a loss for the humorous quip or the soothing remark or the daring proposal when an opening suddenly presents itself. When he meets with someone like Mao Zedong, whom he regards as a titanic historical figure, he can be awed without being overawed. But he is equally capable of taking the proper measure of a lesser personage like Assad of Syria without the condescension that is the surest path to stupidity in a diplomat. A believer in the centrality of power, he nevertheless has a judicious respect for even the least powerful of nations and the sensitivity of an anthropologist to the distinctive features and beauties of even the least imposing of cultures. No wonder he won the answering admiration and affection of so many of the leaders he dealt with, including many who counted themselves enemies of the United States.

If Kissinger ever suffered any anxiety in becoming national security adviser and then secretary of state, or in performing the duties of those offices, it is not recorded in these memoirs. Being (as he would perhaps be willing to admit) human, he cannot be an absolute stranger to anxiety. But as a statesman he was at ease only as a man could be who had found the job that he was clearly born to do.

In this respect, the contrast between Kissinger and Nixon could not have been sharper or more poignant. In one of the most extraordinary passages of these memoirs—it comes toward the end of *Years of Upheaval*—Kissinger describes an automobile trip he took with Nixon and his friend Bebe Rebozo in California during the summer of 1970. What Nixon wanted was to show Kissinger and Rebozo the house where he was born and the town in which he grew up. After pointing out various landmarks of his childhood and his youth, "Nixon suddenly conceived the idea that Rebozo and I should see not only his origin but how far he had come." Accordingly he directed his driver to the place he had lived for two years after losing the presidential election of 1960 and where he had regained his sense of balance. But astonishingly, he was unable to locate it. Thus the president of the United States and his national security adviser spent well over an hour searching "every canyon and the streets leading off them" in the vicinity of the Beverly Hills Hotel, without ever finding the house they were looking for.

Rightly seeing in this episode an allegory of Nixon's life, Kissinger comments: "He was at ease with his youth; he could recount his struggles; he could not find the locus of his achievements. . . . On his way to success he had traveled on many roads, but he had found no place to stand, no haven, no solace, no inner peace. He never learned where his home was."

Henry Kissinger had traveled on many roads, too, but unlike Nixon he did find a home. Quoting Archimedes ("Give me a place to stand and I shall move the earth"), Kissinger remarks that "Nixon sought to move the world but he lacked a firm foothold." Yet Kissinger obviously discovered a firm foothold in the very place that failed to provide one for the poor boy from Whittier who had put him there. Even in the White House Richard Nixon, the man who "lacked a firm foothold," remained "slightly out of focus." For he "had set himself a goal beyond human capacity: to make himself over entirely; to create a new personality as if alone of all mankind he could overcome his destiny." Not Kissinger. Though he does not say so himself, but as we know from the simple fact that this enormously ambitious man trying to make his way in circles not particularly hospitable to foreigners never even bothered to get rid of his accent, Kissinger was guilty of no such "presumption." Therefore he did not pay "the fearful price" he believes the gods exacted of Nixon: "the price of congenital insecurity." And thus it was that the refugee from Fürth, Germany, unlike the refugee from Whittier, California, found a home in Washington, and a firm foothold, and the sharpest possible focus for his talents and his energies, which then proceeded to pour forth in prodigious torrents of virtuoso activity.

Whether he moved the earth is, however, another question. What he attempted to do, always working with and often (it is important to remember) under the direction of Nixon, was to build a new "structure of peace" in the world. This involved, first, arranging for an "honorable" American withdrawal from Vietnam; second, establishing a new relationship with the Soviet Union to be known as détente and to be based on negotiation rather than confrontation; and third, inaugurating an American relationship with Communist China. All this was to be accomplished, moreover, within the context of a diminishing American presence in the world. Indeed, it was precisely because domestic support for American intervention abroad had been eroded by Vietnam that substitutes had to be found to prevent the balance of power, on which Kissinger and Nixon believed that peace depended, from tilting dangerously toward the Soviet Union.

In presiding over what was in effect a strategic retreat, Nixon and Kissinger were trying to make certain above all else that the retreat would not turn—as retreats are always in danger of doing—into a wholesale rout. This consideration in itself precluded a precipitous withdrawal from Vietnam. We had to leave in such a way as to give South Vietnam a fighting chance to save itself from conquest by the Communist North, thus vindicating the purpose of our own intervention and demonstrating the reliability of American commitments.

At the same time, we had to find a way to restrain Soviet expansionism that did not depend entirely or even largely on the use or the threatened use of American military power. This new strategy, as Nixon and Kissinger conceived it, was composed of two tactical strands. The first and more important was to offer incentives (mainly consisting of economic benefits) for Soviet moderation and restraint, and to threaten penalties (mainly consisting of the withdrawal of those benefits) for aggressive or adventurist activity. This, in essence, was what détente meant. Although the rhetoric in which Nixon and Kissinger and their supporters talked about it was usually more grandiose, détente was at bottom an effort to compensate for the loss of American military power (the will to use it as well as the relative edge in hardware) with a more purposeful deployment of economic power. In this scheme, the function of arms control was to keep the military balance stable, both for its own sake and because reducing the influence of the military factor would make the economic factor more effective.

The second tactical strand of the new strategy for containing the Soviet Union at a time of diminishing American power and will was the so-called Nixon Doctrine. This entailed finding regional allies or surrogates who would assume the responsibility for deterring Soviet expansionist moves and, if necessary, resisting them by force. The United States would supply arms for this purpose, but such regional surrogates as Iran under the Shah would do the rest. The opening to China, whatever else it may have been intended to accomplish—and there were undoubtedly many reasons for the move—has to be understood in the first instance as a product of the Nixon Doctrine. For China, too, was to be built up as yet another restraint on Soviet expansionism. No one, certainly not Kissinger, was so foolish as to think of the Chinese as an American surrogate. But playing the China card was undoubtedly part of the overall strategy of finding substitutes for the formerly all but exclusive reliance on American military power to contain the Soviet Union in Asia and indeed everywhere else in the world.

It was, no doubt about it, a brilliant strategic conception, each element consistent with every other and all together blending into an organic whole. That it corresponded with Nixon's instincts and impulses we can be certain, and there is no way of knowing where exactly, in the collaboration between them, Nixon left off and Kissinger began. In general (so Kissinger tells us) Nixon, in effect, saw what had to be done and gave the orders to do it; the details of the execution were left to others—and where foreign policy was concerned, others meant Henry Kissinger.

This is not to suggest that the strategy was all Nixon and the tactics all Kissinger. For it was Kissinger who, at first under the pseudonym "a high official" and later openly in his own voice, took over the job of explaining and articulating the administration's policy—in press briefings, in interviews with influential columnists like James Reston, and in private conversations both with journalists and with congressmen. Thus, the exquisite balance and symmetry in the design of the overall strategy must surely have owed at least as much, and more, to Kissinger the intellectual, the "conceptualizer," as to Nixon the politician.

Whatever the share of responsibility—credit *or* blame—to be assigned to Kissinger, however, one might say of this strategy what Edmund Burke said of Lord North's treatment of the American colonies: "This fine-spun scheme had the usual fate of all exquisite policy." Brilliant though it was in achieving perfect internal coherence, it failed because it misjudged the nature of the Soviet threat on the one side and the nature of American public opinion on the other.

That men like Kissinger and Nixon should have misjudged the nature of the Soviet threat is on the face of it hard to believe. Neither one of them was in the least subject to sentimental illusions about the Soviet Union; neither had any sympathy for the Soviets or any admiration for their leaders. Whereas Kissinger writes about Mao Zedong and Zhou Enlai with a respect bordering on and occasionally crossing over into reverence, he is sardonic about Brezhnev and Gromyko. Nor did Kissinger or Nixon ever doubt that the Soviet Union had expansionist aims or that it was capable of great ruthlessness in the pursuit of those aims.

At the same time, however, while Kissinger here, and Nixon in his own writings, always make their obeisances to the role of ideology in determining Soviet behavior on the international scene, for the most part they saw the Soviet Union as a nation-state like any other, motivated by the same range of interests that define and shape the foreign policies of all nation-states. From this perspective—the perspective of realpolitik—Communist Russia was not all that different from Czarist Russia, the facts of geography, history, and ancestral culture being far more decisive than the ideas of Marx and Lenin.

If this were indeed the case, it would certainly be possible to make a deal of the kind contemplated by the policy of détente. If, in other words, the aims of the Soviet Union were limited, they could be respected and even to a certain extent satisfied through negotiation and compromise, with the resultant settlement policed by means other than, and short of, actual military force.

But what if the Soviet Union is not a "normal" nation-state? What if in this case ideology overrides interest in the traditional sense? What if Soviet aims are unlimited? In short (and to bring up the by-now familiar contending comparisons), what if the Soviet Union bears a closer resemblance to the Germany of Hitler than to the Germany of Kaiser Wilhelm? Wilhelmine Germany was an expansionist power seeking a place in the imperial sun and nothing more than that. Hitler, by contrast, was a revolutionary seeking to overturn the going international system and to replace it with a new order dominated by Germany (which also meant the political culture of Nazism). For tactical reasons and in order to mislead,

Hitler sometimes pretended that all he wanted was the satisfaction of specific grievances, and those who were taken in by this pretense not unreasonably thought they could "do business" with him. But there was no way of doing business—that is, negotiating a peaceful settlement—with Hitler. As a revolutionary with unlimited aims, he offered only two choices: resistance or submission.

All the evidence suggests that the Soviet Union poses the same kind of threat, and the same narrow range of choices, to the West. It has committed itself by word and deed to the creation of a "socialist" world. There is no reason to think that it can be talked out of this commitment or even (as, at bottom, détente assumes) bribed out of it. It may well be, as we are often told, that the Soviet leaders no longer believe subjectively in Communism. But whatever they say to themselves in the privacy of their own minds, they are (to borrow from their own vocabulary) *objectively* the prisoners of Marxian and Leninist doctrines. Without these doctrines, which mandate steady international advances in the cause of "socialism," they have no way to legitimize their monopoly of power within the Soviet Union itself. Hence, even if they wanted to limit their aims and become a "status-quo power," they would be unable to do so without committing political suicide.

What this means is that the conflict between the Soviet Union and the West is not subject to resolution by the traditional tools of diplomacy. Or, to put the point another way, given the nature of the Soviet threat, détente is not possible. Certain agreements may be possible from time to time, but they will invariably cover ground (cultural exchanges, arrangements for travel and communications, and the like) that is peripheral or even trivial from the point of view of the central issue. Where really important ground is touched upon, the agreement will invariably result in a Soviet advantage.

This is not because the Soviets are necessarily better at negotiating than we are or because they will necessarily cheat. They may or may not be better and they may or may not cheat. It is, rather, because in any negotiation between a party with limited aims and a party with unlimited aims, the party with limited aims is bound to lose in the very nature of things. Even a deal that on the surface promises mutual benefits will work out to the advantage of the side pursuing a strategy of victory over the side pursuing a strategy of accommodation and peace.

Thus, for example—as Kissinger himself has had the honesty and the courage to admit—the expanded commercial relations that were supposed to encourage Soviet restraint did not prevent the invasion of Afghanistan or the repression of Solidarity in Poland (not to mention such earlier Soviet moves as the dispatch of Cuban proxies to Angola). But economic "linkages" did work to restrain the American response on each of these occasions and to paralyze the Europeans altogether.

The case of arms control is perhaps less obvious but it is no less telling. What have the SALT negotiations accomplished? SALT I, which Kissinger defends with his customary brilliance (but with uncustomary heat), may well have been the best agreement possible at the time. Nevertheless, whereas it did nothing to limit the buildup of Soviet strategic arms, it did contribute to the slowing down of the American buildup.

Again, this was not because the Soviets cheated (though they may have, just as a roulette wheel may be fixed though the house wins even when it is honest). It was because, as the history of disarmament agreements in this century should have taught everyone, such agreements result in disarming only the party that wants to disarm and not the party that has no intention of doing so. That is what happened after the naval agreements of the 1920s and 1930s, when the United States, the British, and the French did not even build up to their legal limits while the Japanese and then the Germans not only did so but invented ways of exceeding their quotas while remaining within the letter of the law. And it is exactly what happened after SALT I, a period in which the Soviet buildup continued on its relentless course in both quantity and quality while the United States was either standing still or actually cutting back.

Kissinger frequently argues that a tough policy toward the Soviet Union can only enlist the support of public opinion in the United States (and in the West generally) if it is accompanied by a strategy for peace. People, that is, must be convinced that their leaders are doing everything possible to resolve the conflict by peaceful means before they will vote for the increases in defense spending, and before they will back the firm stands against Soviet expansionism, that Kissinger himself has consistently favored as the indispensable foundation of American influence and as a necessary element even of a successful policy of détente.

But the historical record suggests the opposite. In relation first to Nazi Germany and then to Soviet Russia, Western public opinion was lulled by negotiated agreements and was only galvanized at those moments when the nature of the enemy revealed itself unambiguously in action.

Where Hitler was concerned, for example, it was not until the invasion of Poland that the British public finally awoke from the dream of Munich—that great monument to the illusion that Nazi Germany was a state like any other with limited and hence negotiable ambitions. In the case of the Soviet Union, this illusion comes and goes. It was blasted for the first time after the Czechoslovak coup of 1948, only to rise again during the period of de-Stalinization of the fifties until it was blasted by the invasion of Hungary in 1956, only to rise again during the "thaw" of the sixties until it was blasted by the invasion of Czechoslovakia in 1968, only to rise again in the time of détente until it was blasted by the invasion of Afghanistan in 1979.

The trouble is that each time the illusion returns, it seems to grow stronger, fed by fear as the Soviet military arsenal also grows stronger. Now that it is rising again, it is indeed stronger than ever, forming the basis of the most explosive outburst of support for unilateral disarmament yet to erupt in Western Europe, and of an antinuclear hysteria in the United States that is well on its way to becoming a more respectable cover for isolationism than any of the other disguises isolationism has recently assumed.

THE MISREADING OF the nature of American public opinion that underlay détente was thus symbiotically connected to the misreading of the nature of the Soviet Union itself. The American people for better or worse have always been and still are very reluctant to support large standing armies, let alone to use them in combat, merely for geopolitical reasons. In the absence of some higher meaning, the idealistic Wilsonian strain in the American character is likely to be overwhelmed by the ever-present isolationist temptation. Therefore, as I once put it, "by representing the Soviet Union as a competing superpower with whom we could negotiate peaceful and stable accommodations—instead of a Communist state hostile in its very nature to us and trying to extend its rule and its political culture over a wider and wider area of the world—the Nixon, Ford, and Carter administrations robbed the Soviet-American conflict of the moral and political dimensions for the sake of which sacrifices could be intelligibly demanded by the government and willingly made by the people."

In *Years of Upheaval* Kissinger calls this "the subtlest critique" of détente, but the generosity of his characterization does not imply agreement. "The argument that the American people cannot understand a complex challenge and a complex strategy to meet it," he writes, "that unable to handle both deterrence and coexistence it must base its policy on truculence, reflects a lack of faith in democracy."

Having so often been accused—though never by me—of lacking faith in democracy, Kissinger must have taken a special pleasure in thus turning the tables on some of his critics. But the issue here is not democracy; it is, rather, the nature of the American character. Kissinger, who is so good at delineating national character when he talks about other peoples, and whose mastery in practicing the art of diplomacy is so intimately tied to his respect for the limitations and possibilities flowing out of the national character of his opposite numbers, somehow refuses to see that the people of his own country, no less than the Chinese or the Israelis or the Vietnamese, are shaped by the facts of geography, history, religion, and culture and are therefore capable of certain things and not of others. He knows that it is foolish to demand of other nations what the facts of their situation make it impossible for them to give. But he seems not to know that this is equally true of the United States.

Given the nature of the American national character, a very high price had to be paid for the achievement of which Kissinger is perhaps most proud and for which the Nixon administration has been universally applauded—the opening to China. The strategic purpose of striking a de facto alliance with Communist China was to enlist its help in containing Soviet imperialism. But the question arose then, and continues to bedevil us today, of whether a China allied to the United States contributes any more to the containment of the Soviet Union than a China treated with benign neglect. After all, the number of Soviet divisions pinned down on the Chinese border before Kissinger went to Beijing has not increased.

On the other hand, by befriending one of the two great Communist colossi, we have made it harder to explain to ourselves what the struggle with the other is all about. In this way, too, the Soviet-American conflict has been robbed of the moral and political significance without which the dangers and the sacrifices it involves begin to seem pointless. People then begin to wonder why, if we can support Communist China, we should put ourselves at risk to resist Communist Russia. Why not let the Russians work their will in the Persian Gulf, or for that matter in Western Europe? Or, if the only objection to the establishment of Communist regimes in countries like Nicaragua and El Salvador is that they are tied to the Soviet Union, why not woo them away?

Indeed, underlying much discussion of these matters in the United States nowadays is the idea, rarely made explicit, but present in the logic of particular proposals, that the safest course for us is to help sponsor a world of Communist regimes which are independent of the Soviet Union. Instead of making the world safe for democracy, we are urged to make it safe for Titoism.

To the extent that the opening to China was part of the Nixon Doctrine, then, one can say that this component of the new strategy—a strategy, to repeat, aimed at finding substitutes for American military power at a time when that power was in relative decline and when the will to serve as "policeman of the world" was declining even further—rested on the same misjudgment of the American national character as did the détente policy, which represented the other major component of the overall strategy.

Of course the Nixon Doctrine cannot yet be said to have failed the test of China. But it can most definitely be said to have failed the two other tests it has undergone. The first was in Vietnam, when, after the withdrawal of American troops, the United States Congress doomed the South Vietnamese to defeat at the hands of the Communist forces by cutting off military aid even in the midst of an invasion by the North Vietnamese army. The second was in Iran, when we either would not or could not (it makes no practical difference) save the government on which the Nixon Doctrine depended in that region from being overthrown by forces hostile to the United States.

When Vietnam was abandoned, Kissinger was still in office, but his protests and pleas fell on deaf congressional ears; by the time the Shah was abandoned, Kissinger was a private citizen, and his protests were a fortiori of no avail. He blames Watergate, but there are reasons to believe that even without Watergate American public opinion would have opposed continued involvement in Vietnam after the withdrawal of our troops. The case of Iran is harder to judge, but even there one wonders whether American public opinion under any president (even a Nixon undamaged by Watergate) would have countenanced the bloodletting that would have been necessary to keep the Shah in power once the revolutionary mobs had hit the streets.

In short, as a "conceptualizer" Kissinger was very brilliant but for the most part wrong. The "structure of peace" he envisioned was an illusion, based on a misconception of what was possible in the real world. Since such misconceptions are common to intellectuals—who are always in danger of getting carried away by ideas—it is tempting to blame the intellectual in Kissinger for his errors as a statesman. But if he (rather than circumstances like Watergate) is to be blamed at all, it is paradoxically the diplomat rather than the intellectual in him at whom the accusing finger should be pointed.

Kissinger was so good at diplomacy, so great a virtuoso in the negotiating arts, that he may well have come to imagine that he could negotiate *anything;* and this may have led him into the mistake (which the intellectual in him could reinforce with dazzling rationalizations) of trying to negotiate the nonnegotiable. Throughout these volumes, whenever a stalemated negotiation is being described, the vision of the *breakthrough* shimmers in the distance, and when it comes, the sense of achievement is so great and so vividly conveyed that the reader not only shares in it but is in danger of joining Kissinger in forgetting for the moment that in at least two major cases it ultimately turned out to be a mirage. The Paris accords that seemed to end the Vietnam War are one such case of a "breakthrough" in a conflict that could not be settled by compromise or accommodation; the 1972 agreement with the Soviet Union on the Basic Principles of Détente was another.

There is one more great conflict in the world, to which, as it happens, more space is devoted in *Years of Upheaval* than to any other: the Arab-Israeli conflict. Is it also nonnegotiable? Certainly the essential feature of the nonnegotiable conflict is there. One side seeks victory, in this instance meaning not merely the conquest or the domination but the total destruction of the other side, which for its part seeks peaceful coexistence and accommodation. For many years the Arabs were entirely open about the unlimited character of their ambitions with respect to Israel. Nasser proclaimed that he wanted to drive the Jews of Israel into the sea, and the Arab world as a whole was united in the famous three "No's" proclaimed at Khartoum in 1967: No recognition, No negotiation, No peace. So long as this "rejectionist" position held, not even the most talented negotiator— not even Henry Kissinger—could see any chance of real motion toward a settlement. But with the rise of Sadat, and with his decision to inch his way toward a new and therefore potentially negotiable position, possibilities opened up that had not been there before; and at this point even a less perceptive diplomat than Henry Kissinger might have seen the faint glimmerings of a breakthrough at the end of a very long tunnel. Kissinger is frank to admit that he was a little slow in taking the full measure of Sadat, but once he did, there was no stopping him in pursuit of this most prized (because most elusive) breakthrough of all.

It was said at the time, and can still be maintained, that Egypt was egged on to attack Israel in 1973 by the Soviets (who thereby violated the provision in the Basic Principles of Détente calling on the two superpowers to exercise a restraining influence on third parties lest they themselves be drawn directly into the conflict). Kissinger, however, did not and does not see it that way. What he came to believe was that Sadat had launched the

Yom Kippur War, not because of the Soviets, and not in order to destroy Israel, but to establish the psychological precondition for making peace with Israel: the restoration of Egyptian honor. This meant that Egypt must not be subjected to a humiliating military defeat. Thus, while the United States was making certain through the supply of equipment that Israel would not be defeated by a Soviet-armed opponent, and while Nixon and Kissinger were deterring a direct Soviet intervention by putting U.S. forces on alert, their policy simultaneously required that Israel be denied a decisive victory.

The policy, in effect, was to contrive a virtual draw. This would leave Egypt feeling that its honor had been restored and would therefore make dealing with the Israelis psychologically possible; it would leave the Israelis indebted to the United States for saving them from being overwhelmed; it would therefore leave the United States (as Sadat often put it) with "99 percent of the cards," and would also result in a severe diminution of Soviet power in the Middle East. For an inconclusive end to the war would demonstrate that, while the United States would not permit the Arabs to win a military victory over Israel (the only kind of victory the Soviet connection could promise), only American diplomacy could help the Arabs recover territory that they had lost to the Israelis on the battlefield.

The outlines of this overall design were sufficiently clear even while the Yom Kippur War was still going on. They were discerned, for example, by such observers as Walter Laqueur and Edward N. Luttwak who, writing in collaboration, accused Kissinger of dragging his feet in resupplying the Israelis with vital military equipment in order to make the scheme work. Others, including Kissinger himself, blamed the second echelon of the Defense Department for this delay, and I must say that my original belief in the Laqueur-Luttwak interpretation has been shaken by his account of the episode in *Years of Upheaval.*

In any event, the Yom Kippur War *was* concluded in the way the new strategy required: in the end the Israelis were saved by a heroic American resupply effort; Egyptian honor was preserved by American pressure on Israel to spare the encircled Third Army; the Soviets were squeezed out of the ensuing diplomatic play; and the United States, in the person of Henry Kissinger, became the central actor in the Middle East. The military disengagement between Israel and Egypt that Kissinger negotiated in the course of the first example of "shuttle diplomacy" the world had ever seen led ultimately to the signing of a separate peace between the two parties: a stunning breakthrough indeed which, although not arranged directly by

Kissinger himself (he was out of office by then), must be considered the direct progeny of his original achievement.

If the peace holds, Kissinger will have been vindicated; if, however, Egypt, having used American diplomacy to get what it could not win on the battlefield, should return (whether openly or covertly) to the rejection-ist fold, another example will have been added to the Paris agreements on Vietnam of the terrible dangers of contriving a negotiated settlement between a party that wants peace and a party that, although it may at certain moments pretend otherwise, wants only victory.

Whatever happens, however, Kissinger is surely right in saying, as he often does, that the statesman works in darkness, that he is always forced to make choices, not only without foreknowledge of the future, but usually even without adequate knowledge of what is going on in the present. One salient virtue of these memoirs is the sense Kissinger gives us of how the process works from day to day, from hour to hour, sometimes even from minute to minute. We are drawn in, we share in the anxieties and excitements of one crisis after another, we are in suspense while we read, even though we know what the outcome will be.

For myself, even when following Kissinger through the execution of a policy with which I disagree, I find it very hard to fault or blame him. What else could he have done? What better could *anyone* have done? That is the feeling I get as I read, and it is undoubtedly the feeling he wants us all to get. Yet valuable as these memoirs are, they would have been more valuable still if Kissinger—having evoked the circumstances in which he did what he did and having convinced us that there was probably no better alternative available at the time—had added the dimension of hindsight and commented, from the perspective of today, on where and how he nevertheless went wrong.

On the evidence of some of his recent statements, for example, he has changed his mind about détente, or at least certain features of détente (such as the effects of economic linkage), and about arms control (whether there is such a thing as strategic superiority and what can be done with it). But so busy is he here with the effort to explain and justify his earlier views that he scarcely does more than hint at the revisions time and experience have wrought in his thinking. Understandable though this is, it remains a pity. For as the foreign policy of the Reagan administration has revealed, we will never recover from some of the illusions of the past until we arrive as a nation at a franker and more realistic assessment than Kissinger provides here.

For example, in defending himself against those (myself included) who have pointed out that the fate of the Shah has demonstrated that the United States cannot safely rely on surrogates to defend its interests in the Persian Gulf, Kissinger asks what alternative there was to this policy at a time when neither Congress nor American public opinion would have sanctioned the stationing of American forces in the region. But the fact that there may have been no alternative under the circumstances prevailing at the time does not mean that the policy was sound. It may well have been the best we could do, but we now know that even the best turned out to be not good enough.

Perhaps it is too much to expect Kissinger himself, the most interested of all parties, to provide the disinterested critical assessment of the past we so desperately need. On the other hand, there is no one on the face of the earth from whom such a reassessment would come with greater authority.

In the meantime, and despite this deficiency, I think it is important, and especially for one like myself who was and remains opposed to the political strategy in whose defense these memoirs were written, to emphasize that they have already earned a place among the great books of their kind and among the great works of our time.

IF ORWELL WERE ALIVE TODAY

"DICKENS," GEORGE ORWELL once remarked, "is one of those writers who are well worth stealing," which was why so many different groups were eager to claim him as one of their own. Did Orwell foresee that someday he too would become just such a writer? Almost certainly he did not. In 1939, when he wrote those words about Dickens, he was still a relatively obscure figure, and, among those who knew his work at all, a highly controversial one. Only a year earlier, his book about the Spanish Civil War, *Homage to Catalonia,* had been rejected on political grounds by his own publishers in both Britain and the United States; and far from being claimed by contending factions as one of their own, he was closer to being excommunicated and excoriated by them all. Nevertheless, by the time of his death in 1950 at the age of forty-six, he had become so famous that his very name entered the language and has remained there in the form of the adjective "Orwellian." At first, this great status rested almost entirely on the tremendous success, both critical and commercial, of his two last novels, *Animal Farm* (1945) and *Nineteen Eighty-Four* (1949). Thanks to them, all his other books, including several early novels that were scarcely noticed at the time of their publication, as well as literary essays, book reviews, and even fugitive pieces of dated journalism, came back into print and are still easily available. As these earlier works became better known, they gradually enhanced Orwell's posthumous reputation. For example, the much-maligned *Homage to Catalonia* was pronounced "one of the important documents of our time" by Lionel Trilling when it was finally published in the United States after Orwell's death. And when in 1968 *The Collected Essays, Journalism and Letters of George Orwell* came out in four massive volumes, the occasion was seized upon by another American critic, Irving Howe, to proclaim Orwell not only "the best English essayist since Hazlitt, perhaps since Dr. Johnson," but also "the greatest moral force in English letters during the last several decades." Bernard Crick, one of Orwell's most recent British biographers, goes, if possible, even further, placing him with Thomas Hobbes and

Jonathan Swift as one of the three greatest political writers in the history of English literature (greater, in other words, than even Edmund Burke and John Stuart Mill).

This enormous reputation by itself would make Orwell "one of those writers who are well worth stealing." It is, after all, no small thing to have the greatest political writer of the age on one's side: it gives confidence, authority, and weight to one's own political views. Accordingly, a dispute has broken out over what Orwell's position actually was in his own lifetime, and what it might have been if he had survived to go on participating in the political debates that have raged since the day of his death.

Normally, to speculate on what a dead man might have said about events he never lived to see is a frivolous enterprise. There is no way of knowing whether and to what extent he would have changed his views in response to a changing world; and this is especially the case with a writer like Orwell, who underwent several major political transformations. On the other hand, the main issues that concerned Orwell throughout his career are still alive today, often in different form but often also in almost exactly the same form they took when he wrote about them. This is why so many of his apparently dated journalistic pieces remain relevant. Even though the particular circumstances with which they deal have long since been forgotten, the questions they raise are questions we are still asking today and still trying to answer.

If this is true of much of Orwell's fugitive journalism, it becomes even more strikingly evident when we consider some of his major works: *Animal Farm* and *Nineteen Eighty-Four* among his novels, and, among his discursive writings, *Down and Out in Paris and London* (1933), *The Road to Wigan Pier* (1937), and *Homage to Catalonia* (1938), not to mention many of the wonderful essays collected in *Inside the Whale* (1940), *Dickens, Dali and Others* (1946), and *Shooting an Elephant* (1950). So relevant do all these works seem today that to read through them is to be astonished, and a little depressed, at the degree to which we are still haunted by the ghosts of political wars past.

When Orwell wrote his essay on Dickens, the two main groups trying to "steal" Dickens were the Marxists and the Catholics. (That they could automatically be taken as equivalent to Left and Right is one interesting measure of how things have changed in the past forty years.) The two main groups contending over Orwell today are the socialists on the one side and, on the other, the disillusioned former socialists who have come to be known as neoconservatives. The socialists, of whom Crick is a leading representative, declare that Orwell was a "revolutionary" whose values can only be (as Crick puts it) "wilfully misunderstood . . . when he is claimed for the camp of the Cold War." For their part, the neoconservatives deny that Orwell was a revolutionary; they think of him instead as a major critic of revolutionism. And they do indeed claim him for "the camp of the Cold War" in the sense that they see in his work one of the great prophetic warnings against the threat of Soviet totalitarianism. Thus, the Committee for the Free World, an organization made up mainly of neoconservative intellectuals (and with which I am associated), publishes material under the imprint "Orwell Press" and in general regards Orwell as one of its guiding spirits.

As a writer, Orwell is most admired, and rightly so, for the simplicity and straightforwardness of his style. "Good prose," he said, "is like a window pane." He valued such prose for its own sake, on aesthetic grounds, but he also believed that in political discourse clarity was a protection against deceit: "In our time, political speech and writings are largely the defense of the indefensible. . . . Thus political language has to consist largely of euphemism, question-begging and sheer cloudy vagueness." Since Orwell wrote about politics in a language that not only avoided those vices but succeeded marvelously in the art of calling things by their proper names and confronting questions with plainness and precision, one might think that nothing would be easier than defining his point of view. The problem is, however, that he wrote so much and changed his mind so often—mostly on small issues but also on large ones—that plausible evidence can be found in his work for each of the two contending interpretations of where he stood.

As a very young man, Orwell was, by his own account, a "Tory anarchist." But at the age of thirty or thereabouts he converted to socialism and kept calling himself a socialist until the day he died. Crick therefore has no trouble in piling up quotations that support the socialist claim to possession of Orwell. He does, however, have a great deal of trouble in trying to explain away the side of Orwell that has given so much aid and comfort to antisocialists of all kinds. For, avowed socialist though he certainly was, Orwell was also a relentless critic of his fellow socialists from beginning to end.

Thus no sooner did he declare his allegiance to socialism than he began taking it upon himself to explain why so many decent people were put off by his new political faith. "One sometimes gets the impression," he wrote in *The Road to Wigan Pier,* "that the mere words 'Socialism' and 'Communism' draw towards them with magnetic force every fruit-juice drinker, nudist, sandal-wearer, sex-maniac, Quaker, 'Nature Cure' quack, pacifist and feminist in England." Shortly after delivering himself of this observation, and while he still regarded the Communists as comrades in the struggle for socialism, he went to fight against Franco in the Spanish Civil War. There he learned two things: that the Spanish Communists were more interested in furthering the aims of Soviet foreign policy than in making a socialist revolution at home, and that the left-wing press in England (and everywhere else) was full of lies about what was actually going on in Spain. For the next few years, much of his writing was devoted to attacks on the Stalinists and their fellow travelers, who, in those days of the "Popular Front," included almost everyone on the Left.

These attacks were written from what can loosely be described as a Trotskyist or revolutionary-socialist perspective based on, among other things, the proposition that England was hardly, if at all, better than Nazi Germany. But with the outbreak of World War II, a new Orwell was born—Orwell the English patriot. "My Country, Right or Left," he now declared in one of his most memorable phrases, and went on to excoriate the "anti-British" attitudes that had been so fashionable on the Left throughout the 1930s and to which he himself had temporarily subscribed.

Then, toward the end of the war, and with the defeat of fascist totalitarianism in sight, Orwell began brooding more and more on the possibility that Communist totalitarianism might turn out to be the inevitable wave of the future. In *Animal Farm,* written while the Soviet Union was still a wartime ally of the Western democracies, he produced a satire on the Russian Revolution so unsparing that it could be and usually was interpreted as a repudiation of all hopes for a benevolent socialist revolution. Like *Homage to Catalonia* before it, the manuscript was rejected as too anti-Soviet by the first few publishers to whom it was submitted. One of the publishers in this case was no less a personage than T. S. Eliot, whose own aggressive conservatism did not prevent him from doubting that Orwell's was "the right point of view from which to criticize the political situation at the present time."

Finally there was *Nineteen Eighty-Four,* which came out just at the height of the Cold War and very shortly before Orwell's death. In that novel, Orwell portrayed the England of the future as a totalitarian society ruled over by a Communistlike party in the name of "Ingsoc" ("newspeak" for English socialism). He later explicitly denied that in using this term he had intended to cast any aspersions on the British Labor party, of which he was a (highly critical) supporter, let alone that he was attacking socialism itself. Nevertheless, neither in *Animal Farm* nor in *Nineteen Eighty-Four* was there any trace of the idea that a socialist revolution could be accomplished without a betrayal of the ideals of liberty and equality to whose full realization socialism was in theory committed.

No wonder Crick has so much trouble staking the socialist claim to Orwell. No wonder, too, that other socialists of varying stripe like Isaac Deutscher and Raymond Williams have said that Orwell was not really one of them.

If Orwell was a great political writer—and I think he was, though I would not place him quite so high as Crick does—it is not because he was always right in his strictly political judgments. The plain truth is that he was more often wrong than right. For example, he predicted that the British Conservatives (the "Blimpocracy") would never go to war against Hitler; then, when they did, he refused to believe, and he doubted "whether many people under fifty believe[d] it either," that England could "win the war without passing through revolution."

In addition to making many mistaken political predictions, he was also capable of serious errors of political valuation, as when he joined briefly in the fashionable cry of the mid-1930s to the effect that there was no difference between fascism and liberalism. And even after correcting errors of this kind, he was capable of backsliding into such similar absurdities as saying that British rule in India was as bad as Hitler's rule in Europe, or that British policy toward Greece in 1945 was no different from "the Russian coercion of Poland."

Wrong though he so often was about particular events, however, Orwell in every stage of his political development was almost always right about one thing: the character and quality of the left-wing literary intellectuals among whom he lived and to whom he addressed himself as a political writer. More than anything else, the ethos of the left-wing literary intelligentsia was his true subject and the one that elicited his most brilliant work. Indeed, whatever ideas were fashionable on the Left at any given moment were precisely the ones he had the greatest compulsion to criticize. And the fact that he criticized them from within only added authority to the things he said—so much so that I wonder whether this was why he insisted on clinging so tenaciously to his identity as a man of the Left.

It is largely because of Orwell's relation to the left-wing intelligentsia that I believe he would have been a neoconservative if he were alive today. I would even suggest that he was a forerunner of neoconservatism in having been one of the first in a long line of originally left-wing intellectuals who have come to discover more saving political and moral wisdom in the instincts and mores of "ordinary" people than in the ideas and attitudes of the intelligentsia. "One has to belong to the intelligentsia to believe things like that," he wrote in 1945 after listing several egregious examples relating to the progress of World War II; "no ordinary man could be such a fool." This remark has become especially well known in recent years, but it is only one of many passages of similar import scattered throughout Orwell's writings.

Nor was it only on political issues that Orwell defended the "ordinary man" against the left-wing intelligentsia. Even in the mid-1930s, during his most radical period, he attacked Cyril Connolly's novel *The Rock Pool* for suggesting that "so-called artists who spend on sodomy what they have gained by sponging" were superior to "the polite and sheeplike Englishman." This, he said, "only amounts to a distaste for normal life and common decency," and he concluded by declaring: "The fact to which we have got to cling, as to a lifebelt, is that it *is* possible to be a normal decent person and yet to be fully alive."

This streak of populism, always strong in Orwell, became even more pronounced with the outbreak of World War II, when it took the form of a celebration of England and the English character. As a corollary to becoming a wholehearted patriot—and in coming to see patriotism as a great and positive force—Orwell lashed out more ferociously than ever at the British intelligentsia:

> . . . the really important fact about so many of the English intelligentsia [is] their severance from the common culture of the country. . . . England is perhaps the only great country whose intellectuals are ashamed of their own nationality. In left-wing circles it is always felt that there is something slightly disgraceful in being an Englishman and that it is a duty to snigger at every English institution. . . . All through the critical years many left-wingers were chipping away at English morale, trying to spread an outlook that was sometimes squashily pacifist, sometimes violently pro-Russian, but always anti-British. . . . If the English people suffered for several years a real weakening of morale, so that the Fascist nations judged that they were "decadent" and that it was safe to plunge into war, the intellectual sabotage from the Left was partly responsible.

Is it any wonder that the neoconservatives see Orwell as a guiding spirit when everything he says here has been echoed by them in talking about the American intellectuals of today? And when Orwell was charged with "intellectual-hunting" by a leading young pacifist named Alex Comfort (who, as though to confirm Orwell's diagnosis of the phenomenon of which Comfort was a typical specimen, would go on to greater heights of fame in later years as the author of *The Joy of Sex*), he replied in terms that have been echoed in similar arguments by the neoconservatives as well: "It is just because I do take the function of the intelligentsia seriously that I don't like the sneers, libels, parrot phrases and financially profitable back-scratching which flourish in our English literary world. . . ."

Another and related reason for thinking that Orwell would be a neoconservative if he were alive today lies in his attitude toward pacifism. For a very brief period in his youth Orwell flirted with pacifism, but nothing could have been more alien to his temperament and he soon broke off the affair. By 1938 he was writing (and in language that shows how far he was willing to go in speaking plainly, even when euphemism might better have served his own political position):

> If someone drops a bomb on your mother, go and drop two bombs on his mother. The only apparent alternatives are to smash dwelling houses to powder, blow out human entrails and burn holes in children with lumps of thermite, or be enslaved by people who are more ready to do these things than you are yourself; as yet no one has suggested a practical way out.

And again in 1940, when a British defeat seemed likely: "There is nothing for it but to die fighting, but one must above all die *fighting* and have the satisfaction of killing somebody else first."

Moved by such feelings, Orwell came to write about pacifism with an even fiercer edge of scorn and outrage than before. Later he would regret using the term "objectively pro-Fascist," but that is what he now accused the pacifists—or "Fascifists," as he called them—of being (for, "If you hamper the war effort of one side you automatically help that of the other"); he also attacked them for "intellectual cowardice" in refusing to admit that this was the inescapable logical implication of their position; and he said that they were hypocritical "for crying 'Peace!' behind a screen of guns." But in trying to imagine where Orwell would have stood if he were alive today, the key sentence in his attack on pacifism is this: "Insofar as it takes effect at all, pacifist propaganda can only be effective *against* those countries where a certain amount of freedom of speech is still permitted; in other words it is helpful to totalitarianism."

Everything I have just quoted was written at a time when Nazi Germany was the main totalitarian enemy. But here is what Orwell said about pacifism at the very moment when the defeat of Hitler was imminent and when the Soviet Union was about to replace Nazi Germany as the most powerful embodiment of totalitarianism in the world:

> Pacifist propaganda usually boils down to saying that one side is as bad as the other, but if one looks closely at the writings of the younger intellectual pacifists, one finds that they do not by any means express impartial disapproval but are directed almost entirely against Britain and the United States. Moreover they do not as a rule condemn violence as such, but only violence used in defense of the Western countries. The Russians, unlike the British, are not blamed for defending themselves by warlike means. . . .

The "real though unadmitted motive" behind such propaganda, Orwell concluded, was "hatred of Western democracy and admiration for totalitarianism."

It is hard to believe that the man who wrote those words in 1945 would have felt any sympathy for the various "objectively" pacifist antidefense movements of today, about which the very same words could be used without altering a single detail. I can even easily imagine that Orwell would have been still angrier, if he had lived, to see so many ideas that have been discredited, both by arguments like his own and by historical experience, once again achieving widespread acceptability. It goes without saying that he would have opposed the unilateral disarmament that became the official policy of the British Labor party under the leadership of his old journalistic colleague Michael Foot. He understood, after all, that "Despotic governments can stand 'moral force' till the cows come home; what they fear is physical force." But I think he would also have opposed such measures as the nuclear freeze and a unilateral Western pledge of no-first-use of nuclear weapons. Given the conception of totalitarianism he developed in *Animal Farm* and *Nineteen Eighty-Four* as a totally closed system in which lies become truth at the dictate of the party, the notion that a verifiable disarmament agreement could be negotiated with the Soviet Union would surely have struck him as yet another pacifist "illusion due to security, too much money and a simple ignorance of the way in which things actually happen."

As for no-first-use, Orwell surely would have seen this as a form of unilateral disarmament by the West (since it would make Soviet superiority in conventional military power decisive on the European front), as well as a euphemistic screen behind which the United States could withdraw from its commitment to the defense of Western Europe under the hypocritical pretext of reducing the risk of nuclear war.

Nor is it likely that Orwell would have been reconverted to pacifism by the fear of nuclear weapons. As a matter of fact, he thought that "the worst possibility of all" was that "the fear inspired by the atomic bomb and other weapons yet to come will be so great that everyone will refrain from using them." Such an indefinite Soviet-American stalemate, he predicted, would lead to precisely the nightmare he was later to envisage in *Nineteen Eighty-Four* ("the division of the world among two or three vast totalitarian empires unable to conquer one another and unable to be overthrown by an internal rebellion").

This does not mean that Orwell contemplated the possibility of a nuclear war with equanimity, or that he did not on other occasions say that it could mean the destruction of civilization. Nevertheless, in 1947, the very year in which the Cold War officially began, Orwell wrote: "I don't, God knows, want a war to break out, but if one were compelled to choose between Russia and America—and I suppose that is the choice one might have to make—I would always choose America." Later that same year, he made the point again: "It will not do to give the usual quibbling answer, 'I refuse to choose.' . . . We are no longer strong enough to stand alone, and . . . we shall be obliged, in the long run, to subordinate our policy to that of one Great Power or another."

The same essay contains another one of those uncanny passages we so often come upon in Orwell that could be applied to our situation today without altering a single detail:

> To be anti-American nowadays is to shout with the mob. Of course it is only a minor mob, but it is a vocal one. . . . I do not believe the mass of the people in this country are anti-American politically, and certainly they are not so culturally. But politico-literary intellectuals are not usually frightened of mass opinion. What they are frightened of is the prevailing opinion within their own group. At any given

moment there is always an orthodoxy, a parrot-cry which must be repeated, and in the more active section of the Left the orthodoxy of the moment is anti-Americanism. I believe part of the reason . . . is the idea that if we can cut our links with the United States we might succeed in staying neutral in the case of Russia and America going to war. How anyone can believe this, after looking at the map and remembering what happened to neutrals in the last war, I do not know.

So much for Orwell's attitude toward the neutralism that lies at the basis of what in Western Europe is called the "peace movement" today.

To understand the force and the courage of Orwell's forthright repudiation of the idea that there was no significant moral difference between the United States and the Soviet Union, we need only look at the essays by the disillusioned ex-Communists collected in *The God That Failed* which demonstrate that neither anti-Americanism nor neutralism was confined exclusively to the pro-Soviet Left. When Orwell said, "I particularly hate that trick of sucking up to the Left cliques by perpetually attacking America while relying on America to feed and protect us," he could easily have been referring to his friend Stephen Spender's remarks in *The God That Failed* that America "seems to offer no alternative to war, exploitation and destruction of the world's resources" and that, no less than the Soviet Union, the United States was a "force producing aggression, injustice, destruction of liberties, enormous evils." In any event, so far as Orwell was concerned, the people in the British Labor party who openly wanted "to appease Russia" were more honest: they at least understood "that the only big political questions in the world today are: for Russia-against Russia, for America-against America, for democracy-against democracy."

Despite Crick's sophistical protestations, then, there can be no doubt that Orwell did belong in "the camp of the Cold War" while he was still alive. Nor can there be much doubt that, if he were alive today, he would have felt a greater kinship with the neoconservatives who are calling for resistance to Soviet imperialism than with either the socialist supporters of détente or the coalition of neutralists and pacifists who dominate the "peace movement" in Europe and their neoisolationist allies in the United States.

For consider: Orwell's ruling passion was the fear and hatred of totalitarianism. Unlike so many on the Left today, who angrily deny that there is any difference between totalitarianism and authoritarianism, he was among the first to insist on the distinction. Totalitarianism, he said, was a new and higher stage in the history of despotism and tyranny—a system in which every area of life, not merely (as in authoritarian regimes) the political sphere, was subjected to the control of the state. Only in Nazi Germany and the Soviet Union had totalitarianism thus far established itself, and of the two the Soviet variety clearly seemed to Orwell to be the more dangerous.

Indeed, Orwell's loathing for Nazi Germany was mild by comparison with his feeling about the Soviet Union. He was sufficiently serious in his opposition to fascism to risk his life in struggling against it in Spain (where as a soldier he was very nearly killed by a bullet through the neck). Yet he showed surprisingly little awareness of how evil Nazism actually was. Not only did he never write anything like *Animal Farm* about the Nazi regime; there is scarcely a mention in all his writings of the death camps. (Two of his closest friends, Arthur Koestler and T. R. Fyvel, saw a relation between this curious "blind spot" about Nazism and his equally curious hostility to Zionism.)

When Orwell wrote about the dangers of totalitarianism, then, whether in his essays or in *Nineteen Eighty-Four,* it was mainly the Communist version he had in mind. To be sure, he followed no party line, not even his own, and he could always be relied on to contradict himself when the impulse seized him. At one moment he would denounce any move to establish good relations with the Russians, and at another moment he might insist on the necessity of such relations.

But these were transient political judgments of the kind that, as he himself ruefully acknowledged, were never his strongest suit. What he most cared about was resisting the spread of Soviet-style totalitarianism. Consequently, he "used a lot of ink" and did himself "a lot of harm by attacking the successive literary cliques" that had denied or tried to play down the brutal truth about the Soviet Union, to appease it, or otherwise to undermine the Western will to resist the spread of its power and influence.

If he were alive today, he would find the very ideas and attitudes against which he so fearlessly argued more influential than ever in left-wing centers of opinion (and not in them alone): that the freedoms of the West are relatively unimportant as compared with other values; that war is the greatest of all evils; that nothing is worth fighting or dying for; and that the Soviet Union is basically defensive and peaceful. It is impossible to imagine that he would have joined in parroting the latest expressions of this orthodoxy if he had lived to see it return in even fuller and more dangerous force.

I have no hesitation, therefore, in claiming Orwell for the neoconservative perspective on the East-West conflict. But I am a good deal more diffident in making the same claim on the issue of socialism. Like Orwell, most neoconservatives began their political lives as socialists; and most of them even followed the same course Orwell himself did from revolutionary to democratic socialism. Moreover, those neoconservatives who were old enough to be politically active in 1950, the year Orwell died, would still at that point have joined with him in calling themselves democratic socialists. About thirty years later, however, most of them had come around to the view expressed by the philosopher William Barrett in explaining why he had finally given up on his long and tenaciously held faith in "democratic socialism" (the telling quotation marks are Barrett's):

> How could we ever have believed that you could deprive human beings of the fundamental right to initiate and engage in their own economic activity without putting every other human right in jeopardy? And to pass from questions of rights to those of fact: everything we observe about the behavior of human beings in groups, everything we know about that behavior from history, should tell us that you cannot unite political and economic power in one center without opening the door to tyranny.

The question is: would Orwell, in the light of what has happened in the three decades since his death, have arrived eventually at a position similar to Barrett's? Crick is certain that he would not—that he would have remained a socialist, and a militant one. I am not so sure.

Orwell was never much of a Marxist and (beyond a generalized faith in "planning") he never showed much interest in the practical arrangements involved in the building of socialism. He was a socialist because he hated the class system and the great discrepancies of wealth that went with it. Yet he also feared that the establishment of socialism would mean the destruction of liberty. In an amazingly sympathetic review of F. A. Hayek's *The Road to Serfdom*, Orwell acknowledged that there was "a great deal of truth" in Hayek's thesis that "socialism inevitably leads to despotism," and that the collectivism entailed by socialism brings with it "concentration camps, leader worship, and war." The trouble is that capitalism, which "leads to dole queues, the scramble for markets, and war," is probably doomed. (It is indeed largely as a result of the failure of capitalism that the totalitarian world of *Nineteen Eighty-Four* comes into being.)

Suppose, however, that Orwell had lived to see this prediction about capitalism refuted by the success of the capitalist countries in creating enough wealth to provide the vast majority of their citizens not merely with the decent minimum of food and housing that Orwell believed only social-ism could deliver, but with a wide range of what to his rather Spartan tastes would have seemed unnecessary luxuries. Suppose further that he had lived to see all this accomplished—and with the year 1984 already in sight!—while "the freedom of the intellect," for whose future under socialism he increasingly trembled, was if anything being expanded. And suppose, on the other side, he had lived to see the wreckage through planning and centralization of one socialist economy after another, so that not even at the sacrifice of liberty could economic security be assured.

Suppose, in short, that he had lived to see the aims of what *he* meant by socialism realized to a very great extent under capitalism, and without either the concentration camps or the economic miseries that have been the invariable companions of socialism in practice. Would he still have gone on mouthing socialist pieties and shouting with the anticapitalist mob?

Perhaps. Nothing has been more difficult for intellectuals in this century than giving up on socialism, and it is possible that even Orwell, who so prided himself on his "power of facing unpleasant facts," would have been unwilling or unable to face what to most literary intellectuals is the most unpleasant fact of all: that the values of both liberty and equality fare better under capitalism than under socialism.

And yet I find it hard to believe that Orwell would have allowed an orthodoxy to blind him on this question, anymore than he allowed other "smelly little orthodoxies" to blind him to the truth about the particular issues involved in the struggle between totalitarianism and democracy: Spain, World War II, and Communism.

In Orwell's time, it was the left-wing intelligentsia that made it so difficult for these truths to prevail. And so it is, too, with the particular issues generated by the struggle between totalitarianism and democracy in our own time, which is why I am convinced that if Orwell were alive today, he would be taking his stand with the neoconservatives and against the Left.

AN OPEN LETTER TO MILAN KUNDERA

Dear Milan Kundera:

Several years ago, a copy of the bound galleys of your novel, *The Book of Laughter and Forgetting,* came into my office for review. As a magazine editor I get so many books every week in that form that unless I have a special reason I rarely do more than glance at their titles. In the case of *The Book of Laughter and Forgetting* I had no such special reason. By 1980 your name should have been more familiar to me, but in fact I had only a vague impression of you as an East European dissident*—so vague that, I am now ashamed to confess, I could not have said for certain which country you came from: Hungary? Yugoslavia? Czechoslovakia? Perhaps even Poland?

Nor was I particularly curious about you either as an individual or as a member of the class of "East" European dissident writers. This was not because I was or am unsympathetic to dissidents in Communist regimes or those living in exile in the West. On the contrary, as a passionate anti-Communist, I am all too sympathetic—at least for their own good as writers.

"How many books about the horrors of life under Communism am I supposed to read? How many ought I to read?" asks William F. Buckley Jr., another member of the radically diminished fraternity of unregenerate anti-Communists in the American intellectual world. Like Buckley, I felt that there were a good many people who still needed to learn about "the horrors of life under Communism," but that I was not one of them. Pleased though I was to see books by dissidents from behind the Iron Curtain published and disseminated, I resisted reading any more of them myself.

What then induced me to begin reading *The Book of Laughter and Forgetting?* I have no idea. Knowing your work as well as I do now, I can

---

*Since then you have taught me that the term East Europe is wrong because the countries in question belong to the West and that we should speak instead of Central Europe. But in 1980 I did not yet understand this.

almost visualize myself as a character in a Kundera novel, standing in front of the cabinet in my office where review copies of new books are kept, suddenly being seized by one of them while you, the author, break into the picture to search speculatively for the cause. But whatever answer you might come up with, I have none. I simply do not know why I should have been drawn against so much resistance to *The Book of Laughter and Forgetting*. What I do know is that once I had begun reading it, I was transfixed.

Twenty-five years ago, as a young literary critic, I was sent an advance copy of a book of poems called *Life Studies*. It was by Robert Lowell, a poet already famous and much honored in America, but whose earlier work had generally left me cold. I therefore opened *Life Studies* with no great expectation of pleasure, but what I found there was more than pleasure. Reading it, I told Lowell in a note thanking him for the book, made me remember, as no other new volume of verse had for a long time, why I had become interested in poetry in the first place. That is exactly what *The Book of Laughter and Forgetting* did for my old love of the novel—a love grown cold and stale and dutiful.

During my years as a literary critic, I specialized in contemporary fiction, and one of the reasons I eventually gave up on the regular practice of criticism was that the novels I was reading seemed to me less and less worth writing about. They might be more or less interesting, more or less amusing, but mostly they told me more about their authors, and less about life or the world, than I wanted or needed to know. Once upon a time the novel (as its English name suggests) had been a bringer of news; or (to put it in the terms you yourself use in your essay "The Novel and Europe") its mission had been to "uncover a hitherto unknown segment of existence." But novel after novel was now "only confirming what had already been said."

That is how you characterize the "hundreds and thousands of novels published in huge editions and widely read in Communist Russia." But "confirming what had already been said" was precisely what most of the novels written and published in the democratic West, including many honored for boldness and originality, were also doing. This was the situation twenty years ago, and it is perhaps even worse today. I do not, of course, mean that our novelists follow an official "party line," either directly or in some broader sense. What I do mean is that the most esteemed novels of our age in the West often seem to have as their main purpose the reinforcement of the by now endlessly reiterated idea that literary people are superior in every way to the businessmen, the politicians, the workers among whom they live—that they are more intelligent, more sensitive, and morally finer than everyone else.

You write, in the same essay from which I have just quoted, that "Every novel says to the reader: 'Things are not as simple as you think.'" This may be true of the best, the greatest, of novels. But it is not true of most contemporary American novels. Most contemporary American novels invite the reader to join with the author in a luxuriously complacent celebration of themselves and of the stock prejudices and bigotries of the "advanced" literary culture against the middle-class world around them. Flaubert could declare that *he* was Madame Bovary; the contemporary American novelist, faced with a modern-day equivalent of such a character, announces: How wonderful it is to have nothing whatever in common with this dull and inferior person.

In your essay on the novel you, too, bring up Flaubert, and you credit him with discovering "the *terra* previously *incognita* of the everyday." But what "hitherto unknown segment of existence" did you discover in *The Book of Laughter and Forgetting?* In my opinion, the answer has to be: the distinctive things Communism does to the life—most notably the spiritual or cultural life—of a society. Before reading *The Book of Laughter and Forgetting,* I thought that a novel set in Communist Czechoslovakia could "only confirm what had already been said" and what I, as a convinced anti-Communist, had already taken in. William Buckley quite reasonably asks: "How is it possible for the thousandth exposé of life under Communism to be original?" But what you proved in *The Book of Laughter and Forgetting* (and, I have since discovered, in some of your earlier novels like *The Joke* as well) is that it *is* possible to be original even in going over the most frequently trodden ground. You cite with approval "Hermann Broch's obstinately repeated point that the only *raison d'être* of a novel is to discover what can only be discovered by a novel," and your own novels are a splendid demonstration of that point.

If I were still a practicing literary critic, I would be obligated at this juncture to show how *The Book of Laughter and Forgetting* achieves this marvelous result. To tell you the truth, though, even if I were not so rusty, I would have a hard time doing so. This is not an easy book to describe, let alone to analyze. Indeed, if I had not read it before the reviews came out, I would have been put off, and misled, by the terms in which they praised it.

Not that these terms were all inaccurate. *The Book of Laughter and Forgetting* assuredly is, in the words of one reviewer, "part fairy tale, part literary criticism, part political tract, part musicology, and part autobiography";

and I also agree with the same reviewer when he adds that "the whole is genius." Yet what compelled me most when I first opened *The Book of Laughter and Forgetting* was not its form or its aesthetic character but its *intellectual force,* the astonishing intelligence controlling and suffusing every line.

The only other contemporary novelist I could think of with that kind of intellectual force, that degree of intelligence, was Saul Bellow. Like Bellow, you moved with easy freedom and complete authority through the world of ideas, and like him, too, you were often playful in the way you handled them. But in the end Bellow seemed always to be writing only about himself, composing endless and finally claustrophobic variations on the theme of Saul Bellow's sensibility. You, too, were a composer of variations; in fact, in *The Book of Laughter and Forgetting* itself you made so bold as to inform us that "This entire book is a novel in the form of variations." Yet even though you yourself, as Milan Kundera, kept making personal appearances in the course of which you talked about your life or, again speaking frankly in your own name, delivered yourself of brilliant little essays about the history of Czechoslovakia, or of music, or of literature, *you,* Milan Kundera, were not the subject of this novel, or the "theme" of these variations. The theme was totalitarianism: what it is, what it does, where it comes from. But this was a novel, however free and easy in its formal syncretism, whose mission was "to discover what can only be discovered by a novel," and consequently all its terms were specified. Totalitarianism thus meant Communism, and more specifically Soviet Communism, and still more specifically Communism as imposed on Czechoslovakia, first in 1948 by a coup and then, twenty years later in 1968, by the power of Soviet tanks.

Nowadays it is generally held that Communism is born out of hunger and oppression, and in conspicuously failing to "confirm" that idea, you were to that extent being original. But to anyone familiar with the literature, what you had to say about Communism was not in itself new: that it arises out of the utopian fantasy of a return to Paradise; that it can brook no challenge to its certainties; that it cannot and will not tolerate pluralism either in the form of the independent individual or in the form of the unique national culture.

All these things had been said before—by Orwell, Koestler, Camus, and most recently Solzhenitsyn. Indeed, according to Solzhenitsyn, Communism has done to Russia itself exactly what you tell us it has done to Czechoslovakia and all the other peoples and nations that have been absorbed into the Soviet empire. From the point of view of those nations it is traditional Russian imperialism that has crushed the life out of them, but in Solzhenitsyn's eyes Russia itself is as much the victim of Communism as the countries of Central Europe.

In another of your essays, "The Tragedy of Central Europe," you lean toward the perspective of the enslaved countries in fixing the blame on Russia rather than Communism, and you also agree with the great Polish dissident Leszek Kolakowski when he criticizes Solzhenitsyn's "tendency to idealize czarism." Nevertheless, there can be no doubt that *The Book of Laughter and Forgetting* is anti-Communist before it is anti-Russian. It begins not with Stalin but with the Czech Communist leader Klement Gottwald and the coup that brought Communism to power in Czecho-slovakia, and you make it clear throughout that the utopian fantasies in whose service Czechoslovakia is gradually murdered as a nation come from within. It is only when the nation begins to awake and tries to save itself from the slow suicide it has been committing that the Soviet tanks are sent in.

Yet even though in one sense *The Book of Laughter and Forgetting* said nothing new about Communism, in another sense it "discovered" Communism as surely as Flaubert "discovered" everyday life (about which, after all, *Madame Bovary* said nothing new, either). As I have already indicated, I find it very hard to understand how you were able to make the familiar seem unfamiliar and then to familiarize it anew with such great freshness and immediacy. Perhaps the answer lies in the unfamiliar form you created, in which a number of apparently unrelated stories written in different liter-ary genres, ranging from the conventionally realistic to the surrealistic, are strung together only by the author's direct intervention and a common theme which, however, is not even clearly visible in every case.

What, for example, connects Karel of Part II, who makes love simulta-neously to his wife and his mistress as his aged mother sleeps in the next room, with Mirek of Part I, a disillusioned ex-Communist who gets six years in prison for trying to keep a careful record of events after the inva-sion of Czechoslovakia? Then there is the section about the student who rushes off to spend an evening getting drunk with a group of famous poets while a married woman he has been lusting after waits impatiently for him in his room. Why is the fairly straight comic realism of that section imme-diately followed by the grim Kafkaesque parable of the young woman who finds herself living in a world populated exclusively by little children ("angels") who at first worship and then finally torment her to death?

Whatever explanations subsequent analysis might yield, the fact is that those "brutal juxtapositions" make so powerful an effect on a first reading that they justify themselves before they are fully understood; and here, too (at least so far as I personally was concerned), you prevailed against resistance. Nowadays my taste in fiction runs strongly to the realistic, and the enthusiasm I once felt for the experimental has waned as experimental writing has itself become both conventional and purposeless. But just as you have "discovered" Communism for the novel, so you have resurrected formal experimentation. The point of such experimentation was not originally to drive the novel out of the world it had been exploring for so long through the techniques and devices of realism; the point was to extend those techniques to previously unexplored regions of the inner life. What you say of Bartók, that he "knew how to discover the last original possibility in music based on the tonal principle," could be said of what Joyce, Kafka, and Proust were doing in relation to the fictional principle of verisimilitude. It can also, I believe, be said of you.

But since you yourself compare *The Book of Laughter and Forgetting* to a piece of music, it seems appropriate to admit that in reading it I was not so much reminded of other modern novelists as of the tonal modernist composers who, no matter how dissonant and difficult they may be (some of Bartók's own string quartets are a good case in point), are still intelligible to the ear in a way that the atonal and serial composers are not, no matter how often one listens to their works. Bartók, Stravinsky, Prokofiev, Shostakovich, and your beloved Janáček all found new and striking means by which to make the familiar world of sound seem new—to bring it, as we say, back to life. And this, it seemed to me, was what you were doing to a familiar world of experience in *The Book of Laughter and Forgetting*.

A few weeks after I had finished reading it, *The Book of Laughter and Forgetting* was published in the United States, and to my amazement the reviewers were just as enthusiastic about it as I had been. If you are wondering why this should have amazed me, I will tell you frankly that I would not have expected the American literary world to applaud so outspokenly anti-Communist a book. In France, where you have been living since 1975, anti-Communism may lately have come into fashion among intellectuals, but here in the United States it has for some years been anathema to literary people—and to most other people who think of themselves as liberals or as "sophisticated" or both. Very few of these people are actually sympathetic to Communism, but even fewer of them take it seriously as a threat or even as a reality. They are convinced that no one in the Soviet Union, let alone the satellite countries, believes in Communism any longer, if they ever did; and as for the Third World, the Marxist-Leninists there are not really Communists (even to call them Communists is taken as a sign of political primitivism) but nationalists making use of a convenient rhetoric. Hence to be an anti-Communist is to be guilty of hating and fearing an illusion—or rather, the ghost of something that may once have existed but that has long since passed away.

In the view of most American literary people, however, anti-Communists are not merely suffering from paranoid delusions; they are also dangerous in that they tend to exaggerate the dimensions of the Soviet threat. Here again, just as very few of these people are pro-Communist, hardly a single one can be found who is openly or straightforwardly pro-Soviet. Once there were many defenders of and apologists for the Soviet Union in the American literary world, but that was a long time ago. In recent years it has been almost impossible to find a writer or a critic who will argue that the Soviet Union is building a workers' paradise, or who will declare that Soviet domination of the countries of Central Europe is a good thing.

On the other hand, it is now the standard view that in its conflict with the West, or rather the United States, the Soviet Union is more sinned against than sinning. Everything the Soviets do (even the invasion of Afghanistan) is defensive or a reaction to an American provocation; and anything that cannot be explained away in these terms (the attempted assassination of the pope, the cheating on arms-control agreements, the use of poison gas) is denied. The idea that seems self-evident to you (and to me), namely, that the Soviets are out to dominate the world, is regarded as too patently ridiculous even to be debated; it is dismissed either with a patronizing smile or with a show of incredulous indignation. One is permitted to criticize the Soviet Union as a "tyranny," but to see it as a threat is both to be paranoid and to feed Soviet paranoia, thereby increasing the risk of an all-out nuclear war.

Given this frame of mind, most reviewers might have been expected to bridle at the anti-Communism of *The Book of Laughter and Forgetting*. But none of them did. Why? Possibly some or even all of them were so impressed with your novel as a work of art that they were willing to forgive or overlook its anti-Communism. Perhaps. But in any event—and this is a factor I should have anticipated but did not—as a Czech who has suffered and is now in exile, you have a license to be anti-Soviet and even anti-Communist. All Soviet or Central European dissidents are granted that license. By sympathizing with and celebrating dissident or refugee artists and intellectuals from the Communist world, literary people here can demonstrate (to themselves as much as to others) that their hatred of oppression extends to the Left no less than to the Right and that their love of literature also transcends political and ideological differences.

If you ask me what objection I or anyone else could conceivably have to such a lofty attitude, I will ask you in turn to reflect on the price that you yourself are paying for being treated in this way. In a piece about the reaction in France to your latest novel, *The Unbearable Lightness of Being,* Edmund White writes: "When faced with a figure such as Kundera, French leftists, eager to atone for former Soviet sympathies, begin to echo the unregenerate anti-Communism of Gaullists." The opposite has been true of the American reaction to your work. Here it has either become yet another occasion for sneering at "unregenerate anti-Communism" or else it has been described in the most disingenuously abstract terms available. You are writing about memory and laughter, about being and nonbeing, about love and sex, about angels and devils, about home and exile—about anything, in short, but the fate of Czechoslovakia under Communism and what that fate means, or should mean, to those of us living in the free world.

Thus one of your leftist admirers in America assures us that "Kundera refuses to settle into a complacency where answers come easy; no Cold-War scold he. He subjects the 'free world's' contradictions to equally fierce scrutiny; the issues he confronts—the bearing of time, choice, and being— transcend time and place." Neither, according to another of your admirers who also puts derisive quotation marks around the phrase "free world," do you detect any fundamental difference between the fate of literature under conditions of artistic freedom and what happens to it under Communist totalitarianism: "His need to experiment with form is surely connected to his personal vendetta against the puerilities of 'socialist realism' and its 'free world' counterparts." What is being done to you here, I have come to see, bears a macabre resemblance to what has been done posthumously to George Orwell. In Orwell's own lifetime, no one had any doubt that the species of totalitarianism he was warning against in *Nineteen Eighty-Four* was Communism. Yet as we have all discovered from the endless discussions of that book occasioned by the coming of the real 1984, it is now interpreted and taught more as a warning against the United States than the Soviet Union. If the word Orwellian means turning things into their opposites ("war is peace," etc.), then Orwell himself has been Orwellianized—not by an all-powerful state in control of all means of expression and publication, but by what Orwell himself called the "new aristocracy" of publicists and professors. This new aristocracy so dominates the centers in which opinion is shaped that it is able to distort the truth, especially about the past, to a degree that Orwell thought could never be reached so long as freedom of speech existed.

Like Orwell before you, you are obsessed with the theme of memory, and you believe with one of your characters "that the struggle of man against power is the struggle of memory against forgetting." The power you have in mind is the political power of the totalitarian state, but what the case of Orwell so ironically and paradoxically and poignantly demonstrates is that in the democratic West the power against which memory must struggle is the *cultural* power of the "new aristocracy." This power, with no help whatever from the state (and indeed operating in opposition to the state), has taken the real Orwell, to whom nothing was more fundamental than the distinction between the free world and the Communist world, and sent him down the memory hole, while giving us in his place an Orwell who was neutral as between the United States and the Soviet Union and who saw no important differences between life in a Communist society and life in the democratic West.

Now that same power is trying to do the same thing to you. But of course this is an even more brazen operation. Orwell's grave has been robbed; you are being kidnapped.

When I first thought of writing to you about this, I assumed that you would be appalled to learn how in America your work was falling into the hands of people who were using it for political purposes that you would surely consider pernicious. But now I am appalled to learn that you have been cooperating with your own kidnappers. "If I write a love story, and there are three lines about Stalin in that story," you tell the *New York Times Book Review,* "people will talk about the three lines and forget the rest, or read the rest for its political implications or as a metaphor for politics." But in America, once again, the opposite more nearly obtains: you write a book about Czechoslovakia under Communism containing three lines about love and everyone talks about those three lines and says that Czechoslovakia under Communism is a metaphor for life in the "free world" (in quotation marks of course). Or you write a novel, *The Unbearable Lightness of Being,* containing a brief episode in which an anti-Communist Czech émigré in Paris is seen by one of the characters as no different in kind from the Communists back in Prague (both being equally dogmatic), and virtually every reviewer gleefully cites it by way of suggesting that in your eyes Communism and anti-Communism are equivalent evils.

I think I can understand why a writer in exile from a Communist society should wish to turn his back on politics altogether, particularly where his own work is concerned. It is, after all, the essence of totalitarianism to politicize everything, most emphatically including the arts, and what better protest could there be against this distinctive species of tyranny than to insist on the reality and finally the superior importance of the nonpolitical in life? You are, for example, obviously fascinated by erotic experience in its own right and for its own sake, and that is why you write about it so much. Yet it is hard to escape the impression that sex also plays such a large role in your novels because under Communism it became the only area of privacy that remained relatively intact when everything else had become politicized. (Surely, too, you make fun of orgies and nude beaches because they represent an effort to turn sex into a servant of the utopian fantasies that Communism has failed to satisfy.)

But even greater than your passion for sex is your love of Western civilization, and especially its literature and its music. If I read you correctly, nothing that Communism has done, none of the crimes it has committed, not even the Gulags it has created, seem to you worse than the war it has waged against Western culture. To you it is a war that goes beyond the stifling of free expression or the effort by the state to prescribe the very forms in which artists are permitted to work. It is *total* war. It involves the complete cultural annihilation by the Soviet Union of the countries of Central Europe, and this in turn—so you believe—represents the amputation of a vital part of Western civilization.

You make a powerful case in "The Tragedy of Central Europe" for the proposition that the countries of that area are "the cultural home" of the West. From this it follows that in acquiescing since Yalta in their absorption into the alien civilization of the East (alien because "Russian Communism vigorously reawakened Russia's old anti-Western obsessions and turned it brutally against Europe"), the West has shown that it no longer believes in the worth of its own civilization. The unity of the West was once based on religion; then religion "bowed out, giving way to culture, which became the expression of the supreme values by which European humanity understood itself, defined itself, identified itself as European." The tragedy of Central Europe has revealed that "Just as God long ago gave way to culture, culture in turn is giving way." To what? You do not say because you do not know. "I think I know only that culture has bowed out" in the West.

You do not explicitly add here that you for one are refusing to bow out, but you do tell us elsewhere that your supreme commitment is to the heritage of the European novel. You further give us to understand that as a novelist you mean to keep faith with your Central European heritage in particular—a heritage embodied in a "disabused view of history" and "the 'nonserious spirit' that mocks grandeur and glory." Summing it all up, you once responded to someone who had praised your first book as an indictment of Stalinism with the irritable remark: "Spare me your Stalinism. *The Joke* is a love story. . . . [It] is *merely* a novel."

Your love of culture, then, gives you a double incentive to deny the political dimension of your work. You wish to protect it from the "mindlessness of politicization," and at the same time to be antipolitical is a way of *not* forgetting the murdered spirit of Czechoslovakia and the other countries of Central Europe which have now "disappeared from the map."

Even though I do not share your generally sour attitude toward religion, to all this I say: Yes, yes, and again yes. But I ask you, I implore you, to consider that by cooperating with those who have kidnapped your work, you are "bowing out" yourself. The testimony of the dissidents behind the Iron Curtain, whether they languish in prison or now live in the West, has played an immense role in forcing the intellectuals of Europe and America to think about the political values at stake in the conflict between East and West. Now you have come along and forced us all to begin thinking again (or perhaps for the first time) about the *cultural* dimension of this struggle. This has been the distinctive contribution, and the glory, of your work. Why then should you wish to encourage the agents of the very cultural abdication you deplore and mourn and lament? Why should you, of all writers, wish to be co-opted by people who think there is no moral or political—or cultural—difference between West and East worth talking about, let alone fighting over? Why should you allow yourself to provide cover for people who think that Western civilization should not and cannot be defended?

You will perhaps answer in the words with which your essay on the novel concludes: "I am attached to nothing apart from the European novel," and that the "wisdom of the novel" requires skepticism as opposed to dogmatic certainty, the refusal to take sides, the raising of questions rather than the finding of answers. But let me remind you of what you also know—that the novel is devoted to exploring the concrete and the particular. Those on the American Left who have taken you up have been able to do so only by ignoring the novelistic essence of your work, its concreteness and its particularity: by robbing it (to adapt the guiding metaphor of your latest novel) of *weight,* by cutting it loose from the earth and letting it float high into a realm of comfortable abstractions in which all moral and political distinctions become invisible, and everything merges into "the unbearable lightness of being."

In the novel to which you give that phrase as a title, you profess uncertainty as to whether one should choose weight or lightness, but that novel itself, like your writing in general, belies the uncertainty. In your work you have chosen weight, which is to say the burdens of memory and the celebration of a "world of concrete living." Even your flirtation with the irresponsibilities of lightness paradoxically adds to that weight, deriving as it does from the heavy burden you have accepted of keeping the mocking and irreverent spirit of your culturally devastated homeland alive: a spirit that darkens the lightness of the laughter you so value and that throws the shadow of the gallows over the jokes you love to make.

You have declared in an interview that you want all of us in the West to understand what happened at Yalta, that it is necessary for "a Frenchman or an American . . . to know, to reason, to comprehend what is happening to, say, people in Czechoslovakia . . . so that his naiveté won't become his tragedy." It is for the sake of that necessary understanding that I beg you to stop giving aid and encouragement to the cultural powers who are using some of your own words to prevent your work from helping to alert a demoralized West to the dangers it faces from a self-imposed Yalta of its own.

THE TERRIBLE QUESTION OF
ALEKSANDR SOLZHENITSYN

To THINK SERIOUSLY ABOUT
Aleksandr Solzhenitsyn—to immerse oneself in his work, to contemplate
the story of his life—is such a hard thing to do, so unpleasant, so unsettling, that no one without a special reason is likely, once having started, to
persist. The difficulty begins with the sheer quantity of Solzhenitsyn's
work. Even omitting books that remain untranslated, and skipping over
minor works of verse and drama, the English-language reader is still confronted with about five thousand pages, most of them closely printed, and
all of them written with the kind of density that demands unflagging attention: if the mind wanders for so much as a few seconds when reading
Solzhenitsyn, the thread is almost certain to be lost.

To compound the difficulty, Solzhenitsyn's very subject matter is guaranteed to induce a wandering mind. If he is not describing imprisonment
under conditions of hunger, sleeplessness, and cold (or heat) that one
would have thought too harsh to sustain life, let alone endless hours of gru-
eling labor, then he is writing about the horrors of the battlefield, or the
terrors of patients afflicted with cancer, or the humiliations and anxieties of
writers working under the eye of semiliterate censors and KGB thugs. How
is it possible to keep the mind from wandering in search of relief from so
relentless an assault? And how, when it has rebelled by wandering, can it be
brought back? *The Gulag Archipelago* is one of the most famous books ever
written, but I know from asking that very few people have managed to get
all the way through the six hundred pages of the first volume and that
hardly any at all have read the even longer second and the only slightly
shorter third.

As for Solzhenitsyn's novels, their readership, I would guess, again from
asking, has declined with each succeeding one. The first (and the shortest),
One Day in the Life of Ivan Denisovich, has been very widely read, but *The
First Circle* and *Cancer Ward* have proved disappointing to many enthusi-

asts of *Ivan Denisovich,* while *August 1914* and *Lenin in Zurich* have, I believe, been more reviewed than read. Indeed, so far had the public mind wandered from Solzhenitsyn by 1980 that *The Oak and the Calf,* perhaps his most readable book, was hardly noticed when it was published in that year.

But of course by 1980 something had happened to Solzhenitsyn which placed between him and the Western reading public another and even greater obstacle than the length, the density, and the unpleasant subject matter of his books. He had become, to use the usual euphemism, "controversial." And thereby hangs a tale.

Before his expulsion from the Soviet Union in 1974, Solzhenitsyn had been seen in the United States, and in the West generally, as one of the two greatest and most heroic of the Soviet dissidents (the other being Andrei Sakharov). As such, he was also taken to be a "liberal"—which, in a certain sense and in the context of Soviet society, he undoubtedly was. On occasion he even called himself a liberal, meaning by this that he was fighting against the censorship of literature and the arts.

In those days, too, Solzhenitsyn was careful not to overstep certain limits in his challenge to the Soviet authorities. He had originally been arrested toward the end of World War II, while still in the army, when it was discovered that he had made disparaging jokes about Stalin; for this he had been sentenced to eight years in prison camps and another three in internal exile. Yet neither the fact that he was critical of Stalin, nor his bitterness over being imprisoned, at first turned Solzhenitsyn into an anti-Communist. He remained a Marxist and a Leninist in whose eyes Stalin had betrayed the revolutionary heritage of 1917. It was only in the Gulag that he gradually came to see Stalin and Stalinism not as the betrayal of Marxism and Leninism but as their logical culmination and fulfillment.

Having arrived at this realization, however, Solzhenitsyn prudently kept it to himself, even after Stalin's death and Khrushchev's de-Stalinization campaign. By posing as a Leninist who, like so many millions of other loyal Communists, had suffered unjustly for his premature opposition to the "cult of personality," Solzhenitsyn not only could aspire to rehabilitation as a Soviet citizen but could even hope that he might get away with a book that told the truth about Stalin's prison camps.

The strategy worked. *One Day in the Life of Ivan Denisovich* was submitted to the leading Soviet literary journal, *Novy Mir,* itself edited by just such a "liberal" Communist as Solzhenitsyn pretended to be, Aleksandr Tvardovsky (who was also Russia's most highly regarded living poet). Thanks to

Tvardovsky's maneuverings, publication of *Ivan Denisovich* was eventually authorized by Nikita Khrushchev himself; and in November 1962, literally overnight, an unknown forty-four-year-old ex-convict, employed as an elementary-school teacher of math and physics in a small provincial town, became one of the most celebrated writers on earth.

Nevertheless, after *Ivan Denisovich* and a couple of shorter pieces, *Novy Mir* rejected one manuscript after another by Solzhenitsyn—not because Tvardovsky disliked them but because, things having tightened up again, he feared that these manuscripts would be stopped by the censors and that the position of his magazine would thereby be jeopardized. Yet the false dawn of liberalization under Khrushchev had left a trace: these were the years when manuscripts, often copied in a feverish rush, were beginning to circulate through the clandestine network known as samizdat and were also being smuggled out of the Soviet Union and finding publishers in the West. It was via such channels that Solzhenitsyn's books came to light, simultaneously endangering him with the Soviet authorities and protecting him from their wrath. Taking shrewd advantage of this situation, Solzhenitsyn carried on a running battle with the Writers' Union, demanding that it stand up against the censorship of literature by insensitive party functionaries and appealing for support in getting his own novels published in the Soviet Union.

All this time, Solzhenitsyn was thought in the West (in the words of the appendix to the first British edition of *Cancer Ward* in 1968) to be "a loyal and patriotic Soviet citizen [whose] protests were directed against the bureaucracy's excesses and abuses, not against Soviet authority and the Communist society [and whose] aim was to improve and perfect the Soviet system, not to destroy it." And when, in 1970, Solzhenitsyn was awarded the Nobel Prize for literature, he was still the darling (to quote the appendix to *Cancer Ward* again) of "the liberal intellectuals of the West . . . the same people who had for years hoped for the liberalization of the Soviet state and worked hard for the reduction of East-West tensions."

About three years later, the KGB unearthed a hidden copy of *The Gulag Archipelago,* and Solzhenitsyn was finally arrested. But instead of being returned to prison as he had expected, he was stripped of his Soviet citizenship and deported to Germany. Now that he was in the West and beyond the reach of the KGB, Solzhenitsyn had no reason to continue posing as a good Communist fighting for his rights under Soviet law; dissembling would in any event have been impossible after the publication of *The Gulag Archipelago,* in which the origins of Stalin's terror are traced right back to Lenin himself and in which terror in general is seen as the essence of the Bolshevik Revolution. And in case his liberal admirers in the West should somehow fail to grasp the point, Solzhenitsyn proceeded to hammer it home in a series of speeches, interviews, and essays that left no room for doubt or ambiguity.

Evidently Solzhenitsyn's enemies in the Soviet Union had been right in calling him anti-Soviet and his apologists in the West had been wrong; and if it was treason for a Soviet citizen to be an anti-Communist, then Solzhenitsyn was indeed a traitor.

By itself being guilty of treason would not necessarily have damaged Solzhenitsyn's reputation in the eyes of the liberal intellectuals of the West. For one thing, many of them—as witness their attitude toward Alger Hiss, the Rosenbergs, Kim Philby, and Burgess-Maclean—saw nothing overwhelmingly reprehensible in treason. For another, the climate of opinion in the 1970s was very favorably disposed toward any individual defiance of authority in any country for any reason; dissent was the order of the day, never mind its content or direction. Angela Davis here, Solzhenitsyn there: it was all the same.

But Solzhenitsyn *here* turned out to be another story. For not only was he anti-Communist, he was anti-liberal; and not only was he anti-Soviet, he was anti-détente; and not only was he both anti-liberal and anti-détente, but he insisted on bringing the two antipathies together into a scathing denunciation of the West for its failure of nerve in the face of an ineluctable Communist threat. Here was a species of treason that the liberal intellectuals of the West were not quite so ready to forgive. "At one time," writes Michael Scammell in his biography of Solzhenitsyn, "one almost never heard a word against him; he was lionized and idolized"; but now "he is more often denounced as embittered or ignored as irrelevant."

Scammell disclaims any intention "to redress the balance," but the response to his book suggests that he has at least inaugurated a process of reconsideration. Not, to be sure, in all quarters. Thus the late Carl R. Proffer, a specialist in Soviet literature, in a review published in the *New Republic* just after his death, described Solzhenitsyn from beyond the grave as "an old man with the limited education of a convinced Soviet Leninist and the limited life of a totalitarian prisoner," an "amateur" whose work is marked by silliness and stupidity. It is all "claptrap," and yet "for two decades right-wing Russians and others tremblingly call him a prophet." More surprisingly, on the other hand, in such other liberal periodicals as the *Atlantic* (Bernard Levin), the *New York Review of Books* (Aileen Kelly), and the *New*

York Times (John Gross), Scammell's book has called forth pieces in defense of Solzhenitsyn, none written by "right-wing Russians" and all leaning heavily on the word "prophet."

About Scammell's *Solzhenitsyn: A Biography,* there is bad news and good news. The bad news is that it adds yet another thousand pages to the more than five thousand by Solzhenitsyn himself that must be read by anyone wishing to think seriously about him. The good news is that it is a wonderful book, and not the least wondrous of its qualities is that despite its daunting length it makes a serious encounter with Solzhenitsyn easier rather than harder to undertake.

There is a great deal of autobiographical material in Solzhenitsyn's own books, especially the *Gulag* volumes and *The Oak and the Calf,* but it is so disconnected and fragmentary that putting it all together into a coherent account as one goes along is almost impossible. Thus even if Scammell had done nothing but this, his book would have performed a major service to anyone trying to think seriously about Solzhenitsyn.

But Scammell does much more than merely organize Solzhenitsyn's scattered revelations about his own life into an intelligible story; he also checks these occasionally tendentious and self-serving revelations wherever possible against other sources. Further, in addition to subjecting Solzhenitsyn's version of events to critical scrutiny, Scammell is critical of Solzhenitsyn's political ideas from his own unobtrusively expressed social-democratic point of view. Yet the last thing he wishes to do is "expose" or debunk Solzhenitsyn. This is a book written out of the deepest respect for its subject, and it can be said of Scammell that as a biographer he does what Matthew Arnold enjoined the critic to attempt to do in dealing with a literary work: "To see the object as in itself it really is."

Finally, Scammell is himself so good a writer that his book is a pleasure to read. His prose is lucid and elegant; his scholarship is scrupulous, well digested, and lightly carried; and his narrative pace is steady and sure.

BUT IF SCAMMELL truly fulfills Matthew Arnold's injunction in dealing with Solzhenitsyn the man, he does not, in my opinion, do so well with Solzhenitsyn the writer, whom he seems to regard as a major artist in the line of the great nineteenth-century Russian novelists, in some respects resembling Tolstoy and in others Dostoevsky.

This view is very widely shared and is—or at least used to be—the foundation of Solzhenitsyn's enormous prestige. It was as a novelist that he burst upon the Soviet scene, it was as a novelist that he won the Nobel Prize, and it was as a novelist that the world held him in so high an esteem. It was also primarily as a novelist that Solzhenitsyn saw (and sees) himself. Indeed, one of the paradoxically surprising facts about Solzhenitsyn that emerges from Scammell's book is that he was always a literary man—surprising because when *Ivan Denisovich* was published in the West the impression was conveyed that its author was a scientist who had tried his hand at a novel as the best way to tell the world about Stalin's labor camps.

In fact, however, Solzhenitsyn had entertained literary ambitions all his life. "As a young child," says Scammell, "he had decided that he wanted to become one of three things: a general, a priest, or a writer." At the age of nine he was already writing stories, poems, and plays; at the age of thirteen he kept a journal called *The Literary Gazette;* and at the age of fifteen he wrote a novel. Even before reaching eighteen, he had resolved to write "a big novel about the Revolution" modeled on Tolstoy's *War and Peace,* and he even drafted a plan for it. All this time he was also immersing himself in the classics of Russian literature, reading and rereading the works of Pushkin, Gogol, Gorky, and especially Tolstoy. Nevertheless, he decided to study physics and mathematics at the university rather than literature, partly because it would be easier to make a living as a teacher of science.

Then, only days after his graduation, war broke out and Solzhenitsyn joined the army, becoming in due course an artillery officer. So much the writer was he by now that not even combat could stop him. While complaining in letters home that the continuous fighting at the front was keeping him from his "main work," he managed between battles to write several stories, and when he sent a batch of them off to two Soviet writers he admired, he announced to one of his friends that "I'll tear my heart out of my breast, I'll stamp out fifteen years of my life," if they should say that he had no talent.

If war could not stop Solzhenitsyn from writing, neither could imprisonment. In the Gulag, even on those rare occasions when pen and paper were available, to write was literally to risk one's life or at the very least to court more severe conditions and longer sentences. Yet even under those circumstances Solzhenitsyn went on writing, in his head if not on paper, and in verse rather than prose because verse was easier to memorize. In eight years he committed *tens of thousands* of lines to memory, and it was only after his release that he was able to transcribe them and even then only in secret.

A writer, then, from the very beginning and a literary man through and through. The ambitions of this writer, this literary man, moreover, knew virtually no bounds. Not only did he make grandiose plans like the one for a multivolume epic about the Bolshevik Revolution that would be nothing less than a successor to *War and Peace;* he also dreamed of rescuing and reviving the great traditions of Russian literature which were in danger of being forgotten and lost as a result of censorship and the state-imposed corruptions of "Socialist Realism."

It is a measure of Solzhenitsyn's almost incomprehensible single-mindedness that he should actually have stuck with the first of these ambitions, formed when he was only seventeen years old. The original scheme involved a Communist hero, and by the time he started work on the first volume (published here in 1972 as *August 1914*), he had undergone the revolution in his own political perspective that reversed his attitude both toward the Revolution (from positive to negative) and toward the Russia of the czars (from negative to positive). Yet so little did this radical change in point of view affect the overall design that, according to Scammell, "he was able to incorporate some of the scenes written in Rostov nearly thirty years beforehand virtually without altering them."

Since *August 1914* has now been followed by several more volumes, of which only the excerpts concerning Lenin have thus far been translated into English (under the title *Lenin in Zurich*), with more yet to come, it is perhaps unfair to attempt a critical judgment. Nevertheless, it can already be said with confidence that if *August 1914* is a fair sample, *R-17* (as Solzhenitsyn calls this entire work in progress) has nothing in common with *War and Peace* except the superficial characteristics of length and theme.

War and Peace is about Russia during the Napoleonic Wars and *August 1914* is about Russia during World War I; both move back and forth from the battlefield to the home front; and both contain fictional characters as well as historical personages. There, however, the resemblances end. *War and Peace,* one of the greatest of all novels, is alive in every detail, and *August 1914* is, to put it plainly, dead from beginning to end. Neither the fictional nor the historical personages are truly realized, and though the combat scenes are scrupulously rendered, they remain staged set pieces with no power to arouse the emotions or draw the reader in. As for the narrative line, it is driven by the grim energy of the author's will and not by the inner compulsion through which the living organism of a genuine work of novelistic art always unfolds itself.

In short, judging by *August 1914,* Solzhenitsyn's epic of the Revolution fails utterly in its claim to stand beside *War and Peace.* Beyond this, it bespeaks the collapse of the hope that Solzhenitsyn would rescue and revive the great stifled tradition of the nineteenth-century Russian novel.

It was this hope of a rebirth of Russian literature that was aroused in Tvardovsky and his colleagues on the editorial staff of *Novy Mir* when they read the manuscript of *One Day in the Life of Ivan Denisovich*, with its audaciously realistic exploration of life in a forced-labor camp. "They say that Russian literature's been killed," Tvardovsky exclaimed in the course of a drunken celebration over the anonymous manuscript that had been submitted to them. "Damn and blast it! It's in this folder. . . ." And when, finally, *Ivan Denisovich* was published, millions of Russians responded in much the same way. Scammell explains:

> It is hard for Westerners to grasp just how bleak and barren the Soviet literary scene is and was (especially in the early 1960s), how parched and starving Soviet readers are for contemporary literature of any quality. . . . Paradoxically . . . although *Ivan Denisovich* was published in Moscow for avowedly political reasons and was received both there and abroad mainly as a political sensation, it was one of the few Soviet prose works since the war that could stand completely as a work of art and be discussed exclusively in terms of its aesthetic achievement, quite apart from its political qualities. It was a universal statement about the human condition, and it was for this reason that comparisons were made with Tolstoy and Dostoevsky and that hungry readers cherished the book.

Yet, as Solzhenitsyn himself has often pointed out, and approvingly, Russian readers differ from Westerners in making little or no distinction between the aesthetic and the moral or spiritual dimensions of literature. Accordingly, it was not as "a universal statement about the human condition" that *Ivan Denisovich* was read and revered in the Soviet Union, but as a truthful rendering of a particular experience undergone by the Russian people.

This was naturally the case with former prisoners—*zeks,* to use the Russian term—who poured out their thanks to Solzhenitsyn in hundreds and even thousands of letters. Here are some examples: "My face was smothered in tears. . . . I didn't wipe them away or feel ashamed, because all this . . . was mine, intimately mine, mine for every day of the fifteen years I spent in the camps." Or again: "Although I wept as I read it, at last I felt myself to be an equal citizen with the rest. . . ." And again: "Thank you for your tremendous achievement, thank you from the bottom of my heart. I would give you anything, anything. Reading your story I remembered . . . the frosts and the blizzards, the insults and humiliations. . . . I wept as I read—they were all familiar characters. . . ."

Nor was it only former *zeks* who were grateful to Solzhenitsyn for *Ivan Denisovich*. "I kiss your golden hands," wrote one reader; "Thank you for your truthfulness," wrote another; "Thank you for your love and courage," said a third; and speaking for them all, one correspondent declared: "Thank goodness that you exist . . . look after yourself. Your existence is our happiness."

With the help of Scammell's brilliant account of the context, and by the exercise of a little imagination, a non-Russian can understand reactions such as these, even if he finds it impossible to share in them. For while *Ivan Denisovich* is certainly a better novel than *August 1914,* it never really rises to "a universal statement about the human condition," and no more than *August 1914* can it bear comparison with Tolstoy and Dostoevsky.

Yet Tvardovsky, going even further than mere comparison, pronounced *Ivan Denisovich* superior to Dostoevsky's *House of the Dead* because "there we see the people through the eyes of an intellectual, whereas here the intellectuals are seen through the eyes of the people." On this issue, however, even many admirers of *Ivan Denisovich* disagreed, asking why Solzhenitsyn had chosen to write from the point of view of a simple peasant instead of through the consciousness of an intellectual. Solzhenitsyn hotly defended himself against this criticism:

Of course, it would have been simpler and easier to write about an intellectual (doubtless thinking of oneself all the while: "What a fine fellow I am and how I suffered"). But . . . having been flung together with [Ivan Denisovich] Shukhov in the same sort of conditions . . . a complete nobody as far as the others were concerned and indistinguishable from the rest of them . . . I had a chance to feel exactly the same as they.

Scammell, agreeing with Tvardovsky and Solzhenitsyn against the critics, adds that "By making his hero a common peasant, Solzhenitsyn was able to seize the essence of the labor-camp experience and universalize it. An intellectual hero would have been less typical and more particular, diluting the story's power and impact."

Surely, however, the impact of the story is weakened, not strengthened, by being told through a character whose life on the outside has been as full of hardship and deprivation as Ivan Denisovich Shukhov's, and who has therefore become so accustomed to the kind of conditions he is forced to endure in the labor camp that he can end a day of unrelieved horror in a state of happiness over all the luck he has had in not suffering even more ("They hadn't put him in the cooler. The gang hadn't been chased out to work in the Socialist Community Development. . . . They hadn't found that piece of steel in the frisk," and so on). Solzhenitsyn intended this conclusion as a celebration of the resiliency of the human spirit, and so it is. But at the same time it makes identifying with Ivan Denisovich Shukhov (or entering into his skin, to use Solzhenitsyn's image) almost insuperably difficult.

No such problem of identification is presented by *The First Circle,* which is set in the least harsh "island" of the Gulag, a prison (known as a *sharashka*) housing scientists whose forced labor takes the form of research on various projects useful to the state. Here, therefore, all the main characters are intellectuals and they spend a good deal of time arguing about philosophy, politics, and the history of their country.

In moving from the "inferno," as it were, of *Ivan Denisovich* to the *sharashka,* "the first circle" of this prison-camp hell, Solzhenitsyn was trying both to broaden and deepen his fictional exploration of the Gulag. *The First Circle* is thus very much longer than *Ivan Denisovich* and includes a much wider representation of Soviet society, ranging from Stalin himself through various levels of the party hierarchy and down to the depths of the prison system and its inhabitants. In *Ivan Denisovich,* we see Shukhov taking pride in the physical labor he is forced to do, and in *The First Circle* the prisoner-scientists are similarly fired up over a project that, if successfully completed, will enable the KGB to keep even closer surveillance over the population. The difference (tending to vindicate the critical view of *Ivan Denisovich*) is that for some of the characters in *The First Circle* this poses the kind of acute moral dilemma that lies far beyond the range of Shukhov's consciousness.

But if it is easier to identify with the characters in *The First Circle* than with Ivan Denisovich Shukhov, it is harder to sustain an interest in them over the course of this very long novel. As in *August 1914*—and as in *Cancer Ward,* another long and thickly populated novel set in a hospital for patients suffering from cancer—Solzhenitsyn doggedly does all the things a novelist is supposed to do. He constructs plots, he catalogues details of scene and character, he transcribes conversations, he sets up dramatic conflicts, he moves toward resolutions. Yet all to no avail. Edmund Wilson once said of F. Scott Fitzgerald that despite everything that was wrong with his novels they never failed to live. The opposite can be said of Solzhenitsyn's novels: despite everything that is right about them, they always fail to live.

IN MAINTAINING, HOWEVER, that Solzhenitsyn is not a true novelist, let alone another Tolstoy or Dostoevsky, I am far from suggesting that he is not a great writer. On the contrary, in my opinion his two major nonfiction works, *The Gulag Archipelago* and *The Oak and the Calf,* are among the very greatest books of the age. Everything that he tries, and fails, to do in his novels is magnificently accomplished in these works. While the novels never come to life, there is so much vitality in the three volumes of *The Gulag Archipelago* that it threatens to overwhelm, and undermine, the horrors of the material. For never can such stories have been told with such verve, such gusto, such animation, such high-spirited irony and sarcasm as Solzhenitsyn brings to this history of the Soviet prison system.

But to call *The Gulag Archipelago* a history is a little like describing the Talmud as a legal encyclopedia. The reason the Talmud is so hard to describe to anyone unacquainted with it is that there is nothing else quite like it to which it can be usefully compared. The same thing is true of *The Gulag Archipelago.*

In the absence of archives or histories or other published sources, Solzhenitsyn's research at first consisted of collecting reports and stories from former *zeks*—227 of them, to be exact—through secret meetings and carefully concealed correspondence; only later did he have access to such published materials as existed in restricted library collections. Drawing on all these sources, and on his own experience as well, Solzhenitsyn managed, through concrete episodes, biographical and autobiographical detail, historical analysis, and an almost infinite variety of literary modes and devices, to reconstruct the entire history of the Soviet prison-camp system and to convey the experience of the many millions (as many as one hundred million all told, he estimates) who lived and died on the "islands" of the "archipelago." Writing this book, especially under conditions of enforced secrecy, was a stupendous feat of mind, spirit, creative originality, and stamina. It will stand forever as one of the majestic achievements in the history of literature.

Solzhenitsyn himself valued *The Gulag Archipelago* highly enough to resolve that, if his children were kidnapped and held hostage by the KGB as a way of preventing him from authorizing its publication in the West, he would sacrifice them rather than permit the book to be suppressed. But to *The Oak and the Calf* (where we learn about this "superhuman decision" to choose *The Gulag Archipelago* over his own children) he ascribed very little importance indeed. He called it "*secondary* literature: literature on literature, literature apropos of literature, literature begotten by literature," and he apologized in a preface for wasting the reader's time with such inferior stuff: "So much has been written, and people have less and less time for reading: should we, in all conscience, be writing memoirs, and literary memoirs at that?"

The irony is that *The Oak and the Calf* is not only far superior to any of Solzhenitsyn's "works of primary literature" (by which he means his novels), but even exceeds them in the very qualities that are usually thought of as novelistic. For example, there is not a single character in Solzhenitsyn's novels as vividly and fully realized as the character of Aleksandr Tvardovsky in *The Oak and the Calf*. Nor does any of the novels carry the dramatic force—the drive, the pace, the suspense—of *The Oak and the Calf*. Somehow, in telling the story of his own literary career, Solzhenitsyn was able to make far better use of his novelistic skills than he ever could in the writing of actual novels. The result is a great work of autobiography, and one of the most revealing books ever written about life, and particularly cultural life, in the Soviet Union.

Solzhenitsyn is not the only writer in our time who has largely been valued both by himself and the world as a novelist but whose best work has been done in forms other than prose fiction. Norman Mailer and James Baldwin spring to mind immediately as American examples of this phenomenon. It goes without saying that Solzhenitsyn towers over writers like these, but he has in common with them a quasi-religious attitude toward art in the traditional sense: to be a writer means to compose novels, poems, or plays. These are what make up—in Solzhenitsyn's own terms—"primary literature"; everything else is "secondary." But whereas Mailer and Baldwin are merely writers who mistake the nature of their own true talents (encouraged in this by a culture that accords higher status to fiction than to nonfiction), Solzhenitsyn presents a more complicated problem. And it is in trying to grapple with that problem that we immediately run up against the much-vexed issue of Solzhenitsyn the prophet.

There can be no doubt that Solzhenitsyn has come in retrospect to regard himself as an instrument of the will of God. As is clear from many hints and suggestions in *The Oak and the Calf,* he believes that, unbeknownst to himself, he was appointed to rescue from oblivion "the millions done to death" in the Gulag. It was for this purpose that he was sent to the Gulag himself; it was for this purpose that he survived the ordeal; and it was also for this purpose that his life was spared once more after he developed a cancerous tumor that had been diagnosed as fatal. Not only did God mark him out and then spare him for this mission; God also (though, again, he was unaware of it at the time—there were no visions or voices from on high) guided his steps in his struggles with the Soviet authorities, enabling him, a lone individual, to defy the awesome power of a totalitarian state and live to tell the tale.

It is not necessary to accept Solzhenitsyn's interpretation of his own life, or even to share his belief in God, in order to understand how and why he should have come to see himself as an instrument of the divine will. Indeed, one measure of the greatness of *The Oak and the Calf* is that it makes this conviction of Solzhenitsyn's seem at the very least plausible and even a rationally irresistible conclusion from the clear evidence of his life. In any case, whether or not one believes in God, and whether or not one believes that Solzhenitsyn is an instrument of the divine will, *his* belief has produced those "clear effects" to which William James pointed as the "pragmatic" test of a genuine religious experience.

The first, and the grossest, of those effects is to have kept Solzhenitsyn alive when he might so easily have succumbed to the hardships of his years in the labor camps and then to his struggle with cancer. He himself takes the view that "People can live through hardship, but from hard feelings they perish," and that "Cancer is the fate of all who give themselves up to moods of bilious, corrosive resentment and depression." What saved Solzhenitsyn from such mortally dangerous "hard feelings" was his conviction that the millions done to death in the Gulag depended on him to rescue them from yet a second and in some ways an even more terrible death—the death of oblivion. If he weakened, if he faltered, if he himself were to die, they would all sink unremembered, unrecorded, into a silent pit.

Thus, reproaching himself for "the mistaken sense of obligation" that led him to follow Tvardovsky's advice that he hold back for a while after publication of *Ivan Denisovich,* Solzhenitsyn writes:

Let me make myself clear. I did, of course, owe something to Tvardovsky, but the debt was purely personal. I had, however, no right to look at things from a personal point of view and to worry about what *Novy Mir* would think of me. My point of departure should always have been that I did not belong to myself alone, that my literary destiny was not just my own, but that of the millions who had not lived to scrawl or gasp or croak the truth about their lot as jail birds. . . . I, who had returned from the world that never gives up its dead, had no right to swear loyalty either to *Novy Mir* or to Tvardovsky. . . .

After the KGB had found and confiscated a hidden archive of his manuscripts, he reproached himself even more bitterly:

> Just one slip of the foot, one careless move, and my whole plan, my whole life's work, had come to grief. And it was not only my life's work but the dying wishes of the millions whose last whisper, last moan, had been cut short on some hut floor in some prison camp. I had not carried out their behests, I had betrayed them, had shown myself unworthy of them. It had been given to me, almost alone, to crawl to safety; the hopes once held in all those skulls buried now in common graves in the camps had been set on me—and I had collapsed, and their hopes had slipped from my hands.

In these and similar passages, we see the apparently contradictory combination of megalomania and selflessness that come so miraculously together in the making of a true prophet. *Everything* depends on him alone, and yet he himself is nothing: truly nothing, a mere vessel. In the case of Solzhenitsyn, it is only keeping faith with the dead that keeps him alive, and more than alive: capable of feats of endurance, exertion, courage that do indeed seem "superhuman." This is a word he himself, as we have seen, uses in describing his decision to sacrifice his own children, if need be, rather than suppress *The Gulag Archipelago.* But I for one do not hesitate to apply it to the entire story of his life: to his survival, to his capacity for work, and to his defiance of the Soviet authorities. Nor, to repeat, is it necessary to see the hand of God in all this in order to recognize it as in some sense superhuman.

But even if one did see the hand of God in Solzhenitsyn's life, I do not think one would see it in his novels. Reading *War and Peace* or *Anna Karenina,* one is hard put not to regard Tolstoy as superhuman; the young Maxim Gorky, for example, atheist though he was, could not help feeling that Tolstoy was more than a mere human being. But as a novelist, Solzhenitsyn is, one might say, all too human. In the making of novels, he is driven by ordinary and quite conventional literary ambitions. He wants to be a great artist and to write books worthy of the masters of Russian literature. The subject matter of those books is more or less the same as the subject matter of his nonfiction works, but the point, the overriding point, of the novels is to use it for the purposes of the author's artistic dreams and aspirations. In the novels, he is serving himself, he belongs to himself alone, his literary destiny is just his own. How do I know this? I know it from the simple fact that his novels are dead on the page, denied the breath of life that the novelist is only given the power to give when he is able to transcend himself and enter into the experience, the "skin," of others.

The opposite is true of Solzhenitsyn's nonfiction works. Again, the contrast with Tolstoy is instructive. Tolstoy, as we know from Henri Troyat's fascinating biography of him (a biography, incidentally, from which Tolstoy emerges looking like a character out of Dostoevsky), was certainly a megalomaniac, whether writing fiction or religious tracts. But it was only as a novelist that he became capable of selflessness as well; the theoretically impossible marriage of these two opposing qualities in the writing of *War and Peace* and *Anna Karenina* is what makes him seem superhuman. The Tolstoy who later wrote tracts and pamphlets was as little capable of selflessness as most human beings, even though it was this Tolstoy whom the world, with its usual perspicacity, took for a saint and a prophet.

With Solzhenitsyn the position is reversed. It is in *The Gulag Archipelago* and *The Oak and the Calf* that Solzhenitsyn's megalomania merges with selflessness. Here he *is* serving something more than the "purely personal." Here he does *not* belong to himself alone. Here his own "literary destiny" *is* beside the point. Here he does become a vessel through which "the millions who had not lived to scrawl or gasp or croak the truth about their lot" find voices and tongues and are at last able to tell what they know. And therefore, it is here, where he is true to his prophetic vocation, and here alone, that he also becomes a great writer.

As such he succeeds in accomplishing what he only imagines he is doing in and through his novels. To the Russian people he is returning their stolen or "amputated" national memory, reopening the forcibly blocked channels of communication between the generations, between the past and the present; and to other peoples in other parts of the world he is offering "the condensed experience" of his own country "accurately and concisely and with that perception and pain they would feel if they had experienced it themselves." To what end? Why, quite simply, to help them all avoid making the same mistake themselves: the mistake of submitting to Communism.

Here, then, we arrive at the very heart of Solzhenitsyn's prophetic mission: to preach against

the failure to understand the radical hostility of Communism to mankind as a whole—the failure to realize that Communism is irredeemable, that there exist no "better" variants of Communism; that it is incapable of growing "kinder," that it cannot survive as an ideology without using terror, and that, consequently, to coexist with Communism on the same planet is impossible. Either it will spread, cancer-like, to destroy mankind, or else mankind will have to rid itself of Communism (and even then face lengthy treatment for secondary tumors).

It is by preaching so radically anti-Communist a point of view—and in terms allowing for no hope of negotiation or compromise and seeming to threaten another world war—that Solzhenitsyn has made himself more and more unpopular in the West. I am well aware that Solzhenitsyn's Western critics also include a number of staunch anti-Communists who oppose him not because he is a "cold warrior" but because he espouses a species of Russian nationalism that is explicitly antidemocratic and (so they claim) implicitly anti-Semitic. Indeed, several such critics have charged that the latest volume of *R-17*, which has not yet been translated into English, goes beyond implicit into open anti-Semitism in its recounting of the assassination of Stolypin, Czar Nicholas II's prime minister, by a terrorist of Jewish origin.

Others to whom I have spoken disagree, and not having read the book in question, I cannot make a firsthand judgment. But my own impression, based on an acquaintance with virtually everything by Solzhenitsyn that has been translated into English, and confirmed by Scammell's characteristically scrupulous examination of the question, is that the charge of anti-Semitism rests almost entirely on negative evidence. That is, while there is no clear sign of positive hostility toward Jews in Solzhenitsyn's books, neither is there much sympathy. I can well imagine that in his heart he holds it against the Jews that so many of the old Bolsheviks, the makers of the Revolution that brought the curse of Communism to Russia, were of Jewish origin; and in general he also seems to ignore the mordant truth behind the old quip (playing on the fact that Trotsky's real name was Bronstein) that "the Trotskys make the revolutions, the Bronsteins pay the bill." Still, whatever there may be in his heart, there is no overt anti-Semitism in any of his translated works.

There is also this to consider: that Solzhenitsyn has always defended Israel, even to the point of invidiously comparing the courage of the Israelis in the face of their Arab enemies with the appeasement of the Soviet Union by the Western democracies. To be sure, there was a time when it was possible for an anti-Semite to be a Zionist of sorts: the founder of Zionism himself, Theodor Herzl, thought that the anti-Semitic European governments would welcome the establishment of a Jewish state precisely because it would be a good way of getting the Jews out of Europe. But in our own day, Israel has become *the* touchstone of attitudes toward the Jewish people, and anti-Zionism has become the main and most relevant form of anti-Semitism. So much is this the case that almost anything Solzhenitsyn may think about the role of Jews in the past—or even in the post–Communist Russia of his dreams—becomes academic by comparison.

On the other hand, in contrast to his references to the Jews, Solzhenitsyn's speeches and pamphlets are full of overt attacks on the democratic West, whose loss of "civic courage" and whose capitulation to the "Spirit of Munich" ("concessions and smiles to counterpose to the sudden renewed assault of bare-fanged barbarism") he blames on secularism, materialism, and liberalism. It is this, rather than any intimations of anti-Semitism, on which Solzhenitsyn's liberal critics have fastened in trying to write him off. And even to some of us who agree with him about Communism and about the "Spirit of Munich," Solzhenitsyn's brand of Russian nationalism with its authoritarian coloration and its anti-Semitic potential presents the most unpleasant and the most unsettling facet of a serious encounter with his life and his work.

In my opinion, however, we who agree with Solzhenitsyn about Communism would be making the worst of mistakes if we allowed ourselves to join with his critics in dismissing him as a crank or if we ourselves were to ignore him as an embarrassment. His challenge to the Russian people is to liberate themselves from Communism by means of their own spiritual resources and without the help of the West, but no matter how we feel about the form of society he urges upon them in the post-Communist Russia for which he prays, *our* main business is with his challenge to *us*.

For here—it cannot be repeated too often—is a lone individual who, by having successfully stood up to the full power of the Soviet state, has made himself into a living reproach to the West: a parable in action of the very courage in the face of Communist totalitarianism that the West has been unable or unwilling to summon in its own dealings with the Soviet state. Solzhenitsyn's terrible and terrifying question to us is this: is it possible that courage like his own is all that we require to escape from the fate he has come to warn us against? Is it possible that the courage first to see the truth about Communism and then the correlative courage to act upon it can guide our steps to safety as his own courage guided Solzhenitsyn's, that it can make the Soviet leaders back down and ultimately, perhaps, even collapse, just as they did when confronted by Solzhenitsyn himself?

Forcing us to face that terrible question, rubbing our noses in it, has been Solzhenitsyn's prophetic mission to the West. To seize upon the antidemocratic Slavophilia of his message to the Russian people, or even his resentment of the Jews, as an excuse for continuing to evade the challenge of his life and his work would only confirm the worst of his charges against us—the charge that we are cowards. And it would bring us ever closer to the day when we, too, might find ourselves plunged headlong into that pit out of which Solzhenitsyn once clawed his way so that the dead might be remembered and the living might be saved.

The 1990s

Editor's Note

W HEN Podhoretz retired as editor in chief of *Commentary* in 1995, he could look back at three-and-a-half decades of eventful American history: a civil-rights movement that was by turns successful and then twisted; a war in Vietnam that had been nobly begun, but then mismanaged, lost, and misremembered; American support for Israel that had come in the nick of time during two wars but that had wavered during many years of trouble with Palestinian terrorists; and, most important, the end of the Cold War, which on the one hand had vindicated neoconservatism's hard stance against Communist totalitarianism, but on the other had introduced the uncertainties of a multipolar world. Readers who have come thus far in this collection have seen, too, how the decades witnessed Podhoretz's own development—a matter of "breaking ranks" as he quit what the critic Harold Rosenberg had in another context called "the herd of independent minds" always moving Left, and joined the squad of intellectuals, truly (as he sees it, and I agree) independent but self-disciplined and cohesive, now moving Right.

What the present collection should also reveal, however, are the core principles that over the years have endured in Podhoretz's writing, adapted to circumstances, naturally, yet steady enough to be seen as incorruptible. These principles are the free pursuit of happiness, equality of opportunity, and the importance of literature and the arts in exhibiting the variousness with which all human beings, ordinary folk as well as intellectuals, and with manifold degrees of success and unsuccess, have seized their opportunities and realized their happiness. That such moral and cultural commitments should entail a passionately patriotic attachment to America and a correlatively passionate concern for Israel has been a palmary motif throughout his career.

So much is evident in the poignantly brief "Valedictory" he wrote in 1995 on stepping down after thirty-five years as the editor of *Commentary,* and turning the reins over to his long-time deputy Neal Kozodoy. Though I have not included it here, I wish to quote a passage from this piece—a passage that is itself a quotation from a talk Podhoretz had delivered ten years earlier, on the occasion of his twenty-fifth anniversary as editor of the magazine:

> I am . . . proud that I have been able, in and through *Commentary,* to defend my *own*—my own country and the values and institutions for which it stands: my own people and the religious and cultural heritage by which we have been shaped. Like so many of us, I was educated to believe that the *last* thing one ought to be defending was one's own, that it was more honorable and nobler to turn one's back on one's own and fight for others and for other things in which one had no personal stake or interest. This has been a very hard lesson to unlearn, and I am proud to have unlearned it.
>
> *Commentary* has defended America at a time when America has been under moral and ideological attack. *Commentary* has defended the Jewish people and the Jewish state when they, too, and for many of the same reasons, have been subjected to a relentless assault on their legitimacy and even their very existence. For me there has been no conflict or contradiction involved in defending this dual heritage by which I have been formed.

In this short statement, Podhoretz provides a key to his overall perspective. But he gives us a more elaborate account of that perspective in "Neoconservatism: A Eulogy." Here, by way of correcting certain persistent misconceptions about this much misunderstood movement (or "tendency," as he instructs us it more accurately should be called), he traces its history and defines its nature as a new species of conservatism which "came into the world to combat the dangerous lies that were being spread by the radicalism of the 1960s and that were being accepted as truth by the established liberal institutions of the day." Now, after some thirty years, neoconservatism is dead, not because it failed but because it succeeded, and to a greater extent than anyone had once imagined possible. And while "it no longer exists as a distinctive phenomenon requiring a special name of its own," it has left behind a living legacy "of emphasis, of ideas, and of people" that will play an essential part in the "conservative work yet to be done." (This prediction concerning the legacy of neoconservatism would, in the field of foreign policy and especially in the debates over the Second Gulf War, turn out to be far more accurate than Podhoretz clearly expected. But the name, far from being interred, would come to be much more widely used than ever before—so widely, indeed, that it would be applied not only to its true legatees but even to conservatives who had been on the Right all their political lives.)

Neoconservatives in America greatly helped, in the wake of our defeat in Vietnam, to concentrate the minds of politicians and voters on the fact that all countries defend themselves against their enemies, and that the chief enemy of our liberal, capitalist democracy was the Soviet Union. The galvanizing crisis, demonstrating that those Communist totalitarians were still expansionist, was the 1979 invasion of Afghanistan.

Visiting Jerusalem in 1995 for the bar mitzvah of the eldest of the four children born to his daughter Ruthie, who had by that point been living there for eighteen years, Podhoretz in "Israel—with Grandchildren" wonders what crisis would give conservatives in the Jewish state a similar opportunity to concentrate their country's mind. The war-weary Israelis who support the "peace process"—turning over land for a Palestinian state in exchange for fraudulent promises of peaceful coexistence—remind Podhoretz of the self-loathing of many American intellectuals during and after the Vietnam War, for whom our involvement was worse than a blunder or a crime: it was in their eyes "the poisoned fruit of a rotten tree," a country "evil" from the get-go because it had, among other things, been founded on the conquest of Native American peoples. The essay ends movingly, as Podhoretz tearfully worries about his beloved Israeli grandchildren growing up in a country whose dangers, acute enough already, are increased by an intellectual class and a government sunk in wishful thinking.

"*Lolita,* My Mother-in-Law, the Marquis de Sade, and Larry Flynt" is surely one of the best essays Podhoretz has written, even if, at the end, he offers no firm suggestion as to what might be done about the problems he has posed. The pollution of our cultural environment, through pornography in this case, cries out, Podhoretz says, for governmental regulation quite as much as the pollution of our natural environment has done. Only, he goes on, one can't imagine bureaucrats or judges capable of discriminating between, on this side, misogynistic perverts like the Marquis de Sade and Larry Flynt, and on that side, artists like D. H. Lawrence and Vladimir Nabokov. In an earlier age of reticence, bureaucrats and judges were more likely to lump the latter with the former, dirty minds all. Nowadays they are likely to do the reverse, regarding *Hustler* or Vivid Video's manufactures as protected expressions of free speech just like the aforesaid novels. That was the premise of Miloš Forman's *The People vs. Larry Flynt,* the overrated film presenting "the People" as puritan troglodytes, *Hustler* as some "down-market version of *Playboy,*" and Flynt, its editor, as a sweet splicing of Huck Finn and Abbie Hoffman.

Lolita, Podhoretz recognizes, is a "masterpiece" which exhibits "dazzling virtues as a work of art," but the extreme aestheticism of its author raises a difficult issue. Podhoretz is happy to stipulate that aestheticism, also known by its slogan "art for art's sake," helped to free artists from the obligation to create works for the sake of God, morality, society, or a party line—all jobs better done by priests, parents, teachers, journalists, publicists, et al. But at the same time he reminds us that aestheticism risks fostering a hermeticism in the artist, a turning away from "any and all obligations other than those imposed by the laws of his art"—obligations to consider what, for example, children or unstable adults would make of the work he created.

So with *Lolita:* by treating pedophilia so "beautifully," Nabokov had effectually made it, if not beautiful in itself (he did regard it as a perversion), then at least less "unthinkable." Tolerance for it sneaks in under the radar, so to speak. To understand Humbert Humbert's perversion, as Trilling claimed the novel helped him do, is a major step toward forgiving and accepting it. Which, taking the slide down the slippery slope, is to reach that realm where all sex acts are equivalent, and where "liberated" swingers are supposed to enjoy "unalloyed ecstasy." In the place where real people live, however, "it brings the unbearable lightness of being" that Kundera so chillingly depicted, and that we in America face when, deviance having been defined down and down, the Humbert of the hour has become a Woody Allen, scarcely hurt by scandal.

The *"Lolita"* essay makes one think again of the "bloody crossroads." Aesthetes are traveling down one road and don't seem interested in any other. Politicos are traveling down *their* road, and are also uninterested in any other. The first write and read novels like *Lolita,* loftily indifferent to the harm such works may do. The politicos either don't care for art at all, or they want writers, painters, filmmakers, and so on to produce agitprop, which in its cruder forms is actually less dangerous than the likes of *Lolita* because it is so easily seen for the hackwork it is. As a critic, Podhoretz characteristically concerns himself with problems directly *at* the crossroads—the aesthetically successful work of art that embodies ideas about politics, and reality in general, that we need to take note of; or works of art that *claim* to be about nothing outside themselves (art for its own sake), but that in fact *are* about something else—a morally dangerous something in the case of Nabokov, or a theologically momentous something in the case of Bach or Beethoven, about which more below.

Still another case in point is Philip Roth. From the beginning of his career in the late 1950s (which Podhoretz as a young editor helped to sponsor), the greatly talented novelist addressed in "Philip Roth, Then and Now" had high literary ambitions. However, he had no interest in—he was indeed incapable of—rising above his passions and ideas to sculpt some Keatsian cold pastoral. Rather, he wanted "to take stock of the world in which he lived," as Podhoretz says. But for Roth, taking stock of that world meant to "give it the business, as only someone with so wicked a pen and so unforgiving a mind as his could do."

So adept was Roth at catching and laughing at the foibles of Jews in America that older Jewish readers, even those too sophisticated to insist that he write more positively about his people and theirs, could feel as though anti-Semitism had recruited a dirty-mouthed collaborator. More, he seemed during the 1970s and 1980s to have become what Podhoretz called "the laureate of the New Class," the Left-liberal intelligentsia that regarded itself as the nation's "conscience" and was accordingly anti-anti-Communist (which in many instances made it anti-American) and anti-Zionist (which often made it borderline anti-Semitic).

In *American Pastoral,* which Podhoretz considers his best novel, Roth appeared to have reevaluated some of the New Class assumptions, becoming more critical of them than he was before: "Here, for once, it was the ordinary Jews of his childhood who were celebrated—for their decency, their sense of responsibility, their seriousness about their work, their patriotism—and here, for once, those who rejected and despised such virtues were shown to be either pathologically nihilistic or smug, self-righteous, and unimaginative." But then, with *I Married a Communist,* Roth, as though to demonstrate that he hadn't really become a neoconservative, reverted to the "old-time" anti-anti-Communism he had intellectually grown up on. It's a relapse that, however, doesn't negate the achievement of *American Pastoral*—a foretaste, Podhoretz ends by hoping, of yet better novels to come.

"What Happened to Ralph Ellison" connects with two earlier essays in this *Reader:* obviously "My Negro Problem—and Ours" and, less obviously, "The Terrible Question of Aleksandr Solzhenitsyn." It was Ralph

Waldo Ellison, as many readers need to be reminded, even his last name chiming with Emerson. Ellison refused to be ghettoized. He was proud of his American roots, which were no less important to him as a black writer than equally deep national roots were to, say, Bellow, Bernard Malamud, or Roth as Jewish writers.

Like the young Baldwin, Ellison recognized that *mere* "protest novels" were sentimentally, morally reductive. The artful protest novel—think Stendhal's *The Red and the Black,* Dickens's *Bleak House,* or Twain's *Huckleberry Finn*—makes its case while still complicating motives and consequences. Ellison's *Invisible Man* had done just that back in the 1950s, and the novelist had earned enough moral authority, as we saw in the early 1960s, to complicate Podhoretz's own mixed-marriages approach to the race problem in America.

Podhoretz at once got Ellison's point that such marriages would only produce more looked-upon-as-black babies, plus Ellison's other insistence that black culture was based on more than simple oppression, and was richer than, as an outsider, he had thought. It took him longer, though, to understand Ellison's point about the one-dimensionality of protest literature. Influenced by the socialist critic Irving Howe and by a Baldwin who was in the early 1960s reversing his famously negative view of the protest novel, the young Podhoretz wanted black writers to follow suit.

Thirty years on, with the publication of Ellison's posthumous *Juneteenth,* Podhoretz could more coolly assess the novelist's achievements in the aesthetic terms Ellison himself had always appealed to. And, alas, he was to find him wanting, not only in *Juneteenth* but to his surprise also in *Invisible Man.* On a third reading, it now struck him as too mechanically, not to say "gratuitous[ly]" symbolist in method. Further, and more seriously, it lacked the profound universality that might have helped it survive what was so patently "dated" about its main theme. Invisible men? Blacks were no longer invisible, what with affirmative-action placements everywhere and, in the academy, multiculturalist privileging (based on a counting of beans by color, not by intrinsic worth, that Ellison himself deplored). Then again, the novel's hustlers and pimps are tamely "represented as ingenious and admirably resourceful, not as menacing or dangerous," whereas in subsequent decades what has most affected race relations in America is "black violence and criminality, the fear of which has spread even among the most sympathetic white liberals."

Well, there we are. Ellison lived long enough to see and lament these developments, but he never wrote the novel to depict and analyze them.

What he did live to write were essays that, for all their stodginess, seem remarkable to Podhoretz for the bravery of the lonely stands they took on a whole range of issues. Which is where the connection with Solzhenitsyn enters in: like the Russian, Ellison wished to be known as a novelist, but like Solzhenitsyn, too, he wrote only one good novel. (To this I would add, however, that the quality of Ellison's essays surely weighs light on the scale compared to the great Russian's *Gulag* trilogy and *The Oak and the Calf.*)

Similar discriminations are in order when weighing Norman Mailer's books: from a strictly literary point of view, there's nothing in his many novels to match the nonfictional *Armies of the Night.* And what's amiss in the fiction and nonfiction alike, as one sees in "A Foul-Weather Friend to Norman Mailer" (the only item in this section of the *Reader* to have been published previously between hard covers) is the writer's philosophical, moral, and political ideas. When it comes to critical judgment at the cross-roads where literature and politics meet—where, in the best of cases, the literature is truly literature (the right words in the right order, etc.) and the politics, or more generally the ideas, merit consideration—then most of us, including Podhoretz, prefer the books whose understanding of life is close to our own, frequently because our own understanding has been shaped precisely by such books. And when we are friends with an author, as Podhoretz was very intimately a friend to Mailer beginning in the late 1950s, we usually find it impossible to sustain the relationship when his ideas diverge radically from our own.

Not that Podhoretz didn't try, especially during the foul weather marked by Mailer's attraction to drugs and violence, his compulsively "serious" (as against casual) promiscuity, his near-fatal stabbing of his second wife and subsequent couple of weeks at Bellevue for psychiatric observation, and so on. Podhoretz's portrait of his friendship with Mailer is not only unembarrassed in its affection, it's also candidly self-examining. For the salient episode—Mailer's influentially unfavorable review of *Making It* in the pages of the Family's bible, the *Partisan Review*—was far from disinterested. It was an act of almost fraternal betrayal, challenging the betrayed friend, who naturally feels tempted to sulk in resentment, first to understand why the betrayer did it, and second, since so much love has hitherto gone into the relationship, to try if possible to remain friends. But in the end it was "no go," not so much because of the betrayal as because their ideas had grown too far apart. Not to mention the fact that Podhoretz's initial enthusiasm for Mailer's work waned on rereadings, and virtually faded altogether as the years wore on.

Isaiah Berlin was a philosopher and a historian of ideas rather than a novelist, but Podhoretz—exactly as he does with Roth, Ellison, and Mailer—thickens the texture and adds weight to the analysis by drawing upon firsthand experience. In "A Dissent on Isaiah Berlin"—a characteristically rich survey of Berlin's work that flies no less characteristically in the face of generally accepted opinion—Podhoretz argues against the enormous reputation enjoyed by this champion of liberal pluralism (with whom he had been acquainted for many years). He readily acknowledges, with the help of a vivid portrait of the man, that Berlin was "extraordinarily brilliant" as well as "a conversationalist of genius, and the most amusing companion one could ever hope to have"; he also warmly praises several of Berlin's essays. But none of this makes Berlin into a great thinker, and still less—given his refusal to speak out in public on a number of crucial issues about which he fumed in private—a moral hero. For these and other reasons, Berlin cannot serve "as the source of a new moral validation and the fount of a new intellectual vitality" for the contemporary liberal thinkers who have been turning to him in their desperate efforts "to resurrect a point of view grown moribund with softness" and spineless in its relativism.

The tersest of notes about the three short pieces that bring this *Reader* to a close. "My New York" laments the dispersal of the Family of writers that once found the city a center of face-to-face intellectual life, contested of course, but always vital. With the scattering of colleagues came, too, the degradation of the physical environment of the city, but Podhoretz takes occasion to praise Rudolph Giuliani for acting on the now well-known "broken windows" theory and, especially through the police department, making the city safer and more beautiful than it had been in twenty years.

"Was Bach Jewish?" is a jeu d'esprit contrasting the felt spirit of Bach's music (earthbound, law-abiding, and accepting of the mortal human condition) with that of Beethoven's (mystical, antinomian, and defiant toward death): the one essentially Old Testament, the other New (though akin less to Jesus in the Gospels than to Paul in the Epistles). In any event, the essay brings out one of Podhoretz's deepest passions—listening to music.

Finally, a millennium-closing piece from the *Wall Street Journal,* which shows Podhoretz's higher-journalist capacity for summing up big historical movements—here the dialectic between faith and reason over some two thousand years—and which says, in short, that since reason has not succeeded in "killing" God, people should not, through genetic engineering, etc., presume to "play" Him, either.

But I would offer one last, nontheological word. In 1995, at the banquet commemorating Podhoretz's retirement as editor in chief of *Commentary,* the novelist and critic Cynthia Ozick said that "He has written some of the finest and cleanest and most persuasive prose of our time." This collection, restricted as it is to the second half of the twentieth century, does not include any samples of the work Podhoretz has done since the new millennium began and he entered his amazingly prolific seventies—none of his many essays on a typically wide range of subjects, and nothing from the two splendid books he has also produced: *My Love Affair with America* (2000) and *The Prophets: Who They Were, What They Are* (2002).

Though keeping these articles and books out of reach, this collection will, I trust, provide vindication enough of Ozick's celebratory judgment for readers both anciently and now newly familiar with Norman Podhoretz's writings. As Paul Johnson says at the beginning of this volume, he is something of an American prophet. Through all our political and cultural wars he has, as directed by his touchstone in Deuteronomy, "chosen life" and given many of us the courage to do the same. And as the author of "some of the finest prose of our time," he has, in the process of so choosing and giving, added new riches to our national literature that (if I may borrow one last time from Keats) have earned him a place among the American writers.

—TLJ

NEOCONSERVATISM: A EULOGY

IN PROPOSING TO DELIVER A
eulogy in honor of neoconservatism, I am obviously implying that it is
dead. But is it? There are those who think that neoconservatism is still very
much with us; if so, in rushing to eulogize it I could be fairly accused of
staging a scene out of one of those buried-alive horror stories by Edgar
Allan Poe. Others might say that instead of trying to bury neoconservatism
alive, I have come to orate over an empty coffin; maybe neoconservatism is
not dead but only temporarily missing, which would leave us with a kind
of corpus delecti problem.

Among those who deny that neoconservatism is dead are its enemies on
the Right, the so-called paleoconservatives, who have long regarded it as a
sinister force—in both senses of the word sinister. To them, neoconservatism is not only wicked but, as *Human Events* put it recently in an attack
on the new *Weekly Standard* and its editor William Kristol, a "sort of . . .
Trojan Horse . . . , a vehicle for moving the [Republican] party leftward."
Conversely, many of the enemies of neoconservatism on the Left—who,
despite the sectarian animosities that have lately infected the conservative
movement, are much more numerous than its enemies on the Right—see
it as the driving force behind everything symbolized by the name of Newt
Gingrich.

Nor is it only the enemies of neoconservatism who deny that it is dead.
Many of its friends do the same—a denial that in their case is mainly motivated by the wish to deprive its enemies of the joy they must feel at such
wonderful news. But the liberal enemies of neoconservatism have no reason to rejoice at the news of its death because, as I hope to show, the legacy
it has left behind will continue to plague them for a very long time to
come. Which is to say that as between neoconservatism's enemies on the
Right, to whom it is a leftist Trojan horse, and its enemies on the Left, who
can perceive not a dime's worth of difference between the neoconservatives
and Newt Gingrich and his troops, it is its enemies on the Left who are
closer to the truth.

BUT LET ME FIRST explain why I believe that neoconservatism is dead—
by which, reverting from metaphor to straightforward denotation, I mean
quite simply that it no longer exists as a distinctive phenomenon requiring
a special name of its own. And perhaps the best place to begin such an
explanation is with the name itself.

"Neo" of course means new, suggesting that neoconservatism was a new
kind of conservatism; and so it was. But before counting the ways in which
it was new, I want to correct a common error concerning the name itself. I
have no idea who first coined it, but I do know that, despite what almost
everyone seems to think, it was not invented by the late Michael Harrington
toward the end of the 1960s. In 1963, when I was still on the Left, I beat
Harrington to the punch by applying the term to Walter Lippmann, Clinton Rossiter, and a number of others who, I wrote then, were "overim-
pressed with the evil propensities of man and underimpressed with the
possibility of political and social arrangements that would encourage the development of the human potentiality for good instead of concentrating on
restraint of the bad." But early though I was, I cannot claim to be the original author of the term. The *Oxford English Dictionary* traces it back to a
1960 review in the British monthly *Encounter* by G. L. Arnold (the pseudonym adopted for a time by the late George Lichtheim), while a recent letter
in the (London) *Times Literary Supplement* finds an even earlier appearance
in a piece by Dwight Macdonald published in the *Reporter* in 1952.

It is true, however, that the term "neoconservative" only entered into
widespread usage in the late 1960s after Harrington and some of his socialist comrades applied it to a group of intellectuals who had just begun voicing serious doubts about the leftist ideas and policies they themselves had
helped to develop and propagate in the years just past.

The newness of neoconservatism begins, then, with the people who
made up this movement—or tendency, as I prefer to describe it, since it
never had or aspired to the kind of central organization characteristic of a
movement. In talking about those people, it is impossible to avoid Irving
Kristol's definition of a neoconservative as a liberal who has been mugged
by reality. Yet famous though this definition has become, there is something slightly misleading about it.

No doubt a goodly number of the people who came to be known as
neoconservatives had formerly been liberals; but what is often overlooked
under the influence of Kristol's irresistible witticism is that many had also
once been radicals. In fact, the most notable example was Kristol himself,

who had gone through a Trotskyist phase in his youth in the 1930s—a very brief phase, but decisive in his intellectual formation. I am another example. As I have often complained, Kristol and I are widely taken to be the same person; but one of the several ways in which we differ is age. Being ten years younger than he, I was born too late to get involved in the old radicalism of the 1930s. I did, however, make up for this deprivation by becoming intellectually active in the new radicalism of the early 1960s before breaking ranks with it and entering into a de facto alliance with the neoconservatives which in due course became de jure. And in the age cohort about ten years or so below me, a substantial number of latter-day Trotskyists—or should I call them neo-Trotskyists?—known as Shachtmanites drifted closer and closer to the neoconservatives in the late 1960s and early 1970s and ended by becoming indistinguishable from them.

NEOCONSERVATISM is usually identified as a movement of New York Jewish intellectuals, and there is no question that the ex-radicals who became neoconservatives were mostly intellectuals of Jewish birth who came from or worked in New York. But for whatever it may be worth by way of sociological illumination, I would point out that the *liberals* who were mugged by reality into neoconservatism were mostly non-Jews like James Q. Wilson, Daniel P. Moynihan, Jeane Kirkpatrick, Michael Novak, Richard J. Neuhaus, William J. Bennett, and George Weigel. And for whatever additional illumination it may provide, except for Jeane Kirkpatrick and Richard Neuhaus, all were not only Gentile but Catholic—and Neuhaus would later remove himself from the short list of exceptions by leaving the Lutheran Church and going over to Rome.

Most members of this group—along with some of the ex-radicals— tended to reject the label "neoconservative." Not only did they consider it pejorative (in those prehistoric days, people actually regarded the term liberal as an honorific and contended fiercely for possession of it), they also thought it was wrong. So far as they were concerned, they were indeed still liberals, fighting to reclaim the traditional principles of liberalism from the leftists who had hijacked and corrupted it. Most of them also remained members of the Democratic party, supporters of Senator Hubert Humphrey (the liberal anti-Communist Humphrey of the 1950s, not the Humphrey who went Left in the last years of his life) and especially the great cold warrior Senator Henry "Scoop" Jackson who, they vainly hoped, would rescue the party from the McGovernite forces that took it over in 1972 and return it to its old Trumanesque glory.

Nevertheless, nothing these people could say or do prevented them from being called neoconservatives by everyone else, and most of them, with varying degrees of reluctance, eventually surrendered to the name. They did so because despite their best efforts and fondest wishes, the word "liberal" had been so successfully co-opted by the Left that applying it to themselves could only confuse and mislead. Or, as Moynihan recently put it, the neoconservatives were like "good Catholics who were excommunicated and who said, finally, OK, we're Protestants."

BUT THE NEOCONSERVATIVES brought something new to conservatism besides their own persons. They were not converts who earnestly and faithfully and humbly—certainly not humbly—embraced an established faith. If they had been converts of that stripe, there might have been some justification in the speech once delivered by a paleoconservative professor who, upset by all the attention the neoconservatives were getting, declared that while he had nothing against welcoming this repentant whore into the church, he violently objected to turning over the pulpit to her. But the malice here was misplaced, because the neoconservatives were not applying for admission to an established church. They were, rather, caught up in the process of shaping a perspective of their own that differed in important respects from the older varieties of American conservatism.

Thus, in the area of domestic policy, the neoconservatives dissociated themselves from the wholesale opposition to the welfare state which had marked American conservatism since the days of the New Deal. Unlike the older schools of American conservatism, they were not for abolishing the welfare state but only for setting certain limits to it. Those limits did not, in their view, involve issues of principle, such as the legitimate size and role of the central government in the American constitutional order. Rather, they were to be determined by practical considerations, such as the precise point at which the incentive to work was undermined by the availability of welfare benefits, or the point at which the redistribution of income began to erode economic growth, or the point at which egalitarianism came into serious conflict with liberty.

A related distinction between neoconservatism and the older varieties of conservatism lay in their differing attitudes toward the labor movement. The older conservatives were uniformly hostile to labor unions, both in principle and in practice, whereas the neoconservatives remained as friendly to the labor movement as they had been in their days on the Left.

There were many reasons for this, some nostalgic and atavistic, rooted in the working-class background out of which many neoconservatives came. But perhaps the most important reason of all had nothing whatever to do with personal sentiment or domestic affairs. It was the fact that the leadership of the labor movement was so staunchly anti-Communist. Since anti-Communism was the ruling passion of the neoconservatives in foreign affairs, they were naturally drawn into an alliance with the AFL-CIO, which in those days was as passionately anti-Communist as they.

Now it goes without saying that all the older varieties of conservatives were ardently anti-Communist as well. But as Richard Gid Powers points out in *Not Without Honor,* his new history of American anti-Communism, they tended to worry less about aggression from the outside than about the threat of internal subversion; and in tracking down the sources of that threat, they were not, to put it gently, always scrupulous in distinguishing among the various factions on the Left. The truth is that in their heart of hearts most of the older conservatives simply did not believe that anyone on the slippery slopes of the Left, let alone a "labor agitator," could really be an anti-Communist.

Conversely, they found it hard to believe that businessmen who contributed large sums of money to the Republican party and made the right noises about taxes and government regulation could be less than fully committed to the struggle against Communism. Yet, hard to believe or not, the business community did on the whole support the policy of détente with the Soviet Union and the opening to China pursued by the Nixon and Ford administrations. For, as George Will would later say of the bankers during the Polish crisis of the early 1980s, they loved commerce more than they loathed Communism.

The neoconservatives did not love commerce, or anything else, more than they loathed Communism; nor did their allies in the labor movement. Few businessmen, and few Republicans for that matter, had ever met a Communist. Some of them seemed to think that the Soviet Union was one huge regulatory agency, a sort of gigantic Federal Trade Commission armed with nuclear weapons (which was about as close as they could come to an image of absolute evil). Others were so temperamentally remote from and unfamiliar with the phenomenon of ideological fervor that they thought the Soviets could in effect be bribed out of Communism by the right business deals.

No such illusions ever clouded the minds either of the neoconservative intellectuals or of their allies in the labor movement. They had all had first-hand experience of one kind or another with Communism; they knew it for the evil totalitarian system it was; they knew how it operated; and they knew how to contend with it.

IT IS INSTRUCTIVE in this connection to remind ourselves that Ronald Reagan had been a labor leader, and had fought the Communists in that capacity; and Reagan can also be considered one of the first neoconservatives, having been a liberal Democrat for most of his political life and then becoming a Republican only at the age of fifty-one. And it is even more instructive in this same context to ponder a wonderful anecdote, possibly apocryphal, about Ernest Bevin, the British labor leader who became foreign secretary just in time to attend the summit conference with Stalin at Potsdam in 1945. Though Bevin had never before participated in an international negotiation, he had spent years fighting the attempts by the British Communist party to take over the local trade unions. Asked upon returning from Potsdam what the Russians were like, he replied, "They're just like the Communists."

The neoconservatives in America, too, knew that the Russians were just like the Communists they had been fighting for so long (in some instances, after having once been Communists themselves). Among other things, this meant they understood that the Soviet Union was not a "normal" imperial power, merely seeking its place in the international sun, and that it was a great mistake—moral no less than political—to treat it as such.

In other words, the neoconservatives understood that the Soviet Union had more in common with the revolutionary and expansionist pre–World War II Germany under Hitler than with the authoritarian but nonrevolutionary pre–World War I Germany under Kaiser Wilhelm. And so it was they who led the attack against an American policy based on the Wilhelmine model, the policy of détente, and it was they who also took the lead in making the case against the correlative delusions of arms control and for a stronger national defense in response to the great Soviet arms buildup of the 1970s.

Another issue of foreign policy on which the neoconservatives differed from the older schools of conservatism was Israel. Some older conservatives were, for religious reasons, uncomfortable with the idea of Jewish sovereignty in the Holy Land; to others the Jewish state was a parasitical and untrustworthy socialist country. But the neoconservatives saw Israel as a highly vulnerable outpost and surrogate of the West in a strategically vital region, and they interpreted the fierce assault on its legitimacy as part of the ideological offensive against the democratic world led and orchestrated by the Soviet Union. Thus, while their enthusiastic support of Israel was often attributed to the fact that so many neoconservatives were Jewish, the truth was that it had at least as much if not more to do with the fact that they were anti-Communists.

FINALLY, there was the realm of culture. If anti-Communism was the ruling passion of the neoconservatives in foreign affairs, opposition to the counterculture of the 1960s was their ruling passion at home. Indeed, I suspect that revulsion against the counterculture accounted for more converts to neoconservatism than any other single factor.

This revulsion was not only directed against the counterculture itself; it was also inspired by the abject failure of the great institutions of the liberal community to resist the counterculture. First the universities capitulated, then the national media, and finally even the Democratic party. In part the problem was simple moral cowardice, but in part it was the sheer inability of these institutions to defend themselves intellectually when they came under attack. William Phillips, the editor of *Partisan Review,* once told the British critic Kenneth Tynan, who was throwing hoary Marxist arguments in his face, that these arguments were so old he couldn't remember the answers. Well, neither could the great institutions of American liberalism remember the answers when the counterculture assaulted them as bastions of oppression and repression, pillars of a society so rotten that it was beyond help through reform and so far gone that it had to be destroyed before it could be saved.

Here too, as with the strictly political battles involving policy toward the Soviet Union and the Communist world in general, the neoconservatives enjoyed a great advantage over other conservatives in being intimately familiar with the sources of the enemy's arguments and attitudes. In this case the sources were the adversary culture of modernist literature, avant-garde art, and bohemian libertinism, on which many neoconservatives had themselves cut their cultural teeth. Some of *them* may have forgotten the answers; but under the pressure of the countercultural assault, they quickly began to remember, or in some instances to discover for the first time, why American society and its sustaining institutions were worth defending—or, to state it more strongly and more accurately, why the traditional values of the bourgeois democratic order were superior to any of the known alternatives.

Among the sustaining institutions worth defending was capitalism, which needed defending in those days if anything did. So tarnished had its reputation become—even among conservatives, and even among capitalists themselves—that it dared not speak its name. At a time when so many other formerly forbidden practices were noisily coming out of their respective closets and shouting their names from every rooftop and every talk show, the proponents of capitalism were still evasively resorting to euphemisms like "free enterprise" or the "market system" or the "free market." And little wonder: the word "capitalism," like "neoconservatism" after it, was first employed (in the early nineteenth century) mainly as a term of abuse, and still carried strongly pejorative connotations.

It was the neoconservatives who decided that the time had come to drag capitalism out of the closet. In doing so, they defiantly revived the name as part of an aggressive campaign to demonstrate not only that capitalism was far better than socialism at producing wealth, but that it even managed to distribute it more widely; and not only that it was good in itself, being a form of freedom, but that it was also a great bulwark against totalitarianism.

Admittedly, there was at first a limit to the enthusiasm with which the neoconservatives pressed this campaign. Irving Kristol, for instance, could only bring himself to give (in the title of one of his books) *Two Cheers for Capitalism*. But Michael Novak later made up for this in *The Spirit of Democratic Capitalism*, where he gave it the equivalent of four, bringing the neoconservative average up to the full and proper measure of three.*

THIS, THEN, is the list of things that made neoconservatism new and different. It is in looking over the list today that I find it hard to escape the conclusion that this phenomenon no longer exists as a distinctive thing in itself, requiring a special name of its own.

Begin again with the people. If the neoconservatives were new to conservatism when they first appeared on the scene, there is self-evidently nothing new about them today, twenty-five or thirty years later. Irving Kristol is known as the godfather of neoconservatism, but by now he might more accurately be called its grandfather, since there is not only a second generation to the manner born, but yet another hungry generation in the wings already preparing to tread that one down.

Neoconservatism is even old enough to have spawned several genera-

---

*George Gilder, in *Wealth and Poverty*, went Novak at least one better, but never having been on the Left, Gilder was not, strictly speaking, a neoconservative. Nor was Peter L. Berger, who, in *The Capitalist Revolution*, came closer to Kristol's two than to Novak's four or Gilder's five.

tions of defectors. At one end, a few of the founding fathers, including Daniel P. Moynihan and Daniel Bell, have broken with it entirely. Moynihan has reverted to the liberalism he always insisted he had never abandoned, while Bell has gone back to whatever it is he has gone back to. And at the other end, a couple of young people have lately been furthering their journalistic careers by denouncing the neoconservatives who launched those careers in the first place, thereby demonstrating how much nourishment can be had under the right circumstances from biting the hand that has fed you.

In addition to losing its newness simply by virtue of having been around for a long time, neoconservatism has also been losing its ideological distinctiveness. If it originally differed from the older varieties of conservatism in wishing to reform rather than abolish the welfare state, few traces of that difference remain visible today. By now most neoconservatives have pretty well given up on the welfare state—by which, as they see it, American society has been mugged just as surely as they themselves once were by reality. They may disagree with other schools of conservative thought, and with one another, over the best and most humane way to phase out particular features of the welfare state, or over the question of whether states can do a better job than the federal government in administering social policy. But there is hardly any disagreement over the harm the welfare state has done in fostering illegitimacy and all the terrible social pathologies that flow from babies having babies. Nor is there any disagreement over the desirability of working to get rid of the welfare state, or at least as much of it as is politically possible.

There is an instructive parallel here with the defectors from Stalinism in the 1920s and 1930s who became Trotskyists. These Trotskyists regarded the Stalinists as betrayers of the Revolution; they, by contrast, were the true Communists, the true heirs of Marx and Lenin. The Stalinists, for their part, regarded the Trotskyists as thoroughgoing traitors to the Communist cause who were only using Trotsky as a way station into the anti-Communist camp. Of course, the language used by the Stalinists against the Trotskyists was much more violent and vituperative than I have indicated, but in a fair number of cases the substance of the accusation turned out to be justified: many of the Trotskyists did wind up in the anti-Communist camp. Similarly with the analogous charge hurled against the neoconservatives by their former political friends on the Left—namely, that for all their protestations, the neoconservatives were not really the true heirs of pre-1960s' American liberalism but rather apostates on the road to the Right.

Where the welfare state and social engineering in general are concerned, it must be acknowledged that this accusation was on the mark.

On the other hand, with regard to another major issue of domestic social policy—namely, affirmative action—the opposite was true. The neoconservatives fought against affirmative action from the very beginning, and precisely on the ground that it represented a violation of the traditional liberal principle that every individual should be treated on his own merits as an individual and not as a member of a group. Here the neoconservatives really were the true defenders of pre-1960s liberalism in the face of a policy built on the rejection by the Left of a fundamental element of the liberal creed. And here, in contrast to what happened with the issue of the welfare state, it was the older schools of conservative thought that came around to the neoconservative position.

Thus it was that some on the Right who had opposed the civil-rights movement even before it was radicalized in the late 1960s, and who had never had any use for Martin Luther King Jr. when he was alive, later learned under the tutelage of the neoconservatives that one of the most effective weapons they could wield in the fight against affirmative action was King's dream of a world in which all would be judged not by the color of their skin but by the content of their characters. In this way many conservatives came to embrace the ideals which had animated the civil-rights movement during what the late Bayard Rustin called its "heroic period," and which the neoconservatives continued to uphold even when the most vocal leaders of the black community itself had turned to a very different set of ideas. This belated conversion of a large part of the conservative movement, however, again had the effect of robbing neoconservatism of ideological distinctiveness, if from the other direction.

In foreign affairs, neoconservatism has lost not so much its distinctiveness within the larger conservative community as its own internal identity. Among some of the older varieties of conservatism, the end of the Cold War has led to a resurgence of isolationism. This is less surprising than it may seem, since it was only the fight against Communism that drew many conservatives out of their traditionally isolationist shell in the first place (just as it was only the fight against Nazism that drew many liberals out of *their* isolationist shell). With the Soviet Union gone, and with China not yet a threat, these traditionally isolationist conservatives have begun returning, as it were, to normalcy.

On this point, at least, we can say that the neoconservatives are still different. For if there is a neoconservative extant who has become an isolationist, I do not know where to find him. At the same time, though, I can think of only a tiny handful who still advocate the expansive Wilsonian interventionism that grew out of the anti-Communist passions of the neoconservatives at the height of the Cold War, and that repeatedly trumped the prudential cautions of the realists among them. My impression is that today the realists have the upper hand in the neoconservative community, or what is left of it.

But whatever the precise balance of forces may be among these contending schools of thought, in foreign policy it has become impossible to define a neoconservative position. Once upon a time, I could foresee with reasonable assurance where any neoconservative would stand on almost any serious issue in world affairs. Today I am hard put to predict where even some of my closest friends will come out when a contentious issue like Bosnia arises, or on the question of NATO expansion, or on how to deal with China, or on whether to send American troops to the Golan Heights.

As with the Cold War, so with the culture war. Of course, unlike the Cold War, the culture war rages on. But it has moved into a new phase in which the single most salient and most neuralgic issue is abortion; and on that issue a clear neoconservative position is as hard to define as it is in foreign affairs. I would guess that the great majority of neoconservatives consider themselves pro-life. I would also guess that most of them are uneasy with the absolutism of the pro-life movement. But these are only guesses. The fact is that I simply do not know where many of my friends stand on this issue. Despite what the paleoconservatives think, there is no clearly identifiable neoconservative position here.

To be sure, a new front in the culture wars has recently opened on which most neoconservatives do seem to differ from other conservatives, and that is the issue of immigration. The conservative opponents of immigration argue that, unchecked, it will end by destroying the common culture which has given this country its character and held it together in all its diversity. The neoconservatives, myself emphatically included, disagree. In endless hours of private argument with Peter Brimelow and John O'Sullivan, the two leading conservative critics of current immigration policy, I have repeatedly pointed out—to no avail, naturally—that the same cultural anxiety they feel was expressed a century ago by the likes of Henry Adams, John Jay Chapman, and Henry James, and that it turned out to be unwarranted.

For example, in the course of a visit to the Lower East Side of New York in 1905, James persuaded himself that the Yiddish-speaking masses there were an "agency of future ravage" that would topple "the consecrated English tradition" and transform the English language itself beyond recognition: "Whatever we shall know it for," he sighed, "certainly, we shall not know it for English." But the joke was on James, if a joke it was, for perhaps his most devoted, and maybe even his only, readers in the generations ahead would be the children and grandchildren of these agents of future ravage, alarming numbers of whom would go on to produce doctoral dissertations on, precisely, the novels of Henry James.

On immigration, then, we may again have something resembling a distinctive neoconservative position. Nevertheless, important though this issue is, it is not in my judgment enough by itself to bring neoconservatism back to life.

HAVING BEEN A neoconservative for so long that I ought perhaps to be called a paleo-neoconservative, I have good reason to mourn the passing of this movement or tendency. And yet I must confess that its death seems to me more an occasion for celebration than for sadness. For what killed neoconservatism was not defeat but victory; it died not of failure but of success.

Neoconservatism came into the world to combat the dangerous lies that were being spread by the radicalism of the 1960s and that were being accepted as truth by the established liberal institutions of the day. More passionately and more effectively than any other group, the neoconservatives exposed those lies for what they were: expressions of hatred, rooted in utopian greed, for life as it is lived in this country, and weapons in a campaign to deprive it of the will to defend itself against its enemies in the world outside. And more passionately and more effectively than any other group, the neoconservatives undertook the job of rebuilding intellectual and moral confidence in the values and institutions on which American society rests, not to mention the actual physical defenses on which the country's security depends. That effort, extending over a quarter of a century and more, and seeming utterly quixotic when it was launched in the late 1960s, succeeded to so great an extent that the neoconservatives were left, like Othello, with their occupation gone.

Take what I have identified as the two ruling passions of neoconservatism—its anti-Communism and its revulsion against the counterculture. With respect to the former, I would note that, as against the claim that no one foresaw the collapse of the Soviet Union, the neoconservatives, driven by their anti-Communist passions and ideas, argued that the entire purpose of a more determined resistance to Soviet power was to encourage the forces of disintegration that had become visible within the Soviet empire and even within the Soviet heartland itself.

I would not deny that the neoconservatives were as surprised as everyone else by the speed with which the Soviet Union eventually collapsed. But it was they themselves who had held out the promise of just such a collapse, as the ultimate reward of the policy they consistently urged on Ronald Reagan: a military buildup, combined with an ideological offensive, and capped by an active challenge to the widespread notion that the West had an interest in the maintenance of the Soviet empire. (And Reagan, incidentally, though he needed no urging to accept this line of argument, did need a good deal of urging as president to follow through on it.) So, surprised though they were by how fast the Soviet Union collapsed, the neoconservatives were not surprised by the collapse itself. They felt vindicated by it, and rightly so.

As for their other ruling passion, I think we can claim that the defense the neoconservatives mounted of American society and its traditional values against the frontal assaults of the counterculture ended with a victory that in its own modest way resembled the victory of the West over Communism in the Cold War. Who today shies away from the word "capitalism," or denies that it is superior to socialism both in producing wealth and distributing it? Who today celebrates free and easy sex as the road to health and happiness? Who today promotes drugs as the gateway to a higher consciousness? Today family values are all the rage, even among feminists, and indeed even among homosexuals, who have gone from celebrating the "joys of gay sex" to demanding that they be permitted to participate in the joys of married life.

I have no desire to adopt a triumphalist tone, or to suggest that there is no conservative work left to do. On the contrary, in the realm of domestic social policy it is obvious that only a beginning has been made on the work of the conservative revolution—or, rather, counterrevolution. (I prefer the latter term since the purpose of this movement is to dismantle the structures created by the liberal revolution of the past fifty years, and left largely intact even when Republicans came to power, and even after many Democrats had themselves lost faith in them.) But while neoconservatives are deeply involved in the work of the counterrevolution in domestic social policy, they are, as I have already indicated, no longer acting in that area as *neo*conservatives.

And then there is the even more recalcitrant realm of culture. There, the *naked* anti-Americanism which the neoconservatives devoted so much energy to combating has been discredited in its original forms. But at the same time it has mutated into insidious new shapes and thereby acquired a new lease on life, especially in the universities, where the assault on the traditions and values of this society comes disguised, under the name of multiculturalism, as an innocent effort to give their belated due to previously excluded ethnic and sexual minorities.

Nor is the lingering influence of the counterculture confined to the universities. The hostility it bred toward this country—toward its history and toward the values and the moral standards by which it has always tried to live—has been seeping down into secondary- and even elementary-school curricula and classrooms. That same hostility now pervades the mainline churches, the great liberal foundations, and even such formerly staid institutions as the Smithsonian. And in the world of the arts, it enjoys the status of a complacently unchallenged orthodoxy.

Here, too, an enormous amount of conservative work remains to be done—so much, indeed, that in contemplating it I begin to wonder whether I have overstated the extent of neoconservative success in this area. Be that particular accounting as it may, however, there is a big difference between the situation in the period of the neoconservative ascendancy and the situation today. For thanks to the influence of neoconservatism on the conservative movement in general, the philistine indifference to culture which once pervaded that movement is largely gone. Everyone is now so fully alive to the importance of the cultural realm that the neoconservatives are no longer alone on the field of battle contesting ground that to many older conservatives seemed hardly worth taking. We are all Gramscians now.

ANOTHER WAY of putting all this is to say that the conservative work which remains to be done in every realm will be marked and guided and shaped by the legacy neoconservatism has left behind. That legacy has wrought a profound change in the scope and the character and the ethos of American conservatism.

It is a legacy of emphasis, of ideas, and of people. The emphasis is the emphasis on the role of culture and—increasingly as the years have rolled by—on religion as the root and fount of the cultural issues which have moved from the periphery to the center of the national debate. Almost from the moment the neoconservatives appeared on the scene, they began speaking, in Nathan Glazer's famous phrase, of "the limits of social policy," and they began reminding us, in the words of the great couplet from Dr. Johnson that I myself have always loved to quote:

> *How small, of all that human hearts endure,*
> *That part, which laws or kings can cause or cure!*

This reminder was scarcely heeded in a period when everything was being politicized, when all problems were thought to have solutions, and all solutions were believed to lie in the political realm. But today it is finally taking hold, and it will become even more important as the exaggerated expectations once invested in "laws or kings" give way, as they have already started doing, to a new sense of the overriding importance of moral and spiritual factors both in causing and in curing—insofar as they can be cured—the ills of the human condition.

As to the ideas that neoconservatism has left behind, they are ideas about the history and the nature of American society and the American polity—what makes this country tick, and how and why it has managed to provide more freedom and more prosperity to a greater share of its populace than any other on earth. And as to the people, they are people whose intellectual and political skills were developed and sharpened and energized by contact with the special style of discourse that the neoconservatives brought with them from the Left and into the conservative movement.

A word about that style. Hard to describe and harder still to define, it is nevertheless easy to perceive in the primacy it gives and the loyalty it accords to ideas over the details of policy or the demands of party. It is also readily recognizable from the way it synthesizes a number of qualities that are rarely found together, let alone coexisting in such perfect harmony. It is, at its best, exuberantly polemical and combative, and yet always careful to deal honestly with the case against which it is contending; it seeks to marry ideological passion to intellectual disinterestedness; it gives vent to a heated sense of urgency about the present moment while maintaining a sense of historical perspective; and it aims to be simultaneously illuminating to the specialist and accessible to the common reader. Though neoconservatism no longer exists as a unique school of thought, this intellectual style, which has always marked it as unmistakably as the political positions it took, is vibrantly alive in the pages of a classically neoconservative magazine like *Commentary*, and it is already setting its stamp on the *Weekly Standard* where, as I reported earlier, it has been mistaken for a leftist Trojan horse.

———————

Surely nothing is here to make the enemies of neoconservatism happy. Instead, I would say, borrowing from John Milton's lament over the death of Samson:

> *Come, come, no time for lamentation now,*
> *Nor much more cause, Samson . . . hath finish'd*
> *A life Heroic, on his Enemies*
> *Fully reveng'd, hath left them years of mourning.*

And to the veterans of the neoconservative battalions and their friends and heirs, I would say, still borrowing from *Samson Agonistes,* that

> *Nothing is here for tears, nothing to wail*
> *Or knock the breast, no weakness, no contempt,*
> *Dispraise or blame, nothing but well and fair*
> *And what may quiet us in a death so noble.*

But perhaps the tragic Miltonic mode is too elevated for the occasion at hand. In addressing the immediate neoconservative community, then, I will descend from these poetical sublimities and simply express my conviction that it is right and proper and healthy to recognize and openly to acknowledge the end when it comes, the better to make a new beginning in the living spirit of what has passed. I mean to say that this is not a time for mourning or for apprehension or for anxiety, but a time for satisfaction over a just war well fought, and a time for rejoicing in a series of victories that cleared the way and set the stage for other victories in the years to come. In those victories of the future, I believe that the legacy, and the legatees, of neoconservatism, now zestfully thriving all around us, will play as indispensable a part as did the neoconservatives themselves in achieving the victories of the past.

ISRAEL—
WITH GRANDCHILDREN

*T*HE FOLLOWING WAS OBVIOUSLY *written before the black day on which Yitzhak Rabin was assassinated. It is no secret that I have been highly critical of the peace process over which Rabin was presiding, and it should come as no surprise that this caused a personal rupture between us. I first met Rabin in 1967 in Israel, right after the Six-Day War, when he was still chief of staff of the Israeli armed forces. Then, a year or so later, on his way to Washington to take over as the newly appointed ambassador to the United States, he stopped at my apartment in New York where (at the request of the Israeli consul general) I had arranged for him to meet a group of prominent American intellectuals. Though I had not found him exactly endearing in our first meeting in Jerusalem, I was charmed—and also much impressed—by his ill-concealed amazement at some of the incredibly foolish things that were said to him that night. In the ensuing years, I saw him many times, and though we never became close friends, our relations were always relatively cordial. When, however, I began voicing my misgivings over the changes in his thinking that led to the handshake with Yasir Arafat on the White House lawn, he understandably grew cold, and after one very tense accidental encounter in Jerusalem, I never saw him again.*

The article that follows was all but on press when the news came of his assassination, and my immediate inclination—as well as that of the editor of Commentary—*was to suppress it as being out of date, and perhaps also as unseemly. But on further reflection we decided to let it ride as a record of how things stood before Rabin was murdered and as an account of forces that are still at work in Israel and that will continue to make themselves felt even now that he is gone. Given the difficulty in my relations with him, his passing has caused me more personal grief than I would have expected. But personal feelings and political disagreements aside, my judgment is that his assassination was a crime so horrible that it will be remembered as one of the great infamies of Jewish history.*

FRIDAY, SEPTEMBER 1, 1995

Only minutes after we arrive at the airport we get the big news from Noam, the eldest of our four Israeli grandchildren and the one whose bar mitzvah we have come to celebrate: "We have a McDonald's in Jerusalem now—*non*kosher!" From the enthusiasm with which he stresses the fact that this new McDonald's is nonkosher, one might think that Noam was a precocious version of one of those militant secularists who abound in Israel, and especially in Jerusalem where the highly visible presence and power of the ultra-Orthodox *haredim* have provoked among many people a backlash against religion in general. Not at all: his aim is to underline the difference between the new McDonald's and the strictly kosher Burger Ranch (or "*Boorger Rench*," as the Jerusalemites call it) to which on previous visits my wife and I have sometimes taken him and his three younger siblings (Alon, almost ten, and the five-year-old twins Boaz and Avital) for a special treat. This new McDonald's in Jerusalem, Noam wants us to understand, is the real thing—exactly the same as the ones he has come to love so well from previous visits of his own to America.

I will remember this little episode a few days later when watching a clip on CNN (that constant companion of the contemporary American traveler abroad) featuring demonstrations by participants at the UN conference on women in Beijing. None of these demonstrations seems to have anything directly to do with women as such. One, for example, is against American imperialism—a theme I naively thought had gone out with button shoes, or anyway the Cold War, and whose reappearance makes me feel almost nostalgic. Another is directed against the resumption of nuclear testing by the French, reminding me by the novelty of its target country that the Cold War really has ended.

But the most bizarre group of protesters consists of a gaggle of young American women stomping on an effigy of Ronald McDonald and screaming hysterically: "Get out of my backyard! Get out of my country! Get out of my world!" Clearly McDonald's, with its nutritionally incorrect menu and its putatively carcinogenic plastic wastes, has replaced Coca-Cola as the great symbol of a metastasizing American plague in this post–Cold War world—a world more apocalyptic about ecology than about nuclear holocaust and where opposition to nuclear weapons (as the anti-French protests reveal) is itself now based not on the fear of war but on the horror of environmental contamination.

Yet it strikes me that, like Coca-Cola before it, what McDonald's really symbolizes is the universality of human nature. Once, there seemed to be no country and no culture whose people did not fall in love with Coca-Cola the minute they tasted it; and today (to borrow a slogan invented for another product), nobody doesn't like a Big Mac—nobody, anywhere on earth. Where these things are concerned, at least, the dream of Schiller and Beethoven has been realized and all men have already become brothers.

Nor is McDonald's the only sign of progress to which Noam points on the drive from the airport to Jerusalem. "We also have Tower Records and Blockbuster Video," he announces proudly to our granddaughter, his American cousin Sarah ("Nani," to her family). Fresh (and flush) from her own very recent bat mitzvah, Nani has come with us to join in Noam's barmitzvah celebration while getting her first taste of a foreign country.

Eager to sharpen that taste, and forgetting (if I ever really knew, despite having raised four of them) what thirteen year olds are like, I fatuously suggest to Noam that he point out some of the sights to her as we enter Jerusalem. He pauses thoughtfully and then bursts out: "You see that building over there? It's a great place for rollerblading!"

Later, I laugh about this with his mother, our daughter Ruthie, who has now been in Israel for eighteen years, almost half her entire life. She adds to the merriment by informing me that after we were dropped off at the hotel, Noam as an afterthought proposed that Nani visit Yad Vashem, Jerusalem's grim memorial to the Holocaust. "That's what Israel adds up to for an Israeli kid," cracks Ruthie, "McDonald's and the Holocaust."

But once we have had our laugh, she is off on a tirade against the Israeli educational system. As she has told me more than once, secular schools in Israel suffer from all the vices of the "progressive" philosophy of education that was so fashionable in her own childhood in America. Thanks to this system, Israeli kids are largely left to their own devices and taught very little about anything, including their own history. ("If you ask an Israeli kid who the Maccabees are, he'll think you're talking about the local basketball team.") On the other hand, thanks to cable TV, Israeli kids know everything there is to know about America: O. J. Simpson, Michael Jackson, and *NYPD Blue* are more familiar to them than King David or, for that matter, David Ben-Gurion. But this subject soon gets us laughing again at the picture it brings back of Alon, watching television on a visit to New York when he was about six years old and yelling out excitedly in Hebrew to Noam: "Hey; they've got *MacGyver* here, too!" (Along the same lines, this very evening five-year-old Boaz, checking up on the possibilities of cross-cultural communication with his cousin from America, will ask her: "Do you know what means Power Rangers in English?")

SUNDAY, SEPTEMBER 3

Speaking of school, Friday was supposed to be the first day of the new semester, but because of a brief strike by teachers protesting a cut in funds for security guards, the opening is postponed until today (Sunday being an ordinary working day in Israel). Noam is now in high school (they refer to it, European-style, as a *gymnasium*), and out of curiosity to see what the place looks like, I accompany Nadav, my Israeli son-in-law, when he takes time out from his law practice to pick Noam up at the end of the school day.

Having expected something dingy, I am oddly pleased when it turns out to be a fairly new and rather attractive building. But the first thing that hits my eye as we enter is an explosion of graffiti, all of them in English. "FUCK YOU" screams one wall. "FUCK YOUR SISTER" declares another, to which the viewer's attention is helpfully directed by arrows on the floor. And a third, in the largest letters of all, simply says "COOL." This, I gather, is meant as a self-congratulatory comment on the whole project: as Noam, who is completely bilingual himself, explains when I ask why the vandals have used English instead of Hebrew, "English is cool" (so much so that the word itself, pronounced *kul,* has now been imported into Hebrew).

For this we needed a Jewish state? That used to be the all-purpose Israeli mot in the face of anything that departed from pristine Zionist utopianism, and it immediately springs to mind, bringing with it a wry smile at the thought that I, who once made fun of that slogan, should now be involuntarily invoking it in all seriousness myself. And it springs to mind again on a walk we take later that afternoon along a lively pedestrian mall in the center of Jerusalem. It is filled with cafés and restaurants and shops of every variety, including the (to me) now fabled McDonald's, whose presence is announced with a sign reading: "McDonald's—One Minutes [*sic*] Away." (English may be *kul* but it is still a foreign language in the Jewish state.) The mall is also crowded with Israelis of every variety, from *haredim* dressed all in black to a young woman dressed all in black herself except for the words emblazoned in white on her very tight T-shirt which read, "WHO GIVES A SHIT?"

For this we needed a Jewish state? Well, I say to myself, yes. After all, one of the main purposes of establishing a Jewish state was to bring about "the normalization of the Jewish people." Of course, the early Zionist thinkers who developed this concept had something else in view. They envisaged a situation in which Jews, instead of being concentrated overwhelmingly as they were in the Diaspora in a few occupations (and thereby arousing resentment), would like all other peoples work at everything: they would be not only doctors and lawyers and bankers and journalists but also farmers and laborers and soldiers and policemen.

Some early Zionists saw this as one of many ways to cure the "pathologies" and straighten out the "deformations" which, they believed, living in the Diaspora for two thousand years had wrought in the Jewish character: in a sovereign state of their own the Jews would flourish once again and regain the kind of greatness they had shown in biblical times. But there were other Zionist thinkers who cherished the opposite hope: that living in a sovereign state of their own would turn the Jews not into a special or superior breed but into "a people like all other peoples." And so, on the evidence of McDonald's and obscene graffiti and T-shirts and cable television, it has come to pass.

Yet that is far, very far, from the whole story. For one thing, the dream of a "normal" occupational distribution has largely been realized in Israel. Not, to be sure, entirely, since most construction work and many menial jobs are done by Palestinians. Still, Jews now fill most other occupations from which they had traditionally either been barred or which for one reason or another they had avoided in the Diaspora. This is now so commonplace that younger Israelis find it hard to understand a joke that circulated when the state was still in its infancy. It was about a survivor of the Holocaust who cringed at the sight of a policeman in Tel Aviv until he was told that the policeman was a Jew, at which he straightened up and said: "A Jew? Well, to hell with him, then!"

For another thing, the Jews of Israel have developed into a different breed from their ancestors and relatives in the Diaspora. The most spectacular instance is the Israeli army (the Israel Defense Forces, or IDF, to call it by its proper name). Jews in the Diaspora were not notable for their skill in or enthusiasm for the military arts, but the IDF has become one of the best armies in the world. Conversely, in intellectual and scholarly pursuits, an area where Jews might have been expected to excel, the Israelis (despite their accomplishments in technology) are relatively weak: the Hebrew University is not one of the best institutions of higher learning in the world.

Not that its faculty has lacked for great scholars like the late Gershom Scholem, whose pioneering work on Jewish mysticism constitutes one of the towering academic and intellectual achievements of the twentieth century. But it was Scholem himself who once explained to me why the Jewish state should have turned out to be better at fighting wars than at realizing the dream of cultural efflorescence that had converted him, a young German-Jewish intellectual from a highly assimilated family, to Zionism and brought him in the 1920s from Berlin to Jerusalem and eventually to a professorship at the Hebrew University. The Jews, he said (speaking with a wistfulness rooted in his fundamentally pacifist tendencies), are a talented people, and talent goes where it is needed; at this stage of Jewish history it is needed in the army, and so that is where it has gone.

WITH THESE WORDS of Scholem running once again through my head, as they so often have done, I go to meet A., an Israeli friend who in his own person seems to contradict them. He is a professor who has done internationally recognized work in his field, and is at the same time a high-ranking reserve officer in the IDF with a distinguished military record. Contemplating this combination of talents, I say to myself, well, for this we certainly did need a Jewish state.

Yet listening to him talk is enough to make me wonder—and not for the first time—whether the Jewish state we needed, and need, can survive yet another form of "normalization"—the one that goes by the name of the "peace process." No doubt the species of normalization represented by obscene graffiti in English and McDonald's and cable television would have horrified old Zionist theoreticians like Ahad Ha'am and A.D. Gordon, but these things are no threat to the continued existence of the Jewish state. A., however, thinks, as I do, that the peace process will bring not peace but war—a war first with the Palestinians but then drawing in most of the Arab states who will set aside their own internecine conflicts and seize on this one last chance to defeat Israel militarily. Even if Israel should win, the cost would be tremendous, and in a monstrous irony the Israelis would wind up reoccupying the very territories from which their forces would have withdrawn in the hope of achieving peace. But if Israel were to lose, the Jewish state that we needed, and need, would come to a horrible and bloody end.

While agreeing that the peace process is a form of normalization, A. and I disagree about the sense in which it is so. As I see it, negotiations with the

PLO were undertaken by a nation so war-weary that it was becoming as debellicized and as averse to the military arts as all other democratic countries "normally" are.

A.'s take on the negotiations is different. A Labor-party man for most of his life, he nevertheless feels that, under the government of Yitzhak Rabin and Shimon Peres, Israel has revealed itself not as a normal nation, but rather as one still marked by certain of those traditionally Jewish "pathologies" and "deformations" that statehood was supposed to have corrected. A normal nation, he maintains, would never sue for peace when it was powerful and its enemies were weak. Yet this is in effect what Rabin and Peres have done. At the very moment when Israel's armed might remained intact and when the PLO had fallen into total disarray—demoralized, discredited, and bankrupt because its support of Saddam Hussein in the Gulf War had deprived it of its Arab patrons—the Israelis resurrected a politically moribund Yasir Arafat and offered him land and (implicitly) statehood in exchange for a few paper promises and a few honeyed words.

I would find this interpretation more persuasive if it did not overlook the fact that in its last war with the Palestinians—that is, the *intifada*—Israel for all practical purposes lost, largely because it could not and would not continue doing what was necessary in order to win; and it also overlooks the great psychological damage done in 1961 to the Israelis, to their morale and their fighting pride, when they were forced by the United States under George Bush to sit by passively during the Gulf War while Iraq rained missiles on their heads.

In other words, I say, Rabin may justify his policy by talking of the new opportunities for peace that have been opened up by the demise of the Soviet Union, which no longer arms and instigates the enemies of Israel against it; and Peres may prate of a new Middle East in which everyone is more interested in making money than in making war. But in their negotiations with the Palestinians they are acting not like farsighted statesmen or magnanimous victors—or for that matter like "deformed" products of the Diaspora—but like the leaders of a defeated nation; and in that way, too, they are acting normally.

My allusion to Peres's rhetoric prompts A. to tell me about the interview Hosni Mubarak, the Egyptian president, has just given to an Israeli journalist in which he ridicules the idea that there is a new Middle East. Mubarak should know. After all, at the huge international conference convened last year in Casablanca to explore the supposedly new opportunities for investment in the Middle East, the Egyptian delegation showed up with a ninety-page booklet of proposals for joint economic development in which the name of Israel was never so much as mentioned; nor did Israel appear on any of the six maps of the region contained in the booklet. But as A. points out, Jordanian maps do not acknowledge the existence of Israel either—and Egypt and Jordan are the two Arab countries which have signed peace treaties with the Jewish state.

MONDAY, SEPTEMBER 4

I meet with L., an eminent Israeli writer, and the only old friend I have left here from the other side of the political divide. Once upon a time, and even after I had begun the rightward movement that eventually landed me in the conservative camp, virtually all my Israeli friends were to one degree or another on the Left. But until fairly recently being on the Left in Israel did not necessarily involve illusions about the desirability of a Palestinian state run by the PLO and with East Jerusalem as its capital. Nor did it entail a willingness to give up the Golan Heights in exchange for a treaty with Syria. On the contrary, as I have often pointed out to certain critics who accuse me of parroting the Likud line, it was not Menachem Begin or Yitzhak Shamir or their successor as the leader of Likud, Benjamin Netanyahu, who taught me that a Palestinian state would constitute a mortal threat and that Jerusalem must never be divided again and that Israel must never surrender the Golan Heights; it was Labor leaders like Golda Meir and Shimon Peres and Yitzhak Rabin (the last of whom reiterated precisely these positions when campaigning in the last election).

Nor did being on the Left entail the blame-Israel-first mentality that by now has become as widespread among Israeli intellectuals as anti-Americanism was in the United States in the days of Vietnam. In this respect, the Israeli Labor party of old and its supporters in the intellectual community resembled their counterparts in the West during the first phase of the Cold War, when social democrats everywhere recognized Communism as a menace and resolved to hold the line against it. Only later did some of these same staunchly anti-Communist social democrats (typified most vividly by Willy Brandt in Germany) turn almost 180 degrees, adopting a revisionist view of the Cold War according to which the United States was at least as much to blame for starting it as the Soviet Union, and becoming enthusiastic proponents of accommodation with the Kremlin.

Applying Dr. Johnson's famous maxim that the prospect of hanging concentrates the mind wonderfully, I once assumed that the social democrats in a besieged Israel would be immune from the local variant of this disease. No such luck. To cite only one among many telling examples of the spread of the infection to Israel, Shimon Peres, who in a former incarnation did so much to build up the IDF, has become the Willy Brandt of the Arab war against Israel.

The ground of this transformation was assiduously prepared by the intellectual community of Israel. Long before the demise of the Soviet Union, or the putative changes in the Arab world on which Rabin and Peres would later rely in justifying their own change of mind and heart, many Israeli intellectuals were already blaming their country for the murderous hatred it inspired in others. They accused Israel not only of oppressing the Palestinians since 1967, when the occupation of the West Bank and Gaza began, but of primal sins and crimes that called the very foundations of the Jewish state's existence into question. In this, too, they resembled the American intellectuals of the Vietnam period who, not content with attacking the war as a discrete blunder or even a crime, represented it as the poisoned fruit of a rotten tree—just the latest manifestation of the evil endemic to American history and inherent in American society. The difference is that whereas no one in America was going to be driven by such ideas into actually giving the country back to the Indians, Israeli politicians like Rabin and Peres were about to turn over a large swath of territory to the Palestinians.

Most of my other former friends on the Israeli Left have surrendered to these ugly ideas and attitudes, but not L. He supports the peace process, but with ever diminishing enthusiasm, and he does so mainly because he thinks that it is a better alternative than continuing to rule over a million Palestinians, not because he regards Israel as the guilty party in this conflict. Far from buying Peres's vision of a new Middle East in which the lion will lie down and then form a business partnership with the lamb, he looks forward to the opposite: the complete "separation" between Israel and the Palestinians that Rabin sometimes holds out as the true goal of his policy.

"Let them," L. says with clenched teeth, "go their way and we will go ours. The main thing is to rid ourselves of this corrupting occupation." As for my dire predictions of what this course will bring with it, he would love to dismiss them out of hand. Yet even though he trusts Rabin to shed the burdens of the occupation without jeopardizing Israel's security, he is in all honesty unable to deny that the dangers on which I keep harping are real, any more than I can cavalierly wave away the possibility that I may be all wet. And so we can still talk across a divide that has become too great for me and all my other former friends in Israel to bridge.

Since L. is so untypical, I cannot be sure that his growing skepticism about the peace process is indicative of the mood of the camp to which he belongs. But the impression I get from skimming the press is that little remains of the post-Oslo euphoria even among Israeli intellectuals. The intellectual community—concentrated here as in America in the universities, the arts, and the media—had almost to a man persuaded itself that the Palestinians really had changed, that they had given up the dream of wiping Israel off the map, and that they were ready to live in peace alongside a reduced Jewish state. But the increase in terrorism since Oslo has shaken even the intellectuals, as has Arafat's inability or unwillingness to stop it, or to fulfill the other promise he made there, namely, to abrogate the commitment to the destruction of Israel in the Palestinian National Charter. Very likely this is why they have quietly dropped their utopian expectations and fallen back, like L. and like Rabin himself, on "separation" as the most desirable goal.

TUESDAY, SEPTEMBER 5

Public opinion is another matter, as I learn today from G., one of the very few journalists in Israel who opposes the government's policy. Among the general public, he informs me, "separation" is a popular idea, but the wave of terrorism has still eaten into support for the peace process, and therefore for Rabin. Having been way ahead of Netanyahu in the aftermath of Oslo, he now runs about neck and neck with him, except when there is a terrorist attack, at which point Netanyahu forges ahead. But according to G.'s careful analysis of the polls, the political effect of a terrorist attack fades after about two months and then they go back to a 50-50 split. It follows that, other things being equal, the next election (scheduled for 1996) may well be decided by the Palestinians. If they restrain themselves in the weeks before election day, Rabin could squeak through; if not, Netanyahu will become the next prime minister. The problem is that by then it may be too late to stop or reverse the slide down the slippery slope.

R., a close friend and former government official with whom I meet after leaving G., is not so coolly analytic. In fact, he is in despair over Rabin. It was not ever thus with him. When I began expressing my gloomy opposition to the policy of the Rabin government even before Oslo made it official, R. would always counter by assuring me that Rabin, whom he knew well and for whom he had once worked, could be depended upon to hold firm. True, Peres in his view was another matter and would stop at nothing to make a deal (meaning that, for all Peres's denials, he was already prepared to accept a Palestinian state with East Jerusalem as its capital and to withdraw entirely from the Golan Heights); and Peres's deputy Yossi Beilin was even worse (meaning that he was ready to do all this tomorrow). But Rabin would never cross certain "red lines."

Then, when Rabin crossed the first of these lines in accepting the PLO as his negotiating partner, R. was sure he would never cross the second; and when he did so in signing the Oslo agreement, R. simply could not believe that he would go on to the third; and when he did so in ignoring Arafat's violations of the agreement, R. still maintained that he would never go any further; and when he did so in tolerating PLO political activity in Jerusalem and in declaring his willingness to withdraw from the Golan Heights, R. finally gave up. He has not joined the extremists who denounce Rabin as a traitor, but short of that, R. has become the most passionate critic of Rabin I know in Israel.

Having lost his faith in Rabin, R. now relies on reality. That is, instead of insisting at every stage that Rabin will never do whatever Rabin then proceeds to do, he now insists that the peace process will founder on the rock of obstacles in the real world that it keeps ignoring or wishing away. At this moment it is Hebron, which has become the final sticking point in "Oslo 2," the agreement under which Israeli forces are to withdraw from most of the West Bank. R. is certain that the proposed arrangements for protecting the Jewish settlers in Hebron cannot possibly work even if the Palestinians accept them, which they never will. Commenting on the announcement in the press that Rabin and Peres are planning to visit Hebron this afternoon, he says, "Good, let them go and see for themselves and then they will realize how crazy this arrangement is." In a gavotte that we have danced so often that the steps have become second nature to us both, I retort that they will see only what they wish to see, and that if the Palestinians persist in refusing to accept their proposals, they will advance other proposals that the Palestinians will be willing to accept. Nothing, I say for the hundredth time, will be permitted to derail this train from the track until it reaches the end of the line.

But what about Jerusalem? Time was when I felt certain that no Israeli government would ever acquiesce in the redivision of Jerusalem, and on this point even R. still has faith in Rabin. It is a highly tremulous faith, to be sure, and it is undermined a little more every day by the government's de facto toleration of Palestinian political activity in East Jerusalem—activity which constitutes a violation of the Oslo agreement—while pretending to forbid it.

As for me, I have no faith left to be undermined. At the ceremonies the other night inaugurating a yearlong celebration of the three thousandth anniversary of Jerusalem as the Jewish capital, Rabin proclaimed that "undivided Jerusalem is the heart of the Jewish people and the capital of the state of Israel. Undivided Jerusalem is ours. . . . There is no state of Israel without Jerusalem and no peace without Jerusalem undivided." Instead of bucking me up, these words put a chill in my blood. They were so reminiscent in their firmness and confidence of other declarations he had made in the past that I could not help seeing in them the last of the "red lines" he would eventually cross, all the while pretending (perhaps even to himself) that he was doing no such thing.

The way this trick would be pulled off would be through some form of "shared sovereignty" under which Jerusalem would technically remain a single city. There would be no barriers or barbed-wire fences as in the years between 1948 and 1967, but two different nations would call Jerusalem their capital and two different flags would fly over the two halves of the city. Already, indeed, foreign dignitaries pay official visits to the offices of the Palestinian Authority in East Jerusalem while the countries they represent still refuse to recognize the city as the capital of Israel.

These countries include the United States, whose current president declared during his campaign for office (in words reminiscent of Rabin's): "I recognize Jerusalem as an undivided city and the eternal capital of Israel." Yet Bill Clinton's ambassador to Israel, Martin Indyk, could not even bring himself to attend the opening ceremonies of Jerusalem 3000. In contrast to the European ambassadors who refused to participate on the ground that these ceremonies were a political event, Indyk claimed that they were a cultural event and therefore sent his cultural attaché to represent him.

This is the same Martin Indyk who, as the head of a think tank in Washington, wrote a paper advocating that the American embassy be moved from Tel Aviv to Jerusalem. Now, with the tacit approval of the Israeli government—such is the Orwellian world that the peace process has created—he lobbies against this move as harmful to the negotiations, and it is a good bet that he will wind up lobbying for shared sovereignty when it turns out that the Palestinians will accept nothing less. It is an equally good bet, moreover, that Rabin and Peres will go along with an arrangement of this kind rather than derail the policy to which they have committed their political fortunes in the present and their standing in the eyes of Jewish history.

THURSDAY, SEPTEMBER 7

We take Nani, who has thus far spent more time hanging out with her adoring Israeli cousins than seeing the sights of Jerusalem, to the Western Wall. It is a brilliantly sunny day and so hot that our visit lasts only a short time, but still long enough for me to catch the tail end of a bar mitzvah that has just been conducted here. At first I am surprised to see this happening on a weekday, but then I remember that, since the essence of a bar mitzvah is calling the new adult for the first time to the Torah, the ceremony can be held on any day the Torah scroll is read publicly, which in a normal week means Monday and Thursday as well as Saturday.

This is not the bar mitzvah I have come to Jerusalem for, and ordinarily I might not have paid much attention. But I find myself fascinated by the sight of a family of Oriental Jews who seem so alien to me (on closer inspection they turn out to be immigrants from India) engaged in this totally familiar ritual—a familiarity which includes not only the prayers and procedures of the service but even the custom of women pelting the participants with pieces of candy from behind the barrier that, in accordance with Orthodox practice, separates them from the men.

Only the other day I had described to a delighted Ruthie the wicked fastballs that were hurled from the balcony of the Orthodox synagogue of my own childhood by wild-eyed crones who seized on every bar mitzvah as a wonderful opportunity to engage in a little aggression against the male sex. I had thought this custom was purely East European, but now I discover that Oriental Jews practice it, too.

The reason these people seem alien to me is not that they are dark skinned. It is because they do not conform to the atavistic idea of a Jew that neither age nor experience has succeeded in dislodging from my mind and that catches me unawares at unguarded moments like this. As a child, I had the same trouble with German Jews—people who act like that, and who can't even speak Yiddish, are Jews?—and because most of the Gentiles with whom I grew up were Italian, for a long time I was simply unable to believe that there could be such a thing as an Italian Jew: the very term was an oxymoron.

Now, to confuse and complicate matters even further, I notice that the rabbi presiding at this bar mitzvah does conform perfectly to the stereotype of which I have never been able to rid myself. Though by all appearances from Morocco, he is dressed in the traditional black garb of an East European Hasid (a clothing style that dates from eighteenth-century Poland). And not only does he look like my idea of a real Jew, he prays like one, racing at the usual breakneck speed through the blessing he is pronouncing over the head of the bar-mitzvah boy. (Later, I remark to my wife how interesting it was to discover that Oriental Jews pray just as fast as East Europeans. "Naturally," she grins. "All Jews do. The services are so long that if they didn't, they would be at least five hundred years behind.")

And so here I am in front of the Western Wall watching a Moroccan rabbi in the costume of a Polish Hasid speeding through an ancient Hebrew blessing over the head of an Indian bar-mitzvah boy being pelted with candy by women dressed in saris while speaking modern Hebrew— and it is evidently all too much for me. The Jews are too much for me, the mystery and wonder of their ingathering in this country are too much for me, their diversity and their unity as a people are too much for me, and to my amazement, and embarrassment, I feel tears coming to my eyes and spilling over onto my cheeks.

FRIDAY, SEPTEMBER 8

When I see B., another of the handful of Israeli professors who are not on the Left, he wants to know how we American neoconservative intellectuals "did it." How, that is, did we manage to challenge the hegemony of the Left in the world of ideas and not only survive but prevail? His question is not academic or motivated by historical curiosity. What he is looking for is practical guidance that he hopes he can apply to the situation in Israel.

I tell him that, beginning in the late 1960s, we American refugees from the Left mounted as powerful a critique as we could of the ideas and assumptions in which we had lost faith; simultaneously we developed an alternative perspective that was both internally coherent and in tune with the available evidence. Where foreign policy in particular was concerned, this meant challenging the anti-American notion that the United States and the Soviet Union were morally equivalent and the correlative revisionist view that the Cold War could only be settled by a conciliatory accommodation with Moscow.

Obviously, an analogous job needs to be done here, where the leftist interpretation of the Arab war against Israel bears an uncanny resemblance to the leftist interpretation of the Cold War that came to prominence in the wake of Vietnam. But I warn him that a campaign against this interpretation, while absolutely necessary, is not sufficient. It will take a major crisis to turn things around. For us in America, it was the Soviet invasion of Afghanistan in 1979 which overnight convinced almost everyone that our analysis of Soviet intentions was right and that the anti-anti-Communists who had been claiming that the USSR was no longer expansionist, if in truth it had ever been, were wrong. If the structure of ideas we had built up over the years had not been in place and readily available for explaining what had just happened much more convincingly than the Left was able to do, Afghanistan might not have had so enormous a political effect. But if Afghanistan, or something like it, had not occurred, we would not have won the political battle even though we had already demolished our opponents in the realm of ideas.

This account only succeeds in deepening B.'s gloom—and mine as well. For without saying another word, we both understand that the only "Afghanistan" that can be expected here is terrorism and war. Which means that a very high price will have to be paid to persuade the shapers of opinion in Israel that Rabin's "separation" is as much a pipe dream as Peres's "new Middle East"; that the Palestinians will not settle permanently for a state confined to the West Bank and Gaza; that they, and the Arab world in general, are still intent on eradicating the Jewish state; and that they have changed only in shifting to a different way of pursuing that objective.

In the past they put their faith in direct military assault, but this approach having repeatedly failed, they have at last come around to the strategy of "stages" first proposed many years ago by President Habib Bourguiba of Tunisia. It is a shift that has paid off more handsomely than anyone could have expected. The Palestinians are now well on their way to achieving the first stage: a state of their own on land wrested from the Israelis by political maneuvering (with a little help from the *intifada*). There are various possibilities for stages two and three, but in the end the idea is to launch the jihad, the holy war against Israel, that even today Arafat (who sings a different tune when he addresses non-Arab audiences) keeps invoking in his speeches to his own people.

He can do this with impunity, knowing that the Israeli and American governments will dismiss such talk as nothing more than a rhetorical bone thrown to the Islamic fundamentalists of Hamas. He also knows that they will forgive him for it, even though it serves to incite the very terrorists he has pledged to control. And he knows that in the last resort the two governments will even try to deny that he makes such speeches. Thus, when a videotape of one of these speeches was shown in Israel recently, Peres immediately declared that the tape was probably a forgery and only backed down when Arafat himself admitted that it was genuine. But this admission cost him nothing, and within a week or so he was back saying the very same things again in another speech in Gaza.

SATURDAY, SEPTEMBER 9

The day of Noam's bar mitzvah, the day for which we mainly came to Israel, has arrived. At 8 A.M. we amble over to a small Orthodox synagogue in the Baka'a section of Jerusalem where Ruthie and her family live. The bar mitzvah will take place in this synagogue even though the family does not belong to the congregation and is not religiously observant.

Ruthie grew up on the Upper West Side of Manhattan, and she often makes mordant jokes about the sociological resemblances between the place from which she fled and the one in which she has landed. Like the Upper West Side of her pre-Israel life, Baka'a is full of writers, artists, academics, and journalists who are successful enough to afford its relatively expensive apartments and who are, if anything, even more solidly left-wing than the people among whom she was born and raised. It was from people like this—or at any rate from their political opinions and attitudes—that Ruthie ran away, only to wind up among them again.

Today, however, you would never take her for a Baka'a woman. In respectful deference to the Orthodox idea of female decorum, she has put on a long skirt, a blouse that covers her arms, and a kerchief around her head. This costume has a transforming effect. Ruthie is a beauty, and no matter what she is wearing she looks much younger than her age. But seeing her in this getup, you would never believe she is old enough to be the mother of a thirteen year old, or that she could be the same person who dispenses sage and witty advice to troubled Israelis every Thursday in her "Dear Ruthie" column in the *Jerusalem Post*. More likely you would take her for the prettiest girl in a religious settlement on the West Bank.

If Baka'a reminds Ruthie of her childhood in Manhattan, the synagogue in which Noam's bar mitzvah is being celebrated instantly carries me back to my childhood in Brooklyn. It is smaller than the shul in Brownsville I attended every Saturday more than a half century ago and where my own bar mitzvah was held, and the women here are segregated behind a barrier rather than in a balcony (the one from which those hard-candy fastballs were hurled). But the atmosphere is eerily reminiscent of that shul. Indeed, the men here are praying—at, I need hardly mention, breakneck speed—in the selfsame inflections that could be heard back there.

This is stranger than it might seem, for they are all Israelis who, when speaking Hebrew in their daily lives, use the standard Sephardi pronunciation. Yet in reciting their prayers, most of them adopt, or revert to, an Ashkenazi accent, the accent of the East European Diaspora. As a result, they sound not like Israelis but exactly like the kind of congregation in Brooklyn of which I was a member in days of yore. Perhaps this is their way of maintaining a distinction between Hebrew as a holy language and Hebrew as a vehicle of secular life. Or perhaps they suspect that there is truth in the joke about God cocking His ear to an earthly congregation praying in Sephardi accents and complaining to the angels—in Yiddish, of course—that He cannot, for the life of Him, make head or tail of what these Jews are trying to tell Him *("Vos far a loshn redn zey dortn?").*

When, however, Noam is called to the Torah—to the accompaniment, I am relieved to see, of the traditional shower of candy from the women's section—he sounds exactly like the sabra he is. His part is a difficult one even for an Israeli kid, whose native Hebrew bears about as much resemblance to biblical Hebrew as contemporary American English does to Shakespeare. But he chants it flawlessly and with the insouciant confidence that used to be characteristic of the sabra and that now seems to have succumbed, like so much else, to "normalization."

NOAM IS THE FOURTH of our ten grandchildren to have gone through this ceremony in less than two years, and it gets me every time. If I was taken aback when I felt tears welling up the other day at the bar mitzvah of the Indian boy at the Wall, I fully expected them to come up on me today, just as they had for Noam's three cousins before him; and so they do. Never much given to weeping in my younger days, in my incipient dotage I have become something of a blubberer, though for the most part the sappiness is brought out only by my grandchildren. Over any or all of these ten wondrous creatures I can weep at the drop of a hat.

Sometimes I weep with joy and pride and sometimes I weep with worry and anguish. But just now I am weeping with anxiety over the four here in Jerusalem. For all their "normality," for all their easy commerce with McDonald's and Michael Jackson and O. J. Simpson, they are Israelis and I cannot prevent myself from believing that they are living in a condition of terrible danger. When I told one of my Israeli friends that from the minute

I landed here I have been feeling slightly ill, he replied without missing a beat, "Well, of course, this country makes you sick." He was right; it does. It makes me sick with frustration and apprehension as I watch it careering toward a major disaster that nothing seems able to head off and no one seems able to prevent. And there sit Noam and Alon and Boaz and Avital—Noam who flings himself ardently at me whenever we meet or part; Alon who, over my protests, will press his precious fountain pen upon me tomorrow as a farewell gift; Boaz ("the sweet thug" to his grandparents) who will refuse to say goodbye except by punching me angrily as we leave; and Avital (the imperious little "Queen of Jerusalem") who addresses and refers to me always, in English, as "Beloved Grandpa."

Intellectuals would usually rather be right than president—indeed, would rather be right than anything. But not this one, not this time. Weeping silently at the sight of my grandson becoming a full-fledged Jew, I pray to God that I am wildly mistaken in fearing what I fear for him and for all Israel. As I have done over and over again in the last three years, I find myself, here in this shul in Jerusalem, praying that those who see peace and harmony and prosperity ahead for this country will for once in their political lives turn out to be right, and that those of us cursed with visions of disaster and war will be granted the blessing of an outcome that proves us utterly wrong.

LOLITA, MY MOTHER-IN-LAW,
THE MARQUIS DE SADE,
AND LARRY FLYNT

N<small>OT LONG AGO, THE</small> L<small>IBRARY</small> of America put out a beautiful new three-volume edition of the novels and memoirs of Vladimir Nabokov, and I decided to seize upon it as a convenient occasion for reacquainting myself with his work. Which explains why I happened to be reading *Lolita* on the very day a story by Nina Bernstein appeared on the front page of the *New York Times* that cast a horrifying new light on Nabokov's masterpiece. It also brought memories to the surface that had long been buried, and simultaneously forced me into rethinking a number of questions I had up till then considered fairly well resolved. As I was going through this difficult process, I was given a few more pushes by Miloš Forman's movie, *The People vs. Larry Flynt*, and two recently published books, Roger Shattuck's *Forbidden Knowledge* and Rochelle Gurstein's *The Repeal of Reticence*. By the time I was through, my peace of mind had been so disturbed that I was left wishing that those old memories and those settled questions had been allowed to remain in their contentedly slumberous state.

Nina Bernstein's story concerned the unearthing of a list of thousands of children "whose names were secretly compiled, annotated, and stored with a cache of child pornography on a computer used by a convicted pedophile in a Minnesota state prison" just north of Minneapolis. Minneapolis! The mere mention of it in this lurid context prodded the first of those long inert memories back to life. It featured my late mother-in-law, Rose Rosenthal, who in a sociologically unusual wrinkle of American Jewish history was born almost exactly a century ago in Minneapolis's "twin city," St. Paul, and lived there until her death in 1972.

A loyal Jew and a fierce Zionist, Rose Rosenthal was in all other respects so typical a Midwesterner that a character modeled on her would have been entirely at home in one of the novels of her fellow Minnesotan, Sinclair

Lewis. Before meeting her, I had thought I understood—precisely from reading Lewis and many others—what the word "bourgeois" meant, but I soon began to realize that I had never known the half of it. After all, where would I—born and bred in a Brooklyn slum in the 1930s and then moving in the years after World War II from college and graduate school into the milieu of the New York intellectuals—ever have had a chance to encounter a true member of that much-derided species in the flesh?

Obviously I had run into many middle-class people, but such a battering had the "bourgeois" world view taken over the past several decades that they had either given up on it themselves or had lost the nerve to exhibit any of the traditional stigmata of their moral and cultural background. None of them, for example, would have risked appearing so unsophisticated as to condemn a movie star like Ingrid Bergman for flaunting an adulterous affair and then bearing a child out of wedlock. But my mother-in-law did, loudly, and with total confidence in the rightness of her judgment.

Intransigently provincial as she was, the only moral standards she recognized as valid were the rigidly puritanical standards prevailing in the St. Paul of her day. Any violations of those standards outraged her, and the more they were violated by the outside world, the more she felt confirmed in her commitment to them. So far as she was concerned, the rest of the country, and especially New York, was going to hell, while St. Paul, and the Midwest generally, remained an enclave of goodness and purity and rectitude. But surely, I would protest, the things that appalled her must be happening out there, too. "No," she would reply with a stubborn set of the jaw, "not in our part of the country."

Not in our part of the country: it was those words that started ringing in my head as I read the *Times* story about the inmate with "multiple convictions for child sexual assault" sitting in the Lino Lakes Correctional Facility, just a stone's throw away from St. Paul. There, in that prison, this monster had free and easy access to a state-of-the-art computer and a modem, and using that equipment he had compiled a huge database mostly of little girls between three and twelve for circulation on the Internet to other pedophiles.

The names came not from the Internet itself but from local newspapers all over Minnesota, to which he also had free and easy access through exchange subscriptions with a prison newspaper (founded, in a piquant detail, by members of the Jesse James gang in 1887 and still going strong). By combing through birthday announcements and such features as "Citizens of Tomorrow," he was able not only to collect names for his database but also to embellish it with many helpful pointers.

Thus, the *Times* reports, the children "appear by age and location . . . in dated entries that . . . include personal details written as 'latchkey kids,' 'speech difficulties,' 'cute,' and 'Little Ms. pageant winner.'" Even more to the point of my ancient argument with my mother-in-law:

> The towns where the children live are alphabetized and coded by map coordinates, as though on a road atlas to the American Midwest. Most are hamlets in northern Minnesota, places born of the railroad in the last century and bypassed by the highway in this one.

Not in our part of the country indeed.

TO BE SURE, even in the late 1950s, when I first met her, my mother-in-law was wrong and I was right about life in places like St. Paul. Premarital sex, adultery, illegitimacy, homosexuality, and—yes—pedophilia were by no means entirely unknown there. (In the year of her death, the very pedophile who would later use a computer to locate potential victims did the same thing with the more primitive tool of a notebook, and was caught and then convicted for the first time after breaking into a home in St. Paul itself.) Such goings-on, however, were sufficiently rare, or anyway well enough hidden, so that a novel like *Peyton Place* could create a huge sensation merely by revealing their presence in small-town America.

This revelation, like so many others before it in the literature and polemics emanating from the higher reaches of American culture, carried the additional satisfaction of confirming the charge of hypocrisy that invariably accompanied attacks on the moral professions of the middle class. But those who so loved to yell "hypocrite" at the bourgeoisie always seemed to forget that hypocrisy, being "the tribute vice pays to virtue," testifies to the commanding power of the standards being violated, not to their weakness or fraudulence.

As for my mother-in-law, I would bet my life that she was no hypocrite and that she practiced what she preached. But she was without any question a great denier, who simply refused to see what she did not wish to see or to know what she did not wish to know. In thus adopting what amounted to a private form of censorship, she withheld even de facto recognition from anyone or anything that disrupted or challenged the moral order in which she believed with all her heart.

There were millions upon millions like her in America, and their practice of private censorship was mirrored and reinforced by the law. And if this dual system did not work well enough to wall off their "part of the country" entirely from the "bad examples" being set by my part of the country, it did afford at least some measure of protection. Certainly it is hard to imagine the Minnesota of my mother-in-law's day becoming, of all things, the center of a network of child molesters.

Those walls, wherever they were built in America, have all long since been blasted to smithereens, as I first realized when, on a visit to Salt Lake City in the early 1970s, I discovered pornographic books and magazines being sold openly in a drugstore right across the street from the Mormon Temple. It amazed me that even a city dominated by Mormons had given up trying to defend itself against the tidal wave of pornography which had followed in the wake of a series of increasingly liberal court decisions. True, those decisions had still left a bit of room for restrictive local ordinances, but it had evidently become too troublesome and too expensive for local prosecutors to take advantage of them. For all practical purposes, then, the fight against censorship had already been won.

As a young literary critic and as an editor, I had taken part in that fight. It was not a very large part, consisting only in the writing and publishing of a few articles, the delivering of a few lectures, and on one occasion the giving of testimony in an obscenity trial. But this brings me to another cluster of long-dormant memories that rereading *Lolita* in conjunction with Nina Bernstein's story in the *Times* has prodded back to life.

ONE OF THESE is of a talk I gave in defense of pornography at Bard College in the late 1950s. In those days I never lectured from a prepared text and the notes on which I relied have gone the way of all notes, so that now, after nearly forty years, I am a bit hazy as to what exactly I said. But as best as I can reconstruct it, the case I made in defense of pornography began with a literary analysis. Conceding that the purpose of pornography was to arouse lust, I argued that there was no reason why this should be considered any less legitimate than the arousal of such other emotions and passions as anger, sorrow, pity, and so on. Like any other literary genre, pornography could be well written or badly written, and the appeal to lustful thoughts and impulses could be artfully managed or unskillfully and crudely done.

I believe I then went on to claim that, aesthetic considerations apart, pornography had a value all its own. It represented a kind of utopian fantasy of pure sex, sex liberated from consequence and into unalloyed ecstasy ("pornotopia," as my old college friend, Steven Marcus of Columbia, would later call it in a book on pornography in the Victorian era). And this fantasy demanded and deserved recognition for the role it played in attacking—I cringe at the thought that such words ever came out of my mouth, even when I was young—the stifling proprieties and unhealthy repressions of bourgeois society.

The students in the audience at Bard (a "progressive" college, and as such already in tune with the spirit of the 1960s to come) loved it. They applauded wildly when I was through, and their questions in the discussion period were all requests for more of the same. But then Professor Heinrich Blücher, whom I knew slightly through his wife Hannah Arendt, raised his hand. Though overshadowed by her growing fame as a political philosopher, this obscure German scholar was rumored to be working on a (never-to-be-completed) monumental History of Everything that would put her work to shame; and Hannah herself had told me more than once that he possessed one of the great minds of our age. With this reputation adding to the fearsomeness of his aristocratic Prussian bearing, he jumped to his feet and shouted at the top of his lungs in the heaviest possible German accent, "You are taking all the *fun* out of sex!"

I needed a small pause to shake off this stinging left hook, but after a second or two I recovered myself enough to counterpunch with the insistence that it was not necessary for sex to remain hidden in order to be fun. "But," he shot—or rather shouted—back, "don't you know that pornography soon becomes *boring?*" To this I replied that I knew no such thing, and that I was hard put to take people at face value who said they were bored by pornography. Embarrassed, yes; ashamed, yes; repelled, yes; disgusted, yes; but the claim of boredom seemed to me an affectation of superiority to something which only a saint could be superior to.

I now realize that Heinrich Blücher, who had probably grown sated with pornography as a young man steeped in the sexually unbridled culture of Weimar Germany, knew what he was talking about. But unlike the America of today—which has exceeded even Weimar in sexual license and licentiousness, and where pornography can be piped into any home at the click of a mouse or the flick of a television remote or the activation of a VCR*—

---

*In 1996, according to a recent survey in *U.S. News & World Report,* the number of hard-core video rentals in this country reached a total of 665 million, almost all of them from "mom and pop video stores." Americans also spent an additional $150 million bringing "adult" films into their homes on pay-per-view TV, and yet another $175 million "to view porn in their rooms at major hotel chains such as Sheraton, Hilton, Hyatt, and Holiday Inn."

in the America of the 1950s there was still very little of it around. In the world in which I lived, it was easy enough to borrow copies of *Fanny Hill* or the novels of Henry Miller or a few other equally classy pornographic books that had been smuggled in from Paris by friends. But in general, getting hold of pornography was like trying to buy illegal drugs. One had to have a "connection," and one had to venture into seedy and possibly dangerous places to "score."

AS IT HAPPENED, I had such a connection in the unlikely person of an uncle of mine who was more like an older brother to me than an uncle. Unlike *his* brothers, who included my father and who all acted as if there was no such thing as sex, he made no bones about his obsession with it. But so far as I could tell, he indulged this obsession exclusively through the consumption of pornography. (That *acting* on it was not for him was something he discovered to his eternal regret when a friend told him that in order to participate in an orgy, he would have to do certain things that he did not think he could bring himself to do. "But can't I just do what I want?" he asked plaintively. "No," said his friend. "If you want to be a pervert, you have to act like a pervert.")

It was thanks to my uncle that I had seen a pornographic film starring a young woman named Candy Barr (a model who was reputed to be the "moll" of a famous gangster). The film was very short, hardly more than a five-minute clip, but the great beauty of the star and the apparent enthusiasm with which she performed had made it a classic and a collector's item among connoisseurs of hard-core pornography. They were right: even in a very bad print projected by a primitive camera onto a portable roll-down screen that resembled a cheap window shade, it was overwhelming—more so even than the few pornographic books I had read by then, and they were quite overwhelming enough.

Because I had actually seen a pornographic film, I was the envy of my circle, very few of whom had ever had this kind of firsthand experience (not that it stopped them from theorizing endlessly on the subject). And as the only one with a connection, I was under constant pressure to arrange a showing for them. At last I agreed, only to discover that my uncle's supplier had been arrested, and that he himself was very reluctant (justifiably, as it would turn out) to let his precious copy of the Candy Barr clip out of his hands. But when I explained that a group of distinguished writers and critics was eager to see the movie, he gave in out of deference to "educated people" whose readiness to lower themselves to his level simultaneously puzzled and pleased him.

The great event was scheduled for a party at the home of another old college friend, Jason Epstein, then a rising young book editor who would subsequently be active in the ultimately successful campaign to find an American publisher for *Lolita;* and among the many writers and critics who did indeed turn up was Susan Sontag, who would later deliver herself of a famously solemn essay in defense of pornography. By the time I arrived directly from Brooklyn with Candy Barr in the can and my uncle's projector and screen under my arm, the excitement, punctuated by many jokes, was intense. But the biggest and best joke of all was to come. First it emerged that not a single one of these "educated people" knew how to work a projector, and then the person who volunteered to try succeeded only in tangling the film and finally burning it in the heat of the projector's lamp. The sickening smell of smoldering celluloid pervaded the room, and when I thought of confronting my uncle, it sickened me even more. Everyone else was either deeply disappointed or convulsed with laughter at the fiasco which seemed to have a message hidden in it somewhere.

NOT LONG AFTERWARD, I agreed to join another (though somewhat overlapping) group of distinguished writers and critics in traveling to Provincetown, Massachusetts, to testify on behalf of a local bookseller. For stocking a novel by Hubert Selby Jr. entitled *Last Exit to Brooklyn,* which was notorious for the graphic description it contained of a gang rape, this bookseller had been put on trial for violating the local law against the dissemination of obscene materials. But since the Supreme Court had exempted any work that, taken as a whole, possessed literary value, the defense in such cases usually consisted in summoning expert witnesses to grant the necessary certification.

I did not much like or admire Selby's unrelievedly grim novel, but there was no doubt that it was a serious piece of work by a talented writer. Hence I had no problem with testifying as to its literary merit when I was put on the stand. But then the judge, a local magistrate who had been scowling at all these interlopers from New York throughout the presentation of the case for the defense and who seemed to take an especially sour view of my testimony, suddenly decided to cross-examine me himself. "Do you have any children?" he demanded. "Yes," I said. "Any of them girls?" "Three," I replied. He grinned malevolently. "Well, how would you like it if they read books like this?" The question took me by surprise, and I hesitated for a few seconds before coming up with an answer. "Your honor, there are hundreds and hundreds of books in my apartment. I don't forbid my daughters to read any of them, and I don't keep track of the ones they do." To which his honor snorted: "I'll bet."

Strictly speaking, I was telling the truth, but it was not the whole truth and nothing but the truth, given that the few specimens of hard-core pornography I owned were deliberately kept out of the reach of our kids by being placed on the top shelf of a very tall bookcase. Like Heinrich Blücher's charge that I was taking the fun out of sex, the judge's sarcastic remark stayed with me. Whenever I told the story, I would mock him with Menckenesque gusto, and so would my audience. But that "I'll bet" must have given me my first inkling that hypocrisy in these matters was no longer a monopoly of Mencken's "booboisie."

THOUGH the pornographic books I kept up on that high shelf were all of the literate variety usually known as "erotica," they were still hard-core in the sense that their whole point was to provide highly explicit descriptions of sexual activity. To the extent that they made use of genuinely novelistic elements like a plot and carefully drawn characters, the purpose was to set off and heighten the impact of the dirty passages. (And "dirty" was the word that I and every other fighter for the legalization of pornography used in the privacy of our own minds, and indeed everywhere else except in a courtroom or when the politics of the issue required us to mouth the standard liberal pieties.) But a few other books that were not in the least pornographic in that sense were also up on that top shelf, and among them was the original edition of *Lolita,* published in Paris in 1955.

Nabokov had sent the manuscript to Paris with some reluctance and only after numerous rejections had convinced him that he would never find an American publisher for it.* One of those rejections had come from Doubleday, where the fierce battle being waged for its acceptance by Jason Epstein had foundered on his superiors' quite reasonable fear of prosecution. At any rate, it was from Epstein that I first heard of *Lolita,* and it was from him, if I remember rightly, that I got my copy of the cheaply bound and printed edition put out by the Olympia Press, a young company that specialized in erotica written, as *Lolita* was, in English.

English was not exactly a foreign language to Nabokov—he had learned

---

*He finally did in 1958, when Putnam put out the first American edition.

it as a child in czarist Russia from governesses and tutors—but it was still not his own in the way his beloved native Russian was. In fact, before venturing in his forties on a novel in English, he had already written many volumes both of fiction and poetry in Russian (most of them published in Europe after he had been driven into exile by the Bolshevik Revolution). And although he was not the only writer ever to have pulled off this trick of switching to English from a radically different native tongue, he outdid even his closest rival, the great Joseph Conrad, in his amazing mastery of the new language. More: in my judgment, to which I still hold today, he could even give James Joyce, born to English and its most spectacular contemporary virtuoso, a close run for his money.

But as I have now come to understand on rereading Nabokov in the new Library of America edition, there was something less admirable that went along with his linguistic genius and that he also had in common with Joyce: a contempt for his audience. I realize this is a very harsh charge, but how else can one honestly describe the attitude implicit in a style so in love with itself that it often loses sight of what it is supposed to be conveying, and so aesthetically narcissistic that it intransigently refuses to make any concessions whatsoever to the reader, even to the point of often requiring an editor's footnotes to decipher the pyrotechnical wordplay in which it so mischievously indulges?

Discussing this very issue in the course of deigning to engage in the "fatal fatuity" of explicating a series of such allusions, Nabokov was unusually frank about it. "It may be asked if it is really worth an author's while to devise and distribute these delicate markers whose very nature requires that they be not too conspicuous." Who, after all, will notice them or, having noticed, will be able to make sense of them without the help of footnotes? No matter. "In the long run, . . . it is only the author's private satisfaction that counts."

Far from being peculiar to Nabokov and Joyce, this attitude was shared by practically every novelist and poet associated with the modernist movement. In a manifesto issued in Paris in 1926, for instance, a large group of writers declared, among other things, that "The writer expresses. He does not communicate," and ended with "The plain reader be damned." It must further be acknowledged that in arrogant authorial indifference to the reasonable expectations of the reader, "plain" or fancy, Nabokov was a mild sinner when set alongside Joyce. Asked how he expected anyone to understand *Finnegans Wake,* Joyce once replied: "The demand that I make of my reader is that he should devote his whole life to reading my works."

Nabokov never went that far either in theory or in practice (he admired *Ulysses* but not *Finnegans Wake*). Still, as a relentless player of what the editor of the Library of America edition calls "intricate games of deception and concealment" (meaning this, in accordance with good modernist doctrine, as a compliment), a sinner he was nevertheless.

HERE *Lolita* is an exception among Nabokov's novels. It is relatively easy to follow, and the linguistic pyrotechnics, while still on display, are kept under unusually strict control. Yet if *Lolita* is more or less free of this species of modernist sin, it is just as driven as Nabokov's other novels by the radical modernist aestheticism of which their "intricate games of deception" and their stylistic excesses are only one symptom or expression. This kind of aestheticism was once summed up in the slogan "art for art's sake," which was to say, *not* for the sake of God or morality or ideology or society. Often for better (as a protection against the dictates of politics) and sometimes for worse (as an encouragement to mandarinism and hermeticism), the aestheticist creed thus represented a declaration of the artist's independence from any and all obligations other than those imposed by the laws of his art.

No more fanatical devotee of this creed existed than Vladimir Nabokov. There were only two things he cared about as a writer. One was capturing the exact feel and color and shading and texture of a perception or an emotion or a memory, and the other was fooling around with language for the sheer fun of exercising his enormous power over it. The subject matter of a novel was of little importance to him except as an occasion—I might almost say a pretext—for doing these things. Here is how he himself put it:

> For me a work of fiction exists only insofar as it affords me what I shall bluntly call aesthetic bliss, that is a sense of being somehow, somewhere, connected with other states of being where art (curiosity, tenderness, kindness, ecstasy) is the norm. . . . All the rest is either topical trash or what some call the Literature of Ideas. . . .

Whenever he could, Nabokov made sure to disabuse anyone who might be led by the subject matter of his own work to misinterpret it (even sympathetically) as belonging to either of those dread categories. A good example of how he did this was the introduction he provided to a later reissue of *Bend Sinister,* one of his earliest novels in English.

Set in a fictional country that has fallen under totalitarianism, and written by a man who had fled the Soviet regime and clearly hated it with all his heart, *Bend Sinister* was in danger of being taken by the innocent "plain reader" to be about Soviet Russia, much as George Orwell's roughly contemporaneous *Animal Farm* and *Nineteen Eighty-Four* were. But Nabokov repudiated any such reference. *Bend Sinister,* he insisted, had no kinship whatever with "Orwell's clichés" (which he clearly consigned to the category of "topical trash"):

> I have never been interested in what is called the literature of social comment. . . . I am neither a didacticist nor an allegorizer. Politics and economics, atomic bombs, primitive and abstract art forms, the entire Orient, symptoms of "thaw" in Soviet Russia, the Future of Mankind, and so on, leave me supremely indifferent. . . . Similarly, the influence of my epoch on [*Bend Sinister*] is as negligible as the influence of my books, or at least of this book, on my epoch.

In short, despite being interlarded "with bits of Lenin's speeches, and a chunk of the Soviet constitution, and gobs of Nazist pseudo-efficiency," *Bend Sinister* was "not really about life and death in a grotesque police state." Its main theme was the love of a father for his son, and what mattered most in it was certain recurrent images, such as a puddle that appeared at the very beginning and then reappeared at various points later on as an ink blot, an ink stain, spilled milk, and several other similarly interesting mutations.

AS WITH POLITICS, so with morality. "*Lolita,*" Nabokov declared of this novel about a pedophile (Humbert Humbert) who seduces his twelve-year-old stepdaughter (Lolita) and continues forcing himself on her until she runs away, "has no moral in tow." Indeed, those "gentle souls who would pronounce *Lolita* meaningless because it does not teach them anything" are more right than they know. For "the nerves of the novel, . . . the secret points, the subliminal coordinates by means of which the book is plotted" and through which it affords the discerning reader the "aesthetic bliss" whose achievement is the only purpose for which it exists, are not located in the story of a pedophile and his victim, let alone in any lessons that might flow from it. They lie, rather, in

> such images as Mr. Taxovich, or that class list of Ramsdale School, or Charlotte saying "waterproof," or Lolita in slow motion advancing

toward Humbert's gifts, or the pictures decorating the stylized garret of Gaston Godin, or the Kasbeam barber . . . , or Lolita playing tennis, or the hospital at Elphinstone, or pale, pregnant, beloved, irretrievable Dolly Schiller dying in Gray Star (the capital town of the book), or the tinkling sounds of the valley town coming up the mountain trail. . . .

Now, Nabokov was undoubtedly right when he then proceeded to deny that *Lolita* was a work of pornography. While it did, in his words, "contain various allusions to the physiological urges of a pervert," it did not contain obscene language or explicit descriptions of sexual activity. The problem, then, as Nabokov recognized, was not with his treatment of the theme, but with the theme itself. It was, he wrote, one of three "which are utterly taboo as far as most American publishers are concerned," the other two being a successful interracial marriage and an "atheist who lives a happy and useful life, and dies in his sleep at the age of 106."

Yet here, for once, the snobbish sarcasm to which Nabokov was always given outraced his immense intelligence and trumped his normal passion for precision, since the other two themes were not remotely in the same class of the forbidden as the idea of adults molesting children. Nor did they inspire the same kind or degree of horror, assuming they even inspired it at all outside of certain restricted social circles. Hence in telling the story it told, *Lolita* was admitting something truly forbidden into public consciousness, and by doing so it was—whether Nabokov liked it or not—insidiously seducing its readers into "thinking about the unthinkable."

I have borrowed that phrase from the debates over nuclear war which were being conducted around the same time *Lolita* came out in an American edition. It was charged then that strategists like Herman Kahn who speculated about the waging of nuclear war were breaking the taboo against it and thereby making it more likely to happen. Could an analogous charge be lodged against Nabokov's novel about a pedophile? In the case of Kahn and the others, they defended themselves by saying that, on the contrary, they were making nuclear war less likely by teaching us how better to deter it. But no such defense was available to Nabokov. By his own account, he was not trying to teach us anything one way or the other about pedophilia. And while he did not hesitate to label pedophilia a perversion, the way he treated it was emphatically not calculated to deepen our horror over it. Just the opposite. And herein lies a paradox.

Because, as D. H. Lawrence said, the point of pornography is to "do dirt on sex," and because it also depends for its effect on the feeling that sex is dirty, a straightforwardly pornographic treatment of pedophilia would inevitably retain the sense of it as a taboo and would play on the horror attached to violating it. Not so with Nabokov. The very brilliance of his language, the very sharpness of his wit, the very artfulness of his treatment all help to shatter the taboo and thereby to rob pedophilia of its horror. In other words, in aestheticizing the hideous, Nabokov—as I can now clearly see—comes very close to prettifying it.

Worse yet, he comes very close to excusing it. Reviewing the first American edition of *Lolita* in 1958, my old teacher and mentor, Lionel Trilling, began with an acknowledgment of how shocking the book was, but then added:

> And we find ourselves the more shocked when we realize that, in the course of reading the novel, we have come virtually to condone the violation it presents, . . . to see the situation as less and less abstract and moral and horrible, and more and more as human and "understandable." Less and less, indeed, do we see a *situation;* what we become aware of is people. Humbert is perfectly willing to say that he is a monster; no doubt he is, but we find ourselves less and less eager to say so.

It is important to understand that Trilling was saying this not to bury *Lolita* but to praise it for fulfilling what he considered one of the primary *moral* duties of the novel, which was to deepen the reader's sense of the complexity of life. On this point I agreed enthusiastically, but I was also less ambivalent than Trilling about the smashing of taboos, from which—as it seemed to me at that age and at that time—only good could come.

Be that as it may, the sort of effect Trilling described never happens in reading pornography. There are no people to understand in pornography; there is only a succession of graphically represented sexual acts performed by faceless creatures who are driven by lust and nothing but lust. This may arouse the reader's own lustful urges, but at least it can be said that pornography never plunges him into a state of moral confusion—not even on those rare occasions when it tries to do just that.

THE MOST NOTORIOUS instance of a pornographer trying to sow moral confusion is to be found in the eighteenth century and in the person of the Marquis de Sade. "Evil, be thou my good," declares Satan in *Paradise Lost,* and Sade set out to follow that invocation into regions that would have been way beyond John Milton's most lurid antinomian imaginings. For this, Sade's books were banned in his own time. But in ours he has come to be hailed as a great writer, a great philosopher, and a great moralist—the "Divine Marquis," as his countryman, the early-twentieth-century avant-garde poet Guillaume Apollinaire, called him.

I was reminded of all this by the appearance of Roger Shattuck's *Forbidden Knowledge,* which spends many pages refuting the case for the rehabilitation and canonization of Sade. Shattuck does a very good job of it, but as I went through those learned and carefully nuanced pages with their earnest and respectful analyses of the arguments advanced by the (mostly French) intellectuals to whom Sade's work resembles (as one of them actually put it) "the sacred books of the great religions," I could not help thinking—again—of Orwell, and specifically of what he once said about certain obviously ridiculous ideas: "One has to belong to the intelligentsia to believe things like that; no ordinary man could be such a fool."

If Shattuck had been addressing the "ordinary man," he could have won his case simply by juxtaposing the claims made by admirers of the "Divine Marquis" with the samples of Sade's own writings he quotes in *Forbidden Knowledge.* So disgusting are those writings that even today, when anything goes, it is daring of Shattuck to quote them, and even then he (or his publisher) must have thought it the better part of prudence to print a notice at the head of the book warning parents and teachers of material to come that is "inappropriate for children and minors," and still another notice in the chapter on Sade flagging "passages that many people will consider offensive and obscene in the extreme." Why then use them? Here is Shattuck's justification:

> Most writings on Sade and even some anthologies avoid such explicitness and limit their quotations to philosophical discussions of crime, passion, nature, freedom, and the like: To bowdlerize Sade in this fashion distorts him beyond recognition. The actions described in his works directly complement the ideas and probably surpass them in psychological impact.

Except for that "probably"—"most assuredly" or "infinitely" would have been more accurate—this is excellent, and it brings to mind the first time I finally read Sade himself after having read a number of the critics taken on by Shattuck. Encountering Sade in the flesh, so to speak, I was almost as shocked by the mendacity of those critics as by what I found in his books.

First of all, none of them had made clear that for Sade the supreme sexual act is buggery, both of men and of women, but of the latter mainly as an expression of revulsion for the female sexual organs so great that he could imagine—and actually describe with great relish—sewing them up. Though he does include plenty of the whipping and other forms of torture that have come to be associated with his name, buggery is by so wide a margin his favorite sexual activity that the term "sadist" might more precisely have been used as a synonym for sodomite.

I confess that I do not understand why the commentators I read some thirty-five or forty years ago on Sade, who exalted him for his "unfaltering demand for the truth" (Jean Paulhan) and for "daring to look [his dangerous fantasies] in the eye" (Georges Bataille), were so prissily reticent about the homosexual content of those fantasies. Perhaps in passing lightly over the connection in Sade between homosexuality and a loathing of women—who are represented as foul in themselves and foul, too, because they breed (Sade, as Shattuck points out, regarded "propagation of the species as contrary to nature")—his apologists were being protective of homosexuality.*

Another possibility is that Sade's admirers were being protective of *him*, fearing that to call attention to his homosexuality would limit his allegedly universal relevance and compromise their claim that his fantasies are directly relevant to everyone. If so, this would be of a piece with the general bowdlerizing about which Shattuck complains, and which was the second source of my astonishment when I first read Sade after having read some of his defenders. Just as they glided so lightly over Sade's homosexuality that I was amazed to discover how blatantly pervasive it was in his books, so they also failed to convey a sense of what Sade's pornographic scenes were actually like.

Like Shattuck, I believe that the only way to convey such a sense is through quotation and paraphrase, and I now mean to borrow from *Forbidden Knowledge* in doing so. Being less nervy than he is, however, I will for the most part reproduce not Sade's own language but only a small segment of one of Shattuck's summaries, from which in addition I will omit a

---

*I learn from Shattuck that some critics are now finally acknowledging that "the central Sadean doctrine is the primacy of the act of sodomy." Shattuck himself agrees about "the all-pervasiveness of sodomy in Sade's writings," but interestingly enough, both he and the critics he cites, while talking easily about "anal intercourse" and perfectly willing to call it "buggery," still shy away from identifying it as a largely homosexual practice.

few details. Of course, even in this slightly cleaned-up version, the passage remains utterly revolting:

> After a bizarre double wedding ceremony in drag among members of the same sex, . . . the sons are forced to bugger the father, who imitates the shrieking behavior of a young virgin. Whippings begin, blood flows, breasts are ripped off, limbs are broken and dislocated, and eyes are torn out while Noirceuil sodomizes the victims. . . . Brought to extreme arousal by the excruciating torture to death of two female victims, Noirceuil buggers one of his sons while literally eating the boy's heart, which has been torn out of his body by Juliette.

Noirceuil then violently rapes Juliette's seven-year-old daughter ("this disgusting product of the sacred balls of your abominable husband"), after which, with the mother's enthusiastic assent, he throws the child naked into the flames. Sade writes, in Juliette's voice:

> I help him with a poker to arrest her natural compulsive responses to save herself. . . . Others are diddling us and buggering us. Marianne is roasting. She is consumed. Noirceuil discharges. I do the same.

One must indeed "belong to the intelligentsia"—or perhaps the *French* intelligentsia—to see moral value and wisdom in the abstract lectures about freedom and nature with which Sade surrounds such scenes and for which they are supposed to serve as concrete illustrations.

WHAT ROGER SHATTUCK does in discussing Sade is precisely what the director Miloš Forman lacks the honesty and/or the guts to do in *The People vs. Larry Flynt*. As I have already indicated, I caught this movie while I was rethinking the issue of pornography, and quite apart from turning out to be wildly overrated as a work of cinematic art, it nudged me in exactly the opposite direction from the one it wanted me to go.

Flynt is the publisher of a magazine called *Hustler* whose stock-in-trade has been vividly described by Bob Herbert in his column in the *New York Times*:

> A photo of a man driving a jackhammer into the vagina of a naked woman was captioned: "A simple cure for frigidity." One of the mag-

azine's covers showed a disembodied woman's head in a gift box. . . . [Another feature] showed four photographs of women's bodies in various stages of mutilation. The photos are attached to what appears to be charred human skin. Razor blades are scattered about. Nipples and what appear to be clitorises are attached to the skin with fishhooks and safety pins. Some of the women in the photos have been decapitated, or have lost limbs. A dead woman, naked, is shown lying beside a toilet.

Not that you would guess any of this from Forman's movie, any more than you would suspect that a Justice Department report once calculated that children were shown as sexual objects in *Hustler* on an average of fourteen times per issue.

No doubt out of fear that seeing what *Hustler* is really like would alienate the audience's sympathy for Flynt (not to mention the fear of losing money by bringing an X rating down on his head), Forman bowdlerizes his subject much as, mutatis mutandis, the defenders of Sade used to do. Thus, he conveys the impression that *Hustler* is nothing more than a downmarket version of *Playboy*, a bit raunchier perhaps but also more given to prankish humor and satirical high jinks. In fact, a piece of satirical high jinks is precisely how the movie characterizes the notorious *Hustler* cartoon that showed the evangelist Jerry Falwell committing incest with his mother in an outhouse. It was this cartoon which led to the libel suit whose resolution in Flynt's favor by the Supreme Court forms the triumphant climax of the movie.

Forman's cheerleaders—compounding his dishonesty with their own—make a big point of insisting that he never "glorifies" or even "whitewashes" Flynt himself. Yet the plain fact is that through the omission or misrepresentation of many damaging details about Flynt's life and career, he too is bowdlerized—into a high-spirited and mischievous good old boy, a mixture of Huck Finn and Abbie Hoffman. Not only does this likable rogue mean no harm; he is actually a courageous fighter for freedom—sexual freedom and freedom of the press—against the puritanical hypocrites who wish to suppress both. Furthermore, never is there so much as a faint hint that there might exist other kinds of people with other grounds for objecting to the open circulation of a magazine like *Hustler*.

Prominent among these missing people and perspectives are feminists like Catharine MacKinnon and Andrea Dworkin who regard pornography as degrading to women and who are for that reason no less eager than the Christian Right to censor it.* Now I happen to disagree with these feminists about heterosexual pornography in general. In my opinion, what the critic Louis Menand observes about the mass-market pornography which emerged into full public view in the late 1960s and early 1970s—namely, that it was based on the idea "that women enjoyed sex as much as men, and in the same way as men were imagined to enjoy it—that is, actively, promiscuously, and without guilt"—has always been true of heterosexual pornography. This idea may be "just another male fantasy," and it may be false to the sexual nature of women, but it cannot be said to degrade them. (Of course Dworkin and MacKinnon believe that normal heterosexual intercourse, which they regard as almost always indistinguishable from rape, is just as degrading to women as the pornography that describes it.)

Where *Hustler* is concerned, however, I think these feminists have a point. If there is a case of heterosexual pornography that truly does degrade women, it is *Hustler,* in whose eyes they are all filthy sluts who deserve to be brutalized. Flynt, a kind of straight subliterate Sade, also forges the same "association of sexual gratification with malevolence, pain, torture, and murder" that Shattuck identifies as the distinctive mark of the "Divine Marquis."

THERE IS ALSO another opposing perspective whose existence is not acknowledged either by Miloš Forman himself or by the admirers of his movie. Less visible for the moment than the feminist argument but intellectually far more formidable, it is represented by the two recent books I mentioned at the outset. The first, Roger Shattuck's *Forbidden Knowledge,* I have already touched on in discussing Sade (though it covers much more ground). The second, Rochelle Gurstein's *The Repeal of Reticence,* carries the rather unwieldy subtitle *A History of America's Cultural and Legal Struggles over Free Speech, Obscenity, Sexual Liberation, and Modern Art.* Both these books—neither, by the way, written by a conservative—raise troubling questions about the price we have paid for what I myself once

---

*If in making his movie Forman was unaware that such feminists exist, he discovered after its release how influential they could be. A piece on the Op-Ed page of the *New York Times* by Gloria Steinem attacking Forman for glorifying Flynt was credited with damaging the movie's commercial fortunes, and feminist ire was also blamed for the film's failure to be nominated for an Academy Award even though it had been praised to the skies by all the leading reviewers (including the conservative John Simon writing in *National Review*).

applauded: the shattering of all taboos (Shattuck) and the dragging of everything that was once private into full public display (Gurstein).

The great service Shattuck and Gurstein perform is to remind us forcibly that there is more—a great deal more—to say about the legalization of pornography than is dreamed of in the philosophy of the writers and artists for whom unrestrained freedom of expression is the supreme value and civil libertarians for whom the discussion begins and ends with the First Amendment. Here Gurstein is especially relevant. Reaching back to the late nineteenth and early twentieth centuries, she revisits the writings of the mostly forgotten members of the "party of reticence" (among them the once well-known essayist Agnes Repplier, Professor Charles Eliot Norton of Harvard, and William Trufant Foster, the president of Reed College), and shows how much stronger and more intellectually sophisticated their arguments were than almost anyone remembers today.

Those arguments pointed to the deleterious effects of pornography on the moral and cultural environment, on standards of taste and judgment, and on sexual life itself. But the "party of exposure" (whose members included practically every prominent young literary figure of the age, along with sexual reformers like Margaret Sanger and political radicals of every stripe) managed to banish all such considerations from the debate. It did this first through the relentless Menckenesque campaign of ridicule that stigmatized them as hopelessly bourgeois and retrograde, and then by dragging the issue into the courts where, one by one, the objections to pornography registered by the "party of reticence" were ruled out as irrelevant, leaving the narrowly legal question of a given individual's constitutional rights as the only one that mattered.

One could scarcely dream up a more perfect epitome of this process than *The People vs. Larry Flynt*. To Miloš Forman (and most of the reviewers of his movie), The People are all joyless troglodytes who have nothing to say that is worth hearing. As for Larry Flynt, he may not be to everyone's taste but everyone's freedom is nevertheless so inextricably implicated in his that when he wins his fight against Jerry Falwell in the Supreme Court, the ultimate guardian of all rights, he becomes an American hero.

Yet not even so great a victory can allow us any rest: the enemy is still there, and the fight goes on. Thus in a fawning piece, Frank Rich (whose opinion of *The People vs. Larry Flynt* is at the opposite pole from that of his fellow *New York Times* columnist Bob Herbert) writes of Forman's great anxiety over "the growing power of American cultural commissars on the secular and religious Right." "I spent my most sensitive years in two totalitarian regimes," Forman (who was born and raised in Czechoslovakia) tells Rich. "The Nazis and Communists began by attacking pornography, homosexuals—it always starts very innocently."

Never mind that neither the Nazis nor the Communists "began" in this way. (The original paramilitary unit of the Nazi party, the SA, was filled with homosexuals, including its commander, while in the early days of Communist rule in Russia, "free love" was elevated over marriage and the avant-garde dominated the arts.) Never mind that comparing "the secular and religious Right" in America to Nazis and Communists is a vile insult. Never mind that if we do have "cultural commissars" in this country, they are the very critics and reviewers who have cheered Miloš Forman and pronounced his movie a great work of art.

Never mind all that, and never mind, too, that until only yesterday (as Gurstein demonstrates), no one ever imagined that the freedom of speech guaranteed by the First Amendment extended to pornography. So far as Forman and his admirers are concerned, anyone who opposes the likes of Larry Flynt is still backward or wicked or both, and the corrupting effects of pornography on our society and on our culture (if indeed there are any) are still a small price to pay (if indeed a price it is) for our most precious freedom.

I never knew until I read Rochelle Gurstein that one of the original and most influential authors of this line of reasoning, the famous civil-liberties lawyer Morris Ernst, came to have second thoughts about its validity. As far back as 1970, Ernst admitted that he was repelled by the "present display of sex and sadism on the streets" and "sodomy on the stage or masturbation in the public area." Surely, Gurstein comments,

> his lifelong project had miscarried when purveyors of pornography could claim they were completing the movement begun by his own brilliant defense of *Ulysses,* where, as he put it, he had "legitimatized a four-letter word." "I deeply resent the idea . . . that the lowest common denominator, the most tawdry magazine, pandering for profit, to use the Supreme Court's word, should be able to compete in the marketplace with no constraints."*

---

*Ernst was not the only leader of the "party of exposure" who later developed second thoughts. Even Mencken did to some degree, and others like Walter Lippmann and Joseph Wood Krutch also came to feel as they grew older that the complete rout of "the party of reticence" had brought with it unforeseen and unfortunate consequences.

Here, then, we have a third perspective whose existence goes unacknowledged by Forman's movie and its admirers.

OF THE MANY POINTS emerging from these varied perspectives, there are two that have hit me with special force. The first is the emphasis placed by the "party of reticence" on pollution. This is a word we now use only about the physical environment, having forgotten that we also live in a moral and cultural environment that is equally vulnerable to contamination. We have forgotten, too, that our minds and spirits, no less than our lungs, can be damaged when the air they breathe is fouled by pollutants. If we are willing to place restrictions on the manufacturers of material goods in order to protect ourselves against pollution of the physical environment, why should we not be willing to take measures that would offer protection against pollution of the moral and cultural environment?

The second point that has hit me hard has to do with the effect of pornography on sex itself. In this connection, Rochelle Gurstein leans heavily on a phrase that comes from Miloš Forman's countryman and contemporary, Milan Kundera, who used it as the title of one of his novels: "the unbearable lightness of being." This phrase has long been one of my own favorites because it so wonderfully defines what life is like when the burdens of responsibility and consequence are lifted from it. These burdens may seem intolerably heavy, but it is the lightness experienced in casting them off that is really unbearable. And this is what has happened to sex in our time.

Listen to the testimony of Katie Roiphe in her new book *Last Night in Paradise*. A liberated young woman who talks openly and even boastfully about her many affairs, Roiphe has begun to understand on her own pulses what the unbearable lightness of being means:

> We find ourselves living without the pain, reassurance, and clarity of late-19th-century social censure. We are on our own . . . yearning for consequences. Meaning. A tiny ruffling of the social order. If an act has serious social ramifications, . . . then it appears to have transcendent meaning as well. It matters. It changes things. . . . The end of consequences has created a new moral universe in which events such as Anna Karenina's adulterous affair can seem formless and weightless.

It was, I recognize, the sexual revolution, not pornography, that created this state of affairs, but pornography helped trigger that revolution and, accompanying it every inch down the slippery slope, also played an autonomous part of its own. Heinrich Blücher, all those years ago, accused me of taking the fun out of sex by defending pornography, but he might better have charged me with turning it into something weightless. For sex without consequence of any kind is precisely what pornography sells: sex that is cut loose from morality, from love, from pregnancy, from marriage, from jealousy, from hurt. In this "pornotopian" world, sex thus liberated brings unalloyed ecstasy. In the real world, it brings the unbearable lightness of being.

AND SO IT IS that I have fallen to wondering uneasily whether, if we wish to clean up our moral and spiritual environment and at the same time put at least some of the weight back into sex, we should consider a restoration of censorship. Roger Shattuck provides all the materials needed to construct a case for doing just that, but he answers No to Simone de Beauvoir's question, "Must We Burn Sade?" (and a fortiori less extreme variants of pornography). Rochelle Gurstein, after providing a complementary set of materials, ends with a sympathetic account of a book by Harry Clor which forthrightly advocates censorship, but she herself falls short of a ringing endorsement of it.

Daring, then, as Shattuck and Gurstein are in trying to promote a return of the now-repressed arguments for respecting taboos and banishing obscenity from the public square, they are not quite daring enough to drop the other shoe. Neither, if truth be told, am I. This is not, as I have already indicated, because I think that censoring pornography is the first step on the road to totalitarianism. And it is not because I buy the specious historical and legal contention that the First Amendment applies no less to pornography than to political speech. No, the reason I hesitate to come out for censorship is that I cannot conceive of government bureaucrats I would trust to do the censoring. In the past, such officials could detect no difference between the likes of D. H. Lawrence and the likes of Larry Flynt; it seems unlikely that their successors would be any more discriminating.

And yet, having acknowledged that, I also ask myself whether the banning of some genuinely good books would be too high a price to pay for getting rid of the poisons in the moral and cultural air we breathe. Once upon a time, when I was a devotee of the religion of art and a leftist to boot, the very question would have struck me as nothing short of blasphemous. But I ask it of myself today because it is no longer all that obvious to me that my mother-in-law, who certainly would not have been able to tell the difference between *Lolita* and Larry Flynt, was wrong in trying to protect her "part of the country" from both. If we cannot have *Lolita* without taking Larry Flynt, or for that matter the Marquis de Sade, maybe we should refuse the whole package deal.

But what about *Lolita* itself? Must we have *Lolita?* I ask myself this even more blasphemous question because I can no longer dismiss out of hand the possibility that *Lolita* bears at least some share of the blame for the plague of pedophilia that has been raging through this country and that has now hit my mother-in-law's home state with a special vengeance. By helping to make pedophilia thinkable, may not Nabokov have to some indeterminate extent been responsible for the greater toleration that gradually came to be accorded what had previously been regarded as perhaps the most horrible of all crimes?*

Thankfully, not all the horror has been drained out of pedophilia. Child molesters are still excoriated, and the fear of them is still great enough to generate outbreaks of hysteria in which innocent parents and teachers are falsely accused by little children at the prompting of overzealous prosecutors and by grown women with "recovered memories" planted by quack psychotherapists. (I suspect, incidentally, that the credence given to these outbreaks is the displaced and distorted product of an uneasy conscience. After all, with so many little children being guiltily left in day-care centers, it is no wonder that lurid imaginings should arise of the dangers to which they are being abandoned; and it is also no wonder that an escape from guilt should then be sought in the idea that children are as much at risk from their own fathers at home as they are from custodians in nursery school. Even then, there is no escape from the guilt everyone surely feels over doing so little in general to protect the children of this country from the moral poisons in the air.)

In any event, even when the accusations of child molestation are true, these monsters are either sent for "help," which is what usually seems to happen to fathers who have committed incest with a child, or imprisoned

---

**Lolita has by now sold more than fourteen million copies, and a new film version will soon be released. [After being initially rejected by studio executives in 1997, the film was finally released in 1998, more than a year after this essay was written ED.] It will star a first-time actress in her early teens named Dominique Swain (whose saucy photograph recently adorned the covers of both *Esquire* and *Vanity Fair*). Unlike the relatively tame version done by Stanley Kubrick in the early 1960s, or indeed the novel itself, the new *Lolita* will feature explicit scenes of copulation in the nude. Miss Swain reportedly had no objection to appearing nude in those scenes herself, but to avoid running afoul of the kiddie-porn laws, a nineteen-year-old "body double" was used in her place.

with shorter sentences than they deserve. (If it were up to me, they would either be executed or put away for life without possibility of parole, instead of being released after a few years with nothing to stop them from preying again but a sadly ineffective Megan's Law.)

Nabokov's own fictional pedophile, Humbert Humbert, was not so gently let off by his creator, who arranged for him first to lose Lolita and then to die in prison (of a heart attack). But Nabokov stood at the top of this particular slippery slope, down which he did his part to push us. Now, after forty years of sliding, we have landed in a region where the condition of being has become so light and so weightless that the only consequence suffered by a real-life Humbert Humbert like Woody Allen is a short-lived scandal that does not even deprive him of his Lolita or leave him sufficiently disgraced to ruin his career.

LITTLE DID I ever expect that I would wind up on the edge of endorsing the censorship of pornography, and not in my wildest conservative dreams did I ever before entertain the thought that we might have been better off if even a masterpiece like *Lolita* had never been published. But such is the uncomfortable pass to which I have been driven by the dormant memories that were evoked and the settled questions that were reopened by that story about a ring of pedophiles in Minnesota which appeared in the paper just as I happened to be rereading what I now see as a dangerous book paradoxically made all the more dangerous by its dazzling virtues as a work of art.

PHILIP ROTH, THEN AND NOW

I HAVE ALWAYS HAD TROUBLE with the work of Philip Roth. Unless my memory is playing tricks on me—and if so, I have no doubt that someone, though not, if I know anything about him, Roth himself, will correct me—it was I who "discovered" him as a writer of fiction. In early 1957, as a recently hired assistant editor of *Commentary,* I had the job of going through the daily deluge of unsolicited manuscripts known as the "slush pile." Even at a glance it was easy to see that most of these manuscripts were unworthy of publication anywhere, or unsuitable for *Commentary* in particular. But once in a while, even if the manuscript that had been submitted was not in itself much good, the writer might show enough sign of real talent to be encouraged or cultivated; and once in a greater while, I would come upon a piece that was in my judgment actually publishable, and I would then circulate it to my superiors for a final decision.

One of the first such manuscripts I singled out in this way was something called "You Can't Tell a Man by the Song He Sings" by an unknown writer named Philip Roth. I say "something" because it might have been either a memoir or a short story: it was—foreshadowing in this much of the author's later work—hard to tell. And I say "unknown" because, though I recognized Roth's name from a few short reviews he had done for the *New Republic,* I had never before come upon anything else of this nature by him. In any case, I was excited by the literary powers Roth demonstrated here and considered him a real find.

My senior colleagues, though markedly less impressed than I was, still thought well enough of this submission to accept the piece, and it ultimately appeared in the November 1957 issue of *Commentary.* By placing it in a department that used to run in the magazine under the rubric "From the American Scene," and that was devoted mainly to nonfictional accounts of immigrant Jewish life in neighborhoods like the Lower East Side of New York, we were treating it as a memoir (the locale in this case being the Weequahic neighborhood of Newark, to which Roth would never cease returning in his work). So far as I can recall, Roth made no objection to this categorization, but by including "You Can't Tell a Man By the Song He Sings" in his first book, the collection of short stories entitled *Goodbye, Columbus* that appeared about two years later, he himself chose to represent it as a piece of fiction.

It was and still is rare for a writer of fiction to make his debut with a collection of short stories; usually he is able to get such a collection published only after he has produced a well-received novel or two. Even more unusual was—and is—it for a collection by anyone other than a well-established author to attract a great deal of favorable attention, let alone be awarded important literary prizes. Yet more than one reviewer pronounced *Goodbye, Columbus* a masterpiece; it won the National Book Award, whose prestige within the serious literary community was already becoming much greater than the more middlebrow Pulitzer Prize that it had been established to challenge; and the book even sold well, going through innumerable printings both in hard- and softcover editions.

What explained this degree of success was that Roth, from a strictly literary point of view, was so precociously accomplished that in himself he amounted to a phenomenon no less unusual than the circumstances and the reception of his book. Reviewing it for *Commentary*, Saul Bellow put the case with his characteristic brilliance:

> *Goodbye, Columbus* is a first book but it is not the book of a beginner. Unlike those of us who came howling into the world, blind and bare, Mr. Roth appears with nails, hair, and teeth, speaking coherently. At twenty-six he is skillful, witty, and energetic and performs like a virtuoso.

Then, too, there was the Jewish side of *Goodbye, Columbus*. Since the appearance six years earlier of Bellow's own *The Adventures of Augie March* (his third novel) there had been much talk of the flowering of a new school of American Jewish fiction, and Bellow himself had come to be regarded as its major representative. In this capacity he was in effect giving Roth the same kind of imprimatur that had a little earlier been accorded to Bernard Malamud (mostly, as with Roth, on the basis of his short stories, though they had not yet been brought together into a book-length collection). To be sure, all three of these writers, and especially Bellow, would express resentment when they were identified as *Jewish* writers, as though this diminished them and made their work less American or less universal.

Thus, playing on the brand name of a quality men's clothing manufacturer of the time, Bellow would quip that he, Malamud, and Roth had been turned into the Hart, Schaffner & Marx of American literature.

NO SUCH ANXIETY ever seemed to trouble the soul of William Faulkner, or of any of the other prominent Southern novelists whose own flowering had preceded that of the Jews and who by the late 1950s were beginning to be forced to jostle with them for center stage in the upper reaches of the literary culture. Faulkner, for example, believed—and very aggressively so— that it was precisely the particularistic Southernness of his own work that gave it universality.

In theory, Bellow and his younger Jewish colleagues certainly shared Faulkner's belief that in literature the road to universality was through the particular, as did all sophisticated literary people in that period. Indeed, no critical doctrine was more influential in those days than this one. Nevertheless, some lingering trace of doubt seemed to remain in the hearts of the Jewish novelists. Probably this was left over from an all-too-recent past in which a writer with a name like Nathan Weinstein felt obliged to change it to Nathanael West if he was to be taken seriously, and in which fiction about Jewish life was almost always relegated to the literary margin, if it was noticed at all. A very striking and poignant illustration was Ludwig Lewisohn. His early work in the 1920s had attracted the admiring attention of giants like Thomas Mann and Sigmund Freud, but he became a virtual nonperson in the literary world after espousing Zionism and writing in his novels both openly and in a "positive" spirit about Jews and the Jewish experience.

Another saliently cautionary example was *Call It Sleep* by Henry Roth (no relation to Philip). This novel about life among immigrant Jews on the Lower East Side, written in part in an English idiom that managed to mimic the rhythms and locutions of Yiddish, would many years later (and in the wake of the cultural change Bellow and the others helped bring about) be rediscovered and acclaimed as a masterpiece. But *Call It Sleep* was largely ignored upon its publication in 1934 (inducing in its author one of the longest-lived writer's blocks in the history of literature). Much the same fate, and at much the same time, befell Daniel Fuchs's so-called "Williamsburg Trilogy," though unlike Roth, who went to Maine to raise waterfowl, Fuchs responded to the failure of his novels by going off to Hollywood where he became a screenwriter—and, mercifully, a successful one at that.

It was perhaps in response to so unwelcoming a cultural climate that a playwright like Arthur Miller took to pretending, by giving the characters in his plays Waspy names like Biff or ethnically ambiguous ones like Loman, that these people, whose Jewishness was obvious to anyone with eyes to see, were undifferentiated Americans. (When Miller's *Death of a Salesman* was staged in a Yiddish translation, the review of the production in *Commentary* was wickedly entitled "*Death of a Salesman* in the Original.") Similarly, another famous Jewish playwright, Lillian Hellman (who in *The Little Foxes,* which was actually based on her own family, had set a model for Miller's way of washing the ethnic taint out of his characters) thought that the Jewishness of *The Diary of Anne Frank* would limit its appeal on Broadway. Consequently, Hellman advised the playwrights she proposed for the job of dramatizing the diary that they in effect de-Judaize it as much as they possibly could.

But at the same time, and in another part of the cultural forest—the highbrow part—Jewish writers who drew on the Jewish experience for material were becoming all the rage. In this new climate, the poet Delmore Schwartz did not feel the need to change his surname to its Anglo equivalent of Black (in fact, if his parents had changed it to Black, he might well have changed it back to Schwartz). Nor did his great friend and mutual admirer Saul Bellow—however hard he may have found it to erase every single trace of these old pressures from his soul—make any attempt to disguise the Jewishness of his characters. On the contrary, he boldly asserted that they were as American as anyone in the novels of Henry James: "I am an American, Chicago born," declares Augie March in the highly significant first words of the first-person novel that achieved a breakthrough into the mainstream for Bellow himself and for the Jewish novelists who followed in his footsteps.

ACCORDINGLY, in his review of *Goodbye, Columbus,* Bellow did not hesitate to spend most of his time talking about Roth's handling of Jewish material. Invidiously, he compared this young colleague with older Jewish writers like Herman Wouk, "who think that ours [i.e., the ones inhabited by Jews] are the best of all possible suburbs in the best of all possible Americas," and defended him against those within the Jewish community "who feel that the business of a Jewish writer in America is to write public-relations releases, to publicize everything that is nice in the Jewish community and to suppress the rest, loyally."

Roth's early success, in short, was based on more than his remarkable talent. Poor Henry Roth had made his debut within a literary culture that had either no interest in Jews or that regarded them as an unfit subject for American literature, whereas Philip Roth exploded into a culture in which there had developed a new receptivity to fiction about Jews. There were, however, implicit conditions attached to this receptivity. Obviously the work in question had to be sufficiently intimate with the still exotic American Jewish experience to render it convincingly. But the author also had to be sufficiently distanced from this experience to write about it with a critical if not a jaundiced eye. This test Roth passed with flying colors from the word go.

True, the stories of Bernard Malamud, being much more sympathetic to their Jewish characters than Roth's, did not pass, or even sit for, this test. But Malamud's Jews were acceptably and reassuringly *poor,* and he tended to envelop them in a kind of mythological aura that made the "public-relations" question moot or irrelevant. By contrast, the novella from which *Goodbye, Columbus* took its title was the very contemporary and very realistic story of an affair between the protagonist-narrator, a lower-class boy from Newark named Neil Klugman, and Brenda Patimkin, the daughter of an affluent suburban family whose nouveau-riche way of life he gets to know in all its garish detail almost as intimately as he comes to know Brenda in the physical sense.

It was also true that Wouk's *Marjorie Morningstar,* as Bellow went out of his way to emphasize, took a very different—or, if one likes, a more positive—tack from Roth's and also achieved great success: it was well reviewed and became a big best-seller. But in the highbrow literary world (including *Commentary,* where I myself had written a savage piece about *Marjorie Morningstar* upon its publication in 1956), the aggressively antiassimilationist Wouk, like the equally aggressive assimilationist Miller, were looked down upon as inconsequential middlebrows whose great popularity had nothing to do with genuine literary distinction.

So far as this last issue went, I fully endorsed Bellow's assessment of Philip Roth. In reading "You Can't Tell a Man by the Song He Sings" when I had fished it out of the slush pile, I, too, was amazed by how extraordinarily accomplished this young writer already was—and that story (memoir?), as would soon become apparent, was far from one of his best. In "Goodbye, Columbus" itself, and the four other shorter stories that, along with "You Can't Tell a Man by the Song He Sings," made up the book, Roth demonstrated that no one, not even Bellow himself, had so perfectly pitched an ear for the speech of the first two generations of Jews who had come to America from Eastern Europe, or so keen an eye for the details of the life they lived, or so alert a perception of the quirks and contours of their psychological makeup.

In addition to sharing Bellow's admiration for Roth's literary abilities, I also felt the same irritation he did with the uncritically celebratory attitude toward America expressed by Herman Wouk. (Uncompromisingly and puristically stern young critic that I was in my early twenties, I had even accused Bellow himself of the same failing when I reviewed *The Adventures of Augie March* in 1953.) And finally, I was at one with Bellow in his contempt for the philistinism of Jewish readers who regarded it as the duty of Jewish writers to portray their people only, or at least largely, in the most sympathetic and favorable terms.

BUT, AS I SAY, I have always had trouble with Roth, and here is where it first popped up. It was one thing to hold out, as Bellow did in defending Roth against certain of his readers within the organized Jewish community (and this, remember, was still in the relatively innocent pre-*Portnoy's Complaint* days), for the right and the duty of literature to get at reality in its own special way. It was also intellectually shooting fish in a barrel to assert, as Bellow again did, that literature was not a species of public relations. In fact, in the 1950s, the piety toward serious literature—which equaled, and perhaps even exceeded, the standing it had first acquired in the nineteenth century as a substitute or even a replacement for religion, and from which the contemporary attitude originally derived—was so great that making such an argument seemed entirely unnecessary.

Many years later—though before the rise of politically correct speech codes—A. Bartlett Giamatti, then a professor of literature at Yale, would privately tell me that the lengthy and tediously argued demonstrations by his colleague Robert Brustein of the artistic failings of obviously inconsequential Broadway hits seemed to him the critical equivalent of "mugging cripples." So too with the attacks that Bellow and even more so Roth himself—first in dealing with the angry response to an essay he would do for *Commentary* in 1963 entitled "Writing About Jews," and then following the great Jewish storm that would break after publication in 1969 of *Portnoy's Complaint*—launched on the rabbis, the Jewish functionaries, and many ordinary Jews of an older generation. I do not mean to insinuate that these Jews were "cripples," but only that their arguments were so weak and out of touch with contemporary critical dogma that exposing and ridiculing them, as Roth was so easily able to do, bore a certain resemblance to the mugging by the strong of the weak and defenseless.

It went without saying that I was on the side of Bellow and Roth in this "mugging"; otherwise, as the then editor of *Commentary* (which I had become in 1960), I would not have accepted "Writing About Jews." Even so, however, I had an uneasy (if largely hidden, as much from myself as others) sympathy for the Jewish nervousness over Roth's work; and over the years this feeling of sympathy grew deeper.

Yet there were complications and nuances involved here that must be brought in and stressed. On the one hand, I was well aware that Roth could never have achieved so uncanny a degree of accuracy unless he had not only paid close attention to but had taken genuine delight in the world he was evoking. Moreover, he was being perfectly sincere when he declared:

> Not always, but frequently, what readers have taken to be my disapproval of the lives lived by Jews seems to have to do more with their own moral perspective than with the one they would ascribe to me: at times they see wickedness where I myself had seen energy or courage or spontaneity; they are ashamed of what I see no reason to be ashamed of, and defensive where there is no cause for defense.

On the other hand, it was also clear to me that more than a little sophistication in literary matters was required to detect the presence of this delight in Roth's work. As he himself put it, his Jewish critics, in "looking at fiction as they do—in terms of 'approval' and 'disapproval' of Jews, 'positive' and 'negative' attitudes toward Jewish life," were unable to see what his stories were really about. "It is difficult, if not impossible," he complained, "to explain to some of the people claiming to have felt my teeth sinking in, that in many instances they haven't been bitten at all."

IN OTHER WORDS, reinforcing and exacerbating their Jewish defensiveness and sensitivity was an old-fashioned moralistic conception of literature (a conception, by the way, that had been good enough for some very great literary critics like Dr. Johnson and Matthew Arnold, and to which Roth might have paid a bit more respect on that account alone). All they could see was a cruel eye relentlessly being cast on them and theirs, with no other purpose than to sneer and mock and defame; and the better Roth was at this game—the closer he cut to the bone—the worse it was for such readers.

Most of these people, after all, were old enough to have been exposed personally to the kind and degree of anti-Semitism from which Roth's generation (which was also my own—I am about three years older than he) had blessedly been spared. We had grown up in an America where, because the Holocaust had shown that there was literally no limit to the lengths to which anti-Semitism was capable of going, it had become taboo (for white Gentiles, that is) to say anything hostile about Jews. But our parents and grandparents and the organizations that spoke in their defense had not been so blessed. In the light of what they had seen and heard and gone through, either in their own lives or in those of other Jews, how could they *not* expect harmful consequences to follow from the reports that this young "informer"* of genius was broadcasting to the enemy, confirming and reinforcing every hurtful stereotype that they had been struggling so hard to discredit? To them it seemed that with the Gentile anti-Semites finally forced to bite their tongues, a smart Jewish boy with a big dirty mouth had come along to take their place.

In all honesty, I have to add that even if Roth had introduced more "positive" shading or balance into his picture of the first- and second-generation American Jews, it probably would have gone unnoticed within the context of the much richer and more daring fun he was making of them (those "teeth" Bellow said he had been born with, and to which Roth himself alluded, were as large and as sharp as a shark's). But in any event no such balance could be perceived in—to take the most striking instance—his portrait of the Patimkin family in "Goodbye, Columbus." Consumed by their lust for material goods to the exclusion of all else, shrewd about money and business and vulgar about anything cultural or spiritual, armored by a self-satisfaction that no uncertainty could penetrate, the Patimkins were the very glass of the unfashionable and the very mold of bad form (and looking worse and worse with the ethos of the 1960s fast approaching).

Yet the irony was that, in its own way and of its own kind, the self-satisfaction of Philip Roth seemed at least as great as that of the Patimkins. Even at the time, and in spite of my admiration for Roth's literary powers, I wondered how it was that a simple question had never occurred to his protagonist or to him: how could someone like either one of them have possibly emerged from such a milieu and from such a people? Surely they could not have sprung full-blown from the brow of Henry James. Surely there must have been something in the life into which they were born and the culture in which they grew up that made them into such utterly won-

---

*This was Roth's own word for what he suspected his Jewish critics really thought of him.

derful people (and that may even have predisposed them to being attracted to the likes of Henry James). But if so, what was it? And why did not the slightest sign of it show up in the stories? And did not its absence constitute a failing—even an aesthetic failing, an offense against the inner artistic requirements of the stories themselves?

I was bothered by this set of questions, but truth to tell, I evaded their implications as long as I could allow myself to get away with it. For confronting them head-on might have pushed me uncomfortably closer to a position about the relation of literature to things outside itself than I then had any wish to be. Like Roth, I, too, had been educated—he at the University of Chicago, I at Columbia and Cambridge—to believe that there was no higher calling than literature, that it needed no justification from any other enterprise, and that its only responsibility was to itself. Art was not, as the Communists and other leftists had recently been proclaiming, a "weapon"—not in the class struggle and not in any other war, either. Still less were its concerns—as Roth, echoing Bellow, would phrase it himself—those of "a public relations firm." Art was a good in itself, complete unto itself, responsible only to its own inner imperatives and laws.

IN HIS LATEST NOVEL, *I Married a Communist,* Roth puts a more extensive and developed version of this conception of literature into the mouth of an instructor at the University of Chicago named Leo Glucksman who is trying to undo the intellectual damage that has been done to Nathan Zuckerman—the character who by now has been not only Roth's protagonist but his virtual alter ego through many books—at the hands of a Communist mentor Nathan had known as a high-school kid in Newark:

> "Art as a *weapon?*" he said to me, the word "weapon" rich with contempt and itself a weapon. "Art taking the right stand on everything? Art as the advocate of good things? Who taught you all this? Who taught you art is slogans? Who taught you art is in the service of "the people"? Art is in the service of *art*—otherwise there is no art worthy of *anyone's* attention.

But Glucksman's sermon is far from finished, and with mounting fury he goes on:

> What *is* the motive for writing serious literature, Mr. Zuckerman? To disarm the enemies of price controls? The motive for writing serious

literature *is to write serious literature.* You want to rebel against society? I'll tell you how to do it—write *well.* . . . You want a lost cause to fight for? Then fight for the *word.* Not the high-flown word, not the inspiring word, not the pro-this and anti-that word, not the word that advertises to the respectable that you are a wonderful, admirable, compassionate person on the side of the downtrodden and the oppressed. No, for the word that tells the literate few condemned to live in America that you are on the *side* of the word!

The young Philip Roth must have taken this aestheticist creed to heart. "I was," he once said, "one of those students of the 1950s who came to books by way of a fairly good but rather priestly literary education, in which writing poems and novels was assumed to eclipse all else. . . ." I was one of those students, too.

But down deep, both of us had reservations about the aestheticist doctrine, each after his own kind. My own had to do with the growing dissatisfaction I was coming to feel over the hermeticism and Alexandrianism it tended to breed. Under the influence of critics and teachers like Lionel Trilling at Columbia and F. R. Leavis at Cambridge, I was learning that while loyalty to the dictates of its own nature and traditions was certainly the necessary precondition for the creation of a genuine work of art, it was not the only condition, and especially where literature, and more particularly where the novel (as opposed to music and abstract painting or even lyric poetry) was concerned. For the novel could hardly help getting involved in the social, moral, and political milieu out of which it emerged and could hardly evade commenting on the life around it.

I did not for a moment doubt that the political imperialism and the intellectual crudity of the doctrine of "art as a weapon" had to be rejected. And yet I also began to understand that rejecting it did not necessarily mean that the only alternative left standing was aestheticism. By the time I began publishing literary criticism as a very young man in the early 1950s, I had come to accept that while my duty was to arrive at a reasoned and informed judgment of the aesthetic merits of the work, this was not the end of it: other duties then followed. There were—as Leavis so powerfully demonstrated in his own critical writings—moral considerations to be raised. And as Trilling showed in *his* critical essays, social and even political factors could be brought into the discussion without violating the principle that aesthetic factors remained paramount both in the creation and in the response to a work of art. For me this meant that as a critic my job was to show how the aesthetic successes or failings of the work could themselves tell us important things about its surrounding social, moral, and political context.

Roth's reservations about aestheticism, I think, were of a somewhat different order: not so much theoretical as practical. I strongly suspect he would have liked to follow through on Glucksman's concluding adjuration to Nathan Zuckerman to

> achieve *mastery* over your idealism, over your virtue, as well as over your vice, aesthetic mastery over everything that drives you to write in the first place—your outrage, your hatred, your grief, your love! Start preaching and taking positions, start seeing your own perspective as superior and you're worthless as an artist, worthless and ludicrous.

But if, in his own words, the young Philip Roth "imagined fiction to be something like a religious calling, and literature a kind of sacrament," and if he would therefore have wished to work in accordance with Glucksman's creed, he must soon have discovered that he was simply incapable of achieving mastery over the outrage, hatred, grief, and love that drove him to write. By nature he was too judgmental and too passionately tendentious to transcend such motives and feelings. What he wanted to do as a writer, what he *needed* to do as a writer, was to take stock of the world in which he lived and give it the business, as only someone with so wicked a pen and so unforgiving a mind as his could do. How then could he submit to what Leo Glucksman demanded of him? Why should he even try?

But Roth's most serious disability from the perspective of Glucksman's dictates was that he could never stop himself from seeing his own perspective as superior. Superior to the culture of contemporary middle-class America, superior to what he took in his own untutored mind to be the traditions of Judaism and the Jewish people, and superior to all the characters he himself wrote about—except of course the ones like Neil Klugman in "Goodbye, Columbus" or Nathan Zuckerman in most of his later books, who have served as his protagonists. Yet Irving Howe—a formidable critic to whom Roth could not give the back of his hand and with whom he could not wipe the floor in an argument about literature, as he had done with the rabbis who had earlier expressed such anger and anguish over the harm they thought he was causing the Jewish people—

eventually came along to question the ground of this sense of superiority. Quoting with approval another such critic (Baruch Hochman), Howe pointed out that it was "not at all clear how Neil Klugman, who is so offended at the Patimkins, stands for anything substantially different from what they stand for."*

Howe's article, "Philip Roth Reconsidered," was published in *Commentary* in December 1972, just about ten years after Roth's own "Writing About Jews." By then, Roth had followed up *Goodbye, Columbus* with five novels. The first two of these, *Letting Go* (1962) and *When She Was Good* (1967), were very different from his debut volume, and seemed to represent strenuous (and in this sense, I would say, commendable) efforts to broaden his range. Having previously made his mark with short fiction, in *Letting Go* he produced a very long and dense variant on the academic novel; forsaking the exuberantly satiric and comic touch that marked most of the stories in *Goodbye, Columbus,* he now turned unrelievedly grim and depressing in focusing on the unmodulated woes of two young academics at the University of Chicago. And having become known as a member of the Hart, Schaffner & Marx trio, he then went on in *When She Was Good* to write a book about a Midwestern American family in which no Jews appeared.

In sum, what Roth tried to do in his first two full-length novels involved a kind of repudiation of his most authentic gifts, and the predictable result was failure. From a literary point of view, both *Letting Go* and *When She Was Good* had their moments, but neither proved a worthy successor to *Goodbye, Columbus,* and neither was well received.

My guess is that the failure of these two books was one of the factors that emboldened Roth to write *Portnoy's Complaint,* which came out in 1969, about two years after *When She Was Good.* All the qualities that had made *Goodbye, Columbus* so impressive and that he had temporarily abandoned in writing his next two books now returned with hurricane force, given even greater velocity by the freedom Roth was now willing and able to indulge. Previously—as I personally had occasion to witness in the pre-*Portnoy* days—Roth could keep a whole dinner party in stitches when he decided to

---

*Howe did, however, have a good word to say for "Defender of the Faith," one of the stories included in *Goodbye, Columbus,* about a Jewish soldier who insinuatingly tries to take advantage of the fact that his sergeant is also Jewish. This story had done more to upset many Jews upon its original appearance in the widely circulated *The New Yorker* than even "Goodbye, Columbus," which, first published in the quarterly *The Paris Review* with its tiny readership, attracted much less attention outside advanced literary circles.

let loose with a spontaneous comic riff. But it was not until *Portnoy's Complaint* that he felt free to do the same thing as a writer on paper.

This freedom was a personal assertion by Roth while—as I also had occasion to know from direct experience—representing a change in his own sense of propriety. For, hard as it may be to believe, there was a decidedly prissy side to Roth when he was young. Shortly after our first meeting, which took place in 1957 when he came to see me in connection with the imminent publication of "You Can't Tell a Man by the Song He Sings" in *Commentary,* he told a mutual friend that he disapproved of how foul-mouthed I was. It was true that I tended, as was common in literary circles in those days, to use four-letter words quite frequently in private conversation. Roth did not. Perhaps the reason was that such language was frowned upon at the University of Chicago, where he was teaching at the time, and perhaps it was because he still felt uncomfortable with it. Of course, as things turned out, in this respect I could not have held a candle, or even a matchstick, to the author of *Portnoy's Complaint.*

But the new freedom that made *Portnoy's Complaint* possible was also a gift of the 1960s. *Portnoy's Complaint,* published a decade after *Goodbye, Columbus,* took full advantage of the dispensation afforded by the culture of the 1960s really to "let go," to "let it all hang out," to shed any and all inhibitions in the choice of subject matter, the use of scatological language, the explicit descriptions of sex (Roth's great contribution was to bring masturbation, up till then one of the dirtiest and most secret of dirty little secrets, into the realm of serious fiction), and in the expression of disreputable social attitudes (disreputable, that is, by the standards that were still prevalent, at least on the surface, when *Goodbye, Columbus* came out: pretty soon these new standards would become as conventional in liberal circles as the ones they would replace).

ROTH'S NEW BOOK created a sensation in the literary world and was a great success in the commercial realm. And to the Jews who had been so offended by *Goodbye, Columbus,* it in effect said what Al Jolson had once had a habit of announcing to his audiences: "You ain't heard nothin' yet."

Sophie Portnoy, the mother of Roth's new protagonist and narrator Alexander, and her beaten-down husband made the Patimkins look positively genteel, while their son's compulsive denunciations of just about everything and everyone Jewish (except, again, himself and, by extension, his creator) went beyond anything even hinted at in any of the stories of *Goodbye, Columbus.* Yet either out of sheer exhaustion, or out of the same sense of defeat that the culture of the 1960s inflicted upon almost all other established institutions, or out of an unwillingness to go around the track with Roth yet again in a period when their objections were bound to seem even more hidebound and retrograde than before, the defenders of Jewish honor against the even more horrific defamations he was heaping upon it now made (if memory serves) no greater a fuss, and perhaps even a smaller one, than they had over *Goodbye, Columbus* or even "Writing About Jews."

This time, however, they themselves had a few defenders who could present their case in terms that, being at least as grounded as Roth's in the most sophisticated assumptions and ideas of contemporary literary culture, were far more persuasive. Irving Howe was the main such defender, and in running his "Philip Roth Reconsidered" in *Commentary,* I added my own two cents in a little piece in the same issue called "Laureate of the New Class."

Like Howe, I said, I had praised *Goodbye, Columbus.* Like him, too, I had found little to admire in Roth's next two books (the first of which, *Letting Go,* I had in fact written about unfavorably in another magazine). Nor did I find any more to admire than Howe did in the two very short ones that by 1972 had already followed *Portnoy's Complaint—Our Gang* (1971), a satire on Nixon and his administration that managed to be both demagogic and boringly conventional in the orthodoxy of its liberal stance, and *The Breast* (1972), a novella, obviously inspired by Kafka's story about the man who turns into a cockroach, but going its model one better, or perhaps worse, by making the hero suffer a metamorphosis into a female breast. And though I freely admitted rating *Portnoy's Complaint* more highly than Howe did, I also said that I agreed in almost every other detail with his literary analysis of Roth's work in general and of his weaknesses both as a novelist and as a satirist. I agreed, too, that Roth had come to stand very close to the center of the culture as it had developed in the 1960s, and that this had much to do with his steadily increasing reputation among the critics and his growing popularity with the reading public in general.

Here, however, I parted company with Howe in his attribution of this status to a decline in the quality of Roth's work. Lurking below Howe's explanation I spotted an atavistic remainder of the old assumption once shared by leftists and modernists alike that when a serious artist achieves popularity, he must have "sold out" by compromising his own standards and accommodating himself to popular taste and fashion. My own view was that the process had worked in exactly the opposite direction. That is, over the years more and more people had come along who were in tune with the disgust for Americans and American life that had been expressed in Roth's work from the beginning and who hence had in increasing numbers come to recognize him as their own. Because so many of the Americans this Jewish writer dealt with were Jewish, he had been accused of a special animus against his own people or of Jewish self-hatred. But it had become clear from books like *Letting Go, When She Was Good,* and *Our Gang* that his loathing for non-Jewish Americans was scarcely less intense than his distaste for his fellow Jews.

But, I went on, not *all* Americans, whether Jewish or Gentile, were subject to this disgust. Exempted along with himself were the members of his own "gang"—the group of educated people that had come to be known as the "New Class." Roth was their "laureate" in the sense that everything he wrote served to reinforce their standard ideas and attitudes, to offer documentary evidence for their taken-for-granted view that America was a country dominated by vulgarians, materialists, bores, and criminal political leaders. In doing so, Roth was inviting his readers to join with him in snobbishly and self-righteously celebrating their joint superiority to everyone else around them. *They* were what one of their member-admirers (the socialist political writer and activist Michael Harrington) extolled as a "conscience constituency," motivated only by ideas and ideals, whereas the rest of the population was animated only by baser drives. Even the New Class's own baser drives—Alexander Portnoy's sexual lusts, to cite the most blatant example—were a sign of superiority, since they represented a healthy yearning for liberation from the constrictions and limitations of a repressed puritanical society.*

There was, then, I argued, an extraliterary and even a narrowly political dimension to Roth's work and to his popularity as well. Without going as far as the New Left or the counterculture, he nevertheless, and in his own unique style, experienced and gave voice to a hostility as great as theirs to middle-class America and what later came to be called "family values." As he had put it in a famous passage from another article he did for *Commentary* in 1961, "Writing American Fiction":

---

*I should add for the record that, on the issue of whether this group constituted a new and potentially hopeful constituency of political conscience or a New Class pursuing its own interests, Howe was with his fellow socialist Harrington, not me. To put it mildly, he did not much like my use of Roth as a stick to beat a group with which he himself was growing more and more sympathetic, however dimly he may have felt about the literary merits of the work of its "laureate."

[T]he American writer in the middle of the 20th century has his hands full in trying to understand, and then describe, and then make *credible* much of the American reality. It stupefies, it sickens, it infuriates, and finally it is even a kind of embarrassment to one's own meager imagination. . . . Who, for example, could have invented Charles Van Doren? Roy Cohn and David Schine? Sherman Adams and Bernard Goldfine? Dwight David Eisenhower?

As the editor of the magazine in which this piece was published, and as a leftist, I thought at the time that it was a wonderful essay, but from the perspective of my present conservative outlook, the passage I have just quoted seems silly. Who now even remembers some of these characters who struck Roth as so vividly outlandish or wicked that they were "the envy of any novelist"? By that standard, Bernard Goldfine should still be a name as familiar as Raskolnikov, but I myself no longer even know who he was, and I venture to guess that most young people today would say the same of Sherman Adams, Charles Van Doren, and David Schine. And to single out Eisenhower for dishonorable mention among political leaders in a century that had spawned Hitler, Stalin, and Mao? This was indeed an embarrassment to Roth's "meager imagination," though not in the sense he intended.

Naturally I could and should have raised some of these questions even then, but my own general position was still so close to Roth's that they never sprang to mind. Besides, even if they had, I might well have dismissed them as overly fastidious and niggling.

IRVING HOWE, in a remark as hurtful in its own way as anything Roth himself ever wrote, said: "The cruelest thing anyone can do with *Portnoy's Complaint* is read it twice." Well, I once committed that very cruelty and still found the book very funny, at least in certain passages. But though I had already read everything Roth had previously published, and though I would continue keeping up with everything he was subsequently to produce, I confess to having given him only one reading per post-*Portnoy* volume. Even this took a lot of time, since Roth proved to be a very prolific writer—*I Married a Communist* is his twenty-third book—and not all of it turned out to be well spent. I was repelled by *Our Gang*, I was disgusted by *The Breast*, and I was bored both by *The Great American Novel* (1973, about baseball) and, many years later, by the return to scatological extremism in the much-praised and belaureled *Sabbath's Theater* (1995).

Moreover, I was irritated by the literary games Roth took to playing in some of his later, "postmodern" novels. These games consisted in virtually forcing the reader into seeing something as autobiographical and then implicitly rebuking him for doing so (how could anyone be so stupid as not to understand that art "transmutes" reality?). For example, the recurring protagonist Nathan Zuckerman had so much in common with Roth himself (among a myriad of other details, he was the author of a best-selling novel called *Carnovsky,* which was a dead ringer for *Portnoy's Complaint*) that it would have taken a mind set in postmodernist critical concrete not to see him as a thinly disguised version of his creator. But by various means, both within the novels and in pronouncements Roth made to interviewers (including his favorite one, himself) the reader was ridiculed for being such a dodo. Indeed, we were even forbidden, on pain of proving ourselves incapable of understanding the nature of artistic creation, to read *Operation Shylock* (1993) as autobiography, though the hero was actually called Philip Roth and other real people also made appearances under their own names.

In *Leaving a Doll's House* (1996), her memoir about her eighteen-year-long relationship with Roth that began as an extended affair, culminated in marriage, and ended in divorce, the British actress Claire Bloom tells the following story about reading the manuscript of the novel which was eventually published in 1990 as *Deception:*

> I eagerly opened the folder. Almost immediately I came upon a passage about the self-hating, Anglo-Jewish family with whom he lives in England. Oh well, I thought, he doesn't like my family. There was a description of his working studio in London, letter-perfect and precise. Then I reached the depictions of all the girls who come over to have sex with him. . . . As Philip always insisted that the critics were unable to distinguish his self-invention from his true self, I mindfully accepted these . . . seductresses as part of his "performance" as a writer; but I was not so certain.

Her uncertainty on this point was not, however, the worst of it. The worst came when she

> arrived at the chapter about his remarkably uninteresting, middle-aged wife. . . . She is an actress by profession, and—as if hazarding a guess would spoil the incipient surprise lying in store—her name is Claire.

So insulting did she find this portrait of herself and so "completely unacceptable" was his use of her name that she demanded he change it to another one. At first he refused. "He tried to explain that he had called his protagonist Philip, therefore to name the wife Claire would add to the richness of the texture." But for once this fancy pulling of artistic rank failed. When Claire Bloom desperately threatened a lawsuit to have her name removed, Roth finally gave in.

FOR ALL THIS, however, at a certain point a new note had already been entering into Roth's work. Unaided by fresh rereadings, my memory, alas, is no longer good enough to locate precisely when it happened, but I have the impression that the change may have started in earnest with the novels collected into a single volume under the title *Zuckerman Bound: A Trilogy and an Epilogue* (1985). Here I thought I detected a touch of tenderness toward his characters that had never been much in evidence before, and, what was even more startling, the same feeling extended to the Jews he had so relentlessly and exuberantly ridiculed in the books that had first brought him fame. Once upon a time he had made light of anti-Semitism as a problem in the contemporary world, and he (excuse me, Alexander Portnoy) had even gone so far as to advise the Jews, in a typical example of language "transmuted" by art, "to stick your suffering heritage up your suffering ass." But as the quotation above from Claire Bloom suggests, and as *Deception* itself confirms, living in England seems to have led Roth to a change of mind and heart about the persistence of anti-Jewish feeling in the world, and therefore about Jewish security, including the security of Israel.

In *Patrimony* (1991), a book about the death of his father that he wrote within this new phase and that did not pretend to be fictional, he also expressed open affection and indeed love for his own family and for the Jewish world from which it stemmed. Neal Kozodoy, reviewing that book in *Commentary* (May 1991), made several brilliantly telling points about the limitations of this affection, seeing in it the ugly remnants of the same old ignorance about his Jewish "patrimony" and the same old patronizing attitude toward the Jews themselves that had always marked Roth's work. Yet nothing Roth had written before ever came even this close to acknowledging that there might be some virtue other than sheer energy to be found in the history and character of his own people.

Even more unexpected was *American Pastoral* (1997), the novel that immediately preceded *I Married a Communist*. I myself, and many other people, too, detected in this book a born-again Philip Roth whose entire outlook on the world had been inverted. Going far beyond the Zuckerman trilogy or *Patrimony* in this respect, *American Pastoral* set up a contrast between, on the one hand, the middle-class Jews who had once offered such fat targets for his poisoned arrows and, on the other, the counterculture and its academic apologists with whom in his younger days (admittedly never with a completely full heart) he had once identified and to whom he had directed his authorial winks of complicity. But to the delighted astonishment of some of us, and the puzzlement and disappointment of others, he now changed sides in the distribution of his scorn and his sympathies. Here, for once, it was the ordinary Jews of his childhood who were celebrated—for their decency, their sense of responsibility, their seriousness about their work, their patriotism—and here, for once, those who rejected and despised such virtues were shown to be either pathologically nihilistic or smug, self-righteous, and unimaginative.

From a technical standpoint, *American Pastoral* was almost as surprising as the attitudes it embodied and dramatized. Saul Bellow had long ago pointed out that Roth was already a virtuoso performer from the very moment he appeared on the scene, and yet this literary natural, after so many years of practicing his craft with the deftness and sureness that had come to be expected of him, suddenly turned awkward in handling the form of a story-within-a-story in which he chose to cast *American Pastoral*. Because of its problems of construction, the novel was repetitious, and this made it overly insistent and sometimes tiresome. My guess is that the fault lay with Roth's inner resistance to coming right out with a frank and unambiguous mea culpa; if so, the formal flaws of *American Pastoral* amounted, so far as I was concerned, to a felix culpa.

Inevitably a question arose and hung in the air, tantalizingly for some and ominously for others: had Philip Roth turned into a neoconservative? A number of liberal critics who had always admired and defended him, and who were unwilling to believe that one of their own most prized novelistic spokesmen might have defected to the enemy, tried desperately to demonstrate that any such interpretation was simplistic and ideologically tendentious (dread words). While not exactly denying what *American Pastoral* seemed to be saying, they insisted that it was too complex a work to be summed up in political or social terms. So well did they succeed in defending it against itself that *American Pastoral* won another National Book Award for Roth, which it probably would not have done had the literary establishment taken it for what it really was.

ROTH HIMSELF, not previously famous for being reticent about his own intentions as a writer, maintained a prudent silence on this occasion, neither affirming nor denying. But his very next and latest book, *I Married a Communist,* amounts to a reassuring declaration of solidarity with his old comrades within the liberal establishment. Not that this is its only intention, or even its main one. He clearly also wrote it to get even with Claire Bloom for her attack on him in *Leaving a Doll's House* (just as he had done to Irving Howe through the character of Milton Appel in *The Anatomy Lesson*), and to tell his side of the story of their affair and marriage.

Of course (need I even say it?), this aspect of the book has been put through the usual "transmutations" of art. Thus, instead of being a British actress who made her mark on the stage and screen, the Claire Bloom character (called Eve Frame) becomes an American who once starred in silent films and then shifted to radio, and it is not Roth's alter ego Nathan Zuckerman who suffers at the hands of this impossibly neurotic wife but another radio actor, Iron Rinn (né Ira Ringold).

There are other "transmutations" as well. The daughter to whom Claire Bloom was so attached, and who was apparently one of the main sources of her problems with Philip Roth, is a singer in real life (if I may be forgiven for introducing so crude a concept into so aesthetically lofty a context), whereas Eve Frame's daughter is a harpist—that kind of thing. Yet so closely does Roth hew to the details of Bloom's indictment in defending himself against her that it is almost impossible to understand what certain elements of *I Married a Communist* are doing there without first having read *Leaving a Doll's House.*

But the most significant "transmutations" undergone in the Claire Bloom part of the story involve shifting it back from the 1980s and 1990s to the 1950s, making the husband not only into an actor but also into a secret member of the Communist party, and turning the spurned wife's book from the tepidly feminist memoir Claire Bloom published into a vicious McCarthyite denunciation of her husband entitled, precisely, *I Married a Communist* (which then ruins his life). It is through this series of devices that Roth signs a loyalty oath (as one might put it) to the old-time liberal religion from which he seemed to have defected in *American Pastoral.*

And I mean old-time. Every liberal cliché about America at the height of the Cold War is resurrected here—that its fear of the Soviet Union and its hostility to Communism were paranoid, that the Communists at home

posed no threat worth taking seriously, and that the congressional investigations and the blacklists were cynical ploys aimed not at quashing Communist influence but at discrediting liberals and Democrats.

True, there is some slight awareness shown here and there of what we
have learned (or rather what we have had definitively confirmed) from
Kremlin archives since the demise of the Soviet Union, as well as from such
formerly classified American sources as the Venona Papers, about the slav-
ishness with which the American Communist party submitted to the dictates of Moscow, and the efforts it made to control the entertainment
industry and the labor movement (though I cannot recall any allusion by
Roth to the extent of espionage practiced by American Communists in this
country). It is also important to note that neither of Roth's two protagonists—the other is Murray Ringold, Ira's brother and Nathan Zuckerman's
old high-school English teacher, who tells Nathan the story that Nathan
tells us—is a Communist. Both Nathan and Murray reject Communism as
a form of secularized religious utopianism, and both acknowledge that
many Communists, including Ira himself, flat out lied about being Communists. Both recognize as well that the Communist organizer who had
recruited Ira into the party was a nasty piece of work. Nevertheless, the
Communists, they suggest, meant well—after all, what harm did they
do?—and anyway who could blame them for lying at a time when a
McCarthyite lurked under every liberal bed? To put the point another way:
with some qualification, the general tenor here is set by the anti-anti-Communism on which the young Roth cut his political teeth.

Like *Patrimony* and a number of Roth's recent novels, *I Married a Communist* is also much preoccupied with the theme of getting old and sick and
waiting for death to strike. This preoccupation generates the only genuinely powerful passages the novel contains: passages that are wistful without being sentimental, that are lyrical without becoming soupy, and that
are written in the veritably gorgeous prose of which Roth is capable when
the mood is upon him. Yet the point these passages convey—that the vast-
ness of the universe makes everything on earth seem unreal and meaningless—sounds rather narcissistic coming from a writer meditating about
death (quite as though he were saying: "If I have to die, and sooner rather
than later, what difference can anything make?"). And even if we ignore or
forgive their narcissism, they still fail to redeem what is in the end one of
Roth's less successful books.

For me this is a double disappointment. After *American Pastoral*, I
looked forward eagerly to the riches that might be unearthed by the

changes in Roth's sense of life—the broadening of his sympathies, the deepening of his perceptions, and the liberation of his mind from the stifling orthodoxies of the politically correct liberal faith of his youth. What has come out instead is a regression to spiritual pettiness and vindictiveness and another act of political flattery directed at the ideas and attitudes of the audience that had made him its laureate on this very account.

After all these years, then, and after a brief interlude in which I thought my troubles with Philip Roth had finally been resolved, I find myself disturbed by them yet again. But Roth, for all his preoccupation with death, is still only about sixty-five, which means that as things are today he is still a relatively young man with—God willing—long years of writing ahead of him. And to judge by his unfailing literary energies, he is also still full of enough creative juice, discipline, and stamina to produce many more books.

All of which is to say that perhaps the best is yet to come from Philip Roth. I myself think there is a chance that it will. But I also think he will only be able to mine the full lode of riches still buried within him if he can finally summon the courage to "let go" altogether of the youthful habits of mind and spirit from which he seemed to be freeing himself for a while but which, on the evidence of *I Married a Communist,* are still putting up a strong fight to keep him from digging further into the depths that are so dangerous to those very habits and so full of potential reward for him and for the literature of this country.

WHAT HAPPENED TO RALPH ELLISON

WHAT WINSTON CHURCHILL said of the Battle of Britain—"Never . . . was so much owed by so many to so few"—might with appropriate adaptations easily be applied to the American novelist Ralph Ellison. For surely no author ever owed so much to a single book: so much acclaim, so much honor, so many awards.

The novel in question, of course, is *Invisible Man,* which came out in 1952 when Ellison was already thirty-eight years old. Except for a few excerpts that had appeared while the book was still a work in progress, he had previously published only a number of reviews and a few stories of no particular distinction. But this first novel by an obscure Negro writer (to use the term in common currency in those far-off days) was immediately hailed on all sides as a classic, an imperishable masterpiece, perhaps the greatest American novel of the century. Accordingly, Ellison was elevated overnight into the upper reaches of our culture, and for the remaining forty-two years of his life—he died in 1994 at the age of eighty—was treated reverently on the strength of this one book.

Well, not entirely, and not quite by everyone. Even upon its original publication, at least one other Negro novelist, John Oliver Killens, denounced *Invisible Man:* "The Negro people need Ralph Ellison's *Invisible Man* like we need a hole in the head or a stab in the back. . . . It is a vicious distortion of Negro life." Then for a time, especially in the 1960s, black radicals of one stripe or another either ignored or attacked him as, if not exactly an Uncle Tom, then at least an unreliable ally in the struggle they were conducting against white society. Thus, to the poet and playwright Amiri Baraka (who had changed his name from LeRoi Jones upon becoming a fierce black nationalist), Ellison's sin was to elevate aesthetic over political considerations; to other black cultural separatists, it was his dismissal of the need for, or even the possibility of, a special "black aesthetic" and his belief in the universal "laws of literary form" to which all writers—and by extension artists working in other genres—of whatever racial or ethnic group were bound.

In its own right, as well as in its relation to him as a novelist, this aspect of Ellison's career has enormous interest and significance. It also lies at the root of the curious—and to him, if not necessarily to the rest of us, tragic—paradox of his life. But before getting into all that, I want to concentrate for the time being on the strictly literary part of his reputation.

On that side of Ellison's street, it was usually sunny, and hardly any rain ever fell on his parade. Much more typical than the attacks of Killens and Baraka (though echoes of them can sometimes still be heard) was the response of Ellison's fellow novelist, Saul Bellow: "What a great thing it is when a brilliant individual victory occurs, like Ellison's, proving that a truly heroic quality can exist among our contemporaries." It was mainly praise of this high order, and even higher, that came his way, and the few times he was criticized—by me, among others—it was for certain ideas expressed in his essays,* not for any faults or deficiencies that might have been unearthed in *Invisible Man* on a second or third reading, let alone a first.

THE LITERARY CLIMATE has changed very radically since 1952, to the point where many people have come to suspect the operation of a double standard whenever a black author wins the National Book Award or the Pulitzer or some other literary prize. It therefore seems necessary to state bluntly that the admiration Ellison evoked with *Invisible Man* emitted not the slightest whiff of critical affirmative action, and would not have done so even if such a concept had existed then (which mercifully it did not).

This is not to imply that Ellison's race went unnoticed. How could it? The word "novel" means new, and there was a time when the novelist saw it as his job either to bring the news of a world previously unexplored or to find a new way of performing that task on ground that may already have been broken and tilled and ploughed by others before him. In both of these senses—the substantive as well as the technical—Ellison was unmistakably and unabashedly, and proudly, a *Negro* novelist. As he himself defiantly declared: "Who wills to be a Negro? *I* do!"

Moreover, the "invisibility" he was making visible referred not only to the identity of his nameless hero. Even more broadly and crucially, it consisted of his effort to show that Negroes were very far from being an undif-

---

*One collection, *Shadow and Act* (of which I wrote what I now regard as a wrongheaded negative review), was issued in 1964, and a second, *Going to the Territory,* came out in 1986. The contents of both of these volumes, plus some additional pieces, have been brought together posthumously by his literary executor, John F. Callahan, in *The Collected Essays of Ralph Ellison.*

ferentiated mass of suffering victims with no autonomous existence of their own—that they were not, in other words, a people wholly created and determined by forces controlled by the white world. This was how they had been, and still were (and to this day still are), most often portrayed by their own spokesmen, literary as well as political, black as well as white. But as Ellison never grew weary of saying in his essays and interviews, and as *Invisible Man* was written to "prove" in the way that only art can do, Negroes (*even* under slavery, let alone lesser forms of oppression) were fully human.

Human: that was the almost embarrassingly naked word he reverted to time and again in this connection. Being human, Negroes had always retained a degree of inner or imaginative freedom that was "limited only by their individual aspiration, insight, energy, and will." And as such, they had also created a dense and distinctive culture.

In speaking of the culture of the American Negro, Ellison did so first in the anthropological sense:

> Being a Negro American . . . has to do with a special perspective on the national ideals and the national conduct, and with a tragicomic attitude toward the universe. It has to do with special emotions evoked by the details of cities and countrysides, with forms of labor and with forms of pleasure; with sex and with love, with food and with drink, with machines and with animals, with garments and dreams and idioms of speech; with manners and customs, with religion and art, with lifestyles and hoping, and with that special sense of predicament and fate which gives direction and resonance to the Freedom Movement.

Clearly with Henry James's famous observation that it was a "complex fate" to be an American echoing in his head, Ellison went on to apply a version of the same concept to being an American Negro:

> It imposes the uneasy burden and occasional joy of a complex double vision, a fluid, ambivalent response to men and events which represents, at its finest, a profoundly civilized adjustment to the cost of being human in this modern world.

But when Ellison discussed culture, he naturally also had in mind the arts—especially the blues, jazz, and (on its own less self-conscious level) folklore—that had developed to give the deepest expression to the American Negro's special modes of thinking and speaking and being. Such expression was what he had aspired to achieve in *Invisible Man,* and it remained his ambition throughout his whole life.

However, distinctive as the Negro American culture may have been, Ellison—blasting an unbridgeable gulf between himself and the black nationalists whose rhetoric his own could sometimes misleadingly resemble when the celebratory spirit was upon him—also never tired of repeating that this culture was simultaneously American to the core:

> It is not skin color which makes a Negro American but cultural heritage as shaped by the American experience, the social and political predicament; a sharing of that "concord of sensibilities" which the group expresses through historical circumstances and through which it has come to constitute a subdivision of the larger American culture.

To Ellison this was a self-evident truth, although it, too, was "invisible" to most white people, and many blacks as well.

But most "invisible" of all was the correlatively pervasive interpenetration of the Negro culture and "the larger American culture," as well as the degree to which they drew from the same sources and had influenced and shaped each other. This is why he loved juxtaposing Louis Armstrong with the St. Louis born-and-bred T. S. Eliot, both of them children of the Mississippi River. Going even further, he always claimed that while he found Eliot's poem *The Waste Land* hard to understand when he first came upon it (in, as he often made a point of stressing polemically against those liberals who imagined that no such thing was possible, the library of Tuskegee, the black college he attended in the South), he could still detect in its obscure verses a resemblance to the offbeat jazzy rhythms that marked Armstrong's music.

One of the many times Ellison gave passionate expression to this idea of interpenetration was in a piece he did in 1970 entitled "What America Would Be Like Without Blacks" (the name that had by now supplanted "Negro," though Ellison himself never quite gave up on the older usage). Here he began by exploring the various schemes that had cropped up throughout American history for "getting shut" of the blacks. "Despite its absurdity," this "fantasy," he said, was "born not merely of racism but of petulance, of exasperation, of moral fatigue" on the part both of whites (including at one time even Abraham Lincoln, whom Ellison, unlike future revisionists, never ceased revering) and of blacks alike.

But then, having underlined how relentlessly black culture had flowed into the American "cultural mainstream" ("Negro Americans are in fact one of its major tributaries"), he proceeded to challenge the newly influential idea (which had first been propounded most authoritatively a few years earlier by Nathan Glazer and Daniel Patrick Moynihan) that the "melting pot" had not actually melted:

> The problem here is that few Americans know who and what they really are. This is why few [white ethnic] groups . . . have been able to resist the movies, television, baseball, jazz, football, drum-majoretting, rock, comic strips, radio commercials, soap operas, book clubs, slang, or any of a thousand other expressions and carriers of our popular culture.

From here Ellison leaped headlong to a much bolder assertion:

> On this level the melting pot did indeed melt, creating such deceptive metamorphoses and blending of identities, values, and lifestyles that *most American whites are culturally part Negro American without even realizing it.* [emphasis added]

One might even say without too much exaggeration that Ellison had written *Invisible Man* precisely to give novelistic life and flesh to this previously most "invisible" of all the truths he was bent on bringing to light ("Who knows," runs the book's last sentence, "but that on the lower frequencies I speak for you?").

But there was another side to the same coin that has to be displayed if the picture is to be complete—and all the more so at a moment when thinking on these matters, while bearing a superficial similarity to Ellison's, is at the furthest remove from his. If most American whites were, in Ellison's unshakable view, "part Negro American without even realizing it," most Negroes were conversely more American than they or their white countrymen generally understood. There is a saying in Hebrew: "As his name is, so is he," and Ralph *Waldo* Ellison was a very good example of this peculiar phenomenon. That he had been named after one of the quintessentially American writers and sages was something to which he and others often alluded as an amusing and even slightly embarrassing fact. But my own guess is that, deep down, he took it with great seriousness as a mark not only of his Americanness but of his literary destiny and his human fate.

———————

ELLISON had originally set out to pursue a career in music, and though he then had and would maintain a lifelong love affair with, and the profoundest admiration for, the music of the black world—most notably the blues and jazz—his ambition was (characteristically) to become a composer of classical symphonies. Then, when already into his twenties, he met Richard Wright, who with the publication of *Native Son* (1940) was soon to emerge as the leading black novelist of the generation before Ellison's and who encouraged him to try his hand at writing. That did it. The young man's growing suspicion that he was not talented enough to realize his musical ambitions gave way to a more promising and positive intuition: that what he was truly cut out for was a literary career—though in talking about Ellison, a better term would be "vocation."

Yet it is of the utmost importance to emphasize again that Ellison's ambition was to become an *American* writer. As what used to be labeled a "pluralist," he believed in the existence of a common culture, one which the various ethnic and racial groups making up a heterogeneous society like ours steadily enriched by their indigenous contributions. This common culture was a precious heritage that could be claimed by any American of whatever group or color, and to it every American of whatever group or color also owed a debt and an allegiance. Which is to say that Ellison had nothing in common with today's "multiculturalists," who regard the common culture, to the extent that they recognize its existence at all, as nothing more than the heritage of a single group (the white Anglo-Saxon Protestants) and in whose eyes it deserves no special "privilege" with respect to the cultures of other groups. If anything, many multiculturalists even regard it as inferior.

For Ellison, this balkanizing tendency was an ironic reappearance in sheep's clothing of the racial segregation under which he himself had grown up, and even may have been worse. Neither as a Negro kid in Oklahoma nor as a college student in Alabama was he prevented from reading books that opened his eyes and his mind and his imagination to a wider world of possibility; on the contrary, he was urged on, not discouraged, by teachers and other adults to do so. Later, even as a literary novice, he never felt himself to be "limited" in any respect by his race or defined by it as a writer. Hence it was not to other black novelists—not even his first sponsor Richard Wright—that he looked for models to be emulated. Still less did he think that it was their books he should study in trying to learn the new craft—"a very stern discipline," he called it—that he was so fiercely determined to master.

One knows all this from the snippets of autobiography that frequently turn up in Ellison's essays and interviews, and from the resentment always aroused in him by any suggestion that he had been exclusively or even largely influenced by other black writers. For instance, he excoriated his old friend and "sparring partner," the critic Stanley Edgar Hyman, for assuming that the use of folklore in *Invisible Man* was a product of Ellison's race:

> I use folklore in my work not because I am a Negro, but because writers like Eliot and Joyce made me conscious of the literary value of my folk inheritance. My cultural background, like that of most Americans, is dual (my middle name, sadly enough, is Waldo). . . . My point is that the Negro American writer is also an heir of the human experience which is literature, and this might well be more important to him than his living folk tradition.

On numerous other occasions, he also went out of his way to deny that this or that detail of *Invisible Man* had been inspired by Wright or some other black predecessor. A much more powerful literary influence on him when starting out as a writer, he often insisted, had been exerted by a French novelist, André Malraux (and—further to underscore his constant emphasis on the admixture of cultures—he would add that it had been the Negro poet Langston Hughes who had given him two of Malraux's novels to read).

In addition, it had been through three nineteenth-century novels, Emily Brontë's *Wuthering Heights,* Thomas Hardy's *Jude the Obscure,* and Feodor Dostoevsky's *Crime and Punishment,* that the artistic power of fiction had first made an impact on him as an undergraduate at Tuskegee. The American writers he most often cited in his pieces about literature were also all white: Mark Twain, Stephen Crane, Henry James, and Ernest Hemingway. And then—above all, as it would turn out—there was William Faulkner, a Southerner who, though still to some extent infected by racism, had in Ellison's judgment produced more truthful portraits of Negroes than any black or white-liberal Northern novelists had ever succeeded in doing.

YET EVEN IF ELLISON had not told us all this himself, one would have deduced it from his conception of the dual nature of identity in America—his own and that of all others who had arrived on these shores more recently than the *Mayflower.* And it would also have become clear to any perceptive reader of *Invisible Man.*

I am not a good enough scholar of black writing in America to assert with full confidence that *Invisible Man* was the first work of fiction by a Negro about the life of his people to free itself from the disabilities of what another Negro writer, about ten years younger than Ellison, James Baldwin, in an essay of the late 1940s about Richard Wright that brought him a premonitory taste of fame, had dubbed the "protest novel." But if not necessarily the first, *Invisible Man* must surely have been the most successful. Baldwin had criticized Wright's most famous book, *Native Son,* and the tradition out of which it came, for representing its hero, Bigger Thomas, as so purely a creature of white oppression that he is not even responsible for the rape and murder he commits. Like all "protest" literature, *Native Son* thereby for all practical purposes dehumanized the black man, which as James Baldwin then saw it (he would later change his mind, to the great detriment of his own novels) was too high a price to pay, both in life and in literature, in order to do what this literature primarily aimed at—to make whites feel guilty.

As we can tell from his own written comments about Wright, and from many other indications, including *Invisible Man* itself, Ellison agreed with Baldwin's early view of the matter. Admittedly, he sometimes claimed that he did not "recognize [any] dichotomy between art and protest," citing Goya, Dickens, and Twain, and insisting that the problem for Negro writers lay not in the act of protest but in their "lack of craftsmanship and their provincialism." Still, it was in order to move beyond and transcend the limitations of the protest novel as handled by Negro writers before him that he employed the techniques he had learned from careful study of the great masters of the novel. And that this was exactly what he himself hoped to do he made no bones about admitting in 1981 in an introduction to a new edition of *Invisible Man.* There he confessed to the difficulty he had had in "trying to avoid writing what might turn out to be nothing more than another novel of racial protest instead of the dramatic study in comparative humanity which I felt any worthwhile novel should be."

Not that this was a matter of technique alone. For implicit in the novelistic craft itself at the highest reaches to which Ellison aspired was the ambition to represent the realities being portrayed in as full and rounded a form as possible. Which meant, as the great Victorian critic Matthew Arnold had put it in describing literary criticism at its best, striving "to see the object as in itself it really is." And this meant, in turn, eschewing special pleading, apologetics, and any offstage or, for that matter, onstage obeisance to the extraliterary imperatives of ideological militancy. In Ellison's formulation: "The greatest difficulty for a Negro writer was the problem of revealing what he really felt, rather than serving up what Negroes were supposed to feel, and were encouraged to feel."

To be sure, Arnold also spoke of literature as a "criticism of life." But (rather like the kind of protest Ellison defended) this was a criticism arrived at through the special objectivity or disinterestedness which was given only (borrowing a phrase from a poem by W. B. Yeats) to the "cold eye" of the true artist.

On my first reading of *Invisible Man* when it appeared in 1952, I thought that Ellison had pulled off this supremely difficult task. Here was a novel that presented us, in an intensely charged prose that managed (as Gustav Mahler had done in music, and as Saul Bellow would soon go on to do in *The Adventures of Augie March*) to synthesize elements of high style and low vernacular, with a wonderful—and often wonderfully comic—panorama of Negro life in all its American varieties and stretching from the Deep South to Harlem.*

INVISIBLE MAN, written in the first person, is a kind of bildungsroman about an idealistic young Negro (Ellison never gives him a name†) who begins as a student at a black college in the South dutifully hoping to become what once upon a time was known as a "credit to his race." But a naive error leads to his expulsion, and he then makes his way to Harlem. There, instead of eventually finding and forging an identity by which he can be recognized by others, he is subjected to a series of adventures (including a stint in the Communist party, disguised by Ellison for no very good reason as "the Brotherhood") which finally leave him with the realization that he is in fact faceless—that is, invisible—to everyone around him, whether black or white. They all want to make some use of him for whatever ends they happen to be pursuing, but nobody has the slightest desire

---

*In the introduction to a posthumous collection of Ellison's earliest forays into fiction, *Flying Home and Other Stories*, John F. Callahan, the book's editor, makes a point similar to the one I am trying to get at in bringing up the name of Mahler: "The young man who had dreamed of composing a symphony by the time he was twenty-six . . . ended up writing *Invisible Man*, a novel with traces of symphonic form as well as the beat and breaks of jazz." Mutatis mutandis, the same juxtaposition can be found in Ellison's initially bizarre comparison of Louis Armstrong and T. S. Eliot to which I referred above. "Ever loyal to his musician's bent," writes Callahan, "while his eye read Eliot's fragments, his ear heard Louis Armstrong's 200 choruses on the theme of 'Chinatown.'"

†In 1959, James Baldwin, perhaps directly or unconsciously influenced by Ellison's idea, would write an essay called "Nobody Knows My Name"—a title he would then use for the collection in which the piece would be reprinted in 1961.

to see or know him as the individual human being he is. Nor are they any more interested in confronting the realities of the world around them, to which they are as blind as they are to him.

So disillusioned does he become through this realization that he winds up living all by himself in an abandoned cellar. But in the closing pages he decides to end his hibernation and reemerge, as invisible as ever but capable now of telling his imaginary interlocutor "what was really happening when your eyes were looking through."

The Invisible Man's story unfolds in the manner of a classic picaresque novel, as one vivid character after another bursts with such incandescent clarity onto the scene that the reader's eyes are simply prevented from "looking through." These characters are collectively meant to penetrate the stereotypes that have hidden the great diversity of Negro life in America. They thus cover a very broad range: from the apparently meek but cunningly manipulative and malevolent black college president Dr. Bledsoe, with his bewilderingly complicated sense of the only way a Negro can successfully maneuver his way around a hostile white world; to the wildly colorful and semicomic, semisinister black-nationalist demagogue of West Indian origin, Ras the Exhorter; to the handsome and troubled Communist militant Tod Clifton; to the brilliant con man and hustler Rinehart; to the lovingly warmhearted Harlem landlady Miss Mary Rambo.

Swelling this huge cast are many other figures, both major and minor, among them a number of whites like Mr. Norton, the wealthy trustee of the protagonist's college, and the Communist leader Brother Jack, who are portrayed with the same clarity: a clarity that can be arrived at only by the nonapologetic "cold eye" of a true novelist working with all his might to achieve precisely that and nothing else (though the paradox is that he accomplishes much else along the way that escapes writers who go whoring after what, from the perspective of an artist, are always strange gods).

All this was astonishing enough. But what seemed equally amazing for a first novel—and what today, knowing as we now do how great a reader Ellison was and how diligently in learning to write fiction he schooled himself in other books, seems all the more amazing—was how underivative it was. If one looked closely enough, one could detect the influence here and there of this writer or that. But the main quality that struck so many of us on a first reading of *Invisible Man* was its originality: no such voice had ever been heard before in American literature. In some of his earliest stories, now collected in the posthumous *Flying Home,* Ellison was obviously imitating Hemingway's prose, and doing it pretty well. But he eventually got Hemingway out of his system, having discovered that the "teasing" character of such prose, "that quality of implying much more than was stated," was not right for expressing what he "really felt" and was not a flexible enough vehicle for evoking the varieties of experience he wished to represent.

IT WAS ABOUT ten years before I reread *Invisible Man,* and I was still sufficiently impressed to vote for it as the best American novel of the postwar period in a poll of critics conducted, if memory serves, by the Sunday book supplement of the now-defunct *New York Herald-Tribune.* Yet I was disappointed to find that it did not hold up as well as I had expected. Or was it that extraliterary considerations had entered, distorting my judgment?

For by this time I had met Ellison, and was seeing him fairly often around New York. To my great surprise, the humorous touch that was so central a part of his talent as a novelist rarely if ever showed itself in private conversation, or in the essays he published from time to time. But this is putting it too mildly. He actually was, at least in my encounters with him, a bit of a stuffed shirt, tending to speak like a character he himself might have lampooned in fiction. Once, while we were discussing something or other about which we disagreed, the author of *Invisible Man* actually delivered himself of the sentence: "As for me, I have values." It was like that, too, when he gave a lecture or wrote a nonfiction piece. On such occasions his prose was almost invariably pompous and pretentious: just the opposite of what it sounded like in his novel.

For all I know, then, the poor impression I had formed of Ellison personally may have had something to do with the somewhat lessened esteem in which I now held his novel. And what may have influenced my slight change of judgment even more was the obvious dislike Ellison felt for me.

Since he never owned up to this dislike or discussed it openly, I never figured out exactly what it was that bothered him. Maybe I simply rubbed him the wrong way, as he did me. But other possibilities entered my mind. One of them was that, in common with many of Saul Bellow's friends and Bellow himself, he never altogether forgave me for the negative review I had written as a fledgling critic in 1953 of *The Adventures of Augie March.* Another was my fairly close association in the early 1960s with James Baldwin, who had become his closest rival among contemporary black writers.

Out of some motive I could never fathom, Ellison was grudging about Baldwin even when they were on the same side (as against Richard Wright) in the debate over whether the black writer's main responsibility was to be "ideologically militant" or to work at "writing well." The easy explanation of this stingy attitude on Ellison's part was that it stemmed from envy of all the attention and praise Baldwin (whose beautifully elegant prose style certainly exempted him from any criticisms based on deficiency of craft) had already been getting in the 1940s as an essayist before Ellison pulled ahead, far ahead, with *Invisible Man.* A year later, in 1953, Baldwin's own first novel, *Go Tell It on the Mountain,* was published to loud hosannas and even became a best-seller, but no one—myself included—ever thought, or said, that it was in the same class as *Invisible Man.*

In short, Ellison had no apparent cause to envy the early Baldwin. Conceivably the problem was a lack of generosity in Ellison's character—a supposition that is given plausibility by other evidences of that trait that could be detected in his conversation and his essays. But then again the explanation may lie in something personal that was going on between the two men to which I was not privy.

BUT IF I WAS, and remain, a little puzzled by Ellison's lack of generosity toward the early Baldwin, there was no mystery about it once the younger writer's conversion to a species of black nationalism took place in the early 1960s. This new strain then grew more and more virulent in the poisonous attitudes it fostered in Baldwin toward whites (and Jews), as well as in the hectoring and self-pitying tone of the books written under its spell. Such a development could only have repelled Ellison who, after all, identified himself with and spoke for an American Negro tradition "which abhors as obscene any trading on one's own anguish for gain or sympathy." In the spirit of this tradition, he denounced the increasingly fashionable "stance of militancy" as "an easy con-game" for "ambitious, publicity-hungry Negroes."

Ellison did not mention Baldwin's name in this connection, but very likely, as the 1960s wore on, it kept moving closer and closer to the top of his private enemies list.* Therefore my own enthusiastic response to Baldwin's first hesitant embrace of what would soon become a fanatically held point of view—that is, his highly sympathetic essay about the Black Muslims, "The Fire Next Time," a piece I myself had actually persuaded him to write, and which caused nothing short of a sensation when it appeared in 1963—may well have made me guilty by association.

---

*In all fairness, I should note that Ellison did on various occasions make some sort of effort to suggest that he was not hostile to Baldwin. But whenever he did, one could sense that his heart was not in it. Nor can I recall a word of actual praise for Baldwin—I mean Baldwin when he was at his very best—either in private or in any of his published writings.

If so, I soon compounded the guilt, and now on my own hook, when in that same year, partly in response to "The Fire Next Time" and with Baldwin reciprocally egging me on, I wrote an essay entitled "My Negro Problem—and Ours." Of this essay a critic once said that it contained something in it to offend everyone, and where Ellison was concerned, there was more than one such something.

Oddly, he did not complain to me about the passage that in retrospect, having just reread practically his entire published output, I would think would most have outraged him. This was the section in which I declared that unlike the Jews, who wished to survive as a distinct group because "they not only believed that God had given them no choice, but . . . were tied to a memory of past glory and imminent redemption," the American Negro had no correspondingly powerful motives for the same wish. "His past is a stigma, his color is a stigma, and his vision of the future is the hope of erasing the stigma by making color irrelevant, by making it disappear as a fact of consciousness."

Surely Ellison must have been enraged by these words, with their sweeping dismissal of his fervent belief in the great richness and precious value of the American Negro's culture and the inestimable contribution it had made, and was still making, to "the wider American culture" (and, as he invariably added, to American democracy, too, in calling it to account and demanding that it fulfill its best promise). Yet in at least two discussions I had with him about the piece—discussions he was so reluctant to enter that I had to prod him out of his loud silence by asking flatly where he stood in the heated controversy my essay had generated—he said nothing to me about the insult I had hurled at the culture of the American Negro.

Perhaps the reason he kept silent on this point was that he was assuaged by the sentences that came immediately before (the ones that, in as it were equal-opportunity fashion, most offended many Jewish readers of the piece):

> In thinking about the Jews I have often wondered whether their survival as a distinct group was worth one hair on the head of a single infant. Did the Jews have to survive so that six million innocent people should one day be burned in the ovens of Auschwitz?

Or perhaps, as a devout pluralist, he did not consider it worth debating this particular issue with someone who could be so obtuse and impious not just about Negroes but about his own people as well. Or perhaps he felt he had

already taken sufficient care of the matter in the angry reply he had written
to an essay by the socialist critic Irving Howe, "Black Boys and Native
Sons," that was published shortly after "My Negro Problem—and Ours"
and that also used the word "stigma." Knowing I had read that reply when
we talked about my own piece, Ellison may well have assumed that I
understood it as applying with equal, if not greater, force to me and may
have decided not to waste any further breath on it.

Even so, he did let me have it about the notorious last paragraph of my
essay, where—driven by the logic of my prior analysis of race relations in
America—I concluded that the only solution to "the Negro problem" was
the wholesale mixing of whites and blacks through intermarriage. *Don't
you realize,* he asked with a decidedly unfriendly grin but in a completely
civil tone—I am paraphrasing from memory here—*that this would be no
solution to anything, since the babies who would be produced by these inter-
marriages would still be considered black? All you would accomplish would be
to increase the size of the black population, which would probably make things
politically worse.* I must confess that this criticism—which he was the only
one to come up with, though a thousand different objections to the essay
were raised by others—caught me completely off guard and that I had no
answer to it.

WHAT FINALLY TORE IT between us, however, was my review about a
year later (1964) of *Shadow and Act,* his first collection of essays and his
first book of any kind since *Invisible Man* had come out twelve years earlier.
Ellison was as thin-skinned as the next writer, and he could not have taken
kindly to my statement that he had "never mastered the art of the essay
enough for his best qualities to find expression in it." Never mind that I
professed myself a great admirer of his fiction and that I also praised him
"as an extraordinarily principled man, a man of great seriousness, stubborn
rectitude, and intellectual determination." Given his virtually religious
devotion to craft, none of this could have canceled out my attack on the
stilted and awkward prose of *Shadow and Act.*

Nor could he have failed to be angered by the corollary I drew here from
the point I had made in "My Negro Problem—and Ours" about the price
of Jewish survival. By now, largely under the influence of Ellison's own
essays, I was ready—even eager—to concede that the Negro past was more
than a "stigma," and that there were "marvelous qualities" in Negro culture. But I also denied, in the teeth of Ellison's assertions to the contrary,

that these qualities could survive the disappearance of the oppression that "in some awful sense" had produced them in the first place.

As if all this were not enough to finish me off in his eyes, I (now entrenched in the radical phase of my complicated political evolution) devoted a large section of the piece to siding with Howe in his dispute with Ellison. In "Black Boys and Native Sons," Howe had defended Richard Wright and the "protest novel" against both Ellison and Baldwin. It was more incumbent on the Negro writer, said Howe with a vigorous nod from me, to call attention, as Wright had done, to the terrible and inescapable pain suffered by his people in America than to cultivate the aesthetic virtues to which these two black critics of Wright's work attributed a higher importance (though Baldwin, as Howe did not fail to recognize, had already been moving in the other direction—that is, toward Wright's position).

Nevertheless, even if I now had a slightly lower opinion of *Invisible Man,* I still thought it was a very good novel, and better than almost anything else written in that period. No longer, however—and on this, I feel sure, I was exercising a disinterested critical judgment, without any taint of personal pique—did I regard it as a true masterpiece. All the indisputably great works of my acquaintance got better with repeated rereadings over the years: I would discover things in them as I grew older that I had been too young or inexperienced or ignorant to perceive or appreciate or even understand the first time around. With *Invisible Man,* by contrast, the freshness of it had faded somewhat in the ten years since I had last read it, and with that freshness went the illuminating shock of the first reading. The prose was still what it had been—vivid and charged with the energy of the superficially incongruous elements out of which Ellison had brilliantly forged it. The story, too, was still beautifully paced and structured. But now some of the characters had become less interesting, largely because, while still delightfully colorful on the surface, they were rarely examined in depth.

Then, too, there was the problem of the symbolism Ellison had clearly worked so hard to incorporate into the central idea of the hero as an Invisible Man living in a hole in the ground, and also in several much-praised scenes (like the one that takes place in a bizarre paint factory), which now came across as strained and even gratuitous. It was as if this symbolic dimension had sprung more out of deference to the high-literary dogmas and fashions of the 1940s and 1950s than out of the organic imperatives of the narrative. (Not for nothing did Ellison once say that both he and Baldwin had been created as much by the library as by the environments in which they had grown up; and I know from firsthand acquaintance with both men that Ellison read many more symbolically minded critics like Kenneth Burke and Edmund Wilson, and took them more seriously, than Baldwin ever did.)

MEANWHILE, there had arisen the great question of when Ellison's next novel would appear. The word, coming from Ellison himself and his closest friends, was that he had actually started it even before beginning *Invisible Man,* and that he had now returned to this aborted project and was working steadily on it. But since he was a notoriously slow writer (*Invisible Man* had taken him seven years to complete), and since this was to be a much longer book than its predecessor, there was no telling how many more years we would have to wait for its appearance.

Despite the eight excerpts from this work in progress that appeared in various literary magazines between 1960 and 1977, the suspicion spread that Ellison had been afflicted by a writer's block that was preventing him from developing and putting them all together into a finished novel. There was nothing unusual about this: many writers had been known to experience great difficulty in following up on a first novel, especially one so successful as *Invisible Man.* Writing was hard enough under normal conditions, but the inevitable compulsion to satisfy the expectations aroused by an impressive debut was well calculated to induce paralysis, sometimes temporary, sometimes permanent.

Until Ellison came along, the most famous second-novel block in American literature had been the one that silenced Henry Roth, whose *Call It Sleep,* published in 1934, had (like *Invisible Man*) been recognized as a masterpiece by certain critics but (unlike *Invisible Man*) had been a disastrous commercial failure. Unable to finish the second novel he then set out to write, Roth gave up in despair and disgust, becoming, among other things, a poultry farmer. Ellison had no need to seek refuge and income in a territory so distant from the literary world. While working on *his* second novel, he made his living by teaching at one university after another while also collecting the royalties and the prize money that kept pouring in from his first.

But would he ever finish what looked to be an endless project, assuming that he had even made a real start on it? I for one had my doubts, and then came the great disaster that increased those doubts. Here is John F. Callahan on what happened:

In his own mind Ellison was moving toward completion in . . . 1967 as he revised the novel at his summer home . . . in the Berkshires. Then, in the late afternoon of November 29, 1967, Ellison and his wife, Fanny, returned from shopping to find the house in flames. . . . Ten days after the event, he wrote . . . that "the loss was particularly severe for me, as a section of my work in progress was destroyed with it."

The section, he told an interviewer shortly before his death in 1994, had amounted to 362 pages, of which he had no copy. (In another version of the story, he did have a copy of the pages themselves but not of the revisions he had made on the one that perished in the fire.) Even so, he had told another interviewer in 1980: "I guess I've been able to put most of it back together again."*

Saul Bellow also revealed—further refuting my suspicion that the second novel had not even been seriously begun—that in 1959 or 1960 Ellison had given him "a couple of hundred pages, at least" to read. It now appears that by the time Ellison died about five years ago, the still unfinished manuscript consisted of some two thousand pages in all. At one point, around 1970, he had considered publishing the whole thing in three volumes, but then changed his mind because he wanted each volume to "have a compelling interest in itself," which, he feared, would not be the case. And so, for the next twenty-four years, he continued to write and expand and revise without ever completing the book to his own satisfaction.

This may not exactly seem like a block—a word that conjures up the inability to write at all—but it is one of the forms that a block can sometimes take. I know of a novelist who turned out several hundred thousand words without—or rather to avoid—coming to the end, and I would guess that something similar was involved in Ellison's two thousand pages. *Invisible Man* was a very tough act to follow, made tougher yet by the honors

---

*It may be instructive to compare Ellison's experience with a similar disaster that befell Thomas Carlyle more than a hundred years earlier. In March 1834, Carlyle lent the only copy of the manuscript of the first volume of his history of the French Revolution, on which he had been laboring for three years, to John Stuart Mill, whose maid accidentally burned it. Without any notes or earlier drafts, Carlyle still managed to rewrite the entire volume in just four months, and he then went on to complete the entire work with two more volumes by the end of the same year. For Ellison, obviously, putting "most of it back together again" after the fire that destroyed his manuscript did not have the same result that Carlyle so miraculously achieved under comparable circumstances. But as has often been observed, when it came to writing, the Victorians were as different from us as they were in their moral convictions.

that had been heaped upon him; and he simply proved unable to follow it. He differed from Henry Roth, who was rendered mute for a very long time, in that he could produce pages. But what he could never manage to do was produce another finished work that would justify the tremendous fuss made over him as a result of a single book written ages before.

At this juncture, we witness a fascinating reversal of roles between Ellison and Henry Roth. Late in life, Roth found his tongue again (curiously through learning how to use a computer), and proceeded to pour forth what had been pent up for so many years into a very lengthy autobiographical novel (published serially in several volumes) that in my judgment was as wooden and amateurish as his youthful first novel had been alive and precociously accomplished. It was a sad, even pathetic, dénouement to the story of a career that might better have been left in the poignantly and romantically legendary state in which it had previously been frozen.

By sharp contrast, Ellison, with all the makings of a book in hand, was unable to bring it to a conclusion and present it to the world. Now, however, the dedicated and indefatigable John Callahan has carved a fairly short novel out of the two thousand manuscript pages Ellison left behind and issued it under the title *Juneteenth.*

JUNETEENTH takes off from the attempted assassination (apparently in the 1950s) of a race-baiting United States senator named Sunraider who represents a New England state (one of several implausible details in the book through which Ellison must have wanted to say something—probably concerning racism in the North—that he never gets around to saying) by a young black man about whom we never learn anything else here.* Lying in the hospital close to death, Sunraider sends for an old black minister, the Reverend Hickman, who a few days earlier had come to Washington with members of his congregation in order to warn the senator of the danger facing him (though we never find out how they knew), but had been unable to get past his secretary.

---

*However, according to a piece in the *New York Times Magazine* by Gregory Feeley, who has read everything Callahan decided to leave out of *Juneteenth,* there is a great deal about the young assassin in the pages that remain in manuscript. Other pages were omitted, too, that may fill in some of the gaps I mention below. And Callahan also omitted from his edition of *Juneteenth* four of the eight published excerpts mentioned above, among them the much-admired "Cadillac Flambé." Callahan promises, though, to include all this material, along with different versions of some of the sections he chose to use, in a special "scholar's edition" that he will eventually issue.

Now, through a combination of Hickman's soothing discourse to the partly comatose Sunraider and the fevered reminiscences that float through the senator's mind, we learn that this racist politician had as a child been raised in the South under the name of Bliss by "Daddy" Hickman and had worked with him as a boy preacher. One day he had run away, changed his name, and had eventually become a United States senator. Left in suspense is whether Sunraider is a light-skinned Negro who has successfully passed for white, or a white foundling who had in effect been adopted by Hickman. But at least this question is finally resolved.* Not so with Sunraider's story. We long to hear it after getting to know him as a child, but the gaps in the narrative are so wide that the steps of his vast journey are never traced. All we are given is a few pages about one of these steps: at some point, Sunraider had been in the movie business. Yet how and why he got there, and how and why this had led him into politics, remain untold.

By comparison with *Invisible Man,* which teems with a multitude of characters, *Juneteenth* is sparsely populated. A number of female members of Hickman's congregation are vividly drawn, but only Hickman himself and the boy Bliss are evoked with any real fullness. Hickman, in his youth a jazz musician and sinner before converting and becoming a "Revrend," speaks in the marvelously pungent and seductively rhythmic idiom of the best black Southern preachers, but as a character he is too good to be true—so good that the portrait of him verges on sentimentality. So does the sketchier portrait of Sunraider as the boy Bliss.

But these weaknesses of *Juneteenth,* which can mainly be ascribed to its unfinished state, are the least of its problems. I have already noted that one of the most extraordinary features of *Invisible Man* is that, unlike most first novels, it was not derivative. Ellison might have been a creature of the library, and his earliest stories might have sounded like talented imitations of Hemingway, but in writing *Invisible Man* he had triumphantly banished the voices of other novelists from his head and had been rewarded with the discovery of his own style and his own voice. How could it have happened, then, that he would go on to write in *Juneteenth* a novel that is as derivative as the stories of his novitiate?

In the case of *Juneteenth,* the ghost haunting the prose is not Hemingway, however, but Faulkner. The author of the multivolume Yoknapatawpha

---

*That is, as I read the book. Feeley disagrees: he says that the question is left hanging. But as others read it, the answer is the opposite of the one I think Ellison gives. One of these three interpretations should be right, but it is also possible that Ellison never finally made up his mind, and that this is why so much confusion has been generated.

saga is there in Ellison's very desire to produce a multivolume saga of his own, but his presence can be felt even more intrusively in the prose of *June-teenth*. Here is a typical passage:

> Oh, she said. . . . You not from Chicago?
> Never been there, I said. And looking at her nibbling the sandwich, her soft eyes on my face, I thought of some of them. *We had had a rough time, coming through all of that cloudburst of rain, having to avoid the towns where I might have been recognized and the unfriendly towns where the oil rigs pounded night and day, making the trip longer and our money shorter and shorter. Getting stuck in the mud here and having engine trouble there, the tires going twice and the top being split by hailstones the size of baseballs and almost losing all of the equipment off a shaky ferry when we crossed a creek in Missouri.* [italics in the original]

The hands may be the hands of Ellison, but from large elements like the cadences of the italicized interior monologue—sired by James Joyce out of Ireland on another thoroughbred across the ocean and in the American South—down to smaller stylistic details like the omission of quotation marks in the dialogue and the heavy reliance on gerunds, the voice is the voice of William Faulkner.

READING *Juneteenth* under the impression that it was the product of a forty-year gestation by a perfectionist who was laboring without letup to satisfy his own demands on himself, I found this regression to literary derivativeness very puzzling. But then at the end I came to Callahan's afterword, where he informs us that "Except for a very few, very brief passages, written in the early 1990s, the novel is not Ellison's most recent effort." Actually it was mostly composed as early as 1959 and designated as the second of the three-volume saga Ellison had been aiming at.

It is a stretch, then, for its publisher to call *Juneteenth* a "new novel" (as Henry Roth's final series genuinely was) or the product of a forty-year effort. What we have here instead is an unfinished section of a never-to-be-completed larger novel that Ellison wrote in the years immediately after *Invisible Man*. It can thus more accurately be described as an early—or, if one prefers, middle-period—than a late work.

Yet it is still very hard for me to understand how, having succeeded in the immensely arduous job of finding his own voice and staying with it throughout the seven years it took him to complete his first novel, Ellison should have then lost it and become possessed in working on his second by the daimon of another writer. But that the other writer should have been Faulkner is not so mysterious when we consider the deep admiration Ellison had always felt for him even despite the atavistic traces of racism of which the great Southern novelist was never fully able to rid himself.

Other parts of the two-thousand-page manuscript he left behind may prove me wrong, but for now my speculation is that Ellison—a man of great intelligence and literary erudition who had an ear second to none— knew that Faulkner had invaded and taken him over and that this was why he could never finish the book. I can imagine him struggling for forty years to get Faulkner's sound out of his head; I can imagine him searching desperately for the lost voice he had created in *Invisible Man;* I can imagine him trying to fool himself into thinking that he had finally found it again, and then realizing that he had not; and I can imagine him being reduced to despair at this literary enslavement into which some incorrigible defect in his nature had sold him—and to a Southern master, at that!

I offer this theory with sadness in my heart, and I am even unhappier at having to report that after revisiting *Invisible Man* yet again in recent weeks, the faults that had become apparent on my second reading loomed even larger, and its virtues were commensurately diminished. Worse yet, the book now struck me as dated. Let me try to explain why.

Insofar as the central theme of *Invisible Man* is the significance and implications of the black presence in America—which of course it mainly is ("the most complex, multilayered, and challenging novel about race and being and the preservation of democratic ideals in America," in the words of one of its admirers)—its very title, and its defining symbol, has now acquired an almost quaintly archaic aura.

For if Negroes—or blacks or African Americans—were once invisible, today, in the age of affirmative action and multiculturalism, they have become perhaps the most salient group in the American consciousness. If their literary culture was previously held at naught, it is now studied and celebrated beyond what Ellison—judging from his own harsh remarks about the need for his fellow black writers to become better craftsmen— would probably have deemed its intrinsic merits. If the way of life growing out of their oppressed condition was once dismissed as nothing but a stigma and hence demanded to be brought into view with the undeniable force of conviction about its richness that lay behind the picture painted by *Invisible Man,* this way of life has now become a national obsession at which no one ever stops looking and about which no one ever stops talking.

On the other hand—and this dates the book even more—there is hardly a trace in *Invisible Man* of the one aspect of that way of life which has done more in the years since the book was published to affect race relations in this country: black violence and criminality, the fear of which has spread even among the most sympathetic white liberals. Yes, *Invisible Man* contains hustlers and pimps and tricksters and con artists, but (like Rinehart, who embodies them all in his own individual person) they are represented as ingenious and admirably resourceful, not as menacing or dangerous.

BUT COULD NOT the same charge of datedness be leveled against almost any novel written in the past about the past? The answer is no—not, in any event, when we are dealing with those that are truly great. And because Ellison once praised Richard Wright for his eagerness to compete with the best, and because this eagerness was even more intense in Ellison himself, I think it fair to pit *Invisible Man* against such indisputably great novels as—to cite a few very different ones off the top of my head— James's *The Bostonians,* George Eliot's *Middlemarch,* Dostoevsky's *The Possessed,* and Tolstoy's *Anna Karenina.*

In each of these books, the social conditions of the world being portrayed, and the attitudes that underlay and supported them, are dead and gone and so obsolete that one might suppose a reader of our own day would be incapable of identifying with the characters whose plight is determined by them. In *Anna Karenina,* for example, the entire plot hinges on an adultery that is taken with a literally deadly seriousness hardly imaginable to a contemporary American. Yet the human tragedy Tolstoy depicts, fully anchored though it is in social circumstances and moral attitudes that could not be more radically different from our own, reaches so deeply into the never-changing human realities beneath them that the reader is gripped by it from the first word to the last. Something similar happens with all the other novels I have listed. But alas, it does not happen with *Invisible Man.* Good though it is in so many respects, it does not survive this acid test of greatness.

The reason it saddens me to say these things is that I would have wished at this point in my own life to celebrate Ellison, not to denigrate him. For I feel that I owe him a posthumous apology for having, during my sojourn on the Left in the 1960s, taken the side of Howe and Baldwin against him when he was so bravely standing almost alone in resisting the politicization of everything and holding out for the writer's responsibility as a writer to his art above any other consideration.

The upshot is that though Ellison has been diminished somewhat in my eyes as a novelist, studying his essays again has had the opposite effect on my opinion of him as an intellectual and as a man. I cannot tell a lie: much of the prose of those essays has not in my reluctant opinion become any less stilted and awkward and pretentious over the years. But the general position they take has acquired a luminosity and a nobility that were, if not exactly "invisible" to me when I first read them, then much less striking.

Indeed, if *Invisible Man* has been rendered dated by the place to which, for better and worse, we have come in America, many passages in Ellison's essays have acquired a greater power in that very same place than they had when he wrote them. I quoted above from one such passage in another context, but it is so perfect an embodiment of the quality I wish to capture that I am going to quote it again. It comes from the section in which Ellison chides Irving Howe for suggesting (in Ellison's paraphrase) "that unrelieved suffering is the only 'real' Negro experience, and that the true Negro writer must be ferocious." To this Ellison counters with the following little lecture:

> But there is also an American Negro tradition which teaches one to deflect racial provocation and to master and contain pain. It is a tradition which abhors as obscene any trading on one's anguish for gain or sympathy; which springs not from a desire to deny the harshness of existence but from a will to deal with it as men at their best have always done. It takes fortitude to be a man and no less to be an artist. If so, there are no exemptions.

It is in this same reply to Howe that he later speaks (in a sentence from which I also quoted above) of "what an easy con-game for ambitious, publicity-hungry Negroes this stance of 'militancy' has become." If this was the situation in 1964, the name of Al Sharpton alone tells us how much worse things have become in the intervening thirty-five years.

ALL HONOR, THEN, to Ralph Ellison. If *Invisible Man* is not the great novel it has been taken to be, it still ranks among the best we have had in the past half century; and if Ellison falls far short even of that in *Juneteenth,* he is still a magnificent intellectual and moral and political exemplar. It is—and now I arrive at long last to the paradox I mentioned at the beginning—that aspect of his life and work, and not his fiction, which, in looking back at his entire career, now stands out as the most admirable and impressive.

Hearing this would have distressed Ellison no end, and he would almost certainly have felt offended by it, if only because it was to the novel that he committed himself as to a religious calling. It was also as a novelist that he wanted to make his contribution not only to the literature of the America he always loved (even when he was growing up under segregation in Oklahoma) but to the struggle of the Negro people he loved, and "affirmed," with equal intensity. Refusing to be mollified by Irving Howe's praise of *Invisible Man* as "miraculous," Ellison shot back: "If there is anything 'miraculous' about the book, it is the result of hard work undertaken in the belief that the work of art is important in itself, that it is a social action in itself."

I shout Amen to that, but I end with an even deeper and more reverent bow to the proud and self-respecting tradition out of which Ellison spoke and from which he could never be budged: a tradition that exposes the aggressive black nationalists and separatists and mau-mauers who have grown more numerous today than ever for the whiners and braggarts and self-haters Ellison despised them as being. If he had done nothing more than keep that tradition alive by his steady reminders of its existence, he would deserve all the prizes he won, and a few more as well.

Without a doubt Ellison's response to such an estimate of him would have been a furious "No thanks, Jack." Apart from the blow it would have dealt to his pride in *Invisible Man,* he would have seen and gone after it as just another ruse in the elevating of ideology over art; the fact that in this round it was his own ideology being elevated rather than Richard Wright's or Irving Howe's or the later James Baldwin's would have made no difference, or anyway not enough of one to pacify him or keep his dander down.

As for me, having been wrong once before on this issue from the other political side, I would even be willing to say that I was now wrong again—if, that is, and only if, *Invisible Man* were indeed a great novel. But like it or not (and it was, remember, Ellison himself who asserted that in the matter of artistic standards "there are no exemptions"), the thanks we owe him are not so much for *Invisible Man* as for the kind of *visible* man he himself was in the literary, political, and intellectual history of this country.

FROM *EX-FRIENDS:* A FOUL-WEATHER
FRIEND TO NORMAN MAILER

THE HIGHEST COMPLIMENT I
was ever paid by Norman Mailer was when he called me a "foul-weather
friend." He grinned as he said it, pleased with himself for the wit and felic-
ity of the formulation. I grinned back, both because I shared his own
appreciation of the clever way he had put the compliment and because I
knew that, having always stood more steadfastly by him in bad times than
in good, I richly deserved it. Our friendship started in what was an especially rough period for him, and it slowly and gradually began to unravel
when he was once again riding high. I, on the other hand, was in big trouble at that point, and he did not prove to be a foul-weather friend to me.
But there was more—much more—to the story than that, and I would be
false to the reality of it if I created the impression that the rise and fall of
our friendship was, to borrow from Jay Gatsby, "only personal."

By the time I first met him at a party thrown by Lillian Hellman in the
late 1950s, Mailer* had written three novels and a few sections of what
would turn out to be an abortive fourth. The first, *The Naked and the
Dead,* had been a sensation upon its publication in 1948, propelling him at
age twenty-five into bestsellerdom and celebrityhood as the author of what
the popular press took to be "the best and most definitive novel about
World War II." Yet—and here is one large measure of how much things
would change in the decades ahead—the very success of that book made
Mailer as suspect in the eyes of the serious critical community as Lillian's
plays had made her.[†]

From what I learned when I came to know him about ten years later,

---

*I more often called him that than Norman, feeling self-conscious about our shared first name.
He had no such feeling and always called me Norman.

†Their own friendship began when she tried to adapt *The Naked and the Dead* to the stage.
The project failed, but they remained on good terms.

Mailer was shocked to discover that there was a literary world out there whose leading lights were at best dismissive and at worst contemptuous of best-selling books and the people who wrote them. A graduate of Harvard he may have been, but somehow he had managed to get through four years in Cambridge without really coming to understand that in the America of the late 1940s all culture was divided into three parts: highbrow, middlebrow, and lowbrow; that the highbrows more or less automatically dismissed any best-selling novel as middlebrow or lowbrow and therefore beneath notice; and that this tiny and obscure minority, powerless to command or disburse the worldly rewards of big money and national fame, nevertheless mysteriously enjoyed a virtual monopoly over the power to confer true literary status.

There were, to be sure, exceptions to the rule that commercial success debarred a writer from highbrow acceptance or acclaim, the main one being Mailer's god Ernest Hemingway, whose career had probably been responsible for misleading him on these matters. But even Hemingway was only a partial exception, since he had begun by publishing in what had once been called "little magazines" and had established himself as an important experimental writer (with an imprimatur from one of the cardinals of the avant-garde church, Gertrude Stein herself) by the time he broke through to commercial success. Mailer, by contrast, hit it big with no such prior credentials.

To make matters worse, he did so with a novel written straight out of the naturalist tradition against which the avant-garde and the highbrow critics who supported it had been setting their faces for some three decades. Even the few departures Mailer risked from traditional naturalism in *The Naked and the Dead* consisted of techniques borrowed from John Dos Passos, a novelist whose prestige among highbrows, very high though it had been when his magnum opus *U.S.A.* was completed in the 1930s, was already fading and who was soon to be relegated to almost complete critical obscurity. The fall of Dos Passos no doubt had more to do with his move from the radical Left to the libertarian Right than with the alleged decline of his later novels as works of art—not that anyone would admit this at a time when political considerations were not supposed to influence aesthetic judgment. Mailer, by sharp contrast, was emphatically on the Left, but from the point of view of the highbrows, his leftism, like Lillian's, was of the wrong—that is, Stalinist—variety (though unlike her, he was only a fellow-traveler).

In the essay about him on which I had been working when we first met,* here is how I described the politics behind *The Naked and the Dead:*

> In 1948 Mailer—who was shortly to become a leading figure in Henry Wallace's campaign for the Presidency—subscribed to the notion that our postwar difficulties with Russia were the sole responsibility of American capitalism. We had gone to war against Hitler not because the American ruling class was anti-fascist, but because Hitler had shown himself unwilling to play the capitalist game according to the rules, and the next step was to dispose of Russia, the only remaining obstacle on the road to total power. World War II, then, was the first phase of a more ambitious operation, while the army had been used as a laboratory of fascism, a preview of the kind of society that the American ruling class was preparing for the future.

Such blatantly Stalinist views had long been politically unacceptable in highbrow literary circles—just as unacceptable as the middlebrow literary genre through which Mailer put them forward. In fact, there were critics who saw middlebrowism itself as one of the aesthetic faces of Stalinism. Thus, Robert Warshow, writing in *Commentary* a year before *The Naked and the Dead* appeared, drew a direct line between Stalinism and "the mass culture of the educated classes—the culture of the 'middlebrow.'" And without making the connection explicit, Dwight Macdonald, who would later become Mailer's friend and champion, first wrote a devastating exposé of Henry Wallace as a dupe of the Communists and then followed it up a few years later with an equally devastating assault on middlebrowism (or, as he renamed it, "midcult").

Oddly enough, not even in all the hundreds (or was it thousands?) of hours we spent talking after we became intimate friends did I ever ask Mailer when he first fully understood the importance of the highbrow literary community and, in particular, of *Partisan Review.* Nor did I ever find out whether the radical change he went through, both as a novelist and in his political orientation, in the three years between the publication of *The Naked and the Dead* and the appearance of his second novel, *Barbary Shore,* had anything to do with his newfound determination to win the high-

---

*It would appear in *Partisan Review* in 1959 under the title "Norman Mailer: The Embattled Vision" and would then be reprinted in 1964 in *Doings and Undoings.*

brows over even, if necessary, at the expense of another popular success. There is good reason to believe that the influence over him of Jean Malaquais, a Trotskyist who became his French translator and close friend, played a serious part here. Yet my own guess is that in abandoning both the naturalism and the Stalinism of *The Naked and the Dead* and producing, in *Barbary Shore,* a Kafkaesque allegory in celebration of Trotskyism, he was making a bid (whether conscious or half-conscious or unconscious I still cannot say) for highbrow approval.

But if that was what he was up to, he miscalculated badly. *Barbary Shore* was a flop both with the general public, for whom it was too obscure, and with the highbrow critics, who paid it very little attention. The highbrows ignored it partly because he had already been written off as just another middlebrow, and perhaps also because, even though he had lost (or abandoned) his popular touch, he still remained behind the high-culture curve. By 1951, the modernism of *Barbary Shore* was beginning to seem as dated as the naturalism of *The Naked and the Dead.* As for Mailer's politics, from the point of view of the highbrows, becoming a follower of Trotsky was certainly an improvement over being a Stalinist fellow-traveler, but Trotskyism too seemed old hat by 1951. (As my wife paraphrased the review William Barrett wrote for *Partisan Review* of *Barbary Shore,* "Oh, ho hum, now Mailer's taking up *this* stuff.") For this was a time when the highbrow literary world, with a few lonely exceptions, had grown disaffected with revolutionary socialism of whatever coloration. As such, it was in the process of laying a newly possessive claim to "our country and our culture," as the editors of *Partisan Review* entitled the symposium they ran in 1952, in which the changing attitude of their community toward these matters was most saliently registered.

On the other hand, the fact that Mailer was invited to participate in that very symposium meant that *Barbary Shore* had at least made him more of a figure to be reckoned with than before. William Phillips, the coeditor of *Partisan Review,* later admitted that Mailer's inclusion was "a political act" both on the magazine's part and on Mailer's, signifying that he had now become "part of our community"; and Mailer himself said, "In a funny way, the symposium was my coming out."

But being Norman Mailer, he came out swinging. In his contribution, he announced that he was shocked by the assumptions of the symposium, and he scolded the editors of *Partisan Review,* as well as many older novelists (he specifically mentioned Hemingway, Dos Passos, James T. Farrell, William Faulkner, and John Steinbeck) for having "traveled from alienation to varying degrees of acceptance, if not outright proselytizing, for the American Century." There was deliberate provocation, and even a touch of offensiveness, in Mailer's reference to the "the American Century," a term which the head of Time, Inc., Henry Luce, had coined a few years earlier in a famously triumphalist editorial in *Life* magazine. In using this term, Mailer was all but explicitly charging that the writers he named had at the very least associated themselves with, and at the very worst had sold out to, what he regarded as the true and most powerful enemy of everything they had traditionally stood for both in culture and in politics. But this stubborn stance of opposition to American society did not mean that Mailer was destined to remain a Trotskyist or any other kind of Marxist. On the contrary, having moved from Stalinism to Trotskyism, like the editors of *Partisan Review* long before him, he would soon go trailing after them again, this time into a repudiation of Marxism in particular and ideological thinking in general.

In taking this step, however, Mailer embarked on a very different road from the one the ex-Communists and former Trotskyists of *Partisan Review* were now on. So far as most of them were concerned, Marxism, in prophesying the doom of capitalism in the West and the ensuing triumph of a socialist revolution led by an aroused and mobilized working class, had shown itself to be a faulty guide to the future. For here we were in peacetime, when capitalism, which in the view of the Marxists had survived the Great Depression of the 1930s only through being placed on an artificial life-support system by the economic needs of the war, was finally supposed to experience its temporarily delayed collapse. Yet with the plug now pulled, this supposedly moribund system was showing even greater vitality than before. Meanwhile, Marx's revolutionary dreams had turned into a totalitarian nightmare in Russia, and the workers of America, the most advanced of the capitalist countries, were obdurately refusing to play their prescribed role in the Marxist scenario. Instead of rising up in revolt against their exploiters and oppressors, they were expressing great satisfaction with a system that was beginning to realize *their* dreams of prosperity and even of what the economist John Kenneth Galbraith would later famously denounce as "affluence."

This was very far from Mailer's take on the failure of the Marxist revolution, as he made clear in his notorious essay "The White Negro." Improbably, it appeared in the socialist magazine *Dissent,* whose editor, Irving Howe (himself an ex-Trotskyist who still kept faith with elements of Marxist theory), had evidently decided on the basis of the *Partisan Review* symposium that Mailer could be a useful ally in the struggle to revive the waning influence of socialism among the intellectuals. But, if so, Howe, as he eventually discovered, had Mailer all wrong.* In "The White Negro," Mailer spoke of Marxist theory with respect, but he declared that it had failed "in application" because it had been "an expression of the scientific narcissism we inherited from the nineteenth century" and had been motivated by "the rational mania that consciousness could stifle instinct."

For Mailer the alternative was not some form of liberalism (as with Lionel Trilling) or democratic socialism (as with Irving Howe) or anarchism (as with Paul Goodman). It was "Hip," which Mailer rather pretentiously described as the American form of existentialism. In the rise of the "hipster" (who served in this new theory as a kind of substitute for Marx's proletariat), Mailer detected "the first wind of a second revolution in this century, moving not forward toward action and more rational equitable distribution, but backward toward being and the secrets of human energy."

This "second revolution" would not involve political action or the mobilization of masses; it would come about through the pursuit of immediate gratification that was the hipster's only raison d'être and that Mailer saw as the new wave of the future. Never mind that such a pursuit seemed trivial and was moreover disreputable in the eyes of virtually every moral philosopher from Aristotle to John Dewey: Mailer still cavalierly put himself through many intellectual contortions to ascribe a huge metaphysical significance to it. But the real proof of the theory was supposed to be furnished not by his essay but by his fiction, beginning with his Hollywood novel, *The Deer Park,* which appeared just before the "The White Negro" in 1956. *The Deer Park* was a better book than *Barbary Shore,* but it fell very far short indeed of the enormous claims Mailer made for it, and though it fared better than its immediate predecessor with both the critics and the public, he was left feeling frustrated and disappointed.

He then decided that something more daring and more ambitious was needed to fulfill his new vision, and he embarked on the production of "the proper book of an outlaw." So huge a project was this that it would, he thought, take him ten years to complete. Furthermore, resorting characteristically to a sports metaphor (though boxing rather than baseball was the

---

*Howe was, he later said, "delighted" to publish "The White Negro," but "after a while some of the editorial staff [of *Dissent*] began to sense that there was going to be a divergence. It wasn't yet totally clear, but the feeling was that what Norman was doing didn't have much political significance." The wonder is that this "divergence" was not already obvious to Howe and his colleagues in "The White Negro" itself.

sport he usually favored whenever he "got into the ring" with other novelists), he announced that it would represent "the longest ball ever to go up into the accelerated hurricane air of our American letters." This would be "a novel which Dostoevsky and Marx; Joyce and Freud; Stendhal, Tolstoy, Proust and Spengler; Faulkner, and even old moldering Hemingway might come to read, for it would carry what they had to tell another part of the way."

All that ever came of this grandiose project, however, was two self-contained fragments. One of them, "The Time of Her Time," caused a furor because of its very graphic erotic passages (culminating in the achievement of the heroine's first orgasm, when she is forcibly buggered by the hero, with both the active and passive parts of this great event treated with tremendous portentousness by Mailer). The other, "Advertisements for Myself on the Way Out,"* fell almost completely flat in spite of the fact that it was accepted for publication by *Partisan Review* and might on that account alone have attracted more attention among the highbrows than it did.

It was shortly after the appearance of "Advertisements," and only a week or so before we first met, that I finished an early draft of my essay on Mailer. Having heard both editors of *Partisan Review,* Philip Rahv and William Phillips, speak disparagingly of his work, I had been surprised by their willingness to run "Advertisements," and assuming that they had changed their minds about him, I thought they would now also be glad to publish my piece. But when I sent it to them some weeks later, they seemed reluctant to do so, and only agreed after chiding me for taking him too seriously. Phillips: "Rahv and I had reservations about Podhoretz's essay, but the situation was complicated by the fact that Rahv didn't like anybody praised too much. . . . We asked for changes, but we always asked for changes; the particular changes were necessary to mute his praise for Norman."†

Up to that point, Mailer had every reason to think of me as a literary and ideological enemy. I had never reviewed or otherwise written about any of his novels before, but I had taken a very hard swipe in print at his

---

*Not to be confused with his autobiographical book *Advertisements for Myself* (1959), in which this "prologue" to the long novel in progress was reprinted.

†Except where otherwise indicated, the quotations in this chapter (including the one from Irving Howe in a footnote above) all come from Peter Manso's *Mailer: His Life and Times* (1985), a compilation of interviews with Mailer and practically everyone who ever knew or had anything to do with him, myself among them.

celebration of the hipster ("The White Negro" of his title) and of what Mailer himself described as the hipster's psychopathic personality. Like many early readers of "The White Negro," I was fascinated by the sheer intellectual and moral brazenness it displayed, but I was also disturbed by it. I knew that Mailer was not connected either personally or in his literary style and manner with writers like Jack Kerouac and Allen Ginsberg, and yet in their "beatniks" and his hipsters I saw the same pernicious cultural and political implications, and I spelled them out in my attack on the Beats in "The Know-Nothing Bohemians."

In the concluding section of that piece, I quoted Mailer's suggestion about the "second revolution" that would move "backward toward being and the secrets of human energy." Without quite saying it in so many words, I in turn suggested that this kind of talk was reminiscent of fascism ("History, after all—and especially the history of modern times—teaches that there is a close connection between ideologies of primitive vitalism and a willingness to look upon cruelty and blood-letting with complacency, if not downright enthusiasm"). I then went on to charge flat out that the spirit of hipsterism was very close to that of the Beat Generation and that it was this same spirit which animated the "young savages in leather jackets" who had been running amok in recent years with their switchblades and zip guns.

What, I wondered, did Mailer think of those "wretched kids" who were responsible for a veritable epidemic of violent juvenile crime (or "delinquency" in the parlance of the social workers of the 1950s) that seemed to emerge out of sheer malignancy disconnected from the usual motives of robbery or revenge? What did he think of the gang that had stoned a nine-year-old boy to death in Central Park in broad daylight a few months earlier or the one that had set fire to an old man drowsing on a bench near the Brooklyn waterfront one summer's day or the one that had pounced on a crippled child and orgiastically stabbed him over and over again even after he was already dead? Was that what he meant by the liberation of instinct and the mysteries of being? There were, I said, grounds for thinking so, as the following passage from "The White Negro" demonstrated:

> It can of course be suggested that it takes little courage for two strong eighteen-year-old hoodlums, let us say, to beat in the brains of a candy-store keeper. . . . Still, courage of a sort is necessary, for one murders not only a weak fifty-year-old man but an institution as well, one violates private property, one enters into a new relation with the

police and introduces a dangerous element into one's life. The hoodlum is therefore daring the unknown.

I called this one of the most "morally gruesome ideas" I had ever come across and a clear indication of where "the ideology of hipsterism" could lead.

In spite of these powerful misgivings, "The White Negro" had aroused my curiosity about Mailer's novels, which I had (youthful highbrow snob that I was) never bothered reading before. Yet even if I had not been propelled by "The White Negro" into reading them now, I would have found it necessary to do so anyway: I had been toying with the idea of undertaking a book about the postwar American novel that would go beyond John W. Aldridge's *After the Lost Generation* of 1951, and in any such book a consideration of Mailer's work would have to be included. And so I went carefully through the three he had so far published and astonished myself by concluding, as I would soon put it in my essay (intended as a chapter of the book I now was more than ever determined to write), that he was "a major novelist in the making."

UNAWARE OF WHAT I had in the works about him, Mailer eyed me with a leer that mixed menace with irony when we encountered each other in Lillian Hellman's living room, and he immediately assumed the boxer's crouch that I was to learn he loved to affect whenever an argument of any kind threatened to erupt. This was the first time he had ever seen me in the flesh, but I had seen him once before, when he was the featured speaker at a rally in support of Henry Wallace's campaign for the presidency that was held on the Columbia campus in 1948; I was then eighteen and he was twenty-five. A newly minted celebrity and still inexperienced as a speaker, he did such a terrible job (as he would so often do even after a thousand performances on public platforms) that if not for the inclusion on the program of the veteran Communist folksinger Pete Seeger, the occasion would have been a total flop. Looking him over now, I noticed that the skinny young man of 1948 had in the ensuing years gained a fair amount of weight, along with a commensurate increase in self-assertiveness. All traces of the nervousness and the diffidence that had tied his tongue at the Wallace rally seemed to have been replaced by an insistent and dominating presence.

If I had not been armed with the secret of my forthcoming article, I would almost certainly have tried to steer clear of Mailer that evening. The reason was that at a very early stage in my career as a critic, and even before a very rough night in the company of Allen Ginsberg and Jack Kerouac, I had already discovered how unpleasant a face-to-face confrontation could be even with the friends of an author whose work I had panned, let alone with the author himself. Back in 1953, for instance, I had written (for *Commentary*) one of the few negative reviews of Saul Bellow's novel *The Adventures of Augie March,* and though I was lucky enough not to meet Bellow himself until many years later (by which point he had still not forgiven me, and never really would), I did have the misfortune shortly after the piece had appeared to run into the poet John Berryman, who was one of Bellow's most ardent boosters. Staggering drunkenly over to me at a big party in the apartment of William Phillips, he snarled, "We'll get you for that review if it takes ten years."*

In the case of Bernard Malamud, with a rather critical review of whose first novel, *The Natural,* I made my debut in *Commentary,* also in 1953, things turned out differently. When I met him a bit later, he was extremely cold, but as soon as he realized that I was a great admirer of his short stories, he relented a bit; and when I subsequently expressed this admiration publicly in an article in *Partisan Review,* our relations became very cordial. (Until, that is, he too turned into an ex-friend when I broke ranks in the late 1960s with the Left. Malamud was no leftist himself and was less interested in ideological politics of any kind than any writer I knew, but he had a keen sense of *literary* politics and must have felt—accurately—that maintaining an association with me after I had become a persona non grata within the literary community would do his career no good.)

Yet even if I had tried to avoid Mailer that night at Lillian's, it would have availed me naught. Having figured out who I was even before we were introduced, he accosted me—skipping the social pleasantries and getting right down to business—with the inevitable charge of having misunderstood and misrepresented him. I have no clear memory of what I said in my own defense, but I do remember cutting the argument short by telling him that I was working on a long article about his whole body of work and that maybe he ought to hold his fire until he had had a chance to read it. He snorted something to the effect that there was no need for him to wait

---

*Not that Bellow himself remained silent. When my editor, Robert Warshow, who disagreed with my judgment of the book, sent a galley of the review to Bellow, he shot back a long letter, with copies to about a dozen people, denouncing "Your young Mr. P," dismissing Warshow's avowal of admiration for the book, and ending with an admonition from Cromwell: "I beseech you in the bowels of Christ, think it possible you may be mistaken."

since he already had a pretty good idea of what a piece by me about him would say. "You wanna bet?" I grinned, resorting to the lingo of the Brooklyn streets from which we both came. "I'll bet you ten bucks."

Now, Brooklyn once was (and possibly still is) a real place with a distinctive culture of its own that left its mark on everyone who grew up there. Indeed, throughout my entire life, whenever I have found myself developing an instant rapport with someone I have just met, it usually turns out that he (or she) also stemmed from Brooklyn. So it was with Mailer. He was from Crown Heights, an economic step up from the Brownsville of my youth but governed by exactly the same street culture, and we had even attended the same high school. Like me, and practically every Brooklyn boy I had ever known, he was direct and pugnacious and immensely preoccupied with the issue of manly courage.

This "macho" obsession in Mailer has often been attributed to the influence of Hemingway, but it was much more the product of the Brooklyn boy's code of honor and his terror of being thought a "sissy." In Mailer's particular case, the "sissy" problem was aggravated by his reputation in adolescence as being coddled and overprotected by his mother. According to one of his childhood friends: "If you didn't play ball, you were done for. . . . [But] Norman wasn't allowed to play because his mother was afraid he'd be hurt." According to another boyhood friend:

> There was this feeling that he was more subject to doing what his parents said. None of us obeyed our parents; he did. . . . He seemed to be on a shorter leash, more obedient, kind of quiet. . . . In those days none of the kids had any manners. Norm had manners, and he was different from the rest of us, who were like hooligans, real terrors. . . . I never saw Norm in a fistfight, even though we'd fight among ourselves.

Mailer would spend the rest of his life overcoming the stigma of this reputation as a "nice Jewish boy" by doing as an adult all the hooliganish things he had failed to do in childhood and adolescence.

Be that as it may, Mailer was certainly recognizable as a Brooklynite at our first meeting that night. Accepting my offer of a bet, and treating it as a poker player's bluff, Mailer proceeded to speculate on the substance of my article, which, as I recall, took the form of a parody of the literary prissiness he associated with highbrow critics like me. But I refused to rise to the bait. "Just wait," I said, and drifted away to talk to someone else as his (second) wife, Adele, a dark and very sexy beauty who had been standing by silently during our conversation, flashed me a look that was challengingly flirtatious with a touch of contempt thrown in. "I'll make you a bet, too," it said. "I'll bet you don't have the guts to take me on." (She was right, as would be definitively confirmed some years later when, after a particularly vicious spat with him, she would all but openly dare me to go to bed with her.)

Notwithstanding the tension between Mailer and me on that first meeting, we actually hit it off well, and when I left Lillian's party that night, I had the feeling that I would be hearing from him again. Sure enough, in the following weeks we saw each other several times, the initiative usually coming from him. Then, when I finally showed him the galleys of my essay, he was so pleased by it and so happy that it would be coming out in *Partisan Review* that it cemented a friendship already growing deep.

What Mailer liked most was arguing with me about ideas, especially his own ideas, which I continued to find wrongheaded and often foolish even after I had come to admire the power and boldness of his writing. To me this Harvard graduate seemed strangely uneducated (what on earth had they taught him there?), sounding like one of those autodidacts who used to roam around Greenwich Village spouting their big and usually conspiratorial theories. It was no secret to him that this was how I felt, but he never seemed bothered by it in the slightest: he just kept trying to persuade me that I was being too "establishment," too rigid and conventional, in my thinking.

Besides, for all my criticisms of his ideas, he knew that I regarded him as a man who had to go his own way and discover things for himself, and that this necessity was one of the engines of his talent as a novelist. I was someone who could learn from books or from the experience and mistakes of others, but not Mailer: if it did not register directly on his own pulses and in his own nervous system, it was not for him. He was absolutely determined to do everything for himself, to invent the world anew, and because I thought this admirable and courageous, I was careful not to judge him too quickly.

On the other hand, I could not abide his antics: the arm-wrestling contests to which he was always challenging everyone around him, the sudden putting on of accents (especially Irish or Southern) for no immediately discernible reason, the readiness to get into fistfights. (A striking instance came at the famous masked ball Truman Capote threw at the Plaza Hotel in New York in 1965 to celebrate the great triumph he was then enjoying over his "nonfiction novel," *In Cold Blood.* I was sitting at a table with Lillian Hellman and McGeorge Bundy, the former Harvard dean who was now Lyndon Johnson's national security adviser, when Mailer, clearly in his cups, came by. I introduced him to Bundy, who was gracious in his patrician way, but within minutes Mailer invited him outside to settle their differences over Vietnam. When Bundy, declining this invitation to a fistfight, told him not to be so childish, Mailer spat back, "I paid you too much respect.")

Yet he was very careful never to lapse into this kind of thing when we were alone together, perhaps because he, nothing if not perceptive, realized that I would never tolerate it and that it might drive me away. Thanks in part to this self-restraint, our friendship was relaxed, not competitive.* We were drinking buddies, we exchanged intimate confidences, and we generally read each other's writings hot off the typewriter, sometimes aloud. Though I was not exactly the "intellectual conscience" to him that Edmund Wilson had been to F. Scott Fitzgerald in the 1920s, Mailer did pay close attention both to what I said in conversation and to my critical writings (the title he wanted me to give my first collection was *Hanging Judge* but I thought it the better part of prudence to use *Doings and Undoings* instead), and in this way I did occasionally serve as a brake on some of his more extreme flights of fancy.

Moreover, as the critic who had in effect brought him into the Family and given him the imprimatur of what the novelist Terry Southern memorably called the "quality lit biz,"† I felt a certain proprietary interest in Mailer—he was my tiger. Not only that, but I believed something larger was riding on his back. I once ventured the proposition that there was a

---

*For whatever it may be worth, Mailer's longtime secretary Ann Barry saw it differently: "There seemed to be a kind of jousting between them, intellectual jousting. Competitive. Little ripples. Posturing, rooster behavior. Not only intellectual, though, but mixed up with the personal. I knew the two Normans were very close, and they would do funny things together. . . . They'd get involved in little projects, and there'd be lots of telephone calls, arguments about someone misunderstanding or not having the right interpretation or not taking the correct line. . . . Podhoretz was considered a heavy hitter in those days, and I got the sense that Norman considered him in no way his inferior. My impression was that their relationship had to do with discussing the nature of what is a Jew, what is a radical, what is a political person, a writer, an artist."

†The cartoonist Jules Feiffer put the same point in somewhat less colorful terms: "Norman Podhoretz . . . played a very important role for Mailer in terms of the literary community; he legitimized him, made him okay to the *Partisan Review* crowd because Mailer was the outlaw. Podhoretz had his credentials as a Trillingite, and then, of course, he wrote about Mailer and was one of the first to do so."

sense in which the validity of a whole phase of American experience—the move in the 1950s away from "alienation" and toward self-acceptance as an American—was felt to hang on the question of whether or not Saul Bellow, who was in effect enacting that development in his work, would turn out to be a great novelist. In this same sense, Mailer was the anti-Bellow, and the viability of the new radicalism, which he was testing out in *his* work, might conversely depend on whether *he* would turn out to be a great novelist.

MAILER'S ANTICS APART, there were two other problems between us. One was his entourage. Like many famous people, Mailer liked to surround himself with a crowd of courtiers, many of whom had nothing to recommend them that I could see other than their worshipful attitude toward him. A few of them I grew to like well enough—Roger Donoghue, an ex-boxer turned beer salesman; Mickey Knox, a blacklisted minor actor; Bernard Farbar, a magazine editor and aspiring writer. But even in the company of these, Mailer was always at his worst, and with the other hangers-on, who came and went and sometimes stayed, he could be positively intolerable—posing, showing off, bumping heads (another of his favorite sports), bullying, ordering about, and, underneath it all, flattering.

The flattering was especially in evidence with women, not only or even primarily as a means of seduction but mainly as a way of romanticizing and thereby inflating the significance of everything that came into his life. He would inform some perfectly ordinary and uninteresting girl that she could have been a great madam running the best whorehouse in town or that she had it in her to be a brilliant dominatrix, and once the initial shock wore off, she would be delighted. Or he might with similar effect tell some equally vacuous young man that he was a general at heart or a bullfighter or that he had the evil makings of a corporate president.

Mailer's wives especially got this kind of treatment. For example, he decided that Adele (who was born in Cuba and had Peruvian roots but came to Brooklyn at a very young age and grew up there) was a primitive Indian with passions to match, and he encouraged—or, rather, forced—her to live up to that image. One of her close friends described it well:

> [Norman] creates a person, and if the person subjects himself, if the person is vulnerable to that, he or she accepts it. . . . The idea that Latin people are any more passionate or sexual than Jews is not so, of

course, but, still, it was like he was doing an investigation of this kind of passion, something that he was going to practice—practice the hundred ways in which he and Adele could have a fight.

I think I must have witnessed at least a dozen or two of these "hundred ways" both with Adele and several of the wives who followed her, and it was very hard to stomach. Almost as hard to take was the spectacle of Mailer surrounded by his mostly raunchy court, and I tried as best I could to avoid seeing him in those circumstances and to meet him alone instead.

The other big problem was drugs. I was a heavy drinker in those days, but I had no use for drugs. I was, quite simply, frightened by hard drugs like heroin, and even marijuana seemed dangerous to me. As an adolescent with an older friend who was connected to the jazz world on Fifty-second Street, I had tried pot and disliked it. I was also put off by the mystique that came to surround it in the 1950s and that Mailer totally bought. In later years, marijuana would become so common that the kind of talk then circulating about its powers to expand consciousness and introduce the mind into new realms of being would seem overheated. So, too, would the solemnity surrounding its use.

Mailer was always trying to turn me on to pot—for my own good, of course—and one night at a party in the Greenwich Village apartment he and Adele had recently rented, I gave in. The scene in retrospect looks even more ridiculous than it struck me at the time, with a dozen or so people sitting in a circle, passing a joint around, and inhaling it by turns with the reverence of devout Catholic communicants taking the Eucharist. In contrast to the loosening of tongues that drinking customarily caused, everyone in this circle communed only with himself and no one spoke (leading me to remark later that if pot were ever legalized it would never replace liquor at weddings and bar mitzvahs). Suddenly, the girlfriend of a well-known actor (who happened to be starring around that time in a play by Jack Gelber celebrating the glories of heroin) started to throw up all over the place. Yet not even this party-pooping accident disrupted the religious tone of the gathering. Everyone continued to sit in place privately listening—or maybe just pretending to listen—to the music of the spheres through the invisible headphones with which a puff or two had miraculously equipped them. As for me, there was no music of the spheres. All I got was a slight buzz in the head and an unpleasant feeling in the stomach. The next day Mailer scolded me for resisting and thereby allowing the "establishment" side of my character to beat down the radical in me. Very likely he was right. Subsequently, I made two other conscientious but equally unsuccessful attempts to overcome my resistance, and that was that for marijuana and me.

The only other experiment I would try with drugs was on Fire Island in the 1960s, when one of Mailer's courtiers (he himself was not present) persuaded me to sniff an amphetamine capsule. The buzz in my head this time was not at all slight, and the dizziness it brought with it did not live up to its advance billing as an extraordinarily pleasant sensation. I seem to remember Mailer teasing me when I told him about this, though he was not a great partisan of amphetamines or hard drugs in general. Down deep I think he was almost as afraid of them as I was. He gave me the impression that he felt obligated to try peyote and perhaps acid, but so far as I know he never used heroin or cocaine.

THEN THERE WAS SEX. If I was put off by Mailer's constant proselytizing for marijuana, I had an entirely different reaction to his even more obsessive preoccupation with sex. Here there was a complication. On the one hand, I thought Mailer made far too much of sex in his writing. By no means did I think sex was unimportant; on the contrary, in some ways I was just as obsessed with it as he was. But not as an *issue*. There was a part of me that resonated to the crack made by a critic (I believe it was Henri Peyre) that French literature was entirely devoted to something that ought to interest a serious person only ten minutes a week. If this criticism could be leveled at any American writer, it was Mailer (though he would later get a lot of competition from Philip Roth and John Updike). Much as I admired the virtuosic workings of his prose, and much as I was fascinated by the wildly unconventional workings of his mind, I was embarrassed on his behalf by the apocalyptic significance he attributed to sex in general and to kinky or perverted sex in particular. It struck me as callow of him to treat oral sex as such a big deal in *The Deer Park* or to attribute a veritably metaphysical significance to the act of heterosexual anal penetration in "The Time of Her Time."

All this on the one hand. On the other hand, if he wrote and even talked like someone of such limited sexual experience that he lacked all perspective on it, he was certainly creating a false impression so far as the experience itself was concerned. By which I mean simply that he was wildly promiscuous, both in and between marriages (of which he was to have six). One might describe him as a pioneer of the sexual revolution to come, except for the fact that, unlike the counterculture radicals of the 1960s to whom casual sex was the norm, he did not take sex in action any more lightly than he did on paper. No matter how many women he might bed, he rarely went in for one-night stands or anonymous couplings. When Mailer slept with a girl, she was probably in for more than a physical encounter. Before being sent on her way, she could expect a lecture, or a scolding, or a dose of advice on how to become better than she thought she was; and, as often as not, he would arrange to see her again, and then again, and then again. Combining the skill of a professional juggler with the talents of a White House scheduler, he could keep a number of affairs going simultaneously for years, some of them even overlapping with his successive marriages. Where he found the energy and the time for all this while still turning out many pages a day always baffled me. Evidently, living that way fed rather than drained him.

Although I disdained his ideas about sex, I could not help envying his practice of it. Here, too, there was a complication. For while I was just as much "a nice Jewish boy from Brooklyn" as Mailer was, and an even more serious student in school, I also had a secret double life (secret from my parents, that is) as a bad street kid. I liked hanging around with the boys who were, usually with good reason, regarded as bums by the adults in the neighborhood; I frequented poolrooms where older bums, hustlers, and petty criminals held court; I got into fistfights (though never willingly, and only when my terror of being considered chicken overrode my fear of getting beaten up); and I gambled, betting what little money I had on sports events and often shooting craps on street corners, which occasionally led to a brush with the cops. But what was most important in this context was that I had also been much more sexually precocious than Mailer, having started earlier and having enjoyed an amount of success with girls that was unusual for those days, when "getting laid" as an adolescent really was the big deal Mailer would make of it as an adult (when it no longer was).

I had, however, said goodbye to all that by the time I first met him. At the age of (nearly) twenty-eight, I had been married only for about a year, and I believed strongly in marital fidelity. This belief derived not only from high-minded moral ideas about marriage but also from an ideology rooted in an earlier stage of the sexual revolution of the twentieth century. According to this doctrine, sex was good and also necessary to the health of men and women alike, but promiscuity was not the way to achieve true sexual fulfillment. To be promiscuous was to be stuck in an "infantile" or "immature" stage of development, deprived of the depths of erotic experience that could only be plumbed by marital or monogamous sex.

This was not, as people like the Beats and Mailer himself would later assume, the creed of the "square": it was the reflection of a highly sophisticated sense of life preached in various modalities by thinkers and writers from Sigmund Freud to D. H. Lawrence. Admittedly, it involved its own type of solemnity, its own exaggerations, and its own failures of perspective in relating sex to the rest of life. But those of us who held to it prided ourselves on being more serious about what Lawrence had called "the hard business of human relationships." We were convinced that our kind of sex was more profound and even more exciting (leading, not to put too fine a point on it, to better orgasms) than the superficial bohemian variety that Lawrence had also denounced as "sex in the head."

But of course I was young and the blood was hot and the temptations ever present. Resisting them was at least as hard as the "hard business" of building a good and lasting marriage, and my friendship with Mailer made it even harder. He subverted me by explaining that his own marriage to Adele had "in a funny way" (one of his favorite locutions) been strengthened, not weakened, by his infidelities, allowing him to rid himself of the resentment that he would otherwise have felt at being stifled and imprisoned by her. This was no sophistical trick: Mailer was very fond of my wife, he had great respect for her, and he had no wish to damage our marriage. Nevertheless, he thought that fidelity was yet another element of the "establishment" side of my character that would have to be overcome before I could realize my ambition for greatness, which, as I often told him, was just as burning as his.

I would eventually learn that I was wrong about this: my ambition was not remotely a match for his. But Mailer's ambition for greatness, and the naked frankness with which he expressed and pursued it without worrying about looking bad or actually making a fool of himself, was one of the main sources of my attraction to him. In my essay on him, I had quoted a statement he had made to an interviewer about his own intention to explore, as he put it,

the possibility that the novel, along with many other art forms, may be growing into something larger rather than something smaller, and the sickness of our times for me has been just this damn thing that everything has been getting smaller and smaller and less and less important. . . . We're all getting so mean and small and petty and ridiculous, and we all live under the threat of extermination.

AT THIS DISTANCE it is difficult for me to recapture the thrill I felt at the prospect that the arts and the life they reflected would grow "larger," and the conviction I developed that the road to this happy eventuality could be opened up only by breaking through the constrictions and the limits defined by traditional moral and cultural categories. At the same time, I was convinced that this could only be done by working one's way *through* those categories: merely dismissing them contemptuously, as the intellectually philistine Beat writers were doing, could lead into nothing but sterility and nihilism. If a new moral and cultural radicalism was to be born, it would have to be generated in the world of theory by the likes of Norman O. Brown. In his book *Life Against Death* (whose fame I had helped to spread by introducing it to Lionel Trilling), Brown issued a powerful challenge to Freud's doctrine that human possibilities were inherently and insurmountably limited. But he did so not by arguing, as earlier critics like Karen Horney and Erich Fromm had done, that the master's theories had been valid only, or mainly, for the particular kind of society in which he himself had lived. Disdaining the cheap relativism of such tactics, Brown set out to show that Freud's pessimistic sense of human possibility did not necessarily follow from his analysis of human nature, an analysis Brown accepted as sound in all essential respects. The brilliance of *Life Against Death* lay in the amazingly convincing case Brown was able to build for the consistency of that analysis with his own vision of a life of "polymorphous perversity," a life of play and of complete instinctual and sexual freedom.

Brown's vision, of course, jibed perfectly with Mailer's much less rigorous notion about the implications of the hipster's pursuit of immediate gratification, and it scared me just as much. Even so, it gave a highly respectable theoretical justification to the sexual restlessness I could not help feeling and that Mailer was bent—again for my own good!—on encouraging me to act upon. He was especially keen on getting me to participate in an orgy (this exotic species of sexual experience having become a central element of his new philosophy), and I finally did, though without his help or knowledge.

Under the rationalization that going to an orgy was not, strictly speaking, a form of infidelity, I got entrée into one that consisted entirely of people I had never met before. But I was simply not up to it, and it turned out to be a total and humiliating disaster for me. Yet instead of feeling that Mailer had misled me, I decided that I was simply not good enough to break through my own sorry limitations. Naturally, I told him about it, and he shook his head in amazement. That was not, he said, what he had been talking about. What I had gone to was "a concentration-camp orgy," and I was lucky to have gotten out of there alive.

Some weeks later he invited me to spend an evening with him and one of his longtime girlfriends, who lived in another city and was in town for a few days. She turned out to be a beautiful woman who had actually read and liked my stuff, and the three of us had a very good time together over dinner in a restaurant. Afterward, we repaired to her hotel room for a nightcap. The atmosphere was sexually charged, and I began wondering, with a mouth getting dry, what Mailer was up to when he suddenly excused himself and went into the bathroom. A few minutes later he returned stark naked and directed a very serious look straight into the eyes of his girlfriend. It was as if he had decided to make up for having inadvertently misled me by demonstrating what a proper orgy was like. But his girlfriend, totally unprepared for this turn of events, was not having any of it, and she laughed him off with a witty apology to me.

I must admit that I was more disappointed than relieved. But this was not yet the end of the story. About ten years later, she showed up in New York again, and this time the three of us had lunch rather than dinner together. When it was over, she shooed away Mailer (who took this with so little complaint that I suspected it had been prearranged) and asked me to come up to her hotel room for a drink (by which she of course meant, in the parlance of the period, a "matinée"). Alas, her generous effort to make up for having disappointed me the first time around had come too late, and now it was my turn to say no. Not, God knows, in retaliation but because I had by the early 1970s decided that the radical ideas in the sexual realm with which I had been playing around were no less pernicious than their counterparts in the world of politics, and I had now returned for good to my old set of beliefs in marital fidelity and everything that went with it.

BUT IT WAS NOT ONLY over drugs and his ideas about sex that Mailer and I had our differences and difficulties. There was also the issue of loyalty. As a "foul-weather friend," I stood up for him when, in the course of a violent fight with Adele toward the end of a big party at which Allen Ginsberg had yelled at me and that I had already left a few hours before, he stabbed her with a penknife, coming within an inch of killing her. They were then living on West Ninety-fourth Street, and I was just a dozen blocks away in a second-floor apartment that faced onto West 106th Street. After the stabbing, Mailer beat it out of his house and rushed up to mine. It was about 4 A.M. when he stood there under our windows calling out to me, but I was so fast asleep that I never heard him. He then left, and waited until later in the day to telephone and ask me to meet him downtown in a coffee shop near the hospital to which Adele had been taken. Still hiding from the police, he refused to tell me exactly what had happened: if he did, I might have to lie and would then get into trouble myself. But what he mainly wanted was to extract a promise from me that I would do everything in my power to keep them from committing him to an asylum. He would rather go to jail than be institutionalized, he said, because if he were deemed insane his work would never be taken seriously again.

My impression of Mailer's mental condition differed from that of some of our mutual friends, including Diana Trilling, who thought he "needed psychiatric help," and Lillian Hellman, who (at least according to Diana) thought that it was now unsafe to be alone with him.* Unlike them, I did not believe that he was clinically insane, and my opinion was shared by Lionel Trilling, who, Diana later reported, "insisted that it wasn't a clinical situation but a conscious bad act; . . . [that] Norman was testing the limits of evil in himself, that his stabbing of Adele was, so to speak, a Dostoevskian ploy on Norman's part, to see how far he could go." I also agreed with Mailer that institutionalization would make it easier for people to take his work less seriously. And since, finally, I felt that he should be allowed the right to choose jail over an asylum, and that this acceptance of responsibility was more morally honorable than pleading insanity, I promised to help as much as I could.

There was a strategy session by the Mailer family that Sunday evening at which I was among the few outsiders and where I made the case Mailer had persuaded me to make. Then I met him again the next day in the same downtown coffee shop. There he asked me to accompany him to the hospital, where, after visiting Adele, he would surrender to the police. I, too, went in to see Adele, who, although lying there frightened and crying, told me that she had decided not to press charges. Then the police who had

---

*Lillian told me, and also Diana, that Mailer had once tried to break down her bedroom door, which may account for her response to the stabbing. But whether this event, if it actually occurred, took place before the stabbing or after, I cannot recall.

been keeping watch over her room arrested him. Probably because he was a celebrity, they were very polite and even allowed me to go along with them all to the station house on 100th Street, where he was booked.*

They then sent him to Bellevue for psychiatric observation, and eventually a deal was struck, whose terms I never learned, that set him free after a couple of weeks. The day he was released he came to our house for lunch. As my wife would later describe the scene:

> He was absolutely himself, very calm, and definitely not tranquilized. . . . Norman had always had a "court," and when he got out [of Bellevue] he turned up with the doctor who'd been examining him. . . . The doctor had been converted into another courtier.

I have often asked myself whether I did the right thing in acceding to Mailer's request; in a similar situation today, I would almost certainly push for psychiatric help. But in the early 1960s, when electroshock therapy (of which I had a great horror) was the main treatment used, I feared for the effects on Mailer's mind. I was well aware of the streak of craziness in him, but it did not seem to go very deep and for the most part it was under control. I had noticed that Adele had been ragging him all night and that the mood between them was getting very ugly—so much so that the novelist Barbara Probst Solomon, another mutual friend who was there, recalls my telling her that I "didn't like the look of things." Her recollection was accurate. Having been witness to more than my share of nasty scenes between Mailer and Adele, I decided to leave before another one exploded. In any event, my conviction that he was not clinically insane was reinforced by the very fact that he did not blame her for provoking him into the stabbing, that he took responsibility for it, and that he was ready to go to jail. Which was why I felt so uneasy over his escape from punishment and over my secret fear that he might have dishonored himself by allowing money to change hands to get him off. Still, there was no evidence whatever for this suspicion, and I bent over backward in trying to dismiss it as unworthy.

---

*Mailer was very good with children (he had three of his own then and would eventually have another six), and mine, who adored him, steadfastly refused to believe that he had stabbed Adele. One of my daughters, then about ten, assured me that she knew who had really done it. "Who?" I asked. "Leonard Lyons," she answered, referring to the gossip columnist of the *New York Post* who had been writing of nothing else for days now. "Leonard Lyons?! What on earth makes you think that?" "Well," she said, "if he didn't do it, how come he knows so much about it?"

Over the next few months I consistently defended Mailer against most of my Family friends, who did not need him to be institutionalized in order to use the stabbing as a good reason for persisting in their refusal to take his work seriously.

Our friendship accordingly deepened and we saw each other even more often than before. By now I had become the editor of *Commentary*, and I was working very hard in trying to drag the magazine out of the cold-war liberalism in which it had been stuck under Elliot Cohen and to pull it in the leftward direction I myself had already been moving as a critic for the past three years or so.

By mutual agreement, Mailer did not at first figure in this project. For one thing, we both recognized that he was too wild for a magazine sponsored by the most establishmentarian of all Jewish organizations, the American Jewish Committee. As the editor, I enjoyed complete independence, and I was making such full use of it in articles about both foreign and domestic policy that I was already being subjected by the Trillings and other Family friends to accusations of having become too soft on Communism and too hard on America. But I was simultaneously being careful not to jeopardize the institution for which I was now responsible or my position in it by moving too far too fast in a culturally radical direction. This meant, at a minimum, no four-letter words or overly explicit sexual material whether in stories or in essays.

Confirmation that such prudence was necessary came when, even after I had already been running *Commentary* for nearly five years and after it had been well established as a main intellectual center of the new radicalism, I published an article by the psychoanalyst Leslie H. Farber called "'I'm Sorry, Dear.'" This was perhaps the first serious critique of the sexologists Masters and Johnson, and the moral assumptions behind it were actually quite traditional. Yet because it contained a frank discussion of the female orgasm and a description of a film Masters and Johnson had made in which women were shown masturbating, it caused a great deal of trouble for me with the AJC. One prominent member of my board resigned in protest, and a campaign was launched to get me fired.

But if Mailer at first agreed that it was advisable for him to stay out of *Commentary*, he soon began growing a little resentful about it, as I could tell from the remarks he kept making about how tame the magazine was. Then, all of a sudden, he came to me with a proposal. In Martin Buber's *Tales of the Hasidim*, he had decided that there was, as he would soon write, something in Judaism that called out to him—"a rudimentary sense of clan across the centuries." Mailer had grown up in a "modestly Orthodox, then Conservative" family, had gone to a Hebrew school, and had "passed through the existential rite of a bar mitzvah." But none of it had stuck. "I would never say I was not a Jew, but I looked to take no strength from the fact. . . . I left what part of me belonged to Brooklyn and the Jews on the streets of Crown Heights."

Indeed he had. In wiping out every trace in himself of the "nice Jewish boy from Brooklyn," he had done such a good job on the Jewish part that not even I to whom the "Jidas touch" had once been attributed ("Everything you touch turns to Jewish") could detect any lingering odor of it in his personality or his behavior. This man, who saw himself as a fearless spiritual adventurer, was apparently fearful of exploring his own spiritual roots, preferring instead the pretense of being an "existential hero" with no ties to the past.*

But now, perhaps proving that I really did have the Jidas touch, Mailer, of all people, came up with a plan to write a monthly column in which he would reprint stories from Buber and then provide his own personal commentaries on them. If this was his way of overcoming my increasingly irksome resistance to his appearance in *Commentary*, it was certainly very cunning. What idea could be more suitable than this for *Commentary*, one of whose purposes from the very beginning had been to arouse the interest of disaffected Jewish writers and intellectuals in their own origins? And what could be more quintessentially Jewish than a commentary appended to a text?

Nevertheless, I had grave doubts about whether I wanted such a column. *Commentary* was, after all, a magazine which prided itself on the maintenance of serious intellectual and scholarly standards, and Mailer's ignorance of the material he proposed to elucidate was vast. How could I, the editor of a magazine in whose pages Buber himself and Gershom Scholem, the greatest living scholarly authority on Hasidism, sometimes held forth on the subject, allow what they would rightly have called a total *am-haaretz* (illiterate ignoramus) to poach on their territory?

As we sat drinking together in a bar, I tried saying these things tactfully to Mailer, but it was no soap. For the first time in our relationship, he showed real anger toward me, calling me a "delicate bureaucrat," denouncing my disloyalty, and attributing it to the establishmentarian timidity that

---

*I suspected then, and I am still inclined to think, that this fear had much to do with Mailer's failure to realize his full potential as a novelist.

would in the end do me in altogether as a writer. With these charges, to which I was very sensitive, he beat me down (which was what I thought he really wanted to do even more than he wanted to write the column). But I salvaged what self-respect I could by insisting successfully against his initially furious refusal that it be a bimonthly feature instead of appearing every single month.

As part of his preparation for launching the column, he wanted to see some Hasidim in the flesh. He therefore asked me to take him to the Yom Kippur eve service at the synagogue of the Lubavitch sect, which, as it happened, was located in Crown Heights, right around the corner from where he himself had grown up. I was a little edgy about this, knowing that something very unpleasant might occur if Mailer failed to behave himself. So before yielding to his request, I made him promise that he would get himself a hat, put on a proper suit, remove any jingling coins or keys from his pockets, and carefully avoid doing anything that might offend the congregation. With a docility unusual for him, he accepted these conditions, and sure enough he arrived at the appointed time (well before sundown, so as not to risk being caught violating the prohibition against travel on the holy day) with a brand-new fedora on his head and all dressed up in a blue suit and white shirt and tie.

The synagogue was located in the basement of the building that served as the headquarters of the Lubavitch movement, and (in the manner of many Orthodox *shtiblach,* or small houses of prayer) it was very unprepossessing. The room was bare except for very heavy wooden benches, and since the holiday had not yet begun, young *yeshiva* students were standing around smoking and dropping their cigarette butts on the floor. To my great relief, nobody paid much attention to us when we came in (the Lubavitcher, unlike other Hasidic sects, were accustomed to being visited by curious fallen-away Jews), and soon the room grew as crowded as the subway at rush hour. Then, without any advance warning, someone shouted in Yiddish that the rebbe was coming, and miraculously, like the Red Sea for the Israelites fleeing from Egypt, the crowd immediately parted and the two of us were nearly decapitated as the benches were hoisted up with unbelievable swiftness to make a path for the rebbe through the mob.* The services then started without any further ado, but as soon as the opening prayer of Kol Nidre was over, Mailer whispered that he had seen

---

*This was the same Menachem Mendel Schneerson who many of his followers would come to believe was the Messiah.

enough, and asked if we could leave. Once outside, he pronounced himself delighted by how "mean and tough" the Hasidim were. Their attitude, he said (with considerable shrewdness), was "Out of my way, motherfucker," and he was all for it.

"Responses & Reactions," as we called the column, turned out to be something of an anticlimax, neither creating great curiosity nor provoking a scandal. After six installments, Mailer lost interest, and the column was quietly dropped. Yet even though he had won his point against me, the whole episode left a bad taste in both our mouths—in mine because I had given in to his bullying, in his because I had been less than fully loyal to him.

SOON ENOUGH, HOWEVER, I was to commit what was in Mailer's eyes a much more serious act of disloyalty, and one for which he never ever forgave me. Mailer had become obsessed with the Kennedys, and had written a couple of famous pieces for *Esquire* about them. The first, "Superman Comes to the Supermarket," had pleased John F. Kennedy by representing him as a true existential hero (the greatest accolade Mailer could bestow on anyone). But the second, "An Evening with Jackie Kennedy," had offended her deeply (not that that was so hard to do). This bothered Mailer, who wanted very much to be inside the circles of power (though always on his own terms), and I had the impression that he was on the lookout for some way to square things with her.

Some months after the assassination of her husband, Jackie moved to New York, and one Sunday afternoon, as I was sitting around my apartment not doing much of anything, an unexpected call came. It was from my friend Richard Goodwin, who had worked in various capacities for President Kennedy and had somehow managed the trick of staying on in the White House with Lyndon Johnson without being branded as a traitor by the Kennedys (in whose government-in-exile he figured as a leading courtier). Goodwin said that he was in town with someone who wanted to meet me, and asked if they could drop by for a drink. Within minutes, he showed up at my door with a jeans-clad Jackie Kennedy in tow.

She and I had never met before, but we seemed to strike an instant rapport, and at her initiative I soon began seeing her on a fairly regular basis. We often had tea alone together in her apartment on Fifth Avenue, where I would give her the lowdown on the literary world and the New York intellectual community—who was good, who was overrated, who was amusing, who was really brilliant—and she would reciprocate with the dirt about

Washington society. She was not in Mary McCarthy's league as a bitchy gossip (who was?), but she did very well in her own seemingly soft style. I enjoyed these exchanges, and she (an extremely good listener) seemed to get a kick out of them, too.

After a while, she invited me (along with my wife, whom she generally treated as an invisible presence) to a few of the dinner parties she had started to give. At the first of these which my wife and I attended, I arrived from the West Side in what Jackie considered improper attire, and as she ran her big eyes up and down from my head to my toes, she smiled sweetly and said, "Oh, so you scooted across the park in your little brown suit and your big brown shoes." To which the Brooklyn boy still alive in me replied, "Fuck you, Jackie." She liked that so much that I realized how tired she was of the sycophancy with which everyone treated her and how hungry she had become for people who would stand up to her even though she was the most famous and admired woman in the world. And so we became even faster friends than we already were.

Jackie's dinner parties were always star studded, but they rarely included literary types. Obviously, almost anyone she wished to summon was certain to accept, and yet she was oddly reluctant to invite people she had not already met. The upshot was that she asked Dick Goodwin to ask me to arrange a party in my apartment at which I would introduce her to some of the writers and literary intellectuals I had been telling her about. But Jackie herself then told me that I was not to include Norman Mailer, at whom she was still angry for the article he had done about her. If, however, I knew William Styron, whose novels she admired and whom she had already met, it would be nice to see him again. And so I invited the Styrons, along with about a dozen equally eminent writers whom she had never encountered before.

Nearly twenty years later—in accounting for having joined the general assault that had been launched against *Making It* when he wrote a review article about it for *Partisan Review* after assuring me in private that he had liked the book very much—Mailer would refer back to his "bruised feelings" at not having been invited to this party:

Norman P. . . . had had these high hopes that my review was going to turn the day, and so it was a bitter disappointment for him, maybe even crueler than all the others. From his point of view I had betrayed him. And from my own point of view I did betray him to a degree. Yet I also felt, This is fair—he betrayed me with the Jackie Kennedy party. Because not only had he not invited me, he invited Bill Styron, who was then my dire rival. Betraying Podhoretz, therefore, wasn't the world's worst thing to me. Maybe it was my way of saying, "Fuck you back." . . . Deep in me I could've been saying, "All right, now we get you for that Jackie Kennedy party. . . ." So it could have been a double cross.

No foul-weather friend, he, that was for sure.*

Still, neither of us was ready or willing to allow his betrayal of me to cause a complete rupture between us. We got together and talked. I was more hurt and bewildered than angry—my own "bruised feelings" easily being a match for the ones he had suffered over the party—and he was more uncomfortable than I had ever seen him before. He simply claimed that he had reread the book, changed his mind about it, and then had to say what he really thought. He would now have to live with the consequences, though he slyly hinted that he had written the piece in the hope of showing me how and why I had "injured a promising book."

Among the consequences he would have to live with was a new idea about him that began taking shape in my head. We were now in a period when radicalism was coming to enjoy even deeper influence and greater power than it had achieved at its most recent high point in the 1930s, and under these circumstances Mailer once again came into his own. Indeed, he was a much bigger figure at that point than he had been as the wunderkind author of *The Naked and the Dead*. Most of the novelists of his own generation thought of him as (in his own parlance) the one to beat, and almost all the younger writers looked up to him as the Master. Occasionally his bad-boy antics would still get him into trouble, as when the curtain was rung down on him at the Ninety-second Street Y when he insisted on using obscene language during a reading, or when he had another, though minor, brush with the police (in Provincetown, where he owned a summer home). But the times they were a-changing, and the more outrageously Mailer behaved, the more admiration he brought upon himself from the spreading radical culture of the 1960s.

His writing, too, was more and more admired. In 1968, inspired perhaps by *In Cold Blood*, Mailer produced *The Armies of the Night*, which he subtitled (presumably to distinguish it from Capote's "nonfiction novel")

---

*Incidentally, Jackie Kennedy was also so offended by *Making It* that she became an ex-friend herself, and later she and Mailer had some sort of reconciliation.

"History as a Novel—The Novel as History." *The Armies of the Night* was about an antiwar demonstration in which he had participated, and it won both the Pulitzer Prize and the National Book Award.

It also won my admiration, even though I had already begun the process of breaking ranks with the political perspective from which it was written. Most of it was originally published in *Harper's,* which could pay him far more than I could, but he let me have a section for *Commentary* anyway. I considered the whole book a dazzling literary performance, his best work in any genre since *Advertisements for Myself,* which I had called "one of the great confessional autobiographies of our time." (Since this extravagant judgment appeared in *Making It,* Mailer's attack on that book showed either that he was so incorruptible that not even so gratifying an estimate could buy him off or that his lust for revenge—"a dish," as he had once said, "best eaten cold"—was greater than his appetite for praise. Uncharitably, I incline toward the latter explanation.)

But if I admired *The Armies of the Night,* the fiction Mailer was turning out gave less and less warrant to my old estimate of him as "a major novelist in the making." As far back as 1964, when I was still counting on him to fulfill his early promise, I had been very disappointed in *An American Dream,* and though *Why Are We in Vietnam?* (which came out three years later and was actually about hunting in Alaska and had nothing to do directly with Vietnam) was filled with extraordinarily evocative passages of description, I was disappointed in it as well. Then in 1983, long after it was all over between us, came *Tough Guys Don't Dance,* a mystery set in Provincetown which struck me as positively silly. So, in that same year, did his hugely ambitious novel about ancient Egypt *(Ancient Evenings),* into which he poured all his obsessions about buggery. This was followed in 1991 by the equally ambitious but perhaps even sillier *Harlot's Ghost,* the novel in which all his wildly romantic paranoia about the CIA was given full play. Both of these books had their wonderful moments, and they both testified to the aging Mailer's continued possession of large reservoirs of creative energy and talent. But so foolish were the ideas behind them that I simply could not take them seriously. And so embarrassed was I by the whole concept of *The Gospel According to the Son* (1997), in which he rewrote the New Testament versions as he imagined Jesus would have told the story, that I could not bring myself even to read it.

The steady stream of nonfictional works that were interspersed between these novels also bore witness to the tremendous stores of literary energy that Mailer still had in reserve. Yet none that followed *The Armies of the*

Night lived up to the literary standard of that book. *Miami and the Siege of Chicago* and *St. George and the Godfather* (about the presidential nominating conventions of 1968 and 1972) were well enough written, but they left no lasting impression. As for *A Fire on the Moon* (1970), about the astronauts, it was one of the few actually boring books Mailer ever wrote, and *The Prisoner of Sex* (1971) seemed to me a craven effort to appease the ever more powerful women's movement, whose sensibilities he had offended in so many of his earlier pronouncements about sex, while simultaneously pretending to go against it. He redeemed himself somewhat in 1979 with *The Executioner's Song,* his much-acclaimed nonfiction novel about the murderer Gary Gilmore (for which he won yet another Pulitzer Prize), but I thought it still represented a severe falling-off from *The Armies of the Night.*

The same silliness that wrecked most of Mailer's later novels also showed up in much of his nonfiction of the 1970s and 1980s. In his book on Marilyn Monroe, for example, he uninhibitedly indulged his inveterate weakness for confusing great success or power with intrinsic merit, and in the one he did on the "art" of graffiti he reverted to his old confusion between criminality and creativity.* By the mid-1990s my expectations of getting anything worthwhile out of him had grown so weak I could no more bring myself to read the nonfiction books he produced on Picasso and Lee Harvey Oswald in 1996 than I could bear even to look at his version of the Gospel story, which was published about a year later.

I HAVE SEARCHED my soul to find out whether these adverse reactions, which presented themselves to me as disinterested aesthetic judgments, were in reality driven primarily by ideological considerations. Was I, that is, concluding that Mailer had not turned out to be a major novelist only because I had simultaneously been losing my faith in the cultural revolution whose viability I had once thought his work was supposed to confirm? While I cannot dismiss the possibility out of hand, neither can I dismiss the converse possibility: namely, that the weaknesses of his later books actually should be placed in evidence—the special kind of evidence that literature, properly understood and interpreted, provides—against the view of life out of which they emerged and were written to serve.

But whatever may be the case about that issue, I am reasonably sure, after conscientiously probing the region surrounding the lowest depths of

---

*He then acted out the same confusion more dangerously by helping to free a convict writer named Jack Henry Abbott who, no sooner out of jail, went on to commit a murder.

critical integrity, that not even a minor contribution has been made to my harsh judgment of his later work by a lingering resentment over his article on *Making It*. Nor, to give credit where it is richly due, did Mailer ever stoop to making such an accusation against me. Indeed, though our trust in each other would never quite recover from the blows it had suffered from *Making It*, our friendship remained surprisingly strong for nearly another ten years.

Not, to be sure, as strong as it had been before, when, among many other personal involvements, I had even seen him through the next two wives he married after he and Adele finally divorced. First came Lady Jeanne Campbell, the granddaughter of the great British newspaper publisher Lord Beaverbrook and the daughter of the Duke of Argyle. As if her lineage were not enough to arouse the sexual conquistador in Mailer, the fact that in winning her he would be appropriating the former mistress of the head of Time, Inc., himself, Henry Luce, made her completely irresistible (Allen Ginsberg had written, "I'm obsessed with *Time* magazine," but in this he had nothing on Mailer, who, if anything, was even more impressed with its power). Unlike Adele before the stabbing, Jeanne was afraid of Mailer: once in our apartment, when he started to snarl at her, she ran out of the living room, hid under the covers of our bed, and pleaded with us to let her spend the night there.

The marriage to Jeanne lasted just long enough to produce a child, and then came Beverly. Like Adele (but unlike Jeanne, whose attraction lay more in her lineage than in her looks), Beverly was a great beauty, though blond and Southern rather than dark and "Spanish." I was even still around when, after splitting up with Beverly, he married one of his girlfriends, Carole Stevens, to legitimize their child and immediately divorced her to marry Norris Church (to whom, as of 1998, he was still married after about twenty years). By the time Norris entered the picture, however, Mailer and I had already been drifting farther and farther apart. There were three reasons.

First of all, I could never do with Mailer what I had done with Lillian Hellman, whose writings I had once pretended to like in order to keep our friendship going. He continued to care about my opinion of his work, he insisted that I be candid about it, and he took my criticisms with extraordinarily good grace (if not always in good temper). He also insisted on dragging me to see the shooting of the incredibly amateurish movies he began making in the late 1960s, and he never really tried to bully me into saying anything good about them. He was also considerate and tactful enough not to pressure me into supporting him when he ran quixotically for mayor of New York on a platform that included, among other original ideas, a proposal that all disputes between juvenile delinquents be settled by jousting tournaments in Central Park. For all that, however, not even Mailer was entirely exempt from the law that genuine friendship (or perhaps any kind of friendship at all) is impossible with a writer whose work one does not admire. He behaved very well on this particular score, but the resentment inevitably built up in him even as I, feeling that I had fallen into a false position in my relations with him, grew more and more uncomfortable in his company.

Secondly, my patience with his marital storms had been wearing thinner and thinner. Unlike Jeanne, Beverly was not in the least afraid of Mailer: she taunted him constantly and stood up to him when they fought. Several of these fights were staged in my presence, and they were at least as ugly as the ones I had witnessed with Adele (though, thankfully, they never came to real violence). The worst, featuring Beverly seizing a dish of mushrooms Mailer had cooked and hurling it at him while screaming that he was "evil," erupted during a weekend my wife and I were spending with them in Provincetown. When we left, I told her that I had just about had it with Mailer and his wives.

Then, of course, there was politics. At first Mailer could hardly believe that I was serious when I began showing signs of breaking with the orthodoxies of the Left. How could I possibly mean it when I said that America, far from being the "totalitarian" country he had always believed it to be (and more so than ever since the Vietnam War), was the only hope of defeating the real totalitarianism that was being spread by the power and influence of the Soviet Union? How could I possibly mean it when I said that, far from being in the grip of the "military-industrial complex" he so hated and feared, we were in fact falling dangerously behind in our military strength and needed an arms buildup to counter Soviet power? Mailer loved to argue and had never in all the years I had known him avoided a political fight with me. Yet once, in the 1970s while having dinner in my apartment, he got so upset by my incomprehensible new ideas about politics that he announced he was unable to continue the discussion and actually stood up and left the room so that he could pull himself together before going on. Even then, when he returned, he suggested that we change the subject.

Ultimately, however (as with Diana Trilling), it was *Breaking Ranks* that put paid to our twenty years of friendship. By coincidence, I finished writing that book just as Mailer was also finishing *The Executioner's Song,* and he invited us to dinner with Norris for a kind of celebration in his house in Brooklyn Heights. He told me that he thought I would like *The Executioner's Song,* and I told him that he probably would dislike what I had written about him in *Breaking Ranks.* "Well," he said, "you owe me one," and I laughed and replied, "Yes, I do, but we'll see if you still feel that way when you've read the book." It was, my wife remarked to me afterward, a very pleasant evening, and I agreed—adding, however, that Mailer would never forgive me for *Breaking Ranks.*

In telling the story there of how I came to break with the Left, I had to devote a certain amount of space to the reception of *Making It,* which had been a turning point in my relation to the radicalism of the 1960s. Obviously, the part Mailer had played was an important element in this account, and I pulled no punches in laying out the facts and analyzing them. I described carrying the galleys to Provincetown because, having heard so much about the scandal the book had already caused, he was eager to see for himself what the fuss was all about. I then related that when he had read through the galleys, he told me how good a book it was and how unfair and even incomprehensible he found the malicious talk about it which had been going the rounds. I went on to summarize the article he later produced in which the kindest thing he could bring himself to say about *Making It* was that it was "a not altogether compelling memoir" and in which he now blamed the ferocity of the response to it on its own faults and failures. And, finally, I recounted the conversation we had in which his only explanation for what I had every reason to regard as a betrayal by my "old dear great and good friend," as he described himself in the piece, was that he had read the book again and simply changed his mind.

I had eventually come up with a different explanation and I now set it forth in *Breaking Ranks.* I said that the first time Mailer read the book, he had not realized (any more than I myself did until much later) how subversive it was of the radical party line of the day both in its relatively benign view of middle-class American values and, even more seriously, in its denial that the intellectuals and the educated class in general represented a truly superior alternative. But then he made a close study of the reaction to *Making It* in preparing for his piece, and it convinced him that the book had overstepped the line into outright apostasy. To defend it was a more dangerous business than he had counted on, and in the face of that danger, I said, he "simply lost his nerve."

True, as the bad boy of American letters—itself an honorific status in the climate of the 1960s—Mailer still held a license to provoke, and he rarely hesitated to use it, even if it sometimes meant making a fool of himself in the eyes of his own admirers. But there were, I said, limits he instinctively knew how to observe; and he observed them. He might excoriate his fellow radicals on a particular matter; he might discomfit them with unexpected sympathies (for right-wing politicians, say, or National Guardsmen on the other side of an antiwar demonstration); he might even on occasion describe himself as (dread word) a conservative. But always in the end came the reassuring gesture, the wink of complicity, the subtle signing of the radical loyalty oath.

Making It (as even Lionel Trilling had complained) contained no such gesture, no such wink, and for Mailer to defend it was, I went on, to risk "his newly solidified popularity." However, to attack me for having been too bold carried the equally unacceptable risk of looking like a coward, and so what he did instead was attack me for ruining what he characterized as "a potentially marvelous book" *not* by having gone too far but by having failed to go far enough in exposing the Left, which he himself acknowledged had become the new establishment.

This, I admitted, was a clever tactic. It enabled him to pretend to the courage of even greater acts of treason against the cultural ruling class than I had been convicted of committing while, by ratifying the sentence it had passed on me, he was actually submitting with the usual wink of complicity to the now-frightening power of the new establishment. The very fact that even Mailer, one of the founding fathers of the radical culture, had been cowed into submission (like, mutatis mutandis, an old Bolshevik fearful of being denounced as a traitor by his own Stalinist comrades) was a measure of just how powerful that culture had become. It also signified that he "was not perhaps so brave as he thought he was."

I of course recognized that there was nothing—*nothing*—that would offend Norman Mailer more than to be accused of lacking in courage, which was why I was so sure he would never forgive me. And indeed about fifteen years passed before he spoke to me again. Indirectly, through third parties, I received reports of how angry he was, and some years later he tried to turn the tables on me:

> What I find most distressing is that [Podhoretz] never asks himself whether *he* didn't lose his nerve living out on the Left during the sixties. Think of all those ongoing years of alienation, all those simmering fears of the ultimate wrath of the authority.

He, who had once affectionately called me a "hanging judge," now thought that I had become too "judgmental and narrow":

> He was merrier in the old days. He talks too much now of how he took care of me in those old days. I also took care of him. How many people I argued with saying, "No, no, Norman Podhoretz is not really as middle-class as he seems. He's really a great guy, and stand-up." Today he couldn't stand up without having his arms around a missile. He's just as brave and tough as all those other military-industrials.

Well, he too had come a long way from the "old days." Once during the late 1950s, when the two of us were about to go against Arthur Schlesinger Jr., and Mary McCarthy in a debate about the 1930s, he warned me that he intended to appear on the platform in a work shirt and jeans because he would feel uncomfortable in a suit and tie. But now, if I had wound up with my arms around a missile, he had wound up practically living in a tuxedo. So attired, he would appear at least once a week in the society-page photographs, and when I would occasionally bump into him at some party or other, it would invariably be a black-tie event.

By the 1990s he had also mellowed toward me. The first time we met at one of these events, he immediately started chatting. What was I doing here? Did I realize that our hostess was a social lion hunter and that she was paying me a great compliment by having me over? (This was a mistake she was never to make again.) Clearly, he was feeling out the possibility of a rapprochement, but while polite, I kept my distance from him. And that was how it went whenever I ran into him: he would be cordial and I would be cool, he would wish to talk and I would wish to get away.

Thus, at a small dinner party to which we had both been invited by an unwitting hostess, he tried to engage me in an argument over the Soviet Union, where he had just spent several months researching his book about Lee Harvey Oswald. Now that the Soviet Union had collapsed, was I ready to admit that I had been wrong about its power during the Cold War? "In a funny way," I was relieved to see that living in a dinner jacket had not prevented him from sticking faithfully to the left-wing party line, which on this issue held that our victory in the Cold War had resulted from the Soviet Union's internal weaknesses and that Ronald Reagan's policies had had nothing to do with it. But I just smiled back, refusing to be provoked, and then I answered with a "Well, maybe" when he parted by saying that he would like to discuss all this with me someday.

By 1998, when he reached his seventy-fifth birthday, Mailer was not exactly falling back on hard times, but neither did he any longer occupy the special position he had enjoyed in the 1960s. His books, while still commanding huge advances, were not enthusiastically received, and neither did they sell very well. True, he remained a highly respected and even revered figure in certain literary circles—to the point where the fiftieth anniversary of the appearance of *The Naked and the Dead* could be celebrated with the publication of a twelve-hundred-page anthology of his work, entitled *The Time of Our Time,* and a huge party to which the tickets were hot. But—to his great chagrin, I feel sure—they were not remotely so hot as the invitations had been to Truman Capote's black-and-white ball in 1965, and the party itself made hardly a splash. Nor did *The Time of Our Time* get much more than a polite nod from reviewers, and from some of them not even that. One of the unkinder cuts that came his way upon the appearance of the anthology was inflicted by a Columbia professor named James Shapiro writing in the *New York Times Book Review.* There was much praise for Mailer's early works there, but it was radically undermined by the attribution of his decline after 1980 to the "deep conventionality" of the views "about the family, homosexuality and, most of all, the relations between the sexes" that lurked "beneath his surface outrageousness." To this professor, in other words, Mailer was still the nice Jewish boy from Brooklyn he had spent his entire life striving not to be.

It was not easy to imagine anything worse from Mailer's point of view, and I felt for him. I also winced to hear him described as "a laughingstock" by a group of much younger literary intellectuals who sneered even at his early work and wondered how I could ever have thought he was "a major novelist in the making." I had trouble defending myself against this challenge, given that I had never reread the books in which I had found so much promise when Mailer and I were both young (because I did not have the heart to look at them in the light of what came after both for him and for me).

Considering how things were going with his literary career, I suspected that Mailer might again have been able to use the kind of foul-weather friend I had once been to him. This suspicion was intensified when, shortly before the big party, he telephoned me for the first time in about twenty years. Hearing from him was surprising enough, but the reason for the call was even more surprising. It seemed that one of Mailer's sons, whose mother had been a Gentile and who therefore was not Jewish in the eyes of rabbinic law, had fallen in love with an Orthodox Jewish woman and wanted to convert. Could I recommend a suitable rabbi? I could and I did. But I also expressed my astonishment and offered my mock condolences at this unexpected turn of events. It reminded me, I told Mailer, of how a direct descendant of Trotsky had wound up living in Israel as the kind of extremist Orthodox Jew known as a *haredi,* and I imagined that he himself was no less distressed than the old anti-Zionist revolutionary would surely have been. No, Mailer said, for him it was not like that at all. He did not in the least mind or object to what his son was doing. Indeed, as the father of nine children, he found it fascinating to watch them go their separate and different ways. "Well," I responded, thinking of his own lifelong flight from Judaism and Jewishness, "my own take on this, to quote from a different part of the book you recently tried to rewrite, is that 'God is not mocked.'" There was a pause. "Where did I say that?" he asked. "*You* didn't," I laughed, "the New Testament did," and he laughed back.

A few days later, I received an invitation to the forthcoming party, and after a long debate with myself I decided not to go. If it was true that Mailer again needed me as a foul-weather friend, there was not the slightest possibility that I could satisfy that need. In our phone conversation, I had felt bound to say, exactly as I had done so many years earlier at his house when *Breaking Ranks* was on the verge of being published, that I had just written something about him (meaning this essay) that he would not like. Back then he had replied, "Well, you owe me one," and on this occasion his response was that he would not of course have expected anything else from me at this stage of our lives. Nor, he went on pleasantly, would it bother him, so long as it was written "with a clean heart." Yet even having been granted this preemptive pardon (and even assuming that he would stick to it, which he had of course failed to do in the analogous case of *Breaking Ranks*), I had no wish to put myself in the false position of participating in the celebration of a career that had so bitterly disappointed my literary expectations. Besides, having spent the last thirty years and more trying to make up for and undo the damage I did in cooperation with Mailer and so many other of my ex-friends, both living and dead, I simply could see no way back to him, or to them, ever again.

A DISSENT ON ISAIAH BERLIN

BY THE TIME SIR ISAIAH BERLIN died in 1997 at the age of eighty-eight, a thick layer of piety and even reverence had long since come to surround his name, and accordingly the obituaries both here and in England took it more or less for granted that he had been, if not the leading political philosopher of the age, then at least a strong contender for that position. He was celebrated for the brilliance of his mind, for the profundity of his thought, for the depth and range of his learning and—not least—for his steadfast defense of liberal values against their rivals both on the Left and on the Right.

Now, there can be no question that in some ways Berlin was an admirable figure. But there are also grounds for believing that he was overrated as a thinker (whether one classifies him as a political philosopher or more precisely as a historian of ideas). In my judgment, too, he suffered as a person from a serious character flaw that robbed even what many conservatives would consider his best and most valuable ideas of any real force in practice. These ideas were thereby prevented from having the salutary influence they might have exerted at certain crucial and difficult moments.

In due course I will get to my reasons for not joining in the chorus of adulation for Berlin, and why arriving at a more temperate estimate of him seems to me important to our general intellectual health. But I want to dwell first on why, even so, I was hit by a sense of loss when he died and by a great feeling of regret at how few were the hours I got to spend in his company. Sharp as it was at the time, this feeling has now been reignited and exacerbated by a reading of Michael Ignatieff's new book, *Isaiah Berlin: A Life*. This is an official biography in that it was authorized by Berlin, who cooperated in every way. He did not, however, ask for the right to approve the manuscript. On the contrary, he refused to read it and stipulated that the book be published only after his death.

Ignatieff is a very good and a very intelligent writer, and not the least of his literary virtues is that he has been able to digest ten years of taped conversations with a famously voluble subject, a nonstop talker of legendary proportions, and then to recast all this material which, when transcribed, must have run into thousands upon thousands of pages, into a book running to only a little over three hundred. In this mercifully brief space, Ignatieff manages to do an excellent, if understandably quite uncritical, job of covering both the thought and the life of Isaiah Berlin.

One problem faced by Ignatieff is that Berlin never produced a major work conveniently pulling together the various elements of his philosophy. Nevertheless, Ignatieff is able to extract a lucid and coherent account of it from the many scattered essays and lectures through which Berlin most naturally expressed himself. But there was also another kind of problem Ignatieff had to contend with in telling the story of Berlin's life—a life compounded, as Berlin himself once summed it up, of "three strands": Russian, English, and Jewish.

Being himself of Russian ancestry and a longtime resident of England, Ignatieff was well equipped to unravel the first two of these strands. But not being Jewish, he might have been expected to run into a bit of trouble with the third. Yet he almost always gets things right in dealing with its nuances and complexities—a feat that not that many Jewish writers would have been able to pull off with comparable accuracy, particularly when we consider that the strand of Jewishness in Berlin was further complicated by being both familiar and unusual.

The familiar part is the journey of a Jewish boy of eleven from Riga, Latvia (then under czarist rule), where he was born in 1909 and lived until the age of six, and then Petrograd, where he spent the next five years, to the upper reaches of intellectual life in the new country to which his family had been forced to flee. Countless such journeys with similar outcomes were traversed—both earlier and later, and by both rich and poor—to America; young immigrants arriving with little or no English and themselves or their children becoming within an amazingly short time major figures in the culture as writers, painters, composers, scientists, philosophers, professors, journalists.

One tends to assume that there were fewer such instances in England, whose society, being both more stratified and more insular, was less permeable than America's to foreigners of any stripe, let alone Jews. Yet as the economist P. T. Bauer—himself a penniless teenage immigrant "of Jewish origin" from Hungary who, capping a distinguished academic career, wound up sitting in the House of Lords—never tired of pointing out, England was far more welcoming to foreign-born talent than is often imagined. Which is to say that the career of Isaiah Berlin qua intellectual was by no means unique. The faculties of Oxford and Cambridge and the London School of Economics (LSE) had a fair share of immigrant Jews (especially in the physical and social sciences) even before their number was swollen by refugees fleeing from Nazi Germany.

Still—and here we come to the unusual part of Berlin's story—very few even of the foreign-born English Jews who were knighted, and/or made it to the House of Lords, ever ascended the most rarefied heights of English society to anything like the extent that Berlin eventually did. No doubt not all these people had the insatiable appetite for high society that was one of Berlin's ruling passions; some of them may positively have disdained dining with duchesses or becoming frequent guests at Buckingham Palace. But whether or not their ambitions ran in that direction, and whether or not, in one of Berlin's own formulations, they were great "diners-out," the fact of their Jewishness—however faintly they might have borne its stigmata or however distant they might have grown from the mores and practices of their ancestors—remained enough of a disqualification to keep them in their social place.

There may have been more exceptions to this rule than I am aware of, but the only one I happen personally to have encountered who scaled the same social battlements as Berlin was—and is—George Weidenfeld. A decade younger, a publisher rather than an academic, and a post-Hitler refugee from Vienna rather than from Bolshevik Russia, Weidenfeld still had much in common with Berlin. The two men also had a professional association that turned out to be very important. As Ignatieff informs us:

> Weidenfeld had been shrewd enough to see the commercial potential locked up in an obscure essay, "Lev Tolstoy's Historical Skepticism," which Isaiah had published in *Oxford Slavonic Papers* in 1951. By retitling it "The Hedgehog and the Fox," and putting it out for a general readership with additions by Isaiah, Weidenfeld did more for Isaiah's public reputation than any other publisher.

Like many (most?) of their foreign-born English coreligionists, above all in the universities and the intellectual world outside them, both men became thoroughly assimilated into British culture and as Jews they were both frank nonbelievers. Being such, they were also nonobservant, though they might (Berlin much more regularly than Weidenfeld) attend a synagogue on the High Holy Days or a seder on Passover. In Berlin's case, as he himself quipped, "the Orthodox synagogue is the synagogue I am not attending"—except, that is, on the High Holy Days; and "wherever he was in the world on Yom Kippur," we learn from Ignatieff, "he made a point of fasting." Also, "As long as his mother was alive he celebrated the Passover every year in her house." But after her death, Berlin being Berlin, the seder naturally tended to turn into "a grand social occasion, with Lord Rothschild, Lord Goodman, the painter R. B. Kitaj and Murray Perahia, the pianist, in attendance."

YET NONBELIEVING and nonobservant though they were, both Berlin and Weidenfeld were entirely open about and comfortable in the skin of their Jewishness, and both were lifelong and highly dedicated Zionists. One might have thought that this would have denied them access to the most fashionable circles. Which is what happened, for example, to Sir Lewis Namier (1888–1960), a Jew from Galicia and a Zionist activist whose great achievements as a historian of eighteenth-century England were enough to earn him a knighthood and other honors without also securing him entrée (except for purposes of research) into the aristocratic world whose acceptance he yearned for in vain and to whose past he devoted enormous scholarly labor. But no such barrier was erected against Weidenfeld and still less against Berlin.

To be sure, Namier was so acerbic and unpleasant that (as Berlin himself tells us in a touching essay about him) not only was he spurned by the "London clubmen (whom he often naively pursued)" but, even though everyone at Oxford acknowledged his greatness and originality as a historian, he was also even repeatedly passed over for the professorship he coveted there. In the sharpest possible contrast, Berlin and Weidenfeld were so charming and witty and such great raconteurs as to be irresistible companions, whether tête-à-tête or at a large gathering. In combination with these qualities, their Jewishness perhaps lent just the right dose—not too much, not too little—of an intriguing exoticism. Someone once said that if you were in low spirits, there was no one you would rather see walk through your door than Isaiah Berlin. I would say much the same thing about George Weidenfeld, as would many others.

Apart from everything else, Berlin and Weidenfeld had no peers in the realm of classy gossip. Both also specialized in that branch of snobbish Jewish genealogy known in Yiddish as *yiches,* or distinguished family connections. Once, for instance, when on a visit to London I was invited to tea by Berlin at (where else?) the Ritz, I asked him in the course of an inevitably wide-ranging conversation about a Harvard professor with a name that the professor pronounced very differently from the way it was spelled. "Well, you see," Berlin replied with a wicked little smile as he told me how the name actually should sound—a pronunciation that immediately gave away its East European origin—the professor did not really mind its being known that he was Jewish, but he most assuredly wanted it thought that his family was not from Minsk or Pinsk but from an aristocratic Sephardi clan "in Mantua or Nantua, as the case may be." And where Gentiles were concerned, if by chance there were a Jew hidden somewhere in an aristocratic woodpile, Berlin and Weidenfeld would be more certain to have dug him out than the editors of *Burke's Peerage*. The question of converted Jews and the children of converted Jews also fascinated them: one of the best things Berlin ever wrote was an essay entitled "Benjamin Disraeli, Karl Marx, and the Search for Identity."*

Speaking of *yiches,* Berlin had plenty of it, both in his own right and by marriage. Through his father he was related to the Schneersons, the family of the Lubavitch dynasty of hasidic rebbes; and through his wife Aline, the granddaughter of the banker Baron Guenzburg, he was also connected to one of the richest and most eminent Jewish philanthropists in Europe. (Aline's inherited fortune was multiplied by her former marriage to a very rich man.) As a Zionist, he had *yiches* as well: Yitzhak Sadeh, one of the founding fathers of Palmach, the elite striking force of the Haganah, out of which after statehood the Israeli army emerged, was simultaneously his uncle and his cousin.

There was a certain *yiches,* too, in the fact that Berlin's Russian childhood differed radically from that of the vast majority of Jews who emigrated from that part of the world in the late nineteenth and early twentieth centuries. Most of them had lived in dire poverty and in the constricted physical conditions of the Pale of Settlement in Russia and the ghettoized *shtetlakh* of Poland, forbidden or unable to travel outside these areas or to practice certain occupations. But for a variety of historical reasons, the Jews of Riga were exempt from these rules. Berlin's father was a very well-to-do timber merchant, and his mother, while remaining a reasonably observant Jew, was far more highly cultivated than the typical Russian Jewish woman of her generation. She read widely in secular litera-

---

*The essay appeared originally in 1970 in *Transactions of the Jewish Historical Society of England,* and was then reprinted ten years later in *Against the Current: Essays in the History of Ideas,* edited by Henry Hardy.

ture in several languages, and Russian rather than Yiddish was spoken in the household. Berlin, an only child, even had a governess. Indeed, the family left Russia not because of czarist anti-Semitism but because of the Bolshevik assault on the bourgeoisie, the class to which they belonged. In this respect, the emigration of the Berlins resembled and anticipated the later flight of the prosperous Jews of Germany and Austria who succeeded in escaping from Hitler.

In any event, once the Berlins were settled in England, Isaiah was sent to the upscale St. Paul's School in London and then to Oxford, where he studied philosophy and would spend most of his professional life as a scholar and a teacher.

TO MY GREAT good fortune, I have passed many hours in the company of Lord Weidenfeld (as he has been for some years now), but I was not so lucky with Sir Isaiah Berlin (who was both knighted and then decorated with the Order of Merit, or OM, an even higher honor than the life peerage awarded to Weidenfeld). I did, however, see enough of him to get a strong taste of the delights that his company afforded (even one meeting would have sufficed for such a taste). I therefore have no difficulty in understanding why he was sought after as a dinner guest in England by Lady This and the Duchess of That. The same was true of their untitled counterparts in America, whom he first got to know during World War II as a junior official at the British embassy in Washington.

His job in Washington was to write weekly reports on the state of American opinion, to be sent out under the signature of the British ambassador, Lord Halifax. But it was obvious to everyone, including Prime Minister Winston Churchill, that Halifax himself could not possibly have produced such brilliant work, and it soon became widely known that the actual author was, as the Foreign Office reported in response to Churchill's inquiry, a "Mr. Berlin, of Baltic Jewish extraction, by profession a philosopher."

Incidentally, Churchill's discovery of the identity of the author of Halifax's dispatches led to a wonderful comic episode. "In early February 1944," as Ignatieff recounts it,

> Clementine Churchill informed her husband that Irving Berlin was in London, and could he find time to thank him for his war work. On the contrary, the Prime Minister said, he must come to lunch. . . . The guests included Sir Alan Brooke, Commander of the Imperial

General Staff, and the Duchess of Buccleuch. . . . At the head of the table, Churchill kept up a steady stream of talk about the war situation. At the end of lunch, . . . Churchill . . . asked Berlin when he thought the war would end. "Mr. Prime Minister, I shall tell my children and grandchildren that Winston Churchill asked *me* that question." By now thoroughly confused, Churchill asked what was the most important thing that Mr. Berlin had written. He replied, "White Christmas."

It was only after the lunch was over that Churchill's secretary "broke the case of mistaken identity to the Prime Minister," whose bewilderment of course gave way to great amusement. When the "Irving-Winston-Isaiah" story got around, it only served to enhance Isaiah's already rising status.

Being the genius of sociability he was, Berlin also (and, from the point of view of his professional duties, quite legitimately) used his job to make personal contacts. By the time he returned to England, he had gotten to know practically everyone who was anyone in Washington and New York. Enduring friendships were formed not only with upcoming young academics and diplomats of his own generation like Arthur Schlesinger Jr. and George F. Kennan, but also with older public figures like Felix Frankfurter—as well, inevitably, as with great hostesses of the time like Alice Longworth (the notoriously wicked-tongued daughter of Theodore Roosevelt) and future ones like Katharine Graham (who would in due course become the publisher of the *Washington Post* and the American social equivalent of a duchess herself).

As I have already suggested, that this should have occurred is not in the least surprising. For, again with the exception of Weidenfeld—who would later travel in many of the same circles on both sides of the Atlantic—I have never in my life encountered a more effervescent conversationalist than Isaiah Berlin. He was not, as Ignatieff acknowledges, a great wit in the Oscar Wilde mode: he did not toss off epigrams that everyone would remember and quote. But there was wit in every other turn of phrase and in the way he framed the conceptions and descriptions with which he regaled everyone within earshot. Words poured out of him in such profusion and such a rush that his interlocutors sometimes had trouble understanding him, or else complained that they themselves could never get a word in when he was at the other end of a conversation. Yet in my own limited experience, I was always struck by how attentive a listener he could be—much more so than most of the great talkers I have known (and I have known my share). His mind was so quick that he could grasp a point one was making before it scarcely had a chance to get out of one's mouth; and he could give it back in a paraphrase that immediately cut to its intellectual quick.

That Berlin was so awesomely articulate perhaps proved a greater gift to others than to himself. So, at any rate, he seems to have felt. He often denigrated his own achievements, a trait that might be considered the intellectual's equivalent of the unseemly game of a rich person playing at being poor. Yet Ignatieff, who speaks often of this habit, mainly interprets it as "part of a carefully cultivated strategy . . . intended to deflect and disarm criticism." Probably it was. For despite his oft-professed indifference to the opinions others held of his work, or for what posterity might say about it, Berlin was very thin-skinned—as the following story I recently heard sadly illustrates.

On the occasion of his eightieth birthday, when tributes were pouring in from all over the world and the British press could hardly find enough space to report on the encomia coming his way, a lone voice—that of the conservative philosopher Roger Scruton—piped up in one paper with a tribute that was not wholly free of a few mildly critical remarks. The scandal this article created within the British intellectual establishment was so disproportionate—Berlin's friends being as thin-skinned on his behalf as he was on his own—that a man who had been close to Berlin for many years was puzzled: what, he was heard to wonder at a private dinner party, was so terrible about Scruton's piece? This question was immediately relayed by the drumbeaters in the London jungle to Berlin, who responded to it the very next day with an eighteen-page handwritten letter full of hurt feelings and accusations of betrayal. Berlin even compared Scruton to Goebbels, and refused to retract when challenged by his morally stunned correspondent.

I TELL THIS STORY not in order to expose Berlin as a hypocrite for pretending not to care about his reputation, but rather as a suggestive piece of evidence for the genuineness of the self-doubt that afflicted him—an affliction that I would guess was caused by his inability ever to write anything that for dazzle and sweep could match his extemporaneous talk. This was a problem he tried to solve by dictating his essays, and his legion of admirers assured him and everyone else that he had succeeded. But Berlin himself, I suspect, knew better, which was why it was only after much persuasion from young disciples that he allowed those essays to be published—some for the first time—in a series of collections that were issued in his later years.

I gather from Ignatieff that Berlin was also tormented by his failure to write the big book, the great book, that was expected of him. When, in those same later years, he made a sustained effort to satisfy this expectation with a major study of Romanticism—a subject upon which he had touched in many of his essays—he spent much time reading and taking notes but, like a graduate student getting bogged down in a doctoral dissertation, he finally had to give it up.

Berlin, of course, was not the only great talker or lecturer whose written work never measured up to his spoken word. For example, anyone who reads Samuel Taylor Coleridge's *Biographia Literaria* is bound to wonder why he was held in such intellectual awe by his contemporaries in the early nineteenth century; and one might well have felt the same way about Dr. Samuel Johnson's reputation among his own contemporaries a century earlier if there were only his *Lives of the Poets* to go by and James Boswell had never come along to record his table talk.

Good as Ignatieff's biography is, he is no Boswell. He therefore cannot help ill-serving his subject, who could really have used a Boswell, all the more so in that Berlin's published writings, even at their best, are not in the same league as those of Coleridge or Johnson. Coming closer to home for another case in point, I would also cite the American art historian Meyer Schapiro, a Lithuanian-born Jew whose lectures and conversation were in their own style as exhilarating and scintillating and rich in texture and context as Berlin's, but who similarly had trouble capturing it all on paper and could equally have benefited from a Boswell of his own.

Interestingly, Berlin himself makes a very similar observation about the nineteenth-century Russian revolutionary Alexander Herzen, who was "a brilliant and irrepressible talker . . . always in an overwhelming flow of ideas and images; the waste, from the point of view of posterity . . . , is probably immense: he had no Boswell . . . to record his conversation." Yet there was compensation for posterity in Herzen's memoirs, *My Past and Thoughts,* which Berlin considered "a literary masterpiece worthy to be placed by the side of the novels of his contemporaries and countrymen, Tolstoy, Turgenev, Dostoevsky." Never having read this book, I cannot say for certain that Berlin's praise is more than a bit extravagant, though I strongly suspect that it is. Be that as it may, Berlin himself left behind nothing that even his most fervent admirers would think of placing on so high a plane.

Herzen was not Jewish, and neither of course were Coleridge and Johnson. Furthermore, neither Berlin nor Schapiro ever had a truly extensive Jewish education. Nevertheless I cannot help wondering whether there may not have been something deeply rooted in Jewish culture that produced the problem with writing experienced by them and a few other great Jewish talkers I could name. What I have in mind is the intimidating effect that talmudic pedagogy has sometimes had on those who have aspired to its deepest levels. Serious students of the Talmud have often been made to feel that they have no business saying anything at all until they have swallowed not only the vast "ocean" of the talmudic text itself but everything the commentators have said about it over the centuries, by which time they discover that anything they might have to add has been said already, and better, by some ancient forebear.

It is true that enough young people overcome the inhibitions this ethos creates to keep the enterprise alive and kicking; and there are those who are able to move with perfect authority into other areas as well. Being educated almost entirely at a Lithuanian yeshiva, for instance, did not prevent Harry Wolfson of Harvard from going on in later life to produce huge and definitive works of subjects as far afield from the Talmud as the early Fathers of the Church and the great medieval Islamic theologians. Still, all exceptions and qualifications duly noted, rereading Berlin's essays, with their incessant and compulsive references to the thinkers of the past, I got the sense that something like the inhibition that has stymied many Jewish scholars—imbibed, I would suppose, by osmosis as a child—was operating in him and that he was sincerely bothered by the conviction that he himself had nothing original to add.

I would exempt from this generalization his essay on Machiavelli, which begins with a breathtakingly concise survey of just about every interpretation ever offered of that notorious writer, and only then ventures on a new one of his own. Yet even here, revealingly, Berlin feels constrained to apologize:

Where more than twenty interpretations hold the field, the addition of one more cannot be deemed an impertinence. At worst it will be no more than yet another attempt to solve the problem, now more than four centuries old.

Whether or not there is any validity in my speculation,* rereading Berlin was a disappointment. Not that this came as a shock, since my very first introduction to him as a thinker about forty-five years ago also resulted in disappointment. He was then (1953) teaching at Oxford, his home base for most of his academic life, and I was a student at "the other place" (that is, Cambridge), but the occasion was a lecture he gave at LSE. The lecture followed hard upon a series of six hour-long talks he had delivered in as many weeks on BBC Radio on the general theme of "Freedom and Its Betrayal." These talks had become famous not so much because they were difficult and devoted to relatively obscure thinkers like Helvétius and de Maistre as because they were done extemporaneously, from notes, without so much as a pause or a stammer. It was, as Ignatieff rightly says, a "prodigious feat of studied verbal improvisation," and it drew hundreds of thousands of listeners, turning Berlin, then about forty years old and not yet known outside academic circles, into a veritable national celebrity.

I never heard these lectures, but I did hear about them, and when I discovered that Berlin would shortly be speaking at LSE, I wangled an invitation through a friend who was studying there. The auditorium was packed, with the front rows occupied by all the great eminences of the LSE faculty (including Karl Popper, then at the height of his fame as the author of *The Open Society and Its Enemies*) and a large pack of highly distinguished academics who had come down from Oxford and Cambridge.

The excitement in the air was intensified by two titillating circumstances. One was that Berlin was to be introduced by Michael Oakeshott, the leading conservative thinker in England who, to the dismay and even horror of the socialists at LSE and elsewhere, had recently been chosen to succeed one of their main intellectual leaders and heroes, the late Harold Laski, as professor of politics. Obviously Oakeshott, the great critic of liberalism, would not wish to praise Isaiah Berlin, the great exponent of liberalism; but how would he get around the problem? And, since this was the first in a series of lectures that had been endowed to honor the memory of Auguste Comte— who a century earlier had, among other things abominable in Oakeshott's eyes, invented the idea of sociology as a science—Oakeshott would need to figure out how to avoid celebratory words about him as well.

---

*And I should make it clear that Berlin would have dismissed it as "absurd," just as he did, conversely, when his father (as Ignatieff writes) would "attribute his son's memory and scholarly achievements to his rabbinical ancestors." The same is true of the subject of *yiches*. Fascinated though he was by it, in his view, as summarized by Ignatieff, to take pride in one's origins was "to surrender to the dubious determinism of the blood."

A great hush, charged with suspense, thus descended upon the auditorium as Oakeshott approached the podium. Glancing around with what seemed a look of disapproval bordering on contempt at the size and composition of the audience for this speaker on this subject, he welcomed us all to the first Auguste Comte Memorial Lecture with the reminder that it had been a hundred years since Comte had burst upon the intellectual scene. At this point he paused and again swept the room with a disdainful glance before continuing: "And what a century it has been for *him!* "

Even Oakeshott's enemies, who far outnumbered his fans in this crowd, were forced to laugh appreciatively at so masterful a stroke, made even more telling by being left to stand alone with no further elaboration. But now it was Berlin's turn to get the Oakeshott treatment, and while it did not go down so well with this audience as his handling of Comte, it was also masterful. How fortunate we were, Oakeshott said, to have as our first Comte Memorial Lecturer the man who had so recently dazzled us all with the virtuosity of his performance on the BBC; so great was Mr. Berlin's virtuosity, indeed, that one might call him "a very Paganini of ideas."*

This was a very tough put-down to overcome, and Berlin did not do well. Although I was a liberal in those days, and on his side, I came away wondering why so much fuss was being made about him. The lecture was an attack on historical determinism, with which I entirely agreed but which seemed to me obvious, platitudinous, and—most unexpectedly—labored. Nor was I alone in my disappointment. Ignatieff:

> The fame he had acquired from "Freedom and Its Betrayal" guaranteed a full turnout; his nervousness was increased by Oakeshott's barbed encomium to his skills as a lecturer; and he had ludicrously overprepared. The text was much too long for delivery and he began abridging it as he went, wildly putting pages aside, struggling to keep the argumentative thread together, talking in an ever faster, high-pitched gabble. When he staggered to a conclusion, the reactions were perfunctory and polite and he came away, not for the last time, with the uneasy feeling that his peers were asking themselves whether his reputation was deserved.

---

*In Ignatieff's version, the phrase Oakeshott used was "Paganini of the platform," but I am pretty certain that my version is the correct one. I did not know, however, that (again according to Ignatieff) T. S. Eliot, another conservative, had earlier come up with a barbed compliment of his own in congratulating Berlin for the "torrential eloquence" of the BBC lectures. Good, but in this case I would award the palm to the political philosopher rather than the poet.

Eventually Berlin turned the lecture into a long paper entitled "Historical Inevitability," which Ignatieff characterizes as "an impressive statement of his most fundamental beliefs." That it is a statement of his most fundamental beliefs is certainly true; but "impressive"? Reading it today in a much fuller version than the one I heard in 1953, I was prepared to discover that I had been wrong about it back then. Instead, I was struck by how academic it is, how internal to the professional concerns of historians and other scholars, if somewhat less so than some of the other papers he wrote during this phase of his career demonstrating the fallacy of using the physical sciences as a model for history and philosophy—papers like "The Concept of Scientific History" and "Does Political Theory Still Exist?" (These can be found, along with much else that came later, in *The Proper Study of Mankind,* a recently published anthology of his essays.) What struck me even more forcibly is how little—for all its many references to the world outside—it really touches upon the living impact of the main ideas with which it deals.

In making this judgment, I am saying exactly the opposite of what is always said by those who see Berlin as one of the major thinkers of the age. They praise him precisely for addressing himself (as one of them has put it) to "the general reader," for being "erudite but . . . not academic"; or (in the words of another) for the "everyday practicality" of his writings, and for bringing abstract ideas to life by confronting them through "the people who conceived them." Yet to borrow a phrase Berlin himself borrowed in another context from his friend and Oxford colleague, the philosopher A. J. Ayer, much that he wrote amounted to nothing more than "a dramatized tautology." At one point in "Historical Inevitability," he remarks, "All this seems too self-evident to argue." I could not agree more. That is how it seemed to me in 1953 and how it seems to me today.

But just as I would maintain that his essay on Machiavelli represents a rare escape from the inhibitions that may have undermined him as a thinker, there are two essays I would exempt from the strictures I have directed at "Historical Inevitability" and the other pieces like it.

The first is the famous "Two Concepts of Liberty." Here Berlin begins as usual with brilliant summaries of what all the other commentators have said about his subject over the centuries. But this time the survey of past opinion serves directly to clarify a distinction—between negative liberty and positive liberty, the former consisting of freedom from external obstructions to one's will, the latter of the freedom to pursue a goal defined as the one and only true good—that is anything but academic, having instead the greatest bearing on how different societies have organized themselves politically.

It is also in this essay that he offers what may be the most effective and passionate defense he ever gave of his commitment to "pluralism." In Berlin's usage of the term, "pluralism" signifies that "human goals are many, not all of them commensurable, and in perpetual rivalry with one another." The human fate is to choose among these goals, without the comforting certainty that they have "eternal validity." But this, he insists, is at least better than the various species of "monism," according to each of which there is only one ideal we must aspire to and attain through reason or scientific method or revelation or some other means. "There is little need to stress the fact that monism, and faith in a single criterion," Berlin writes, "has always proved a deep source of satisfaction both to the intellect and to the emotions." But, he adds, it has also been used to justify "the a-priori barbarities of Procrustes—the vivisection of actual human societies into some fixed pattern dictated by our fallible understanding of a largely imaginary past or a wholly imaginary future."

To put Berlin's point a little less abstractly, "monism," sometimes disguised as "positive liberty," often leads to totalitarianism, while "pluralism" is at the basis of political freedom and its strongest guarantee.

THEN THERE IS the even more famous essay, "The Hedgehog and the Fox," to whose publishing history I have already alluded. Contrary to what is often assumed, Berlin did not invent this image: as he tells us in the very first sentence, it comes from the Greek poet Archilochus, among whose surviving fragments is the line: "The fox knows many things, but the hedgehog knows one big thing." Nor is this mainly another essay about the superiority of pluralism (here represented by the fox) over monism (the hedgehog). Berlin does of course take up that theme and elaborates upon it once again with formulations that he has used before, and will use again, along with some that are new. But as its subtitle informs us, and as we know from the title of the original paper that Weidenfeld persuaded him to elaborate, "The Hedgehog and the Fox" is actually "An Essay on Tolstoy's View of History."

This is an accurate description as far as it goes, but it is also too modest, since Berlin uses Tolstoy's view of history—set forth in those large sections of *War and Peace* that so many readers have found irritatingly boring interruptions of the book's narrative section—as a point of entry into the mind and spirit of arguably the greatest novelist who ever lived. Describing the qualities and powers that made Tolstoy great brings out the best in Berlin (as writing with unfailing generosity in appreciation of the genius of others always did):

> No author who has ever lived has shown such powers of insight into the variety of life—the differences, the contrasts, the collisions of persons and things and situations, each apprehended in its absolute uniqueness and conveyed with a degree of directness and a precision of concrete images to be found in no other writer.

Going on in these breathless cadences, Berlin picks up even more speed:

> No one has ever excelled Tolstoy in expressing the specific flavor, the exact quality of a feeling—the degree of its "oscillation," the ebb and flow, the minute movements . . . —the inner and outer texture and "feel" of a look, a thought, a pang of sentiment, no less than of a specific situation, of an entire period, of the lives of individuals, families, communities, entire nations.

And finally:

> The celebrated lifelikeness of every object and every person in his world derives from this astonishing capacity of presenting every ingredient of it in its fullest individual essence, in all its many dimensions, as it were: never as a mere datum, however vivid, within some stream of consciousness, with blurred edges, in outline, a shadow, an impressionist representation; nor yet calling for, and dependent on, some process of reasoning in the mind of the reader; but always as a solid object, seen simultaneously from near and far, in natural, unaltering daylight, from all possible angles of vision, set in an absolutely specific context in time and space—an event fully present to the senses or the imagination in all its facets, with every nuance sharply and firmly articulated.

Having delivered himself of this spectacularly unerring account of Tolstoy as a novelist, Berlin then abruptly, and without even a sentence of transition to soften the shock, asserts that "what [Tolstoy] believed in was the opposite." In other words, it was not enough for Tolstoy to be perhaps the greatest "fox" since Shakespeare (a writer he came to despise and disparage); what he wanted was to be a "hedgehog." In consequence, he himself

> preached not variety but simplicity, not many levels of consciousness but reduction to some single level— . . . some simple, quasi-utilitarian criterion, whereby everything is interrelated directly, and all the items can be assessed in terms of one another by some simple measuring-rod.

I once joked after reading a biography of Tolstoy (the one by Henri Troyat) that he emerges from it looking like a character out of Dostoevsky. Berlin goes even farther—in my opinion, much too far: "Beside Tolstoy, Gogol and Dostoevsky, whose abnormality is so often contrasted with Tolstoy's 'sanity,' are well-integrated personalities, with a coherent outlook and a single vision." But this presupposes, among other things, that Dostoevsky actually was, as Berlin classifies him (on the basis, I suppose, of his religious beliefs), a hedgehog. I, however, would argue that all great novelists, no matter what convictions they may hold or how single-mindedly they hold them, must necessarily be foxes, and that anyone who lacks the qualities of the fox cannot possibly succeed as a novelist; conversely, very few other kinds of writers can match the foxiness of the novelist.

Which is why I think Berlin spoils this otherwise splendid essay by bringing in Joseph de Maistre as another example of a fox who wanted to be a hedgehog. He spoils it in two ways: first by dwelling at length on the question of whether Tolstoy was more influenced by this eighteenth-century French counterrevolutionary, often considered the intellectual father of the French Right and of French chauvinism, than he was by Stendhal's novel *The Charterhouse of Parma*. But unless something more is done with it than Berlin does here, the question of influence is one of those truly academic issues of no great interest to anyone but professional scholars, and it is a weariness to the "general reader" (this one included) to whom Berlin's work is supposedly addressed.

The other way in which de Maistre's presence damages "The Hedgehog and the Fox" is that he does not enjoy the stature that would entitle him to costar with a giant like Tolstoy. Emboldened by having learned from Ignatieff that Berlin was capable of discoursing with an air of authority about books into which he had only dipped, I am willing to admit that my own acquaintance with de Maistre is strictly of the dipping kind—and that, moreover, it took place many years ago. But surely it cannot be wrong to assume that he belongs in a lesser and lower realm than Tolstoy, and that speaking of the two of them as though they existed on the same plane undermines the unsurpassed tribute Berlin pays to Tolstoy himself.

BERLIN'S ESSAYS, then, could be undeniably impressive, and scintillating to boot, even if they do not seem to me to merit the hymns almost universally sung to his work and his ideas. He certainly deserves great credit for having liberated himself from the sterilities of the logical positivism on which he cut his intellectual teeth, turning his attention instead to the great moral and political questions that had been dismissed as meaningless by his friends and colleagues who belonged to that philosophical school. Coming when and where it did, this in itself was an intellectual achievement, and even a brave one, quite apart from the results it produced.

Possibly the most significant and consequential of those results was to have taught the educated English class, including the radically empiricist and even anti-intellectual historians and philosophers within it, that ideas are of supreme importance in human affairs. Berlin attributed his own appreciation of "the vast and sometimes sinister power of ideas" to his Russian origins, for "Russia is a country whose modern history is an object-lesson in the enormous power of abstract ideas" both for good and ill. It was a lesson the English, much more than the French or the Germans or the Americans, needed to be taught, and some of the adulation that came to Berlin in his adopted country probably originated in gratitude to him for having taught it. (The other side of the coin was that this same stubborn empiricist resistance to big abstract or metaphysical ideas, as Berlin saw it, made England the most civilized and the most politically admirable country in the world.)

He had other impressive qualities as well. No one could surpass him in the extremely difficult enterprise of summarizing and tracing the pedigree of an idea and in cutting to the core of another thinker's point of view. And he was especially good in dealing with thinkers like de Maistre whose opinions, though repugnant to him, he could invariably summon up the intellectual imagination to describe with sympathy and great insight. His portraits of major Jewish—or formerly Jewish—figures like Marx, Disraeli, Moses Hess, and Chaim Weizmann are also as delightful as they are illuminating.

But what, substantively, does it all add up to? The answer Berlin's admirers give is that, in an age when fascism and Communism were rampant and sometimes seemed destined to triumph, he developed a profound defense of liberal pluralism that escaped the great pitfall of relativism which (at least in its more extreme forms) he supposedly found just as (or anyway almost as) objectionable as the determinism of such monistic philosophies as Marxism. Yet for the life of me, I cannot perceive any solid logical or philosophical ground in his work for exonerating him from the charge of relativism. He recognizes that relativism, though it can be animated by a spirit of tolerance for and generosity toward other points of view and is thus an antibody to the dangerous disease of fanaticism, is nonetheless vulnerable to a disease of its own: namely, the spinelessness that can develop from the rejection of any absolutes and the correlative failure to develop rock-bottom convictions. But neither his writings nor his own behavior bear out the claim of muscularity that he and others made for his kind of liberalism as compared with some of the other schools of liberal thought emerging from the Enlightenment that he criticized and from which he dissociated himself.

In the last paragraph of "Two Concepts of Liberty," Berlin approvingly quotes the twentieth-century economist Joseph Schumpeter: "To realize the relative validity of one's convictions and yet stand for them unflinchingly is what distinguishes a civilized man from a barbarian." Or again, in praising one of his heroes, the great Zionist leader Chaim Weizmann, Berlin writes:

> Weizmann had all his life believed that when great public issues are joined one must above all take sides; whatever one did, one must not remain neutral or uncommitted, one must always—as an absolute duty— . . . take part in the world's affairs with all the risk and blame and misrepresentation and misunderstanding of one's motives and character which this almost inevitably entails.

Yet, time after time, it was precisely this "absolute duty" that Berlin failed to discharge. Thus, when the universities—the institution to which he had devoted the better part of his life and which, with all its faults, came closer than any other to embodying the values he so volubly professed—came under assault by the radicals of the Left in the mid- and late 1960s, where was Berlin? To put it charitably, he was nowhere to be seen on the field when the fight was raging most intensely. So much for his willingness to stand, in accordance with Schumpeter's noble dictum, unflinchingly for his convictions. When push came to shove, it was the relativism that won out over the convictions.

But there is more. I read in Ignatieff that Berlin's "distaste for the fashionable intellectuals of the 1960s . . . deepened into something approaching intellectual despair when he surveyed the student revolutionaries themselves." Ignatieff also tells us that "The whole experience of the 1960s made him uneasily aware that he had not understood the nihilist consequences of the Romantic esteem for sincerity and authenticity." He expressed this and kindred sentiments privately in letters to friends (e.g., "I feel depressed by the rapid growth of barbarism . . . among our young men," whom he then proceeds to compare unfavorably with the "revolutionaries of his own day"), but I personally cannot recollect, and Ignatieff gives no examples of, any pronouncements of this nature by Berlin in public. Just the opposite: in those very years of his "despair," he became a regular contributor to the *New York Review of Books,* in which the radicalism and/or barbarism that so distressed him in private were regularly accorded the greatest respect and found their most sophisticated intellectual defense.

ONE EVENING during this period—just when, disillusioned with the radical Movement that I, too, had in recent years been defending, I felt constrained to break with it altogether—I attended, along with my wife, a small dinner party given for the visiting Berlins by my former teacher Lionel Trilling and his wife Diana in New York; the only other guest was one of Berlin's oldest and closest friends, the British poet and critic Stephen Spender. To the delight of the Trillings, who had never approved of my association with the Left of the 1960s and were pleased by my growing disaffection with it, I seized upon the occasion to ask Berlin why he was willing to collaborate so closely with the *New York Review.* Though Spender, too, was writing regularly for it, I did not address this question to him, because I knew that he, as Ignatieff puts it, prided himself on "communing with the young" (he had even had himself hoisted into one of the buildings occupied by the radicals at Columbia where, of course, Trilling was the great luminary of the faculty). Yet along with everyone else in the room, Spender joined in what turned out to be one of the best and most serious discussions I have ever participated in. Contentious issues and their many ramifications were explored with frankness on both sides, without any rancor, and with everyone trying to do justice to the position against which he was arguing instead of reducing it to an easily ridiculed caricature.*

My challenge to Berlin, however, did not focus only on the issue of student radicalism; it also concerned Israel. "You still consider yourself a Zionist, don't you?" I asked him. "Certainly," he replied. "Then," I pressed on, "why do you lend your prestige and support to a paper that regularly publishes enemies of Israel like Noam Chomsky and I. F. Stone?" This question seemed to take Berlin by surprise and for once in his life he did not have a ready riposte. But after a few seconds he responded, and with the friendliest possible smile: "I see. You are accusing me of being a fellow-traveler of a fellow-traveler."

He did not follow up this witticism with a defense either of the *New York Review* or of himself. There was, after all, no denying that Stone (in that period of his life) and especially Chomsky were bitter enemies of the Zionism to which Berlin had been committed all his life. This commitment even formed the basis of his understanding that nationalism was ineradicable (an understanding not common among liberals of his era, who mostly regarded it as the major cause of Nazism and lesser evils), and that utopian efforts to ignore or wipe it out in pursuit of the ideal of an internationalist brotherhood were doomed to fail. Such efforts, he warned, were even as likely to lead to mass murder as nationalism in its more aggressive phases could and did.

Instead, therefore, of trying to justify his connection with the *New York Review,* Berlin stood pat on his witty remark and sat for a while giving my question what looked like thoughtful consideration as we moved on to the general question of student radicalism. Yet as time went on, and as the attacks being mounted in those years by the Left against Israel became ever more ferocious, he remained as silent as he did about its assault on the universities and the liberal ethos embodied in them.

In Ignatieff's interpretation, Berlin comforted himself with the thought that as an exponent of "liberal moderation," he was following the example of his beloved Ivan Turgenev, the great nineteenth-century Russian novelist who in his own day had incurred the disfavor both of the Left and the Right. Turgenev, says Ignatieff,

---

*To my astonishment and, if truth be told, disgust, I later learned that in reporting back to their friends in England on this discussion, Berlin and Spender said that they had spent a whole evening being berated by the editor of *Commentary* (as I then was) merely because they wrote for a rival publication. No wonder Berlin was (so Ignatieff reveals) sometimes accused of being "feline" as a gossip.

was accused throughout his career of ingratiating himself with the authorities and revolutionaries alike, and of securing the trust of neither side. Even Herzen, who respected his literary genius, thought Turgenev an equivocating old maid in politics.

Having supplied this softening and rosy context, Ignatieff gets to the most serious criticism that can be made of Berlin:

> Such, in crude terms, was the charge whispered behind Berlin's back throughout his steady ascent through the upper reaches of English life: . . . All of these failings amounted to the single indictment that he lacked the existential courage to stand and be counted.

Ignatieff makes a valiant, if unsuccessful, effort to show that Berlin was innocent of the whispered charge. But Berlin himself was honest enough to recognize how much truth there was in the indictment, for (as Ignatieff himself emphasizes) "the charge of cowardice bothered him all his life" and "caused him real anguish." As well it should have done, considering how fearful he was of taking public political stands that might jeopardize his ever-growing intellectual and social prestige, or that might—to throw his own words on Weizmann back at him again—expose him to "the risk of blame."

A PARTICULARLY DISTASTEFUL example of his aversion to such risks concerned the writer Goronwy Rees, who had been Berlin's dear friend for many years. Some time after Guy Burgess, a mutual friend of theirs, escaped to Moscow just as he was about to arrested as a Soviet agent, Rees published a series of articles about his now notorious old companion in a sensationalist tabloid. There he gave details of Burgess's libertinism as an incorrigible drunk and a wildly promiscuous homosexual, and strongly intimated that other spies like him were still at large in the British establishment. (He meant the art historian Anthony Blunt, who had not yet been exposed.)

For turning on dear old Guy in this vulgarly anti-Communist way, Rees was excommunicated by virtually the whole intellectual establishment of the country, most of whom, though loyal Englishmen themselves, found a certain merit in the novelist E. M. Forster's declaration that, given the choice, he would rather betray his country than his friend. But even Berlin, a principled and passionate anti-Communist who, Ignatieff assures us, "never had any difficulty thinking of himself as a cold warrior, as a liberal defender of the capitalist world and its freedoms," joined in the anti-Rees orgy. More unlovely yet, when Berlin ran into the left-wing journalist Tom Driberg at the Indonesian embassy in Moscow and heard that Driberg would be seeing Burgess, he asked him to send the traitor "his warmest love" and to tell him that "none of us are speaking to Goronwy." This, despite the fact that Berlin's stated reason for being angry with Rees in the first place was that he thought Rees had hintingly accused him of having once been in cahoots with Burgess.

The two men later had something of a reconciliation, and the day after Rees died, Berlin wrote in a letter of consolation to Daniel Rees that "Your father's death is a deep grief to me"—so deep that he would be unable to speak at the memorial service: "too much painful feeling." Later, however, when he was invited to speak anyway, he begged off on the ground that he did not know how to deal with Rees's own suspected involvement in espionage. More likely the truth was that he did not wish to make so public a gesture of identification with a man who had come to be regarded as a renegade by much of the world Berlin lived in.*

ZIONISM and the fruit it bore in the state of Israel might seem to have prodded Berlin with the chance to show some bravery; and at two points, at least, they did. Being an outspoken Zionist did indeed require courage in the England of the 1930s and then again during the period of fierce anti-Zionism of the Attlee-Bevin government that came into power right after the war and that was aggravated by the Jewish struggle to drive the British out of Palestine. This was especially true in the social circles in which the young Berlin aspired so passionately to move as a full-fledged member. But his loyalty to the Jewish people was so solid and unswerving that it overcame his social ambitions and anxieties.

As, however, the account I have just given about the evening at the Trillings demonstrates, the same loyalty—which I have not the slightest doubt Berlin continued to feel—was not enough to loosen his world-famously loose tongue when it took even greater courage to defend Israel,

---

*Neither the story about the message Berlin sent to Burgess through Driberg nor the one about his refusal to speak at Rees's memorial service comes from Ignatieff (who skates hastily over Berlin's relations with Rees on the one side and Burgess on the other). I found them in Jenny Rees's fascinating book about her father, *Looking for Mr. Nobody: The Secret of Goronwy Rees.* Her sources were Driberg's autobiography, *Ruling Passions,* and the letters she found among her father's papers.

this time not only in high society but also in the universities and among intellectuals in general. Or rather, it loosened his tongue to the opposite effect. Here is how Ignatieff describes Berlin's decision to make a rare public pronouncement about Israel toward the end of his life:

> Like his hero Turgenev who, when dying of cancer, had dictated "A Fire at Sea" . . . to acquit himself of a charge of cowardice, Berlin dictated a public appeal for political compromise in Israel. On 16 October 1997, on no one's initiative but his own, he composed a statement imploring Israelis to accept a final partition of the land with the Palestinians. . . . The alternative, he warned, was an interminable cycle of terrorist chauvinism on both sides and savage war.

Incredibly, Berlin thought, and Ignatieff agrees, that this statement showed courage. Of course, the fact is that it merely put Berlin solidly in line with the opinion being voiced by practically everyone else in the world. I am not suggesting that these were not his true sentiments. After all, in what may well have been the only time in his life he ever did such a thing, he had once refused to shake the hand of Prime Minister Menachem Begin because, as head of the Irgun in the prestate period, Begin had been responsible for the bombing of the King David Hotel, which then served as the headquarters of the British mandatory forces. And if a rumor going the rounds can be believed (it seems plausible enough), Berlin declared after Benjamin Netanyahu became prime minister that he had never hated anyone so much in his life.

In making the case for Berlin's greatness as a philosopher of liberalism, Ignatieff argues that

> empathy was, for Berlin, the core liberal attitude—the capacity to be open, receptive, unafraid in the face of opinions, temperaments, passions alien to one's own. . . . The result was a moral psychology of liberal life which, while unsystematic, was as deep as anything within the liberal canon since Adam Smith's *Theory of Moral Sentiments.*

Well, while such empathy could be summoned forth by Berlin for the extreme rightist views of a Joseph de Maistre, it clearly ran smack up against its limits where the hawkishness of the Israeli Right was concerned.* Nor did his commitment to and capacity for toleration extend to serious religious belief:

> Happy are those who live under a discipline which they accept without question, who freely obey the orders of leaders, spiritual or temporal, whose word is fully accepted as unbreakable law; or those who have, by their own methods, arrived at clear and unshakable convictions about what to do and what to be that brook no possible doubt. I can only say that those who rest on such comfortable beds of dogma are victims of self-induced myopia, blinkers that may make for contentment, but not for understanding of what it is to be human.

Admittedly, Berlin seems to have been thinking here more about the follower of fascist leaders than about Roman Catholics or hasidic Jews like his own Lubavitcher cousins. Nevertheless, in this statement, so violently discordant for an apostle of tolerance to let slip from his pen, he makes not the slightest effort to distinguish between the "spiritual" and the "temporal." All the more outlandish do I find this when I read in Ignatieff that

> For all his skepticism . . . he was repelled by the callow anti-clericalism of the Voltairian Enlightenment and had traced most of the evils of the 20th century to the idolatry of secular reason. "Stone-dry atheists," he once wrote, "don't understand what men live by."

Yet the very same person who could write and think such things was capable of denying to the truly religious an understanding of "what it is to be human" (!) and to lump them together with fascists and Communists.

AN EXTRAORDINARILY brilliant man, then, a conversationalist of genius, and the most amusing companion one could ever hope to have, but not the

---

*Namier once ranted (in Berlin's paraphrase) that "The Jews of England were victims of pathetic illusions—ostriches with their heads in some very inferior sands. . . ." For Namier, this was typically intemperate, but as always with him, there was something to it. Witness the fact that English Jews like Isaiah Berlin, who could write so movingly about Churchill, and even Churchill's own biographer Martin Gilbert, have been advocates of a "peace" policy toward the Arabs that in the European context they would not have hesitated for a second to denounce as appeasement or to predict could only lead to war.

great thinker he is so often taken to be. Even less is Berlin the moral hero that his biographer tries to make of him in an effort to cover over the spinelessness that the relativistic core of liberalism, even in its most sophisticated and civilized form, invariably brings out when determined challenges are posed to it, especially from the Left.

We see this once again today in the supine response of liberals to "multiculturalism," which can be understood as a diseased mutation of the pluralism that Isaiah Berlin never ceased extolling. Pluralism as Berlin expounded it had real force when fascism and Communism were riding high, and when, to its eternal honor, it formed one of the crucial elements making the case for bourgeois democracy as the superior alternative. But today, when "multiculturalism" is all the rage in England as well as in America, it can be of no help and may even do harm in the struggle to prevent the balkanization of our common culture and the dissolution of its intellectual and academic standards.

This is a process that I cannot believe Berlin himself would have wished to encourage. For to give credit where credit is due, he knew very well that pluralism was vulnerable to such diseases. Yet because he also knew that he had never really found a philosophical way of immunizing it against the ravages of relativism, and because he could never bear to be unpopular or to overcome the need to ingratiate himself—a need of which he was entirely aware and that he sometimes thought stemmed from his Jewishness—he made no contribution to the fight against multiculturalism while he was alive, and ideas like his still bear a certain responsibility for its spread.

A few months ago, at a symposium in New York on his work, critical questions of a kind rarely heard before were raised by a number of political theorists, mostly of the Left. It is much more common, however, for liberal intellectuals—in trying desperately to resurrect a point of view grown moribund with softness—to seek inspiration in the apparent solidity and strength of Isaiah Berlin's conception of liberalism. But they are misleading us when they inflate the importance of this great equivocator and they are kidding themselves when they look to his writings as the source of a new moral validation and the fount of a new intellectual vitality.

MY NEW YORK

SOMETHING EVIL IS GOING ON
in New York. But in order to justify resorting to this strongest of all epithets, I need to tell the story of the twists and turns I personally have witnessed and experienced as a native and lifelong resident of the city.

Perhaps as good a place as any to begin is with a phone call I received
some years ago from a woman doing publicity for the Brooklyn Public
Library system. From her broad Midwestern accent alone, I could tell that
she came from neither Brooklyn nor anywhere else in New York, but even
without that detail, the question she asked me would have proved definitively that she knew next to nothing about the city.

The question was this: As one of a number of "prominent people" born
and bred in Brooklyn, would I be willing to have my picture included in a
brochure celebrating an upcoming anniversary of the library? I would be
honored, I said; just send the photographer up to my office. "Oh no," she
answered, "we want to take your picture in front of the local branch you
used as a kid."

I had to pause before replying with a laugh that I had no objection to
this arrangement provided they could send me in a tank, or at least with a
police escort. And they had better do the same for the photographer. Even
if the branch from which I had regularly borrowed books many years earlier was still standing—which I doubted—the neighborhood surrounding
it had become a war zone, and any middle-class white who ventured into it
would be lucky ever to get out in one piece, if at all.

It was clear from her hemming and hawing that she was trying to decide
whether to take this as a piece of especially extravagant hyperbole or a
shameless display of racism; and since I never heard from her again, I concluded that she had opted for the latter. Yet I was exaggerating only slightly
about the danger of setting foot in the 1970s or 1980s into the Brownsville
section of Brooklyn, where I had spent the first twenty years of my life
(1930–50), during most of which Fiorello H. La Guardia was the mayor of
New York.

Admittedly, it was not exactly a peaceable neighborhood even then. In my own corner of it, immigrant Jews from East Europe lived side by side with Italian immigrants from Sicily, and Negroes from the rural American South who, if they were not strictly speaking immigrants, were no less foreign to the ways of the big city than their white neighbors. In these three groups, the adults had as little to do with one another as physical contiguity permitted. But their children (most of them, like me, born in America) all went to the nearby public school together, except for those who were sent either to Catholic or Jewish schools.

Throwing the children into the same educational "melting pot" unquestionably worked to reinforce the process of Americanization that would eventually differentiate us in ways both large and small from our parents. Yet as opposed to what school "integrationists" would naively have expected, there was scarcely any lessening among the kids of the ethnic and racial suspicions and hostilities pervading the immigrant generation. On the contrary: animosity was still strong enough in the second generation to erupt periodically in fistfights or turf wars. By the murderous standards of the future, these battles were relatively tame. Never did they involve guns and only rarely knives (though stones, bottles, and baseball bats could be pretty lethal themselves).

But what I want to emphasize is that such intergroup and interracial clashes were confined almost entirely to the kids. Among the adults, the only violence that ever broke out was black on black, usually (in a carryover from the Southern tradition) on Saturday nights in and around the bars in which no white person was ever seen. Yet (in another carryover from the South) neither was any white passerby ever assaulted.

My father's experience was typical. He worked all night long delivering milk, and on his way home from the subway, he had to pass those bars. Usually this was about 7:30 in the morning when they were still closed, but every Saturday he spent the whole day collecting the week's bills from the customers on his delivery route and did not get back until dark. And so as he walked past the bars and the clusters of drunks invariably hanging around outside them, the pockets of his uniform would be bulging and jingling with the coins that would remain in his care until he could turn them over to the company on Monday. Yet even at the height of the Great Depression of the 1930s, never once was he mugged or robbed.

Subsequently, in the late 1940s, I myself commuted daily by subway from Brownsville to the Columbia campus in uptown Manhattan. Two nights a week I also attended the academic division of the Jewish Theological Seminary, which was somewhat farther north than Columbia and only three short blocks from Harlem. Even then, a group of us—including a number of girls—thought nothing of saving some time after classes were over by cutting across a very dark Morningside Park at 10 o'clock at night to a subway station in Harlem itself.

When precisely it become almost suicidally foolhardy to do such a thing I cannot say. Almost certainly, like so much else by which we have been cursed, the new danger was born in the 1960s. At any rate, I can remember going to a Harlem nightclub as late as the late 1950s without feeling fearful or unwelcome. But I can also remember looking back on that experience a short time afterward with incredulity. By then I was married and living on the Upper West Side of Manhattan, and the menace in the air of my childhood in Brooklyn was now becoming palpable in my present neighborhood as well.

For example, after parking my car at night in the nearest garage, I would feel as though I were traversing a minefield while walking the five blocks to my apartment. Did the group of young Puerto Ricans hanging out on the corner ahead seem more dangerous than the one across the street or the cluster of blacks looming a block farther up? Should I cross here, and take my chances there, or would it be more prudent to keep going?

This was not paranoia or "racial profiling": I was in fact accosted once in a while. But growing up in the wilds of Brooklyn turned out to be good basic training in the techniques of brazening my way out of danger, and except for the rancid taste of fear and the humiliation it brought with it, I always got away unscathed. Others with softer backgrounds were not so lucky, and stories of muggings became the staples of neighborhood lore and conversation.

One consequence was the formation of block associations that would hire private security guards to patrol at night. This reliance on what I sardonically named a bunch of low-rent Wyatt Earps was decided upon, remember, in one of the most liberal parts of New York, where practically everyone believed that nothing could be done about violent crime until its "root causes"—that is, discrimination and poverty—were eliminated.

I raised four children in the neighborhood, and I very nearly bankrupted myself sending them to private schools because, beyond the lower grades, the local public schools were even less safe than the ones I had attended in Brooklyn. But I do not wish to exaggerate. Though a couple of my kids were robbed or roughed up on the streets by blacks or Hispanics a number of times, nothing worse than that happened to them or any of my neighbors' kids in the twenty years I lived on the Upper West Side.

Nevertheless, the point had long since been reached where all New Yorkers were increasingly wary of going out at night; and no one with any sense would venture into the parks after dark. Yet the paradox was that this thickening apprehension manifested itself in tandem with a great hopefulness about the new possibilities of racial harmony. In the late 1950s and early 1960s, the civil-rights movement, still in its benevolent integrationist phase, was under the leadership of advocates of nonviolence like Dr. Martin Luther King Jr. and great believers (like Roy Wilkins of the NAACP and Whitney Young of the Urban League) in the courts and the Congress as instruments of peaceable reform.

There was, however, a dark side to this integrationist optimism. It consisted in the readiness of many white New Yorkers to tolerate behavior from "minorities" (a new solecistic euphemism that had crept into the language) that only yesterday had been regarded as intolerable coming from anyone at all.

I FIRST BECAME AWARE of this development through what may seem a ridiculously trivial event—the sight of a black man lighting a cigarette on a subway train. At this distance, it is hard to convey how extraordinary it then was for anyone to smoke on the subway. Never before in all the thousands of hours I had spent traveling the subways in New York had I seen anyone light up inside one of the cars. I cannot explain why this particular rule had always been observed so punctiliously; but the fact was that it always had been, and to see it being violated—without anyone, including me, daring to protest—was so shocking that it seemed like the beginning of the end of civil order in New York.

Hysterical as my reaction now sounds, this violation turned out to be a clear foreshadowing of what, where far more serious matters—up to and including violent assault and murder—were concerned, was to become the norm in New York. So much so that when in the 1970s (or 1980s?) a number of New Yorkers were asked by a magazine to isolate the single most important problem afflicting the city and what it would take to solve it, I answered that so long as we continued "tolerating the intolerable," we would go on sliding down the slippery slope onto which we had fallen. I ended by wondering when, if ever, we would allow ourselves to reach bottom. Surely there must be a limit to our willingness to accept conditions that were so recently and so universally regarded as intolerable. Or was there?

For a long while, it looked as though the answer was no. The assassination of Martin Luther King in 1968 set off a series of veritably volcanic eruptions in black neighborhoods all over the country, but even in the preceding three years there had already been riots in many of the major American cities. Among blacks themselves, the burnings and the lootings were accompanied by a resurgence of various forms of anti-white black nationalism, with their repudiation of nonviolence in favor of "mau-mauing" or even "taking up the gun," and their rejection of integration in favor of separatism. And among white liberals, there arose a disposition to justify not only the riots but also any outrages committed under the auspices of this great ideological sea change.

In New York, the shift in attitudes among both blacks and whites more or less coincided with the mayoralty of John V. Lindsay (1965–73), a liberal Republican who ultimately made an honest man out of himself by becoming a liberal Democrat. But probably just as significant was the accession in that same era of McGeorge Bundy to the presidency of the Ford Foundation in New York.

Before his appointment to this job in 1966, Bundy had been national security adviser to Presidents John F. Kennedy and Lyndon B. Johnson, and had played a key role in the American decision first to intervene in Vietnam and then to escalate our involvement in the hope of winning the war. But by the time he left the waning Johnson administration, Bundy had evidently come to believe that it had been a mistake to resist the Communist Vietcong in the first place.

On the basis of the policy he immediately adopted as the new president of the Ford Foundation, I used to joke that no sooner had he arrived there than he summoned his staff and demanded that they bring him the Vietcong. The Vietcong? In New York? At so uncomprehending a reaction, as I imagined the scene, a derisive sneer formed on the lips of this famously arrogant New England patrician who knew as much about New York as the publicity lady at the Brooklyn Public Library (or as he himself had known about Vietnam when he plunged into it). "I mean the black radicals, the militants," I could hear him snarling at his underlings. "Get them up here, because this time, instead of fighting them, we're going to give them all grants."

But whether or not any exchange even remotely resembling this ever actually transpired, my imaginary scenario captures precisely how Bundy proceeded to deploy the great wealth and power of the Ford Foundation. In New York at that moment, the main objective of the radicals was to take over the public schools through a system known as "community control." Bundy threw the resources of the Ford Foundation behind this objective and the people pursuing it, while Lindsay more discreetly (being an elected official) added his own weight to the new strategy of appeasement.

Naturally, Bundy and Lindsay and their hordes of cheerleaders on the Left did not think of themselves as engaging in a cynical maneuver, and certainly not as the cowardly victims of a novel species of protection racket. In their own eyes, they were supporting programs designed to bring about a greater degree of social justice.

Similar programs instituted with the same rationale had already been set into motion by Johnson's "War on Poverty" and were constantly either being added to or funded more lavishly than ever (even after Richard Nixon replaced Johnson as president in 1969). And all the while, New York City became a more and more dangerous and unpleasant place to live.

Thus, thanks to an "enlightened" policy of releasing psychiatric patients from the institutions in which they had been hospitalized, New Yorkers soon found themselves tolerating hordes of raving lunatics—white as well as black—screaming and sometimes lunging at them with knives or other weapons, or pushing them off subway platforms into the path of oncoming trains.

The swelling population of the "homeless" who had taken to sleeping (and urinating and defecating) on the streets was made up in some part of these "deinstitutionalized" victims of a theory that was as delusional as their own psychotic fantasies. (The theory was that their illnesses could be treated adequately on the outside by medication, assuming that they were even really ill rather than rebels against a society that was itself insane and therefore eager to pin that label on anyone who refused to conform to its demented conception of rationality.)

But many of the homeless were also incorrigible alcoholics and junkies—again, both white and black—of the type who had once been confined by the police to the Bowery (New York's skid row). Now, however, their spillover into every part of the city was winked at by the police for the simple reason that no public outcry was raised against this intolerable situation.

The upshot was that beggars—a class mainly composed, like the homeless with whom they overlapped, of deinstitutionalized psychiatric patients, and drug addicts and alcoholics—now abounded everywhere a New Yorker went. Their pleas for money were often made with glowering eyes and threatening gestures. Or they might station themselves at intersections where cars were forced to wait for the light to change and start to "clean" the windshields with filthy rags and squeegees, for which service most drivers considered it the better part of prudence to shell out a "tip."

Any effort to cease tolerating these intolerable conditions was invariably frustrated by the courts. I remember in particular a federal judge named Leonard Sand ruling that it was a violation of the First Amendment to ban begging in the subway. Other judges decided that trying to hospitalize several out-of-control lunatics was an infringement on their civil liberties (or was it their civil rights?).

And all this is not even to mention the horrific increase in crimes of assault, rape, and murder whose numbers rose to hitherto unthinkable levels. As Daniel Patrick Moynihan would point out, the gunning down of seven mobsters in Chicago in 1929 became known as the St. Valentine's Day "massacre." Now, however, seven murders were hardly enough to make the evening news, and if the murderers were actually caught, chances were that they would be back on the street in very short order.

No wonder, then, that almost everyone had become sour on the city by the mid-1970s. Once upon a time, Americans from other parts of the country would say that New York was a nice place to visit, but they wouldn't want to live there. Increasingly, however, New Yorkers themselves were saying the same thing, while non–New Yorkers were no longer so sure that it was even a nice place to visit.

True, most of the great museums and concert halls were still located in the relatively safe areas, but the Broadway theaters in the Times Square area were now surrounded by some of the worst concentrations of the ills that had infected other parts of town: filthy streets, aggressive beggars, junkies and their suppliers, prostitutes of both sexes (often children), transvestites, pornographic movie theaters and stores.

Mostly here I have been talking about Manhattan, but in certain parts of the other boroughs it was even worse. The war zone my old neighborhood in Brooklyn had become was matched and even trumped by the South Bronx, whose very name evoked an image of urban decay at its most extreme. An occasional improvement would be announced, and perhaps even effected, through some initiative or other. But more commonly, well-intentioned interventions either collapsed or only made things worse.

In general, no one seemed to know what to do about the deterioration, and morale sank to a lower level than I had ever seen it go. Amazingly, even very prosperous New Yorkers who could enjoy the glamorous life—the great restaurants, the star-studded parties, the hugely expensive apartments on the Upper East Side—began to talk of leaving the city.

IN THE INTELLECTUAL community, which was my milieu, people to whom anywhere in America but New York had once been "Nowheresville" now also not only talked of leaving but actually left, most often for Washington. Indeed, so many intellectuals started moving there in the late 1970s that articles began to be written claiming that Washington, replacing New York, was becoming the intellectual as well as the political capital of the country.

The most formidable such article came from none other than my old friend Irving Kristol. Long regarded as the quintessential New York intellectual, Kristol of all people had pulled up stakes and relocated in Washington, taking the magazine he edited, *The Public Interest,* with him. So portentous did Kristol's desertion of New York seem, and so persuasive was the case he made for its decline as an intellectual center, that I—considered another quintessential New York intellectual—was suddenly getting calls from reporters who wanted to know whether I agreed with him and whether I intended to follow him down there. My answer was that I thought he was right about the decline of New York as an intellectual center, but way off in claiming that Washington would or could replace it.

The problem, I said in a piece I then decided to write in reply to Kristol, was that Washington was a company town. As Detroit was to automobiles, and as Los Angeles was to the movie business, so Washington was to the one great industry for which it had been created. No matter how many think tanks might set up shop there, or how many veterans of New York's ideological wars might join them, Washington would remain umbilically tied to the affairs of the federal government.

As such, it would always strangle any idea that could not immediately be translated into a legislative proposal or a political scheme. But for ideas that aimed "only" at analyzing or synthesizing the realities around us so that we could comprehend or appreciate them better, Washington had little patience and less time. Which meant that it could never provide an environment for a genuinely serious intellectual community.

The New York I had once lived in was a world made up mainly of writers and critics and magazine editors like myself, with an admixture of painters and musicians, who saw one another on a regular basis and who spent much of their time arguing with great heat and seriousness about the arts and politics. The politics in question did not as a rule involve the issues that usually agitated elected officials or that arose in electoral contests. For none of us cared all that much about Democrats and Republicans ("Tweedledumb and Tweedledumber," as one well-known New York intellectual, Dwight Macdonald, once dismissed them). It was politics in the ideological sense that preoccupied us almost exclusively.

This meant arguing about Karl Marx and which of his latter-day disciples, if any, was the legitimate carrier of his analysis and his vision. It meant (since we all agreed that Stalin had betrayed the cause of socialism for which the Russian Revolution had been fought) arguing about whether a change of regime in the Soviet Union could make a difference, or whether the crimes of Stalinism were the logically inexorable consequence of the Communist system, or even (a breathtakingly bold idea) of Marxism itself.

But it also meant arguing about America. Was this country nothing more than the embodiment of a materialistic, plutocratic, puritanical, and philistine culture? Intellectuals not only on the Left but also on the Right (like Henry Adams and the "Southern Agrarians" of the 1930s) had been saying so for at least a century now. Yet some of us (the ones who ultimately became known as "neoconservatives") were beginning to believe that America was the single greatest bastion and defender of freedom and prosperity in a world menaced by murderous totalitarian tyrannies. About this, too, furious debate raged on and on.

On that level, we were very passionate about politics. And we were equally passionate about the arts. I had seen grown men nearly come to blows over the merits of a book of poems (the publication of Robert Lowell's *Life Studies* in 1959 was one such occasion), and I myself (in 1953, at the age of 23!) was threatened with ruin by another famous poet, John Berryman, for what to him was the unforgivably bad critical judgment I had shown in writing an unfavorable review of Saul Bellow's novel *The Adventures of Augie March*. I had also known people who ceased speaking to each other because one of them was convinced that Jackson Pollock was the wave of the future in painting, and the other was betting on Willem de Kooning.

Yes, *that* New York was pretty well dead and gone by the mid-1970s. It had already been weakened by the dispersal of its members to universities all over the country, and then it was killed off by the assault on its foundations that came from the New Left and the counterculture of the previous decade. Hence the intellectual life of the city was now conducted almost entirely on paper, with very few face-to-face encounters to give it an extra lift and a heartier dose of spice.

Nevertheless, New York, I thought, still constituted a better environment for thinking and writing about important matters, including even political matters, than Washington. According to Kristol, the ruling passion of New York had become the pursuit of money. Not that he had anything against this. Though he did not quote Dr. Johnson—"there are few ways in which a man can be more innocently employed than in getting money"—his own attitude was much the same. But the pursuit of money did not, in his view, give as much food for thought as the ruling passion of Washington, which was the pursuit of power. But there, in my opinion, Kristol was mistaken.

As I saw it, the ruling passion of New York was the ambition for success, of which the acquisition or possession of money was merely one of many different forms. Unlike political power, success could be sought in so great a variety of fields that the obsession with it made for a more multifarious and therefore more intellectually interesting world than was dreamed of in the monomaniacal philosophy of our most monolithic company town.

"So," I said in conclusion, "I wish my old friend well in his new surroundings, but for *this* surviving remnant of the moribund New York intellectual community, Manhattan is the only place to be."

I WAS PERFECTLY SINCERE when I wrote these words, but they were incomplete in that they did not touch upon the disgust I shared with so many other New Yorkers about the overall condition of the city. Nor was this disgust significantly lessened by the fact that I had by now moved from the Upper West Side of Manhattan to the Upper East Side. There one felt—and in fact was—safer, but even in this most prosperous and privileged part of Manhattan, people were permitted to sleep on the streets at night and to accost one by day with pleas (or rather demands) for money. Even there, in other words, toleration of the intolerable was still the regnant ethos.

Some improvement seemed to be in the offing when Edward I. Koch became mayor in 1978 and began offering public resistance to what he called the "poverty pimps." Koch even tried hard to get the homeless off the streets and into shelters, but for a host of reasons—not least the opposition he ran into from the courts and liberal organizations like the ACLU—he failed. Therefore, while Koch's colorful rhetoric helped create a better atmosphere, the actual condition of the city remained dismal. Moreover, the outspoken mayor's candor about race, though refreshing to some of us, simultaneously played, as opportunity arose, into the hands of black demagogues like Al Sharpton and Sonny Carson and their white fellow-travelers.

It all went even farther downhill when David Dinkins, New York's first black mayor, succeeded Koch in 1990. The gentlemanly Dinkins, a standard product of the old Democratic machine in New York, was not himself cut from the same cloth as the likes of Sharpton. Yet being black, he was much more subject than Koch to the pressures coming from such quarters. The result was that he permitted Carson, in violation of a court order, to stage a boycott in Brooklyn against a Korean grocery store that went on for weeks with, at most, token interference from the police. Dinkins was also very slow to respond when blacks in the Brooklyn neighborhood of Crown Heights rioted against their Orthodox Jewish neighbors, and a rabbinical student was set upon by a mob and stabbed to death.

It was incidents such as these that led to Dinkins's defeat in 1993 at the hands of Rudolph Giuliani, a Republican who (unlike Lindsay) was not a liberal Democrat at heart. Having voted for Giuliani, I obviously figured that he would be better than Dinkins. Yet neither I nor anyone else ever dreamed that the new mayor—or any other person occupying that office—would be able to turn the city around, let alone that he would do so almost overnight. How wrong we were.

Our error arose from a failure to anticipate two things that would previously have seemed out of the question. One was the application of an academic theory for fighting crime that—perhaps for the first time in the history of academic theories of social policy—not only worked but did so almost from the minute it was put into practice. This was the so-called "broken windows" thesis originally developed by George L. Kelling and James Q. Wilson.

Simply described, the thesis held that neglect of very minor infractions of public order encouraged and engendered larger and more serious crimes that were much more difficult to tackle. Under the influence of this idea, the Giuliani administration concentrated on apparently trivial "quality-of-life" offenses. In a flash the squeegee wielders were gone from the intersections in which they had formerly stationed themselves; suddenly there was hardly a derelict sleeping on the streets by night and begging by day; all at once, youths avoiding the payment of fares by jumping over subway turnstiles ran into the waiting arms of cops on the other side. This last tactic, to the amazement of everyone but (I daresay) Kelling and Wilson, brought a bonus in the arrest of a very large number of youths who were packing guns and were wanted for some graver charge.

All by itself, this campaign effected an enormous transformation. From a city that even a stubborn holdout like me had started wondering whether to leave, New York was turning into a place in which it was again a pleasure simply to walk. It was by no means a paradise, and certainly it helped that the economy—fueled by the Wall Street boom and engendering such improvements as the cleanup of Times Square—was doing so well.

But it was itself stupid to imagine that the change in New York could all be credited to "the economy, stupid." The truth was that a majority of New Yorkers—including even liberals whispering to one another at dinner parties, if rarely in public—had finally answered my question about whether the point would ever be reached when New Yorkers would stop tolerating the intolerable. That this point had indeed been reached was what put Giuliani into City Hall and gave him a mandate to see whether a crackdown would actually bring results even while at least some of the "root causes" of crime remained in place.

The second unexpectedly fruitful course Giuliani adopted in following through on this mandate was to enlarge the NYPD's "street crime" unit. This was an elite force of plainclothes policemen who were sent to high-crime areas (which were invariably populated by blacks and Hispanics) and empowered to take measures that would prevent crime instead of just pursuing perpetrators after their crimes had been committed. Such measures included stopping suspicious-looking types and frisking them in the hope of confiscating concealed weapons.

It was four officers in this unit who in February 1999 pumped nineteen bullets into an innocent young immigrant named Amadou Diallo from Guinea, under—so far as we know—the impression that he was a serial rapist for whom they had been searching and that he was about to pull a gun on them. Here was the golden opportunity Al Sharpton had been waiting for to launch what Arch Puddington, in a recent article in *Commentary,* aptly described as "The War on the War on Crime." It was also the perfect cue for the temporarily silenced "root cause" crowd to find its voice again. Daily demonstrations were held featuring famous politicians and even more famous actors and actresses who demanded that federal investigations be launched. No comparably garish a show of "radical chic" had been seen in New York since Leonard Bernstein's notorious party for the Black Panthers in 1970. Never mind that, as George Kelling himself put it, under Giuliani "last year New York had 0.48 fatal shootings per 1,000 officers, the lowest figure since 1985." Never mind that "in 1992, when David Dinkins was mayor, more than 2,200 people were murdered in New York City—a high proportion of them minorities," as compared with just 600 under Giuliani in 1998 ("fewer," added Kelling, "than in Chicago, whose population is barely one-third of New York's"). Never mind that "sixteen hundred more New Yorkers would have died last year alone had crime remained at Dinkins-era levels."

In spite of all this, the demonstrators shouted themselves hoarse spreading the egregious lie that police brutality and trigger-happiness had run amok under Giuliani. The reduction in crime, went their mantra, had been achieved by a systematic violation of the rights of innocent "minorities."

Here, finally, I come to the reason I think that "evil" is not too strong a word to describe what is going on in New York. To quote Kelling again, this time on what might be characterized as the multiplier effect of the sixteen hundred lives saved by Giuliani's crime-fighting policies: "Calculate the . . . families spared grief, youths not imprisoned, and we are talking about thousands of New Yorkers whose lives have been immeasurably improved. . . ." I contend that "evil" is precisely the right word for a campaign whose purpose is to undo so much good in order to resurrect a discredited ideological position and to reap a crassly partisan political advantage.

But will this evil drive succeed? Will New Yorkers once again allow themselves to be intimidated into tolerating the intolerable? I would guess not, and I hope not, if only because the taste of a better city is still fresh in their mouths. And yet so resolute is the evil will that has come into play here that I fear the worst.

If the worst were to happen, I myself might at long last give up on New York. Unlike Irving Kristol, I managed to remain here despite the loss of the intellectual community that made up *my* New York, and his, and I eventually built up a new life in new surroundings and with new friends. As befits the rapid advance of my age to three score and ten, and also suits my correlatively more reclusive habits, it is a less exciting and much less eventful life than I led when I was young.

Still, in the past few years, there has been compensation in the resurrected pleasures of wandering about this great city that is my birthplace without having to avert my eyes from the signs of degradation that daily afflicted them not so long ago, or to look nervously over my shoulder after dark at the sound of approaching footsteps from behind, or to glance apprehensively at every street corner ahead.

"I'll take Manhattan/The Bronx and Staten/Island too./It's lovely going through/The zoo," sang Rodgers and Hart once upon a time. Once upon a time, too, Fred Astaire danced in Central Park under the lamplight at night, crooning as he leaped from bench to bench something like, "I like

New York in June/How about you?" And later Gene Kelly and Frank Sinatra jumped all over the place singing (in the words of Comden and Green and to the music of Bernstein), "New York, New York, it's a wonderful town/The Bronx is up and the Battery's down/The people ride in a hole in the ground."

Alas, we have not yet arrived back at that romantic Technicolor pass, and perhaps never will. Yet at the moment, just strolling in that same Central Park on a sunny Sunday in the spring is to encounter so many delights—the kids scampering, the dogs running, the roller bladers skating, the joggers jogging, the cyclists biking, the boaters rowing, the girls sunbathing, the musicians performing, and all with nary a frown in view— that it is hard to believe how dangerous this place (where an 80 *percent* reduction in serious crime has occurred in the past six years) so recently was.

If, then, the evil designs of Al Sharpton and his ilk should prevail, New York might finally lose me. And that would of course be the least of so great a calamity.

WAS BACH JEWISH?

I ONCE SHOCKED A DEVOUT Lutheran friend by telling him that Johann Sebastian Bach was really Jewish. I knew perfectly well, of course, that Bach had been a Lutheran—indeed, the greatest glory of that Christian denomination—and I was mainly being provocative. Then I added that, compared with Bach, Ludwig van Beethoven was the true Christian. Here again I knew that Beethoven, although a Catholic and capable of composing the *Missa Solemnis,* had not been so deep a believer as Bach. Yet I was being at least half-serious in assigning Bach to Judaism and Beethoven to Christianity.

A similar thought must have occurred to whoever originally described Bach's *Well-Tempered Clavier* as the Old Testament of keyboard music, and Beethoven's piano sonatas as the New. So far as I know, this analogy has never provoked surprise or outrage; the very fact that it stuck suggests that my own more outlandish extrapolation of it has some basis in a widely shared intuition about the two composers.

Still, I will concede that "outlandish" is the right word to describe my position. For a start, Lutheranism may be at a further remove from Judaism than any other Christian denomination. From a theological point of view, indeed, they are almost polar opposites.

Judaism puts its stress not on belief or faith, but on action—what Christians call "works." To be an Orthodox Jew means to dedicate one's life to following the Law or (in Hebrew) the Torah as handed down by God to Moses on Mount Sinai. The Torah consists of a written text (the Bible, or what Christians call the Old Testament) as interpreted in enormous detail by what was originally an oral tradition. After the fourth century it was set down in writing as well, and became known as the Talmud.

Perhaps the best secular analogy to the relation between the Bible and the Talmud is the one between the U.S. Constitution and the entire corpus of Supreme Court decisions, including all the dissents from those decisions. But whereas the compendium of Supreme Court rulings does not include the congressional debates preceding them, the Talmud does reproduce the exegetical arguments among the rabbis, leading up to their final decisions.

Taken together, all this falls under the rubric of the halakhah, a Hebrew word meaning "the way," but understood to refer to the statutes and rabbinical rulings which govern the behavior of an observant Jew. From the minute he rises in the morning until he goes to bed at night, just about every action he is likely to perform falls under the aegis of these laws.

What seems most strange about Judaism to many Christians is how small a role faith plays in this religious scheme. At Mount Sinai, on agreeing to abide by the Law, the ancient Israelites said, "We will do and we will hear," which was interpreted to mean that action came before belief, and that belief (even if absent) would come and grow through such action. Thus theology never played the kind of role for Jews that it did for Christians and Muslims. There was only a handful of Jewish theologians who busied themselves with faith, but of commentators performing exegeses on the Law there was—and is—no end.

It goes without saying that observant Jews believe in and love God as the creator of the world and as the giver of the Law whose "yoke" they take upon themselves as a blessing and a joy. It is also true that the greatest of all Jewish theologians, Maimonides (who lived in the Middle Ages), laid down thirteen principles in which Jews are supposed to believe. Nevertheless, Judaism is a religion of "works" rather than faith. Good Jews are good by virtue of the commandments they follow, not the theological niceties they accept.

I heard an anecdote illustrating the force of this ethos from an Israeli friend who had become an atheist in his teens and whose father was Orthodox. One day, while having an intense argument about the existence of God, my friend's father looked at his watch and said to his son: "Well, God may or may not exist, but it's time for the evening prayers."

A devout Christian could never say that. And of all the Christian denominations, Lutheranism is perhaps *least* well equipped to understand such a perspective. For it is precisely through faith and not through works that, according to Luther, salvation must be sought. Bach's cantatas— many of them settings of hymns by Luther himself—are pervaded by this doctrine.

As if this were not enough to refute my thesis about Bach, there is the anti-Semitism—no softer term will do—with which Martin Luther came to be infected. So fierce was his hatred of Jews that some have even seen him as the ultimate source of Nazi anti-Semitism. Bach did not, so far as I am aware, share this attitude. Yet in the *St. John Passion,* his setting of the Fourth Gospel, he omitted many passages but not the nasty outbursts which disfigure this most anti-Jewish book of the New Testament.

So how can I suggest that Bach was really Jewish? There is no evidence that Bach himself or any of his ancestors was Jewish; I do not for a moment entertain any such fantasy. What am I talking about, then? The answer lies in the nature of Bach's music and the fundamental principle it embodies, which is strict adherence to the established rules of the art in his day. So law-abiding was Bach—so joyously did he shoulder the "yoke" of the musical laws which had been handed down to him—that he fell out of fashion as other composers came along, including some of his own sons. The music critic Samuel Lipman once described the rebellion against their father by his two most talented offspring—Carl Philipp Emanuel Bach and Johann Christian Bach—as tantamount to saying: "Let's just listen to the pretty tunes now."

Pretty tunes abounded in their father's huge output. To cite just one example, the aria "Erbarme dich" from the *St. Matthew Passion* is arguably the most beautiful melody in the history of Western music. Yet it was embedded in so traditional a composition that for a very long time no one could bother to listen to it. Moreover, not even the fact that the *St. Matthew Passion* as a whole may be the greatest single piece of music ever written could save it from oblivion. It was lost for almost a century until Felix Mendelssohn rediscovered it. Mendelssohn was a Protestant, but he descended from a Jewish family (his grandfather, Moses Mendelssohn, was an eminent Jewish scholar), and he remained attached to his roots. I have always wondered whether it was the connection he maintained with Judaism that opened Mendelssohn's ears to the greatness of the *St. Matthew Passion*—whose words were the words of the New Testament but whose music, in its strict fidelity to the laws governing the art, was the music of the Old.

The same applies to such strictly secular works of Bach as the preludes and fugues of the *Well-Tempered Clavier,* the sonatas and partitas for violin, the pieces for solo cello, and so on. Incidentally, his last work, the unfinished and mysteriously sublime *Art of the Fugue*—a final exploration of the most strictly orthodox of traditional musical forms—suffered an even worse fate than the *St. Matthew Passion.* The only extant manuscript was found by one of his sons after Bach's death, wrapped around a fish.

But to explain why I think all these works are also "Jewish," I must introduce another concept central to biblical Judaism. The rabbis of the

Talmud managed through ingenious hermeneutical digging to extract from certain obscure phrases in the Bible a belief in an afterlife. This is why the resurrection of the dead came to be affirmed in the Jewish liturgy and why it ended up as one of Maimonides's Thirteen Principles of the Faith. But in the Bible itself, no such belief is clearly visible. Biblical Judaism concerns itself with life in this world; it prescribes a way of living such a life which will ensure that it be both long and prosperous. If you choose to live in accordance with God's commandments, you will be rewarded with "length of days" and much prosperity—not in heaven, but here on earth.

That this promise was—and is—honored at least as often in the breach as in the observance did not escape the notice of the ancient Israelites. Many biblical passages and an entire book—the Book of Job—are audacious enough to call God to account, demanding an explanation of why the virtuous so often suffer and the wicked so commonly prosper. The explanation usually consists of a variation on "You are incapable of understanding," yet pious Jews have generally accepted this as sufficient. They have continued to believe that in some sense beyond the powers of the human mind to grasp, God does keep His promise.

I would argue that encapsulated in the music of Bach is what may be the most convincing demonstration ever offered of this biblical proposition: far more convincing than the voice from the whirlwind in the Book of Job. Bach's music does not sweep away the doubts raised by God's promise in the Bible. Instead, it shows that remaining within the finite limits of the Law is the way of infinite riches.

Without seeking for novelty or new forms, Bach was able to pour forth an endless succession of pieces whose reach was as deep as the human mind has ever plunged, as wide as the human heart has ever extended, as high as the human spirit has ever soared. Everything within the universe of human experience is there. And just as every human being born into this world is simultaneously the same as all others of the species and also a unique individual, so almost every one of Bach's pieces is at once free of innovation and also entirely new and original.

Within the confines of the law, Bach uncovered so much complexity, so broad a range of emotion, that the performer of his music can scarcely capture it all or the listener take it all in. But capture it the performer can— and the attentive ear is quite capable of hearing it. In that respect it is like the Law of the Bible itself, which, we are told, is within the grasp of everyone.

In Deuteronomy, the identification between the Law and life is made explicit: "I have set before thee life and death . . . : therefore choose life." But the life we are here enjoined to choose is life on this earth, and we are to choose it by obeying the Law. To make this choice is to escape the curse of death—a living death, not the condition of mortality to which all, saints and sinners alike, are inescapably subject.

This was the bone which stuck in the throat of Saul of Tarsus, a Jew like Jesus himself, who on the road to Damascus had a vision of Christ crucified which transformed him into the man who became St. Paul. It is (is it not?) fairly obvious from the Gospels that Jesus and his disciples had no intention of founding a new religion. They differed from their fellow Jews chiefly in their conviction that Jesus was the Messiah who, upon being resurrected, would eject the Romans from the occupied Holy Land and restore the Davidic dynasty and the rule of God. Far from rebelling against the Law, they dreamed of conditions that would make for a more perfect observance of it than had been possible under the Romans. For had not Jesus himself said: "Think not that I am come to destroy the law. . . . I am not come to destroy but to fulfill"?

To St. Paul, however, the advent of Jesus had effected a cosmic revolution. Whereas the other earliest Christians continued to obey the Law of Judaism, St. Paul proclaimed that it had been abrogated. When he cried out, "Who shall deliver me from the body of this death?" the only answer Judaism returned was, in effect: "No one can rescue you from death, but if you live according to the commandments, you will enjoy all the life there is to live."

Yet this, said St. Paul, was impossible for him. Despite his best efforts, he could not obey the commandments because, although the spirit was willing, the flesh was weak and corrupt by its very nature as an inheritance of the original sin of disobedience committed by Adam and Eve.

The answer St. Paul needed was the answer he understood Jesus (whom he had never known personally) to have given: by the grace of God, manifested in the sacrifice of His only Son, the old Law was no longer binding, and the foremost among its abrogated components was its very foundation: death itself. Mortality had been conquered and abolished: "Death is swallowed up in victory," he wrote. "O death, where is thy sting?" With mortality thus vanquished, eternal life was established—not as the reward of fulfilling the commandments (which was beyond the corrupted human creature anyway), but as a loving gift to those who believed in Christ: "For as in Adam all die, even so in Christ shall all be made alive."

The technical term for hostility to law is antinomianism. There has been much controversy among theologians over how antinomian St. Paul was. Yet I cannot imagine how a disinterested reader of his Epistles could fail to see that a strong strain of antinomianism runs through them. Nor is it easy to miss the link between this attitude to the Law and the ambition to transcend the mortal limits of the human condition.

Which brings me to Beethoven. In his classic work, *Beethoven: His Spiritual Development*, J. W. N. Sullivan writes: "Of Beethoven's religious beliefs we know very little, except that they were not orthodox." Fair enough. But not even Sullivan could deny that Beethoven was some kind of believing Christian; and no one who has listened to the *Missa Solemnis* could doubt it. In characterizing Beethoven as Christian, however, I am not talking about his specific beliefs or his day-to-day conduct. As in the case of Bach, it is the nature of his music that I have in mind.

To Sullivan, on the other hand, the "spiritual development" reflected in Beethoven's music has nothing to do with Christianity. Rather, this development grows out of Beethoven's heroic struggle with the Fate that he had "seized by the throat." It culminates in his achievement of a state beyond struggle—one in which he arrives at an unearthly peace with suffering as an essential component of life. Sullivan even seems to think that to conceive of Beethoven's music in religious terms is to limit it: "The man who has sincerely accepted a religious scheme in which all the major problems of life are provided with solutions is likely to go through life without ever experiencing the direct impact of those problems. That is, in fact, the weakness of Bach as compared with Beethoven."

Sullivan was a mathematician with a great love of music. While not influenced by the vulgar materialism of some of his colleagues, he was enough of a secularist—and sufficiently ignorant of religion—to write the above sentence. How then could he have been expected to know that in denigrating "Bach as compared with Beethoven," he was echoing ancient Christian denigrations of Judaism which went back to St. Paul? (When he says that Bach, "who may be likened to Beethoven for the seriousness and maturity of his mind, lost himself at the end in the arid labyrinths of pure technique," I catch an echo of the charge that Judaism is merely and exclusively legalistic.)

Sullivan's praise of Beethoven—for him, the greatest artist who ever lived—is based less on the composer's heroic struggle against Fate (the same Fate that robbed him of his hearing) than on his refusal to remain bound by the laws of the musical tradition he had inherited. Beethoven's earliest work was, in the main, traditional, but beginning with his third symphony, the *Eroica,* he grew increasingly dissatisfied with the restrictions to which earlier composers had submitted.

Sullivan interprets this refusal as the supreme example of the old-fashioned conception of the artist as the Romantic rebel, shaking his fist at the heavens and asserting the value of his own individuality: "So much of what Beethoven expresses is unique" and his last quartets were "different in kind from any other music that he or anybody else ever wrote." In the school of Romantic thought, by which Sullivan was influenced, no higher praise could be sung.

By contrast, my (almost serious) theory is that this uniqueness testified to an antinomian streak in Beethoven analogous to, and ultimately stemming from, Pauline Christianity. Sullivan, borrowing a line from Wordsworth, declares that Beethoven was "Voyaging through strange seas of Thought, alone" and that in embarking on those seas, Beethoven achieved "superhuman knowledge" and a "superhuman life." In other words, Beethoven's aim was to transcend the human condition as defined by the mortality which to St. Paul was inseparable from the Law.

In using the term "superhuman," Sullivan is also saying that Beethoven realized this aim in his last works, especially the string quartets and most particularly the one in C sharp minor. I do not agree—although I do not challenge the view that Beethoven was a giant among composers. My own knowledge of music comes strictly through the ear—I neither play any instrument nor read scores—but I am an addicted listener. As such, I have tried at least a hundred (or is it a thousand?) times to discern what Sullivan hears in Beethoven's last quartets and piano sonatas. In vain. I must confess to the heresy of hearing in Schubert's String Quintet in C major more of the quality Sullivan finds in Beethoven's String Quartet in C sharp minor.

More heretically yet, as against his last quartets and sonatas, I even prefer the works of Beethoven's middle period (the Seventh Symphony, the "Harp" string quartet, the *Missa Solemnis,* and the first three movements of the Ninth Symphony), in which he has not yet—at least not entirely—devoted himself to overcoming the limitations of the laws of music and thereby "the body of this death."

Might it be the Jew in me who resists the products of this quintessentially Christian ambition, as it may have been the atavistic Jew in Mendelssohn whose ears were opened to Bach's *St. Matthew Passion*—a work which, notwithstanding that its libretto is mostly drawn from one of the most sacred of all Christian texts, I cannot help finding quintessentially Jewish?

Let me give the last word to Thomas Mann. In *Doctor Faustus* there is a scene in which Kretzschmar, a lecturer on music, informs his students that Beethoven's contemporaries doubted he could write a successful fugue. To silence these doubts, Beethoven wrote the *Grosse Fuge,* which puzzled his contemporaries, but which by Kretzschmar's time had come to be seen as one of his most miraculous compositions.

To Kretzschmar himself, however, the issue was more complex. Mann writes: "He would be bold . . . perhaps even stick his foot in it, by declaring that in such a treatment of the fugue one could see hatred and violation, a thoroughly unaccommodating and problematical relationship with the art-form, a reflection of the relationship, or lack thereof, between the great man and one still greater . . . Johann Sebastian Bach."

Emboldened by Kretzschmar, I will stick my foot in even deeper. I will speculate that the idea Mann puts into Kretzschmar's mouth about Beethoven's attitude toward Bach may have some bearing on "the relationship, or lack thereof," between Christianity and Judaism in (let us hope) days gone by.

GOD AND THE SCIENTISTS

THE SINGLE MOST IMPORTANT phenomenon of the millennium just ending was the dog that didn't bark. But the second most important was the dog that did.

As to the dog that barked: it was, surely, the development of modern science. This process started not at the beginning of the millennium but halfway through it, getting seriously under way with Copernicus in the middle of the sixteenth century and picking up steam in the early seventeenth. Yet in the four centuries since Copernicus proved that the Earth revolves around the sun rather than the other way around, more has been learned about the natural world than was known in all the ages of human existence that came before them.

This seems, when one pauses to reflect on it, very odd. After all, there can be no doubt that some of the greatest intellects ever to appear on earth were active two thousand years ago and earlier. Among the ancient Hebrews and the ancient Greeks alone, there were thinkers who have never been surpassed in profundity, originality, vision, and wisdom.

Some of these ancient peoples even applied themselves to mathematics and the sciences, and up through the Middle Ages their work continued to exert a mighty influence on Jewish, Christian, and Muslim philosophers and theologians alike. Thus Scholasticism, the school of thought rejected by modern science (the "new philosophy," in the parlance of the time), was almost as deeply rooted in the Greeks, especially Aristotle, as in the Bible. Indeed, the most formidable of the Scholastics, St. Thomas Aquinas, dedicated himself to reconciling reason (equated with Aristotle) and revelation (the Scriptures). And in the course of pursuing this enterprise, Aquinas had much to say about the physical nature of the universe.

What, then, can explain why most, if not all, of what these great minds thought they knew about the nature of the material world was wrong? Conversely, how did it happen that Copernicus, and then Kepler and Galileo (the two giants who came right after him), and those who followed in their footsteps all the way to the present day, got most, if not all, of it right?

One might imagine that so huge and consequential a question would be hard to answer. But no. Galileo himself answered it. The Scholastics, he clearly recognized, were interested only in explaining *why* things were as they were, and their explanations (with more than a little help from Aristotle) took the form of logical deduction from the truths they already possessed through revelation. Galileo's revolutionary aim, by contrast, was to discover *how* things were by observing and measuring them.

Galileo never claimed that these new experimental procedures could uncover anything about the cause or the origin of the forces being measured and observed. But through such procedures, he could and did find evidence that the Scholastics, and Aristotle before them, were wildly mistaken about the physical universe. Speaking of phenomena that he had spotted through the telescope he built—phenomena that were ruled out by the prevailing Scholastic theory—Galileo declared: "We have in our new age accidents and observations, and such, that I question not in the least, but if Aristotle were now alive, they would make him change his opinion."

Well, Aristotle might, but the professor at Padua was no Aristotle. He declined even to look through the telescope Galileo had built. Why bother? So far as he was concerned, nothing he might see could shed light on the human purposes it served.

Galileo took the opposite tack. It was, he argued, beyond the power of the human mind unaided by revelation to penetrate those purposes. Therefore, it would be better for people "to pronounce that wise, ingenious, and modest sentence, 'I know it not,'" and not (like the Scholastics) "suffer to escape from their mouths and pens all manner of extravagance." Even though Galileo, while famously forced by the Church to recant his belief in the heliocentric cosmology of Copernicus, held on privately to that belief, he did not reject Christianity. He also contended that science did not contradict the Bible as properly understood. But he did, willy-nilly, sever the connection forged most fully by Aquinas between reason and revelation.

To the great English poet John Donne, who lived in the early days of this intellectual revolution, it was a disaster:

> *And new philosophy calls all in doubt,*
> *The element of fire is quite put out;*
> *The Sun is lost, and the earth, and no man's wit*
> *Can well direct him where to look for it. . . .*
> *'Tis all in pieces, all coherence gone. . . .*

However, Donne's fellow countryman and near contemporary, Sir Francis Bacon, saw it all very differently. In Bacon's view, the new philosophy was no threat—not to religious faith, not to the wit of man and not to the social order. By separating out "the absurd mixture of matters divine and human" that the Scholastics had concocted, all the new philosophy did was "to render unto faith the things that are faith's." To understand the word of God, we now had to "quit the small vessel of human reason, and put ourselves on board the ship of the Church, which alone possesses the divine needle for justly shaping the course." Furthermore, in submitting to the limits of human reason, we would lay bare the true wonders of God's creation, and we would thereby ultimately be led to worship Him all the more.

This prediction may have been sincere or, more likely, a clever piece of apologetics, but in any case it turned out to be wrong about the effect of the new philosophy on religious belief. As science progressed, faith in the old sense grew correspondingly weaker, and by the eighteenth century—which was not dubbed the Age of Reason for nothing—it had been diluted into the depersonalized generalities of deism.

In the meantime, the human mind unaided by revelation was showing such enormous power that even a poet like Alexander Pope (who was a Roman Catholic) fell into a state of veneration as before a saint in contemplating the figure of the preeminent scientist of his day, Sir Isaac Newton:

> *Nature and Nature's law lay hid in night;*
> *God said, "Let Newton be," and all was light.*

The paradox was that this apparently unlimited power had been unleashed precisely by the willingness of reason to become (in Galileo's term) more "modest." In restricting itself to what it was capable of discovering, instead of presuming to answer the ultimate questions that were beyond its ken, the human mind had rapidly acquired a vaster store of knowledge about the physical universe than it had managed to gather in all the years gone by.

By the nineteenth century, with the advent of Charles Darwin, the new philosophy had descended from the planets to the apes. And with this shift, the so-called war between religion and science, which Bacon had denied would ever occur, heated up to a veritable frenzy. Like so many of the scientists who had come before him, Darwin protested that he was not a nonbeliever and he insisted that his discovery of the descent of man from the apes did not refute the essential truths of religion.

But to little avail. There were (and still are) desperate efforts by many Christians either to refute Darwin or to find a way of maintaining their faith in the biblical account of creation in the teeth of his work. Great outpourings of religious enthusiasm even occurred here and there. And yet when the German philosopher Friedrich Nietzsche proclaimed toward the end of the nineteenth century that God was dead, he was expressing a very widespread feeling, often secretly held, that few others had the nerve to articulate so boldly.

Nietzsche welcomed the death of God as a necessary precondition for the fruition of human greatness. But his older Russian contemporary, the great novelist Feodor Dostoevsky, like John Donne before him, was appalled by the consequences that the victory of science over religion were likely to bring with it. If God was dead, he said (through the mouth of one of his characters, Ivan Karamazov), then everything was permitted.

At this point in the story, we run into another fascinating paradox. While it was in becoming "modest" that the human mind seemed to have grown to superhuman proportions, it soon forgot, in the headiness of its accomplishments, the respect for its own limits that had made the gigantic accomplishments of reason possible in the first place. Now the idea spread that reason in the form of science had shown that it, not God, was omnipotent and was on its way to usurping the divine attribute of omniscience as well.

And so it came about that modesty was replaced by the puffed-up pride the Greeks called hubris. The likes of the Marquis de Condorcet in the eighteenth century and then Auguste Comte in the nineteenth asserted that science need not even be restricted to the physical world; it could be adapted to the social world just as successfully. "Social science" could design plans for an ideal society, and in implementing them, it could at the same time—or so the most utopian of these social engineers expected—reshape and perfect human nature itself.

If, according to Dostoevsky, the death of God meant that everything (evil) was now permitted, the new worshipers of reason believed that everything (good) was now possible. But Dostoevsky was a better prophet than the utopian rationalists on the other side, as the grisly horrors perpetrated by the two main totalitarian systems that sprang up in the twentieth century would demonstrate.

For both Communism and Nazism were forms of social engineering based on supposedly scientific foundations. The Communists who took over in Russia in 1917 explicitly saw themselves as "scientific socialists," carrying out the hitherto hidden laws of History as unearthed by the mind of Karl Marx and creating as they went along the "new Soviet man." As for the Nazis, they justified their slaughter of Jews and others as part of a program of putatively scientific eugenics that would purify the human race and create the higher breed foreseen by Nietzsche in his vision of the superman.

To be sure, few worshipers of reason detected in the horrors of totalitarianism the fingerprints of their triumph in the war between science and religion. Quite the contrary. Many scientists and other devotees of what has aptly been described as "the religion of science" even supported the Soviet "experiment" (the use of this word was itself significant) and apologized for or denied the crimes it entailed. Conversely, they placed the blame for Nazism not on anything connected with reason or science but on the atavistic influence of religion and the forces of irrationality and superstition that allegedly always accompanied it.

Hence totalitarianism failed to make a dent in the hubris of the religion of science. But the atom bomb did manage to trigger a recoil among the physicists who had invented it. In yet another of the paradoxes that keep cropping up here, this most vivid demonstration of the seemingly limitless power of science brought about something of a return to Galileo's modesty. Scientists like J. Robert Oppenheimer, who had supervised the project, took to agonizing over what science had wrought and were beset by doubts about its role in the total scheme of things.

In yielding to these doubts, Oppenheimer and others had been preceded by scientist-philosophers, of whom the most eminent was probably Alfred North Whitehead. In *Science and the Modern World* (1925), Whitehead, from within a generally scientific worldview, raised deep questions about the idea that science provided an exhaustive account of reality. "Religion," he wrote approvingly, "is the vision of something which stands beyond, behind, and within, the passing flux of immediate things."

During this same period, there were also literary figures like T. S. Eliot who carried forward and modernized the tradition of resistance to the imperialistic claims of reason and science as against those of imagination and religion. Finally, to Eliot and Whitehead were added theologians like Jacques Maritain who, resurrecting and reconceiving lines of argument from St. Thomas Aquinas that had once been thought dead and buried forever, undertook to show that the truths of science did not refute or negate the truths of religion.

Then, too, within the realm of science itself, new discoveries were made, particularly in cosmology (where the whole thing had started) that further encouraged a return to Galileo's modesty. In 1992 the distinguished astronomer Robert Jastrow, while describing himself as an agnostic, wrote a book entitled *God and the Astronomers* concluding that "it is not a matter of another year, another decade of work, another measurement, or another theory; at this moment it seems as though science will never be able to raise the curtain on the mystery of creation."

But the very last sentence of Mr. Jastrow's book was even more astonishing: "For the scientist who has lived by his faith in the power of reason, the story ends like a bad dream. He has scaled the mountains of ignorance; he is about to conquer the highest peak; as he pulls himself over the final rock, he is greeted by a band of theologians who have been sitting there for centuries."

Evidently, reports of the death of God have been greatly exaggerated. I am not here referring to the fact that in the U.S. approximately 95 percent of the population professes to believe in God. No doubt this is impressive, but its impact is somewhat lessened by the highly secularized way of life that so comfortably coexists with it.

What strikes me as more impressive is the almost complete disappearance in recent years of any talk about the war between science and religion. We do talk of a "culture war," but that battle has been raging on an entirely different front. As for science and religion, these two formerly passionate enemies have for the moment reached an accommodation on the ground. It is an unwritten armistice, based (perhaps unconsciously) on the conception of the relations between the two that was advanced by Galileo and Bacon, who rendered unto each its own sphere of truth: to science the *how* of material things, and to religion the *why* of them.

As Mr. Jastrow sees it, this is where the story ends. But alas, he is correct only for the older breed of natural scientists. A new breed, which did not yet exist in the seventeenth century, has come along in the latter part of the twentieth and seems likely to reignite the war between science and religion. This new breed, made up of geneticists, molecular biologists, and biotechnologists, is in only the early stages of its work. Like their predecessors in other scientific fields, they have gone very far very fast, but they have neither begun with nor yet acquired any sense of the limits of what they can do.

A good illustration is provided by two leading pioneers of the "new philosophy" of our own day, Francis Crick and James D. Watson, who jointly won the Nobel Prize for discovering the structure of DNA. So confident were these men of their powers that in the early 1970s they entertained the idea of administering genetic tests to newborn infants who, if they failed, were to be put to death. At the time this idea was so shocking that Mr. Crick prudently refused to allow publication of the BBC interview in which he had floated it, while Mr. Watson confined his endorsement to private conversation (with me, among others).

Of course they defined "failure" as a likely predisposition to certain diseases, so that the infanticide it entailed wore a reassuring therapeutic mask. Yet what was to prevent the future inclusion of standards of height or beauty or intellectual potential as necessary qualifications for the right of a newborn to go on living?

By now, even with this terrible question still hanging in the air, we have a philosopher like Peter Singer throwing all caution to the winds and developing a rationale for an allegedly benevolent program of infanticide. Mr. Singer's reward for his brazen outspokenness has been an appointment as professor of bioethics at the Princeton University Center for Human Values (!). In response, the resistance within the religious community is heating up at a rapid clip.

But wait. Thanks to the progress of genetic engineering, which assures us it can rectify defects in advance, infanticide may prove unnecessary. This sounds wonderful, but wait again. As the political theorist Francis Fukuyama has written, the biotechnical revolution is "on the brink" of being able to custom-design creatures who will resemble humans but will not be governed by human nature as we have always known it.

Unlike his namesake Francis Bacon, who greeted the first stage of modern science with hope and enthusiasm, Mr. Fukuyama looks forward with fear and trembling to this next stage. "To the extent that nature is not something given to us by God or by our evolutionary inheritance, but by human artifice, then we enter into God's own realm with all of the frightening powers for good and evil that such an entry implies."

I tremble even more violently than Mr. Fukuyama, but I cannot believe that the new scientists will succeed in replacing God any more than their predecessors managed to kill Him off. That dog didn't bark in the millennium just ending, and my guess—or perhaps I should say my prayer—is that it will also fail to bark in the one just ahead.

Index

About the Authors

Norman Podhoretz, the author of nine previous books on subjects ranging from contemporary literature to foreign policy, was editor in chief of *Commentary* for thirty-five years and is now the magazine's editor at large. A graduate of Columbia and Cambridge Universities, as well as of the Seminary College of Jewish Studies, he has been awarded a Pulitzer Scholarship, a Kellett Fellowship, a Fulbright Fellowship, the Francis L. Boyer Award from the American Enterprise Institute, and five honorary doctorates. He lives in New York City with his wife, the writer Midge Decter.

Thomas L. Jeffers teaches English and American literature at Marquette University. He holds a doctorate from Yale University and has published widely on Victorian and modern figures in such journals as *Commentary, Yale Review,* and *Hudson Review.* He has published a short book on the Victorian Samuel Butler, and has recently finished a long one on the Anglo-American bildungsroman. Before coming to Marquette, he taught at Cornell and Harvard. He lives in Milwaukee, Wisconsin.

Paul Johnson, the eminent British historian, political commentator, and social critic, is the author of, among many other books, *Modern Times, A History of the American People, A History of the Jews, Intellectuals, Enemies of Society,* and, most recently, *Art: A New History.*